SELECTED STUDIES IN

Marriage and the Family

SELECTED STUDIES IN

Marriage and

he Family

Edited by

Robert F. Winch
Robert McGinnis

NORTHWESTERN UNIVERSITY

HENRY HOLT AND COMPANY, New York

Preface

As WE BEGAN to think about putting this book together, we were mindful of the difficulty which besets many anthologies—a lack of organization and—all too frequently—a lack of coherence. Accordingly, we began with the organization and, after agreeing on this, we searched widely for articles which would fit our outline. We are presenting, therefore, those articles which we have adjudged the best available for the purpose of presenting a coherent and organized set of readings in marriage and the family.

In the first chapter we try to summarize some of the elements of scientific procedure and to relate them to problems involved in studying the family. We are convinced that, as with other classes of phenomena, durable knowledge about the family can be achieved only through the use of scientific method. We hope that the first chapter will provide the reader with a set of criteria for judging the contributions in the rest of the book.

After chapter 1 the organization of this book is rather similar to, although not identical with, Winch's *The Modern Family*. After placing the modern family in its historical context, we note the arguments of those who view the family with various moods—from black despair to sanguine hope. (See chapter 2.) Then in presenting comparative materials we have deviated from the practice of drawing upon a variety of cultures. Rather we have ventured to present a more complete elucidation of a single culture which, though exotic to American eyes, is quite literate and has undergone a telescoped industrial revolution. (See chapter 3.)

In chapter 4 we are ready to present some theoretical formulations about families in general (or about *the* family), and we follow this with a discussion of the changing functions and structures in the

American family. Because the concept of *the* family, and indeed of *the* *American* family, conceals so many differences, we have endeavored to suggest in chapter 5 the degree of variation in American families with respect to the variables of social class, rural-urban residence, ethnicity and race.

Viewed in the large, the family cycle is endless. We break it arbitrarily by taking the viewpoint of the young married couple contemplating parenthood. After some observations on differential fertility in the United States, we present a paper on cultural and other considerations which tend to reward and to punish prospective parents for having children. (See chapter 6.) It is our hypothesis that the attitude of ambivalence which these conditions generate influence the attitude which parents express toward their children and hence leave their mark upon the personalities of the young. In quite general theory we can see that attitudes and patterns of response are shaped by the child's experiences in the family. If, then, we think of personality as an organization of attitudes and response patterns, it follows that parents influence the personalities of their children. In chapter 7 we see such influences at work on the fetus, infant, and child, and we have also a report on the effect of being reared outside the family. Some of the emotions surrounding the belief that parents influence their children's personalities are examined in chapter 8. The latter part of the same chapter considers what we know and what we do not know about the way in which this influence operates and the kind and duration of its consequences.

With the passage of time the child enters the limbo of adolescence in American society, and upon achieving adulthood, he moves from the parental family into the world of occupation and marriage. (See chapters 9 and 10.) In American society to be aged frequently means to be dependent upon none-too-willing children. Ultimately, however, the extension of pension programs will reduce the total volume of dependency. (See chapter 11.) The single paper in chapter 12 constitutes a summary of much of chapters 6-11.

If we may regard the child's period of socialization within the family as the first stage of an affectional cycle, the second stage consists of falling in love, marrying, forming a new family, and thus completing the family cycle. After a review of the concept of romantic love (chapter 13), we present some materials on dating and courtship (chapter 14). Following this, there are several papers which support the hypothesis that mate-selection in the United States is far from a random matter. (See chapter 15.)

Marital adjustment has received considerable attention from the standpoint of empirical studies. In chapter 16 we present summaries of the findings of several major studies, and in chapter 17 some critical discussion of two of these studies. Scholars in this field have been much more interested in marriage than in divorce, but we do have two papers which give information on trends in, and attitudes following, divorce. (See chapter 18.)

As children, we develop attitudes toward mother, father, brother, and sister. To some degree, it appears, we carry these attitudes through life and re-enact them in relation to people who stand in relationships to us which are roughly analogous to the key-figures in our parental families. Although this is hinted at in various papers throughout the book and is somewhat clearer in the article by Henry (chapter 10), we close the book with a chapter (19) which is explicitly devoted to the persistence of attitudes and behaviors learned in the family.

R. F. W.

R. McG.

Evanston, Illinois

February 10, 1953

List of Contributors

Howard W. Beers, Professor and Head of the Department of Sociology and Rural Sociology, University of Kentucky

Hugo G. Beigel, Assistant Professor of Psychology, Long Island University

Ernest W. Burgess, Professor Emeritus and Former Chairman of the Department of Sociology, University of Chicago

Paul J. Campisi, Associate Professor of Sociology, Washington University

Theodore Caplow, Associate Professor of Sociology, University of Minnesota

Leonard S. Cottrell, Jr., Russell Sage Foundation

Allison Davis, Professor of Education, Committee on Human Development, University of Chicago

Kingsley Davis, Professor of Sociology, Columbia University

Robert M. Dinkel, Professor of Sociology, Guilford College

Albert Ellis, Consulting Psychologist and Marriage Counselor, New York City

John F. Embree, Late Associate Professor of Anthropology, Yale University

Sibylle Escalona, The Child Study Center, Yale University

Joseph K. Folsom, Professor of Sociology, Vassar College

E. Franklin Frazier, Professor and Chairman of the Department of Sociology, Howard University

Else Frenkel-Brunswik, Lecturer in Psychology and Research Associate in the Institute of Child Welfare, University of California

Paul C. Glick, Chief, Social Statistics Section, Population and Housing Division, U. S. Bureau of the Census

William J. Goode, Associate Professor of Sociology, Columbia University

Roy R. Grinker, Director, Institute for Psychosomatic and Psychiatric Research and Training, Michael Reese Hospital, Chicago

Robert J. Havighurst, Professor and Chairman of the Committee on Human Development, University of Chicago

William E. Henry, Associate Professor of Psychology and Vice-Chairman of the Committee on Human Development, University of Chicago

A. B. Hollingshead, Professor of Sociology, Yale University

Paul H. Jacobson, Population Statistics Section, Statistical Bureau, Metropolitan Life Insurance Company, New York

Adelaide M. Johnson, Sections of Neurology and Psychiatry, Mayo Clinic, Rochester, Minnesota

Harold E. Jones, Professor of Psychology and Director, Institute of Child Welfare, University of California

Clifford Kirkpatrick, Professor of Sociology, Indiana University

Marvin R. Koller, Assistant Professor of Sociology, Kent State University

Mirra Komarovsky, Associate Professor and Chairman of the Department of Sociology, Barnard College, Columbia University

Thomas Ktsanes, Fellow of the U. S. Public Health Service at Northwestern University

Virginia Ktsanes, Research Associate, Social Psychological Laboratory, Northwestern University

Emanuel Landau, Chief, Family Statistics Unit, Social Statistics Section, U. S. Bureau of the Census

Harvey J. Locke, Professor of Sociology, University of Southern California

George Peter Murdock, Professor of Anthropology, Yale University

Raymond J. Murphy, University Fellow in Sociology, Northwestern University

William F. Ogburn, Sewell L. Avery Distinguished Service Professor Emeritus of Sociology, University of Chicago

Talcott Parsons, Professor of Sociology and Chairman of the Department of Social Relations, Harvard University

Robert F. Peck, Research Associate, Committee on Human Development, University of Chicago

Margaret Redfield, Desplaines, Illinois

Helen Ross, Administrative Director, Institute for Psychoanalysis, Chicago

Julius A. Roth, Committee on Human Development, University of Chicago

Robert R. Sears, Professor and Chairman of the Department of Psychology, Stanford University

L. W. Sontag, Director, Fels Research Institute for the Study of Human Development, Yellow Springs, Ohio

John P. Spiegel, Associate Director, Institute for Psychosomatic and Psychiatric Research and Training, Michael Reese Hospital, Chicago

René A. Spitz, New York Psychoanalytic Institute

Etsu Inagaki Sugimoto, Late Lecturer in Japanese Language and History, Columbia University

Lewis M. Terman, Professor Emeritus and Former Head, Department of Psychology, Stanford University

Willard Waller, Late Associate Professor of Sociology, Barnard College, Columbia University

Paul Wallin, Professor of Sociology, Stanford University

William H. Whyte, Jr., Assistant Managing Editor, *Fortune*

Contents

CHAPTER 1

Editors' Introduction:
Scientific Method and the Study
of the Family

THE REPORTS to be found in this volume are from the logbooks of a strange breed of explorers—the social scientists. They do not travel through unknown places but remain on paths so familiar that the word "explorer" may appear ridiculous. Their searches lead to Main Street, Skid Row, and Suburbia, into mansions, apartments, and tenements well charted in any city directory. And yet, in a sense, they are explorers because they view these familiar scenes in a novel way—through the eyes of science.

Beyond prying about and assigning curious names to ordinary things, social scientists claim to offer some eventual hope of making life more pleasant and rewarding. They maintain that by understanding more fully our daily activities we can extend our control over them and eventually mold them to our liking. The researches described in this book are concerned with a particularly common and, at times, uncommonly troublesome aspect of our life—the business of living intimately with other human beings in the family. Where necessary, editorial comment is provided to assist the reader in his task of translating the peculiar dialects of sociology and psychology in which the reports frequently appear.

Such a collection of articles in one volume provides convenient access to a series of recently derived answers to questions concerning marriage

1

and the family. For some readers, however, answers are unnecessary for others, answers alone are inadequate. It is the reader whose pattern of thought lie undisturbed in the traditional mold for whom answer are unnecessary—indeed, for him the questions may not exist. The following discussion is directed to the skeptic for whom a set of answers standing alone is inadequate.

The skeptic will wish to be provided with some means of assessing conclusions. But to assess conclusions is to be faced with an ancient dilemma arising from the fact that for each interpretation of a given phenomenon there is generally another opposing interpretation. Frequently this fact results in confusion and ultimately in fads and in conflicting "schools" of opinion. Since no interpretation is correct simply because it appears in print, the reader should ask with respect to each article in this volume: is this interpretation correct? Or more practically is the conclusion accurate enough that I may accept it as tentative truth and use it in my life as a guidepost?

It seems clear that in the study of the family, as in other fields, there is need for a way of obtaining knowledge so that it is little affected by personal bias or social fad. Thus far man has discovered only one such way which gives promise of succeeding. This is known as the scientific method. Students of the family look to this system as their only hope of escape from the dilemma of too many answers and too little knowledge.

SCIENCE

In this section we shall deal with two major questions: what is science? and, how do social researchers utilize scientific method in studying marriage and the family? The purpose of this discussion is to enable the reader to answer for himself the question raised previously: is this or that conclusion accurate enough that I may accept as tentative truth?

Although facts are highly useful, the goal of science is not the collecting and classifying of facts. Rather the objective is the development of a completely general and systematic set of theories from which hypotheses are deduced and verified and in terms of which the structures and changes of the animate and inanimate phenomena of the universe may be explained.

The objective of the scientist is to obtain satisfactory answers to *why* questions: why do structures appear as they do, and why do they undergo the processes of change which characterize them?[1] Before the scientist can even learn how to ask the *why* questions properly, however, he must first ask and answer another set—the *how* questions. Before one can begin to explain why phenomena exist and change as they do, one must know how they are structured and how slowly or rapidly they change. To phrase it differently, before a scientist tries to explain a phenomenon, he should have an accurate description of that phenomenon. The proper logical sequence, then, is first to ask the *how* questions and then the *why* questions. We may label the procedures of answering these two types of questions *descriptive* and *analytical* processes respectively.

Theories, then, are answers to *why* questions, and ideally the *why* questions are asked only after the relevant *how* questions are answered. The *how* questions themselves are not involved with theory. For this reason such descriptive studies as Paul C. Glick's "The Family Cycle"[2] are not final science. Since description is the logical antecedent of analysis, however, such studies are invaluable to social scientists. We can evaluate descriptive studies in terms of sample design and measuring instruments. Presently we shall discuss these criteria.[3]

Analytical Studies

Before discussing analytical researches, we should make a few observations about scientific theory, the presence of which distinguishes these studies from the descriptive. A scientific theory is a statement of the way in which abstract variables are related and from which verifiable

[1] Needless to say, our use of the word *why* does not imply questions of ultimate causation which are answerable only on theological grounds.

[2] See pp. 81-92 below.

[3] We have asserted that descriptive studies describe and that analytical studies explain. The neatness of this dichotomy is blurred by the contention of some writers that in the scientific sense explanation is also description. Such a point of view follows from the operational concept of science. (See, *e.g.*, P. W. Bridgman, *The Logic of Modern Physics*, Macmillan, New York, 1932, esp. p. 37.) The apparent confusion, however, is merely a consequence of the differences in meaning with which writers have endowed these words. Order can be restored by pointing out that a descriptive study describes the characteristics of a phenomenon, and an analytical study describes associations between phenomena.

hypotheses are deducible. This is a mouthful, but one worth chewing on.

The meat of the matter is in the term "verifiable." Although a theory may be suggested by an insight, an intuition, a dream, or any other bit of experience, to satisfy the requisites of science it cannot end there. It must culminate in a statement from which testable hypotheses are deduced, tested, and verified or rejected before we can accept or reject the theory. Thus, the term "verifiable" in our definition of a scientific theory frees us from any obligation to regard as scientific knowledge any conclusion based exclusively on insight, intuition, or revelation.

Let us consider an example of the level of scientific explanation in the field of marriage and the family. One study concludes that there is a "rough *inverse* correlation between economic position and tendency to divorce. . . ."[4] It has also been tentatively established that the incidence of divorce is positively correlated with brevity of engagement.[5] In the present state of our knowledge it seems certain that an unknown number of other factors are also related to the incidence of divorce. We may summarize these observations by asserting that in recent times (say, over the past fifteen years) the incidence of divorce in the United States has been a function of factors *a* (economic position), *b* (brief engagement), *c* (unknown) . . . *n* (unknown).[6] The statement is incomplete because the factors from *c* through *n* have not been identified. What remains is to discover what these factors are and how they are related to divorce.[7]

Single-Factor and Multi-Factor Theories

In the last paragraph we said in effect that the theory accounting for the incidence of divorce in the United States is incomplete. With rea-

---

[4] W. J. Goode, "Economic Factors and Marital Stability," p. 535 below. (Italics in original.)

[5] Harvey J. Locke, "Predicting Adjustment in Marriage," p. 486 below.

[6] And possibly of interaction among these factors.

[7] The reader should be warned that if there is a significant correlation between *X* and *Y*, this fact does not tell us that *X* causes *Y* or that *Y* causes *X*. All it tells us is that for every increment of change in *X* there is on the average some degree of change in *Y*. We use the phrase "spurious correlation" to denote correlation between variables when we are unable to relate the variables to each other in any scientifically meaningful way. For example, the incidence of cancer in the United States is positively correlated with the exportation of rice from China. It is not thought that either one of these causes the other, but only that both are correlated with time.

sonable security we may generalize to all of social science the observation that no complete theory exists. Instead, we find theories which are in various stages of development, *i.e.,* those which contain statements of varying degrees of complexity. The least complex type of theory may be labeled the "single-factor" theory. Such theories attempt to explain variation in a class of phenomena in terms of the operation of a single variable. Koller's analysis of mate-selection in terms of the factor of residential propinquity is illustrative of this type.[8]

From the work of Koller and others who have studied the relation between mate-selection and propinquity, then, we can predict that men will tend to marry women who live near them rather than those whose residences are remote. But from the work of Hollingshead[9] and Reeves[10] we can also predict that men are more likely to marry women similar to themselves with respect to race, religion, ethnic grouping, social class, and age group than they are to marry women who differ from themselves in these social characteristics. When we consider all of these factors together, we have a "multi-factor" theory, and we are able to go considerably farther toward the goal of predicting who marries whom than we could have gone by considering any one of these factors by itself. Or, in slightly different words, the greater the number of relevant factors in a theoretical system (*i.e.,* the more complex the system), the more complete will be the explanation.

Since the goal of science is to explain as much about a given phenomenon as is practically possible, one may wonder why all theories are not considerably more complex. One important reason is that the more complex the theory, the more difficulty the researcher has in subjecting it to empirical test and in using it for predictive purposes. With single-factor hypotheses one may use simple techniques of analysis,[11] but for every added factor, the methods of testing hypotheses become more difficult and tedious.

While the articles in this volume contain conclusions, it must be real-

[8] M. R. Koller, "Residential and Occupational Propinquity," pp. 429-34 below.

[9] A. B. Hollingshead, "Cultural Factors in the Selection of Marriage Mates," pp. 399-412 below.

[10] R. J. R. Kennedy, "Single or Triple Melting-Pot? Intermarriage Trends in New Haven, 1870-1950," *American Journal of Sociology,* 58 (1952), 56-59, 201.

[11] Such as the *t* test and the zero-order *r*.

ized that these conclusions are far from complete. And like the conclusions in all scientific fields, they are certainly not final. These studies consist largely of (non-theoretical) description or of single-factor theories. This indicates the present status of family studies. But a scientific discipline cannot reach maturity without first acquiring a fund of descriptive knowledge and an understanding of simple associations.

Making Hypotheses Researchable

Theories consist of statements of relation between *abstract* categories. Abstraction is a process of reducing heterogeneous data to a homogeneous core. The "average man," for example, is an abstraction. It is quite probable that no human being is statistically average in every respect. Yet the idea of an average man is useful in that it gives us a statistical norm from which we may measure deviations in specific cases. An abstraction is an abbreviation of nature created in order that man's limited mind may be able to deal with the great variation of phenomena to be found in the universe.

Since the variables in scientific theories are abstract, it is impossible to find data which will directly verify or reject a theory. Before verification is possible, the theory must be related to something concrete which we can measure or count. This step is accomplished by means of the logical process called "deduction."[12]

The essence of deduction is ". . . the derivation of conclusions *necessarily* involved in the premises . . ."[13] To illustrate, if we set forth the premises (1) that all men are mortal and (2) that William Jones is a man, then we must conclude that Mr. Jones is a mortal because this conclusion is a necessary consequence of the premises. Deductive logic is important to scientists because it is by means of deduction that they proceed from abstract theory to concrete data.

The researcher uses deduction in the following manner. The first premise is a statement of a relationship among abstract variables. The second premise contains indexes of the abstract variables in the first

[12] For a discussion of deduction, see Morris R. Cohen and Ernest Nagel, *An Introduction to Logic and Scientific Method*, New York, Harcourt, Brace, 1934, esp. chs. 7 and 14.

[13] *Ibid.*, p. 273. (Italics in original.)

premise.[14] From these premises he deduces hypotheses which can be tested empirically. For example, if we wish to test Hollingshead's idea that family stability is a function of class position,[15] we might state our premises in this manner: (1) Family stability is positively correlated with position in the class structure. (2a) Divorce is an index of the absence of family stability (or is a negative index of family stability). (2b) Income is an index of social class position. From these premises we should hypothesize that divorce is negatively correlated with income. Thus by using incidence of divorce and income as indexes of the abstract variables (family stability and class position, respectively) in the first premise, we are able to test the statement of relationship between abstract variables. The adequacy of our test depends in part upon how good (or "valid") the indexes are and in part upon the adequacy of the experimental design.

Counting and Measurement

Hypotheses concern characteristics of individual members of classes of phenomena. We speak of these classes of phenomena as populations (or universes) whether or not the units of observation are human beings. Verification involves counting or measuring. In the crudest case the scientist counts individuals to determine the number who do and who do not have a given characteristic. If the characteristic can be measured, the scientist will ordinarily prefer to measure the degree to which each individual possesses it.

Scientific measurement involves considerably more than Geiger counters and oscilloscopes. It may include any technique of recording the phenomenon in question with a minimum of fluctuation resulting from human idiosyncrasies. It may depend upon a multi-million dollar cyclotron or a man standing on a street-corner counting passers-by. Criteria of the worth of a scientific instrument are: relevance, validity,

[14] A strict operationist would label the second premise an "operational definition." For a discussion of operationism, see Gustav Bergmann and Kenneth W. Spence, "Operationism and Theory Construction," in Melvin H. Marx (ed.), *Psychological Theory*, New York, Macmillan, 1951, pp. 54-66.

[15] A. B. Hollingshead, "Class Differences in Family Stability," pp. 105-15 below. The above statement is an over-simplification of Hollingshead's actual position since he states that the "new upper-class family" is more stable than the "nuclear upper-middle-class family."

and reliability. By relevance we mean an affirmative answer to the question: does it measure what the scientist happens to be interested in? By validity we mean the degree to which it measures what it is supposed to measure. Reliability refers to the degree to which the instrument gives constant measurements of an unchanging entity on different occasions.

Sampling

Because of the expense involved it is usually impossible to count all the individuals who do or do not have a characteristic in an entire population, or to measure a characteristic for the entire population. For example, if we wished to test our illustrative hypothesis concerning divorce and income for the population of the United States alone, we should have to contact more than 72 million married persons, more than 3.5 million separated persons and more than 2 million divorcees.[16] For a social scientist working on a typical research budget, such a procedure would be out of the question.

The compromise of the scientist (both social and natural) is to draw a sample of the population which he tries to make as representative of the whole population as he can. The importance of representativeness of the sample cannot be overemphasized. If the sampling procedure breaks down on this point, the results of an otherwise rigorously done experiment are meaningless. As one statistician has observed: ". . . even a large sample confined to a portion of the population is devoid of information about the excluded portions."[17] Thus from a knowledge of the incidence of some social characteristic among American college students we should be able to conclude nothing about the incidence of the same characteristic among the Japanese or among non-college people in the United States.

Design of Research: The "Classical" Experiment

From the discussion to follow we shall see that the conclusions which we may draw from a piece of research are determined in part by the way in which the study is set up—or, to use the more technical term,

[16] "Some Statistics Concerning Marriage and the Family in the United States," pp. 93-95 below.

[17] G. W. Snedecor, *Statistical Methods* (4th ed.), Ames, Collegiate Press, 1946, p. 460.

are dependent in part on the "design" of the research. Although it is frequently impossible to use such a rigorous and ideal design in social research, we shall first consider a classical design of experiment. Then we shall note the ways in which certain practicable designs diverge from the ideal and with what logical consequences.

The simplest design which contains the essentials of the experimental method is as follows. A sample is divided into two groups, one called the "experimental" group, and the other, the "control" group. At this stage the two groups should be as much alike as possible in all relevant respects. If the assignment of individuals from the original sample to the two groups is done in a random manner, then the experimental and control groups should be sufficiently similar, and both groups should be representative samples of the population.[18]

After the two groups have been formed, every individual in each group is measured with respect to the index of the variable under study. Or, if the variable cannot be measured, a count is made in each group to determine how many individuals possess or lack the attribute in question.

Next the experimental group—but not the control group—is subjected to a certain controlled condition (sometimes called "treatment"). After the experimental group has undergone the treatment, measures are obtained from both groups with respect to the variable about which the experimenter is concerned.

We now have two measurements (before and after treatment) in each of the two groups (experimental and control). Concerning these four measurements the researcher sets up what he calls "null hypotheses." A null hypothesis asserts that the obtained difference is *no greater than might reasonably have occurred by chance alone.*

The first of these null hypotheses is employed in a comparison of the experimental-before and control-before measurements. The researcher hopes that here the test will sustain the null hypothesis because such an outcome is evidence that the two groups were initially similar. When the difference between the experimental-after and the control-after cells is greater than might reasonably be imputed to chance, this

---

[18] While random assignment to the two groups is probably the usual procedure, if conditions are favorable, the matched-pair method is more efficient.

difference is interpreted to mean that the experimental treatment has resulted in a measurable effect.

Now let us summarize in schematic form this discussion of what we shall call the "four-fold" or "four-cell" experimental design:

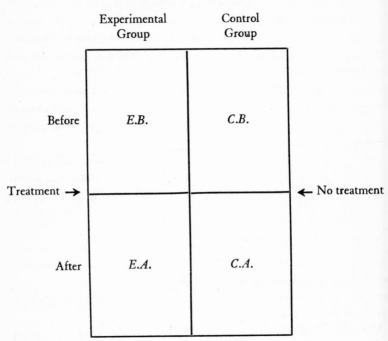

Figure 1.   Schematic diagram of four-cell experimental design

1. A representative sample of some specified population is drawn.
2. By random assignment or some other procedure the sample is divided into two sub-samples, called "experimental" group and "control" group.
3. Every individual in each group is measured with respect to the inde of the variable under study. Or, if the variable cannot be measured and only a "present" or "absent" discrimination can be made, count of the incidence in each group is taken. The counts or meas urements are entered in cells "E.B." and "C.B." of the four-fold tabl in Figure 1.

4. The two groups are compared with respect to the incidence or average degree of the variable measured. Since the two groups are intended to be alike at this stage, it is expected that the difference between them as revealed by the measure will be no greater than might reasonably be expected by chance; *i.e.,* it is expected that the null hypothesis will be accepted.

5. The experimental group is subjected to some controlled condition, stimulus, or treatment. The control group does not have this experience.

6. Every individual in both groups is again measured with respect to the index of the variable under study. The counts or measurements are entered in cells "*E.A.*" and "*C.A.*" of the four-fold table in Figure 1.

7. Again the two groups are compared with respect to the incidence or average degree of the variable measured. Since this comparison is made after the treatment and since the two groups were alike before treatment, a greater than chance difference at this point (*i.e.,* a rejection of the null hypothesis) is interpreted as an effect of the treatment.[19]

Statistical Assessment of Results

To determine the probability that an observed difference might have arisen by chance alone, or, as statisticians say, to measure the significance of the difference, statistical techniques such as chi-square (χ^2), the critical ratio (*C.R.*), and the *t* test are applied. When an author uses the expression "$P < .05$," he is telling us that, for a sample of the size used, a difference as great as that obtained could have occurred by chance alone less than five times out of 100.[20] This knowledge makes

---

[19] The term "experiment" has been used by various writers with a variety of denotations. The editors of this volume regard the following as necessary conditions for a study to be regarded as an "experiment": experimental and control groups, controlled treatment or stimulus, and observations made both before and after treatment. Accordingly, the four-fold design is the simplest prototype of what we call the "experimental method."

[20] A critical ratio of 1.96 is always significant at the .05 level, and a critical ratio of 2.58 is always significant at the .01 level. The significance of an obtained *t* or chi-square, however, varies with the degrees of freedom involved. Tables of areas of the normal curve (for interpretation of the critical ratio), of *t*, and of chi-square are available in Herbert Arkin and Raymond R. Colton, *Tables for Statisticians*, New York,

us reasonably certain that the difference is not a chance occurrence, but the evidence would be more compelling if $P<.01$ or if $P<.001$. Some conclusions appear more nearly certain than others, but we can never be entirely certain. Evidence never leads to absolute certainty in science.

Interpretation of Findings

If the results of a research are statistically significant[21] and in the direction hypothesized, they are interpreted as supporting the hypothesis. Then the researcher tentatively concludes (draws the generalization) that whenever a representative sample of the population studied is subjected to the same treatment under the same conditions, the result will be approximately the same. This conclusion is of course qualified: (a) by the fact that, no matter how small the *probability,* the *possibility* always exists that the result might have occurred by chance; (b) by the assumption that the sample was representative of the population to which the result is to be generalized; and (c) by the assumption that all relevant conditions remain constant or else vary with predictable consequences.

Such a generalization is founded on one of the assumptions basic to science: that *there is uniformity in nature,* or in other words, that what results today from a particular combination of elements under specified circumstances will result tomorrow from an identical combination of elements under duplicated circumstances. This assumption is not demonstrable with any finality, either logically or empirically. Since scientists do seem capable of making better than chance predictions of some kinds of future events, however, the assumption is pragmatically tenable. We must emphasize that an act of faith is involved in the scientist's assumption of uniformity in nature.

Barnes and Noble, 1950. Discussion of the application of such tests to social data is presented in such standard statistical texts as Margaret J. Hagood and Daniel O. Price *Statistics for Sociologists* (rev. ed.), New York, Holt, 1952. The symbol "*P*" above stands for probability.

[21] What constitutes statistical significance is largely a matter of convention in the various disciplines. In fields where it is difficult to produce significant results, scientists are frequently satisfied if the probability that the observed result might have arisen by chance is no more than 1 in 20; in other disciplines 1 in 100 or 1 in 1000 may be the minimum chance probability for a result to be regarded as significant.

Approximations to the "Classical" Experiment

In a sense the experimental method described above is an ideal design of research. As we shall see, there are many problems both in natural and in social science wherein the utilization of this design is impossible. Accordingly research designs have been established which constitute approximations of the ideal. We can readily note the difficulty of applying the four-fold experimental design in sociological problems. For example, let us assume that we wish to test the hypothesis that the incidence of divorce is inversely related to level of income. In this case the treatment would consist of manipulating family income. We should have to keep our experimental families in poverty for a "reasonable" period, which for this kind of problem could probably not be less than ten years. And for the same period we should have to maintain very strict control over the activities of all families in our sample—both experimental and control. Naturally it is difficult to obtain representative samples willing to undergo such experimental treatment over such a prolonged period. This difficulty has led sociologists to seek other designs of research which are less onerous to their subjects and still yield scientifically useful information.

Such an approximation is represented by a study cited by Goode[22] in which families are classified by income, and the incidence of divorce is computed for each income class. The resulting analysis shows income to be negatively correlated with the incidence of divorce. Logically, this design is roughly comparable to the use of only the two bottom cells in the four-fold table, *i.e.,* the experimental-after and the control-after. The similarity is only rough because instead of having one group which has been subjected to poverty (the experimental group) and another in comfortable circumstances, the income distribution is broken down into more than two classes. But the important logical difference is that both "before" cells are missing.

Because of the absence of "before" cells we can never be certain that the obtained correlation is a consequence of the supposedly differentiating factor (income) or whether it is more meaningfully associated with some other factor for which the sample was not controlled, *e.g.,*

[22] *Op. cit.,* pp. 530-43 below.

level of adjustment in engagement. The four-fold method gives us this assurance, telling us that the groups were alike before the treatment was administered. Because the two-cell design never enables us to conclude that the observed variation is a consequence of the variable under study and of that variable only, results obtained from this design are necessarily less conclusive than those obtained from the four-cell method.

Because of the frequency of its appearance in the literature of social science we should also mention what we may call the "one-cell" design or the "clinical" method. To illustrate this method let us assume that a psychiatrist sees a number of juvenile delinquents in a child guidance clinic and from his observations concludes that juvenile delinquency is a consequence of broken homes.

Now let us look at the four-cell design to interpret what the psychiatrist has done. He has seen a group of subjects who are probably not in any way a random sample of any population. These subjects all present a common characteristic (delinquency) which the psychiatrist regards as the effect of some "treatment." His job in this clinical setting is to try to determine what the treatment was. Note that he does not have a group of subjects whose homes were not broken, and hence he does not have the control-after cell. Nor within the design of this problem has he observed these subjects or any control subjects before the homes were broken, *i.e.,* before the treatment. Therefore, both the experimental-before and the control-before cells are missing. His observations are confined to the experimental-after cell, and it is for this reason that we speak of this as a one-cell design.

In addition to the logical limitation of the two-cell design, the clinical method has the further logical limitation associated with the loss of the control-after cell. We have already noted that the logical limitation of the two-cell design is that we are never able to conclude that the observed difference (between the two "after" cells) is a consequence of the variable (or treatment) under study and of that variable only. The additional limitation resulting from the loss of the control-after cell is that the researcher has no way of knowing how great a difference he should try to explain, or, indeed, whether or not the difference which he is trying to explain exists. In this case, for example, the psychiatrist's explanation assumes that the incidence of broken homes is significantly greater among delinquents than among non-delinquents, but the lack of the control-after cell means that he lacks any evidence that this is true.

Before concluding our remarks about the clinical method, let us note one further way in which it is frequently used. This is the one-cell method with a single case. In some fields it is not unusual to find articles in which some general proposition is advanced and that the evidence offered in support of that proposition is from a single case. To continue with our example of the delinquents, we should have an illustration of this procedure if the psychiatrist had seen just one delinquent child, had discovered that the child came from a broken home, and then had presented this finding as a generally valid proposition.

What may we say about the logical status of this kind of evidence? We may note that all the logical limitations of the clinical method are of course still operative and that one more has been added. This limitation results from the fact that with only one case the investigator does not know that the treatment which he has identified as causative is common to individuals showing the experimental effect. To refer to our example again, simply because he had seen one delinquent who had come from a broken home, the psychiatrist would be completely unjustified in concluding that all or most delinquents had come from broken homes.

It is commonplace that it is extremely hazardous to generalize from a single case. From this analysis we can see that the hazard consists in all the limitations of the two-cell design, plus the additional limitations of the one-cell design, plus the lack of evidence that the association noted is even generally true of the individuals in the one remaining cell.

Assessment of Research Designs

Earlier we observed that there were two types of research: descriptive and analytical. We have remarked that the descriptive is the logical antecedent of the analytical in that descriptive studies provide factual information out of which hypotheses are generated and that the hypotheses are then tested by analytical studies.

Our consideration of designs of research has been from the standpoint of analytical studies. When we view as our objective the testing of hypotheses, it is clear that of the designs which we have discussed the four-cell experimental method is best. If, however, our objective is the generation of new hypotheses, there is much to be said for these other methods, especially the clinical method. When it is at all empirical, for example, the Freudian literature consists almost entirely of clinical (or one-cell) designs and frequently with but a single case. The foregoing logical analysis shows that such studies can never be conclusive in establishing hypotheses. On the other hand, the Freudian literature has been remarkably fruitful as a source of new hypotheses. An important reason for the great value of the clinical type of study in the generation of hypotheses is that although it may involve only one or a very few cases, such cases are generally studied in great detail and thus they enable the reader to view the processes of change through time. An ethnographic description of a single culture, moreover, is logically a clinical or one-cell design based on a single case.[23] Although such studies can never establish propositions which are generally valid in any cross-cultural sense, they have provided social scientists with many ideas for hypotheses. Finally, we may note that the single case may be presented to facilitate communication, *i.e.*, to *illustrate* (but of course not to prove) a proposition. This is the purpose of the case presented by Ktsanes and Ktsanes.[24]

Utilizing the Scientific Outlook

We have just concluded a discussion on the use of scientific method in social research. Our purpose has been to provide the reader with some means of evaluating the papers to follow. We, the editors, regard these articles as being among the best studies of marriage and the family. In view of the scientific immaturity of social science generally, however, the reader need not be surprised in discovering that none of

[23] When describing a culture, the anthropologist is concerned with a single case (the culture in question) despite the possibility that thousands or even millions of individuals may participate in that culture. To take an example from the present volume, John F. Embree's "Family and Household in a Japanese Village," has the logical status of a clinical study based upon a single case. (See pp. 47-56 below.)

[24] See pp. 435-53 below.

these studies employs the four-fold experimental design and that many of them will prove vulnerable to criticism from the standpoint of ideal scientific procedure. As a consequence of the foregoing discussion, we hope that the reader will examine the following papers with such questions as the following in mind: How sound are the premises? How representative is the sample? Of what population is it alleged to be representative? How rigorous is the design of research? Do the conclusions necessarily follow from the design and the data? Over what range may the conclusions be generalized? What are the probable consequences of the conclusions? If the article is not an empirical study, does it offer hypotheses which are amenable to test? Can we move from abstract variables to concrete data without too much logical violence? Such questions are in order with respect to each article in the book. For that matter, such questions are in order whenever some-one asserts: "The truth is that . . ."

CHAPTER 2

The American Family in a Changing
Society

WHETHER OR NOT the family as an institution is disintegrating, it has certainly been in flux for the past century or two. The small urban family with its somewhat tenuous relationships stands in marked contrast to the earlier family which was large and highly interdependent and was characteristic of the self-sufficient family farm. In the *Life* article we shall see the views of Zimmerman, who interprets this change as nothing short of disintegration; in the same piece there is a presentation of Folsom who sees the trend as an adjustment— although painful, to be sure—to the changed conditions in which the institution of the family is operating. Further remarks, both pro and con, appear in the papers by Redfield and Burgess.

We may look ahead in the volume and note that the kind of change discussed in the present chapter is not uniquely American. In Japan we can see one sign of this transition from a vignette on the way a man selects a wife. (See "Old Love and New" in chapter 3.) The meaning of these changes is translated into the more formal analysis of the structure and function of the family as an institution in chapter 4.

THE AMERICAN FAMILY IN TROUBLE*

. . . the U. S. family, deep in the millrace of social and technological change, is itself deep in trouble. The root of the trouble is found in

* Adapted and reprinted by permission of the publisher from *Life*, July 26, 1948, 83-99.

another fact: in the last 100 years the pattern of American life has profoundly altered. A century ago the U. S. was largely agricultural, there were few great cities and industrialization was in its infancy. The average family lived on a farm or in a small town. The need for many hands to do the work produced large families of a type called by sociologists the trustee family. Life was not always easy, but economic interdependence and common interests formed a hard base for close family unity. But the trustee-type family could not withstand the march of industrialization. Its extra members went packing off to the booming cities to evolve a new family type, the so-called domestic family—smaller, no longer self-sufficient but still closely knit. Instead of making their own shoes and soap, individuals found they could buy these things with their high industrial wages and have time left over to develop a variety of social interests both within and outside of the family group.

Today the forces of social change have further broken down the family. It is now tiny—a husband, a wife and one or two children. Its members do little more than sleep and eat together. They buy everything—food, laundry, entertainment—and produce nothing but the money for these purchases. The outward pull of movies, automobiles, bridge clubs, and Elks constantly threaten what little family unity remains. The individual now looks outside his home for his interests. He is atomistic, an individualized fragment rather than a part of a unified whole . . .

The Future of the Family Is a Matter of Serious Debate

There are several divergent theories as to where the American family is going next now that it has reached its atomistic state and stands at a kind of sociological crossroads. As a matter of fact there is a great deal of disagreement among the experts even as to where it *ought* to go from here. Two of the leading men in the field of family sociology, Professor Carle C. Zimmerman of Harvard and Professor Joseph Kirk Folsom of Vassar, represent the major conflicting theories on the latter question. They both agree that the family is changing profoundly, but their books and speeches are diametrically opposed as to what values should be maintained as the changes take place.

In a book published last year, called *Family and Civilization** Professor Zimmerman first gave the labels trustee, domestic and atomistic

* New York, Harper & Brothers, 1948.

to the main types of families which have been developed by Western civilization over centuries of social change. He then went on to sketch the development of each type as it had taken place twice before, among the Greeks and Romans. The moral of his history lesson is that the decline of each civilization to its collapse went hand in hand with the parallel disintegration of the Greek and Roman families from trustee to domestic to atomistic to chaos.

Zimmerman thinks he can see exactly the same signs of decay within the American family as plagued the ancients: the growing concept of marriage as a personal affair rather than one having real religious significance; the increased use of "causeless" divorce (for minor or meaningless grounds); the decreasing number of children per family (the average now is only about two); the "revolt of youth" against their parents and the growth of a youth class with idols and customs of its own; the rise of juvenile delinquency; the growing acceptance of sexual perversion. All of these signs Zimmerman lists as evidence of recurring atomism—of things which have happened before and which are happening again now. And atomism, he believes, is a chain-reaction breaking down of our society that will not stop with the family unit but will spread throughout the entire social structure until the modern world goes the dismal way of Greece and Rome.

Zimmerman has some immediate remedies for this danger. First of all he thinks the average family must begin having more children, preferably three or four, in order to reproduce itself. He would also like to see a revival of family spirit and activity among the learned and leadership classes, who were the first to weaken under the competition of outside forces like the school, the country club and the sacrosanct adult bridge table. "We have on the one hand an institution which is breaking up because (people believe) it is not needed and, on the other hand, a great many juveniles who are breaking up because they do not have the proper family backgrounds." He does not expect the family to revert to the trustee form, for he regards that unit as having been most useful when the nation was young and struggling and so weak in the way of law and order that it depended upon the family to make and maintain its own laws. But he does think that the family should be pegged at least at the domestic level of united mutual interests and authority. As for the atomistic family, it is not so bad in itself, but it is a symptom of something which will wreck the society if it is not replaced by a strong family system, and the something is unbridled individualism. "There is little left now within the family," he warns, "or the moral code to hold (it) together. Mankind has consumed not only the crop but the seed for the next planting as well. The very continuation of our culture seems to be tied up with this nihilism in family behavior."

To all this Professor Folsom of Vassar answers that the American family is not really disintegrating at all, but simply changing its form and its value to keep up with the permanent changes taking place in the society of which it is a part. "Something called 'the family' has survived all the revolutions of history. We need not worry about its continued existence," he writes in his book, *The Family and Democratic Society.** Folsom's reason for believing this is that the family fills too important a need for the people to allow it to collapse completely under the pressure of outside interests. With the increased mobility and complexity of our society, cooperation between individuals becomes more important and lifelong friendships with people outside the immediate family become difficult to maintain. The family will be preserved for the companionship it affords, if for nothing else.

"The problems of the modern family," he continues, "are similar in some respects to some which existed in Roman times. Does Roman history teach us any lessons by which we can profit? Some seem to think so, saying that we must not behave as the Romans did or we shall suffer their fate. But the conditions are different. The Romans lacked modern science. Our solution is not to preach against tendencies which cannot be checked but to do something additional which the Romans failed to do. Our job is to keep adjusting."

By this Folsom means that family atomization need not worry us into a frenzy or reform. Instead "when family members become more *independent* of one another economically and morally, their *dependence* upon one another for love may involve less frustration. It may be that further decline of the family as an economic unit may strengthen it as an emotional unit." The same holds true, he believes, for family authority. When family love was tied closely to authority and the parents ruled supreme, a threat to that authority brought anger and rebellion and love was smothered. When love is fully divorced from authority and coercion it may become more loyal and permanent. Even divorce comes in for a revaluation by Folsom. To make his point he tells the story of a cruel king who, as punishment to two

* New York, John Wiley & Sons, Inc., 1934.

lovers, ordered them tightly bound together for a period of several days. "It is said the lovers came to hate each other. We cannot verify the fact, but we know that it is quite in accord with known psychological processes. Thus does society, in the supposed interest of institutions called marriage and the family, sabotage that upon which modern marriage must rest: love."

The signs of change, therefore, which so worry Zimmerman, do not bother Folsom. In fact the very signs which worry Zimmerman the most—the splitting off of family members, the early growing up and moving away of the children, the growing strength of individualism—all these are to Folsom proof that the American society is actually progressing and reaching its goal of freedom. If the family as a unit is to be so sacrosanct as to stand in the way of allowing a growing child to develop his own contacts freely, to roam in search of fresh, private experiences and to strike out when he is ready to conquer his share of the world—then it has ceased to fulfill the functions for which it is intended in a democratic society.

That is why Folsom thinks that the atomistic atmosphere need not be harmful to children but will probably be healthier for them in the long run, despite the looseness of family ties and the present high incidence of divorce. He believes that the continued lessening of formal discipline (which leads to friction in the home) will result in an increase of parental affection and understanding, and hence to an increased feeling of responsibility. Says Folsom, "When parents respect the private world and personal values of their children, they may safely demand greater respect for their own needs. The mother will find she can afford to delegate some of her work and be physically absent from the home for longer periods in order to enrich other aspects of her own personality if she has more sympathetic insight into the child's needs when she is present.

"The family is our most important primary group," he continues. "In large measure it determines personality development. If we believe in democracy we must promote freedom in the family and help parents build young personalities which will not sabotage democracy in the larger world through their frustrations and pent-up hostilities. This is the real significance of the family in modern society."

Folsom believes, finally, that if the American family is in deep trouble it is only because it has not realized the real meaning of American democracy. When the people who show up in the divorce statistics learn how to live together and get along with themselves and their children the family will begin to find the changes taking place around it less disorganizing and confusing. "The modern family doesn't think of itself as 'atomistic.' People just don't live that way. Their strongest desires are to live together, and when they learn to do so the American family will be here to stay."

THE AMERICAN FAMILY: CONSENSUS AND FREEDOM*

MARGARET PARK REDFIELD

As an organization of parents and offspring meeting the universal necessity to rear the young, the family seems simple, basic, and easily comprehensible. Yet we know that family relationships vary widely from one culture group to another with varying effects upon the resulting personalities. Nor are the functions of the family universally the same. In traditional China the role and scope of activity of the individual was defined almost exclusively by the family, while in some tribal groups the influence of the immediate blood kin appears scarcely greater than that of other individuals in the community. The American family—parents and children—appears on the surface as a simple conjugal type with no important or formal connections with remoter kin, no rituals of ancestor worship (except, perhaps, in the case of the D.A.R.'s), and no intricate economic ties. It is a small, compact group of two generations, bound together by ties of affection and functioning to care for the young until they reach years of maturity and can repeat for themselves the process of family rearing.

Nevertheless, there exists among students of society, in spite of this simplicity or perhaps because of it, a wide disparity of opinion as to just how this family is functioning. Sorokin and Burgess represent widely divergent views. We find Sorokin stating: "As it has become more and more contractual, the family of the last few decades has grown ever more unstable, until it has reached the point of actual disintegration."[1] Burgess, on the other hand, finds that the modern

* Adapted and reprinted by permission of the author and publisher from *The American Journal of Sociology*, 52 (1946), 175-83.
[1] Pitirim Sorokin, *The Crisis of Our Age,* New York, E. P. Dutton & Co., 1941, p. 187.

type of family which permits freedom to the individual is "dynamic, adaptable, and creative—characteristics suited for survival and growth in a society in process of rapid social change."[2]

All agree, however, that many of the functions of the family have been taken from it and transferred, either successfully or unsuccessfully, as the point of view may be, to other institutions. Something without doubt is happening to the family, but there is some difference of opinion as to just what it is. In the numerous newspaper accounts of the growing casualness of family life, of children left alone in unheated flats, abandoned in taverns, or brutally treated by one or both parents, we find evidence which supports Sorokin's thesis that the family as we have known it is collapsing. It has often been pointed out that in our society, especially in the wildernesses of our cities, there is little to reinforce family ties and much to break them down and to weaken the mores which sustain them. Family living is made more difficult by obviously hard conditions of life: overcrowding, the nervous fatigue caused by the swift pace of living and the easy accessibility of commercialized distractions which lead away from rather than to home activities. Even under more favorable conditions, the respectability of the divorce court as a solution to family troubles and the high premium placed on romantic and individual freedom rather than on the preservation of the home contribute further to the instability of family life.

Yet a tendency to instability does not necessarily mean complete disintegration. It is, in fact, this very absence of rigidity which Burgess finds admirable in the modern family, the ideal type of which he finds most closely approximated in families living in the apartment-house areas of the city. Such groups, many of which may appear to the outsider to come close to having no family life at all, represent to Burgess the "new" or "companionship" type of family, embodying the "ideal . . . of democracy as to the way of life, of the equality of men and women, and of personality as the highest human value."[3]

How can we resolve these different points of view? One difficulty in doing so seems to lie in the fact that the family is not clearly or consistently defined. Does an aggregate of individuals living together in one household constitute a family to the sociologist as it does to the

2 Ernest W. Burgess, "The Family," in *American Society in Wartime,* ed., W. F. Ogburn, Chicago, University of Chicago Press, 1943, p. 39.

3 *Ibid.,* p. 39.

census taker? Is it the form or the content or both which make a family, and what are the criteria for judging them? And, the family once defined, what is the role it plays in present-day society as contrasted with the part it should have in the world we are trying to build? Sorokin, in emphasizing the need for consensus and a revival of older forms, and Burgess, in advocating individual freedom and presenting a glowing picture of the future, give but indirect answers to these questions. We need, it appears, not only to come to an agreement as to what we should like but also to know something more of what, under present conditions of life, it is possible to have. The starting point will be a more definite and realistic picture of the attitudes and practices of Americans. Superficially viewed, at least, American family life among the great middle class, which constitutes the majority of our citizens, appears neither as degenerate nor as "modern" as it has been painted.

Common knowledge provides the outlines of the general American ideal of family life. This conception includes having a home of one's own with a yard and vegetable garden; a husband who, in some senses, is less free than husbands in many other countries since he is expected not only to support the family but also to remain faithful to his wife, help with the dishes, and play with the children; a wife and mother who combines the practice of outside activities, social, political, or patriotic, with the provision of scientifically planned diets, attractive home furnishings, and modish clothing for the family; and children who, with a minimum of discipline, grow up to be better men and women than their parents. How this last end is to be attained is not clearly understood, nor is there understanding of the responsibility of the family for attaining this end. Schools and, to a lesser extent, churches are looked to, but without any clear analysis of their function. The family is thought of not as an organic structure to be handed on from generation to generation but rather as the individual creation of each generation and enduring rather less than a lifetime. As put by a working-girl with a rather conservative attitude toward the freedom of woman: "You got to love your fella enough to leave your family for him, although you had to love them enough to stay with them until he came along. Then you got to love your babies enough to leave everyone (including your husband if necessary) to raise 'em. But don't go and expect much in return, for they are just getting ready to go off and leave you with somebody *they* meet at a picnic or dance."[4]

In line with our romantic and individualistic ideal, the selection of a life-partner should, it is felt, be left wholly to the judgment of the two young people, no matter how young and inexperienced they may be. Angelo Patri states the general point of view when he writes: "The choice of a marriage partner is a peculiar, personal, almost instinctive one, and only the person most concerned can make the decision. Nobody else can possibly know."[5] American young people are convinced, and often rightly, that their elders, loved as they may be, possess no basic wisdom. They prefer to trust their own impulses, or, among the more sophisticated, may resolve doubts by having recourse to "psychology" or "marriage counseling." The employment of such agencies represents a breakaway from the old romantic tradition. But it has not gone on long enough, or become so generally popular, that we can yet know its effect.

As contrasted with even a generation ago, today's young people reveal a growing tendency toward freedom of individual action. Frank describes the situation in older America as follows:

To marry, have children, acquire property, gain a position of respect and dignity in the community, share in the common body of beliefs and affirmations about the universe and man's place therein—these made up a way of life to which the teachings of family, school, and church, and the sanction of government and religion were all directed. Young people grew up in a society where the patterns appropriate to their way of life were ready-made and while they often criticized their stodgy parents and revolted against their demands, middle age often found them more or less settled into the ruts of conformity, since there were no socially sanctioned alternatives.[6]

But the modern world is characterized not only by the breakup of families but also by the weakening of community life. The present day world is full of a multitude of socially sanctioned alternatives and even nonsocially sanctioned behavior is far less severely penalized than formerly. Conformity based on intimate impressions made in early youth and related to ultimate traditional values of life has come more and more to be replaced by the need for holding one's own in

[4] Eleanor Rowland Wembridge, *Life among the Lowbrows*, Boston, Houghton Mifflin Co., 1931, p. 64.

[5] Chicago *Daily News*, September 14, 1944.

[6] Lawrence K. Frank, "Social Change and the Family," *Annals of the American Academy of Political and Social Science*, CLX, March, 1932, 99.

a world of comparative strangers and for conforming to values derived largely from the newspaper, radio, advertisements, and moving pictures. Values derived from these commercialized sources are secular rather than sacred, superficial rather than deeply rooted, unstable rather than long-lived. In this world the individual is, in a sense, free to make choices. But if he has not acquired a sound basis for judgment, he may become a prey to any influence which happens to come along. Much of the freedom of American life appears, in fact, to be of this sterile and empty sort, the understandings derived from casual association being too slight and impermanent to provide a basis for common action.

Conceptions of the family which go no further than individual liberty would appear, therefore, inadequate for a society which is to be organized on the basis of concensus. Consensus is important, and, if we wish to know what role the American family plays in creating it, we shall have to do more than study it from the point of view of conflict and accommodation in marriage and of the formation of personality in the young. "Family culture" is a recognized but little explored concept in sociology. This is the very aspect of family living in which one would expect the sociologist, as distinguished from the social psychologist, to be interested. Nevertheless, in spite of the masses of material on the family, statistical, historical, ethnological, except for a few brief discussions of families among certain marginal groups such as the mountaineers[7] and the Mexican migrant families, there is little or no concrete material on American family life from this point of view. It is true that there are studies of family disorganization, but where are the studies on the organizing elements, such as family morale, family rituals, family jokes and language? Yet for those interested in the content rather than in the formal organization of American life, the lack of these elements of cultural integration may mean not only that the family is weak, but that in an important sense it is not a family at all. We may ask again, when is a family not a family but simply an aggregate of individuals? The view here is that unless there is some form of cultural organization relating the members of a household to each other, there is no family in the sociological sense.

On the whole, we have tended not to question or examine very closely our own system of family organization. We have recognized

[7] Carle G. Zimmerman and Merle E. Frampton, *Family and Society*, New York, D. Van Nostrand & Co., 1935.

the sense of personal insecurity which a "broken home" may create
in the individual. Moreover, psychiatrists, once concerned with difficulties arising from over-attachments in the family, now seem to be
turning their attention to the results of insufficient paternal affection.
Anna Freud, in her studies of institutionalized infants in wartime
England, emphasizes the importance of identification with the mother,
or substitute mother, in bending the young child's will toward socially
accepted behavior—which becomes the basis for moral character.[8]

But, as sociologists, we have not been concerned with the question
of whether the exceeding casualness of some present-day homes does
for their members that which families in the past did for theirs—
namely, provide a sense of security derived from status in a group of
which they are permanent members, initiate into a consistent mode
of procedure so that there may be some standards for action
and principles of right and wrong, and create an attachment to certain
rituals which not only give color to life but also supply in certain areas
of existence sacred rather than secular values. The answer to this question is important, for it concerns a function of the family which,
unlike the service functions, cannot, it appears, be very successfully
transferred to other agencies. That it is a function of first importance
remains to be demonstrated, however. For if adaptability is rated the
prime virtue in family organization, then a continuous dilution of
family culture, in line with the weakening of cultural patterns generally,
is desirable. An understanding of family culture in the United States
today can be most easily gained by applying the general concept of
culture to its analysis.

How do cultures arise in the first place? They do not burst forth full
blown, but, as in the case of plants, from many small beginnings only
a few, to whom chance has given specially favorable conditions, will
grow, develop, and at length flower. What are the conditions which
favor cultural development? At the risk of restating the familiar, it
may be said that a first necessary condition is that of a continuing,
intimate relationship among a number of individuals, a number which
shall be large enough to allow for the building up of an organization
of some degree of complexity but not too large to prevent full communication and the handing on of traditions to all its members. A
helpful condition for culture growth is that the group be attached to

[8] Anna Freud and Dorothy T. Burlingham, *Infants without Families: The Case for and
against Residential Nurseries,* New York, International Univ. Press, 1944.

a fixed position on the earth's surface. This not only aids in the preservation of the continuity of the culture but tends to create an intimacy with the natural environment so that at length the ways of living of the individuals of the group become adapted to and even expressive of their habitat. The physical environment is then a common basis for sentiment as well as for traditional behavior. In order that a culture may acquire a distinctive form, a certain amount of isolation from outside influence is needed. The culture group is an in-group: its members value their own ways beyond those of outsiders and are united against them. On the other hand, under too great conditions of isolation there is no stimulus for development and expansion. It is a commonplace that the great civilizations of the world have resulted from the contact and fusion of many cultural elements. But the new elements must be introduced slowly enough so that they can be absorbed and adapted to the existing structure without any sharp breakdown of sacred traditions. For it is of the essence of culture that it builds up values and traditions which are sacred, which are expressed in special symbols, and which are reinforced and reanimated by great festivals in which all members of the group take part.

In the light of these well-known ideas, it may be asked how the modern American family, as we normally see it, conforms to these conditions. Generally speaking, it is a small group, except in the case of some families of the lower incomes. No scientific study has been made, I believe, of the relation of a vigorous family life to the size of the family. It is clear that not all large families are well organized from the fact of size alone. Yet those who have had personal experience with larger family groups will testify that, other conditions being favorable, one finds here a more highly developed and active community life than in a small family group. In a large, well-organized family it is the older children who tend to bring up the younger, especially in the matter of family traditions, for children are essentially conservative in these matters. In the large family each individual derives status and a measure of security from his position in the family, the elder generally enjoying a sense of responsibility and the prestige of superior knowledge and experience, the younger the sense of lowered responsibility and somewhat more indulgence. In the small family the individual may have greater freedom of movement, but he will tend to lack the experience of a rich and interesting communal life. In the American culture small families and high standards of living are generally assumed to be the better choice.

As for attachment to the earth's surface, American families are notably mobile. Although we may sentimentalize about the "old plantation" and "down on the farm," few individuals actually possess an old homestead to return to if they would. A city apartment cannot even be sentimentalized about. In urban neighborhoods, before the shortages of wartime housing, Moving Day on the first of May was a recognized day in the calendar, and many moved from one apartment to another every year or so. Attachment to a neighborhood, or to a city as a whole, such as the New Yorker's feeling for New York, or to a region such as the South, the East, or the West Coast is probably greater than to any specific building or location, but even this does not appear to be of very great importance. Sentiment for the small town of one's origin appears to be considerable (Margaret Mead comments on this in *And Keep Your Powder Dry*), but it is not enough to keep people from moving away and settling elsewhere.

Even where families appear to have made the effort to take root by buying land in a country location and building their own home, a new turn of events or a profitable financial arrangement will easily lead them to sell and move on. The influence of the frontier in American life, as Turner pointed out, has been such as to give a fluid and expansive character to American institutions. In those sections of the country, such as New England and the old South, where the influence of the frontier was less powerful and less movement took place, property was passed down from one generation to the next and family life and family feeling, pride, and traditions were also more highly developed. In present-day society, however, the old order has been largely broken up and sectional differences are no longer very marked.

That cultural traditions tend to be broken up by the mere act of moving from one environment to another is clear from the history of our own country. For man's very survival, old habits have had to be changed and new ones, better suited to the situation, adopted. Only a homogeneous culture with strongly developed family life, one in which traditions are supported by strong religious sanctions, seems able to survive the test of transplantation. And even this culture will crumble in time and tend to conform to the world about it unless the community is segregated by religious or other doctrine or through prejudice. Families, small cells in a larger organism, can only rarely, under the guidance of specially strong-minded individuals, survive the impact of disintegrating forces from the outside. In general, although the older generation of an immigrant people clings to the old ways, in an expanding world it lacks sufficient strength and prestige to combat the indifference or hostility of the younger generation. Often the continuity of tradition is broken by the fact that the grandparents are no longer close at hand to keep the family memories vivid. In periods of rapid change, rational and pragmatic or, on a lower level of morality, opportunistic attitudes toward life necessarily develop. As a nation of immigrants who have enjoyed great material and geographic expansion, we have fallen heir to many tag-ends of custom and belief but to few sacred values. Of our national holidays, only Christmas and, to a lesser extent, Thanksgiving retain the character of genuinely holy days. And even the significance of the rituals retained here may be minimized as originating in "the desire of parents to please children and to repeat in the lives of their own children some of the incidents upon which the idealized memories of their own childhood are based"[9] rather than viewed as the handing on of important sacred traditions. Mother's Day, originally promoted by the florists, and still a source of profit to them, has its whole point in an organization of society in which parents and children lose touch with one another. American family life, even when well established, has never been inclined to face inward—witness the American front porch and unenclosed back yard as compared with the Englishman's walled garden.

In England, side by side with the passionate wish to preserve the integrity of the family, there is the determination to keep it as a whole as *separate* as possible from other families and from any outside intrusion. There was for a long time in this country an inherent dislike of flats amongst the rich and poor alike, because to share a staircase or lift with another family, to have another family overhead or underneath was considered a violation of that privacy which is the family's inalienable right. . . . . This is not a prejudice only of the poor. There is hardly a garden in England which is not surrounded by wall or hedge or railing, the obscurer the better. There is hardly a London Square garden which is not protected from the public by padlock and key. There is hardly a window in any family house which is not curtained effectively to obscure the view of the inquisitive passerby.[10]

9 Willard Waller, *The Family, A Dynamic Interpretation*, New York, Cordan Co., 1938, p. 478.
10 Margery Spring Rice, *Working Class Wives*, Harmondsworth Middlesex, England: Penguin Books, 1939, pp. 15-16.

American families, on the other hand, strive neither for privacy nor for that family unity which would get in the way of the free movement of their members. In other societies than our own the lack of firm family ties is often made up for by a strong community organization. But community organization is for the most part lacking in America. It is true that in our small towns one is likely to find more orderliness and safety, less juvenile delinquency, and fewer divorces than in the urban environment. In such communities individuals become more "socialized" in the sense in which the nursery schools use this term: trained to get on with their fellows. But pressures here too often are toward a superficial conformity toward an outmoded "middle-class morality" rather than toward building an adherence to moral principles adapted to the expanding universe. As a result, only the more backward and less aggressive have tended to accept the domination of the small community. Forward-looking individuals find new values in the freer atmosphere of the city, but these values tend not to be integrated one with another or with the traditional values of the past. Family life in our large cities is, as Burgess points out, adapted to its environment. In admitting this, one also admits that it is largely adapted to chaos. Culture, in the sense of a body of common understandings enabling the group to act effectively toward the realization of recognized values, is largely lacking both in families and in communities. This lack has come to be so marked that it is even recognized by city planners who, starting with architectural reforms, have now moved on to the more primary problem, as they see it, of reorganizing and re-creating social groups.

The culture of a family or strongly organized community provides, then, to the individual an intimate personal attachment to a way of life as well as to other human beings, a sense of participation in and personal responsibility for the activities of the group, and ultimately a conviction as to what constitutes the values in life worth living and dying for. That we do have some culture in this sense in America seems clear from the existence of a well-defined and generally accepted "American Creed"—the dignity and worth of the individual. But the fact that we tend rather to pay lip service than to take effective action in accordance with this creed points to a divorce of principles from practice. Morality rests not merely upon a rational acceptance. It requires an emotional attachment which can be effectively established only early in life. A moral order cannot be built by passing a law, as we continue to find out to our cost, nor can social values often be effectively taught by precept in school to children who have had no experience of them at home. Weakness in the family, therefore, unless some adequate substitute be supplied, means a weakening of the whole social structure. The problem of right family relations becomes a more complex one than that of merely allowing full freedom of expression to all the members. Nor can we simply return to older, more rigid forms of family organization. A narrow family or group loyalty which lays the basis for humanity does not necessarily enable a man to function well in a changing world. As in the re-creation of democracy generally, we must have more than mere freedom of action—rather a freedom defined within freely accepted limits. It is a task of social science to define these limits as well as to set up a goal for future planning. We may mention in the following paragraphs some of the more obvious limitations which our present social organization and ideals seem to impose upon family development.

In the foregoing pages there is some account of elements which tend to lead to a strong family organization: a large family attached to a homestead, with a rich heritage of tradition, enough cut off from others to develop a distinctive form of life, having to experience no sudden change. How can we expect to realize any of these conditions at the present time? Lewis Mumford, in advocating a revival of family life, urges the larger family and the spacious house, but we can hardly expect any but those in certain small favored groups to respond (thereby reversing the phenomenon that people with small incomes have large families and vice versa). Children have generally ceased to be an economic asset and thus, unless we expect greatly to reduce our standards of living, we cannot expect a notable increase in the size of families. Nor will the owning of one's own home come to be more practical in the future than it is today, we may suggest, for the masses of our urban population. The rebuilding of our cities in such a way as to create smaller and more intimate communities focused around neighborhood centers should do much to encourage family life as well as to improve living conditions generally. Given half a chance, the unsophisticated human being seems to enjoy a family. Cities have tended to break up families. Yet, the *anomie* and loneliness of the city have created a special need for the warmth of intimate response. Given community centers and a more intimate community life, community ceremonials and festivals might, as in village life, supplement the bareness of individual family existences.

With the diversity of America's cultural origins, we have no lack of traditions to build upon. A relaxation of the pressure from commercial interests to throw away the old and buy the new (even in the war year of 1943 Marshall Field's was advertising "Your Home is not a Home unless it is Changing") might open the way toward developing some sense of the enduring value of the old and familiar. If we are to have impermanent home sites, let us at least preserve some Lares and Penates. Laura Ingalls Wilder, in a series of accounts of her childhood in a pioneer family, tells how, in the log cabin in the forests of Wisconsin, the sod hut in Indian territory, and the frame house on the prairies of Dakota, the children knew that when the fiddle and the Bible were taken out and the china shepherdess put on the shelf of the carved corner cupboard, they were again at home. Perhaps even the modern architect, with his somewhat rigid ideas of functionalism, may come to see the function of certain nonrational aspects of life which involve a clinging to the past. And though we can hardly hope in this country for the introduction of the family shrine, the preservation of family pictures and family records may come to be seen as sometimes based on a deeper impulse than that of mere snobbishness.

American family life has suffered not only from physical limitations but also from lack of prestige. The annual selection of the "Mother of the Year" is an exceptional attempt to focus attention upon the homemaker; more energetic and able American women tend rather to win recognition by competing with men. Moreover, unless she takes over the rearing of her grandchildren, the mother of several children will have a number of years—perhaps two-thirds of her life, including the years before marriage—in which she is not functioning as a mother. The active mother-in-law is a stock figure of fun, and, although the grandmother has a place in the family circle, she rarely grows to be a matriarch.

Others have commented on the fact that although American women are freer than most other women, they have often not known what to do with their freedom. This seems to come from the fact that beyond the roles of glamour girl and nursemaid, the part to be played by women is but vaguely defined in our society. Even in the matter of bringing up a family, the definition tends to be negative rather than positive. In the past, the conviction that they were engaged in a worthwhile task gave to parents strength and stimulation. Child psychologists, however, while, on the one hand, aiding parents by increasing the store of knowledge of the needs of childhood have, on the other hand, partly tended to destroy their self-confidence. The "divine right of parents" has been replaced by the fear of creating harmful complexes. Timid parents feel helpless and inadequate and tend both to be dominated by and to create insecurity in their offspring. An emphasis on the duties rather than on the joys of parenthood often makes an already difficult task still more so. Parents who continually do things *for* their children rather than *with* them may enjoy the pleasures of self-sacrifice, but neither they nor the children will experience the deeper satisfaction which comes from a genuinely developed family life. Family life, to repeat, develops not merely from physical proximity nor from kind attentions but from the sharing of common aims, pleasures, and understandings. Suppressed boredom is no substitute for genuine parental enthusiasm. Learning to enjoy family life —singing around the piano, walking in the woods, reading a well-loved book, even listening to a favorite radio program or going to a good movie together, but particularly celebrating family events, birthdays and holidays—seems to be one of the prime requisites for creating a healthy and effectively family life. Thus is created the store of family memories which in times of crisis reinforce the ties of natural affections. Bare as American family life is of ritual, it has tended to have a good deal of this sort of family fun.

But family life is not based simply upon the sharing of pleasures. It also derives its strength from a sense of standing together as a group, of struggling against difficulties, economic or otherwise, of standing for something. American families, except for a few on farms, do not generally work together to build up the family income. In the easy, comfortable life of our middle class there has been little need for promoting a sense of responsibility in all family members for the maintenance of the home. Basically, in most homes, there is less to be done now than in the past and thus less need for sharing the labor.

More fundamental than this sort of participation is the need for sharing a common goal. Most American parents, unsure of just what they do stand for, or even of what they want from life, pass on to their children no more than a vague adherence to an "American Way," in which democratic ideals are often obscured by prejudiced practices and the maintenance of a high standard of living is confused with the traditions of the forefathers. Young people in Gary, Indiana, discussing racial prejudices in the schools, decided that it was hopeless to try to educate their parents. So long as parents lag behind in both their realistic and idealistic approach to problems, so long will parental authority decline. The rapid changes in our civilization are in a sense more difficult for the older than for the younger generation to assimilate. But basic principles of conduct need not vary from generation to generation. These it is which it has always been the function of the older generation to transmit and which constitute an important part of the cultural heritage.

The discussion of parental inadequacies is a well-worn theme. Yet the basic causes of such inadequacies are not always recognized. Men are able to transmit to others only that which they themselves possess. Parents who were themselves never given clear principles for right conduct will be handicapped in defining such principles for their own children. Nor can those who never had a pattern of home-making placed before them be expected to be expert in constructing one for themselves. With the disappearance of the more rigid controls of an older society, authority in the modern family rests upon a consensus which is often lacking. Juvenile delinquency grows year by year. Yet sociologists, fearing the crushing of individuality and the loss of freedom of expression, warn of the "psychic dangers of family integration."

Although in our society over-integrated families appear to be rarities, we may assume that such dangers do exist. Being born into a family group does not necessarily assure the newcomer congenial company— and the deviator in any well-organized group will suffer. Cherishing as we do the concept of the individual, we shall never wish to accept a rigid control. It seems unlikely, however, unless a radical change takes place, that American family organization will develop in the direction of holding on to members who wish to escape. Many of the unadjusted persons in our modern society now appear to be not so much the products of an overdeveloped familism as of having grown up in an incomplete or only partially functioning family. A successfully integrated individual experiences compulsion without suffering from it since he finds the highest expression of his own personality in reinterpreting and reshaping the fundamental pattern offered to him. Moreover, a family formed by the democratic process, in which all members contribute to its shaping and policy, seems to offer in a sense greater freedom than do the pressures of mass organization. We may ask, to what extent can the individual ever really be free? To live in society at all is to accept a series of limitations upon action. Those whose personality has not been shaped by intimate attachments appear not only less human but also more vulnerable. Our complex civilization requires, it seems, a balance between the detachment which makes for adaptability—a detachment aided by the processes of mechanization, standardization, and secularization—and that inward attachment which gives some fixed values and creates some sort of moral order for the individual in spite of rapid changes in the environment. Social scientists, by relating the ideal to the possible, can help to establish this balance. In so doing, however, they will be obliged not only to systematize knowledge but also to set up explicit standards of value in place of the implicit standards with which they now tend to work.

THE FAMILY IN A CHANGING SOCIETY*

ERNEST W. BURGESS

. . . In this country the patterns of family life are so numerous and varied that it appears more appropriate to speak of American families rather than of any homogeneous entity, as implied by the term *"the American family."*

Never before in human history has any society been composed of so many divergent types of families. Families differ by sections of the country, by communities within the city, by ethnic and religious groups, by economic and social classes, and by vocations. They are different according to the family life-cycle and by number and role of family members. They vary by the locus of authority within the family and by widely different styles of life. There are the families of the Hopi Indian (primitive maternal), of the old Amish of Pennsylvania (patriarchal), of the Ozark mountaineers (kinship control), of the Italian immigrant (semipatriarchal), the rooming-house (emancipated), the lower middle class (patricentric), the apartment house (equalitarian), and the suburban (matricentric).

* Adapted and reprinted by permission of the author and publisher from *The American Journal of Sociology*, 53 (1948), 417-23.

Unity in Diversity

With due recognition of all the diversity in American families, it is still possible and desirable to posit the concept of *the* American family. In a sense it is an ideal construction in that it attempts to concentrate attention upon what is distinctive of families in the United States in comparison with those of other countries. These differential characteristics are largely in terms of process rather than of structure and represent relative, rather than absolute, differences from families in other cultures. Chief among these distinctive trends are the following:

1. *Modifiability and adaptability* in response to conditions of rapid social change
2. *Urbanization,* not merely in the sense that the proportion of families living in cities is increasing but that rural, as well as urban, families are adopting the urban way of life
3. *Secularization,* with the declining control of religion and with the increasing role of material comforts, labor-saving devices, and other mechanical contrivances like the automobile, the radio, and television
4. *Instability,* as evidenced by the continuing increase in divorce, reaching in 1945 the proportion of one for every three marriages
5. *Specialization,* on the functions of the giving and receiving of affection, bearing and rearing of children, and personality development, which followed the loss of extrinsic functions, such as economic production, education, religious training, and protection
6. The *trend to companionship,* with emphasis upon consensus, common interests, democratic relations, and personal happiness of family members

These distinctive trends in the American family will not be elaborated. Certain of them, however, will receive additional comment at appropriate places in this paper.

The Family and Society

With all the variations in American families, it is apparent that they are all in greater or less degree in a process of change toward an emerging type of family that is perhaps most aptly described as the "companionship" form. This term emphasizes the point that the essential bonds in the family are now found more and more in the interpersonal relationship of its members, as compared with those of law, custom, public opinion, and duty in the older institutional forms of the family.

The point is not that companionship, affection, and happiness are absent from the institutional family. They exist there in greater or less degree, but they are not its primary aims. The central objectives of the institutional family are children, status, and the fulfillment of its social and economic function in society.

The distinctive characteristics of the American family, as of the family in any society, are a resultant of (1) survivals from earlier forms of the family, developing under prior or different economic and social conditions; (2) the existing social and economic situation; and (3) the prevailing and evolving ideology of the society.

1. Survivals. The American family has had a rich and varied historical heritage, with strands going back to all European countries and to the religious ideologies of the Catholic, Jewish, and Protestant faiths. What is distinctive in the American family, however, has resulted from its role, first, in the early rural situation of the pioneer period, and, second, in the modern urban environment.

The growth of democracy in the family proceeded in interaction with the development of democracy in society. Pioneer conditions promoted the emancipation both of women and of youth from subordination to the family and to the community. Arrangements for marriage passed from the supervision of parents into the control of young people.

The rural family of the United States before World War I, however, had progressed toward, but had not achieved, democratic relations among its members. Control was centered in the father and husband as the head of the farm economy, with strict discipline and with familistic objectives still tending to be dominant over its members. Children were appraised in terms of their value for farm activities, and land tenure and farm operations were closely interrelated with family organization and objectives.

2. The Evolving Urban Environment. The modern city, growing up around the factory and serving as a trade center for a wide area, provided the necessary conditions for the development of the distinctive characteristics of the American family. It still further promoted the equality of family members and their democratic interrelationships, initiated and fostered to a certain degree by the rural pioneer environment. In the urban community the family lost the extrinsic functions which it had possessed from time immemorial and which continued, although in steadily diminishing degrees, in the rural family. The urban family ceased to be, to any appreciable extent, a unity of economic production. This change made possible a relaxation of authority and regimentation by the family head. Then, too, the actual or potential employment of wife and children outside the home signified their economic independence and created a new basis for family relations. In the city the members of the family tended to engage in recreational activities separately, in their appropriate sex and age groups. Each generation witnessed a decline of parental control over children.

This increased freedom and individualization of family members and their release from the strict supervision of the rural neighborhood was naturally reflected in the instability of the family. The divorce rate has averaged a 3 per cent increase each year since the Civil War.

Urbanization involves much more than the concentration and growth of population. It includes commercialization of activities, particularly recreational; specialization of vocations and interests; the development of new devices of communication: telephone, telegraph, motion picture, radio, the daily newspaper, and magazines of mass circulation. All these still further promote the urbanization and secularization of families residing not only in cities but even in remote rural settlements.

3. The Ideology of American Society. Democracy, freedom, and opportunity for self-expression are central concepts in the American ideology. The frontier situation favored their expression in the social, economic, and political life of the people. As they found articulation in the American creed, they reinforced existing tendencies toward democracy and companionship within the family.

Urban life in its economic aspects provided less opportunity than did the rural environment for the exemplification of the American ideology. For example, the development of big business and enormous industries decreased the opportunities for the husband and father to run his own business. But the city greatly increased the economic freedom and independence of the wife and children by providing employment outside the home. The social conditions of the modern city led to the emancipation of family members from the institutional controls of the rural family. The urban family tended to become an affectional and cultural group, united by the interpersonal relations of its members.

The Family in Process

The paradox between the unity and the diversity of the American family can be understood in large part by the conception of the family in process. This means, first of all, that it is in transition from earlier and existing divergent forms to an emergent generic type and, second, that it is in experimentation and is developing a variety of patterns corresponding to the subcultures in American society.

1. The Family in Transition. Much of what is termed the "instability" of the American family arises from the shift to the democratic companionship type from the old-time rural family of this country and the transplanted old-world family forms of immigrant groups.

Many of the current problems within the family are to be explained by the resulting conflicting conceptions in expectations and roles of husbands and wives and of parents and children. The husband may expect his wife to be a devoted household slave like his mother, while she aspires to a career or to social or civic activities outside the home. Immigrant parents attempt to enforce old-world standards of behavior upon their children, who are determined to be American in appearance, behavior, and ideas.

2. The Family in Experimentation. The changes taking place in the family have constituted a vast experiment in democracy. Hundreds of thousands of husbands and wives, parents and children, have participated in it. Couples have refused to follow the pattern of the marriages of their parents and are engaged in working out new designs of family living more or less of their own devising. This behavior has been fully in accord with the ideals and practices of democracy and has exemplified the American ideology of individual initiative and opportunity for self-expression.

This experiment in family formation, while apparently proceeding by individual couples, has been essentially collectivistic rather than pluralistic behavior. Each couple has naturally cherished the illusion that it was acting on its own. To be sure, individual initiative and risk-taking were involved.[1] Many individual ventures have ended in disaster. But actually it has been a collective experiment in the sense that the couples were acting under the stimulus of current criticisms of family life and were attempting to realize in their marriage the new conceptions of family living disseminated by the current literature, presented by the marriages of friends, or developed in discussion by groups of young people.

[1] See Floyd Dell, *Love in Greenwich Village,* New York, Doubleday, Doran & Co., Inc., 1926.

Adaptability versus Stability

In the past, stability has been the great value exemplified by the family and expected of it by society. This was true because the family was the basic institution in a static society. American society, however, is not static but dynamic. The virtue of its institutions do not inhere in their rigid stability but in their adaptability to a rapid tempo of social change.

The findings of two recent studies underscore the significance of adaptability for the American family. Angell began his study of the family in the depression with the hypothesis that its degree of integration would determine its success or failure in adjustment to this crisis.[2] He found, however, that he needed to introduce the concept of adaptability to explain why certain families, highly integrated and stable before the depression, failed, and why some moderately integrated families succeeded, in adjusting to the crisis. A restudy of these cases indicated that adaptability was more significant than integration in enabling families to adjust to the depression.

Another study[3] arrived at a similar conclusion. In predicting success and failure in marriage, data were secured from couples during the engagement period. Certain couples with low prediction scores were later found to be well adjusted in their marriage. The explanation seemed to lie in the adaptability of one or both members of the couple, which enabled them to meet and solve successfully difficult problems as they developed in the marriage.

Adaptability as a personal characteristic has three components. One is psychogenic and represents the degree of flexibility in the emotional reaction of a person to a shift from an accustomed to a different situation. The second component is the tendency of the person as culturally or educationally determined to act in an appropriate way when entering a new situation. The third component of adaptability is the possession of knowledge and skills which make for successful adjustments to a new condition.

Successful marriage in modern society with its divergent personalities, diversity of cultural backgrounds, and changing conditions depends

[2] Robert C. Angell, *The Family Encounters the Depression,* New York, Charles Scribner's Sons, 1936.

[3] See E. W. Burgess and Paul Wallin, "Engagement and Marriage," chapter on "Adaptability" (unpublished manuscript).

more and more upon the adaptability of husbands and wives and parents and children. The crucial matter, then, becomes the question of the adaptability of the family as a group, which may be something different from the adaptability of its members.

The growing adaptability of the companionship family makes for its stability in the long run. But it is a stability of a different kind from that of family organization in the past, which was in large part due to the external social pressures of public opinion, the mores, and law. The stability of the companionship family arises from the strength of the interpersonal relations of its members, as manifested in affection, rapport, common interests and objectives.

Flexibility of personality is not sufficient to insure adaptability of the family to a changing society. Its members should also be culturally and educationally oriented to the necessity for making adjustments. For example, the prospects of successful marriage would be greatly improved if husbands on entering wedded life were as predisposed in attitudes as are wives to be adjustable in the marital relation. Finally, adaptability in marriage and family living demands knowledge and skills on the part of family members. These are no longer transmitted adequately by tradition in the family. They can be acquired, of course, the hard way by experience. They can best be obtained through education and counseling based upon the findings of social science research . . .

CHAPTER 3

The Japanese Family in a Changing Society

Chapter 2 presented the cataclysmic change which has occurred in the family in America and in industrialized areas throughout the rest of Western society. Such change, however, is not unique to the Occident. It is discernible in Japan, which began this transition more recently than did the nations of the West. This transition is captured in the two vignettes by Sugimoto—a betrothal arranged in the traditional manner, and a defiance of tradition in the form of an escape from an arranged marriage.

The remaining articles concern the traditional Japanese family. Embree's contribution is a detailed description of it. He reports that this type of family was usual in the villages and in the upper classes before World War II. Winch summarizes some of the most representative literature tracing the impact of the traditional Japanese family upon personality development in Japan.

OLD LOVE AND NEW*

ETSU INAGAKI SUGIMOTO

The Honourable All Ordains

This family council was the largest that had been held since Father's death. Two gray-haired uncles were there with the aunts, besides two other aunts, and a young uncle who had come all the way from Tokyo on purpose for this meeting. They had been in the room for a long time, and I was busy writing at my desk when I heard a soft "Allow me to speak!" behind me, and there was Toshi at the door, looking rather excited.

"Little mistress," she said with an unusually deep bow, "your honourable mother asks you to go to the room where the guests are."

I entered the big room. Brother was sitting by the *tokonoma,* and next to him were two gray-haired uncles and the young uncle from Tokyo. Opposite sat Honourable Grandmother, the four aunts, and Mother. Tea had been served and all had cups before them in their hands. As I pushed back the door they looked up and gazed at me as if they had never seen me before. I was a little startled, but of course I made a low, ceremonious bow. Mother motioned to me, and I slipped over beside her on the mat.

"Etsu-ko," Mother said very gently, "the gods have been kind to you, and your destiny as a bride has been decided. Your honourable brother and your venerable kindred have given much thought to your future. It is proper that you should express your gratitude to the Honourable All."

I made a long, low bow, touching my forehead to the floor. Then I went out and returned to my desk and my writing. I had no thought of asking, "who is it?" I did not think of my engagement as a personal matter at all. It was a family affair. Like every Japanese girl, I had known from babyhood that sometime, as a matter of course, I should marry, but that was a faraway necessity to be considered when the time came. I did not look forward to it. I did not dread it. I did not think

* Adapted and reprinted by permission of the publisher from *A Daughter of the Samurai,* New York, Doubleday, Doran & Company, Inc., 1928, pp. 55-8, 88-9.

of it at all. The fact that I was not quite thirteen had nothing to do with it. That was the attitude of all girls. . . .

The Honourable All Defied

I must have been very young when my brother went away, for though I could distinctly recall the day he left, all memory of what went before or came immediately after was dim. I remember a sunny morning when our house was decorated with wondrous beauty and the servants all wore ceremonial dress with the Inagaki crest. It was the day of my brother's marriage. . . .

Ishi and I wandered from room to room, she explaining that the bride for the young master would soon be there. . . .

. . . The "seven-and-a-half-times" messenger in his stiff-sleeved garment . . . had returned from his seventh trip to see if the bridal procession was coming, and though the day was bright with sunshine, was lighting his big lantern for his last trip to meet it halfway—thus showing our eagerness to welcome the coming bride. . . .

Then suddenly something was wrong. Ishi caught my shoulder and pulled me back, and Brother came hurriedly out of Father's room. He passed us with long, swinging strides, never looking at me at all, and stepping into his shoes on the garden step, he walked rapidly toward the side entrance. I have never seen him after that day.

The maiden my brother was to have married did not return to her former home. Having left it to become a bride, she was legally no longer a member of her father's family. This unusual problem Mother solved by inviting her to remain in our home as a daughter; which she did until finally Mother arranged a good marriage for her.

In a childish way I wondered about all the strangeness, but years had passed before I connected it with the sudden going away at this time of a graceful little maid named Tama, who used to arrange flowers and perform light duties. . . . Tama was not a servant. In those days it was the custom for daughters of wealthy tradesmen to be sent to live for a short time in a house of rank, that the maiden might learn the strict etiquette of *samurai* home life. The position was far from menial. . . .

The morning after my brother went away I was going, as usual, to pay my morning greetings to my father when I met Tama coming from his door, looking pale and startled. She bowed good morning to me and then passed quietly on. That afternoon I missed her and Ishi told me that she had gone home.

Whatever may have been between my brother and Tama I never knew; but I cannot but feel that, guilt or innocence, there was somewhere a trace of courage. . . . In that day there could be only a hopeless ending to such an affair, for no marriage was legal without the consent of parents, and my father, with heart wounded and pride shamed, had declared that he had no son.

It was not until several years later that I heard again of my brother. One afternoon Father was showing me some twisting tricks with a string. . . . A maid came to the door to say that Major Sato, a Tokyo gentleman whom my father knew very well, had called. . . . I shall never forget that scene. Major Sato, speaking with great earnestness, told how my brother had gone to Tokyo and entered the Army College. With only his own efforts he had completed the course with honour and was now a lieutenant. There Major Sato paused.

My father sat very still with his head held high and absolutely no expression on his stern face. For a full minute the room was so silent that I could hear myself breathe. Then my father, still without moving, asked quietly, "Is your message delivered, Major Sato?"

"It is finished," was the reply.

"Your interest is appreciated, Major Sato. This is my answer: I have daughters, but no son."

FAMILY AND HOUSEHOLD IN A JAPANESE VILLAGE*

John F. Embree

The Family

In Japan, as in all countries, the basic social unit is the family. Where Japanese society differs from American is in the fact that the Japanese family group is usually larger and the network of rights and duties between the members is more clearly defined. The European family system as found in prewar France resembled that of Japan in many ways.

* Adapted and reprinted by permission of the publisher from *The Japanese Nation,* New York, Farrar & Rinehart, 1945, pp. 152-62.

The Japanese family consists of the family head and his wife, the eldest son of this couple and his wife and children and any unmarried children of the head. Thus the "normal" Japanese family living in one household includes two elementary family units.

In addition to this basic or "immediate" family there is the extended family group consisting of the brothers and sisters of all male members of the house, and children of the family head who may have married or been adopted out. This extended kin group assembles on the occasion of weddings and funerals and may form a mutual-aid group in the event that one or another member needs assistance either in labor or in money.

Family ties are reinforced by emphasis on ancestral worship, *i.e.,* maintenance of ancestral tablets, and Buddhist memorial services for deceased family members. Until the Meiji restoration only families of the *samurai* and noble classes used family names. Farmers and workers legally and officially had only personal names and for identification were referred to by their occupation or place of abode. Every family today has its own name and its own crest, which is reproduced on the formal *kimono* worn by family members, and in wealthy families may be found on its lacquer ware and chests for clothing.

The family name is a very important thing in Japan, something to be kept always shining. In feudal times one of the worst punishments was for a *samurai* to have his house, *i.e.,* his family name, extinguished, and today the fear of a bad record being placed in one's official record (*koseki*) is a serious matter even in poor families and those which have acquired names since Tokugawa times. It is a disgrace not only to one's own character but to the good name of the family, deceased, living, and yet to be born.

Rich and noble families have their own family codes governing the behavior of members, and all important decisions such as financial investments, foreign travel, and in some families even marriage and divorce are subject to the approval of a family council consisting of the older family heads of the chief and branch families, sometimes also including the widows of deceased family heads. Thus in the upper classes there is a family government by consultation and group decision.

The roles of the various family members are well defined. The male head of the house is the final authority within his family. His family rank is recognized by his being the first to be served at mealtime, the first to use the family bath, but not the first to arise in the morning.

He is the sole owner of most of the family property and income and he dispenses money to the various members of his family as they may need it. The house head represents his family in dealings with outsiders and with the local and national government. While he has the various rights just outlined, he also has heavy responsibilities and must look to the prosperity of the house and welfare of its members.

The wife is mistress in her own house, being in charge of the servants, the household budget, and the family shopping. She is the one to look after the children's needs, and such family matters as preschool education and marriage arrangements. All domestic work is done by the wife of the head assisted by her daughters and maidservants. If the eldest son of the head is married, the daughter-in-law is expected to take over much of this work. Since the daughter-in-law is dominated by the older woman, friction may develop which in turn may lead to a divorce, especially in the early stages of a marriage. The wife does not get out of the home so much as her husband and in middle-class urban areas her social life is largely limited to family affairs and women's groups.

The eldest son, as heir to the headship, is usually trained in the occupation of his father, taught respect for the family ancestors, and inculcated with a sense of responsibility to fit him for succession to his father's estate and position. Younger sons must not only obey and respect their father but also their elder brother as prospective head of the family. On the other hand, their responsibilities are fewer and they have a freer choice of profession.

Daughters, lowest in the family hierarchy, learn the domestic arts from their mother and acquire attitudes of respect for their parents and brothers. In general, age rank is important, older family members having greater rights than younger ones and in turn having obligations to look after the welfare of younger brothers and sisters.

A family head and his wife when they reach the age of sixty may wish to resign as active members of the family and go into retirement. This procedure and state of retirement is known as *inkyo*. The retired persons may dwell in a separate room or even a separate small house free from the duties and responsibilities of running a family and household, participating only in family festivals, weddings, and funerals.

Social status in a community is dependent on family status. In an upper-class family the eldest son maintains the status of his father, but a younger brother who establishes a branch family has as a rule a somewhat lower social standing. A daughter's status depends ultimately on that of the man she marries and this in turn may affect that of the family into which she was born.

Adoption

The importance of the family name is reflected in the widespread custom of adoption. Through adoption the maintenance of the ancestral tablets is assured, as well as the continuity of the family itself.

If a couple have no son they solve the problem by adopting one, frequently a younger son of the family head's brother. If a couple have a daughter but no son, a son may be adopted to marry the daughter. Occasionally, in the event of no children, but as a means of maintaining the family line, a daughter, often a niece, is adopted and then a son to marry her. Still another form of adoption is one whereby a man with no sons may adopt as a son his own younger brother who is fifteen or twenty years his junior. In business families, if the own son of the head of the firm does not take to commerce, a son may be adopted from among the more promising men in the firm.

The primary function of adoption is to insure heirs, but an associated function is to insure the prosperity and good name of the family; hence the prospective son is carefully chosen, frequently from among the children of one's relatives. Attention is paid to his character, his health, and his general aptitude. Since adopted sons have all the rights and privileges of a real son, adoption by a prosperous business superior or uncle provides a means of rising in the social scale.

Adoptions to be legalized must be recorded in the *koseki*. They may be dissolved if they prove unsatisfactory, a procedure which also requires a legal change in the *koseki* unless, as sometimes happens, the adoption has not yet been recorded.

The custom of adoption in Japanese society makes possible the maintenance of the family independent of the procreative powers of the parents. While family lines may die out from a biological point of view, adoption insures the perpetuity and stability of the family lines as institutions.

The basic family pattern here outlined is found in every town and village; furthermore, it is equally important among the upper classes and in other aspects of Japanese society. Big business houses are conducted on the basis of the head as a father to his employee; in the army older soldiers play the role of elder brothers to newcomers. The nation itself is conceived of as one great family with the Emperor as the head and benevolent father. . . .

The family also attempts to maintain its solidarity and there are in Japan, as in most countries, social and religious sanctions to maintain its integrity. The strong social and economic interdependence of the family members in Japan helps to give solidarity to the family and, through this, stability to the nation. Just as all three forms of social control are united in the Emperor on the national level, so they are again united in the individual family. The master of the household is the civil head and responsible for the good behavior of his family, . . . and his religion serves to unite the family and the nation in a common bond of respect for ancestors—he must not behave in any way to bring disrespect to them or to the family name.

Home and Household

In an earlier day, and even today in rural areas, the important unit of a community was not the individual or even the small family but the household consisting of the immediate family, perhaps an old grandparent or two, and the family servants living together in the home almost as part of the family.

The house in which this household dwells is far more than a simple shelter. Often it has great age and character and always it is under the beneficent protection both of the ancestral spirits whose tablets are kept in some sacred alcove and of various kitchen and household deities to whom flowers or rice and tea are daily offered.

In its physical aspects the Japanese home varies greatly from the simple thatch-roofed house of a farmer to the elegant tile-roofed town and city dwellings with expensive interior woodwork and sliding screens decorated by talented artists. There are a number of basic traits of all Japanese domestic architecture—the houses are of plain unpainted wood with unimposing exteriors, usually of one story, sometimes of two, with a restful horizontal line predominating both inside and out.

The rooms of the house are measured according to the number of three-by-six-foot straw mats or *tatami* they contain. In the parlor or *zashiki* where guests are received, there is a special alcove or *tokonoma* in which is hung a scroll painting (*kakemono*) often set off by a simple-looking but carefully constructed flower arrangement proper to the season or the special occasion. In the *tokonoma* is often hung a picture scroll of the Emperor and of some Shinto or Buddhist deity.

The *tokonoma* is in the "upper" part of the room, the place where honored guests are seated. By observing which guests are seated by the *tokonoma* and which below, one can estimate their relative social rank. In small communities the mayor or headman and the schoolmaster hold high rank as do visiting dignitaries. Older male members of well-to-do local native families also rank high. It is good form to decline the host's first offer of a place by the *tokonoma*.

Sleeping rooms, smaller than the *zashiki,* contain no beds and when night comes, quilts are brought out of a closet and laid on the quiet resilient mats to form mattress and covers. In the kitchen, part of which is often dirt floored, may be found stoves, pots, and jars of various sizes containing supplies of pickled radish, soy bean paste (*miso*), and a kitchen sink of stone or metal-covered wood. In rural areas the stoves are usually brick, heated by wood or charcoal, in the towns oil stoves are coming into use, and in cities oil and gas stoves had tended to replace charcoal ones before the war. The stove is placed at the side of the kitchen away from the rest of the house, probably as an old safety measure. A poster saying beware of fire, given out by the firemen's association, may be pasted somewhere on the wall.

In rural districts, rooms are heated by a fire pit (*irori*) and portable charcoal heaters (*hibachi*). In cities, *hibachi,* oil, gas or electric stove are used. A very popular heater in both rural and urban areas is the *kotatsu,* a lattice-like wooden structure placed over the *irori* and covered with a heavy blanket or quilt. People of all ages like to sit around this heater with their folded knees under the quilted covering. The fire pit and *hibachi* is the center of sociability, the source of heat for the ever present tea kettle, and the place to relight interminably one's diminutive pipe.

The various rooms are separated by sliding screens which may be removed on special occasions, such as a wedding banquet, to double or triple the expanse of a room.

In rural areas there are separate outhouses for toilet and bath but in urban areas these are part of the main structure. Modern plumbing is generally lacking so far as the toilet is concerned, human excreta being used as fertilizer. In most cities this "night-soil" is collected regularly and sold to the farmers. Once when the Tokugawa were thinking of making a government monopoly of this business a local Patrick Henry proposed that, as a protest, the people cease production.

The Japanese bath (*furo*) has its own etiquette, often but poorly understood by foreign visitors. The usual time for the bath is in the early evening either before or after dinner. Before stepping into the deep and very hot water one is expected to wash and rinse oneself— the aim of the deep hot water being not to clean but to warm and relax one. After the guest has bathed, the head of the house may follow, then the wife and children and finally, late in the evening, the servants. In hotels and public baths, several people may occupy a large bath at once, talking and relaxing together in pleasant sociability.

At night wooden shutters are pulled to, to keep out both robbers and night air, and at an ungodly hour of the morning the wife or maidservant noisily opens them again.

Physical privacy is not obtainable in the ordinary Japanese dwelling and there is an accepted household etiquette to provide for privacy by proxy—one simply does not observe people under certain circumstances such as when they are undressed or otherwise not presentable. The closeness of home life, whereby small children are rarely left alone, may have something to do with the adult Japanese tendency to do things together and in groups.

Marriage

Marriage in Japan, as in France, is primarily a family matter and marriages are made on earth to insure the future perpetuation of the family in its proper social class. The primary function of marriage is to provide for heirs to carry on the family name. Equally important is the establishment of an economically interdependent household unit whereby certain occupations are performed by the husband, others by the wife. The lone individual is at both a social and an economic disadvantage in such a society. In accord with this situation whereby the social and economic functions of marriage so far outweigh matters of mere personal fancy, the individual does not take the initiative but rather awaits his family's decision as to a proper spouse.

Since the joining of two families in marriage involves many delicate issues of family background and financial status, great reliance is placed on a go-between or *nakōdo*. When, let us say, a young man's family feels that the time for marriage has arrived, the matter will be discussed with some family friend who may act as go-between. This man and his wife may suggest a number of suitable young ladies of proper social status, and finally, on the suggestion of the boy's parents, they will undertake marriage negotiations with one of these. The initial call of the go-between on the girl's parents will be of the most tentative nature, the subject of a possible marriage being suggested in passing. A good deal will depend on the initial reaction of the girl's family, and if they are opposed to the match, the whole affair may be dropped then and there with no loss of face to anyone concerned.

If all goes well, the go-between will continue his good offices and the girl's family may also find a friend to serve as their representative in the negotiations. In addition to working out the plans of the wedding itself, the go-betweens have the ticklish job of negotiating a suitable dowry, of investigating family backgrounds to discover whether or not there are any family skeletons such as leprosy, insanity, or tuberculosis, and whether there are any particularly evil crimes recorded in the family's *koseki*. All of this is work that by Japanese etiquette the families themselves could not do directly since it could all too easily lead to embarrassing face-to-face situations. The go-between, being a member of neither family, can smooth over any difficult situations that may arise.

The families concerned have definite obligations to the go-between. The bride- and groom-to-be must conduct themselves with propriety if they were to act in any improper way before the marriage arrangements were completed the go-between would lose face by having his efforts nullified. Any direct contacts between two families during this period would also undermine the position of the go-between.

The wedding itself is strictly a family affair to which are invited many relatives of both the bride and the groom. The wedding ceremony proper usually takes place at the groom's home and consists of a ceremonial drink exchange of rice wine (*sansankudo*) between the bride and groom. The go-betweens and their wives are present at this ceremony, which corresponds in ceremonial sanctity to a church service in European countries. The ceremony is followed by a sumptuous banquet at the end of which the bride serves tea to the parting guests— a symbol that she is now the housewife in her husband's home.

In cities some families now have the wedding ceremony in a Shinto shrine according to Shinto rites but this is a post-Meiji development, weddings being traditionally a purely family arrangement. Another urban development is that of holding the wedding banquet in a hotel.

Legal registry of the marriage takes place sometime following the wedding and in rural areas there may be a lapse of many months or even a breakup of the marriage before such registry takes place.

Usually the recording is done sometime before the birth of the first child to insure its legitimacy.

Shortly after the wedding the bride and groom call on the go-between with a gift, partly in return for his good offices and partly in return for his wedding gift. The duties of the marriage go-between do not cease at marriage. In the event of any difficulties between bride and groom he steps in as peacemaker, and, like a relative, he is invited to family affairs such as the naming of the first child or the funeral ceremony after a death.

The new wife now faces a difficult period of adjustment for which her early training in patience stands her in good stead. She must learn the many little customs of her husband's family, she must adopt his family's Buddhist sect, she must please her mother-in-law with her good housekeeping, and finally she must show herself to be a good mother. After the birth of a child, especially a boy, the new wife's status improves considerably, and the bonds of the marriage are greatly strengthened.

At marriage a girl symbolically leaves her family of birth, in some regions even being dressed in white *kimono,* and her name is blotted out of the *koseki* of her parents and entered into that of her husband. Despite all of this, however, a girl usually maintains close ties with her parents, going home the first New Year's after her marriage to visit them. If her husband or his family mistreats her, she may in extreme cases return home. If her parents are of as good or better social standing than those of her husband, the fact that an insult to the girl is also an indirect insult to her family serves to protect her interests.

In the event of a marriage by adoption the whole procedure is re-versed—negotiations are initiated by the girl's family, the marriage takes place in her home and the husband takes her name and is blotted out of the *koseki* of his parents. The personal problems of an adopted husband are greater than those of a bride since he has not had the same training in patience.

A young woman who has a clandestine affair, even though she becomes pregnant, is not because of this fact likely to marry the man of her desire. He may be of the wrong social class and, furthermore, it would be difficult to find a man to sponsor such a match by acting as go-between since his role has been flouted by the couple in question. The usual fate of the unmarried mother is to marry somewhat below the social class of her birth and for her child to be adopted either by her husband or by some other family. Sometimes a couple may elope, with the result that both families are likely to disown them and so make life for the newlyweds most difficult—or the lovers may commit *shinjū*—double suicide.

SOME OBSERVATIONS ON PERSONALITY STRUCTURE IN JAPAN*

Robert F. Winch

In contemporary social psychology it is an article of faith that variation in conditions of living—and hence in experience—are correlated with variation in personality structure, and ultimately in behavior. It is a commonplace, moreover, that various peoples have different cultures and hence different living conditions. Accordingly, we should expect some variation in personality as we move from one culture to another. Such considerations underlie a field of investigation which has come to be known by the title "personality and culture." Military exigency during World War II pressed us to learn as much as possible about our erstwhile enemies, and hence during the early 1940's several attempts were made to describe German and Japanese "national character." More intensive and systematic efforts in the same tradition resulted in Kardiner's concept of the "basic personality structure."[1]

* Original manuscript.

[1] On German "national character" see: H. V. Dicks, *The Psychological Foundations of the Wehrmacht*, London, Directorate of Army Psychiatry, Royal Army Medical Corps, 1944; E. H. Erikson, "Hitler's Imagery and German Youth," in Clyde Kluckhohn and H. A. Murray (eds.), *Personality in Nature, Society, and Culture*, New York, Knopf, 1948, pp. 485-510; D. M. Levy, "The German Anti-Nazi: A Case Study," *American Journal of Orthopsychiatry*, 16, 1946, 507-15; David Rodnick, *Postwar Germans: An Anthropologist's Account*, New Haven, Yale University Press, 1948; Bertram Schaffner, *Father Land: A Study of Authoritarianism in the German Family*, New York, Columbia University Press, 1948; "Germany After the War, Round Table—1945," *American Journal of Orthopsychiatry*, 15, 1945, 381-441. The following are representative studies of Japanese "national character": Ruth Benedict, *The Chrysanthemum and the Sword: Patterns of Japanese Culture*, Boston, Houghton-Mifflin, 1946; Geoffrey Gorer, "Themes in Japanese Culture," *Transactions of the New York Academy of Sciences*, Series II, No. 5, March 1943, 106-24; Douglas G. Haring, "Aspects of Personal Character in Japan," *The Far East Quarterly*, 6, 1946, 12-22; Weston LaBarre, "Some Observations on Character Structure in the Orient: The Japanese," *Psychiatry*, 8, 1945, 319-42. The concept of "basic personality structure" is developed in two books by Abram Kardiner:

Very cogent criticisms have been levelled against such studies: *e.g.,* that the actual observations have generally not been made by persons skilled in psychological techniques, that not enough attention has been paid to intra-cultural variations in behavior, personality, and culture; that the studies have been so poorly designed that it has been virtually impossible for the researchers to subject their hypotheses to critical tests.[2] The impatient reader may conclude from these criticisms that he should dismiss such studies as valueless. To the writer such summary dismissal is a sophomoric solipsism. It is well to beware a portrayal based upon the observations and interpretations of a single writer. And it is pertinent to bear in mind that some statements are more inferential (*e.g.,* those concerning "basic dynamics") than others (*e.g.,* those concerning overt behavior). Since knowledge is so hard to come by and so expensive to develop, therefore, the writer is inclined to accept as tentatively valid evidence and interpretations about "national character" or "basic personality structure" of a people where there is a reasonable degree of consensus between two or more qualified writers. We should give heed to one final note of caution regarding the range of applicability of the following description. For the most part, the studies on which the following report is based have centered upon the more rural and traditional loci of Japanese culture. For this reason the following observations undoubtedly portray more accurately the situation in rural (pre-occupation) Japan than in contemporary urban Japan.

The ethos of Japanese culture differs radically from that of American culture. With us the goals of life are defined in terms of the pursuit of "good," and "good" is conceived in the twofold manner as the opposite of evil and as the source of personal gratification. Not only does Japanese culture deplore personal gratification as a life goal, but it omits the conception of there being any struggle between the forces of good and evil. Rather than the individualistic end of self-validation, the Japanese pursues his course of fulfilling the many obligations of various kinds imposed upon him by his system. Physical pleasures are not condemned.

The Individual and His Society, New York, Columbia University Press, 1939, and *The Psychological Frontiers of Society,* New York, Columbia University Press, 1945.

[2] Representative critiques of studies in culture and personality: Otto Klineberg, "Recent Studies of National Character," in S. S. Sargent and M. W. Smith (eds.), *Culture and Personality,* New York, Viking Fund, 1949, pp. 127-38; A. R. Lindesmith and A. L. Strauss, "Critique of Culture-Personality Writings," *American Sociological Review,* 15, 1950, 587-600.

On the contrary they are sought and valued, but the culture dictates that indulgence in sensual pleasures, which are regarded as being in "the circle of minor relaxation," must not intrude upon the circle of major obligations which constitute the serious business of life.[3] Chief among the physical pleasures defined in Japanese culture are the hot bath, sleeping, eating, drinking, and sex (heterosexual, homosexual, and autoerotic).

In the life of the typical Japanese, Ruth Benedict describes the periods of freedom and indulgence in terms of a U-shaped curve.[4] Thus it is in childhood and in old age that the individual finds his greatest gratifications. On the other hand, after the individual, either male or female, enters adulthood, he is confronted with an imposing array of obligations: to the emperor, to parents, to affinal family, to other relatives, to one's name, etc.

Children are greatly desired by the father for the purpose of assuring continuity of the family line and by the mother because they provide her with the means of rising from a position of subordination (to her mother-in-law) to one of superordination (over her daughter-in-law). It is traditional that the daughter-in-law is submissive, but that she becomes despotic upon acquiring the status of mother-in-law.[5] Since divorce is common, the wedding ceremony gives little assurance that the marriage will be permanent. The birth of the first child, however, is interpreted as a sign of the stability of the marriage. Frequently marriages are not entered in the village records until the wife is pregnant. It is not until she has born her first child that the wife achieves full-fledged membership in the status of married woman. From this time on she may enjoy the privileges of smoking, drinking, and telling sexual jokes.[6]

For the infant the world is indulgent. Whenever he cries, he is given the breast. Not only is he seldom left alone, but he is almost always in contact with the body of his mother or nursemaid.[7] By the age of four months, however, toilet-training may be begun, and the infant may get his first taste of the rigors of Japanese discipline.[8] As he

[3] Ruth Benedict, *op. cit.*, pp. 177, 184-87.

[4] *Ibid.*, p. 254.

[5] *Ibid.*, pp. 124, 255-56.

[6] J. F. Embree, *Suye Mura: A Japanese Village*, Chicago, University of Chicago Press, 1939, p. 182.

[7] *Ibid.*, p. 184; D. G. Haring, *op. cit.*, pp. 16-17.

[8] Geoffrey Gorer, *op. cit.*

begins to walk, not only does he lose the reassurance of bodily contact with mother or nursemaid, but he is rapidly subjected to more and more of the prohibitions of his culture: to eat sparingly and to observe frugality generally, never to show the inside of his mouth, to show respect—by learning at an early age to bow before his elders and to avoid the place of honor in the guest room. Despite the rigors of his early discipline, the infant is not ordinarily weaned for several years unless the mother becomes pregnant sooner.[9]

Training in sex-typed behavior begins at an early age and is especially evident with respect to the expression of aggressive impulses. There is no person toward whom the small girl may act aggressively without incurring strong disapproval. Although the male baby may not express aggression toward older males (authority-figures), he is not forbidden to express it toward all females. By the age of four the boy may be engaging in insolence and physical aggression toward girls and toward his mother. In view of the acceptance of male superiority in Japanese culture, the female's only defenses are cajolery and bribery.[10] Accordingly, mother and sisters indulge and obey the growing boy who learns that it is unmanly to express tenderness and affection toward them, and that it is his right to feel superior to any female.[11]

In school the emphasis has been more upon moral than upon intellectual instruction. Because of the shame which failure in school would bring upon the child's family, teachers in the rural schools see that practically every child is promoted. The consideration of "face" is seen also in scholastic athletic contests where all entrants are accorded prizes.[12]

Irrespective of their social class, it is anticipated in respectable families that the parents will select a son's wife. Considerations of money and genealogy make the choice of a wife a concern of the family rather than of the individual.[13] Marriage is essentially a social and economic arrangement between two families,[14] and the ends of marriage are defined as procreation and continuity of the family line.[15] Thus it is

9 Haring, *op. cit.,* p. 17. Maloney even reports that the babe in arms is put through the motions of paying respect to his father: ". . . the mother pushes the head of the suckling into a bow as the father enters the room." J. C. Maloney, "A Study in Neurotic Conformity: The Japanese," *Complex,* Spring, 1951, 26-32. (Quotation is from p. 26.)

10 Haring, *op. cit.,* p. 18; Weston LaBarre, op. cit., p. 335.

11 Haring, *op. cit.,* pp. 19-20.

12 J. F. Embree, *op. cit.,* p. 188.

13 Benedict, *op. cit.,* pp. 120-21.

14 Embree, *op. cit.,* p. 203.

15 Benedict, *op. cit.,* pp. 184-87.

culturally consistent that one's obligations to his parents should include unquestioning acceptance of the selected spouse.[16]

Romantic love is a "human feeling" which the Japanese cultivate but which is inconsistent with their form of marriage or with their obligations to family.[17] Because of the system of arranged marriages it is not assumed that a couple engaging in sexual relations will be married even if the girl becomes pregnant. In such a case the girl's parents would try to arrange for her marriage before the pregnancy goes to full term. Since it is difficult to arrange a quick marriage for a pregnant daughter, the outcome might well be that she would marry a widower or a man of inferior social status.[18] In view of the approved system of arranged marriages, it is not assumed that there will be any deep bond of affection between man and wife. One writer reinforces this point by stating: "Mutuality in love is excluded by the dogma of female inferiority . . ."[19] Accordingly, the culture dictates an elaborate formality in the marital relationship, and children seldom or never observe any manifestations of marital affection. In childhood, age-groups of the same sex form close relationships which tend to last throughout life. The culture defines these relationships as being closer than those of marriage.[20]

The Japanese husband regards his marital responsibilities as one rather distinct area of a segmented life. His erotic pleasure is another distinct area. Both are open and aboveboard. It is assumed that the husband will seek his erotic pleasure outside the home by supporting a mistress if he can afford one, or else by patronizing a prostitute.[21]

The culture is less considerate in providing techniques of gratifying the wife's unsatisfied erotic impulses. The mode of life in the Japanese household renders difficult a liaison between the wife and another man. It appears that she is expected to gratify her unmet erotic needs by masturbation.[22]

[16] *Ibid.,* pp. 120-21.

[17] Double love-suicides, which constitute a favorite theme in writing and conversation, are viewed as the logical outcome of an unconventional passion which challenges the family system. (Cf. Benedict, *op. cit.,* p. 183; Haring, *op. cit.,* p. 20.) This is similar to the medieval concept of romantic love. (Cf. Winch, *The Modern Family,* New York, Holt, 1952, pp. 370-71.)

[18] Embree, *op. cit.,* p. 195.

[19] Haring, *op. cit.,* p. 20.

[20] Benedict, *op. cit.,* p. 269.

[21] *Ibid.,* pp. 184-87.

[22] Embree states: "The most frequent difficulty of women involves not their social but

For the male, marriage marks a transition in status from "father's son" to "man," and the transition is really completed when the male becomes a father.[23] To the girl, entering into marriage signifies the beginning of a period of subordination to her mother-in-law whom she must seek to please in all respects. If the mother-in-law is not satisfied with the performance of her daughter-in-law, she may order her son to divorce his wife, and irrespective of his degree of satisfaction with her, he is obliged to execute his mother's order. The more satisfied he is with his wife, and, therefore, the more reluctance he might be expected to show over losing her, the greater is his honor for executing his mother's order to divorce her.[24]

Early in this paper we noted Benedict's statement to the effect that infancy and old age are the periods in which the gratification of impulses is relatively free of cultural constraint, and we have already discussed the indulgence shown the young infant. Concerning the later period, Embree notes that in Suye Mura a man or a woman holds a party on attaining the age of sixty-one. This party marks the passage of the individual into the oldest age group, which is regarded as a second childhood. From this time on old people may behave more individualistically; they may demand, and their demands will be met; they may engage in more ribald conversation than would be appropriate for younger persons; they "may do and say what they like without fear of criticism."[25]

It has been observed before that the goal of life is the fulfillment of obligation. The pursuit of this goal involves self-denial perhaps even to the point of suffering. Such self-denial, however, is not regarded as a basis for self-pity, and the Japanese characteristically profess their inability to comprehend the Christian concept of self-sacrifice. Their view is that the suffering and self-denial involved in the fulfillment of obligations tend to strengthen will and character and lead to virtue, and that this is a worthy objective in itself. Hence, self-pity is not an

---

their sexual lives. Many cases of insanity and most of *hysteri* are clearly due to sexual maladjustments. The term *hysteri* is applied to all women who are known for their instability, nervousness, or promiscuity. Occasionally, talking of a man famous for his sexual freedom, a woman will say that 'he has *hysteri*.'" *Op. cit.,* p. 175. Of the Japanese wife Benedict asserts: "when her husband looks elsewhere, she may have recourse to the accepted Japanese custom of masturbation, and, from the peasant village to the homes of the great, women treasure implements for this purpose." *Op. cit.,* pp. 284-85.

23 Embree, *op. cit.,* p. 213.
24 Benedict, *op. cit.,* p. 208.
25 Embree, *op. cit.,* p. 214.

appropriate sentiment. Perhaps the most illuminating statement concerning the difference between the Japanese and American culture is Benedict's assertion that in Japan "strength of character, they think, is shown in conforming not in rebelling."[26] Thus, the son's acceptance of his mother's order to divorce his wife becomes intelligible as an element in ego-enhancement.

Summary

To a considerable degree the contrasts between Japanese culture and that of middle-class America may be summarized in the observation that the former discourages individualism, whereas individualism is at the heart of the American ethos and is the *leitmotif* of the American dream. The goal of life of the Japanese is to fulfill the many obligations he has to family, clan, and state. To the American it is to "make something of himself," and this is generally understood to mean that he should strive to improve the socio-economic status inherited from his parents by performing well and obtaining rewards in the occupational system.

While infancy is a period of relative indulgence in both cultures, the "tapering-off" process appears to begin earlier in Japan with the early introduction of toilet-training and other disciplines. The Japanese strongly emphasize the difference between masculine and feminine behavior. At an early age the Japanese child encounters strong pressures to achieve the appropriate sex-type. Boys have a considerable range of relationships in which they are expected to express aggression and hostility. Girls are trained in passivity and docility. In America males are expected to be somewhat more aggressive than females, but boys are encouraged to sublimate hostile impulses into competitive striving, and the overt expression of hostility is discouraged in both sexes. Whereas in America the Puritan heritage is still evident in our devaluation of sexual and other physical pleasures, the Japanese regards such pleasures without any twangs of conscience.

In individualistic America young adulthood is regarded as the golden period in life. It is then that one has great energy with which to embark upon a career of achievement and that one is at the height of physical attractiveness and is expected to engage in romantic affairs leading to marriage. In familistic Japan the advantages of old-age are emphasized. The elders have fulfilled their obligations. They are en-

[26] Benedict, *op. cit.,* p. 207.

titled to deference, and they are accorded special privileges. It is consistent with their familistic system that not only marriages but also divorces are arranged by the families. Consistent also is the difference in the route to the status of full adulthood: in Japan, marriage and parenthood; in America, chronological age and financial independence of the parents.

Finally, virtue in America consists in internalizing morality, in possessing a highly developed sense of right and wrong, and in rebelling against authority when one's conscience dictates that authority is in the wrong. The emphasis in the handling of self-control in Japan is not so much on the basis of internalized and private morality as upon the fear of ridicule and the loss of "face." Accordingly, the accolade of virtue is bestowed upon conformity.

CHAPTER 4

Structures and Functions of the Family in General and in America

As we turn from one culture to another, we see that the structure and function of the family present great variation. After examining descriptions of 250 societies, Murdock gives a presentation of the structural and functional elements which these family forms have in common. From reports compiled by the Bureau of the Census we find statistical evidence for important changes which have occurred in the structure of the American family since 1890, such as the trends toward earlier marriage and smaller families. Glick reports a change which has come about with urbanization and the rise in level of living and, more precisely, with the decrease in the death rate. This is an increase in the length of the family cycle. Whereas in 1890 it was usual for at least one parent to die before all the children were raised, in 1940 the average parents had several years of life together after the children were reared. Ogburn notes the changes in the family's functions consequent upon a shift from a rural to an urban-industrial social organization.

STRUCTURES AND FUNCTIONS OF THE FAMILY*

GEORGE PETER MURDOCK

The family is a social group characterized by common residence, economic cooperation, and reproduction. It includes adults of both sexes, at least two of whom maintain a socially approved sexual relationship, and one or more children, own or adopted, of the sexually cohabiting adults. The family is to be distinguished from marriage, which is a complex of customs centering upon the relationship between a sexually associating pair of adults within the family. Marriage defines the manner of establishing and terminating such a relationship, the normative behavior and reciprocal obligations within it, and the locally accepted restrictions upon its personnel.

Used alone, the term "family" is ambiguous. The layman and even the social scientist often apply it undiscriminatingly to several social groups which, despite functional similarities, exhibit important points of difference. These must be laid bare by analysis before the term can be used in rigorous scientific discourse.

. . . The most basic type of family, called herewith the *nuclear family,* consists typically of a married man and woman with their offspring, although in individual cases one or more additional persons may reside with them. The nuclear family will be familiar to the reader as the type of family recognized to the exclusion of all others by our own society. Among the majority of the peoples of the earth, however, nuclear families are combined, like atoms in a molecule, into larger aggregates. These composite forms of the family fall into two types, which differ in the principles by which the constituent nuclear families are affiliated. A *polygamous*[1] *family* consists of two or more nuclear families affiliated by plural marriages, *i.e.,* by having one married

---

* Adapted and reprinted by permission of the author and publisher from *Social Structure,* New York, The Macmillan Company, 1949, pp. 1-13.

[1] The terms "polygamy" and "polygamous" will be used throughout this work in their recognized technical sense as referring to any form of plural marriage; "polygyny" will be employed for the marriage of one man to two or more women, and "polyandry" for the marriage of one woman to two or more men.

parent in common.[2] Under polygyny, for instance, one man plays the role of husband and father in several nuclear families and thereby unites them into a larger familial group. An *extended family* consists of two or more nuclear families affiliated through an extension of the parent-child relationship rather than of the husband-wife relationship, *i.e.,* by joining the nuclear family of a married adult to that of his parents. The patrilocal extended family, often called the patriarchal family, furnishes an excellent example. It embraces, typically, an older man, his wife or wives, his unmarried children, his married sons, and the wives and children of the latter. Three generations, including the nuclear families of father and sons, live under a single roof or in a cluster of adjacent dwellings.

. . . The nuclear family is a universal human social grouping. The reasons for its universality do not become fully apparent when the nuclear family is viewed merely as a social group. Only when it is analyzed into its constituent relationships, and these are examined individually as well as collectively, does one gain an adequate conception of the family's many-sided utility and thus of its inevitability. A social group arises when a series of interpersonal relationships, which may be defined as sets of reciprocally adjusted habitual responses, binds a number of participant individuals collectively to one another. In the nuclear family, for example, the clustered relationships are eight in number: husband-wife, father-son, father-daughter, mother-son, mother-daughter, brother-brother, sister-sister, and brother-sister. The members of each interacting pair are linked to one another both directly through reciprocally reinforcing behavior and indirectly through the relationships of each to every other member of the family. Any factor which strengthens the tie between one member and a second, also operates indirectly to bind the former to a third member with whom the second maintains a close relationship. An explanation of the social utility of the nuclear family, and thus of its universality, must consequently be sought not alone in its functions as a collectivity but also in the services and satisfactions of the relationships between its constituent members.

The relationship between father and mother in the nuclear family is solidified by the sexual privilege which all societies accord to married

[2] Cf. M. K. Opler, "Woman's Social Status and the Forms of Marriage," *American Journal of Sociology,* XLIX, 1943, 144; A. R. Radcliffe-Brown, "The Study of Kinship Systems," *Journal of the Royal Anthropological Institute,* LXXI, 1941, 2.

spouses. As a powerful impulse, often pressing individuals to behavior disruptive of the cooperative relationships upon which human social life rests, sex cannot safely be left without restraints. All known societies, consequently, have sought to bring its expression under control by surrounding it with restrictions of various kinds. On the other hand, regulation must not be carried to excess or the society will suffer through resultant personality maladjustments or through insufficient reproduction to maintain its population. All peoples have faced the problem of reconciling the need of control with the opposing need of expression, and all have solved it by culturally defining a series of sexual taboos and permissions. These checks and balances differ widely from culture to culture, but without exception a large measure of sexual liberty is everywhere granted to the married parents in the nuclear family. Husband and wife must adhere to sexual etiquette and must, as a rule, observe certain periodic restrictions such as taboos upon intercourse during menstruation, pregnancy, and lactation, but normal sex gratification is never permanently denied to them. . . .

As a means of expressing and reducing a powerful basic drive, as well as of gratifying various acquired or cultural appetites, sexual intercourse strongly reinforces the responses which precede it. These by their very nature are largely social, and include cooperative acts which must, like courtship, be regarded as instrumental responses. Sex thus tends to strengthen all the reciprocal habits which characterize the interaction of married parents, and indirectly to bind each into the mesh of family relationship in which the other is involved.

To regard sex as the sole factor, or even as the most important one, that brings a man and a woman together in marriage and binds them into the family structure would, however, be a serious error. If all cultures, like our own, prohibited and penalized sexual intercourse except in the marital relationship, such an assumption might seem reasonable. But this is emphatically not the case. Among those of our 250 societies for which information is available, 65 allow unmarried and unrelated persons complete freedom in sexual matters, and 20 others give qualified consent, while only 54 forbid or disapprove premarital liaisons between non-relatives, and many of these allow sex relations between specified relatives such as cross-cousins.[3] Where pre-

---

[3] A cross-cousin is the child of a father's sister or of a mother's brother. The children of a father's brother and of a mother's sister are technically known as "parallel cousins."

marital license prevails, sex certainly cannot be alleged as the primary force driving people into matrimony.

Nor can it be maintained that, even after marriage, sex operates exclusively to reinforce the matrimonial relationship. To be sure, sexual intercourse between a married man and an unrelated woman married to another is forbidden in 126 of our sample societies, and is freely or conditionally allowed in only 24. These figures, however, give an exaggerated impression of the prevalence of cultural restraints against extramarital sexuality, for affairs are often permitted between particular relatives though forbidden with non-relatives. Thus in a majority of the societies in our sample for which information is available a married man may legitimately carry on an affair with one or more of his female relatives, including a sister-in-law in 41 instances. Such evidence demonstrates conclusively that sexual gratification is by no means always confined to the marital relationship, even in theory. If it can reinforce other relationships as well, as it commonly does, it cannot be regarded as peculiarly conducive to marriage or as alone accountable for the stability of the most crucial relationship in the omnipresent family institution. . . .

In view of the frequency with which sexual relations are permitted outside of marriage, it would seem the part of scientific caution to assume merely that sex is an important but not the exclusive factor in maintaining the marital relationship within the nuclear family, and to look elsewhere for auxiliary support. One such source is found in economic cooperation, based upon a division of labor by sex.[4] Since cooperation, like sexual association, is most readily and satisfactorily achieved by persons who habitually reside together, the two activities, each deriving from a basic biological need, are quite compatible. Indeed, the gratifications from each serve admirably to reinforce the other.

By virtue of their primary sex differences, a man and a woman make an exceptionally efficient cooperating unit.[5] Man, with his superior physical strength, can better undertake the more strenuous tasks, such as lumbering, mining, quarrying, land clearance, and housebuilding. Not handicapped, as is woman, by the physiological burdens of pregnancy and nursing, he can range farther afield to hunt, to fish, to herd, and to trade. Woman is at no disadvantage, however, in lighter tasks

[4] See W. G. Sumner and A. G. Keller, *The Science of Society*, New Haven, 1927, III, 1505-18.
[5] *Ibid.*, I, 111-40.

which can be performed in or near the home, *e.g.,* the gathering of vegetable products, the fetching of water, the preparation of food, and the manufacture of clothing and utensils. All known human societies have developed specialization and cooperation between the sexes roughly along this biologically determined line of cleavage.[6] It is unnecessary to invoke innate psychological differences to account for the division of labor by sex; the indisputable differences in reproductive functions suffice to lay out the broad lines of cleavage. New tasks, as they arise, are assigned to one sphere of activities or to the other, in accordance with convenience and precedent. Habituation to different occupations in adulthood and early sex typing in childhood may well explain the observable differences in sex temperament, instead of *vice versa.*[7]

The advantages inherent in a division of labor by sex presumably account for its universality. Through concentration and practice each partner acquires special skill at his particular tasks. Complementary parts can be learned for an activity requiring joint effort. If two tasks must be performed at the same time but in different places, both may be undertaken and the products shared. The labors of each partner provide insurance to the other. The man, perhaps, returns from a day of hunting, chilled, unsuccessful, and with his clothing soiled and torn, to find warmth before a fire which he could not have maintained, to eat food gathered and cooked by the woman instead of going hungry, and to receive fresh garments for the morrow, prepared, mended, or laundered by her hands. Or perhaps the woman has found no vegetable food, or lacks clay for pottery or skins for making clothes, obtainable only at a distance from the dwelling, which she cannot leave because her children require care; the man in his ramblings after game can readily supply her wants. Moreover, if either is injured or ill, the other can nurse him back to health. These and similar rewarding experiences, repeated daily, would suffice of themselves to cement the union. When the powerful reinforcement of sex is added, the partnership of man and woman becomes inevitable.

Sexual unions without economic cooperation are common, and there are relationships between men and women involving a division of

[6] See G. P. Murdock, "Comparative Data on the Division of Labor by Sex," *Social Forces,* XV, 1937, 551-3, for an analysis of the distribution of economic activities by sex in 224 societies.

[7] Cf. M. Mead, *Sex and Temperament in Three Primitive Societies,* New York, Morrow, 1935.

labor without sexual gratification, *e.g.,* between brother and sister, master and maidservant, or employer and secretary, but marriage exists only when the economic and the sexual are united into one relationship, and this combination occurs only in marriage. Marriage, thus defined, is found in every known human society. In all of them, moreover, it involves residential cohabitation, and in all of them it forms the basis of the nuclear family. Genuine cultural universals are exceedingly rare. It is all the more striking, therefore, that we here find several of them not only omnipresent but everywhere linked to one another in the same fashion.

Economic cooperation not only binds husband to wife; it also strengthens the various relationships between parents and children within the nuclear family. Here, of course, a division of labor according to age, rather than sex, comes into play. What the child receives in these relationships is obvious; nearly his every gratification depends upon his parents. But the gains are by no means one-sided. In most societies, children by the age of six or seven are able to perform chores which afford their parents considerable relief and help, and long before they attain adulthood and marriageability they become economic assets of definite importance. One need only think here of the utility of boys to their fathers and of girls to their mothers on the typical European or American farm. Moreover, children represent, as it were, a sort of investment or insurance policy; dividends, though deferred for a few years, are eventually paid generously in the form of economic aid, of support in old age, and even, sometimes, of cash returns, as where a bride-price is received for a daughter when she marries.

Siblings[8] are similarly bound to one another through the care and help given by an elder to a younger, through cooperation in childhood games which imitate the activities of adults, and through mutual economic assistance as they grow older. Thus, through reciprocal material services sons and daughters are bound to fathers and mothers and to one another, and the entire family group is given firm economic support.

Sexual cohabitation leads inevitably to the birth of offspring. These must be nursed, tended, and reared to physical and social maturity if the parents are to reap the afore-mentioned advantages. Even if the burdens of reproduction and child care outweigh the selfish gains to

[8] The term "sibling" will be employed throughout this work in its technical sense as designating either a brother or a sister irrespective of sex.

the parents, the society as a whole has so heavy a stake in the maintenance of its numbers, as a source of strength and security, that it will
insist that parents fulfill these obligations. Abortion, infanticide, and
neglect, unless confined within safe limits, threaten the entire community and arouse its members to apply severe social sanctions to the
recalcitrant parents. Fear is thus added to self-interest as a motive for
the rearing of children. Parental love, based on various derivative satisfactions, cannot be ignored as a further motive; it is certainly no more
mysterious than the affection lavished by many people on burdensome
animal pets, which are able to give far less in return. Individual and
social advantages thus operate in a variety of ways to strengthen the
reproductive aspects of the parent-child relationships within the nuclear
family.

The most basic of these relationships, of course, is that between
mother and child, since this is grounded in the physiological facts of
pregnancy and lactation and is apparently supported by a special innate
reinforcing mechanism, the mother's pleasure or tension release in
suckling her infant. The father becomes involved in the care of the
child less directly, through the sharing of tasks with the mother. Older
children, too, frequently assume partial charge of their younger siblings,
as a chore suited to their age. The entire family thus comes to participate in child care, and is further unified through this cooperation.

No less important than the physical care of offspring, and probably
more difficult, is their social rearing. The young human animal must
acquire an immense amount of traditional knowledge and skill, and
must learn to subject his inborn impulses to the many disciplines pre-
scribed by his culture, before he can assume his place as an adult
member of his society. The burden of education and socialization
everywhere falls primarily upon the nuclear family, and the task is,
in general, more equally distributed than is that of physical care. The
father must participate as fully as the mother because, owing to the
division of labor by sex, he alone is capable of training the sons in the
activities and disciplines of adult males.[9] Older siblings, too, play an
important role, imparting knowledge and discipline through daily interaction in work and play. Perhaps more than any other single factor,
collective responsibility for education and socialization welds the various relationships of the family firmly together. . . .

Agencies or relationships outside of the family may, to be sure, share

[9] Cf. R. Linton, *The Study of Man*, New York, 1936, p. 155.

in the fulfillment of any of these functions, but they never supplant the family. There are, as we have seen, societies which permit sexual gratification in other relationships, but none which deny it to married spouses. There may be extraordinary expansion in economic specialization, as in modern industrial civilization, but the division of labor between man and wife still persists. There may, in exceptional cases, be little social disapproval of childbirth out of wedlock, and relatives, servants, nurses, or pediatricians may assist in child care, but the primary responsibility for bearing and rearing children ever remains with the family. Finally, grandparents, schools, or secret initiatory societies may assist in the educational process, but parents universally retain the principal role in teaching and discipline. No society, in short, has succeeded in finding an adequate substitute for the nuclear family, to which it might transfer these functions. It is highly doubtful whether any society ever will succeed in such an attempt, utopian proposals for the abolition of the family to the contrary notwithstanding. . . .

Table 1.

Relative (of man)	PREMARITAL INTERCOURSE		POSTMARITAL INTERCOURSE		MARRIAGE	
	Forbidden	Permitted	Forbidden	Permitted	Forbidden	Permitted
Mother	76	0	74	0	184	0
Sister	109	0	106	0	237	0
Daughter	—	—	81	0	198	0

Perhaps the most striking effect of family structure upon individual behavior is to be observed in the phenomenon of incest taboos. . . . Despite an extraordinary variability and seeming arbitrariness in the incidence of incest taboos in different societies, they invariably apply to every cross-sex relationship within the nuclear family save that between married spouses. In no known society is it conventional or even permissible for father and daughter, mother and son, or brother and sister to have sexual intercourse or to marry. Despite the tendency of ethnographers to report marriage rules far more fully than regulations governing premarital and postmarital incest, the evidence from our 250 societies, presented in Table 1, is conclusive.

The few apparent exceptions, in each instance too partial to appear in the table, are nevertheless illuminating, and all those encountered will therefore be mentioned. Certain high Azande nobles are permitted to wed their own daughters, and brother-sister marriages were preferred in the old Hawaiian aristocracy and in the Inca royal family. In none of these instances, however, could the general population contract incestuous unions, for these were a symbol and prerogative of exalted status. Among the Dobuans, intercourse with the mother is not seriously regarded if the father is dead; it is considered a private sin rather than a public offense. The Balinese of Indonesia permit twin brothers and sisters to marry on the ground that they have already been unduly intimate in their mother's womb. Among the Thonga of Africa an important hunter, preparatory to a great hunt, may have sex relations with his daughter—a heinous act under other circumstances. By their special circumstances or exceptional character these cases serve rather to emphasize than to disprove the universality of intra-family incest taboos.

A major consequence of these taboos is that they make the nuclear family discontinuous over time and confine it to two generations. If brother-sister marriages were usual, for example, a family would normally consist of married grandparents, their sons and daughters married to one another, the children of the latter, and even the progeny of incestuous unions among these. The family, like the community, the clan, and many other social groups, would be permanent, new births ever filling the gaps caused by deaths. Incest taboos completely alter this situation. They compel each child to seek in another family for a spouse with whom to establish a marital relationship. In consequence thereof, every normal adult in every human society belongs to at least two nuclear families—a *family of orientation* in which he was born and reared, and which includes his father, mother, brothers, and sisters, and a *family of procreation*[10] which he establishes by his marriage and which includes his husband or wife, his sons, and his daughters.

[10] For these very useful terms we are indebted to W. L. Warner.

THE CHANGING FUNCTIONS OF THE FAMILY*

William F. Ogburn

The dilemma of the modern family is due to its loss of function. Throughout the period of written history the family has been the major social institution. Indeed, in the long period of prehistory, as well as in historical times, the family has been a larger social institution than it is in the Twentieth Century in the United States and western Europe.

Prior to modern times the power and prestige of the family was due to seven functions it performed:

Foremost was the economic function. The family was the factory of the time. It was a self-sufficient unit, or nearly so. The members of the family consumed only what they produced. Hence money, banks, stores, factories were not needed. A wife was a business partner, a good foreman, or competent worker.

As a result of this economic function the family became a center of prestige and gave status to its members, its second function. A member of a family was less an individual and more a member of a family. It was the family name that was important, rather than the first name. Most families stayed for generations on the same pieces of land in or near a small community and hence had an opportunity to establish reputations. It was important to marry into the right family, as well as to marry the individual. The family name was a badge and had to be guarded at all cost and at all times.

The nature of the household economy was such as to make the home the center for education, not only of the infant and child of pre-school age, but also the youth for his vocational education, physical education, domestic science, and so on. The higher education was often obtained by employing a tutor who lived with the family.

A fourth function was that of protecting the members. The husband protected the wife by virtue of his physical prowess, a protection now furnished by the police. The elders found a place readily in the house-

* Adapted and reprinted by permission of the author and publisher from "The Changing Family," *The Family*, 19, 1938, 139-43.

hold of the child to spend the twilight of their lives. Children were an old age insurance.

The family exercised a religious function, also, as evidenced by grace at meals, family prayers, and the reading together of passages in the Bible. Husbands and wives were supposed to be members of the same church.

Recreation in those days was not a function of industry; that is, it was not commercialized. There was some community recreation but it was often at the homestead of some family. Recreation centers outside the home were few.

A final function was that of providing affection between mates and the procreation of children.

These seven functions—economic, status giving, educational, religious, recreational, protective, and affectional—may be thought of as bonds that tied the members of a family together. If one asks why do the various members of the family stay together instead of each going his way, the answer is that they are tied together by these functions. If they didn't exist, it is not easy to see that there would be any family.

The dilemma of the modern family is caused by the loss of many of these functions in recent times. The economic function has gone to the factory, store, office, and restaurant, leaving little of economic activity to the family of the city apartment. About half of education has been transferred to the schools, where the teacher is a part-time or substitute parent. Recreation is found in moving pictures, parks, city streets, clubs, with bridge and radio at home. Religion doesn't seem to make as much difference in family matters as formerly, grace at meals and family prayers are rare. As to protection, the child is protected at home, but the state helps also with its child labor laws and reform schools. The police and social legislation indicate how the protective function has been transferred to the state, as has the educational function. Family status has been lost in marked degree along with these other functions in an age of mobility and large cities. It is the individual that has become more important and the family less so. On the other hand the family still remains the center of the affectional life and is the only recognized place for producing children.

From this survey it may be seen that at least six of the seven family functions have been reduced as family activities in recent times, and it may be claimed that only one remains as vigorous and extensive as in prior eras.*

The loss of these functions from the family institution does not mean that they have been lost to society. They have not disappeared from society as they have from the family. Rather they have been transferred from the family to other institutions, schools, factories, stores, clubs, commissions, and so on. What is the family's loss is the gain of the state and of industry.

One other point may be noted as to these changes in the family. Their causes can be traced largely to the inventions using steam as power. The old family existed with the handicrafts in the city and with subsistence farming in the country. Steam power made possible cities, factories, modern transportation, mass production, and specialization, which are part of the process of the transference of functions away from the family.

There are a number of consequences of the uses of this power. One is the increase in separation and divorce. A sample of the census of 1930, weighted slightly in favor of cities, showed about one in ten families broken by separation, annulment, or divorce. It is well known that one in every five or six marriages contracted will end in a divorce court.† The reason is clear. The bonds that hold married couples together are weaker and fewer. Hence husbands and wives fall apart. Women can get jobs outside the home, and men can get meals and mending done elsewhere. The one function remaining more or less as strong as formerly, the affectional tie, however, is not as strong alone as the seven ties together. The affectional bond snaps and there follows separation and divorce.

The situation is affected not only by steam but by one other invention, the contraceptive. It seems that this invention increases the amount of marriage and promotes early marriage, rather than the contrary as is sometimes claimed. But it would also tend to result in

* ". . . it may be said that the affectional function is still centered in the family circle and that no evidence is recorded of any extensive transfer elsewhere. The evidence of increased separations and divorces does not prove that husbands and wives now find marriage less agreeable than their ancestors did. It may mean only that certain functions and traditions which once operated to hold even an inharmonious family together have now weakened or disappeared. . . . The future stability of the family will depend . . . [largely] . . . on the strength of the affectional bonds." William F. Ogburn, "The Family and Its Functions" in *Recent Social Trends*, McGraw-Hill, 1933, pp. 663-708.—*Eds.*

† For more recent figures concerning divorce, see p. 95 and pp. 520-30 below.—*Eds.*

more families without children. Divorce is many times as frequent among couples without children as with them.*

Another consequence of the transfer of functions from the family is the decline of the authority of the family. There are no longer families that dominate societies as was once the case. Much greater authority rests with state and industry. So also authority in the family declines. The husband's authority over the wife is not what it used to be. The state challenges the authority of the parent over the child, for instance, as to its education and as to its labor. The child grows up accustomed to authorities, many of them elsewhere than at home. The respect which a child has for its parents rests more upon their personalities than upon authorities they possess. So the respect one member has for another is not bolstered up by powers and sanctions. So if the respect is not based upon personality it is not likely to exist.

Another result of the shift of functions from the family to other institutions is the change in the nature of marriage. Marriage was at one time a semi-business proposition, which parents and elders realized fully and the young people realized in part. The young man looked for a good home-maker, who was diligent, thrifty, and capable. It was worth while for a young woman to have a reputation among the neighbors in this regard. The young man was certainly expected to be a good provider, to come from a good family, and to have status. If either had property, that was an item of consideration. Under this framework there was a chance for some romance, unless the marriage was arranged by the parents and unless dowries were of overshadowing importance. Marriage was viewed as an institution, a business. On the other hand, romantic love alone was another thing. It came and went. You were in love today but not tomorrow. It was not considered a phenomenon stable enough upon which to erect a business, to raise and rear a family. There must be something else, efficiency and ability.

With the shift of functions away from the family, romantic love has taken over marriage, aided by moving pictures and the pulp magazines. Whether the wife is a good cook is a secondary consideration. It is not necessary that she be a good seamstress any more than she needs to know how to spin and weave. Hence, there are more hasty marriages. It has become necessary for states to pass laws requiring a certain

---

* On this point see Paul H. Jacobson, "Differentials in Divorce by Duration of Marriage and Size of Family," pp. 520-30 below.—*Eds.*

amount of time to elapse between the purchase of a license and marriage.

Another result of the decline of the family functions is the conflict between the new conditions of family life and the old attitudes surviving from an earlier type of family life. Thus the older philosophy said that woman's place was the home. True enough it was when she made soap, wove cloth, and prepared medicine from herbs. But the maxim is not so clear for women with no children living at home. . . . Often these women live in small apartments quite unsuitable for economic activity. Besides, one in every 8 or 9 married women helps out the family income by drawing wages for work done outside the home. Many men feel it reflects on them to have their wives work for wages. Others feel that they are head of the house, a position that had more significance under the household economy. The conflict is apparent in the case of girls, who do not know whether to prepare for marriage or for jobs. It is not only difficult to do both, but there is also a psychological conflict between the new economic freedom of self-support and the lifelong devotion to husband, children, and home.

One effect of the invention of the contraceptive has been a loss of a family function rather than a transfer of that function to another social institution. I refer to childbearing. No other social institution produces children and illegitimacy is probably on the decline. Thus, at the time when the American colonies won their independence from Great Britain, 10 wives bore 78 children; one hundred and fifty years later 10 wives bear only 23 children. The cost of rearing a child, especially in the city, is great today. Not many fathers could provide opportunities for education and health to seven or eight children, especially when the law forces the family to care for them until they are almost twenty years of age. Fewer children mean, then, more advantages and opportunities, and no doubt better food, less illness, and superior physical well-being.

But the gain on the psychological side is not so clear. The only child and the oldest child are a much larger percentage of all children now than formerly. They receive relatively more attention than middle children. They are with adults more. These conditions cause more geniuses but also more failures. They are said to be more narcissistic and exhibitionistic. It is claimed by psychoanalysts that neurotics are drawn proportionately more from the only, oldest, and youngest children. Indulgent parents are more likely to "spoil" an only child than those of a large brood. Anxious mothers are more likely to inculcate anxiety in an oldest child than in a middle child. Such problem children in youth are a responsibility of the family and school in wealthy neighborhoods. But in poor neighborhoods, where mothers work away from home and where the streets are the playground, such problem children become a responsibility of the state, for their gang life leads to delinquencies of various kinds that may bring them up against the law.

The problem of the family rearing of children in a modern city is due in part to the survival of the older attitudes which are in a practical way incompatible with modern urban conditions, and to the absence of a definite pattern of guidance in a changing society for parents whose intelligence quotients may not be very high. No ethic has as yet risen to take the place of the one followed in the Victorian era.

Not all the difficulty is due to conditions within the family. The conditions outside the family make successful family life difficult. For the family does not exist in a vacuum, as the saying goes, but is a part of society. The inventions which have so changed the institution of the family have also changed society. These changes in society that impinge on the family, often with disastrous effects, may be summarized by the word heterogeneity. There are in a modern city many groups to which the members of a family belong. Formerly they were members of the church, and of perhaps two or three clubs. Now the men of the family belong to a business group, to a church, to a union or trade association, and to some clubs. The wife may belong to a business group, a card club, a church, a social club. The children belong to a school group, perhaps a play group, and perhaps a club.

The meaning of these various memberships lies in the important role the group plays in shaping one's conduct. We conform to the folkways and mores that are set by the group. We become like the group within which we live. We cannot long resist the pressure of Main Street. A man does not rise much above the level of the group in which he lives, nor does he fall much below this level. Our self is really what the group influences make it. Hence, personality is a social product.

Now in modern times the group influences that determine the character of the members of the family do not flow from the family alone, or from just one group. The members of the family belong to many groups, each one having its own folkways and social evaluations.

The boys' gang has a set of standards different from those of the school children, or of the family, or the church. Often these values conflict. Pavlov is said to have produced a neurosis in a dog. He did it by conditioning the dog to respond positively to a great circle of light thrown on a screen. The same dog was conditioned to respond negatively to a great ellipse of light thrown on the same screen at another time. Then when the great experimenter changed the light from a circle and an ellipse to a midway type of figure, the dog did not know what to do, and broke down in a fit of trembling. The conflicting values and standards of the different societies, business associations, churches, athletic groups, and pleasure groups may produce somewhat similar conflicts.

There is a competition with the family by other groups for the control over its members. The family no longer holds sway. The nature of family life is such that it is necessarily important, but it often breaks down under the competition with other groups. Parents thus lose control over their children, husbands and wives lose influence with each other.

This situation is affected by one other condition, namely, city life. When the village is small, consisting of a few hundred persons, and there is little travel and communication with the outside, everyone knows everything about everybody else. Life is in a goldfish bowl. The result is a homogeneity. The set of values for a particular club or association perforce conforms to a general village pattern.

But under city life, the members of the different groups do not know one another. They often come from different neighborhoods, one may never see another member of a club except when the club meets. Hence, city life presents isolation and heterogeneity. In addition communication from the outside world brings—via magazine, radio, and moving picture—the folkways of other places and other lands. The result is an individualization of the members of the family. The individual no longer has his moral problems solved for him by the family group. The heterogeneity of society and the rapidity of social change make impossible specific formulae which tell one what to do in different situations. Right and wrong have to be figured out by the individual, which calls for a high I.Q. and some ability to think in an emotional situation.

Such are some of the consequences following from the loss of functions by the family due to modern invention.

THE FAMILY CYCLE*

Paul C. Glick[1]

From its formation until its dissolution, a family passes through a series of stages that are subject to demographic analysis. Typically, a family comes into being when a couple is married. The family gains in size with the birth of each child. From the time when the last child is born until the first child leaves home, the family remains stable in size. As the children leave home for employment or marriage, the size of the family shrinks gradually back to the original two persons. Eventually one and then the other of the parents die and the family cycle has come to an end.

During the life of the typical family, important changes occur not only in the composition but also in many other measurable characteristics of the group. The family is likely to move to one or more new locations in the process of adjusting to new housing requirements or of improving employment opportunities. A home may be purchased; the rental value of the living quarters may change. The probability of employment of the husband and of his wife will differ from one phase of the family cycle to another. Occupational shifts and corresponding variations in earnings are usually experienced during the lives of the average family's breadwinners.

In treating these subjects, this paper falls into three parts: first, a presentation of the ages at which American married couples usually reach the several stages of the family cycle; second, an analysis of changes in family composition during the life span of the average family; and third, a description of changes in residence and in economic characteristics of the typical family between its establishment and its disestablishment.

The analysis of family composition and characteristics will be limited, where possible, to families of the "husband and wife" type in which

* Adapted and reprinted by permission of the author and publisher from the *American Sociological Review*, 12 (1947), 164-74.

[1] The author wishes to thank Wilson H. Grabill for permission to use certain unpublished data which he had compiled on stages of the family cycle and to thank Elizabeth A. Larmon for assistance in preparing the table and other statistical data.

both members of a married couple are living together in their own private living quarters. About three-fourths of all households contain a family of this type. Groups not included in this analysis are married couples who are living with an established family, persons living alone, broken families, and households maintained by single (unmarried) persons. Likewise excluded are the residents of institutions, transient hotels, and of large lodging houses. . . .

Stages of the Family Cycle

Marriage.   Half of the men in this country who marry for the first time do so before their 25th birthday and half of the women before their 22nd birthday, according to data from the 1940 Census. More specifically, . . . the median age at first marriage for men was 24.3 years and for women, 21.6 years.[2] The average couple marrying 50 years ago was a little older than the average couple in current times. Results derived from the 1890 Census showed that the median age at first marriage was 26.1 years for men and 22.0 years for women at that time. Thus, the average married man of 1940 was his wife's senior by about three years, whereas his grandfather was likely to have been senior by four years.

Men on farms tend to marry at relatively older ages than those not on farms. The decline since 1890 of nearly two years in the median age of men at first marriage may be attributed in part, therefore, to the decline in the proportion of farm people in the United States. Another factor may be the more widespread knowledge today of means of family limitation. In the earlier period postponement of marriage was probably more often relied upon as a means of limiting family size.

It should be recognized, of course, that not all couples establish a separate home when they marry. In ordinary times, approximately one couple out of every five moves in with relatives or lives in rented room as lodgers for a while after marriage. The proportion of couples living in this manner declines sharply until middle age and reaches a low point of about 3 per cent for couples in their 50's.[3]

Over a considerable period of time there has been a growing tendency

[2] Wilson H. Grabill, "Age at First Marriage," Bureau of the Census, Series P-45 No. 7, May 28, 1945.

[3] Based on a comparison of the number of married women with husband present in the household and the number of such women who were wives of heads of households in 1940. See Tables 9 and 11 in Part I, Volume IV, of the 1940 Census Bureau report on population, *Characteristics by Age*, Government Printing Office, Washington, 1943.

for married couples to make their homes with an established family. There is evidence in unpublished data from the Censuses of 1930 and 1910 that smaller proportions of couples at these earlier dates than in 1940 were failing to maintain their own households. A survey made in June, 1946, showed an increase of only 9 per cent since 1940 in the number of private households as compared with an increase of 40 per cent in the number of couples living doubled up in private households.[4] The latter increase developed, no doubt, as a consequence of the lack of housing facilities to accommodate the great numbers marrying during, or since the end of, the war.

Child Bearing. Following marriage, about a year elapses before the average mother bears a child. This interval has not varied greatly since 1917, when the Bureau of the Census first published national figures on children by order of birth.[5] The median age of mothers bearing their first child in 1940 was 22.6 years. In 1890 it probably was about 23.0 years. Between 1940 and 1942 it remained practically unchanged in spite of a rather large increase in the proportion of first births among all births.

For women who had married and had reached the end of their reproductive period (45 to 49 years old) by 1940, the average number of children born per woman was approximately 3.1.[6] Statistics on children by order of birth indicate that these 3.1 children were born two years apart, hence a period of only about four and one-half years elapsed between the birth of the first and the last child, as a rule. The typical mother had, therefore, borne her final child at the (median) age of 27.2 years.

Because families were so large two generations ago, the average woman at that time had twice as long an interval between the birth of her first and last child as does the woman of today. She had borne

---

[4] "Marital Status of the Civilian Population and of Heads of Families: June, 1946," cited above. For a statistical description of married couples and parent-child groups who do not maintain separate homes, see "Characteristics of Secondary Families in the United States: February, 1946," Bureau of the Census, Series P-S, No. 15, February 5, 1947.

[5] *Vital Statistics of the United States,* Government Printing Office, Washington, reports for 1917 to 1944. For selected, highly fertile groups the interval may be less than one year, on the average. See the article by Harold T. Christensen, "The Time-Interval between Marriage of Parents and the Birth of their First Child in Utah County, Utah," *American Journal of Sociology,* Volume 44, No. 4, pages 518 to 525, January, 1939.

[6] See Table 3 of the 1940 Census Bureau report, *Differential Fertility, 1940 and 1910 —Fertility for States and Large Cities,* Government Printing Office, Washington, 1943.

5.4 children[7] with an estimated interval of 9 years between the first and the last. Not until the age of about 32 years had she given birth to the last child.

At this point it is appropriate to mention in passing, at least, those women who have never borne any children. Among women who had married and completed their period of fertility (45 to 49 years old) by 1940, 15.4 per cent had had no children. For 1890 the corresponding figure was only half as large, 7.9 per cent.

Children Leaving Home.   From the time the last child is born until the first child leaves home, the size of the family usually remains stable. Probably a majority of children depart from the parental home for a new permanent place of residence within less than a year from the time they marry.

Let us assume as a reasonable approximation, therefore, that the average (ever-married) woman of completed fertility (45 to 49 years old) in 1940 had had three children who grew to maturity, married, and left home at the same age that their parents married. The decline in the number of children living at home would accordingly have taken place when the mother was between the ages of 45 and 50 years. By way of comparison, the average woman of her grandmother's era would have been 47 to 55 years old, if she had lived as long as that, when her five surviving children were leaving home.

Dissolution of the Family.   This brings us to the final stage of the family cycle, when first one then the other of the parents is expected to die. For the average couple who married in 1940, the chances are 50-50 that, under mortality rates observed at that time, they will survive jointly for about 39 years.[8] At the end of that period the wife would be 61 years old and the husband 64. They would have lived together for 11 years since the last of their three children married. By comparison, the typical couple of two generations ago could have expected to survive together for only 31 years after marriage, that is, until the wife would have attained age 53 and the husband 57. This is two years short of the time when their fifth child would have been expected to marry.

Thus, the decline in size of family and the improved survival pros-

[7] *Ibid.*, Table 4.

[8] Survival rates for the general population were used. Married persons, particularly married men, have slightly better chances of survival than other persons, but they represent such a large majority of all persons between 25 and 65 years of age that the survival factors for married persons, if available, would probably differ very little from those for the general population. . . .

ects of the population since 1890 not only have assured the average parents of our day that they will live to see their children married but also have made it probable that they will have one-fourth of their married life still to come when their last child leaves the parental home. This represents a remarkable change since 1890. It is one of the most dramatic, and at the same time one of the most significant changes from the viewpoint of the life experiences of the parents, of all changes

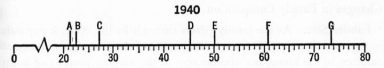

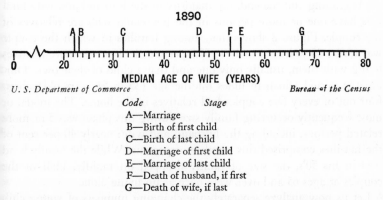

U. S. Department of Commerce   Bureau of the Census

Code	Stage
A—Marriage	
B—Birth of first child	
C—Birth of last child	
D—Marriage of first child	
E—Marriage of last child	
F—Death of husband, if first	
G—Death of wife, if last	

Figure 1. Stages of the family cycle in the United States.

in the family cycle in the last 50 years. It has a multitude of social and economic implications.

The wife would ordinarily be expected to survive longer than her husband, partly because she is usually younger and partly because mortality rates are more favorable for women than for men, age for age. In the typical situation, therefore, the period of joint survival of husband and wife is terminated with the death of the husband. In this case, the average wife would be expected, under present conditions of mortality, to live on after her husband's death for about 13 years, to age 74; 50 years ago, she could have looked forward to living until age 68. In the less common situation, the period of joint survival is broken by the death of the wife. In that case, the average husband, under mortality conditions of today, would be expected to live on for 6 years, to age 70, whereas 50 years ago he would have been likely to live until age 66.[9]

With the dissolution of the family by the death of both spouses, the end of the last stage in the usual family cycle has been reached.

Changes in Family Composition

Family Size. As the family passes through its life cycle, it expands in size and then contracts, not only because of the changing number of children in the home, but also because of the varying number of adult relatives in the household who have not formed separate families or have moved in with the family after a period of living elsewhere.

At all stages of the family cycle, except perhaps for brief periods at the beginning and the end, the majority of the husband and wife families have one or more persons in the household who are relatives of the couple. Figure 2 shows that, among families in which the couple was under 25 years old in 1940, 57.0 per cent had one or more relatives living with them, usually only one and that a child of their own. During the period which includes middle age (35 to 54 years old) about four out of every five couples had relatives in the home. The modal or most frequently occurring family size during this phase was 5 or more related persons, including the husband and wife; nearly 40 per cent of the families comprised this number of persons. While the family head was in his 50's, the size of family dropped off rapidly. Half of the couples at ages 65 and over were once again living alone.

Let us now analyze separately the changing numbers of young children and of adult relatives who make their homes with the family.

Children Living at Home. Forty-one per cent of the husband and wife families in 1940 had no young children under 18 years of age living in the home who were related to the couple. Nearly half of those families in which the husband was under 25 years old were childless. By the time the husband reached his upper thirties slightly more than one-fifth, 21.7 per cent, were still childless or their children who had

---

[9] The ages at death reported in this paragraph are based on chances of survival of each spouse from the median age at marriage. See Thomas N. E. Greville, *United States Life Tables and Actuarial Tables, 1939-1941*, Government Printing Office, Washington, 1946, and James W. Glover, *United States Life Tables, 1890, 1901, 1910, and 1901-1910*, Government Printing Office, Washington, 1921.

not passed their 18th birthday had either left home or died. At that time there were more families with 3 or more children under 18 than with any smaller number. At ages beyond 40 years, an increasing proportion of couples no longer had young dependents in the household. This proportion passed the one-half mark between the ages of 50 and 60 and the seven-eighths point above the age of 75.

Until the husband and wife reach middle age, nearly all of the children living at home are sons or daughters of the couple. In 1940, 11 out of every 12 relatives under 18 years old in the average family were own children of the family head. The remaining one-twelfth consisted very largely of grandchildren. After the couple pass middle age, the children in the home may represent a combination of own children and grandchildren. The husband and wife are likely to reach a point in their 50's when their grandchildren represent the majority of the young children in the household.

Adult Relatives in the Home. Sixty-four per cent of the husband and wife families in 1940 had no adult relatives 18 years old and over living in the home. Very few, about one-eighth, of the families in which the husband was under 35 years of age contained any of these additional adults. At each age of the husband above 45, however, roughly one-half of the families furnished living quarters for one or more adults besides the family head and his wife.

Let us note who these adult relatives were. Nearly three-fifths of them in 1940 were single sons or daughters of the couple who had not yet left home, of whom most were between 18 and 34 years old. This group included about half again as many young men as young women, largely because of the fact that it is customary for men to marry at older ages than women.

About one-eighth of the adult relatives were married, widowed, or divorced sons or daughters and their spouses, if any, who were living with their parents or parents-in-law.

About one-tenth of the relatives were parents of the husband or his wife. Of these parents, about 30 per cent were fathers or fathers-in-law and about 70 per cent were mothers or mothers-in-law. One-fourth of the fathers or fathers-in-law were still married, but only about one-tenth of the mothers or mothers-in-law were still married. The preponderance of mothers among the parents living with established families is in large part a reflection of the lesser tendency for widows than widowers to remarry, the greater chances of women than men to survive to old age, and the greater economic dependency of older women than older men.

Thus, all but about one-fifth of the adult relatives were children or parents (own or in-law) of the family head or his wife. Of this one-fifth, a large proportion were brothers or sisters, including brothers- and sisters-in-law, of the family head or his wife.

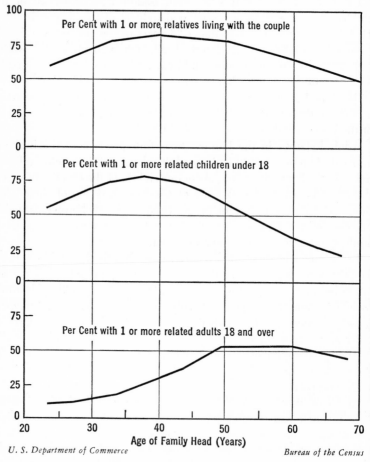

U. S. Department of Commerce   *Bureau of the Census*

Figure 2.   Composition of husband and wife families: U. S. 1940.*

* Derived mainly from Census Bureau data in two sources, Tables 3 and 8 of *Types of Families*, Government Printing Office, Washington, 1943, and Table II of Part I of Volume IV of the 1940 reports on population cited above.

Changes in Residence and in Economic Characteristics

Residential Shifts. In ordinary times, about four out of every five couples establish a home apart from their parents when they marry. Furthermore, many of those who have established a home are likely to move to another location with more adequate living space when the size of their family increases. . . .

Families of young couples are not only more likely to move within a county but are also more likely to migrate between counties. Those in which the husband was under 35 years of age in 1940 were more than three times as likely to have moved into another county (or city of 100,000 or more) during the preceding five years as the group 55 years old and over.[10]

Home Ownership. Closely related to residential shifts is tenure of home. In fact, a large part of the movement of families is occasioned by the purchase of a home. Few indeed of the young couples in separate living quarters own their homes. Only 12 per cent of those under 25 years of age were home owners in 1940 but by the age period 35 to 44 years more than three times that proportion, or 39 per cent, were home owners. At each advancing age of the family head the proportion owning homes increased until, at age 65 and over, 69 per cent were owners.[11]

Monthly Rental Value of Home. Changes in the expenditure for housing space are marked by sharp increases in the earlier stages of the family cycle, for obvious reasons, and decreases in the later stages that are much less sharp. Couples under 25 in 1940 occupied homes with a median rental value of less than half as high as that for couples 45 to 54. The latter age group had homes with the highest median rental value. Quarters occupied by couples who had reached 65 or over had median rental values only about 15 per cent below the peak.[12] These and other available facts indicate that the amount of expenditure for living quarters in the later years of life is only roughly correlated with need, in terms of family size.

[10] For data on migration of heads of private households within a State and between States (not classified by age of head), see the Census Bureau report, *Internal Migration, 1935 to 1940—Social Characteristics of Migrants,* Government Printing Office, Washington, 1946. For recent statistics on the migration of heads of husband and wife families by age of head, see "Migration of Families in the United States: April, 1940, to February, 1946," Series P-S, No. 14, December 26, 1946.

[11] See Table I of *Types of Families* cited above.

[12] *Ibid.,* Table II.

Family Income. The pattern of change in family income for wage-earner families very closely resembles that of rental value. Husband and wife families in which the husband was under 25 years old in 1940 had just about half as large a median family income during 1939 as those aged 45 to 54, the latter representing the peak group. Families in which the husband was in the oldest age group, 65 and over, had a median family income approximately 25 per cent below that in their prime.[13]

The larger median incomes were generally found among those groups of families in which the chief earner had attained the age when he could perform with the maximum skill and usefulness in his trade or profession. Furthermore, higher family earnings were found, other things being equal, among those groups of families in which adult rela · tives were most common.[14] The earnings of these relatives helped to make possible larger payments for housing accommodations and thus also help to explain the correlation between the rental value and family income curves.

Employment of the Husband. All but 1 or 2 per cent of the family heads under 45 years old in 1940 were classified as members of the labor force. At ages 55 to 64, nearly 90 per cent were still working or looking for work. Above the age of 65, only slightly over half, 52 per cent, of the husbands who were family heads reported themselves as workers. Of those in this oldest age group who were still employed, more than 40 per cent were farmers or farm laborers.[15]

Employment of the Wife. Among the wives of family heads in 1940, 12 per cent were actively engaged in work for pay or profit, other than their home housework, or were seeking such work. The maximum percentage of wives in the labor force, 16.5 per cent, was found among those whose husbands were 25 to 29 years old. At each succeeding age thereafter the proportion of wives in the labor force steadily declined. At ages of husbands above 65, only about 5 per cent of their wives were reported as workers.[16]

---

[13] See Table 9 of the Census Bureau report, *Family Wage or Salary Income in 1939*, Government Printing Office, Washington, 1943. See also the article by T. J. Woofter, Jr., based on this report, entitled "Size of Family in Relation to Family Income and Age of Family Head," *American Sociological Review*, Volume 9, No. 6, pages 678 to 684, December, 1944.

[14] See Table 8 of *Size of Family and Age of Head* cited above.

[15] See Tables 13 and 19 of the Census Bureau report, *Families—Employment Status*, Government Printing Office, Washington, 1943.

[16] *Ibid.*, Table II.

Concluding Statement. In the foregoing analysis, we have described a number of significant stages in the family cycle and have demonstrated that characteristics of the average family vary widely from one

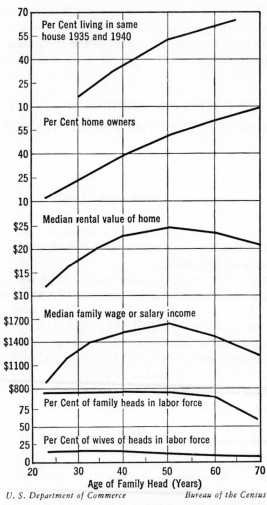

U. S. Department of Commerce   Bureau of the Census

Figure 3. Economic characteristics of husband and wife families: U. S. 1940.

stage of the cycle to another.[17] The existence of these wide variations should be kept in mind in comparing the characteristics of families in two or more areas or social classes. For example, if a person is studying differences in home ownership among family heads in the several occupational levels, he might well limit his analysis to families with heads in a restricted age range or standardize his basic data in some manner for duration of the family as a group. This practice is already quite common in the analysis of data on fertility. It would seem to be a step in the right direction to encourage the application of similar techniques in the analysis of other types of family differentials.

SOME STATISTICS CONCERNING MARRIAGE AND THE FAMILY IN THE UNITED STATES*

Number and Size of American Families: 1890-1951†

The proportion of single persons in the United States declined to the lowest level on record in 1951. . . . Only 19 out of every 100 females 14 years old and over in April 1951 were single, as compared with 28 at the time of the 1940 Census and 34 in 1890, when tabulations by marital status were first made.

The corresponding trend for males is affected by the fact that the survey largely excluded members of the armed forces, most of whom were single. About 24 out of every 100 males 14 years old and over in the civilian population in April 1951 were single. If all the armed forces had been included, the figures for 1951 would probably have shown that about 26 out of every 100 males 14 years old and over were single, as compared with 35 in 1940 and 44 in 1890.

During each decade since 1890, the proportion of single persons has declined. The long-range decrease has been due in part to gradually

[17] Even within each stage there is, of course, more or less variation from the average or median family on the characteristics shown. This type of intra-stage variation could be shown by presenting first and third quartile values, as well as medians, for age at first marriage, age at birth of first child, etc. Furthermore, data are available in the sources mentioned above for the analysis of many of the changes during the family cycle by color, regions, and urban and rural areas.

* Adapted and reprinted from publications of the Bureau of the Census.

† From Bureau of the Census, *Current Population Reports: Changes in Number of Households: 1890 to 1951*, Series P-20, No. 35, Nov. 28, 1951.

rising marriage rates and in part to an increasing proportion of the population in the older age groups where single persons are relatively few. Since 1940 the trend has been greatly accelerated by unusually high marriage rates and by the sharp decline in population in the teens where single persons predominate. Children in their teens in 1950 were born in the 1930's when birth rates were low.

The number of married couples and the number of families have both increased by about one-fourth since 1940. Of the 36 million married couples in the United States in April [1951] 1.7 million, or about 5 percent, were sharing the living quarters of other persons or living in hotels, rooming houses, or other quasi households. The proportion of couples not maintaining households of their own was lower [in 1951] than in 1940 or 1930, when the corresponding figures were 6.8 percent and 6.1 percent, respectively. The number of married couples living together and sharing others' quarters was relatively low in 1951 partly because of the fact that many husbands were away from home in the armed forces.

The average (mean) size of the 39.8 million American families in 1951 was 3.5 persons, as compared with 3.8 persons in 1940.

The number of households was about 44.6 million, according to the survey of April 1951, as compared with 34.9 million according to the 1940 Census, 29.9 million in 1930, and 12.7 million in 1890. The average annual increase in number of households since 1940, roughly 875,000, is far in excess of the average annual increase of about 504,000 between 1930 and 1940 and of 430,000 between 1890 and 1930. The average size of household declined from 4.9 persons in 1890 to 3.7 in 1940 and 3.3 in 1951. The creation of small new households has proceeded so rapidly during recent years that the decline in the average size of household has continued in spite of the extraordinarily large number of births occurring during the war and postwar years. . . .

Number and Size of American Families: 1951*

The 110.8 million persons 14 years old and over covered in the survey in April 1951 are called for convenience the "civilian" population, but this number also includes 610,000 members of the armed forces living off post or with their families on post in the United States. About 23.9 million, or 22 percent of this civilian population were single; 72.1 million

* From Bureau of the Census, *Current Population Reports: Marital Status and House-hold Characteristics: April, 1951*, Series P-20, No. 38, April 29, 1952.

Table 1. Households, Families, and Married Couples, for the United States: 1890, 1930, 1940, and 1947 to 1951

| Date | HOUSEHOLDS[1] | | FAMILIES | | MARRIED COUPLES | | | |
| | Number | Average population per household[2] | Number | Average population per family | Total | With own household | Without own household | |
							Number	Percent
April 1951	44,564,000	3.34	39,822,000	3.54	35,998,000	34,252,000	1,746,000	4.9
March 1950	43,468,000	3.39	39,193,000	3.57	35,925,000	33,928,000	1,997,000	5.6
April 1949	42,107,000	3.42	38,537,000	3.58	35,323,000	33,167,000	2,156,000	6.1
April 1948	40,720,000	3.49	37,280,000	3.64	34,289,000	31,834,000	2,455,000	7.2
April 1947	39,138,000	3.55	36,240,000	3.67	33,406,000	30,545,000	2,861,000	8.6
April 1940	34,948,666	3.67	32,166,000[3]	3.77[3]	28,516,937	26,570,502	1,946,435	6.8
April 1930	29,904,663	4.01	(4)	(4)	25,174,000[5]	23,649,000[5]	1,525,000[5]	6.1[5]
June 1890	12,690,152	4.93	(4)	(4)	(4)	(4)	(4)	(4)

[1] Statistics for 1930 to 1951 include (private) households only; those for 1890 include the small number of quasi households.
[2] Averages for 1930 to 1951 were obtained by dividing the population in households by the number of households. The average for 1890 was obtained by dividing the total population by the number of households (including quasi households). Had the averages for 1930 to 1951 been based on the total population, they would have been about 0.1 person higher.
[3] Estimate based on revised definition.
[4] Not available.
[5] Estimated.

or 65 percent, were married persons living together; 3.5 million, or 3 percent, were married persons who were living apart from their husbands or wives; 9.3 million, or 8 percent, were widowed; and 2.1 million, or 2 percent, were divorced, at the time of the survey. . . .

Table 2. Marital Status of Persons 14 Years Old and Over, by Sex, for the United States: Civilian Population, 1947 to 1951, and Total Population, 1890 to 1940

Date and sex	NUMBER Total, 14 years old and over	PERCENT Single	Married	Widowed	Divorced
MALE					
April 1951	53,420,000	24.3	69.9	4.1	1.6
March 1950	54,287,000	26.2	68.2	4.0	1.6
April 1949	53,448,000	26.1	68.2	4.1	1.6
April 1948	53,227,000	27.7	66.5	3.9	1.9
April 1947	52,350,000	28.2	66.2	4.1	1.6
April 1940	50,553,748	34.8	59.7	4.2	1.2
April 1930	45,087,507[1]	35.8	58.4	4.5	1.1
January 1920	37,953,960[1]	36.9	57.6	4.6	0.6
April 1910	33,361,779[1]	40.4	54.2	4.4	0.5
June 1900	26,415,042[1]	42.0	52.8	4.5	0.3
June 1890	21,501,030[1]	43.6	52.1	3.8	0.2
FEMALE					
April 1951	57,354,000	19.1	66.5	12.4	2.1
March 1950	56,635,000	19.6	66.1	12.1	2.2
April 1949	56,001,000	20.0	66.1	11.8	2.2
April 1948	55,364,000	21.0	64.6	12.1	2.2
April 1947	54,806,000	22.0	64.2	11.6	2.1
April 1940	50,549,176	27.6	59.5	11.3	1.6
April 1930	44,013,048[1]	28.4	59.5	10.8	1.3
January 1920	36,190,483[1]	29.4	58.9	10.8	0.8
April 1910	30,959,473[1]	31.8	57.1	10.3	0.6
June 1900	25,025,494[1]	33.3	55.2	10.9	0.5
June 1890	20,297,979[1]	34.1	54.8	10.6	0.4

[1] Includes "marital status not reported," not shown separately.

The widowed population constituted about the same proportion of the population in 1951 as in 1940, but the ratio of widows to widowers increased slightly. There were about three widows for every widower in 1951. The excess in the number of widows relative to the number of widowers is attributable to several factors: husbands are usually older than their wives and are therefore less likely to outlive them; men have higher mortality rates than women, age for age; men have had a less rapid decline in mortality rates than women; and older men have higher remarriage rates than older women. In 1951 farm areas had the smallest proportion of widows. This fact may indicate that widows generally leave the farm after becoming widowed.

About 600,000 men and 1,100,000 women were reported as separated because of marital discord. The difference between the number of separated men and women is due in part to the fact that some separated men were not included in the survey, because they were members of the armed forces either living in barracks in the United States or stationed outside the country. It probably also reflects some difference in the way in which marital status was reported for men and women. Separated persons represented 1.5 percent of the population 14 years old and over and about half of all married persons who were not living with their husbands or wives. The proportion separated for the nonwhite population was considerably greater than that for the white population, 6.1 percent for nonwhites and 1.1 percent for whites.

Results of the survey indicated striking differences in income for persons in the several marital status categories. The median money income in 1950 for married men ($2,930) was much higher than that of men in any other marital status. Among women with income the highest median incomes were those for the divorced ($1,555) and the single ($1,333). The lower median income of separated men ($1,750) as compared with that for divorced men ($2,242) is evidence that separation is often a substitute for divorce for those who are financially unable to bear the expense of obtaining a divorce. The median income for men was greater than that for women in the same marital status except in the case of single persons. To some extent differences in income by marital status are associated with differences in age; because of the limitations imposed by the size of the sample, only broad age groups were tabulated separately. In general, nonwhites had considerably lower incomes than whites, but differences related to marital status seem to be about the same for the nonwhite as for the white population.

The distribution by marital status for nonwhites differed somewhat from that for the white population. Married couples living together represented a smaller proportion (about 55 percent) of the adult population among nonwhites than among whites (66 percent). Persons who were married but not living with their spouse comprised a greater proportion of the nonwhite than of the white population, about 9 percent for nonwhites, compared with 3 percent for whites. Among nonwhites, about 70 percent of those married but not living with their spouse were reported as separated, as compared with 41 percent for the white population. There were also somewhat higher proportions of the nonwhite population in the widowed and divorced categories.

Table 3. Median Age at First Marriage, for the United States: 1890 to 1951
(Estimated from census data on marital status by age)

| Year | MEDIAN AGE AT FIRST MARRIAGE | |
	Male	Female
1951	22.6	20.4
1949	22.7	20.3
1947	23.7	20.5
1940	24.3	21.5
1930	24.3	21.3
1920	24.6	21.2
1910	25.1	21.6
1900	25.9	21.9
1890	26.1	22.0

It would appear that the chances of ever marrying are greater for nonwhites than for whites, since the percentage of persons 65 and over who had ever been married was 97 for nonwhites, compared with 92 for whites. Statistics obtained in the 1940 Census likewise showed a higher percentage of persons ever married among nonwhites. . . .

The age at which people enter their first marriage was lower for both men and women in 1951 than in 1940. The median age at first marriage dropped from about 24.3 years for men and 21.5 years for women, as indicated by 1940 Census figures, to about 22.6 years for men and 20.4 years for women, as indicated by the 1951 survey figures, supplemented by data on men in the armed forces obtained from other sources.

Definitions and Explanations. *Household and quasi household.* A household includes all of the persons who occupy a house, an apartment or other group of rooms, or a room that constitutes a dwelling unit. It includes the related family members and also the unrelated persons, if any, such as lodgers, maids, or hired hands who share the dwelling

Table 4. Marital Status of Persons 14 years Old and Over, by Age and Sex, for the United States: Civilian Population, April 1951

(In this report, the "civilian population" includes about 610,000 members of the armed forces living off post or with their families on post, but excludes all other members of the armed forces. In reports in Series P-25, the civilian population excludes all members of the armed forces. Percent is not shown where less than 0.1)

Year, marital status, and sex	Total, 14 years and over	14 TO 19 YEARS			20 to 24 years	25 to 29 years	30 to 34 years	35 to 44 years	45 to 54 years	55 to 64 years	65 years and over
		Total	14 to 17 years	18 and 19 years							
Male	53,420,000	5,990,000	4,260,000	1,730,000	4,964,000	5,706,000	5,438,000	10,216,000	8,686,000	6,828,000	5,592,000
Percent	100.0	100.0	100.0	100.0	100.0	100.0	100.0	100.0	100.0	100.0	100.0
Single	24.3	97.8	99.7	92.9	51.7	20.5	12.5	10.3	8.5	7.2	7.6
Married	69.9	2.1	0.1	6.9	47.6	78.2	85.3	86.7	86.3	83.1	66.8
Wife present	67.4	2.0	0.1	6.7	45.4	75.5	82.8	83.5	82.6	80.5	64.6
Husband in armed forces	1.0	0.3	...	1.0	2.5	2.8	2.6	0.6	0.3	0.1	...
Other	66.4	1.7	0.1	5.7	42.9	72.7	80.2	82.9	82.4	80.4	64.6
Wife absent	2.5	0.1	...	0.2	2.2	2.7	2.5	3.3	3.7	2.5	2.3
Separated	1.2	...	...	...	1.2	1.2	1.3	1.6	1.5	1.3	0.9
Other	1.4	0.1	...	0.2	1.0	1.5	1.3	1.6	2.2	1.3	1.3
Widowed	4.1	0.1	0.1	0.1	0.3	0.1	0.4	0.8	2.3	7.5	24.4
Divorced	1.6	...	...	...	0.3	1.3	1.8	2.1	2.9	2.2	1.1
Female	57,354,000	6,332,000	4,222,000	2,110,000	5,766,000	6,210,000	5,970,000	10,846,000	8,952,000	6,986,000	6,292,000
Percent	100.0	100.0	100.0	100.0	100.0	100.0	100.0	100.0	100.0	100.0	100.0
Single	19.1	86.1	95.3	67.9	31.2	11.0	9.4	7.3	7.1	7.6	7.7
Married	66.5	13.7	4.6	31.9	67.3	85.7	85.9	85.3	77.6	63.6	36.3
Husband present	62.8	11.7	4.0	27.0	61.7	80.1	81.0	80.9	74.1	61.5	34.6
Husband in armed forces	0.9	1.4	0.2	3.7	2.4	2.5	1.5	0.5	...	...	...
Other	61.8	10.3	3.8	23.3	59.3	77.6	79.5	80.4	74.0	61.5	34.6
Husband absent	3.7	2.1	0.6	4.9	5.5	5.6	4.9	4.4	3.5	2.1	1.7
Separated	1.8	0.6	0.2	1.4	1.8	2.3	2.8	2.6	2.2	1.1	0.9
Husband in armed forces	0.7	0.9	0.2	2.2	2.4	1.8	0.9	0.3	...	...	...
Other	1.2	0.6	0.2	1.3	1.3	1.5	1.2	1.5	1.3	0.9	0.8
Widowed	12.4	...	...	...	0.3	1.1	1.8	4.2	12.3	26.7	55.0

Table 5. Percent Distribution of the Nonwhite Population by Marital Status, by Age and Sex, for the United States: Civilian Population, April 1951

Age and sex	Total	Single	Total married	MARRIED Spouse present	Spouse absent Total	Separated	Other	Widowed	Divorced
MALE									
Total, 14 years and over	100.0	25.7	66.3	58.9	7.4	4.6	2.8	5.8	2.2
14 to 19 years	100.0	97.3	2.7	2.7	...	...	...	...	...
14 to 17 years	100.0	99.5	0.5	0.5	...	...	...	...	...
18 and 19 years	100.0	92.3	7.7	7.7	...	...	...	...	...
20 to 24 years	100.0	41.5	56.3	49.5	6.9	5.1	1.8	0.7	1.4
25 to 29 years	100.0	23.4	74.3	65.1	9.3	5.2	4.1	0.4	1.9
30 to 34 years	100.0	13.6	81.1	74.9	6.2	4.9	1.2	2.9	2.5
35 to 44 years	100.0	11.1	84.3	73.6	10.7	7.5	3.2	2.5	2.0
45 to 54 years	100.0	7.8	82.0	72.1	9.9	4.2	5.7	6.3	3.9
55 to 64 years	100.0	6.7	76.9	70.6	6.3	2.9	3.4	12.2	4.2
65 years and over	100.0	4.2	64.6	57.1	7.5	5.7	1.9	30.2	0.9
FEMALE									
Total, 14 years and over	100.0	19.9	62.0	52.0	10.0	7.5	2.5	15.6	2.5
14 to 19 years	100.0	80.2	19.6	14.1	5.5	2.3	3.1	...	0.3
14 to 17 years	100.0	92.1	7.9	5.9	2.0	1.2	0.8	...	...
18 and 19 years	100.0	56.6	42.6	30.2	12.4	4.7	7.8	...	0.8
20 to 24 years	100.0	33.6	63.3	53.0	10.3	7.3	3.0	0.6	2.4
25 to 29 years	100.0	9.2	82.3	71.1	11.2	9.5	1.7	4.1	4.4
30 to 34 years	100.0	9.9	84.3	69.3	15.1	11.1	3.9	3.6	2.1
35 to 44 years	100.0	5.6	79.4	66.3	13.1	10.7	2.4	11.3	3.8
45 to 54 years	100.0	5.0	65.6	55.7	10.0	8.1	1.9	26.1	3.3
55 to 64 years	100.0	2.9	55.7	50.0	5.7	4.8	1.0	39.0	2.4
65 years and over	100.0	0.9	31.6	27.0	4.7	2.8	1.9	67.0	0.5

Table 6. Median Money Income in 1950 of Persons 14 Years Old and Over with Income, by Marital Status, Color, and Sex, for the United States: Civilian Population, April 1951

(Medians computed on base of persons reporting income of $1 or more rather than for all persons; not shown where base is less than 100,000)

| Color, age, and sex | Total | Single | MARRIED | | | | | Widowed | Divorced |
| | | | Total | Spouse present | Spouse absent | | | | |
					Total	Separated	Other		
TOTAL									
Male, 14 years and over	$2,570	$1,160	$2,930	$2,959	$1,886	$1,750	$2,056	$1,045	$2,242
14 to 44 years	2,677	1,079	3,087	3,105	2,294	2,181	2,422	2,321	2,509
45 to 64 years	2,854	1,940	2,980	3,015	1,664	1,383	1,889	2,042	2,167
65 years and over	986	765	1,208	1,225	...	...	...	769	...
Female, 14 years and over	953	1,333	956	938	1,098	995	1,281	754	1,555
14 to 44 years	1,135	1,260	1,037	1,042	1,125	996	1,333	1,121	1,617
45 to 64 years	1,083	2,022	969	959	1,163	1,083	1,344	920	1,500
65 years and over	531	710	393	382	...	...	...	570	...
WHITE									
Male, 14 years and over	$2,709	$1,206	$3,058	$3,074	$2,078	$2,071	$2,083	$1,135	$2,324
Female, 14 years and over	1,060	1,496	1,083	1,052	1,313	1,281	1,354	791	1,683
NONWHITE									
Male, 14 years and over	$1,471	$859	$1,661	$1,677	$1,523	$1,346	...	$707	...
Female, 14 years and over	474	474	454	412	733	720	...	494	$833

unit. A person living alone or a group of unrelated persons sharing the same living accommodations as partners is counted as a household. Quasi households, such as groups of persons living in institutions, hotels, and large rooming houses, are not counted as households. The number of households, as shown in this report, may be regarded as comparable with the number of "families" or "private households" shown in the reports published by the Bureau of the Census on the 1930 and 1940 Censuses. The instructions used for identifying a household in 1951 were more explicit than those used in the 1930 and 1940 Censuses, but this difference in the instructions probably did not have a significant effect on the number of households shown.

Family. The term "family," as used here, refers to a group of two or more persons related by blood, marriage, or adoption and residing together; all such persons are considered as members of one family. A family may comprise persons in either a household or a quasi household. A lodger and his wife who are not related to the head of the household, or a resident employee and his wife living in, are considered as a separate family and not as part of the head's family. Thus, a household may contain more than one family. However, if the son of the head of the household and the son's wife are members of the household, they are treated as part of the head's family. A household head living alone, or with unrelated persons only, is regarded as a household but not as a family. Thus, some households do not contain a family.

The meaning of the term "family," as used here, differs from the meaning of the term as used by the Bureau of the Census before 1947. The new definition excludes the large number of household heads with no relatives in the household who would have been classified as families under the old definition; on the other hand, the new definition includes the small number of groups of mutually related lodgers or employees in households and of mutually related persons in quasi households who would not have been classified as families under the old definition. The net effect has been to decrease the number of families.

Married couple. A married couple, as defined for census purposes, is a husband and his wife enumerated as members of the same household or quasi household. The married couple may or may not have children living with them. The expression "husband-wife" before the term "household," "family," or "subfamily" indicates that the head of the household, family, or subfamily is a married man whose wife lives with him. For example, a husband-wife family is a family with a head who is "married, wife present."

Age. The age classification is based on the age of the person at his last birthday.

Marital status. The marital status classification identifies four major categories: single, married, widowed, and divorced. These terms refer to the marital status at the time of the enumeration.

The category "married" is further divided into "married, spouse present," "separated," and "other married, spouse absent." A person was classified as "married, spouse present" if the husband or wife was reported as a member of the household even though he or she may have been temporarily absent on business or on vacation, visiting, in hospital, etc., at the time of the enumeration. The April 1951 survey was the first in which the category "separated" was used. Persons reported as separated included those with legal separations, those living apart with intentions of obtaining a divorce, and other persons permanently or temporarily estranged from their spouse because of marital discord. The group, "other married, spouse absent," includes married persons employed and living for several months at a considerable distance from their homes, those whose spouse was absent in the armed forces, in-migrants whose spouse remained in other areas, husbands or wives of inmates of institutions, and all other married persons (except those reported as separated) whose place of residence was not the same as that of their spouse.

Husband in armed forces. For women who were reported as married but whose husband was not enumerated in the same household or quasi household, an additional inquiry was made to determine whether their husband was in the armed forces. For women who were reported as separated, the additional question was not asked.

Median age at first marriage. The median age at first marriage, as shown in this report, is an approximation derived indirectly from tabulations of marital status and age. In computing this median, several steps are involved. First, the expected proportion of young people who will ever marry during their lifetime is determined. Second, one-half this expected proportion is calculated. And third, the current age of young people who are at this halfway mark is computed. From the assumptions made and the procedures used, it follows that the date of the survey is also the date when this halfway mark is reached. Half of the young people of the given age had married prior to the survey ate and half are expected to marry in years to come. It should be noted, however, that the bulk of first marriages occur within a rather limited age range and hence within a period of only a few years on each side of the survey date.

Color. Persons of Mexican birth or ancestry who are not definitely Indian or of other nonwhite races are classified as white. The group designated "nonwhite" consists of Negroes, Indians, Chinese, Japanese, and other nonwhite races.

Size of family or subfamily. "Size of family" includes the head of the family and all other persons in the living quarters who are related to the head of the family by blood, marriage, or adoption. "Size of subfamily" includes the head of the subfamily, his wife (if any), and their single sons and daughters under 18 years of age. If a primary family has a subfamily among its members, the size of the primary family includes the members of the subfamily. In census reports before 1947, the term "size of family" included the head of the household and all other persons in the dwelling unit who were related to the head.

Own children and related children. "Own" children in a family are sons and daughters, including stepchildren and adopted children, of the family head. Similarly, "own" children in a subfamily are sons and daughters of the subfamily head. "Related" children in a family include own children and all other children in the household who are related to the family head by blood, marriage, or adoption. All children shown as members of subfamilies are own children of the subfamily head.

CHAPTER 5

Cultural Pluralism and the American Family

IN EARLIER CHAPTERS we have seen that the form of the family varies from one society to another and further that important changes in the organization of a society (*e.g.,* the shift from rural to urban-industrial organization) produce modifications in the structure and function of the family. We are now ready to consider the consequences for the study of the family of the additional proposition that cultures of complex societies are not homogeneous. The typical farm family differs from the typical urban; the typical lower-class family from the typical upper-class; the typical Negro family from the typical family of Italian ancestry. We must bear in mind, moreover, that no family is *merely* rural or urban. Each family also has religious, ethnic, and numerous other social characteristics, all of which are related to the structure, function, and stability of the family.

Hollingshead relates the stability of the family to its position in the class structure. Through increasing contact with urban culture the farm family impressionistically described by Beers is changing from a "familistic" to a "semi-familistic" form. The similar transition described by Campisi is complicated by the fact that the Italian families are engaged in a double shift from a European culture which is rural to an American culture which is urban. Frazier interprets the differentiating characteristics of the Negro family as consequences of slavery and segregation but believes that the differences between Negro and white families are diminishing.

CLASS DIFFERENCES IN FAMILY STABILITY*

August B. Hollingshead

Sociologists in recent years have become aware of the interdependence that exists between the family and status systems in American society, but no studies have been focused on the analysis of the problem of class differences in family stability. Consequently, there is no comprehensive body of either quantitative or qualitative data that we may draw upon for a statement of similarities and differences in family stability and instability in the several classes found in our society. Official city, county, state, and national statistics on marriage and divorce do not recognize the existence of social classes, so these data are not appropriate for our purposes. In view of these limitations this paper will merely outline some of the major differences in family stability revealed by studies of social stratification at the community level.[1] However, before we turn to a discussion of the problem of family stability and the status structure, a few paragraphs of theoretical orientation are in order.

Relation of Family and Class Systems

The nexus between the family and class systems arises from the fact that every individual is simultaneously a member of both systems. He is created in the family and placed in the class system whether he wills it or not. However, the functions of the two systems are essentially different; the family is the procreative and primary training institution, whereas the class system functions as a ranking device. The two systems are interwoven at many points in ways that are too intricate for us to

* Adapted and reprinted by permission of the author and publisher from *The Annals of the American Academy of Political and Social Science,* 272 (1950), 39-46.

[1] W. Lloyd Warner and P. S. Lunt, *The Social Life of a Modern Community,* New Haven, Yale University Press, 1941, pp. 60-61, 92-104; James West, *Plainville, U.S.A.,* New York, Columbia University Press, 1945, pp. 57-69, 115-41; Allison Davis, Burleigh B. Gardner, and Mary R. Gardner, *Deep South,* Chicago, University of Chicago Press, 1941, pp. 59-136; August B. Hollingshead, *Elmtown's Youth,* New York, John Wiley and Sons, 1949, pp. 66-126, 335-88, 414-36; August B. Hollingshead, "Class and Kinship in a Middle Western Community," *American Sociological Review,* vol. 14 (Aug. 1949), pp. 469-75.

unravel here. It is sufficient for present purposes to point out that ea
individual's original position in the class system is ascribed to him o
the basis of a combination of social and biological characteristics i
herited from his family through genetic and social processes. I
position may be modified, and in some cases changed sharply, duri
the course of the individual's life; but the point of origin in the stat
system for every individual is the family into which he is born.

The nuclear group of husband, wife, and dependent children co
stitutes the primary family and common household unit througho
our society. This group normally passes through a family cycle[2] whi
begins with marriage and extends through the childbearing and chi
rearing years and on into the old age of the parental pair. It is t
maintenance of the family cycle from marriage to old age that we w
take as our criterion of a stable family. Each marriage of a man a
a woman brings into being a new family cycle. Upon the birth of the
first child the nuclear pair becomes a family of procreation, but f
the child this family of origin is his family of orientation.[*] Thus, ea
individual who marries and rears children has a family of orientati
and a family of procreation. He also has an ascribed status which
inherits from his family of orientation, and an achieved status whi
he acquires in the course of his life. His achieved status may be d
ferent from his ascribed status, but not necessarily, particularly fro
the viewpoint of class position; but his family of procreation, of nec
sity, is different from his family of orientation. In the case of a ma
his achieved status normally becomes the status of his wife and of l
children during their early years.

Each nuclear family is related to a number of other nuclear famil
by consanguineal and affinal ties.[†] Also, each family in the kin gro
occupies a position in the status system. All nuclear families in a k
group may be in the same class or may be in different class positic
from others. The latter situation is produced by mobility on the pa
of some individual families, while other families remain in the appro
imate status position ascribed to them by their family of orientatic
This movement of the individual nuclear family in the status syste

[2] For a discussion of this concept see Paul C. Glick, "The Family Cycle," pp. 81
above.

[*] See George Peter Murdock, "Structure and Functions of the Family," p. 73 ab
—Eds.

[†] See George Peter Murdock, op. cit., pp. 65-66 above.—Eds.

while it is approved, and often lauded as "the American way," has important effects on kin group relations.[3]

With these considerations in mind, we turn to the discussion of class and family stability. We wish to warn the reader, however, that the statements presented in the following analysis are based on a few community studies in different parts of the Nation, and therefore the bases of the generalizations are fragmentary; heuristic observations are made in the hope that they will draw attention to this area of the social structure, and that they will give readers new insight into these facets of our society.

The Upper Class

Families in the upper class may be divided into two categories on the basis of the length of time they have occupied upper-class position: (1) *established* families, which have been in the upper class for two or more generations; and (2) *new* families, which have achieved their position through the success of the present adult generation.

Who one's ancestors were, and who one's relatives are, count for more in the established family group than what one has achieved in one's own lifetime. "Background" is stressed most heavily when it comes to the crucial question of whom a member may or may not marry, for marriage is the institution that determines membership in the family group. Indeed, one of the perennial problems of the established family is the control of the marriage choices of its young men. Young women can be controlled more easily than young men, because of the sheltered life they lead and their passive role in courtship. The passivity of the upper-class female, coupled with sex exploitation of females from lower social positions by upper-class males that sometimes leads to marriage, results in a considerable number of old maids in established upper-class families. Strong emphasis on family background is accompanied by the selection of marriage mates from within the old-family group in an exceptionally high percentage of cases, and if not from the old-family group, then from the new-family segment of the upper class. The degree of kinship solidarity, combined with intra-class marriages, found in this level results in a high order of stability

[3] The effects of a nuclear family's mobility, both upward and downward, on its relations to the kin group will be explored in a forthcoming paper by the author, published elsewhere.

in the upper class, in the extended kin group, and in the nuclear family within it.

The established upper-class family is basically an extended kin group, solidified by lineage and a heritage of common experience in a communal setting. A complicated network of consanguineal and affinal ties unites nuclear families of orientation and procreation into an in-group that rallies when its position is threatened by the behavior of one of its members, particularly where out-marriage is involved. Each nuclear family usually maintains a separate household, but it does not conceive of itself as a unit apart from the larger kin group. The nuclear family is viewed as only a part of a broader kin group that includes the consanguineal descendants of a known ancestral pair, plus kin that have been brought into the group by marriage.

An important factor in the extended established family's ability to maintain its position through several generations is its economic security. Usually a number of different nuclear families within a kin group are supported, in part at least, by income from a family estate held in trust. Also, because of the practice of intramarriage it is not unusual for a family to be the beneficiary. . . .

The In-Group Marriage Test.   The tradition relative to Protestant intra-upper-class marriages had a severe test in recent years. A son in one family, who had spent four years in the armed services in the late war, asked a middle-class Catholic girl to marry him. The engagement was announced by the girl's family, to the consternation of the Scotts.[4] The Scotts immediately brought pressure on the boy to "break off the affair." His mother "bristled" at the very idea of her son's marriage; his father "had a talk with him"; his 84-year-old paternal grandmother snorted, "A Scott marry a Flaherty, never!" A great-aunt remarked icily, "No Scott is dissolute enough to *have* to marry a Flaherty." After the first shock of indignation had passed, the young man was told he was welcome in "any Scott home" without that "Flaherty flip." A few weeks later his maternal grandfather told him he would be disinherited if he "demeaned" himself by marrying "that girl."

After several months of family and class pressure against the marriage, the young man "saw his error" and broke the engagement. A year later he married a family-approved "nice" girl from one of the other "old" families in the city. Today he is assistant cashier in his

---

[4] All names are pseudonyms; they are used because some of the quotations have meaning only in terms of them.

wife's family's bank, and his father is building him a fine suburban home.

Nancy Flaherty, when the storm broke over her engagement, quit her job as a secretary in an insurance office. A few weeks later she left home to seek a job in another city. After the engagement was broken she quit this job and went to New York City. Today she is unmarried, living alone, and working in New York.

This case illustrates a number of characteristics typical of the established upper-class family. It is stable, extended, tends to pull together when its position is threatened—in this instance by an out-marriage—exerts powerful controls on its members to ensure that their behavior conforms to family and class codes, and provides for its members economically by trust funds and appropriate positions.

The New Family. The new upper-class family is characterized most decisively by phenomenal economic success during a short interval of time. Its meteoric rise in the economic system is normally the personal triumph of the money-maker. While its head is busy making a "million bucks," the family acquires the purchasable symbols associated with the wealthy American family: a large house, fine furniture, big automobiles, and expensive clothes. The new tycoon knows the power of money in the market place, and he often attempts to buy a high position in the status system. The new family is able to meet *the means test,* but not *the lineage test* of the established families. Consequently, it is generally systematically excluded from membership in the most prestigeful cliques and associations in the community. This is resented, especially by the wife and children; less often by the tycoon.

The new family is very unstable in comparison with the established family. It lacks the security of accepted position at the top of the local status system—a position that will come only through time; it cannot be purchased. The stabilizing influence exerted on the deviant individual by an extended family group, as well as friends, is absent. (Many upwardly mobile families break with their kin group as part of the price they pay for their mobility.) Then, too, the new family is composed of adults who are self-directing, full of initiative, believe in the freedom of the individual, and rely upon themselves rather than upon a kin group. The result is, speaking broadly, conspicuous expenditure, fast living, insecurity, and family instability. Thus, we find divorces, broken homes, alcoholism, and other symptoms of disorganization in a large number of new families. Because new families are so conspicuous in their consumption and behavior they become, in the judgment of the general population, symbolic of upper-class actions and values, much to the detriment, and resentment, of established families.

The Middle Classes*

The nuclear upper-middle-class family, composed of husband, wife, and two or three dependent children during the major years of the family cycle, is a very stable unit in comparison with the new upper-class family and the working-class family. Divorce is rare, desertion by the husband or wife is most infrequent, and premature death rates are low.

During the past half-century changes that have taken place in American society have created a demand for technically trained personnel in such large numbers that the old middle class could not provide enough recruits to fill the new positions. Concomitantly, our educational institutions expanded enormously to meet the need for professionally, scientifically, and administratively trained personnel. A vast area of opportunity opened for boys and girls in the lower-middle and working classes to move upward in the economic and status structures. Thus the majority of upper-middle-class persons now above thirty-five years of age are upward mobile. Their mobility has been made possible by education, self-discipline, and opportunity in the professional and administrative channels of our economic system.

Geographic mobility has been a second concomitant in this process. The man—or woman—who is now in the upper-middle class more often than not left his home community as a young adult to attend college. After his formal schooling was completed he generally took a job in a different community from the one where he was trained, and oftentimes it was in a different one from his home town. If he began his adult work career with a national business firm, the chances are high that he was transferred from one city to another as he moved up the job ladder.

Geographic movement is typical of an upward mobile family, even when it lives out the family cycle in its home community. In a large number of cases, when a mobile couple is newly married, both partner

* Whyte discusses in detail the effects of social and spatial mobility on the role of the wife in up-moving middle-class families. See William F. Whyte, "The Wife Problem," pp. 278-95 below.—Eds.

work. The couple often lives in an apartment or flat in a residential area that is not desirable as a permanent residence. As the husband achieves a higher economic status, the new family generally moves to a small single-family house, or a two-family one, farther from the center of the city, where there are yards and trees. Often about this time the wife quits work and the first of two or three children is born. A third or fourth move, some years later, into a six- to eight-room single-family house on a well landscaped lot in the better residential areas of the city or the suburbs normally completes the family's odyssey. While it is moving from house to house, many of its social contacts change as the husband passes through the successive stages of his business or professional career.

Even though there is a high prevalence of social and geographic mobility, and no extended kin group to bring pressure on the family, there is a negligible amount of instability. Self-discipline, the demands of the job, and the moral pressures exerted by friends and associates keep the nuclear family together. The principal family goals are success in business or a profession, a good college or university education for the children, and economic security for the parents in their old age. These goals are realized in the vast majority of cases, and the family is generally a happy, well-knit group.

The Lower-Middle Class. The lower-middle-class family, like the upper middle, is a stable unit for the most part. In fact, there is no essential difference between these two levels of the status system in so far as family stability is concerned. In Elmtown 85 per cent of the upper-middle (class II) and 82 per cent of the lower-middle families (class III) were intact after fifteen and more years of marriage.[5] Oren found in an industrial city in Connecticut that 93 per cent of the lower-middle families with adolescent children were unbroken after eighteen and more years of marriage.[6]

Probably a higher proportion of lower-middle-class individuals have achieved their positions through their own efforts than is true of any other status level except the new family group in the upper class. The majority of lower-middle-class adults have come from a working-class background; many have an ethnic background of recent immigrant origin. Through ability, hard work, and an element of luck they have

[5] Hollingshead, *Elmtown's Youth, op. cit.,* note 1 *supra,* p. 99.
[6] Paul Oren, "Becoming a Milltown American," unpublished doctoral dissertation, Yale University, 1950.

founded small businesses, operated by the family members and a few employees, or acquired some technical training which has enabled them to obtain clerical, sales, and minor administrative posts in industry and government.

The major problems of the lower-middle-class family are connected with the security of its economic position and the education of its children. Parents generally have high educational aspirations for their children, but income limitations often compel them to compromise with less education than they desire, and possibly a different kind from what they would choose. Parents acutely see the need for a good formal education, and they make heavy sacrifices to give their children the educational training that will enable them to take over positions held by persons in the upper-middle class. By stressing education for the child, parents many times unwittingly create conflicts for themselves and their children, because the educational goals they set for the child train him in values that lead him away from his family. This process, while it does not have a direct bearing on the stability of the nuclear family, acts as a divisive factor that splits parents and children apart, as well as brothers and sisters who have received different amounts of education and follow different job channels.

The Working Class

The family cycle is broken prematurely in the working class about twice as frequently as it is in the middle classes. Community studies indicate that from one-fourth to one-third of working-class families are broken by divorce, desertion, and death of a marital partner, after a family of procreation has been started but before it is reared. This generalization does not include families broken before the birth of children or after they leave the parental home. In Elmtown I found that 33 per cent of the working-class families (class IV) had been broken after fifteen and more years of marriage;[7] Oren[8] reported that 29 per cent of his working-class families with adolescent children were broken ones. The norm and the ideal in the working class are a stable family but broken homes occur with such frequency that most parents realize that they are, along with unemployment, a constant hazard.

Family instability is a product of the conditions under which most working-class families live. In the first place, they are completely de-

[7] Hollingshead, *Elmtown's Youth, op. cit.,* note 1 *supra,* p. 106.
[8] *Op. cit.,* note 6 *supra.*

pendent on the swings of the business cycle in our wage-price-profits system, for the working-class family is almost invariably supported by wages earned by the hour, the piece, the day, or the week. Ideally its wages are earned by the male head, but in a considerable proportion of families the wife too is employed as a wage earner outside the home. When a working-class wife takes a job it is for a substantial reason, usually necessity, rather than the desire for "a career."[9]

Factors of Stress. The home is the center of family life, and the hope of most working-class families is a single-family dwelling with a yard; but from a fifth to one-half are forced to live in multiple dwelling units with inadequate space for family living. Added to this is the working-class *mos* that one is obligated to give shelter and care in a crisis to a husband's or wife's relatives or to a married child. Thus, in a considerable percentage of these families the home is shared with some relative. Then, too, resources are stringently limited, so when a family is faced with unemployment, illness, and death it must turn to someone for help. In such crises, a relative is called upon in most instances before some public agency. The relative normally has little to offer, but in most cases that little is shared with the family in need, even though grudgingly.*

While crises draw family members together, they also act as divisive agents; for when a family has to share its limited living space and meager income with relatives, kin ties are soon strained, often to the breaking point. One family is not able to give aid to another on an extensive scale without impairing its own standard of living; possibly its own security may be jeopardized. In view of this risk, some persons do everything short of absolute refusal to aid a relative in distress; some even violate the "blood is thicker than water" *mos* and refuse to give help when it is requested. This ordinarily results in the permanent destruction of kin ties, but it is justified by the belief that one's own family's needs come first.

Although the principle is stressed here that the working-class family lives very close to the limits of its economic resources at all times, and when a crisis comes its effects upon family stability are profound, we should not overlook the fact that moral, personal, and emotional fac-

---

[9] See Floyd Dotson, "The Associations of Urban Workers," unpublished doctoral dissertation, Yale University, 1950, for an excellent analysis of urban working-class culture.

* See Robert M. Dinkel, "Attitudes of Children Toward Supporting Aged Parents," pp. 315-28 below, for a discussion of this point.—*Eds.*

tors contribute to family instability. It is possible that these factors are as important as the economic ones, but this and other observations made here need to be verified by field studies. Actually, while we know that the family at this level of the status structure is susceptible to instability, we have little knowledge derived from systematic research to tell us what cultural conditions are associated with unstable, in contrast to stable, families. A carefully planned series of studies of stable and unstable families with class level held constant is needed. Until this is done, we can only guess about the factors which condition stability and instability in family life.

The Lower Class

Lower-class families exhibit the highest prevalence of instability of any class in the status structure. If we view the lower-class family in terms of a continuum, we find at one end stable families throughout the family cycle; at the other end, the nuclear family of a legally wedded husband and wife and dependent children has given way to a reciprocal companionate relationship between a man and a woman. This latter relationship, in most cases, is the result of their personal desire to live together; it is not legally sanctioned. A companionate family is often a complicated one. It may include the natural children of the couple, plus the woman's children from a previous legal or companionate relationship; also there may be dependent children of the man living with the woman. Normally, when the lower-class family is broken, as in the higher classes, the mother keeps the children. However, the mother may desert her "man" for another man, and leave her children with him, her mother or sister, or a social agency. In the Deep South and Elmtown, from 50 to 60 per cent of lower-class family groups are broken once, and often more, by desertion, divorce, death, or separation, often due to imprisonment of the man, between marriage, legal or companionate, and its normal dissolution through the marriage of adult children and the death of aged parents.[10]

Economic insecurity is but one of a number of factors that give rise to this amount of instability. Lower-class people are employed in the most menial, the poorest-paid, and the dirtiest jobs; these jobs also tend to be seasonal and cyclical, and of short duration. Moreover, from one-half to two-thirds of the wives are gainfully employed outside the

[10] Davis, Gardner, and Gardner, *Deep South, op. cit.,* note 1 *supra,* pp. 118-3 Hollingshead, *Elmtown's Youth, op. cit.,* note 1 *supra,* pp. 116-20.

home; in many cases they are the sole support of the family. However, the problem of economic insecurity does not account for amoral behavior that ranges from the flagrant violation of conventional sex mores to open rebellion against formal agencies of social control.

The very nature of our society may be responsible, in large part, for the number, the intensity, and the variety of social problems associated with the lower class. Such cultural values as individualism, wealth, position, and power must be considered in an analysis of social problems from the viewpoint of the class system. Ours is a competitive, acquisitive society where individuals successful in the competitive arena are admired by most other Americans; they achieve positions of prestige and of power desired by many and attained by few. Less successful individuals may struggle as hard but not be able to do more than hold the status in which they were born; their goal may be to avoid the sorry drift toward lower-class existence. Other individuals may fail in the struggle and sink to the bottom. To be sure, some were born there and failed to rise from the unenviable position they inherited at birth.

Research Needed

The interdependence between the family and status systems sketched here needs to be studied systematically before we can draw definitive generalizations that may be used as the basis for an action program to increase family stability. Isolated community studies indicate that there are functional linkages between the types as well as the amounts of family instability at different levels of the status structure. These indications ought to be analyzed by carefully designed research. If and when this is done, I believe we shall gain some valuable new insights into family and individual stability and instability.

A PORTRAIT OF THE FARM FAMILY IN
CENTRAL NEW YORK STATE*

HOWARD W. BEERS

Pictures of the grandparents or great-grandparents hang today besid
needlework samplers and faded hair flowers in heavy frames on th
walls of an occasional farmhouse parlor. Heirlooms now, they typif
a cultural period that had also its characteristic patterns of socia
arrangement. The early designs for living are heirlooms, too, but no
yet as completely relegated to the walls of memory as are the painting
and the handwork in those parlor frames. Sometimes, indeed, we hav
nostalgic urges to recall them entirely from the past to play again the ol
roles of certain status in the present period of greater social confusior
But cultural systems change and if there were to be any permanenc
of role and status it would be too often a kind of social *rigor morti*
Specific patterns of family life are therefore neither universal nor pe
manent. Our pictures of the farm family, as of every other social grouµ
ing, must be adjusted at intervals to cultural change in each locale an
in each social stratum.

A classic picture of the early farm family in New York State ha
been worded by James Mickel Williams.[1] The figure in his portrait i
an English puritan family reaching New York via New Englanc
gradually reshaped by the conditions of pioneering, but with basi
patterns enduring throughout the period of subsistence farming an
continuing even into the recent periods of commercial agriculture an
contemporary metropolitan dominance. The pioneer American famil
was large, biologically vital, and of strong social texture. It was "th
beginning and the end of rural social organization."[2] Family group
were geographically isolated, economically self-sufficient and sociall
self-contained. Parents were often "the school, the church, in extrem

---

* Adapted and reprinted by permission of the author and publisher from the *America
Sociological Review*, 2 (1937), 591-600.

[1] James Williams, *Our Rural Heritage*, New York, A. A. Knopf, 1925, pp. 46-80.

[2] P. A. Sorokin, C. C. Zimmerman, and C. J. Galpin, *A Systematic Source Book i
Rural Sociology*, University of Minnesota Press, 1931, vol. II, p. 4.

cases the state."[3] Fathers were austerely dominant. Wives were obedient, faithful, subordinate in person and in law. Strict obedience was required of children. Actually, the subjection of wife and children to the father exemplified their common submission to natural processes, never completely understood, always uncertain. The common and paramount interest of family members in the outcome of the farm enterprise necessitated agreement on all matters. Farming and living were synonymous. There was need for an executive in each family who could give direction to the process of living. The natural executive was the father, hence our usual judgment that the farm family was patriarchal. There followed from these conditions a strong family pride and exclusiveness, rigid adherence to custom. Self-restraint, thrift and industry were predominant in attitude and in action. There were strong standards of modesty and morality. There was respect for authority, whether parental, religious or legal.

The matrix of rural custom in which these family-forms were set has been only stiffly flexible, yielding slowly to urban encroachment. The very strength of its original position has not only retarded change but it has added to the discomforts of change. Social confusion is in proportion to the rate of change of the mores. Life is well-ordered and relatively easy when standards and rules are fixed, commonly known and commonly unchallenged. The psychological strains and tensions accompanying rapid social change are most acute where there has been greatest reliance on precept and formula. The potentialities for intragroup conflict, therefore, have recently been great in the farm family. City folk were earlier inured to the presence in one family group of widely variant interests and activities than were farm people. Perhaps this is why Burgess found evidence that adolescent-parent relationships are less well adjusted in the rural than in the city home.[4] Alterations of farm family life may be occurring today in a maximum-discomfort stage of cultural change.

The family type described by Williams was at one time common in many parts of the northeastern hay and dairy sections. It was the biological and social ancestor of present day farm families in Central New York State. These families are living today on family-size farms which

[3] J. F. Brown, *Psychology and the Social Order,* New York, McGraw-Hill Book Co., 1936, p. 224.

[4] White House Conference on Child Health and Protection, *The Adolescent in the Family.* Report of the sub-committee on the Function of Home Activities in the Education of the Child, E. W. Burgess, chairman, New York, D. Appleton-Century Co., 1934.

they own or rent and from which they derive their chief income. In the sample studied,[5] all members are native born.

... The husbands average ... 43.5 years in age, two years older than the wives. The parents were married an average of 18 years ago. An average of 3.6 children have been born per family. An average of 2.7 of these children per family are living with their parents at the time of observation. The families have been settled on their present farms an average of 10.8 years. Three-fourths of the wives and four-fifths of the husbands were born on farms. The families are similar, then, with respect to race, general culture, and occupation. They differ among themselves with respect to age, stage of family development, economic status and other factors. There are many interfamily varia-tions like the individual differences among persons. The family patterns in this group are only once or twice removed from those of native white families in town, for they all stem from the early patriarchal type. The country cousin, however, remains biologically more vital than its urban kin. Even though farm birth rates have declined, per-haps more rapidly than city birth rates, the farm family still is formed earlier and is larger.[6] The age of marriage in the United States has been increasing among classes of higher economic status, but it has been declining among farm people, as among other low income classes.

This portrait of contemporary farm families in a particular area will emerge more distinctly if one model sits against the background of descriptive data for all the families studied. Excerpts from a case narra-tive will help to clarify the outlines of our discussion.[8]

The X family lives eight miles from a village of 2500 people in a rugged south central dairy section of New York State. To reach their home, one drives out through the broad valley and up a winding black-top road through the Gully. Turning right into an uphill lane, one stops between the frame house (straw yellow with white trimmings) and the unpainted barns. A flashlight beam points the way through a dark, rainy night to the back entrance.

[5] Howard W. Beers, *Measurements of Family Relationships in Farm Families of Central New York*, Ithaca, N. Y., Cornell Univ. Agr. Exp. Station Memoir 183, 1934, p. 38.

[6] Dwight Sanderson, "The Rural Family," *Journal of Home Economics*, 29, Apr 1937, 223.

[7] Dwight Sanderson, *ibid.*, p. 223.

[8] The case excerpts included with the text of this article are all drawn from the narrative of one family, sufficiently representative to illustrate general statements.

This has been their home for 17 years. Mr. X is 43 years old, and his wife is 41. Both were born and reared on nearby farms. He finished common school. She attended the village high school for two years. Neither has had any occupational experience other than farming, and the farm is now their sole source of income.

Four children have been born to the mother, but the first boy died of pneumonia in his second year. The second boy, now eighteen, is a sophomore at college. The next child is a boy of eleven, in seventh grade. The youngest, a daughter of six, is in school for the first time—four born, three living, and two at home.

When married 20 years ago, Mr. and Mrs. X lived for three years with Mr. X's parents, working the homestead on shares. Then they bought their present farm of 96 acres, going in debt for the full cost. Their small cash reserve was invested in repairs to buildings.

An average season's work on this farm involves handling 15 acres of hay, 12 of spring grain, five of ensilage corn, seven of buckwheat, three of potatoes, one acre of field beans, two acres of wheat, four of alfalfa, the care of nine milk cows, some young stock and 100 hens. Mr. X is now rated by local leaders as a careful and successful farmer.

The basic differences between early farm and city families were due both to rural isolation and to occupation. Today we find the kind of work that families do is becoming relatively more important than their place of residence. The social length of a physical mile varies from moment to moment. Farmers in central New York State undoubtedly knew of the Hindenburg Zeppelin disaster before the flames were extinguished. Certainly, many of them while at breakfast took vicarious part in the coronation of a British King. Furthermore, as the influence of distance declines and the influence of occupation becomes more marked there comes increasingly into the picture a third differentiating factor, namely, that of economic status. Socio-economic differentiation within the rural community is becoming more pronounced. It is less and less possible to portray sharp contrasts between "the rural" and "the urban" family because of greater social heterogeneity within both rural and urban groups. Hitherto rural people in America have belonged largely to the middle classes. Recently, increasing numbers have moved into social positions of lessened status. As this happens it is important to note that "the climbing of the ladder of gentility" [successfully accomplished by Mr. X] "has suddenly become a much more difficult task than has heretofore been the case."[9]

[9] Roy H. Holmes, *Rural Sociology*, New York, McGraw-Hill Book Co., 1932, p. 73.

Underlying or accompanying the vital and economic changes of the farm family, there are changes in psychosocial relationships, changes in status and role. One factor basic to the definition of status is the division of labor among family members. Hence, any change in work pattern is significant. . . . In the farm family of today, specialization is more marked than it was during an earlier period. Formerly, it was not unusual for girls to help with the outdoor work and for boys to help in household routines. Today, however, the processes of economic production have largely left the house for field and barn. . . .

Child labor is traditional on farms and it has been reduced in quantity more by compulsory school attendance than by any shifts in rural attitude. This is well evidenced by nation-wide rural negation of the proposed constitutional amendment regulating the labor of children. In an earlier time, custom allowed rural fathers the privilege of getting all the work they could from their sons while the latter were legal minors. Social maturity was recognized at 21, but not before. This father-son work relationship is still almost unique to the farm family. It constitutes a type of vocational training inherent in family farming. . . .

Although there is greater division of labor in today's farm home, many activities are still shared, and propinquity still fosters family solidarity. Farm families vary in these customs, but the X family is representative for central New York.

The family members are all home together an average of six evenings per week. When asked what the family usually does in the evening to pass time pleasantly, Mrs. X said, "Well, when the boys are home they like to have Mr. X play checkers with them or something like that. I read a great deal. Mr. X reads as much as he can with his poor eyes. Then we have music, too. Lots of times we get around the organ and sing." The family always gathers at meal time with the exception of luncheon on school days when the children are not at home. But when the family is at home each waits for the others to assemble before starting to eat. Reading aloud is customary, as it was in both of the parental homes. The Bible is read aloud once each day. As a rule, shopping in town is a family activity. There is family observance of the usual holidays. On Christmas the family goes to the home of Mrs. X. On Thanksgiving they go to the home of Mr. X. On New Year's Day they observe a holiday at home. On Decoration Day they go to the cemetery to decorate the graves of their first-born and their dead kin. Birthdays are always celebrated with at least a cake . . .

Daily Bible readings and strong social dependence upon church activity appear in the case of the X family. Neither they nor their neighbors follow the old custom of "saying grace" at meals. Yet every one of the marriages among these farm families were performed by a minister of religion rather than by a civil officer. Wives in particular declared that they "would not feel married unless a minister had performed the ceremony." The marriage mores of rural life are still intimate with institutional religion, but family activities are affected less directly by religion than they were in an earlier period.

The shared activities, propinquity and group rituals in these families are not ordinarily accompanied by overt demonstrations of affection. Here, as elsewhere, traditions of restraint and habits of emotional control are vestiges of the pioneer attitude. It is likely, however, that practices with respect to shared activity, demonstration of affection or family ritual vary more from family to family now than they would have varied three generations ago in the same area.

Along with propinquity and the patterns of work and leisure, division of executive authority in the home is equally basic to family structure. As Sims has written, "Although the rural family inclines to the patriarchal type, it often manifests noteworthy democratic traits."[10] It might now be argued that the farm family inclines more and more to the democratic type of organization. The old conditions of risk and uncertainty in agriculture have not been entirely supplanted but there is now less mystery about the processes of production. Uncertainties of biology and weather, although replaced by uncertainties of the market, are no longer so insistent that each family group have a patriarchal head.

The present importance of markets, and the consequent emphasis upon intense, specialized production is introducing certain new influences on role and status within the family, giving some impetus to the democratic trend.

On a check list, which Mr. and Mrs. X completed independently, each gives the other credit for helping earn the family income. Each of them reports it to be earned by "father and mother together." Mrs. X is responsible for buying food. Purchasing children's clothing is a shared responsibility. Borrowing money is a matter that rests largely with Mr. X, although both parents discuss any problem of this sort before action is taken. If a problem directly concerns the children, they are called into council. Buying

[10] N. L. Sims, *Elements of Rural Sociology,* Thomas Y. Crowell Co., 1934, p. 434.

machinery is a matter for Mr. X's decision. He decides what crops to plant, when and where to plant them. If there is any remodeling to be done in the house, a joint decision is made. Contributing to the church is a matter for consensus. Mr. and Mrs. X select together the papers to which they will subscribe. Writing checks is done only by the husband. He buys the insurance, although whether or not it shall be taken is first agreed upon. Training the children is shared; seeing that children study lessons is also shared. Giving the children permission to leave the home or to go away is joint; punishing children is done by both. Both parents give the children spending money. Both of them help in planning the children's education, although Mrs. X said, "Now some of these things, like choosing the children's vocation, neither one of us ever thought that was our place."

There is little evidence here of uncompromising paternal dominance. The husbands in these families rarely take upon themselves the sole responsibility for making decisions, even when problems of business are up for solution. A discussion involving at least the husband and wife precedes the reaching of a decision in seven homes out of eight. In nearly half of the homes, children also are consulted. However, the importance of family discussion varies according to the kind of problem awaiting solution. Questions relating primarily to the farm business are more likely than others to be decided by the husband without consulting the wife. Decisions about the purchase of machinery or what crops to plant are of this type. On the other hand, if the question is whether or not to borrow money, to buy insurance, or to buy a car, there is likely to be a family discussion before any final action is taken. These questions relate directly to family welfare rather than solely to the farm business. If money is borrowed, thrift is forced upon the members of the family. If insurance is purchased, other things will have to be foregone. A new car will be either liked or disliked by each family member, hence each one has an interest in the decision.

The tendency for husbands to be solely responsible for financial decisions is more marked in families on large than on small farm enterprises. There is a suggestion in the evidence that as standards of competitive business efficiency enter farming, the splitting of executive responsibility into home and farm divisions may become more pronounced. The prophets of chemurgy as well as the discoveries of conservative research point to extreme and imminent changes in the practices and skills of agricultural production. The rate and final extento which country life may be deruralized, of course, cannot even be conjectured, but even now milk-dresses and bathtub-tomatoes are more than pure fantasy.

There are also some new problems of financial administration in the home. In the days of family self-sufficiency, production and consumption were one dual process, begun and finished on one farm unit. Cash was unimportant. Now, however, the medium of exchange has a new significance to each family member. How do families meet the problem of an equitable or satisfactory distribution of cash among the separate members? There is little evidence of any one answer sufficiently extant to be called a folkway, but it is likely that low income or disagreement over distribution of income is a new source of tension in the farm family.

Some phases of the parent-child relationship have been mentioned above. In the X family, we found each child attending school, the oldest boy in college. This illustrates an attitude frequently voiced by mothers who want to educate their children into white-collar strata. We found each child with a definite place in the work pattern, a place of responsibility increasing with age, and allocated to house or field and barn on the basis of sex. We found parents and children playing as well as working together. We found children included occasionally in family councils, we found the boys with property and money of their own, we found ritualistic observance of the children's birthdays. (The manner of giving money to children in the X family is not general in the area studied. Irregular amounts of spending money are more customary in other families.) We found both parents sharing some responsibilities for guidance and control, yet allowing children relative freedom in such matters as choice of vocation. However, we still find that unfailing obedience is expected.

"Mr. X, how do you get the children to do what you ask them to do?"

"Why, we just tell them." Mrs. X added, "we never believed in bribing them or paying them to do things." Mr. X continued, "We always calc'late that if they are told to do anything they are s'posed to do it."

"What methods of punishment do you use?"

"Oh, the whip and the strap. Often we deny them something they want. But we always make it clear to them just why we are doing it."

The changed status of wife and mother is at once cause and effect of changing family relationships. It has been only recently that a writer of syndicated newspaper features could, with impunity, advise a farm wife to "calmly announce to your husband that unless you can have a maid on your farm next year you will refuse to do any canning, gardening or chicken raising. Plan to cut down your work at least 40 percent."[11]

But women have been enfranchised. The law now recognizes their property rights. Educational levels have been raised. They participate freely in the organizational life of communities. Their roles with respect to household and farm work have changed. Some of these things have tended to give them a social status both within and out of the home that is more than ever like that of their husbands. The relationship of the mother's position to patterns within the family has been recognized in the foregoing discussion. It is related also to the role of the family in the community, a role that has changed since the days of pioneering. Mrs. X does not operate the family car but 43 percent of the farm wives in neighboring homes are licensed drivers.

The organized participation of the family centers largely in the church. All members of the family attend church and Sunday School regularly. They have not joined the Grange. Mr. X belongs to the Farm Bureau and Dairymen's League. Mrs. X is a faithful attendant at meetings of the Missionary Society. They have not been to a moving picture since they were married. Mr. X goes to the village or a nearby city about twice a week and Mrs. X not more than once a month. Entertainments take them out not more than once a month. Mrs. X visits with neighbors on the telephone from one to three times a day. Mr. X confesses, however, that he probably does just as much visiting if not more than his wife. He meets neighbors on the road and stops to chat with them or he exchanges work with his neighbors and gossips while he works. Once a year they have friends from the city who come to spend a week or a few days with them. Mr. X has been on the church board; he has been a church steward and has been on the church building committee. Mrs. X teaches Sunday School and is vice-president of the Missionary Society. Mr. X is now collector and school trustee of the school district.

The proportion of husbands who did not participate in any organization (15 percent) is greater than for wives (12 percent). Similarly husbands attended an average of only 2.6 organizations while the wives attended an average of 3.2 organizations. This is a reversal of pioneer customs. Commercial recreation is infrequent. The husbands

[11] Garry C. Meyers, *The Parent Problem.* (Syndicated newspaper column, Dec. 11, 1936.)

and wives attend moving pictures only about once in two months. Town contacts were twice as frequent for husbands as for wives because of business trips.

The local leadership of their communities comes from these families. Three-fourths of the men and over half of the women had a record of some past or present office in an organization. This changed community role of the farm wife, however, has not yet removed her from the family group enough to threaten the integration of the home, for wives with leadership records were found in those homes in which there are many shared activities. Furthermore, this activity in organizations often helps mothers to cope with current change. "Parent-teacher associations, child study clubs, and similar organizations render an important service in establishing norms of child behavior and strengthening the morale of the associated members in their efforts to maintain them."[12]

Although the strength of the great family as a rural social control has weakened materially we find the kinship group still important. One-fourth of the households studied included some relative whose only home was with the family group.

In many respects, then, the portrait of today's farm family in Central New York could well hang on the same wall with needlework samplers and framed hair flowers. In other respects, it would not be out of place in a modern mural. It is a modification of old patterns, a partial acceptance of new patterns. It is smaller than the pioneer family, yet it is still among our chief sources of population increase. The rural social organization of the area is no longer familistic, but it is at least "semi-familistic."[13] The roles of parent and child are less fixed in the mores. There is a definite heritage of paternal dominance, but the outlines of the heritage become progressively more dim. Obedience and subjection of children stand forth still as parental goals but with less and less filial recognition. Specialization and education have affected the division of labor, but shared work and shared leisure are still formative of the family pattern. Propinquity continues to foster solidarity, resisting the centrifugal effects of urbanization. There has been definite democratization in the changes of role and status. That is evidenced particularly in the joint executive function of mother and father. The

---

[12] Dwight Sanderson, "Trends in Family Life Today," *Journal of Home Economics*, 24, April 1932, 317.

[13] Dwight Sanderson, *op. cit., Journal of Home Economics*, 29, April 1937, 223.

rate at which this change occurs accelerates with the advance of business efficiency and industrialization in agriculture. Both rate and direction of future change in the farm family pattern are, therefore, quite as likely to depend upon larger economic and social influences affecting agriculture as upon the dictation of tradition.

THE ITALIAN FAMILY IN THE UNITED STATES*

PAUL J. CAMPISI

The changes in the Italian family in America can be visualized in terms of a continuum which ranges from an unacculturated Old World type to a highly acculturated and urbanized American type of family. This transformation can be understood by an analysis of three types of families which have characterized Italian family living in America: the Old World peasant Italian family which existed at the time of the mass migration from Italy (1890-1910) and which can be placed at the unacculturated end of the continuum; the first-generation Italian family in America, which at the beginning of contact with American culture was much like the first but which changed and continues to change increasingly so that it occupies a position somewhere between the two extremes; and, finally, the second-generation Italian family which represents a cross-fertilization of the first-generation Italian family and the American contemporary urban family, with the trend being in the direction of the American type. Consequently, the position this family assumes is near the American-urban end of the continuum.

Since there are significant differences between the northern Italian and southern Italian families and since there are even greater differences between peasant, middle-class, and upper-class families, it seems expedient to single out one type of family for discussion and analysis, namely, the southern Italian peasant family. During the period of mass migration from Italy the bulk of the immigrants were from southern Italy (including Sicily).[1] These immigrants came mostly from small-village backgrounds as peasant farmers, peasant workers, or simple artisans,

* Adapted and reprinted by permission of the author and publisher from "Ethnic Family Patterns: The Italian Family in the United States," *The American Journal of Sociology*, 53 (1948), 443-49.

[1] During the decade of 1900-1910, of the 2,045,877 Italians who came to America, the majority were from southern Italy.

relationships with the parents as well as with immigrant relatives are affectionate and understanding. A third form which the second-generation family takes is of orientation inward toward an Italian way of life. This type of family generally prefers to remain in the Italian neighborhood, close to the parental home. Its interaction with the non-Italian world is at a minimum, and its interests are tied up with those of the Italian community. Of the three, the second type is the most representative second-generation Italian family in America. This is the family depicted in Table 1.

Table 1 reveals the movement of the first- and second-generation Italian families away from the Old World peasant pattern and toward the contemporary American family type. In this persistent and continuous process of acculturation there are three stages: (1) the initial-contact stage, (2) the conflict stage, and (3) the accommodation stage.

The Initial-Contact Stage

In the first decade of Italian living in America the structure of the Old World family is still fairly well intact, but pressures from within and outside the family are beginning to crack, albeit imperceptibly, the Old World peasant pattern. Producing this incipient distortion are the following: the very act of physical separation from the parental family and village culture; the necessity to work and operate with a somewhat strange and foreign body of household tools, equipment, gadgets, furniture, cooking utensils, and other physical objects, in addition to making an adjustment to a different physical environment, including climate, urban ecological conditions, and tenement living arrangements; the birth of children and the increasing contact with American medical practices regarding child care; the necessity to work for wages at unfamiliar tasks, a new experience for the peasant farmer; the attendance of Italian children in American parochial and public schools; the informal interaction of the children with the settlement house, the church associations, the neighborhood clubs, the neighborhood gang, and other organizations; the continuing residence in America and increasing period of isolation from the Old World; the acceptance of work by the housewife outside the home for wages; the increasing recognition by both parents and children that the Italian way of life in the American community means low status, social and economic discrimination, and prejudice; and the increasing pressure

Table 1. Differences Between the Southern Italian Peasant Family in Italy and the First- and Second-Generation Italian Family in America

Southern Italian Peasant Family in Italy	First-Generation Southern Italian Family in America	Second-Generation Southern Italian Family in America
A. *General characteristics:*		
1. Patriarchal	Fictitiously patriarchal	Tends to be democratic
2. Folk-peasant	Quasi-urban	Urban and modern
3. Well integrated	Disorganized and in conflict	Variable, depending on the particular family situation
4. Stationary	Mobile	High degree of mobility
5. Active community life	Inactive in the American community but somewhat active in the Italian neighborhood	Inactive in the Italian neighborhood, but increasingly active in American community
6. Emphasis on the sacred	Emphasis on the sacred is weakened	Emphasis on the secular
7. Home and land owned by family	In the small city the home may be owned, but in a large city the home is usually a flat or an apartment	Ownership of home is an ideal, but many are satisfied with flat
8. Strong family and community culture	Family culture in conflict	Weakened family culture reflecting vague American situation
9. Sharing of common goals	No sharing of common goals	No sharing of common goals
10. Children live for the parents	Children live for themselves	Parents live for the children
11. Children are an economic asset	Children are an economic asset for few working years only and may be an economic liability	Children are an economic liability
12. Many family celebrations of special feasts, holidays, etc.	Few family celebrations of feasts and holidays	Christmas only family affair, with Thanksgiving being variable
13. Culture is transmitted only by the family	Italian culture is transmitted only by family, but American culture is transmitted by American institutions other than the family	American culture is transmitted by the family and by other American institutions

Table 1. (Continued)

Southern Italian Peasant Family in Italy	First-Generation Southern Italian Family in America	Second-Generation Southern Italian Family in America
14. Strong in-group solidarity	Weakened in-group solidarity	Little in-group solidarity
15. Many functions: economic, recreational, religious, social, affectional, and protective	Functions include semi-recreational, social, and affectional	Functions reduced to affectional, in the main
B. *Size:*		
1. Large-family system	Believe in a large-family system but cannot achieve it because of migration	Small-family system
2. Many children (10 is not unusual)	Fair number of children (10 is unusual)	Few children (10 is rare)
3. Extended kinship to godparents	Extended kinship, but godparent relationship is weakened	No extended kinship to godparents
C. *Roles and statuses:*		
1. Father has highest status	Father loses high status, or it is fictitiously maintained	Father shares high status with mother and children; slight patriarchal survival
2. Primogeniture: eldest son has high status	Rule of primogeniture is variable; success more important than position	No primogeniture; all children tend to have equal status
3. Mother center of domestic life only and must not work for wages	Mother center of domestic life but may work for wages and belong to some clubs	Mother acknowledges domestic duties but reserves time for much social life and may work for wages
4. Father can punish children severely	Father has learned that American law forbids this	Father has learned it is poor psychology to do so
5. Family regards itself as having high status and role in the community	Family does not have high status and role in the American community but may have it in the Italian colony	Family struggles for high status and role in the American community and tends to reject high status and role in the Italian community

Table 1. (Continued)

Southern Italian Peasant Family in Italy	First-Generation Southern Italian Family in America	Second-Generation Southern Italian Family in America
6. Women are educated for marriage only	Women receive some formal education as well as family education for marriage	Emphasis is on general education with reference to personality development rather than to future marriage
7. The individual is subordinate to the family	Rights of the individual increasingly recognized	The family is subordinate to the individual
8. Daughter-in-law is subservient to the husband's family	Daughter-in-law is in conflict with husband's family	Daughter-in-law is more or less independent of husband's family
9. Son is expected to work hard and contribute to family income	Son is expected to work hard and contribute to family income, but this is a seldom-realized goal	Son expected to do well in school and need not contribute to family income
D. *Interpersonal relations:*		
1. Husband and wife must not show affection in the family or in public	Husband and wife are not demonstrative in public or in the family but tolerate it in their married children	Husband and wife may be demonstrative in the family and in public
2. Boys are superior to girls	Boys are regarded as superior to girls	Boys tend to be regarded as superior to girls, but girls have high status also
3. Father is consciously feared, respected, and imitated	Father is not consciously feared or imitated but is respected	Father is not consciously feared. He may be imitated and may be admired
4. Great love for mother	Great love for mother but much ambivalence from cultural tensions	Love for mother is shared with father
5. Baby indulgently treated by all	Baby indulgently treated by all	Baby indulgently treated by all with increasing concern regarding sanitation, discipline, and sibling rivalry
E. *Marriage:*		
1. Marriage in early teens	Marriage in late teens or early twenties	Marriage in early or middle twenties

Table 1.   (Continued)

Southern Italian Peasant Family in Italy	First-Generation Southern Italian Family in America	Second-Generation Southern Italian Family in America
2. Selection of mate by parents	Selection of mate by individual with parental consent	Selection of mate by individual regardless of parental consent
3. Must marry someone from the same village	This is an ideal, but marriage with someone from same region (*i.e.,* province) is tolerated; very reluctant permission granted to marry outside nationality; no permission for marriage outside religion	Increasing number of marriages outside nationality and outside religion
4. Dowry rights	No dowry	No dowry
5. Marriage always involves a religious ceremony	Marriage almost always involves both a religious and a secular ceremony	Marriage usually involves both, but there is an increasing number of marriages without benefit of religious ceremony
F. *Birth and child care:*		
1. Many magical and superstitious beliefs in connection with pregnancy	Many survivals of old beliefs and superstitions	Few magical and superstitious notions in connection with pregnancy
2. Delivery takes place in a special confinement room in the home; midwife assists	Delivery takes place generally in a hospital; may take place in home; family doctor displaces midwife	Delivery takes place almost always in a hospital; specialist, obstetrician, or general practitioner assists
3. Child illnesses are treated by folk remedies; local physician only in emergencies or crises	Child illnesses are treated partially by folk remedies but mostly by the family doctor	Child illnesses are treated by a pediatrician; much use of latest developments in medicine (vaccines, etc.)
4. Child is breast-fed either by the mother or by a wet nurse; weaning takes place at about end of 2d or	Child is breast-fed if possible; if not, it is bottle-fed; same practice with variations regarding weaning	Child is bottle-fed as soon as possible; breast-feeding is rare; no weaning problems

Table 1. (Continued)

Southern Italian Peasant Family in Italy	First-Generation Southern Italian Family in America	Second-Generation Southern Italian Family in America
3d year by camouflaging the breasts		
5. No birth control	Some birth control	Birth control is the rule
G. *Sex attitudes:*		
1. Child is allowed to go naked about the house up to the age of 5 or 6; after this there is rigid enforcement of the rule of modesty	Variable, depending on the individual family's situation	This is variable, depending on the individual family; development of modesty is much earlier than in Old World peasant family
2. Sex matters are not discussed in family	Sex matters are not discussed in family	Sex matters increasingly discussed in family but not as freely as in "old" American family
3. Adultery is severely punished by the man's taking matters into his own hands	Adultery results in divorce or separation	Adultery may result in divorce or separation
4. Chastity rule rigidly enforced by chaperonage; lack of it grounds for immediate separation on wedding night	Attempts to chaperon fail, but chastity is an expectation; lack of it is grounds for separation, but there are few cases of this kind in America	No chaperonage; chastity is expected, but lack of it may be reluctantly tolerated
5. No premarital kissing and petting are allowed	No premarital kissing and petting are allowed openly	Premarital kissing and petting are allowed openly
6. Boys and girls attend separate schools	Schools are coeducational	Schools are coeducational
H. *Divorce and separation:*		
1. No divorce allowed	No divorce allowed, but some do divorce	Religion forbids it, but it is practiced
2. Desertion is rare	Desertion is rare	Desertion is rare
I. *Psychological aspects:*		
1. Fosters security in the individual	Fosters conflict in the individual	Fosters security with some conflict lags
2. The family provides a specific way of life;	Family is in conflict, hence cannot provide	Family reflects confused American situation

Table 1.   (Concluded)

Southern Italian Peasant Family in Italy	First-Generation Southern Italian Family in America	Second-Generation Southern Italian Family in America
hence, there is little personal disorganization	a specific way of life; yields marginal American-Italian way of life	does not give individual a specific way of life, but marginality is weakened
3. Recreation is within family	Recreation is both within and outside the family	Recreation is in the main outside the family; this is variable, depending on individual family situation

by American legal, educational, political, and economic institutions for the Americanization of the foreigner.

Nonetheless, the first-generation Italian family in this phase is a highly integrated one, as in the Old World. The demands of the American community are not seriously felt in the insulated Italian colony, and the children are too young seriously to articulate their newly acquired needs and wishes. The Italian family is stabilized by the strong drive to return to Italy.

The Conflict Stage

In this period the first-generation family experiences its most profound changes and is finally wrenched from its Old World foundation. It is now chiefly characterized by the conflict between two ways of life, the one American and the other Italian, and by the incompatibility of parents and children. This phase begins roughly during the second decade of living in America—specifically, when the children unhesitatingly express their acquired American expectations and attempt to transmit them in the family situation and when the parents in turn attempt to reinforce the pattern of the Old World peasant family. Conflicting definitions of various family situations threaten to destroy whatever stability the family had maintained through the first period. This is the period of great frustration and of misunderstanding between parents and children. In this undeclared state of war between two ways of life it is the parents who have the most to lose, for their complete acceptance of the American way of living means the destruction of the Old World ideal.

The first-generation Italian family is also constantly made to feel the force of external pressures coming from outside the Italian colony. It is inevitable that the family structure should crumble under the incessant hammering. Not able to draw upon a complete culture and social system to support its position, the family pattern, already weakened, now begins to change radically: the father loses his importance, the daughters acquire unheard-of independence; in short, the children press down upon the first-generation family an American way of life.

Accommodation Stage

This period begins with the realization by parents and children that the continuation of hostility, misunderstanding, and contraventive behavior can result only in complete deterioration of the family. The ambivalent attitude of the children toward the parents, of great affection, on the one hand, and hostility, on the other, now tends to be replaced by a more tolerant disposition. This stage begins when the offspring reach adulthood and marry and establish households of their own, for by this time the control by the parents is greatly lessened.

Among the many factors which operate to bring about a new stability in the family are the realization on the part of the parents that life in America is to be permanent; the adult age of the offspring; the almost complete dependence of the parents on the offspring, including use of the children as informants, interpreters, guides, and translators of the American world; recognition on the part of the parents that social and economic success can come to the offspring only as they become more and more like "old" Americans; the conscious and unconscious acculturation of the parents themselves with a consequent minimizing of many potential conflicts; the long period of isolation from the Old World which makes the small-village culture and peasant family seem less real; the decision by the parents to sacrifice certain aspects of the Old World family for the sake of retaining the affection of the children; the acknowledgment by the children that the first-generation family is a truncated one and that complete repudiation of the parents would leave them completely isolated; the success of the first-generation family in instilling in the offspring respect and affection for the parents; and the gradual understanding by the children that successful interaction with the American world is possible by accepting marginal roles and that complete denial of the Old World family is unnecessary.

The accommodation between parents and offspring permits the second-generation Italians to orientate themselves increasingly toward an American way of life. The second-generation household, therefore, tends to pattern itself after the contemporary urban American family. Considerable intermarriage, the advanced age of the parents, the loosening of ties with the Italian neighborhood, and the development of intimate relationships with non-Italians make the transition of the second-generation family comparatively easy.

THE NEGRO FAMILY IN THE UNITED STATES*

E. Franklin Frazier

As the result of the manner in which the Negro was enslaved, the African cultural heritage has had practically no effect upon the evolution of Negro family life in the United States. The destruction of the African family system began in Africa, where the slave-traders gathered their human cargo, consisting largely of young males. The process of "breaking" the Negroes into the slave system and the scattering of them on numerous and relatively small plantations and farms left little opportunity for the slaves to reknit the threads of their ancestral culture. Memories of the homeland were effaced, and what they retained of African ways and conceptions of life ceased to have meaning in the new environment. There were no longer marriages according to African customs; hence mating became subject to individual impulses and wishes and to the control of the white masters. The type of family system which developed was determined by the requirements of the slave system. Likewise, in later stages of its development, the character of the Negro family was shaped by social and economic forces in American life.

Under the system of slavery the Negro family emerged first as a natural organization based upon the physical and emotional ties

* Adapted and reprinted by permission of the author and publisher from "Ethnic Family Patterns: The Negro Family in the United States," *The American Journal of Sociology*, 53 (1948), 435-38.

between the mother and her offspring. The father and husband played a less important role in family relations because his interest in the family was less fundamental and his relations with his wife and children were influenced to a larger extent by the fortunes of the slave regime. The attitudes of both "husband" and "wife" toward "marriage," which had no legal basis, were influenced by the degree to which they had assimilated the sex and family mores of the whites. The process of assimilation proceeded most rapidly with the house servants who lived in close association with the whites and shared in the lives of the latter. Where slavery became a settled way of life, and the plantation became a social as well as an industrial institution, the slave family was likely to acquire considerable stability. Moreover, in the organization of the plantation there was a division of labor and social distinctions among the slaves which tended to reinforce the family mores of the whites.*

The process of assimilating the family mores of the whites was facilitated and accelerated by racial amalgamation under the slave system. The very fact of white ancestry tended to make the mixed-blood identify himself with the whites. Largely as the result of race mixture, a class of free Negroes came into existence, especially in those areas of the South where the economic basis of slavery was being undermined. Among the half-million free Negroes, nearly 40 per cent of whom were of mixed blood, there was a substantial element with a secure economic position, especially in the South. It was among this element that the Negro family acquired an institutional character with traditions of conventional sex and family mores.

The social upheaval occasioned by the Civil War, emancipation, and reconstruction tended to destroy the customary forms of family relation that had taken root during slavery. Moreover, the stability and privileged position of the mixed-blood families were affected by the emergence of Negro communities composed largely of Negroes with a background of slavery. From emancipation to the first decade of the

* Herskovits disagrees with Frazier concerning the interpretation to be placed upon the weak bond between the father-husband on the one hand and the wife and children on the other. Frazier believes that the African cultural heritage was lost and that the phenomenon in question resulted from the conditions of slavery. Herskovits, however, sees the weak husband-family bond as an outgrowth of the polygynous origins of the African Negro. For more comprehensive discussions of this point, cf. E. F. Frazier, The Negro Family in the United States, Chicago, University of Chicago Press, 1939, pp. 23, 41, 61, 107; M. J. Herskovits, The Myth of the Negro Past, New York, Harper, 1941, pp. 167-86, esp. p. 181.—Eds.

present century, two general tendencies are apparent in the development of the Negro family. In the families which had acquired considerable stability during slavery, the father's position was more firmly established, especially if he became a landowner or a homeowner. This class grew in importance during the first fifty years of freedom and together with the descendants of the free Negro with whom they intermarried formed what represented the conventional and stable elements in the family life of the Negro. On the other hand, among the great mass of rural Negroes, who became accommodated to a modified form of life on southern plantations, there developed a form of family life based largely upon mutual interests and mutual sympathies. It lacked an institutional basis, since both legal marriage and divorce were not generally observed. The family often grew out of unmarried motherhood and the common interests which developed from the association of men and women in the struggle for existence.

Around the opening of the century public attention was focused upon the widespread family disorganization among Negroes in the cities of the country. Hundreds of thousands of Negroes had gradually drifted into the seven hundred or more cities of the South. Then came World War I, which carried nearly a million Negro migrants, with their simple family folkways, to the metropolitan regions of the North. The small Negro communities in the North were overwhelmed, and race riots often ensued as the Negro communities spilled over into the adjacent white areas. Following World War I the northward migrations continued, along with the cityward movements of Negroes in the South. By the outbreak of World War II nearly half of the Negroes were in cities. As the result of urbanization and widening contacts, Negro family life had to adjust to a new social and economic environment. The type of family life which took shape among the rural folk in the South could no longer function in the urban environment. There has been much disorganization, but at the same time the family has adjusted itself increasingly to the demands of city living.

In order to secure a true picture of familial relations among Negroes, it would be necessary to study groups of families in the cultural and economic life of the various communities of the country. Statistics on family relations for the general population obscure the important differences among Negroes. Nevertheless, when one studies the distribution of whites and Negroes in households for 1940, certain differences, significant in view of the social history of the Negro family, appear (see Table 1). It should be noted, first, that about 5 per cent more white males than Negro males are heads of households. This is in accord with the fact that 28 per cent of white males as compared with 32 per cent of Negro males fourteen years old and over were single in 1947.[1] A more important difference between the races is indicated by the fact that 10.3 per cent of the Negro females in comparison with 6.5 per cent of the white females were heads of households and 9 per cent

Table 1.* Percentage Distribution of Population in Private Households by Relation to Head and by Color and Sex for the South, 1940

	NONWHITE		WHITE	
Relationship to head	Male	Female	Male	Female
Head	39.5	10.3	44.4	6.5
Wife	. . .	31.9	. . .	40.9
Child	41.5	38.2	45.2	40.8
Grandchild	5.4	4.8	2.1	1.9
Parent	0.6	2.4	0.9	2.5
Other relative	6.3	6.7	4.1	4.3
Lodger	6.2	4.8	3.1	2.3
Servant or hired hand	0.5	0.9	0.2	0.5

* *Sixteenth Census of the United States: 1940*, Vol. IV: *Population*, Part I: "Characteristics by Age," p. 114.

fewer Negro females were wives in households. The fewer Negroes than whites who are children of the head of the household is not so significant as the larger proportion of Negroes than whites who are grandchildren to the head of the household. This is undoubtedly related to the fact that Negro families, especially in rural areas, include several generations. Moreover, very often in the Negro maternal households the grandmother becomes the head of the family. Probably this also accounts for the larger proportion of male parents of heads of white households than males who stand in the same relation in Negro households.

The larger proportion of the Negro population than the white population classified as "other relatives" is indicative of what has been called the "amorphous" character of the Negro family. The amorphous character of the Negro family is owing to the fact that it has retained many of the characteristics of a purely primary group. It is likely that

[1] Bureau of the Census, *Current Population Reports* ("Population Characteristics," Series P-20, No. 10), p. 12.

the term "other relatives" includes not only uncles, cousins, and other persons related by "blood," such as illegitimate children, but even adopted children. The larger proportion of servants and hired hands in Negro households than in white households would be misleading if one took these terms literally. Among the rural Negroes servants and hired hands are more likely to represent those who are taken into the household because of human sympathy and share the responsibilities of the household. The larger proportion of lodgers in Negro households than in white households confirms what all statistics show concerning the housing of Negroes in cities.

Although these figures provide a rough index to the general characteristics of Negro families, they do not show some of the important differences between rural and urban families. There is no indication of the large number of childless couples among urban Negroes and the smaller number of children in urban families. Then in regard to female heads of families it is found that in the rural South between a ninth and an eighth of the Negro families have a female head, while in the rural nonfarm areas between a fifth and a fourth have a woman as head.[2] On the other hand, nearly a third of the Negro families in the cities of the South have a woman as head of the family. In the rural areas the landlords want families with an adult male; thus Negro men and women gain mutual advantages in marriage and family relations. In the rural non-farm areas Negro women are able to earn a living for themselves and their children without a husband or father. In the urban areas, family desertion on the part of the men and the opportunity for employ for women, especially in domestic service, swell the number of families with female heads.

Nor do the figures on the distribution of Negroes in households reveal the important differences in the character of the Negro family which are related to the class structure of the Negro community. As the result of urbanization the class structure of the Negro community has become more complex, and there are three fairly well-defined socio-economic classes. Among the lower class, which comprises between 60 and 70 per cent of the Negro population, family relations still reflect the influence of rural folk traditions. It is among these that one finds the majority of families with female heads. The statistics on the marital status of the female heads of Negro families indicate the loose family

2 *Sixteenth Census of the United States: 1940, Population and Housing, Families,* "General Characteristics," p. 31.

ties among this class. Although a larger proportion of owner families—24.5 per cent as compared with 20.9 per cent—have female heads, the marital status of the owners as given in the statistics indicates that there is greater conformity to legal and conventional relations.[3] Among the female heads who are tenants 25.4 per cent of the husbands are absent, 12.7 per cent of the women are single, and only 56.5 per cent are widowed. On the other hand, 77.4 per cent of the female heads who are owners are widowed, 11.5 per cent have husbands absent, and only 7.7 per cent are single. These figures provide only a rough index of the absence of stable and conventional family relations in the lower class.

It is in the middle class, which is assuming greater importance in the Negro community, that one can note the increasing stabilization of Negro family life under the new conditions of city life. The increase in the size and importance of the middle class is the result of the increasing opportunities for employment and education in the city and the integration of the Negro into institutional and associational life of the city such as churches, lodges, and labor unions. Their stability and conventionality of family relations among this class rest partly upon the desire to achieve and maintain respectability. It is among this class that family traditions are built up and merged with the traditions of stable family life already established among the descendants of Negroes free before the Civil War and the more steady elements that emerged from slavery. The middle class constitutes from 25 to 30 per cent of the Negro population. Because of the social mobility in the Negro community, this group merges with the upper class, which is becoming more sharply differentiated from the middle class on the basis of money and style of life. The upper class is relatively small in the Negro group, but it has a style of life and values similar to those among the white upper class. There are relatively few children, and there is considerable emphasis upon conspicuous consumption and leisure. There is intermarriage among prominent families whose aim is to conserve their wealth and maintain their status and family name. Such families are circumscribed both by the limitations placed upon the earning capacity of Negroes and by the fact that the upper class represents an artificial growth behind the walls of segregation.

The deviations in the character of the Negro family from the dominant American patterns have been owing chiefly to the social isolation and economic position of the Negro. As the Negro acquires educa-

[3] *Ibid.*

tion and enjoys greater economic opportunities and participates in all phases of American life, he is taking over the American patterns of behavior characteristic of different classes and regions. His family life increasingly conforms to the American pattern, which is becoming a part of his cultural heritage.

CHAPTER 6

Parenthood and Childlessness in the United States

IN PRECEDING CHAPTERS we have been concerned with the family as a universal institution and with its cultural and subcultural variations. We shall now begin an analysis of the American family in terms of those functions which are most characteristically performed within the family: reproduction and socialization. To provide a background against which to project this discussion McGinnis presents some statistical data on the reproductive performance of the American population as a whole and of certain of its segments. The significance of the American culture and of some of its subcultures for coloring attitudes toward parenthood is the subject of Murphy's paper. In chapters to follow we shall trace the new member of the family from conception through infancy, childhood, adolescence, and into adulthood. Still later chapters will trace the lasting effects of his childhood experiences in the family as he enters business, forms a new family, and finds himself in combat.

PATTERNS OF FERTILITY IN THE UNITED STATES*

ROBERT MCGINNIS

I. Trends in Fertility

During the past few centuries the occidental family has undergone many remarkable changes in structure and function. The most conspicuous of these has been the change in family size. It has been estimated, for example, that at the close of the eighteenth century the average American wife bore more than eight children during her lifetime. In the decade of the 1930's the average was less than two.[1] In less than 150 years, then, reproduction rates in the United States decreased by more than 75 percent.

Figure 1 dramatically depicts the downward sweep in American fertility since 1800. The figure also shows that correlated with the marked decrease of the fertility rates there has been a corresponding reduction in the proportion of rural people in the total population. (This correlation will be discussed below.) It should be noted that the reduction in fertility rates underlies the decline in family size.[2] The declining fertility rates and consequent diminution of family size constitute the demographic underpinning of Ogburn's treatment of changing family functions.[3]

This paper will describe facts underlying these propositions rather than the propositions themselves. The paper does not purport to be exhaustive even as a description, but it should serve to indicate that the degree of fulfillment of the reproductive function has varied drastically through time and, today, varies among different segments of the population.

Fertility: 1940-50. Figure 1 shows that during the decade 1940-50 there was a marked reversal of the general trend of declining fertility.

---

* Original manuscript.

[1] Inter-Agency Committee for the National Conference on Family Life, *The American Family: A Factual Background*. Washington, D. C., U. S. Government Printing Office, 1948, p. 24.

[2] See "Some Statistics Concerning Marriage and the Family in the United States," pp. 92-103 above.

[3] See "The Changing Functions of the Family," pp. 74-80 above.

While it is too early to know definitely whether this shift indicates a permanent reversal of the downward trend, there is some evidence for the view that it is a temporary phenomenon resulting from the

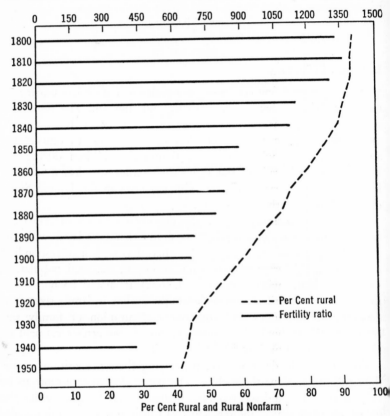

Figure 1. Fertility ratio and per cent of rural population by censal years, United States, 1800-1950.*

* Fertility data from P. K. Whelpton, *et al., Forecasts of the Population of the United States, 1945-1975.* Washington, D.C., U.S. Government Printing Office, 1947, p. 16. Data on percent rural are from Bureau of the Census, *Sixteenth Census of the United States: 1940, Population Vol. I, Number of Inhabitants.* Washington, D.C., U.S. Government Printing Office, 1942, p. 20. Data for 1950 are from Bureau of the Census, *1950 Census of Population, Preliminary Reports: General Characteristics of the Population of the United States: April 1, 1950.* Washington, D.C., February 25, 1951. Since final tabulations are not available, the percent rural for 1950 is an estimate. In 1950 the Bureau of the Census adopted a new definition of "rural," but, in order to make these data comparable, the pre-1950 definition was used throughout.

war-time marriage boom. Unless each fertile woman bears more than two children on the average, the increase in the birth rate cannot be permanent. Figure 2 indicates that, during the last decade, the increase has been most marked in first-order births (births to women who have

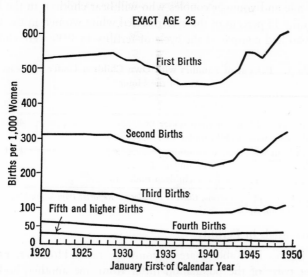

Figure 2.   Trends since 1920 in numbers of births of specified order occurring prior to age 25 per 1,000 white women surviving to this age on January 1 of specified calendar year.*

* Adapted from Clyde V. Kiser, "Fertility Trends and Differentials in the United States," *Journal of the American Statistical Association,* 47 (1952), p. 30.

had no previous children), that there was little increase in third-order births (births to women with two previous children), and practically no change in fourth order and higher. We may ask whether or not the upswing noticeable in first- and second-order births will continue and eventually affect the trend in third- and higher order births. For a definite answer to this question we must wait until this generation (the 1949 cohort) passes through the childbearing period (*i.e.,* until the women in this cohort have become 40 to 50 years of age).[4]

[4] One of the most recent predictions of the trend in the 1950's is that made by P. K. Whelpton in his forthcoming monograph *Cohort Fertility: Native White Women in the United States* (Princeton University Press). Whelpton believes that continuation

Children in Families: 1951. In Table 1 we see that nearly as many American families have no children of their own under 18 in the home as have one or more children. This table should *not* be interpreted to mean that 46.7 percent of the nation's families are permanently childless since many of these are older couples with children beyond 18 years of age and younger couples who will bear children in the future. In fact, only 15 percent of the ever married white women in the United States who had completed the cycle of fertility in 1940 were childless.[5]

Table 1.   Percent of Families with Own Children Under 18 Years of Age in the Home*

All families	100.0
Percent with no children under 18	46.7
Percent with 1 child under 18	21.5
Percent with 2 children under 18	17.0
Percent with 3 children under 18	8.3
Percent with 4 or more children under 18	6.5

* Source: Bureau of the Census, *Current Population Reports: Population Characteristics,* Series P-20, No. 38, April 29, 1952.

II. Differentials in Fertility

The figures in Table 1 are nation-wide rates. However, rates for different parts of the population differ from one another, and hence nation-wide rates do not necessarily reflect the rates of segments of the population. In this section we shall see that reproduction rates differ among people of different residence, social class, race, and nativity.

Residence and Fertility. Figure 1 depicts the downward trend in fertility through time. It indicates also that the rural proportion of the population has been diminishing and by implication that the urban proportion has been increasing. It appears that these trends are closely related and that the link between them consists of a rural-urban difference in attitude toward family limitation.[6] It is evident from Figure 1

during the 1950-59 decade of 1940-49 trends would require a combination of circumstances which is unlikely to occur. For a discussion of the point, see Clyde V. Kiser, "Fertility Trends and Differentials in the United States," *Journal of the American Statistical Association,* 47 (1952), 25-48.

[5] See *The American Family: A Factual Background,* Washington, D.C., U.S. Government Printing Office, 1948, p. 24.

[6] The sheer fact that contraceptives are more readily available in urban areas undoubtedly accounts for some of the correlation apparent in Figure 1. People not only

that an urban milieu is more conducive to small families than is a rural way of life.[7] The small family appears to have originated in the city and seems still to be more prominent there than in the country. Figure 3

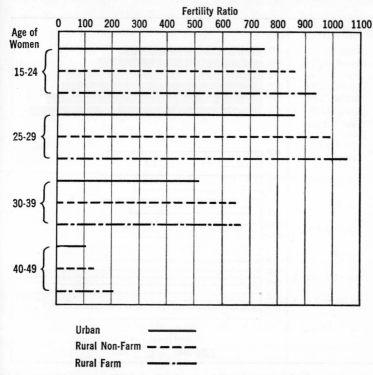

Figure 3. Own children under age 5 per 1,000 married women by age and residence of women in the United States: April, 1950.*

* Bureau of the Census, *Current Population Reports: Population Characteristics*, Series P-20, No. 27, February 3, 1950, p. 7. The above fertility ratios are 1000 times the quotient of the number of children under 5 years of age divided by the number of women in the specified age groups.

supports the notion that residence is an important category of differentiation so far as fertility is concerned. It shows that, in April, 1949,

must have access to means of contraception, however, they must also be willing to use them.

[7] For an analytical discussion of family limitation from the motivational point of view, see Raymond J. Murphy "Motivational Factors Affecting Fertility," pp. 156-70 below.

in all age groups, rural non-farm female residents (*i.e.,* women who lived in communities of less than 2,500 inhabitants) bore more children than did urban females (*i.e.,* women who lived in incorporated places

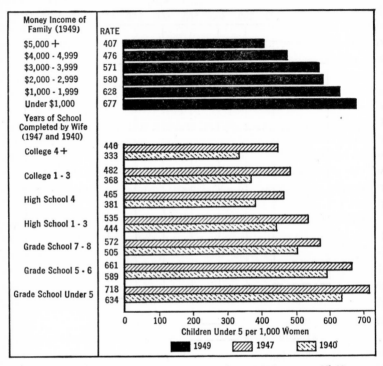

Figure 4. Number of own children under 5 per 1,000 women 15-49 years of age, married and husband present, by total money income of the family, 1949 (top section), and by years of school completed by the wife, 1947 and 1940 (lower section). Rates standardized for age.*

* Clyde V. Kiser, "Fertility Trends and Differentials in the United States," *Journal of the American Statistical Association,* 47 (1952), p. 43.

of 2,500 or more inhabitants) and female farm residents bore more than did the rural non-farm females.

It is tempting to conclude from these data that the city as a way of life has been and will continue to be different from the country. Another and perhaps more plausible interpretation is that rural-urban differences are becoming less marked. Rural dwellers not only are being subjected more and more to the same media of mass communication which influence urbanites, but many farms are coming to resemble urban-industrial organizations. It seems certain that electrification, "factories in the field," modern machine techniques of farming are having far-reaching effects on the structure of rural families. Although the data in Figure 3 indicate that as recently as 1949 rural families were typically more fertile than urbanites, it is doubtful that the difference will remain as great in the future.

Social Class Differences. Whether a group is rural or urban it is subdivided by some form of class structure, and social class is another factor which we might expect to be correlated with differences in fertility. Social class is an abstract concept which cannot be measured directly. There are available, however, several concrete variables which we can regard as indexes of social class and which, therefore, we can correlate with fertility. Here we shall be concerned with three commonly used indexes of social class: income, education, and occupation.[8]

Figure 4 reveals differences in fertility in different income and educational levels. The patterns in this figure show that the fertility ratio is inversely related to social class (*i.e.,* the higher the fertility ratio, the lower the level of income and of education). The only exception to this trend is provided by the "College 1-3" group, but the fact that this does not appear in the data for 1940 may indicate that the exception is temporary.

The most striking feature about Figure 5 is the absence of the decided inverse relationship present in Figure 4. Since occupational category also is a presumed index of social class, the absence of a clear pattern in this figure forces us to reassess the hypothesis that position in the class structure is inversely related to fertility.[9] If we conclude that social

---

[8] See Editors' Introduction for a discussion of the relation of concrete variables to abstract concepts.

[9] If we disregard momentarily the findings based upon income and education and assume that occupation is *the* index of social class, we may explain the lack of pattern evident in Figure 5 by anyone of the three following hypotheses: (1) Occupational categories are not related to social class; hence, if class and fertility are related we should not expect the fact to be revealed by the figure. For a development of the position that occupation and social class are not closely related, see Llewellyn Gross, "The Use of Class Concepts in Sociological Research," *The American Journal of Sociology,* 54 (1949), 409-21. (2) Occupational categories are closely related to social class; hence, Figure 5 indicates that fertility is not related to social class. Kiser develops a hypothesis akin to this while discussing the lack of relation revealed in the data of Figure 5. He suggests

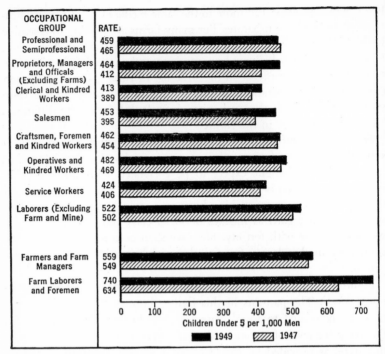

Figure 5. Number of own children under 5 per 1,000 men 20-59 years of age, married and wife present, by major occupational group. Rates standardized for age and relate to civilian employed males in the United States, April, 1947 and 1949.*

*From Clyde V. Kiser, "Fertility Trends and Differentials in the United States," *Journal of the American Statistical Association,* 47 (1952), p. 42.

class and fertility are inversely related, the lack of a clear pattern in Figure 5 means that we are still faced with the problem of describing more clearly the specific nature of this relationship.

There are at least two hypotheses which purport to do this. Accord-

that class differentials are diminishing and that perhaps the apparent relations of fertility with education and income levels result more from lack of control over the residential factor than from a real relation between social class and fertility. See Clyde V. Kiser *op. cit.,* pp. 41-45. (3) Social class is related to fertility, and occupation is related to social class; the lack of pattern in the figure results from inadequate occupational categorization and failure to control other factors. For a defense of this position, see Paul K. Hatt, "Occupation and Social Stratification," *The American Journal of Sociology,* 55 (1950), 533-43.

ing to one, the relationship is linear (Figure 6), that is, for every increment in social class there is a constant decrement in fertility. According
to the other hypothesis, the relationship is curvilinear (Figure 7). This
means that starting at the bottom and running over most of the range
of social class, as social class goes up, fertility goes down. At some class
positions, however (possibly in the upper class or in the upper fringe
of the middle class), the relationship shifts, and from here on, the
higher the social class, the higher the fertility. Proponents of the latter
hypothesis believe that in the upper social strata fertility is positively
correlated with social class.

At this point we have three sets of relationships and two alternate

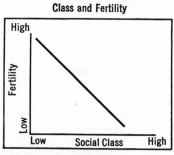

Figure 6. Hypothesis I: Linear
relation between social class and
fertility.

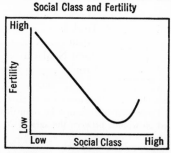

Figure 7. Hypothesis II. Curvilinear relation between social class
and fertility.

hypotheses by which they may interpreted. If we accept the linear
hypothesis (Figure 6), two sets of data (education and income) appear
to fit, but the third (occupation) does not. If we accept the curvilinear
hypothesis (Figure 7) the occupational data begin to fit, but this leaves
the linear relations unsatisfactorily explained. It may be that the first
two relationships actually are curvilinear and that the curve does not
appear because of inadequate categorization. It should be noted that
all groups with annual money incomes of more than $5,000 are lumped
together in our data. This holds true as well for the upper educational
groups, since college graduates are not distinguished from those who
have gone on to professional schools. The few empirical studies which
have made more refined break-downs in the upper income and educa-

tional levels have yielded evidence to support the curvilinear hypothesis.[10]

Race Differences. Table 2 summarizes race differences in reproduction between the white and non-white segments of the urban, rural-non-farm, and farm populations in 1950. Within residential categories, non-whites were more productive than whites. But we can see that the extent of differences between whites and non-whites is less in rural non-farm residence than in farm residence. Moreover, the difference is smaller in urban residence than in either of the other two categories.

Table 2.   Children Under 5 Years of Age Per 1,000 Women Between the Ages of 15 and 49, by Color and Residence of Women in the United States: 1950*

	White	Non-white
Total	418†	472†
Urban	382	394
Rural Nonfarm	489	520
Farm	492	739

* Bureau of the Census, *1950 Census of Population, Preliminary Reports: General Characteristics of the Population of the United States: April 1, 1950*, pp. 7-8.

† These total rates cannot be compared with those of Figure 1 because the latter are based on women between the ages of 20 and 44.

When reproductive differences between races were first studied empirically, no attempts were made to control for such variables as residence; thus the tables included only information comparable to that found in the "Total" row of Table 2. When differences such as these were first discovered, they were interpreted to mean that non-whites had a higher biological capacity to reproduce than whites. More recent interpretations have been based on refined analyses controlling for residence, income, and other social characteristics. These more recent studies have indicated that, when such factors are held constant, the supposedly inherent characteristics are drastically reduced or disappear altogether.

Nativity Differences. The final social category which we shall consider in relation to human fertility is that of nativity, or differences between the foreign-born and native-born. Figure 8 indicates that,

[10] For a presentation of data which seem to support this hypothesis, see Robert F. Winch, *The Modern Family*, New York, Henry Holt and Co., 1952, pp. 118-21.

when occupation and age are controlled in the urban group studied, foreign-born have a higher rate of fertility than either non-white or native-born white except among the professional group.

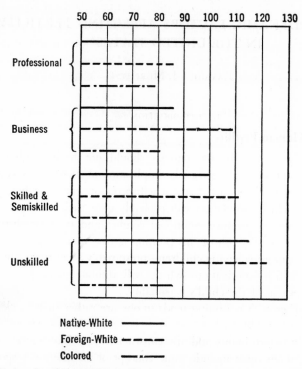

Figure 8. Age-specific fertility rates among wives in the National Health Survey, 1935, by occupational class of the head of family, and by nativity and color of the wife.*

* Adapted from Clyde V. Kiser, *Group Differentials in Urban Fertility*, Baltimore, Williams & Wilkins Co., 1942, p. 63.

Conclusions. From 1800 American reproduction rates declined to a low point in the middle 1930's. There is serious question whether or not the rise in the birth rate since the depression can continue indefinitely.

Fertility rates vary with residence (*i.e.,* urban, rural non-farm, and rural farm), race, nativity, and probably with social class—certainly with education and income. The most plausible interpretation of these differences is that they result from different cultural values rather than from different innate characteristics.

PSYCHODYNAMIC FACTORS AFFECTING FERTILITY IN THE UNITED STATES*

RAYMOND J. MURPHY

I. INTRODUCTION

Needs and Human Fertility

Occasionally one reads that parents should not have children to satisfy their own personal needs. The implication of such a view is that such parents want children because of selfish reasons, and, further, that parents with selfish motivation will probably treat their children in a fashion destined to produce emotional conflict and neurotic disturbances. Another implication of this position is that there is some other kind of motivation for having children—presumably an altruistic, but at least a non-selfish—motivation—which will militate toward a beneficial development of the child's personality.

To this writer such reasoning tends to obscure rather than to clarify the issues in the problem. If we are to operate on the assumption that there are any determinants and any consistency in behavior, then our theoretical system must include some concept of an internal responding, controlling, and impelling "mechanism." (And if we do not assume determination and consistency, there is no basis for a science of psychology.) Most current "dynamic" theories (*i.e.,* theories which attempt to account for motivation) are hedonic (or "hedonistic") in nature. In its simplest expression this means that men, and animals as well, seek to engage in pleasurable experiences and to avoid the painful. In more technical language we speak of pleasurable experiences as tension-reducing or gratifying or rewarding, and the painful experiences as tension-increasing or frustrating or punishing.[1] We can

---

* Original manuscript.

[1] It should be kept firmly in mind that our present use of the term hedonic does not have reference to the philosophy of "eat, drink and be merry," but rather to the fact

conceive also of a middle-ground which is neither pleasurable nor painful, neither rewarding nor punishing, but as non-rewarding and non-punishing.

From this theoretical position it follows that any sort of goal-directed behavior becomes statable in terms of the person's "motives," "drives," or "needs." Since any sort of goal-directed behavior may be stated in the language of motivation or needs, then a person's desire for children or wish to avoid parenthood may be expressed in these terms. Frequently it appears, moreover, that a person may wish both to have and not to have children and thus may have ambivalent attitudes toward parenthood. It is for these theoretical reasons that it seems futile to decry parents who desire children for "their own needs." It is vastly more to the point to analyze the nature of the needs of the person which impel him toward or away from parenthood[2] and to try to trace the consequences of such motivation in his or her interaction with the child.

It seems wise to pause for a moment in our discussion in order to caution the reader about the logical status of the analysis presented in this paper. The generalizations which we make are based on none too adequate descriptions of cultural and subcultural patterns and human personality from which a body of as yet only partially verified theory has been developed. In tracing some of the consequences of such theoretical statements we are making generalizations which must be thought of as propositions of a hypothetical nature yet to be verified in a scientific manner. According to the best available opinion such statements seem to be highly plausible, yet they are presented here as suggestive comments only and as in no way constituting final proof of the influence of psychodynamic factors on fertility.

Properties of Needs

Before proceeding to a discussion of human needs and fertility, let us stop to point out several properties of needs as the source of motivation.

1. Needs May Be Classified as Organic and Social. Needs may be broadly classified as to whether they relate to innate "primary" physiological processes within the body (need for nourishment, regulation of body temperature, need for oxygen, etc.) or to learned "secondary"

---

that the human organism seeks to establish a tension-free relationship to its environment, both internal and external.

[2] Or both toward *and* away, as in the case of the ambivalent person.

processes arising from the life of the individual in a social group. Some authors have thus distinguished between "viscerogenic" and "psychogenic" needs. It is with this second category, the learned or social or psychogenic, that we shall be concerned in this paper since generally in the American society the organic needs of the individual are sufficiently gratified so as to constitute no particular problem requiring detailed analysis. These derived or learned needs originate and are sustained through social interaction. Though this distinction between organic and social needs may help us in our analysis of human motivation, in reality both categories of needs interact. Clinicians, for example, have reported cases in which persons who were denied the satisfaction of the need for affection sometimes compensate for this frustration with a tendency to overeat to the point of obesity.

2. Needs May Change.   Some needs change through time with differing situations in the life of the individual. On the other hand, some of the individual's needs created by his family in his earliest years of life persist throughout his life.

3. Needs May Be Unconscious.   There is strong evidence that many needs are not consciously recognized by the individual. They reside in the realm of unconscious. As elements in the total personality they seem to exert a powerful influence on the development and patterning of behavior. The most dramatic evidence we have of the strength of the unconscious forces operating in the human mind is the formation of neurotic and psychotic symptoms. It seems true, however, that many of the needs of all people are unconscious and this fact must be taken into consideration in our discussion of the complexity of motivation toward parenthood. Thus in the following discussion of the social variables influencing the needs of the individual we must keep in mind the unconscious nature of many such motivations.

As we have indicated, the social needs of an individual are a product of social interaction. It is through association with others in social groups that we learn how to behave, what is regarded as right and wrong, worthless and valuable, and what others expect of us. In other words, social interaction is the basis for the transmission of cultural and subcultural patterns of a society. Once these values and expectations have been learned, they govern future behavior and serve to motivate the individual. In the following section we shall pay some attention to the cultural, subcultural, and idiosyncratic experiences which influence need-structure. These three classes of experience represent different levels of abstraction useful for the purpose of analysis. In reality, however, every individual is influenced by experiences at all of these levels. Individuals are not just farmers or city dwellers, not just upper-class or lower-class, not just Roman Catholic or Protestant, but of course each individual embodies a wide variety of these character-istics. With this point in mind let us attempt to analyze the influence of social needs on human fertility.

II. FERTILITY AND SOCIAL NEEDS

The Socio-cultural Setting

The general value system of a society as a part of the cultural heritage of a people probably exerts an important influence on the specific question of whether or not children are desirable, and hence directly or indirectly regulates the reproductive behavior of a population. Through the learning of such values we develop patterns of striving toward or against goals which are positively or negatively evaluated by the culture.

Some cultures function to create a very strong desire for children by creating potent rewards for parenthood. In other cultures the rewards of parenthood may be nearly balanced by the penalties. It seems safe to assert that no society could long survive in which the cultural penalties of parenthood clearly outweighed the rewards. Cultural con-ditions which would appear to induce strongly positive attitudes toward parenthood are exemplified by the following: fully adult status is not accorded to those who are childless; marriage is not regarded as com-plete until the wife becomes pregnant or bears a child; there is strong emphasis upon the importance of carrying on the family line; children begin while quite young to make a substantial economic contribution to the family. Conditions such as these are characteristic of numerous cultures in which the reproduction rates are high. In traditional Japa-nese culture, for example, these conditions seem to have operated to produce the high birth rate still characteristic of the rural villages of Japan.

Now let us consider some conditions which appear to conduce to a negative orientation toward parenthood. Although there does not appear to be any culture in which parenthood is regarded as disap-proved or disgraceful under appropriate conditions,[3] it is not difficult

[3] It is obvious that in many cultures parenthood is disapproved if the father and mother are not married. In American culture, moreover, there is some disapproval

to find a culture which provides manifest penalties for parenthood. For many socio-economic levels in America children are clearly not economic assets but liabilities. Economically they are not "hands" but "mouths." To young married couples the coming of children heralds not only a new set of responsibilities, economic and otherwise, but also a brake on various kinds of social and recreational activities to which they have become accustomed while childless. Both the economic cost and the limitations on social activities may be viewed by prospective parents as handicapping them in their goal of "getting ahead."

As noted above, however, any culture presenting nothing but penalties for parenthood would undoubtedly be doomed to early extinction. And so in America we find that couples with children are regarded as fulfilling an important duty or mission to contribute to the next generation, as assuring themselves of a source of comfort in old age, as manifesting a socially useful and approved stability. And in America the terms "father" and "mother," especially the latter, are laden with the positive connotation of respect and deference.[4]

What we have been saying is that with respect to parenthood as with respect to other aspects of life, generalized cultural values elicit learned drives or needs. For example, in traditional Chinese culture where final acceptance of the bride was delayed until she had born a son, we should expect that most girls would look forward eagerly (and hence would be positively motivated) to becoming mothers of sons. Or in cultures where motherhood is thought to have damaging effects on the highly valued feminine figure, we might expect girls to view motherhood with some misgiving, and hence to be negatively motivated. The influence of cultural values, then, is considerable on attitudes concerning the desirability of children.

Subcultural Variation

Not only is the need-structure of the individual influenced by society-wide cultural factors, but also by the subcultural variations found in all complex societies. We shall now consider three kinds of subcultural variations: those of rural-urban locality, social class, and religious belief.

---

accorded to married couples who have children without having sufficient financial resources to support them in accordance with their economic station. From some quarters, moreover, criticism is levelled at couples having children while living in cramped quarters, while the wife is employed, or when other conditions obtain which are believed to be deleterious to the optimum development of the children.

[4] Despite the recollections of many of those lying on psychoanalytic couches that parents are ogres.

Rural-Urban Differences. The preceding paper has indicated that variation in fertility exists with respect to rural and urban locality. On the average the farm family is larger than the urban, hence we should expect to find some difference between country and city in the values regarding children.

As social scientists, however, we cannot be absolutely sure about the nature of this differential fertility. Because it is difficult to control the economic and other variables, we are not sure how much of the difference in fertility is due to the fact of residence alone. One study has shown that the fertility ratios of the rural farm and rural non-farm populations are higher than that of the urban population when all three populations are equated for monthly rental value.[5] This one index of income (monthly rental value), then, does not suffice to account for the higher rural fertility. Historically, we may assume that differences in the way of life on the farm and in the city probably have fostered a greater desire for children in rural areas. The increasing urbanization of rural areas would seem to lessen such differences. While it seems probable that such differences are diminishing, therefore, the latest information available seems to imply that they have not as yet entirely disappeared.

In rural areas children seem to have been an asset to the family. They shared in the production of food and the chores of the farm and hence were contributors to the rural economy. Rural marriage was typically thought of not only in terms of emotional companionship, but also as an economic partnership in agricultural production, and children were welcomed as extra hands. In general, the members of the rural family seem to have worked and played together as units to a greater degree than is true of the city. Individual interests were closely related to family interests, and the strength of the bonds of kinship was great. Even today in a few rural areas the community is synonymous with the extended family.[6]

[5] Clyde V. Kiser and P. K. Whelpton, "Fertility Planning and Fertility Rates by Socio-Economic Status," *The Milbank Memorial Fund Quarterly,* 27 (1949), p. 360. (This is one in a series of reports on "Social and Psychological Factors Affecting Fertility.") Another study, also controlling monthly rental value, reports that as recently as 1947 the rural non-farm fertility ratio was still higher than the urban. See Clyde V. Kiser, "Fertility Trends and Differentials in the United States," *Journal of the American Statistical Association,* 47 (1952), p. 44.

[6] For a description of such a community in rural Kentucky, see James S. Brown, "Conjugal Family and Extended Family," *American Sociological Review.* 17 (1952), 297-306.

The city, on the other hand, with its industrialization, specialization, concentration of population, etc., creates a different social atmosphere for the family. As Kingsley Davis puts it:

Urbanism affects not merely the externals, such as the size of the home but also the very nature of the family. It forces individuals to cooperate with countless persons who are not kinsmen . . . It substitutes legal controls for primary ones, and in contrast to the conventionalized intimacy of the family creates rationalized, impersonal associations on the one hand and unconventionalized intimacies on the other.[7]

Moreover, the city presents the individual with a wide range of interests and role possibilities. He has to learn to budget his time and pattern his activities so as to permit adaptation to a broad arc of stimulation. Because of the many alternate cultural values presented by the urban environment, the individual develops a multiplicity of social goals. Often times these goals are contradictory and opposed, for example, the goal of Christian ethics with its admonition to "Love thy neighbor as thyself" is somewhat at odds with the goal of modern business to outdistance the nearest competitor. Such inconsistency in social goals seems to engender in the individual a feeling of tension. From such conflict an attitude of ambivalence is likely to occur. By the term ambivalence we mean the simultaneous presence within the individual of mutually opposed feelings, such as love and hate, which are directed toward the same person or object. In the present context we refer to the coexistence of feelings of desire and reluctance when the possibility of bearing children is considered by prospective parents. Such ambivalent feelings would seem to have possible consequences both for the personalities of the parents and for those of any possible children they may have. The negative pole of ambivalence may engender a feeling of guilt, especially when the culture emphasizes the desirability of having children. That is to say, prospective parents may feel guilty over their reluctance to bear children. On the positive side, the desire for children may be complicated by a conflict in the choice of goals, children being only one of several aspirations of the couple. These negative feelings of ambivalent couples may engender in their children feelings of rejection. The children may come to feel that they are not wanted. Thus, although the purpose of this paper is to relate

[7] Kingsley Davis, "Reproductive Institutions and the Pressure for Population," *The Sociological Review*, 29 (1937), pp. 295-96.

the attitude of ambivalence to fertility, its implications for personality development should also be kept in mind.

In the city, in many cases, children seem to be an economic liability and a social handicap. Because of the time and expense they involve, children may place a barrier on upward mobility. Because of the attention they demand, they may seriously interfere with the other needs and interests of the parents. Quoting Davis again:

> Children tend to prevent the mother's entering an occupation, and if she has a career, they check her professional proficiency. Children, moreover, are an inconvenience in every sphere of activity—a hindrance to travel, parties, unencumbered living quarters, etc. All of these things are difficult and pointless to estimate in terms of cash, but they are, along with the desire for social advancement, powerful forces against the wish for children.[8]

These characteristics which distinguish urban from rural life represent, in considerable measure, penalties for parenthood. At present we do not have enough detailed information to warrant our asserting that there is a direct connection between these urban characteristics and the low fertility in cities. The fact that urban characteristics coincide with low fertility, however, suggests a causal relationship.

The Subcultures of the Social Classes. Another source of cultural variation is that which occurs as a result of socio-economic class position. The studies of Warner and his group and of others have revealed that there are marked differences in outlook, valuation, and behavior among the social classes in cities. We cannot devote a detailed analysis to these differences, yet at the risk of oversimplification a few words should be said about the "style of life" of the three broad strata in our society: the lower, middle, and upper classes.[9]

1. The lower class. Being close to the threshold of survival in terms of satisfying the requirements of food, clothing, and shelter, the members of this class present a picture of insecurity. Because of this problem of survival the immediacy of gratifying everyday needs seems to be

---

[8] *Ibid.,* p. 303.

[9] The following discussion is based largely upon the description of social classes reported in the following monographs: W. L. Warner and P. S. Lunt, *The Social Life of a Modern Community,* New Haven, Yale University Press, 1941; A. B. Hollingshead, *Elmtown's Youth: The Impact of Social Classes on Adolescents,* New York, Wiley, 1949; R. J. Havighurst and Hilda Taba, *Adolescent Character and Personality,* New York, Wiley, 1949; and Allison Davis, B. B. Gardner, and M. R. Gardner, *Deep South,* Chicago, University of Chicago Press, 1941.

an emphasis of the lower class. The ideas of thrift and rational planning have little meaning in an environment which offers little hope
for a better future. As a result, a philosophy of life seems to have
developed which stresses the importance of enjoying life while it is
possible and gives little thought to tomorrow. This outlook is evidenced
in the lower-class patterns of economic consumption and sexual
activity.[10]

When money is available it is spent freely. Much to the chagrin of
the social worker, it is often spent for such luxury items as television
sets, automobiles, etc. At the same time sexual impulses are more freely
expressed, and children are conceived without consideration of such
matters as spacing, the health of the mother, etc. Quite often children
are welcome because they are needed to contribute to the support of
the family and assume this responsibility at an early age. Since advanced
education is expensive and interferes with financial contribution to
the family, it is not encouraged. Because of economic necessity, mutual
aid within the family is a lower-class characteristic. Upward mobility
is not important, all that matters is survival; striving is dedicated to
this end. All in all, the insecurity of the future, the stress on immediate
gratification, and the utilitarian importance of children operate jointly
to encourage parenthood and place a high value on large families.

2. *The middle class*. Middle-class values play a dominant role in
the American culture. The middle classes in our society are composed,
by and large, of people characterized by a high degree of status consciousness and a desire to move upward on the social ladder. It is this
segment of our population which places great stress on the necessity
for savings, hard work, the desirability of long-range planning, and on
the importance of maintaining or improving the current level of living.
These people are also the "joiners" in our society who recognize the
necessity of maintaining the "right connections" in order to reach their
future goals. It is in this stratum where children are often considered
a definite liability to parental advancement. This fact, plus the middle-
class desire that children shall be given every chance in life for higher
education and a better style of living, tends to make the small family
an ideal as well as a practical necessity. The American dream of social

---

[10] Allison Davis comments on the lower class practice of gluttony as a protection
against physical disease and as a reaction to the fear of hunger and insecurity in lower-
class life. See W. Allison Davis, "Child Rearing in the Class Structure of American
Society" in *The Family in a Democratic Society*, Anniversary Papers of the Community
Service Society of New York. New York, Columbia University Press, 1949, pp. 56-69.

and economic advancement may be said to be a middle-class value, and since it appears that the urban middle-class family is becoming the prototype for the American family, the values of the middle class may well become those of the family of the future.

3. The upper class. Although less is known of upper-class values and behavior, the work of Warner and his associates in "Yankee City" has given some indication of life at this level of our society.[11] The members of the upper class look with disdainful conservatism on the striving behavior of the middle class. Although membership in select clubs and charitable organizations is favored, these people are not the "joiners" of the middle class. Their emphasis is upon the preservation rather than the achievement of high status. Conscious of tradition, they show great pride and reverence for the history of their families. The influence of the ancestors is considerable, and a proof of descent from genteel forebears is a social asset. Because of the emphasis upon continuing the family line parenthood is considered desirable. Children are not a burden either socially or economically. Thus, there is probably less conscious effort to limit the size of the family among the higher income levels of our society. This conclusion seems to be borne out by studies which indicate that family size increases at the higher income levels of our society.

Religious Belief. Differences in religious belief and behavior may result in varying attitudes toward parenthood. Such religious groups as the Mormons and Roman Catholics place heavy emphasis on large families by stressing the importance of parenthood as conforming to the will of God and by considering any artificial means of interfering with conception or birth (contraception, abortion) as sinful and taboo. Such religions appear to motivate the devout toward having large families. On the other hand, there are some religious sects (the Shakers, Millerites, Megiddos, Koreshans, etc.) which believe in the imminence of the day of judgment and hence look upon procreation as contrary to the wish of God.[12] For example, the Koreshans believed that rein-

---

[11] See W. Lloyd Warner and Paul S. Lunt: *The Social Life of a Modern Community,* New Haven, Yale University Press, 1941.

[12] For a general description of some of these religious sects, see Elmer T. Clark, *The Small Sects in America,* Nashville, Cokesbury Press, n.d. Although some of these sects (*e.g.,* the Millerites and the Koreshans) are primarily of historical interest, they are considered here because they demonstrate the effect of religious belief on reproductive behavior.

carnation was the basic law of life. To become immortal in the flesh was possible only if one ceased to reproduce. Thus, celibacy was regarded as a positive value, especially for the higher ranks of the church membership.

Idiosyncratic Behavior

Thus far our discussion of individual motivation regarding parenthood has been in terms of cultural and subcultural values shared by the members of a group. It is a matter of common observation, however, that there is variation in personality and therefore in motivation among members of the same social group, as well as among the members of different groups. Such individual differences among persons within a group presumably spring from both hereditary and experiential sources. Examples of such idiosyncratic motivation are as follows. One man who in his youth had been very rivalrous with his siblings was eager to present his parents with their first grandchild. One woman had learned that at the time of her birth her mother had earnestly hoped that she would have a boy. For years this woman had felt that she had failed her mother in turning out to be a girl rather than a boy. On being married she was eager to redeem herself with her mother by presenting her with a grandson. When it developed that her firstborn was a girl, this woman was disconsolate for several days until her mother came and "forgave" her.[13] A marine who had seen much combat duty in World War II had developed strong feelings of guilt over having killed a number of enemy soldiers. He looked forward to parenthood and the creation of new lives as a penance for the lives he had taken. When his wife's first pregnancy terminated in a still birth, he developed a psychosis.[14]

To be sure, the latter two cases are exaggerated to the point of morbidity. All three do, however, indicate kinds of motivation which are probably present in each of us to some degree. Although it would be expected that each of these persons strives toward culturally determined goals, yet in these instances we have motivation which seems idiosyncratic in intensity. Since both idiosyncratic and culturally conditioned behavior must presumably be learned, we should hypothesize

[13] Case reported in M. E. Fries, "The Study of the Emotional Development of Children," *The Medical Women's Journal*, August 1936, Reprint unpaged.

[14] Case reported in Therese Benedek, *Insight and Personality Adjustment*, New York, Ronald, 1946, p. 277.

that these individuals must have been exposed to situations more or less unique out of which these motivations developed.

In summary, the social needs of the individual are cultural, sub-cultural, and idiosyncratic in origin, and they are a product of social interaction. Cultural and subcultural patterns are learned in social interaction in the family and the play group and with other persons and groups both in childhood and in later life. The subcultural patterns which we have considered relate to differences in social class, location or residence, and religion. Experiences shared with other members of social groups plus experiences which are unique (and we all have such experiences) contribute to the structure of one's need pattern. One's need pattern will determine whether children will be regarded as desirable or undesirable. Our culture—especially the sub-culture of the urban middle class—contains both rewards and penalties for parenthood and hence appears to be conducive for the development in parents of ambivalent attitudes toward children.

To illustrate how a variety of factors influences human needs and hence attitudes toward parenthood, let us consider a case history from a social worker's notebook.

III.   THE CASE OF MRS. ANDREWS

Mrs. Janet Andrews is a reasonably attractive young woman of 22. As a child she got along very well with her father, reasonably well with her sister, but very poorly with her mother. She speaks of having a "wonderful father" who has had a real sympathy for her from the beginning. Her mother, on the other hand, is reported as a very religious, dogmatic person who has always sought to keep Janet from normal social relationships. When other girls of Janet's age began to date, Janet's mother forbade her to date. Janet met this disapproval with surreptitiousness. She crawled out her bedroom window to meet her dates and discovered to her surprise that her father did not disapprove of this activity. Probably to show her rebellion against her mother, Janet dropped out of high school and went to work as a waitress although she continued to live with her parents. This exacerbated her mother's disapproval; the mother refused to eat at the table with her, saying, "I won't sit down with a common waitress."

As might be expected, Janet's mother had strong negative attitudes regarding sex and never provided Janet with any information on this subject. When Janet began menstruating at the age of 10, Janet thought she had injured herself in some way. Knowing that her mother regarded sex as evil, Janet feared to tell her mother of her plight. In a few days her mother discovered what was happening, gave Janet a pad and sanitary belt, and said, "Now be careful. You can become a mother now if you're not careful." Janet was mystified by the advice. She did not know how one became a mother, and hence did not know how to be careful to avoid such an eventuality.

As Janet grew older and her mother realized she could not permanently prevent her dating, the mother began to accuse Janet of having sexual relations on her dates. In recalling this, Janet commented, "If people keep thinking you're no good, it's not much incentive to be good. You shouldn't treat a young girl the way my mother treated me."

When she was 20, Janet became acquainted with Jerry Andrews, a sailor stationed at a naval base near her home. Despite her parents' objections, Janet and Jerry were married. Janet became pregnant and miscarried. Shortly thereafter Jerry received orders for a tour of duty at sea. Their brief period of married life together had not proved smooth. They had had few common interests. Jerry loved to dance, but Janet had never learned how. Jerry proved to be somewhat unstable and in Janet's eyes he drank too much.

With Jerry out of the country and her parents still not reconciled to her marriage, Janet felt very alone in the world. At this juncture Janet sought the help of a social worker. She poured out her history and especially her resentment against her mother. As to her hopes for the future, she looked forward to the time when her husband would return and she could become pregnant again and have a child. Realizing Janet's marriage had not achieved a desirable level of stability, the social worker inquired why she wanted a child.

As to many people, this struck Janet as an unusual question. "Why," she said, "I just want a child. How can you say *why* you want a child?"

Granting that it was a difficult question, the social worker encouraged Janet to reflect on it. Then she said, "If I had a child, it would bring my mother back to me. . . . I love children. I would like to have children. . . . I think my wish for a child has something to do with my sister. She has three. The last time she had a baby she called me to come over and take care of the kids when she had to go to the hospital I had the strangest feeling when I got there. I felt as if it was me that was having the baby and after my sister left for the hospital, the kid stayed with me and acted as if I was their mother. It wasn't that I wa jealous of my sister. I have never been jealous of anyone. It was just that I thought it would be awful nice to be having a baby. . . . You go to the hospital and all your relatives and friends come there and bring you things. That would be nice. . . . It would be nice to have a baby because I'm so lonesome. I haven't anything to do all day. It would be something that would keep me occupied, and I wouldn't have my mind so much on myself. . . . Some people have children to make their marriages happier—that is, I mean, if they're not getting along well. Maybe that would help. . . . I didn't know you could think this way about having a child. When Jerry comes home, I'm going to ask him why he wants a child."

Despite the fact that Janet's problem represents a particular set of circumstances, it indicates the influence of social needs on attitudes toward parenthood. Thus, before considering Janet's particular reasons for having a child we shall briefly indicate some of the social factors influencing her need-structure. Her mother's attitude toward sex, probably derived in part from her strict religious training and belief, left Janet confused in matters pertaining to physiological functioning and made it difficult for her to develop normal social contacts with young people of her own age. As we have seen, this restriction led Janet to rebel and to seek escape from the confines of her home. Undoubtedly, then, in her marriage she was looking for respect, affection, and understanding. The marriage was not entirely satisfactory and these social needs were still not adequately satisfied. It is through the birth of a child that Janet hopes to achieve the fulfillment of these needs.

As we reflect on Janet's specific reasons for wanting a child, we can see that they may be broken down into the following headings:

1. She feels that having a child would be a means of restoring her relationship with her mother. Subsequently, however, she has decided that this is probably not correct since she regards the relationship between herself and her mother as hopelessly ruptured.

2. It would reassure Janet of her adequacy vis-à-vis her sister with whom she has felt rivalrous. This point too appears to be related to her seemingly futile hope for better relations with her mother.

3. The baby would provide her with an interest and hence would reduce her sense of loneliness and of having an empty life.

4. The period of confinement at the hospital would enable Janet to become dependent, to be given presents, and to be the center of attention and care of her friends and relatives.

5. In some magical way the baby might improve her relationship with Jerry.

Although Janet has experienced a rough childhood and although her relationship with her mother has been laden with a considerable amount of overt conflict, still there is nothing in the foregoing account which would lead one to regard Janet as a seriously disturbed young woman. The goals she is seeking seem reasonable enough, and it seems clear that many others share her belief that the coming of a child would ensure their eventuating. Yet it seems doubtful that the coming of a baby could produce the results which Janet desires.

Once Janet had surmounted the notion that one does not think about why one wants a child, she began to express a number of reasons. For our purposes the importance of her remarks lies in the fact that all of her reasons were statements of her own needs; to be loved and accepted by her mother; to be as adequate as her sister; to be attended and cared for by her friends; to have a new interest; and to have a closer relationship with her husband. Thus Janet has illustrated the thesis of this paper; that people desire to have—or not to have—children because of needs in their own personalities.

IV. SUMMARY AND CONCLUSIONS

Needs, or motives, may be either conscious or unconscious. Social needs are learned by the individual as he interacts with members of the group or groups to which he belongs. The social needs of an individual affect his attitudes generally, including of course his predispositions regarding children. Where cultural rewards and penalties for parenthood are evenly balanced, we should expect parents to show attitudes of ambivalence toward children.

Social needs are influenced by such subcultural considerations as social class, location of residence, and religious affiliation. Historically, the conditions of rural life rewarded couples for having children. As the rural areas become progressively urbanized, the penalties of parenthood—so apparent in urban middle-class life—will probably become more evident there also. In the city, the penalties are more evident in the middle class than in either the upper or lower class. To members of some religious groups procreation is the will of God; in other groups it is contrary to divine will. Finally, idiosyncratic experiences result in individual differences in attitude toward parenthood.

CHAPTER 7

Parent-Child Relationships:
The Development of Personality

ONE OF THE MAJOR BELIEFS in the psychology of personality is that the way in which a child's personality develops is determined (in whole or, at least, in large part) by the way in which his parents—and especially his mother—interact with him.[1]

Some of our "old wives' tales" concern the notion that by their activities during pregnancy mothers can "mark" the children they are carrying. In the way in which such notions have been conceptualized they have been quite thoroughly discredited. Here Sontag presents a new and more scientifically tenable exposition of the view that mothers' experiences can influence the personalities which will develop from the fetuses they are carrying. Ross and Johnson give a quite orthodox Freudian interpretation of the effect of family interaction on the personality of the infant and child. Whereas the emphasis in the clinical literature seems generally to be that the effect upon the child of the family (and again, especially of the mother) is all too frequently to engender neurosis, Spitz concludes that the child who receives no "mothering" is much less privileged than the child who receives normal maternal care. We find the theme of sub-cultural variation recurring in the article by Davis and Havighurst who describe class and color

[1] In view of the fact that no study known to the editors which bears on this proposition has been of the four-fold design (see Chap. 1), the point must be regarded as tentative. In the next chapter Sears assesses the state of our knowledge in this field.

171

differences in weaning, toilet-training, and other childhood disciplines, and trace their implications for personality development.

WAR AND THE FETAL-MATERNAL RELATIONSHIP*

Lester Warren Sontag

In the many discussions of the subject of war's impact on children, there has been little mention of the fact that such impacts may irreparably injure a child even before he is born. I shall try to present to you a very brief summary of some of what is known of maternal-fetal relationship and even a little bit of that which is not known, but which existing evidence indicates may be true. I shall also indicate to you how a war environment may change certain of these fetal environmental factors and how such changes may be expected to alter an individual's structure and function throughout life. What is fetal environment and what are its components? I shall discuss some of them under the headings of nutrition and maternal endogenous factors.

Nutrition

One does not ordinarily consider nutrition as a part of an individual's environment, although I am not sure that it should not so be considered. During fetal life, however, nutrition is derived from the mother's blood stream, which with its food, endocrine products, waste products, drugs, etc., must be considered a major part of the fetus' environment. How then may this fetal nutritional environment vary as a result of changes in quality or quantity of food the mother eats? In what way may the fetus be affected by that change?

For years obstetricians attempted to control the birth weight of infants by limiting expectant mother's caloric intake, in order to insure an easier labor. They have been unsuccessful because it is the level of sugar in the mother's *blood* which determines how much will filter over through the placenta to the fetus, to be synthesized into fat, and this factor is relatively independent of her caloric intake. The fact that the weight of a new-born infant is not ordinarily influenced by

* Adapted and reprinted by permission of the author and publisher from *Marriage and Family Living,* 6 (1944), 3-4, 16.

the mother's weight or food habits has lulled us into complacency about the possible importance of other prenatal dietary factors. Such factors can, however, be extremely important. Vitamin deficiencies promise to be particularly significant. Children born of mothers whose diet is deficient in Vitamin D do not ordinarily have rickets at birth, but in a recent study of two hundred such children almost two-thirds were found to have developed a full-blown and active rickets when they were a month old. Infants born of mothers on an adequate Vitamin D diet always remain immune from rickets for at least two or three months because of the Vitamin D they have stored during fetal life. The same facts apply to scurvy, in infants born of mothers on a diet deficient in Vitamin C. Children of Vitamin D deficient mothers have soft baby teeth, and show a higher incidence of decay at five or seven years of age. Rats fed on a diet deficient in some of the vitamins and proteins produce young who have body deformities, usually a marked shortening of the bones of the forearm and leg, and deformity of the growth of the jawbone. New-born pigs from sows whose diet was grossly deficient in Vitamin A had eyes which had failed to develop and were totally blind. Such effects have not been demonstrated in human infants but neither have they been excluded. In extremely severe cases of malnutrition during pregnancy, occurring during famines, reductions in birth weight, fetal rickets and a high infant mortality have been found. More recently investigators in Toronto compared the records of two different groups of infants. The mothers of both groups of infants had lived during pregnancy on diets which were poor from the standpoint of vitamins, proteins and minerals. One group of mothers had, however, had their pregnancy diets supplemented by large amounts of vitamins. The infants of this group showed better growth during the first year of life and much less illness, and in general were healthier children than those of the mothers whose diets had not been supplemented by vitamins. An additional fact of interest was that the labors of the mothers on the supplemented diets were easier and shorter than those of the women whose diets were unsupplemented.

Endogenous Factors

So far I have talked only about substances which a mother takes into her body and which subsequently become a part of the fetus' chemical environment. What about maternal endogenous factors—

changes in fetal environment due to changes in physiology from maternal emotions, fatigue, endocrine function, etc.? While our knowledge in this area is still fragmentary, certain facts have been recognized. Emotions, as you know, have a physiological component. Rage or fear or anxiety is not just a state of mind, it is also a state of body. During such emotions, chemicals such as acotylcholine and epinephrine, which are stimulants to certain parts of the nervous system, are liberated in quantities into the blood stream. These products apparently pass through the placental filter into the fetus' blood stream and some of them act as stimulants to the nervous system of the fetus. Thus, maternal emotional stresses of various sorts may indirectly affect the fetal nervous system. Some of these effects are manifested by a marked increase in body activity and heart rate of the fetus.

My co-workers and I have observed an increase of several hundred percent in the body movements of fetuses whose mothers were undergoing emotional stress. Such fetal responses usually last several hours, even when the maternal emotional distress is of short duration. During periods of emotional disturbance lasting weeks, hourly averages of fetal movement during the entire period remain greatly increased. This is an interesting observation, you may agree, but what, if any, are its consequences? We think we know some of them, although the civilian bombings during the war should eventually tell us much more. The immediate effect of prolonged maternal emotional stress evident at birth is a reduced birth weight, although birth length is maintained. This reduced birth weight is a simple matter of energy expenditure—carbohydrates which are used for energy to produce movement cannot be used for conversion into fat. Our fetus has employed a common method of weight reduction—exercise without increase in food intake. Since he does not use minerals for energy production, his skeleton may make its normal growth, but he can put on less fat and consequently weighs a pound or two less at birth.

During World War I the average birth weight of war babies dropped significantly. It was at that time generally presumed that this weight reduction was a matter of reduced maternal nutrition due to war food shortages. In view of the lack of success of the medical men in reducing birth weight by limiting food intake, it seems uncertain whether enough actual starvation of mothers occurred to account for it. The mechanism may very well be in part this emotional factor—in this instance war fears and anxieties and a resulting increased activity level of the fetus.

Another change which is apparent at birth in infants of mothers undergoing severe emotional stresses is in behavior, in total activity level. Such an infant is from the beginning a hyperactive, irritable, squirming, crying child who cries for his feeding every two or three hours instead of sleeping through his four hour feeding. Because his irritability involves the control of his gastro-intestinal tract, he empties his bowels at unsually frequent intervals, spits up half his feedings and generally makes a nuisance of himself. He is to all intents and purposes a neurotic infant when he is born—the result of an unsatisfactory fetal environment. In this instance, he has not had to wait until childhood for a bad home situation or other cause to make him neurotic. It has been done for him before he has even seen the light of day. In certain instances of severely disturbed maternal emotion which we have observed—for example, one in which the father became violently insane during his wife's pregnancy—the infant's bodily functions were so disturbed that a severe feeding problem resulted. The child was unable to retain food and became markedly emaciated and dehydrated. Experience with other similar cases suggests that many of the feeding problems which pediatricians experience with young infants arise from an abnormal fetal environment.

While disturbed maternal emotion is the more clearly demonstrated prenatal environmental influence, severe maternal fatigue, unusual abdominal pressures, violent and repeated sounds are also capable of producing immediate fetal movement responses and may in certain instances be an important part of fetal environment.

The long and fatiguing hours spent in war plants and in the fields by women of Germany, the occupied countries, and perhaps England, have constituted a change from the usual fetal environment. Aside from the fact that such changes are known to be capable of causing an immediate behavior response in the fetus in the form of increased activity, we cannot appraise their effects. They do, however, form an interesting field for speculation. The sound factors of the terrific bombings to which German and British cities have been subjected constitute another aspect of abnormal fetal environment. From such stimuli I should expect somewhat the same type of unstable nervous system of pre-natal neurosis as results from disturbed maternal emotion. Indeed in this instance the sounds of the bombings and the disturbed maternal emotions would be inseparable as causes for the development of an unstable nervous autonomy of the fetus. I should expect the same disturbed autonomic functions at birth with a high incidence of feeding disorders, etc.

In summary, there is evidence that fetal environment is an extremely important factor delineating the original structure, function and behavior patterns of human beings. The alterations in fetal environment most important in war are perhaps in nutrition and in the chemical-physiological changes in the mother's body brought about by maternal emotion, and possibly fatigue. Alterations in these factors may produce infants more susceptible to disease, to rickets and scurvy, to dental decay, and children whose growth progress is slower. It is conceivable that there may be gross alterations in skeletal structure and that alterations in the structure of such organs as the central nervous system, may limit the ultimate potentialities of individuals. The chemical-physiological aspect of severely disturbed maternal emotions may be responsible for the birth during wartime of children exhibiting a high incidence of unstable behavior and functional disorders, particularly of the gastro-intestinal system.

How irreparable and how permanent are the handicaps which adverse fetal environment may create? The matter of early and severe decay of deciduous teeth might be considered unimportant, since these teeth are all replaced eventually by permanent teeth. However, the orthodontist will tell you that the premature loss of deciduous teeth from decay is a major factor among the causes of malocclusions and their resulting facial deformities—factors which are extremely important in the whole problem of personality adjustment. What about nutritional anemias, rickets, excessive illness, and a generally low physical status during the first two or three years of life? Such circumstances may distort normal parent-child relationships; they may create oversolicitous parents; they may create a rejection situation through constant unfavorable comparison of the physically inadequate child with other more robust and attractive ones. The child's energy level and therefore his ability to compete with other children his own age will have profound effects upon his developing personality and social adjustment.

As to the final life significance of the kind of bad start in life I have pictured, I must leave for you to interpret. We may conclude, however, that an unfavorable fetal environment is an important factor in the creation of constitutionally inadequate infants—infants who do not have an optimum structure, nutritional storage, and response patterns to negotiate most successfully those early years.

A PSYCHIATRIC INTERPRETATION OF THE GROWTH PROCESS IN THE EARLY YEARS*

HELEN ROSS AND ADELAIDE M. JOHNSON

. . . Personality is an outgrowth of the relationship between the child and the parents. . . . The first question in psychiatry becomes: why do human beings behave as they do, or what makes people tick? The infinite variation in human personality, even within groups of people who are brought up in much the same manner—indeed, the wide difference between members of one family—calls for explanation beyond the old belief, "They were born that way." With due respect to the importance of inheritance, psychiatry is more concerned with what *happens* to individuals. When something goes wrong, the psychiatrist tries "to do something about it."

Since the first event in life is birth, how the parents feel about the coming of a child even before it is born is important. This does not mean the "prenatal influence" of old wives' tales; for example, if a rabbit frightened the expectant mother, her baby would be born with a hare-lip. It means, rather, that the attitudes of parents are the first influences the child meets when he comes into the world and that they shape the child's feelings about everything in life.

Food and Love

Since the first service to the child is to give him food, let us examine what happens when he is fed. If the mother fondles him, puts him to the breast gently and lovingly, and patiently helps him to learn to suck, his first adjustment to another person is a good one and he learns to expect other people to be friendly, too. If, on the other hand, she forces her breast or the bottle into the tender mucous membrane of the infant's mouth, she may hurt him and throw him into a state of panic,

* Adapted and reprinted by permission of the authors and publisher from *Journal of Social Casework*, 30 (1949), 87-92.

which he will show with random motor activity and inability to suck
He will become afraid and refuse to nurse; he may even come to feel
that his mother is his enemy. This is not "thinking," since the infant's
mental processes are not developed, but it is the body's way of defending itself. Sometimes these distressed infants vomit recurrently. Often
they are thought to have a stoppage in the digestive tract, and an
operation may be performed, when in reality they are simply in a state
of nervous tension brought on by the handling of an anxious, or perhaps unloving, mother. The effect of such an early painful experience
may carry over for a long time, either in physical symptoms or in
evidences of lack of confidence in everyone. A girl of 6, for example,
was brought to the clinic because she had vomited since birth, although
no organic reason for this symptom could be found. She cried a great
deal and was afraid of people. It was discovered that her mother was
unaware of the impatient, tense manner in which she had always dealt
with this child in regard to food. Eating was no fun for her child
(as it should be), but a painful, frightening ordeal. This mother had
been treated in much the same way by her mother. . . .

Hunger is a painful experience. We all love and have confidence in
the person who can ease our pain. The infant develops affection for the
mother who relieves his distress. The child who found eating painful
or who, for some reason, did not get enough food in the first days of
his life, may show the effect of this lack of satisfaction in nagging
demanding ways. It is as if he fears that he will never get enough
of anything. Early hunger may also produce quite the opposite type of
person, one who is shy, apathetic, discouraged, as if he feels there is
no use in trying to get enough. What happens to the infant in his first
activity, eating, may lay down the basic pattern of his character. When
the child has a basic confidence in people, he no longer needs to waste
his energy in trying people out, but can turn his interests to creative
productive pursuits. While breast feeding has advantages in that the
mother has opportunity to be closer to the baby and thus to express her
friendliness, bottle feeding can accomplish the same if the mother really
loves her child and gives freely of her time and interest.

Levy's[1] experiments with puppies have shown that there is great
satisfaction in sucking, aside from relieving hunger. The puppy that is
fed too fast will continue sucking movement long after it has finished

[1] D. M. Levy, "Experiments on the Sucking Reflex and Social Behavior of Dogs,"
American Journal of Orthopsychiatry, Vol. IV, 1934, p. 203.

the bottle. A baby who does not have enough sucking time at feeding may turn to thumb sucking or some other form of mouth play.*

The infant, animal or human, strives to complete a phase of growth when the normal growth process is interfered with. Every phase of growth seems to demand its own span of time for completion and although these phases follow in the same sequence for every individual, there is great variation in tempo. The wise and observant mother is sensitive to the rhythm of her child and does not push him beyond his capacity at the moment. Neither does she hold him back. When he is ready for the next step, such as holding the spoon or cup himself, she helps him. In this way, she assists him to grow toward the independence which our culture expects of every normal person.

Sometimes we see the effects of an unhappy, unsatisfied infancy in grownups around us. Some of these are depressed people who have never recovered from their early discouragement with life. Some are selfish, suspicious, and bitter because they have always felt cheated and neglected, and often try, sometimes unconsciously, to cheat or take advantage of others. There are others whose physical symptoms tell us the story of infantile unhappiness: those who constantly eat too much and are obese; those who never have any appetite, eat with difficulty, and vomit frequently.

Every phase of personality development produces its own stresses which may become reflected in the body or may show themselves in some type of personality disturbance, or both. Stomach ulcers are thought to have their psychological origin in the unsatisfied need to be loved and cared for. Many people are ashamed of such longings and so try to seem highly independent, although they hunger for love. To the infant, love and food are a psychological equation. So when a person allows himself no dependence on a loved person in his daily life because he thinks it childish, his stomach takes up the cause and behaves just as it did when he was an infant: it gets ready for food. This constant stomach wish keeps the gastric juices flowing to an excessive degree, irritation sets in and an ulcer may result. Such an illness is called psychosomatic, meaning that the body functions are influenced

* A well-controlled study to determine the consequence of not rewarding sucking activity in human infants (through feeding them by cup) shows generally nonsignificant results, except that infants who sucked at the breast developed a stronger sucking reflex than did those who either sucked bottles or were fed by cup. *Cf.* H. V. Davis, R. R. Sears, H. C. Miller, and A. J. Brodbeck, "Effects of Cup, Bottle and Breast Feeding on Oral Activities of New Born Infants," *Pediatrics,* 3 (1948), 549-58.—*Eds.*

by psychological tensions. In the realm of personality disturbances, an example is the "infantile character." Some people just do not grow up in a psychological sense; they wish to remain forever dependent on others, to have no responsibility in life.

First Steps in Learning

Anyone who has observed infants carefully knows that they enjoy everything associated with their bodies, including the excreta, which to them are a part of their bodies. But the infant reaches the time (normally toward the end of the first year) when he is ready to learn bowel and bladder control. It is highly important that this learning is not forced upon him before his sphincter muscles are strong enough to do what is expected: to control his elimination until he has reached the toilet. Just as his stomach develops its rhythm for intake of food and digestion, so his bowels and bladder establish their rhythm, each child according to his own make-up. If the mother notes this, she can help him to form habits of cleanliness, but she must have his willingness if the lesson is to be well learned. Children can be taught to conform under fear of punishment, but learning through fear is not economical; since it brings no pleasure, the child relapses easily or fails completely. When his sphincters are ready, he will give up his primitive gratification in soiling himself in return for his mother's approval. If the mother fails to note his readiness to participate in his own training, the child may remain untrained and thus fail to comply with a fundamental demand in social living.

The effects of training a child too early or too severely are seen regularly in both the medical and the behavior clinics. Constipation, diarrhea, and other intestinal complaints are the psychosomatic illnesses that may be induced by interferences with this phase of growth. Stubbornness is a common result of the parents' efforts to force their will on the child; this sometimes develops even to the point of the child's not talking. Or a child may be made unduly anxious over dirtiness and become a slave to cleanliness for the rest of his life. Or he may become so preoccupied with his body functions that there is no psychic energy left for a colorful, creative life.

During the "training" period, the child often feels hostile toward those who are teaching him. The mother, who was at first only the good, indulgent provider and caretaker, has to become the interpreter of society's demands. This means she must not continue to give in o the child's primitive wishes; in his frustration, the child responds with anger. Such anger should be met by the parent with firm, consistent handling; if the parent returns hostility to the child, he only makes the child fearful and guilty and drives the angry feelings inward, where they fester and break out later in some other form. Sometimes a child's anger shows itself in destructive acts, which the parent should treat with firmness and restraint; this the child needs and wants. To allow him to destroy things is to make the child fearful of himself as well as of other people. Little children have to be helped constantly to know what is acceptable behavior. It is not true, of course, that parents or any other individuals can "turn on" suitable feelings or that appropriate responses are automatic. The parent was shaped by his own experiences; he, too, had parents. It may be that a parent has been so much hurt by his own past that he needs the sympathetic counsel of a trained person to help him make those responses that will in turn help his children to be happy and normal.

Destructiveness, however, is not always hostile. As the world of little children is enlarged by their ability to creep or to walk, it becomes more interesting to them; they begin to get into things, to explore, to examine. When this time comes, the play pen is no solution; the child should be allowed to run about, to exercise his large muscles, and to get acquainted with his bigger world. Taking things apart is one means of investigation. Since the child cannot be expected to know the value of things around him, the wise parent moves the destructible, valuable things out of reach. This investigative interest extends to people as well as to things. The little child who has been loved and so has learned to love people wants to be with people. The confinement of the nursery bores him; he wants to be with his father and mother; he wants to know what they do. As soon as he can talk, he asks questions.

The great curiosity of the little child should be welcomed; it is the mainspring of learning, the foundation of all thinking. Only dull children or frightened children do not ask questions. A child of 3 years pays no attention to time or place when some new awareness prompts him to find out more. "Where did I come from?", he may ask in the middle of a busy street.

The little child is curious first about his own body, then about the bodies of others. What the body does is to him endlessly interesting; about it he has none of the guilt and shyness often seen in the adult.

These queries should be answered as they come, but not amplified beyond his questions. He will take in what he can understand and, if the parent has built up confidence, he will come back for more when he is ready. The parts of the body and the functions should be given names and referred to naturally, without shame or undue interest. Evasiveness on the part of parents will leave a child not only unsatisfied, but sensitive and anxious, and because of anxiety, even more curious. Condemnation of his sexual curiosity will drive his interests underground and he will have to fight the thoughts he thinks are bad.

The First Emotional Triangle

At 2 or 2½ years, the normal child is making his own observations and developing his own theories about where he came from. He should have a room apart from his parents, if possible, from birth. The habit of some parents of going nude about the house is questionable. When the little child becomes conscious of his own body, particularly of the sexual characteristics, he suffers from comparison with the adult body and he may become preoccupied with this subject. A time comes when the little child gives indication that he wants his privacy; this should be respected by the parents.

Although the first loved person is usually the mother, by the age of 3 the child has developed a strong affection for both parents and he wants them both for himself. This is the first emotional triangle. But he discovers that the father and the mother belong to each other as well as to him. If he has no brothers or sisters, this is his first experience in sharing love with another, and the emotional outcome of this discovery will determine much of his attitude toward love for his whole lifetime. Even if he has brothers and sisters, he must work out this father-mother-child relationship.

The little girl begins at 3 to be more feminine than formerly; she loves to "dress up"; she watches the mother's attitude toward the father; she imitates the mother's preparation for the father's return from the office; she wants to do everything with the father that the mother does and this includes, in her logic, going to bed with the father. The boy of 3 begins to try to act like the father in respect to the mother; as an infant, he imitated primarily his mother. Now, he becomes jealous of the father's attention to the mother and tries to keep her to himself. Jealousy is natural and unavoidable in these efforts of children to be loved and should be allowed expression. Parents should not be too severe or too lenient toward little children's jealous behavior, but rather accept it as belonging to their growing up.

The child has two problems at this age—to become like the parent of his own sex and at the same time to be loved by both. He competes with one for the love of the other, and this makes him feel hostile or discouraged. Sometimes children turn away from their normal striving to become like the parent of their own sex; as a result, they may try to be like the other sex. The girl may try to be masculine to escape her failure as a girl; the boy may turn to feminine ways, hoping to find himself more adequate and more acceptable in this role. The normal outcome of this phase, known to psychiatrists as the *oedipal period,* is an identification with one's own sex and a strong affectional tie to the other sex. The girl comes to realize that the father belongs to the mother; at the same time, she realizes she, too, will grow up and find a husband. In her rivalry with her mother for her father's attention, she has seen that nothing terrible happened, even if she did want her mother to be out of the way. She will, therefore, be prepared later on in life to compete with other women for her own mate. The same emotional triangle exists for the boy; he gives up the mother as belonging only to him and learns that even though he felt jealous and competitive, he was still loved. He is thus set on the way for his later quest of a wife. This is the expectation of our culture and as such is a part of the foundation for a well-adjusted personality.

Brothers and sisters belong in the family picture, too. How the child feels about them, older or younger, and how these feelings develop have much to do with his growth. It is easier for the child of 3 or older to share the mother with the "new baby" than it is earlier. At 18 months, for example, the child still needs the concentrated attention of his mother and often finds it so difficult to give up that he regresses to infantile behavior. He may return to wetting and soiling himself, begin to suck his thumb, become querulous with the mother, or show other signs of trying to reclaim what he feels he has lost. The youngest child may remain the baby, the object of envy; the oldest may always feel cheated because he had to share the parents' love, particularly the mother's, with another child, or maybe with several others. Jealousy of siblings is normal—each child unconsciously wants to be loved the most. Some learn to share the parental love, as well as material things; others, handled with less understanding, may feel discriminated against always.

Growth of the Conscience

Children usually try to please their parents; they try to be good in order to be loved. This is how the conscience grows; it is made up of all the prohibitions and permissions which the child learns. The earliest foreshadowing of conscience is probably the infant's first response to the frown of the mother. In the period of habit training, he becomes more aware of what his parents, indeed, all the small world around him, expect, and if the parents are loving, he tries to conform. If they are unkind, he becomes anxious, fears punishment, and, even more, fears he will lose the love and care of his parents. The child learns gradually to take the standards and wishes of the parents into himself; the parental voice comes slowly to be the "still, small voice" inside the child so that even when the parents are not in his presence, the child desists from doing things he knows would not meet with their approval.

How to live on friendly terms with one's conscience, which should be neither too restrictive nor too indulgent, is one of the great accomplishments of the developing personality. But this is not always an easy process. To escape the discomfort that arises when there is a conflict of one's wishes with one's standards, people resort to various methods which are technically called *defense mechanisms*. Most common is *repression*. This is putting out of the conscious mind those things that are unpleasant or disturbing. These repressed thoughts and feelings remain in the memory and can be called back into consciousness, as was first discovered by Freud in his early experiments with hypnotism. On this basic discovery, Freud developed the therapeutic method of psychoanalysis. He found that neurotics (he began with hysterical people) could recall in a hypnotic state those painful experiences which had been put away from consciousness but he learned at the same time that the sufferer had to become aware of them in a conscious (not a hypnotic) state in order to deal with them. He therefore gave up hypnosis as a method and developed his own, that of helping patients to unlock the unconscious by recalling what they had tried to forget. . . .

MOTHERLESS INFANTS*

RENÉ A. SPITZ

In the following an extremely condensed report on our findings on psychosocial factors in infant development will be presented. To call attention to the function of such factors in infancy appears to us an urgent need, for it is not generally appreciated that at this age influences of a psychosocial nature are more startling in their consequences for development than at any other period of childhood in later life.

The reasons for this are manifold. At no later period is the development so rapid, so turbulent and so conspicuous. It involves, more obviously than at any later period, the somatic as well as the psychological aspects. Any variation in the development will be manifested in both these sectors, with the result, as will be shown further on, that such variations caused by psychosocial factors can literally become matters of life and death.

In a certain sense development at this age is facilitated by certain peculiarities which infancy does not share with later stages. In infancy development takes place from a quasi-animal level to the human level. This involves the problems of adaptation and communication which arise toward the end of the first year of life. Any anomaly in the solution of these problems will be particularly conspicuous.

Another peculiarity of infancy is that in it environment, in the widest sense of the word, is extraordinarily restricted. The radius of the infant's physical environment is extremely narrow. The social environment in the life of the normal infant is restricted practically to one single person: the infant's mother. This concentration of the infant's habitat and of its social contacts permits the investigator exceedingly close insight into the psychosocial factors operative in the infant's life.

A further facilitation in the study of our problem is offered by another peculiarity of infant life. The single infant can be studied in its family and also in large groups, in institutions. Nevertheless, our

* Adapted and reprinted by permission of the author and publisher from "The Role of Ecological Factors in Emotional Development in Infancy," *Child Development,* 20 (1949), 145-55.

proposition that the infant's environment is restricted to one person, the mother or her substitute, remains substantially unchanged (unless the institution in question should entrust the care of the infants to a number of different persons). For during the largest part of the first year of life no interaction takes place between one infant and the others, such as would be the case between the inmates of institutions at later ages. This makes it possible to study infants of different races and of different hereditary endowment under identical environmental conditions, keeping a large number of variables constant. . . .

A few brief statements will clarify our position on the question of emotional development as observed in the course of our work.

Emotions are not present ready-made from birth. Like any other sector of the human personality they have to develop.

We usually conceive of emotions as paired: friendliness and anger, love and hate, pleasure and displeasure, gay and sad, are the terms in which we think of emotions. But at birth the first emotion visible is a state of diffuse excitation in the nature of displeasure and no pleasurable emotion is observable as its counterpart, only a state of quiescence. A variety of emotions develops from this beginning in the further course of the first year of life. We have been able to correlate the progressive development of specific emotions to definite age levels.

Two distinct emotional responses are differentiated in the course of the first two months of life. They appear to correspond to pleasure and displeasure, and they seem to appear in reaction to physical stimulation.

A response to psychological stimulation seems to present itself for the first time in the third month, when the infant smiles in response to a human partner's face (6).

Somewhat later displeasure also is manifested in response not only to physical, but also to psychological stimulation. It can be observed in the reaction of the infant to being left alone when its human partner goes away.

After the sixth month negative emotions take the lead. Anxiety is differentiated from the displeasure reaction. We assume that a minimum of ego development is the prerequisite for the development of anxiety and find ourselves in agreement on this point with E. Hilgard (3).

In the following two months possessive emotions toward toys are manifested. Jealousy appears in the ninth and tenth months; between the tenth and twelfth months disappointment, anger, love, sympathy, friendliness, enjoyment and a positive sense of property become observable. The age levels mentioned should not be considered as definite limits. They designate approximate ages at which these emotions appear and may vary widely both according to individuals and circumstances.

The significant part of this emotional development is that during the whole of the first year emotional discrimination is manifested approximately two months earlier than any other form of perception. The three months' smiling response, which is the infant's smiling recognition of the human partner's face, appears at an age at which no other object is recognized. Even food, the most familiar object in the baby's life, is recognized only more than two months later. The displeasure which the infant manifests at four months when left by its partner, appears two months earlier than the displeasure shown by the child when its toy is taken away. The eight months' anxiety shown by the child when confronted with strangers is a sign that it has achieved the capacity to discriminate between friend and stranger. This appears two months earlier than the child's capacity to differentiate toys and other objects from each other. Thus, emotional development acts as the trailbreaker for all other perceptive development during infancy. . . .

A brief summary of the first investigation made by us may serve as an illustration for the other ones of which only the results will be given.

The investigation in question (4, 5) was carried out in two institutions which we had the opportunity to observe simultaneously. Both institutions had certain similarities: the infants received adequate food; hygiene and asepsis were strictly enforced; the housing of the children was excellent; and medical care more than adequate. In both institutions the infants were admitted shortly after birth.

The institutions differed in one single factor. This factor was the amount of emotional interchange offered. In institution No. 1, which we have called "Nursery," the children were raised by their own mothers. In institution No. 2, which we have called "Foundlinghome," the children were raised from the third month by overworked nursing personnel: one nurse had to care for from eight to twelve children. Thus, the available emotional interchange between child and mother formed the one independent variable in the comparison of the two groups.

The response to this variable showed itself in many different ways.

Perhaps the most comprehensive index of this response is offered by the monthly averages of the developmental quotients of these children.

The developmental quotient (1, 2) represents the total of the develop-

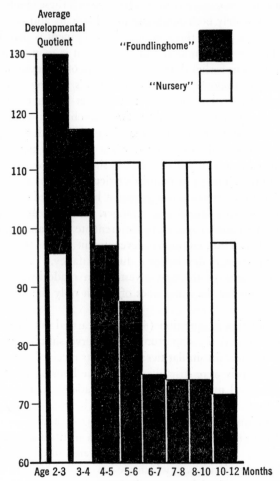

Figure 1.   Comparison of development in "nursery" and "foundlinghome."

ment of six sectors of the personality: mastery of perception, of bodily functions, of social relations, of memory and imitation, of manipulative ability and of intelligence. The monthly averages of the developmental quotients of the children in the two institutions over a period of twelve months are shown in Figure 1.

The contrast in the development of the children in the two institutions is striking. But this twelve months' chart does not tell the whole story. The children in "Foundlinghome" continued their downward slide and by the end of the second year reached a developmental quotient of 45. We have here an impressive example of how the absence of one psychosocial factor, that of emotional interchange with the mother, results in a complete reversal of a developmental trend. This becomes still clearer in Figure 2.

It should be realized that the factor which was present in the first case, but eliminated in the second, is the pivot of all development in the first year. It is the mother-child relation. By choosing this factor as our independent variable we were able to observe its vital importance. While the children in "Nursery" developed into normal healthy toddlers, a two-year observation of "Foundlinghome" showed that the emotionally starved children never learned to speak, to walk, to feed themselves. With one or two exceptions in a total of 91 children, those who survived were human wrecks who behaved either in the manner of agitated or of apathetic idiots.

The most impressive evidence probably is a comparison of the mortality rates of the two institutions. "Nursery" in this respect has an outstanding record, far better than the average of the country. In a five years' observation period during which we observed a total of 239 children, each for one year or more, "Nursery" did not lose a single child through death. In "Foundlinghome" on the other hand, 37 per cent of the children died during a two years' observation period (Figure 2).

The high mortality is but the most extreme consequence of the general decline, both physical and psychological, which is shown by children completely starved of emotional interchange.

We have called this condition marasmus, from the picture it shows; or hospitalism according to its etiology. The ecological background of marasmus is the orphanage and the foundling home which were current in our country in the last century. This ecological background leads to the picture of a developmental arrest which progressively becomes a developmental regression. Its earliest symptoms are developmental retardations in the different sectors of personality. Changes occur in the emotional development, later the emotional manifestations become progressively impoverished, finally they give way to apathy.

In those cases which survived we have found, alternating with the apathetic children, a hyper-excitable personality type. This personality

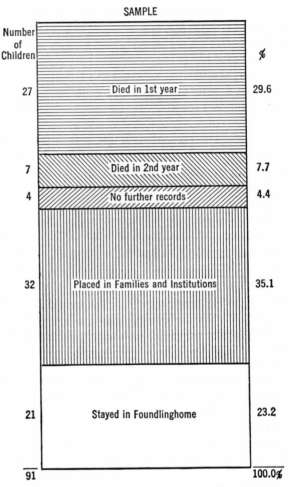

Figure 2.   Mortality rate of children in "foundlinghome" during a two-years' observation period.

type is on the lines described by Wallon as "l'enfant turbulent" (8)
We have called this, for want of a better term, the erethitic or agitated
type.

The results of this study caused us to focus our attention on the mother-child relation in all our further research on infants. We strove to examine whether in less spectacular conditions also it was truly such an all-important influence. Closer investigation bore out this impression. We could establish, in the course of our further research, with the help of statistical methods, that the regularity in the emergence of emotional response, and subsequently of developmental progress both physical and mental, is predicated on adequate mother-child relations. Inappropriate mother-child relations resulted regularly either in the absence of developmental progress, emotional or otherwise, or in paradoxical responses.

This is not a surprising finding for those who have observed infants with their mothers; during the first year of life it is the mother, or her substitute, who transmits literally every experience to the infant. Consequently, barring starvation, disease or actual physical injury, no other factor is capable of so influencing the child's development in every field as its relation to its mother. Therefore, this relationship becomes the central ecological factor in infant development in the course of the first year. On the other hand, development, particularly in the emotional sector, provides an extremely sensitive and reliable indicator of variations in the mother-child relationship.

A few of the further findings made by us in this respect will follow. If our first example showed the complete deprivation of emotional interchange, the following ones will present other and less striking modifications of the mother-child relation.

If, for instance, the deprivation of emotional interchange starts at a later date, in the third quarter of the first year, a condition can develop which greatly resembles the picture of depression in the adult. The psychic structure of the infant is rudimentary and can in no way be compared to that of the adult. Therefore, the similarity of the symptomatology should not induce us to assume an identity of the pathological process. To stress this difference we have called the condition anaclitic (7) depression.

As the name implies, the presenting symptom is a very great increase in the manifestations of the emotions of displeasure. This goes to the point where anxiety reactions in the nature of panic can be observed. Children in this condition will scream by the hour; this may be accompanied by autonomic manifestations such as tears, heavy salivation, severe perspiration, convulsive trembling, dilation of pupils, etc.

At the same time development becomes arrested (see Table 1). The arrest is selective: the least involved is the social sector which remains relatively advanced.

Table 1.

NURSERY	INFLUENCE OF SEPARATION FROM MOTHER ON DEVELOPMENTAL QUOTIENT
	SEVERE DEPRESSION
Duration of separation in months	*Changes in points of DQ*
Under 3	*−12.5
3 to 4	−14
4 to 5	−14
Over 5	−25

One peculiarity of this condition is that the re-establishment of favorable emotional interchange will rapidly re-establish the developmental level. However, this is only true for separations which do not last longer than three months. If the deprivation lasts longer than five months no improvement is shown. On the contrary, the developmental quotient continues its decline, though at a slower rate, and it would seem that a progressive process has been initiated (see Table 2).

Table 2.

NURSERY	INFLUENCE OF SEPARATION FROM MOTHER ON DEVELOPMENTAL QUOTIENT
	SEVERE DEPRESSION
Duration of Separation in months	*Reversibility of decline in points of DQ*
Under 3	+25
3 to 4	+13
4 to 5	+12
Over 5	− 4

Conclusion

. . . We believe . . . that the central psychosocial factor in the infant's life is its emotional interchange with its mother.

The particular ecological significance of this finding lies in the fact that this emotional interchange is largely governed by culturally determined mores and institutions on one hand, by social and economic conditions on the other. To give one example: marasmus was a frequent condition up to 1920 in our country, as foundling homes were still in general use. Today such conditions are difficult to find unless we look for them in countries where foundling homes are still the rule. In the United States placement in foster-homes has taken the place of foundling institutions.

Less extreme conditions, however, like anaclitic depression and the others described above can be readily found at present here too. Our social institutions do not encourage the mother to spend much time with her child—at least in the population at large. Industrial civilization tends to deprive the child in early infancy of its mother. I have recently learned that in another industrial country a financial premium has been introduced for mothers who return earlier to factory work after having delivered their child. The earlier they abandon their baby the more substantial the tax reduction they receive. We can be convinced that the consequences of these socio-economic measures will make themselves felt in a distortion of these children's psychological development, although a dozen or more years must pass before the change becomes evident.

Still less consideration is given in our social institutions and in our present-day mores to the question of how to prepare the future mother's personality for motherhood. From the influence on child development exerted by mood-swings in the mother, by the mother's infantile personality or by her neurosis, it is obvious that attempts to remedy such conditions should begin early. . . . I have stressed that preventive psychiatry should begin as early as possible, at birth at least, but preferably before delivery.

I have attempted to show in this paper that such preventive psychiatry will have to begin by applying measures which are largely of an ecological nature. These measures will have to include a re-arrangement of legislation, making it possible for mothers to stay with their children; of education to prepare our female population for motherhood; and they will have to comprise the introduction of social psychiatry to remedy in expectant mothers psychiatric conditions apt to damage their children.

BIBLIOGRAPHY

1. Buehler, Charlotte, and Hetzer, H. *Kleinkinder Tests.* Leipzig: Johann Ambrosius Barth, 1932.
2. Hetzer, H., and Wolf, K. Babytests. *Z. Psychol.,* 1928, 107, 62-104.
3. Hilgard, E. Human motives and the concept of the self. *Amer. Psychologist,* 1949, 4, 375-382.
4. Spitz, R. A. Hospitalism: an inquiry into the genesis of psychiatric conditions in early childhood. *The Psychoanalytic Study of the Child,* New York: International Univ. Press, 1945, 1, 53-74.
5. Spitz, R. A. Hospitalism, a follow-up report. *The Psychoanalytic Study of the Child,* New York: International Univ. Press, 1946, 2, 113-117.
6. Spitz, R. A., and Wolf, K. M. The smiling response: a contribution to the ontogenesis of social relations. *Genet. Psychol. Monogr.,* 1946, 34, 59-125.
7. Spitz, R. A., and Wolf, K. M. Anaclitic depression: an inquiry into the genesis of psychiatric conditions in early childhood. *The Psychoanalytic Study of the Child,* New York: International Univ. Press, 1946, 2, 313-342.
8. Wallon, H. *L'enfant turbulent.* Paris: Librairie Felix Alcan, 1925, p. 642.

SOCIAL CLASS AND COLOR DIFFERENCES
IN CHILD-REARING*

ALLISON DAVIS AND ROBERT J. HAVIGHURST

In recent years, cultural anthropologists and social psychologists have made intensive studies of the relationships between personality and socialization.[1] They have arrived at a methodological distinction which

* Adapted and reprinted by permission of the authors and publisher from the *American Sociological Review,* 11 (1946), 698-710.

[1] See Margaret Mead, *Sex and Temperament in Three Primitive Societies,* in *From the South Seas,* New York, William Morrow and Co., 1939; Allison Davis and John Dollard, *Children of Bondage,* Washington, D.C., American Council on Education, 1940; W. Lloyd Warner, Buford Junker, and Walter A. Adams, *Color and Human Nature,* Washington, D.C., American Council on Education, 1941; Cora du Bois, *The People of Alor,* Minneapolis, The University of Minnesota Press, 1944; Abram Kardiner, *The Psychological Frontiers of Society,* New York, Columbia University Press, 1945.

has proved helpful in the analysis of personality. In the light of their comparative data on the socialization of individual children in different societies, they have set up the operational principle that personality can best be studied in terms of two basic interacting systems of behavior.

One system of actions, feelings, and thoughts is (1) cultural. It is learned by the individual from his basic social groups: his family, his age-groups, his sex group, his social-class group, and so on. The other system of responses is (2) individual, or "idiosyncratic," or "private." It derives in part from (a) genetic factors and in part from (b) learning. These learned individual traits are responses to (a') organic, (b') affectional and (c') chance factors, and likewise to (d') the particular deviations of a child's training from the standard cultural training for his group.

The of use this hypothesis and its various derivative forms seems likely to bring some order into the chaotic field of personality-studies. As a methodological distinction, it is useful both in the exploration of the life-history, and likewise in the cross-sectional study of personality-traits in a population. As a method of securing and organizing data, it has the virtue of directing the researcher's attention to increasingly *smaller systems* of behavior in his search for the formants of personality. As an hypothesis about the dynamics of personality, this distinction between the cultural and the individual "personalities" leads to the useful effort to understand "adjustment" and "maladjustment," or "normal" and "neurotic" behavior, in terms of the degree of "fit" between a person's *individual* motivation, and the *cultural* demands made upon him to adhere to those roles and those traits approved by his particular society.

The research whose findings will be summarized below is concerned primarily with the cultural aspects of personality. In a later report on a second part of our research, the development of individuality in children will be approached through intensive studies of the development of siblings. In this report, however, our purpose is to describe differences in the *cultural training* of children whose families are of different social and cultural status. . . .

The social class of the child's family determines not only the neighborhood in which he lives and the play-groups he will have, but also the basic cultural acts and goals toward which he will be trained. The social-class system maintains cultural, economic, and social barriers which prevent intimate social intermixture between the slums, the Gold Coast, and the middle class. We know that human beings can learn their culture only *from other human beings,* who already know and exhibit that culture. Therefore, by setting up barriers to social participation, the American social-class system actually prevents the vast majority of children of the working classes, or the slums, from learning any culture but that of their own groups. *Thus the pivotal meaning of social class* to students of human development is that it defines and systematizes different learning environments for children of different classes.[2] It is a fact that the specific form of the American language used, or of clothes, or of food, or of house, or even the social definition of a monogamous relationship varies by social class.

It has been assumed generally that the basic *areas* of training young children were very similar in all social strata, including weaning, toilet-training, property-training, etc. This seems to be true. Our purpose, however, was to determine to what extent *the methods, the timing,* and *the pace* of this early training differed in the various social classes. We attempted to make the same comparison with regard to the training demands in middle childhood.

Throughout this research, we have conceived of personality as an organization consisting of (1) learned responses (habits, thoughts, feelings, values, goals), and (2) the genetic factors of organic irritability, growth tempo, fatigue rate, etc. *The CULTURAL aspects of personality are the responses learned in conformity with the incentives and demands of a human group (a family, a gang, a social class). The INDIVIDUAL aspects of personality include genetic factors, and in addition all other traits which distinguish between men who have been trained in the same culture, but whose responses to this training have varied according to the particular conditions under which the training took place.*

The primary questions which this research attacked were: (1) What are the training demands exerted upon the white and the Negro child in lower class and middle class in Chicago, and (2) What is the extent of the difference in the time of beginning, the length of, and the other conditions surrounding the training? The part of this study dealing with

---

[2] Allison Davis, "Socialization and the Adolescent Personality," Chapter XI in the *Forty-Third Yearbook of the National Society for the Study of Education,* Part I, 1944, pp. 198-216.

the differences between middle-class and lower-class white families in their child-rearing practices has been reported by Ericson.[3] . . .

Procedure

The study consisted of holding guided interviews with mothers of young children, recording their responses on a schedule, and making

Table 1.   Data on Families in the Study

| | MIDDLE CLASS | | LOWER CLASS | |
	White	Negro	White	Negro
Number of mothers	48	50	52	50
Median age of mother at marriage	23	21	20	18
Median age of father at marriage	25	25	25	21
Median age of mother at interview	33	29	29	29
Median age of father at interview	35	33	33	32
No. of children at time of interview	107	109	167	184
No. of families with 2 children only	34	28	12	14
No. of families with 3 or more children .	11	14	34	32
Median age of children at interview	4	4	6	6

Table 2.   Median Ages in Months for Various Aspects of Feeding and Toilet Training

| | WHITE | | | | NEGRO | | | |
| | Middle | | Lower | | Middle | | Lower | |
	N	Median	N	Median	N	Median	N	Median
Breast feeding finished	75	3.8	114	4.9	88	8.5	159	9.4
Bottle feeding finished	95	10.7	123	12.9	74	12.5	99	12.6
Sucking finished	99	10.5	147	12.8	104	12.0	177	12.2
Bowel training begun	99	7.5	158	10.2	105	5.5	172	8.5
Bowel training complete	91	18.4	152	18.8	95	13.4	160	18.6
Bladder training begun	93	11.2	156	12.2	102	9.2	124	11.1
Bladder training complete	81	24.6	139	24.0	76	18.0	143	19.0

a statistical analysis of the data from the schedules. All the mothers were residents of Chicago, and most of them lived on the South Side.

There were fifty mothers in each of four groups, white middle-class, white lower-class, Negro middle-class, and Negro lower-class. Data on the ages of the mothers and fathers, the number of children, and

[3] Martha C. Ericson, "Child-Rearing and Social Status," *American Journal of Sociology,* 53, 190-192 (Nov. 1946).

the ages of their children are given by class and race in Table 1. . . .

The families were classified into middle and lower social classes by using data from the interview which have been found to be closely correlated with social-class placement as defined and described by Warner and Lunt[4] and by Davis, Gardner, and Gardner.[5]

Table 3. Proportions of Children with Certain Kinds of Feeding and Toilet-Training Experience

| | WHITE | | | | NEGRO | | | |
| | Middle | | Lower | | Middle | | Lower | |
	No/Total	%	No/Total	%	No/Total	%	No/Total	%
Children breast fed only	5/106	5	28/163	17	32/107	30	80/179	45
Children bottle fed only	31/100	31	49/151	32	19/106	18	20/179	11
Children both breast and bottle fed	63/ 99	64	90/147	61	58/104	56	84/174	48
Children breast fed one month or more	76/106	72	118/163	72	90/107	83	164/179	92
Children breast fed longer than 3 months	34/106	32	66/163	41	63/107	59	145/179	81
Children sucking longer than 12 months	21/ 99	21	66/147	45	32/104	31	51/177	29
Children fed when they seemed hungry	3/106	3	53/153	35	6/108	6	87/175	50
Children having pacifiers	1/107	1	22/167	13	8/105	7	17/184	9
Children held for bottle or breast fed only	53/ 79	67	72/166	43	78/108	72	99/179	55
Children weaned sharply	20/101	20	23/154	15	7/105	7	39/182	21
Children who sucked thumb	54/105	51	30/166	18	50/104	48	54/183	30
Bowel training begun at 6 mo. or earlier	48/ 99	49	36/158	23	91/105	87	49/172	29
Bowel training complete at end of 12 mo.	25/ 91	28	31/152	21	46/ 95	49	37/160	23
Bladder training begun at 6 mo. or earlier	17/ 95	18	22/157	14	4/102	40	22/124	18
Bladder training complete at end of 18 mo.	26/ 81	32	67/139	48	51/ 76	67	73/143	51
No. of children who have masturbated	56/104	54	27/162	17	30/102	29	27/182	15

[4] W. Lloyd Warner and Paul S. Lunt, *The Social Life of a Modern Community,* New Haven, Yale University Press, 1941.

[5] Allison Davis, Burleigh B. Gardner, and Mary R. Gardner, *Deep South,* Chicago, University of Chicago Press, 1941.

The principal factors used in making the classification were occupation of parents and their siblings, education of parents, their siblings, and grandparents, property ownership, membership in churches and other associations, and section of the city. One of the authors (A.D.) discussed these data with the interviewer in each case, and made the classification. There was seldom any doubt as to the proper classification. For the Negro group, the criteria were parallel to those for the classification of the white families, but shifted systematically because of restrictions on opportunity for Negroes in American society. For example, where the occupation of mail carrier would have suggested lower-class status for a white man, it suggested middle-class status for a Negro. . . .

The sample was not secured by a random procedure. Rather, it consisted mainly of people who had children in certain nursery schools, some private, and some war nurseries supported mainly by public funds. The South Chicago group consisted mainly of people who lived in the neighborhood in which one of the interviewers had grown up. The Woodlawn lower-class group was obtained by calling at random in certain areas where housing was obviously poor, and passing from one family to another with whom the person being interviewed was acquainted. Any systematic bias introduced by these procedures lay probably in the direction of getting a middle-class group which had been subjected to the kind of teaching about child-rearing which is prevalent among middle-class people who send their children to nursery schools.

Results

Summary of Class Differences and Color Differences.* There are a large number of reliable differences between classes and between colors. The following tables report the differences between classes and colors

---

* Elsewhere Professor Davis has written on other differences between the living conditions of lower-class people and those of middle-class persons, and he has traced the correlates of such differences in personality structure. For example, one such difference concerns the orientation toward food. Because they eat regularly, Davis asserts, middle-class people do not generally develop an anxiety about food. Indeed, they seem to be more concerned over the consequences of eating too much than they are about not having enough to eat. The poverty of the lower class, however, renders the regularity of the food supply uncertain. This, he holds, results in an anxiety concerning food, a disposition to overeat whenever the opportunity arises, and to regard obesity as a form of social security. Similarly, the combination of irregular employment and the "needs" test for relief provides little reward for habits of thrift in the lower class. Accordingly, it

on certain parts of the schedule. Those differences which are statistically reliable are summarized in Table 4 and 5. . . .

Table 4.   Class Differences in Child Rearing*

Feeding and Weaning

More lower-class children are breast-fed only.

More lower-class children are breast-fed longer than 3 months (Negro only).

More lower-class children are fed at will.

Weaning takes place earlier (on the average) among middle-class children (white only).

More lower-class children suck longer than 12 months (white only).

More lower-class children have pacifiers (white only).

(c) More middle-class children are held for feeding.

(c) More lower-class children are weaned sharply (Negro only).

Toilet Training

Bowel training is begun earlier (on the average) with middle-class children.

Bladder training is begun earlier (on the average) with middle-class children.

Bowel training is completed earlier by middle-class children (Negro only).

More middle-class parents begin bowel training at 6 months or earlier.

More middle-class parents begin bladder training at 6 months or earlier (Negro only).

More middle-class parents complete bowel training at 12 months or earlier (Negro only).

More middle-class parents complete bladder training at 18 months or earlier (Negro only).

(c) More lower-class parents complete bladder training at 18 months or earlier (white only).

Father-Child Relations

Middle-class fathers spend more time with children.

Middle-class fathers spend more time in educational activities with children (teaching, reading, and taking for walks).

Lower-class fathers discipline children more (Negro only).

Occupational Expectations for Children

Middle-class expect child to help at home earlier.

* The letter (c) indicates that the finding contradicts the general tendency of the results.—*Eds.*

---

is not surprising to find that when they have the money persons who live under such conditions spend freely for television sets, expensive clothing, automobiles, etc. (*Cf.* W. Allison Davis, "Child Rearing in the Class Structure of American Society," in *The Family in a Democratic Society: Anniversary Papers of the Community Service Society of New York,* New York, Columbia University Press, 1949, pp. 56-69, esp. pp. 59-64.)—*Eds.*

Educational Expectation (Length of Education)

More middle-class children expected to go to college.

Age of Assuming Responsibility

Middle-class expect higher occupational status for children.
Middle-class girls cross street earlier (whites only).
(c) Lower-class boys and girls cross street earlier (Negro only).
Middle-class boys and girls expected to go downtown alone earlier.
Middle-class girls expected to help with younger children earlier.
Middle-class girls expected to begin to cook earlier (white only).
Middle-class girls expected to begin to sew earlier (white only).
Middle-class girls expected to do dishes earlier (Negro only).
(c) Lower-class children expected to get job after school earlier.
(c) Lower-class children expected to quit school and go to work earlier.

Strictness of Regime

Middle-class children take naps in daytime more frequently.
Lower-class boys and girls allowed at movies alone earlier.
Middle-class boys and girls in house at night earlier.

Table 5.   Color Differences in Child Rearing

Feeding and Weaning

More **Negro** children are breast-fed only.
More **Negro** children are breast-fed for three months or more.
More **Negro** children are fed at will (lower class only).
More **Negro** children have pacifiers (middle class only).
More white children are weaned sharply (middle class only).
Weaning takes place earlier (on the average) among white children (middle class only).
(c) More white children suck longer than 12 months (lower class only).

Toilet Training

Bowel training is begun earlier with Negro children.
Bladder training is begun earlier with Negro children.
Bowel training is completed earlier with Negro children (middle class only).
Bladder training is completed earlier with Negro children.
More Negro parents begin bowel training at 6 months or earlier (middle class only).
More Negro parents begin bladder training at 6 months or earlier (middle class only).
More Negro parents complete bowel training at 12 months or earlier (middle class only).
More Negro parents complete bladder training at 18 months or earlier (middle class only).

Father-Child Relations

White fathers spend more time with children (lower class only).
White fathers teach and play more with children (lower class only).
Negro fathers discipline children more (lower class only).

Educational Expectations (Length of Education)

More Negro children expected to go to college (lower class only).

Age of Assuming Responsibility

Negro boys and girls cross street earlier (lower class only).
(c) White girls cross street earlier (middle class only).
Negro boys go downtown alone earlier (lower class only).
Negro girls expected to dress selves earlier.
Negro girls expected to go to store earlier.
Negro girls expected to begin to cook earlier (lower class only).
(c) Negro children expected to quit school and go to work later.

Strictness of Regime

Negro boys allowed to go to movies alone earlier.
(c) White girls allowed to go to movies alone earlier.
White boys and girls in house at night earlier.

Table 4 summarizes the class differences which are statistically reliable at the five per cent level, while Table 5 summarizes the color differences which are statistically reliable at the same level. It will be seen that the differences tend to go together; a letter (c) indicates that the finding contradicts the general tendency of the results. For example, the general tendency is for lower-class children to be treated more permissively than middle-class children with respect to feeding and weaning. Contradictory to this tendency, however, more middle-class children are held for feeding. . . .

Discussion

The answer is clear to the principal question which this study was designed to answer. There are considerable social class differences in child-rearing practices, and these differences are greater than the differences between Negroes and whites of the same social class.

Personality Implications of Social Class Differences in Child-Rearing. Middle-class families are more rigorous than lower-class families in their training of children for feeding and cleanliness habits. They generally begin training earlier. Furthermore, middle-class families place more emphasis on the early assumption of responsibility for the self and on individual achievement. Finally, middle-class families are less permissive than lower-class families in their regimen. They require their children to take naps at a later age, to be in the house at night earlier, and, in general, permit less free play of the impulses of their children.

Generalizing from the evidence presented in the tables, we would say that middle-class children are subjected earlier and more consistently to the influences which make a child an orderly, conscientious, responsible, and tame person. In the course of this training middle-class children probably suffer more frustration of their impulses.

In the light of these findings, the data with respect to thumb-sucking are interesting. Three times as many white middle-class children are reported to suck their thumbs as white lower-class children, and almost twice as many Negro middle-class children do likewise. Thumb-sucking is generally thought of as a response to frustration of the hunger drive, or of the drive to seek pleasure through sucking. Since middle-class children are fed less frequently and are weaned earlier, the higher incidence of thumb-sucking would be expected. The Negro middle-class children are treated much more permissively than the white middle-class children with respect to feeding and weaning, but much more rigorously with respect to toilet-training. Yet the proportion of Negro middle-class children reported as sucking their thumb is almost the same as the proportion of white middle-class children so reported. *Perhaps thumb-sucking is a response to frustration of any sort, rather than to frustration in the feeding area alone.*

The data with respect to masturbation are also of interest in this connection. Three times as many white middle-class as compared with lower-class children are reported as masturbating. Twice as many Negro middle-class children as compared with Negro lower-class children are reported as masturbating. The meaning of these findings is obscured by the possibility that some lower-class mothers may not have understood the question. Or it may be that some of them did not watch as carefully for masturbation as middle-class mothers do, or some lower-class mothers may have been more hesitant than middle-class mothers in admitting that their children followed this practice. Yet none of these explanations seems probable, and perhaps the data should be taken at their face value. Perhaps masturbation is much more common among middle-class infants than among lower-class infants. If this is true, it might be explained in terms of the hypothesis that masturbation is in part a palliative to frustration. Children who are frustrated more would masturbate more, according to the hypothesis. . . .

Personality Implications of Color Differences in Child-Rearing. The striking thing about this study is that Negro and white middle-class families are so much alike, and that white and Negro lower-class families are so much alike. The likenesses hold for such characteristics as number of children, ages of parents when married, as well as child-rearing practices and expectations of children.

There are, however, some very interesting color differences. The major color differences are found in the areas of feeding and cleanliness training.

Negroes are much more permissive than whites in the feeding and weaning of their children. The difference is greater in the middle class. Negro babies have a markedly different feeding and weaning experience from white babies.

The situation is reversed with respect to toilet-training. Here the Negro parents are much stricter than white parents, both in middle- and lower-class circles. For example, 87 per cent of Negro middle-class mothers said they commence bowel training at 6 months or earlier, compared with 49 per cent of white middle-class mothers; and the comparable figures for bladder training are 40 and 18 per cent.

If feeding, weaning, and toilet-training have much influence on the personality, we should expect systematic differences between Negro and white people *of the same social class,* though it is not at all clear just what these differences should be, since one group is more rigorous in its training in one area while the other group is more rigorous in the other area.

There is another noticeable color difference. Negroes of both classes tend to give their girls an earlier training for responsibility in washing dishes, going to the store, and dressing themselves. This is probably traceable to the fact that Negroes of both classes have less outside help in the home than whites do and consequently the help of the girls is more urgently needed. It is noticeable, also, that middle-class Negro girls are not allowed to play across the street or to go to the movies alone as early as white middle-class girls. This may be due to the fact that most middle-class Negroes are forced to live in much less desirable neighborhoods, from their point of view, than those in which middle-class whites live.

Personality Implications of Intra-Family Differences. The questionnaire was designed to get information on personality characteristics of children as they might be related to birth order, training experience, and kinds of discipline used. Very few pronounced relationships appeared. This may have been due to several factors. Perhaps the interview method as we used it is not suited to getting information on individual personality characteristics. Again, perhaps such relations as exist are too complicated to be seen clearly in a study like this with a relatively small number of subjects. Nevertheless, there were a few interesting intra-family relationships.

For instance, the relation of "activity when young" to other characteristics is of considerable importance, since the degree of physical activity when young may be taken as an index of native vitality and of whatever inborn drive there may be for exploration or for physical activity. As we should expect, those "most active when young" were reported as most frequently punished, and as most active now. They were also reported as fighting most now, and as least neat. They were reported as happiest, except in the case of the white middle class. In general, it appears that various types of expressive, impulsive behavior tend to go together, and to characterize the happy child. An exception must be made of the white middle class, where happiness is reported by the mothers as associated with quietness rather than activity in the young child.

There are only a few characteristics clearly related to generosity and selfishness, though happiness and absence of fighting seem to be tied up with generosity. On the basis of simple Freudian principles one might expect selfishness and neatness to go together, but this hypothesis is not borne out by the data.

The data on birth order in relation to personality characteristics show some interesting trends. The first child in middle-class families of two children tends to be more jealous and more selfish than the second child. This may be taken as evidence in favor of the hypothesis of downward sibling rivalry as strongly influential in personality formation. Still, it is well to remember that mothers of young children, when there are only two in the family, may report the older as more jealous and selfish merely because the older is bigger and more able to assert himself. The second child was reported as happier and more generous, and also as more punished.

Conclusions

This study has given clear evidence of the following things:

1. There are significant differences in child-rearing practices between the middle and lower social classes in a large city. The same type of differences exist between middle- and lower-class Negroes as between middle- and lower-class whites.

2. Middle-class parents are more rigorous than lower-class parents in their training of children for feeding and cleanliness habits. They also expect their children to take responsibility for themselves earlier than lower-class parents do. Middle-class parents place their children under a stricter regimen, with more frustration of their impulses, than do lower-class parents.

3. In addition to these social-class differences, there are some differences between Negroes and whites in their child-rearing practices. Negroes are more permissive than whites in the feeding and weaning of their children, but they are much more rigorous than whites in toilet-training.

4. Thus, there are *cultural differences* in the personality formation of middle-class compared with lower-class people, *regardless of color,* due to their early training. And for the same reason there should be further but less marked cultural differences between Negroes and whites of the same social class.

5. In addition to the cultural differences between individuals due to early training experience, there are individual personality differences between children in the same family. These are probably due to physiological differences and to differences in emotional relationships with other members of the family.

CHAPTER 8

Parent-Child Relationships:
The Development of Personality

(Continued)

It SEEMS that in most societies mothers "know" how to rear their young. Their "knowledge" is not necessarily valid in the scientific sense of having experimental verification that the procedures used will lead to the child's developing approved patterns of response. Rather their "knowledge" is secure in the sense that it is defined in the culture as the "right" and "proper" way to bring up children. Mothers passed the lore along to their daughters, and grandmothers are repositories of such wisdom.

One of the concomitants of the industrial revolution—even preceding it—has been the scientific revolution with its implication that science rather than the wisdom of the elders is the arbiter of the proper ways of meeting the gamut of human problems. As science succeeds folk wisdom among the *au courant,* "child expert" displaces grandmother in knowing how to handle Junior. And mother learns how to raise children not from her mother, but from classes, books, and articles.

The situation has been further complicated by the fact that "expert" advice has been subject to change practically without notice. One generation of mothers was indoctrinated in the idea of John B. Watson[1] that the proper maternal attitude was one of objective aloofness. But

[1] *The Psychological Care of Infant and Child,* New York, Norton, 1928, pp. 81-82.

less than a generation later Margaret Ribble[2] and her followers were exhorting mothers to be warm and affectionate and to fondle their infants as much as possible.

Like women's clothing, then, the subject of child-rearing has become subject to the swings of fashion. No doubt an important reason for the pendulum-swings in the advice of the "experts" is that their "knowledge" has never been grounded in solid scientific method.[3] It appears that an important consequence among more literate mothers has been a progressive insecurity concerning the "correct" ways of rearing children. As grandmothers became "old fogies," they clearly lost their authority. But since the "experts" have been shifting their advice, mothers can seldom be sure that the advice they receive is the "latest" and the most "authoritative."

In the present chapter Escalona analyzes the current view of "experts" in this field and examines some of the implications of this view. Then we turn to Sears who, assessing the state of our knowledge, points out certain propositions which seem to be fairly well established and indicates areas in which further research is necessary.

A COMMENTARY UPON SOME RECENT CHANGES IN CHILD-REARING PRACTICES*

SIBYLLE ESCALONA

. . . In this country and in modified forms in other countries we have, within a rather short period of time, witnessed a remarkable change in cultural attitudes toward specific child-rearing practices. Now as formerly it is true that the United States (more than other parts of Western civilization) is characterized by the fact that children, their

---

[2] *The Rights of Infants*, New York, Columbia University Press, 1943.

[3] As pointed out in chapter 1, the more studies fall short of the four-fold design, the less scientifically conclusive they are. Most studies in this field have been of the clinical or one-cell design. For a criticism of Ribble's work see S. R. Pinneau, "A Critique on the Articles by Margaret Ribble," *Child Development*, 21 (1950), 203-28.

* Adapted and reprinted by permission of the author and publisher from *Child Development*, 20 (1949), 157-62.

health and education, possess a very high cultural value. In all likelihood this has something to do with the fact that to Americans the future is more important than past or present. Historically, the United States has stood for the realization of concrete, workable, realistic fulfillment—if not here and now, then in the foreseeable future—whereas many other cultures seem to stand primarily for a noble tradition or for more abstract ideals. The importance of children to our society has not markedly changed, but the ways in which society deals with children, the way in which parents, teachers, physicians and others behave toward children, has changed a great deal.

Ten years ago and less, authoritative public opinion subscribed to sentiments and rules which may be characterized as follows: Bodily and mental health is based on an orderly, strictly scheduled existence from early childhood onward. Prescribed formulae are superior to breast feeding, chiefly because the ingredients are known and nutrition becomes, therefore, a controlled process. When babies or children cry without recognized legitimate cause it is best to let them cry it out. It is the responsibility of adults to teach children what is "right" and what is "wrong" in regard to meal times, sleeping hours, play interests and most other activities. The standards for "rightness" in such matters were derived from a combination of adult patterns of living and scientifically established facts about the physical growth of children. At the time, this seemed a highly rational approach. It goes with the concept of a stable, orderly and ultimately predictable universe which characterized the early decades of the 20th century. From the vantage point of the present, it is difficult to recapture the feelings and expectations on which such convictions about child-rearing practices were based. The extraordinary advances made in the natural sciences and their application to almost all facets of living—from the building of bridges to airplane travel, and from routine inoculations to pre-cooked baby cereals—provided for dominant groups in our culture a sense of certainty and power. It was somehow felt that—in principle at least— the external forces of nature had been overcome. The future was ours to master. It is no wonder that such a background of attitudes would lead us to expect that bigger and better children could be produced— much like automobiles or washing machines—through specific, rather mechanical, prescribed procedures. It is well to remember that mothers who forced exactly six ounces of formula down a baby's throat exactly every four hours, nursery school teachers who handed out gold stars to the child who didn't raise his voice nor fight for a toy, and teachers who taught arithmetic by drill and drill alone performed these acts with as much or as little love and devotion for their children as is felt by any mother who feeds her baby on self-demand, and by any teacher teaching self-expression through rhythm games. Mothers dealing with their children flexibly and indulgently today, as well as the mothers who raised their children rigidly and sternly ten years ago, are and were supported by a strong sense of doing what is best for the child in accordance with expert opinion.

In the course of recent years we have lost the naive sense of mastery in regard to the world in which we live. Not only scientists but people in general have ceased to believe that technological advances will solve the problems of human existence. Quite the reverse, we are afraid of the consequences of the split atom and of other devices which release and manipulate natural forces. At the same time a generalized feeling of uncertainty emerged: even on the surface we no longer possess a stable value system. Such changes in cultural atmosphere have, of course, recurred many times in history. They characterize post-war and be-tween-war periods, and are often described as periods of decadence or disintegration.

In one respect, however, the cultural milieu which forms the matrix in which our children presently grow and develop differs from previous times in social crisis. Scientists and everyone else now tend to regard human nature itself as the main source of threat to future security and well being. The fear of the gods, of enemies and of natural forces has been replaced by the fear of the unconscious, or of whatever it is that determines human actions. Psychoanalysis has done more than any other theory to illuminate the seemingly irrational aspects of human behavior. Occasionally it is claimed that the findings of psychoanalysis have helped to undermine the stability of our attitudes and values, and have therefore partially caused the current confusion. It is our impression that the reverse is true. In other words, the writer believes that the enormous impact which psychoanalysis has had upon popular thought, its influence on medicine, education, literature and even the moving picture, are a consequence of the loss of a stable value system rather than the other way around.[1]

---

[1] Neither of the alternative views stated in the text fully reflects the intended meaning. The effect of psychoanalysis upon popular thought and practice, and its relationship to the cultural state, must be reciprocal. The formulation of psychoanalytic theory required

We have referred to the rigid scheduling, the careful dosing of manifest affection and the orgies of formula prescription which constituted authoritative opinion on child rearing practices until recently. The totality of these attitudes and practices we have regarded as of a piece with a social-cultural milieu the stability and cohesiveness of which rested on a sense of technical mastery. What of the present-day philosophy of child rearing? To select a few representative items: It is now thought that it is up to us as adults to meet the needs of the younger child, rather than to expect early adaptation from him. To wit, self-demand schedules and all that goes with them.* Among the needs of the young child we recognize the need for affection and for an intimate relationship with the mother as of very great importance, tending to evaluate it as more crucial than the need for good physical care. We prize self-expression, sincerity of feeling and spontaneous interest above good manners, self-restraint, or intellectual accomplishment. So far so good; each culture has the right and the obligation to determine the educational goals for which to strive, and the above goals appear to adequately represent what we as a group want our children to be.

Let us look, however, at the means we adopt in trying to reach these new goals. Not so much the child-rearing authorities themselves as their interpreters (in the press, the Well Baby Clinics, the case work agencies, the Public Health Departments, etc.) have created a philosophy which by and large makes it seem as though contentment and even normal development for the child can be attained only at the cost of great self-denial on the part of the parents. The mother, especially, must subordinate her need for sleep, for recreation, for getting the housework done or for pursuing nondomestic interests at all times. Moreover, she is expected to do so with a sense of deep satisfaction and happiness. If, for a moment, we disregard all that has been learned about personality development (which led to these new methods) and consider only the vague ideological orientation of many parents and others who apply these new principles—one outstanding feature of the spectacle is that the adults are uncomfortable in many ways. Room-

---

cultural forces which demanded it; the initial resistance against analytic findings and the subsequent popularization of these findings were largely determined culturally; yet during the process the culture changed, partially by virtue of having absorbed new "facts" and new ideas from psychodynamics; the whole process being intricate and dialectic in nature.

* As is implied in the context, the "self-demand schedule" involves feeding the infant when he seems to desire it. This stands in contrast to the practice of feeding the infant by the clock, *e.g.*, every four hours, every six hours, etc.—*Eds.*

ing-in requires the mother to take active charge of the baby at a time when previously she would have rested and been waited upon hand and foot.* Self-demand, especially when the baby is breast-fed or when it is believed that close contact between mother and child at feeding time is important, mean that all other activities must be adapted to the child's rhythm and makes it almost impossible to get away from home. Giving the child free scope to explore the world means endless patience and labor in cleaning up messes and in countless other ways.

If one wishes to establish a relationship between broad cultural trends and child-rearing practices, observations like those above, however correct, would be of very limited significance if they related to this one area alone. Yet even a most superficial survey of accepted attitudes and practices in altogether different areas suggests a similar trend toward making things tough for adults. For instance: after operations people used to have weeks of bed rest—currently they are made to walk about during the first few days. The usual length of hospitalization for childbirth has dropped from ten days to six days. An infection, which in the old days would have been good for several weeks, now, with the use of penicillin and other drugs, will be cleared up in a matter of days. If one breaks a leg plastic braces make it possible to walk again within a few days. If a person be too tired to work, benzedrine will fix him up almost at once. Obviously, penicillin, plastic braces, and the rest represent invaluable advances and constitute essential progress in human knowledge. Similarly, our new and more complete understanding of the needs of children is valuable and has become indispensable knowledge. It remains true, however, that, in our culture, it has become exceedingly difficult for adults to find legitimate channels of indulgence. Where passive needs are concerned even minimal satisfaction is difficult to attain without cultural criticism.

Such a state of affairs is of course multi-determined. If our previous speculation is correct, however, *i.e.,* if it is true that we now tend to ascribe the responsibility for wars and other disturbing events to the

* "Rooming-in" involves placing the infant with the mother shortly after birth. In accordance with this procedure the mother becomes directly responsible for caring for the infant within a few hours after delivery. This stands in contrast to the practice of removing the infant from the mother, of having the hospital staff assume prime responsibility for caring for the infant in a separate section of the hospital, and of having the infant assume with the mother the role of occasional visitor. For a discussion of this and other innovations in the regimen of early infancy see Herbert Thoms, *Training for Childbirth: A Program of Natural Childbirth with Rooming-In,* New York, McGraw-Hill, 1950.—*Eds.*

"human element" rather than to outside forces, this fact may be considered as one among many which have brought on the present attitude of severity toward the needs of adults. Roughly stated our thought is that if we, collectively, assume responsibility for having created our social existence, we automatically assume moral responsibility and hence guilt for the state of affairs in which we find ourselves. In addition it follows that hopes for a better world rest with our ability to make our children more rational, more competent, and more capable of maintaining an orderly existence than we have been.

Such an attitude is reasonable enough, except perhaps for the element of guilt. It is precisely this element which is reflected in some of our child-rearing practices. In the case of individuals we know that feelings of guilt are likely to lead to self-defeating action, designed more to appease the individual's anxiety than to remedy the situation which caused the guilt feeling. It is barely possible that collectively, as a culture, we are doing the same thing. It is as though our recognition of the fact that the better we learn to control events the greater our responsibility for these events implied an apologetic state of mind toward our children. As though we not only regretted that we have not done better by them, but also felt that we must "make up to them," so to speak by extra indulgence and also by punishing ourselves.

It is not suggested that individual parents, or any other persons who deal with children, are apt to consciously and clearly experience the pattern of thought suggested above. Yet, for the moment, we may assume that some such undercurrent exists in our society and motivates and/or activates some of our behavior toward children. What would it mean for the development of the children who grow up amidst such attitudes?

A real discussion of this point would require more time than is available, but the following may suggest the trend of our speculation. It is generally true that as we deal with children, individually and collectively, we communicate to them not only our conscious intention, but also our feelings and attitudes (conscious or unconscious) which accompany these intentions. It is reasonable to assume that if our behavior toward children is in part motivated by anxiety and guilt— as has been suggested in the body of this paper—children will absorb the fact that such attitudes are maintained toward them. This in turn can be expected to affect their developing concept of the self and of the world about them. As is often the case, psychopathological material may provide clues as to the meaning of behavior observations that are made with normal children. Available clinical observations can be interpreted in such a way, it is believed, as to show that in indirect ways children acquire a sense that something is owed them. Moreover, and related to this, the awareness of the adult's insecurity, anxiousness and guilt would seem to operate as a barrier toward developing the trust and confidence in the strength and the superior judgment of adults which children require if they themselves are to feel secure and confident.

In this discussion we have not attempted to evaluate or criticize the recent ideology concerning child care. Nor have we wished to assess the merits of any of the specific methods or practices which were referred to and which resulted from a new philosophy concerning children. In fact, it may not be amiss to mention that in large measure we consider the new pediatric and educational practices as the practical application of valid and useful insights into the nature of personality development.

Rather, we wish to call to your attention the manner in which many of the facts provided by psychoanalysis, child psychology, etc., have been interpreted and applied. It is thought that the application of our new insights has often been made in such a way as to make many of the recommended child-rearing practices the vehicle of our group anxieties and collective guilt. We do not regard this as a logical necessity. Instead we should like to consider it as a comprehensible social-psychological phenomenon which may perhaps be modified and minimized through conscious recognition. Cultural emphasis on the psychological implications of child-rearing practices is likely to continue, and it is desirable that it should. However, a modification in some of our accompanying attitudes is also thought desirable. Increasing awareness of the less rational elements in our behavior—of unconscious motivations and of the intrinsic connection between feelings, beliefs, and actions— is useful to the extent to which it enables us to better control these elements and to master ourselves as we have mastered the physical world. It would be both ironic and tragic if, in the very act of removing some of the frustrations and limitations to optimal psychic development, we ran counter to the very nature of our understanding about the emotional needs of children by unnecessarily burdening them with our historically and socially understandable terrors and uncertainties

PERSONALITY DEVELOPMENT IN THE FAMILY*

Robert R. Sears

The family is the basic social unit that determines both childhood and adult personality. The reason for this lies in the nature of the learning process by which the motivational characteristics of man are formed. Although the newborn infant possesses a complex set of potential action systems which will assist him in adjusting to his environment, none of these is of sufficient effectiveness to enable him to live in the absence of help from adults. Even the fundamental requirements of his metabolic system can be met only by aid from others, and he has but the most rudimentary reflexes with which to protect himself from external dangers or to overcome hazards that prevent him from securing needed satisfactions. It is this basic dependency on others that forces the family into the role of a personality determiner, for the learning process by which the child develops an ability to help himself also produces those properties in him which are characterized as personality. To understand the intimate influence of the family in this matter, one must consider briefly the nature of the learning process and the way in which the conditions of learning determine what the child learns.

The molar unit of individual behavior is the instigation-action sequence. This is a segment of behavior which begins with some definable stimulation and ends with a response that reduces the strength of that stimulation. The stimuli, or instigators, are of two general kinds. The first are the drive stimuli which are sufficiently powerful to impel the child to action of some kind. Initially, in the newborn infant, these actions are determined by reflex pathways laid down in the nervous system as a part of biological development. The second class of stimuli is composed of those which impinge on the child's sensorium from outside, lights, sounds, smells, and touches. Drive stimuli may also arise from outside, as in the case of superficial pain,

---

* This memorandum on research planning in the field of family life was prepared in 1948 at the request of the Committee on Family Research of the Social Science Research Council. The references have been brought up to date for the present publication.

and incidental instigators may arise from inside, as in the case of muscular sensations. The chief difference between drive and non-drive stimuli is in their strength and the degree to which they impel action.

At the other end of the instigation-action sequence is the goal response. This is an action that puts an end to the drive stimuli, or at least reduces their strength. In the case of hunger, the drive stimuli arise from a complex set of physico-chemical conditions within the body (which can most often be effectively measured by specifying the time since food was last ingested), and the goal response can best be described as "eating." Between the occurrence of drive stimulation and the appropriate goal response, there must necessarily be a series of actions which are instrumental to putting the child in such context with his environment that he can make the goal response. These instrumental acts serve to create certain environmental events that must exist for the goal response to occur. In the case of hunger, a young child may cry and thrash his arms about until his mother appears, evaluates the situation, and offers him food. In this instance the crying and thrashing might be termed instrumental acts and the appearance of the mother with food would be the environmental event.

The carrying through of such a sequence has another important effect besides the reduction of drive strength and putting an end to the striving activity. It also reinforces the instrumental activities and increases the probability that they will occur on subsequent occasions when the same stimulus conditions are presented. Thus, the child's crying may be a purely reflex response to the pain of hunger, but if he is consistently allowed to cry before food is offered, he will eventually respond to all painful stimulation with a cry. And because there is a mechanism by which he can learn to "anticipate" the consequences of his instrumental acts, the cry will also develop into a technique by which the mother can be brought to his side for other drive-alleviations than hunger-feeding.

A third effect of the repeated occurrence of instigation-action sequences is the development of secondary drives and their accompanying goal events. Originally, only the final goal response had drive reduction value, and only the inborn primary drive could initiate activity. But with the repetition of such a sequence, the instrumental activities take on the properties of goal responses in their own right, and the presence of the various cue stimuli that have previously been associated with the primary drive stimuli become appropriate to arouse a drive to perform those particular instrumental acts. Their occurrence then can serve to reinforce other new instrumental acts that may be introduced into the new sequence. Thus, the child who originally cried to get his mother to feed him may learn to cry apparently just for pleasure, and the crying may be excited by any of the stimulus conditions that were originally associated with his feeding. Further, the original goal event was getting food into his mouth, but with the constant association of his mother's presence with this form of drive-reduction, he now comes to value his mother's presence in its own right. The phrase "a child wants his mother" refers to the fact that his mother has been sufficiently often associated with primary drive reduction that she has become a secondary goal herself and the child will now respond to any stimulus that suggests her possible presence by performing those acts necessary to effect it.

So far the only social aspect of the learning that is going on is the more or less fortuitous fact that it is the mother who provides primary gratification. It could as well be a mechanical device operated by someone else who never came in sight or sound of the child. In such case, the child would undoubtedly develop the same secondary drives as with the mother, but the secondary goal event would relate to the presence of the robot.

The social influence enters in connection with the psychological properties of the other persons who, in fact, do come in contact with the child and are instrumental in his primary drive reduction. It is clear from what has been said above that the kinds of things a child learns to want, the kinds of objects he loves and fears, the kinds of social situations that give him learned satisfactions, are a function of the arrangement of his environment at the times he makes his goal responses. If his mother is consistently smiling and beaming when she feeds him, changes his diapers, washes him, snuggles him into a warm bed, and kisses and fondles him, a smiling mother will be the necessary environmental event for the various secondary drives established in these situations. If, on the contrary, she is tired or tense, if she is the wife in a marital pair that has failed to make a satisfactory marital adjustment, the child will learn to expect, and to require, in fact, that expression for the satisfaction of his new drives. The myriad complexities of behavior in the adults who surround the child inevitably determine the kinds of behavior which in the future will serve as the necessary conditions for the gratification of his secondary drives. Thus the family, with all its varieties of behavior, its nuances of feeling, its manneristic modes of expression, its uniqueness of structure, will determine the kinds of secondary motivational systems to be established in the new baby. It is these secondary motives that comprise what is commonly called "personality." It is they which determine what kinds of persons can give gratification, what kinds of persons will be loved, which, in effect, specify the destiny of the child's emotional life and his social adjustment as soon as he is born into a living family.*

The mechanics of this learning process are by no means simple; they are the main subject-matter of the psychology of learning as it is currently being investigated in numberless laboratories. More detailed treatments of the basic principles will be found in Hull (1943), Miller and Dollard (1941), and Mowrer and Kluckhohn (1944). It is clear even from such a simplified description as this, however, that the primary determinants of the *content,* or socially relevant *quality,* of human behavior are the *conditions* of learning, the properties of the human environment that reward some actions and non-reward others, that guide this way or that, that provide this or that kind of secondary goal-object as a necessary part of new drives and motives, that enforce learning of actions and ideals congenial to the rewarding and punishing persons who control the child's experiences. The nature of these conditions of learning is determined by the family. It is the family's behavior that specifies what the new child shall do, or can do, to achieve comfort or happiness, and it is the family which therefore establishes his personality. The technical ramifications of this situation have been analyzed in greater detail elsewhere (Sears, 1951), but enough has been said here to explain why most investigators of childhood personality, and the personality adjustment of adults, have approached the matter from a developmental point of view, and why they have concentrated heavily on the influence of family relationships as an antecedent condition for the variables of personality development.

---

* The state of affairs to which Sears refers above is regarded by Winch as the "beginning of infantile love." The helplessness of the infant renders him incapable of ministering to many of his own needs. If he were able thus to care for himself, he would be able autonomously to achieve the pleasurable state of tension-reduction. Being dependent upon the mother or nurse, he comes to associate the pleasure of tension-reduction with her presence, and it is the positive affect thus produced toward her which is infantile love. (*Cf.* R. F. Winch, *The Modern Family,* New York, Holt, 1952, pp. 210-13.) An extension of this same theoretical scheme into the relations between men and women in adulthood provides the basis of Winch's theory of complementary needs in mate selection. (*Cf.* pp. 435-53 below.)—*Eds.*

Socialization of the Primary Drives

The various primary drives—hunger, evacuation, fatigue, and sex—represent primitive action systems for the satisfaction of important needs in the young infant. These systems are primitive in two senses, one in the technical sense of being early forms of action in the ontogenetic life of the child, and the other in the more colloquial sense of being crude and undifferentiated. Demands for food or desires to evacuate exist without reference to the environment's facilities for providing the needed assistance; the child has no conception, at the start, of regulation or modification of his needs in terms of the needs of others. One of the important functions of the family is to provide the appropriate learning experiences for the child during his first few years whereby the primary drives will elicit socially acceptable behavior. The child must learn to satisfy his needs in a culturally conforming manner.

The hazards involved in this learning are great. There is abundant psychiatric evidence to show that improper training, involving serious frustration or the arousal of anxieties or inconsistent over-permissiveness, can create motivational distortions that will prevent a normal and healthy personality development in later childhood and adult years. The consequences of such distortion not infrequently manifest themselves most seriously in the breakdown of interpersonal relations depending on love and the adoption of mature and responsible emotional roles in marriage. On the other hand, effective training leads to secure personalities whose capacities for adjustment to the needs of others is sufficient to ensure wholesome and mutually satisfying relationships throughout life.

While the importance of this early socialization process has been amply attested by clinical studies, the objective data available for guidance in appropriate training methods is painfully scanty. Psychoanalytic practice and theory have been rich sources of hypotheses for the probable relationships between various types of feeding, sex and evacuation control and the consequent personality developments, but few have been critically tested or subjected to the evaluation of objective and experimental procedures. The literature through 1941 has been reviewed by Sears (1943).

Feeding

Research on feeding in relation to personality has been oriented toward two main problems, method of feeding and the weaning process. Both problems are aspects of a more general one concerning the influence of rewards and frustrations on this most fundamental of all human drives. For research purposes, however, some sub-questions must be distinguished.

1. Breast Feeding. Although artificial devices for the feeding of infants were known in ancient Egypt, the wet nurse was the principal substitute for the biological mother until the nineteenth century, when rubber nipples were introduced and bottle feeding became commonplace. Pediatric skill developed milk formulas that in all major ways served as acceptable, or even preferable, substitutes for mother's milk. With the increased participation of married women in economic roles outside the home, the desirability of artificial feeding has become greater and greater in recent years, from the standpoint of many mothers. Although its medical effects are of little consequence, the psychological consequences of bottle feeding have recently been rather vigorously deplored by a number of psychiatrists (Moloney, 1947).

In the absence of objective data, the discussion can only remain on a speculative basis. It has been argued that bottle feeding is a device adopted by mothers whose fundamental, and perhaps unconscious, attitude toward their children is one of rejection. In part, this rejection is believed to derive from a failure of the awakening of the nurturant or maternal impulses which develop most healthily when the infant feeds at the mother's breast regularly. The effects on the child are believed to be of considerable psychosomatic significance. Digestive difficulties have been reported to follow insufficient fondling by the mother, and breast feeding is conceived as important because of its influence on the mother's motivation (Ribble, 1944). The available data on these points, however, are insufficient to verify the conclusions (Pinneau, 1950).

2. Weaning. The importance of the weaning process was first emphasized in the theoretical formulations of the oral component of the libido by Freud (1905). Freud's observations of the pervasiveness of non-nutritional sucking in infants and young children led him to include an oral drive as a part of the newborn baby's native motivational equipment. This drive was believed to be reducible only by stimulation of the sensitive oral zone, and it was believed to persist as the main source of the child's gratification until this position of primacy was taken over by the anal-urethral drive component sometime in the second or third year of life.

If this theory were true, early weaning would represent a frustration of pleasure-seeking at a time when the child had few alternatives for securing gratification. Such frustration would create a state of generalized inhibition and would leave a continuing demand for oral stimulation that could be satisfied only by substitute forms of stimulation such as thumb-sucking. Further, if the weaning were performed with some severity, anxiety would be established as a response to the hunger drive and to all activities relating to food-seeking.

Research on these problems has been directed largely to an analysis of the oral drive and behavior presumably resulting from it. Levy (1928) studied the relationship between thumb sucking in young children and the adequacy of their experiences with nutritional sucking. He found that a history of inadequacy was followed by definite problem behavior in the thumb-sucking category. To get a somewhat purer sample of this relationship, he compared the non-nutritional sucking of litter-mate puppies who were given different opportunities for sucking in the first few weeks of life (1934). He obtained results which were in agreement with those from the children; the less the opportunity for extensive sucking in connection with food-taking, the greater was the degree of non-nutritional sucking.

While these studies substantiate clearly the original hypothesis that babies possess a strong oral drive, they are insufficient to demonstrate its native character. More recently, studies by Davis, Sears, Miller and Brodbeck (1948) have shown that infants fed from birth by a cup do not develop as strong a sucking reflex during their first ten days as do children who are fed at the breast. This suggests that the oral drive may be largely influenced by experience, and that although an oral drive is virtually universal, its presence may be a product of an almost universal method of feeding—namely, by letting the child suck.

The question as to the effects of severity of weaning has been studied by Whiting and Child (1952). By an ingenious compilation of data from a large number of primitive tribes, they have shown that in those cultures which have severe methods of interrupting infant feeding, adults most commonly explain their illnesses as resulting from food-poisoning, the eating of the wrong kinds of foods, and other food-connected activities.

The Research Problems. The procedures used by the mother in feeding her child are of undeniable importance. The feeding situation is one of the most intimate social activities of the child during the first few months of his life, and the attitudes and methods of the feeder become a part of the elaborate goal events involved in the child's secondary motivations. The emphasis on breast feeding reflects clinical awareness of this relationship.

It is not improbable, however, that the important variables are more subtle and complex than the method by which milk is gotten into the stomach. While much needs to be discovered about the exact origins of the sucking drive, and the consequences to the child of interrupting or satisfying it, some approach must soon be made toward the emotional consequences of the mother's attitudes toward the child. Plenty of healthy happy children have been reared by bottle and even by cup; plenty of breast fed babies have developed inadequate personalities. Nevertheless, the investigators who have fixed on these correlated variables are hammering at a general problem of profound significance.

Major areas that require research are: (1) the origin of the oral drive and methods by which it can be modified; (2) motivational consequences of frustration of the hunger drive in early infancy; (3) effects of different kinds of parental personality on the feeding behavior of the child; (4) cultural correlates of various feeding procedures; (5) influence of anxiety-evoking experiences in connection with feeding; and (6) relation of parental attitudes of affection and rejection to the development of those motivational systems which stem from or are influenced by early feeding experiences.

Sex

The sex drive is so intimately bound up with social behavior and with the development of secondary motivational systems that involve interaction with other persons that it can hardly be dealt with in the same way as the hunger drive. For purposes of research planning, two main areas can be distinguished. One is that of the interrelation between various forms of infantile pleasure-seeking, the sensitivity of the erotogenic zones and the relation between them, and the effects of frustration or satiation on the drive strength of the so-called libidinal components. The other involves the social aspects of sex development with reference to the growth of affectional attachments to parents, siblings and other persons. The present section is devoted to the first problem only.

Freud's theories of sex development (1905) are too well known to require detailed summary. In brief, he was led to the conclusion that the infant is born with a capacity to secure pleasure from stimulation of various erotogenic zones and that he has a drive to obtain such pleasure. These zones were believed to be related to one another in such a way as to permit substitute gratification of one through another. Differentiation between them is incomplete during early childhood and hence the frustrations, anxieties, or satisfactions obtained for one drive component generalize to the others in some degree, and later socialized development of any given component therefore must assimilate the early response systems established to the others. This interdependence is seen in the adult as a confusion of childhood memories and associations that relate to the different components, and as a transferring of excitation and inhibitions from one system to another. In psychoanalytic practice with adult neurotics, these confusions and transferrals have been found to be prominently displayed in sexual behavior. The consequences for sexual and marital adjustment are frequently disastrous.

Much of the Freudian theory was a brilliant interpretation backward, chronologically speaking, from the symptomatic behavior of adults to an hypothesized motivational structure and experiential sequence in childhood. Research data on the erotogenic complex of variables in infants and young children is scanty (cf. Sears, 1943). Observations by Halverson (1938) have established clearly that there is a close relationship between reflex activities involving sucking, elimination and erection of the penis in male infants. This juxtaposition of behavior deriving from stimulation of these three erotogenic zones can be interpreted either as evidence of a biological connection between them or as a more or less fortuitous fact that permits of an early association through the learning process. Beyond this, there are but scattered and casual observations that lead to the general conclusion that children secure a good deal of satisfaction from stimulation of their erotogenic zones, that they learn new forms of behavior in order to secure such gratification, that they show evidences of frustration when such behavior is interrupted, and that there is no sharp demarcation line between behavior instigated by eliminative and genital drives.

The natural extension of this area of study is into the problem of socialization. As in the case of feeding, the importance of childhood experiences lies not in the detailed physical manipulations that occur to the child, but in the kinds of affectional relationships that are established within the family. Whatever may be the fundamental sources of the drives that lead to a striving for organic pleasure and satisfaction, the ways in which such pleasure-seeking behavior is handled and modified to be acceptable within the family and the society at large are the sources of those attributes of personality which determine the effectiveness of the individual's later adjustment within such social institutions as the family, the school, the church and the economic structure of society.

However, the study of socialization, the gradual controlling and directing of behavior toward socially approved ends and by approved means, can go forward only if there is simultaneously some attack on the problems of the origin of the drives which produce the to-be-socialized behavior. Such investigation will begin with newborn infants and will be directed to tracing the conditions which, ontogenetically, determine the relative strengths of the various drives, the nature and kind of associations between them, and the effects of various types of non-reward and punishment on their modification.

Other Drive Systems *Secondary*

The influence of various types of toilet training has been widely studied by child psychiatrists. Adult psychotic patients not infrequently have elaborate involvement of the elimination function, with symptomatic distortions of normal functioning; adult neurotics often recall disturbances in the development of their childhood control over elimination, and present complex symbolic involvement of the processes. Problem children examined in child guidance clinics have a high incidence of emotional disturbances recorded in their histories as related to bowel training (Huschka, 1942). Clinical experience, in other words, suggests that the socialization of this action system is intimately related to the development of powerful emotional responses and, in some instances, to distortions of normal personality.

There is little objective research of consequence in this field. Freud's theory of anal character formation has led to a testing of the interrelationship between certain adult traits that Freud hypothesized as deriving from coercive training (*cf.* Sears, 1943), but no careful analyses other than Huschka's exploratory studies have been made with children. Clinical experience has clearly indicated the importance of the problems here, as it has in connection with feeding, sex and fatigue, but the basic research approach to socialization remains to be undertaken.

The effects of fatigue have been more widely studied, but the orientation of such research has commonly been toward the immediate effects of loss of sleep or other fatiguing experiences rather than toward the process of secondary drive development based on the rewarding character of fatigue reduction. Since middle-class American culture provides for an extensive association of parental activity with the going-to-bed behavior of the child, it is evident that this is one of the major opportunities for the creation of socially relevant motivational systems in the child. Again, clinical experience supports the theoretical expectations; anxieties related to sleeping and resting are common among children referred to guidance clinics, and such reactions are often related to maternal rejection, sibling rivalry, and other sources of frustration or threat.

Research on Socialization

Although there is a certain arbitrary quality to the distinction that has been made here between socialization of primary drives and the elaboration of more complex secondary motives such as aggression and dependency, there are sound research reasons for dealing with the problems separately. The socialization of primary drives involves manipulation and control of action systems that are already in existence in the child at birth. To study the processes by which the family does this controlling, and to evaluate the influence of it on the child, requires extensive understanding of the native hierarchy of responses and drives the child possesses. This is in part a biological problem and students who undertake such investigation must be adequately prepared in human biology and especially embryology. They must be experienced in the handling of infants and in the day to day activities involved in working in the hospital setting.

This is not to imply that the development of the more complex social secondary drives is less dependent on human biology, but simply that the effects of learning in the family can be studied with less immediate reference to biology than can the socialization of drive-response sequences that have their immediate qualitative character determined at birth. This means, in turn, that the qualifications for investigators appear to include a heavier emphasis on sociological and anthropological knowledge and techniques in the case of the secondary motivational systems. In the sections which follow, it will be apparent that the most crucial contemporary research problems involve social and psychological analysis of the family and parent-child relations, while in the summary below of research problems in primary drive socialization it is evident that much emphasis is given to analysis of the child's native equipment.

There are three main types of problem that should receive priority in this area. *First,* studies must be made of the native hierarchy of responses the child possesses at birth. While there has been some investigation of the sucking reflex and its development during the first months of life, there are few comparable data on the eliminative process, sexual responsiveness or sleep and fatigue. Before a great deal can be done to discover the most effective ways of family handling of these primary action systems, detailed understanding must be secured of the baby's own equipment.

Second, and of more immediate relevance to family behavior, there must be extensive investigation of the effects on the child of various types of control and training. Freudian theory has placed undue emphasis on somewhat molecular aspects of such control; this is especially true of the psychoanalytic prepossession with the sucking response. Clinical experience with children suggests that the methods of control have pervasive influences beyond the immediate responses they are designed to control. Personality characteristics of the parents are exemplified in the techniques by which weaning is accomplished, for example, but there is reason to believe that the same attitudes in the parents make themselves known to the child in many other ways, some perhaps so subtle that they have escaped the observation of clinicians who must rely on parental report of child-rearing practices.

This area of research will involve thorough study of actual practices in the home, within the family milieu. Interviewing methods provide certain kinds of data with great accuracy, but attention must be turned in the future to more direct observation of the details of parental behavior as they occur, as well as to the filtered parental reports of what occurs. Perhaps the most serious research needed in the whole field of family-child relations is careful methodological study of such observation procedures.

The kinds of problems which seem most significant at present fall into two categories. One relates to the effect of different methods of training on the child's immediate behavior. This is important because it is the immediate characteristics of the child's emotional and motivational conditions that determines in part what effect any given subsequent experiences will have. The second aspect of the research has to do with the ultimate consequences of various methods of training. Undoubtedly the adult personality is partly dependent on the kinds of learning experiences of childhood. Just which ones of the adult traits or motivational systems evolve from these early experiences is still largely a matter of speculation. It is in this set of problems that the anthropologist, with his comparative analyses of culture, can make a most important contribution (Whiting and Child, 1952).

Third, there must be investigation of the personality characteristics of adults with reference to the types of adjustment they make to their children. Methods of child-rearing are not commonly chosen, by parents, with a strictly intellectual approach to the matter. What they do with their children is a function of their own highly elaborated motivational systems, some of which stem from background experiences in their own childhoods. The personality structure that exists in the mature adult, however, can be analyzed independently of its life history origins, and it is such analyses that are needed in order to provide a clear indication of what types of education or reeducation are needed as part of a preparation-for-parenthood program.

Socially Determined Secondary Drives

In addition to the personality characteristics produced by particular methods of controlling and modifying primary drive behavior, there are many motivational systems that result from the sheer fact of social living. Such motives as aggression, dependency, self-reliance and competition are in part the products of parental reinforcement or extinction of the child's efforts to control his environment. For example, the child faced by frustrations resulting from his parents' refusal to assist him may use aggressive techniques for securing their compliance. If his efforts succeed, and they often do, his aggressive behavior is reinforced and he adds one unit of increment to the strength of a secondary drive of aggression. The reason for defining this as a socially determined secondary drive lies in the fact that the aggressive behavior relies for its effectiveness on the biological fact that adults as well as children withdraw from pain and seek to avert it, sometimes by complying with the demands of the person who is producing the pain.

Comparable situations exist with the various other secondary drives. To some degree they represent an irreducible minimum of motivational repertory that derives from family living. All children must be nurtured during their first few years or they would die. Hence, every child goes through the experience of being helped and thereby having his needs fulfilled or his anguish relieved. Thus, every child develops some kind of dependency drive. Every family possesses some materials or some personal relationships which are unshareable, which require competition with other family members. Hence, every child develops a competitive drive. To the extent that human relationships create social associations at the time of sexual gratification, specific secondary sexual attachments are developed.

The modal behaviors of parents from different cultures differ in respect to the methods by which compliance, nurturance, competition, and love are expressed. There are therefore gross differences in the quality and relative strength of the various motives in different societies. Furthermore, within any one cultural group, there are great individual differences among children in the quality and strength of these various drives. Different methods of child-rearing, different affectional values within the family, produce children with different kinds of motivational systems and different styles or qualities of affectional behavior. Ultimately, certain types of motivational quality conduce to healthy social adjustment. It is to the discovery of just what these types are, and just what kinds of parental treatment produce them, that research in the field of socially determined secondary drives must be oriented.

Research efforts in this field have been of three main kinds. First, there has been life-history analysis of adolescent or adult persons. Such analyses have been devoted to discovering the origins, in early family relationships, of personality characteristics noted or measured in the later ages. This is the basic method from which Freud secured the information on which he based his theory of personality development. It is the method of the clinic. It is also the method used in more formal studies of personality variables whose full outlines can be discerned only in adults. For example, sexual adjustment in marriage (cf. G. V. Hamilton, 1929; Terman, 1938) can only be evaluated after there has been an opportunity for adjustment. Research by this method has varied from pure case analysis, in which adult personality (the behavior *consequent*) has been simply a matter for explanation in terms of any detectable *antecedent,* to quantitative measurement of specific and systematically cogent adult variables and a seeing of life-history data relevant to some specific theory of personality development. The former studies outnumber the latter and have been responsible for the great bulk of hunches, intuitions and hypotheses concerning the childhood origins of adult motivation.

Second, there has been a technically different but theoretically similar procedure in which children's personality characteristics are measured and antecedents of them are sought. The logic of these two methods is the same; in each type of study there is measurement of some variable of behavior and then a seeking for any possible explanation or cause of it. In practice, the studies of children provide more immediate access to the family situations and offer far better opportunity for accurate measurement. The various errors associated with life-history material are circumvented. Good examples of this kind of research are to be found in Jones (1943) and Goodenough (1931).

The third method reverses this procedure and seeks the consequences in child behavior of certain specifiable family relationships. Studies by Symonds (1939) and Baldwin, Kalhorn and Breese (1945) exemplify this approach.

Although the first method, the analysis of life-history material, has been magnificently fruitful of hypotheses, the most serious need in contemporary research is for investigations that combine the second and third methods. Effectively to tease out the significant antecedent-consequent relationships, however, requires careful definition of the variables on both sides of the equation. Recent approaches to personality through projective techniques have not infrequently relied on vague and intuitionistic variables having little predictive value for behavior. Not every personality variable needs to be defined in terms of overt behavior—indeed, the naive operationism represented by the cliché that "the variable *is* what the test tests" is as useless as anything in science can well be—but every variable must be related in an internally consistent and logical manner with other variables that do compose a systematic analysis of behavior. Furthermore, there appears to be little gain in research that seeks to explain the total consequences, the whole personality, resulting from a given kind of family relationship, or conversely, to explain the totality of influences that have led to a particular child's personality. The "understanding of the whole child" is a necessary procedure for the practical manipulator of a child's life, a physician, teacher, social worker or parent, but it has comparatively little value as a research procedure. The current need in research is for analyses of the specific motivational consequences of specific kinds of learning experiences in the family.

Aggression

One of the most important motivational systems, from the standpoint of both social adjustment and mental health, is aggression. While considerable attention has been given to both the systematic (Dollard et al., 1939) and descriptive-dynamic (Fite, 1940) aspects of aggressive behavior, relatively little effort has been made as yet to discover the exact conditions under which children develop various kinds and amounts. From a systematic standpoint, there is reason to believe that frustration plays an important role not only in eliciting aggression at any given moment, but also as a necessary precursor in the learning of the aggressive response in early childhood (Sears, 1948).

Goodenough (1931) has shown that, in the early preschool years, the most common sources of anger are situations in the home that interfere with some fairly obvious goal-striving of the child. The theoretical derivation of aggression suggests that its origin lies in the effectiveness of producing pain in others as a method of removing their interference with goal-directed behavior. For example, if the mother fails to provide the child with food when he is hungry or with attention when he is seeking affection, he may strike her or cry loudly enough to make her uncomfortable. In order to eliminate this pain or discomfort, she may then give the child food or offer it affection. This reward act not only reinforces the early, and perhaps more or less random, acts of injuring the mother, but it does two additional things. First, it establishes the act of hurting, as exemplified by the mother's expressions of dislike or pain, as a secondary drive. Increasingly thereafter, with continuing reinforcement, the child therefore secures pleasure from injuring other persons. Second, the immediate stimulus situation that accompanied the rewarding act becomes an effective stimulus for eliciting the acts he used at that time. In other words, the child who is rewarded for his injurious acts develops a secondary drive of aggression (*i.e.,* to make a goal response of injuring others, the necessary environmental event being to see the expressions of pain), and he learns to repeat the act when he is frustrated.

Goodenough also found, as have a number of other investigators, that not every aggressive or angry act was immediately preceded by a discernible frustration. This suggests that other stimulus aspects of the frustrating situation besides the fact of frustration itself, *i.e.,* the mother, meal-time, cross talk between parents, are sufficiently often associated with frustration to become the instigators to aggression. Some support for this view is found in Levy's studies of sibling rivalry (1937). Using a doll-simulated family situation, Levy found that young children possessed vigorous, though not always openly displayed, jealousy and antagonism toward doll symbols of the sibling. Even children who lacked siblings of their own reacted with hostility to the implied threat of a competitor for the mother's affection. The sibling may be presumed to have been sufficiently often associated with frustration that it became the instigator to aggression in its own right, although it is the mother, who fails to pay attention to the child, who is the main source of frustration in the sibling rivalry situation.

In an effort to secure somewhat more immediate and quantitative measures of maternal behavior and child reaction, Merrill (1946) observed mother-child interaction during two half-hour periods of free play. She recorded the salient characteristic of their interaction every five seconds. Within a group of thirty mother-child pairs, she found a positive relationship between the frequency of restricting and controlling behavior by the mother and irritable or complaining behavior by the child. It is evident that there are individual differences in the frequency of reinforcements of aggressive behavior. The children who were most commonly restricted by their mothers also showed a tendency to be more complaining when they played for two half-hour periods with an unfamiliar young woman. This suggests both that the experiences with the mother served to establish habits that could carry over into other social situations, and that other young women could, by a process of stimulus generalization, serve as the effective instigators for eliciting the appropriate behavior, aggressive in this instance.

Within any one culture there are many varieties of parental attitude toward children, and these attitudes are associated with different ways of behaving toward them. Some parents are docile and easy-going, permitting their children great freedom and restricting them little. Others are more rigorous in child control. Some parents cannot tolerate the expression of aggression and others not only expect it but view its development as a sign of an effective personality. These kinds of differences inevitably create different motivational systems among the children. In a recent study, Gewirtz (1948) has made extensive observations of several types of aggressive behavior in 45 preschool children, and has found that there is some degree of consistency for a given child in the types he expresses, but that the children differed greatly from one another. He had no information about the home situations in which these variations presumably were developed, but the fact of wide differentiation is in accord with theoretical expectations.

One salient research problem is that of measuring both parental and child behavior in the home itself. Given such differences among children as Gewirtz has found, the question must be raised as to whether it is possible to discover consistent and specifiable parental behavior that is responsible for the differences.

Another problem lies in the area of sibling relationships. There is need for careful analysis of intra-familial activities, with special attention to different types of pattern of such relationships, as these influence the hostility reactions between sibs. Exact information on the nature of sibling frustrations, and methods by which parental behavior toward children could minimize the frustrations, would be exceedingly valuable.

A third area of research on aggression involves the problem of anxiety. Once the conditions that produce an aggressive drive have been elucidated, the next matter that will need attention will be that of the sources of anxiety about possessing aggressive motivation. No society can tolerate great amounts of in-group aggression, even though such behavior is adaptive in the sense that it often alleviates frustrations; every society has devices and procedures for controlling or inhibiting aggression. Some methods of control appear to induce disabling anxieties, however, while others leave the individual reasonably free to express himself in socially acceptable, though aggressive, ways. Research is needed on these methods.

There are two main procedures that should prove useful for work of this kind. One is the direct observation of behavior in the home. The other involves the use of comparison groups whose cultural backgrounds differ sufficiently, and in clearly enough specifiable ways, that the behavior of the children in the groups can be compared. Such cross-cultural investigation may be done either with primitive groups or with subgroups within our own culture. Class differences in the handling of aggression have been described by Davis and Havighurst

(1947), for example, that would be correlatable with modal child behavior in different classes. Other possible differences are those of sex and ordinal position. A number of investigations, both of realistic and fantasy behavior, have shown that both type and amount of aggression differ in boys and girls. While there may be some biological predispositions toward the difference in *strength* of aggressive drives, the differences in *type* of aggression characteristic of the two sexes seem likely to be derived from certain consistently different ways in which parents rear boys and girls, together with differences in the formulated values for the two sexes.

Dependency

The physical helplessness of the newborn infant provides the appropriate conditions for the establishment of secondary drives based on the helping behavior of other family members, particularly the mother. The quality and strength of these drives become important in later childhood and adulthood because so many social activities involve the cooperative interaction of people who must secure mutual satisfaction from their behavior in order to maintain an interactive relationship. In marriage, for example, the husband-wife relationship is one in which two people must be dependent on each other and each must therefore serve as a nurturant agent for the other. Any disturbance in the delicate balance between succorant and nurturant behavior can destroy the effectiveness of the marriage as a support and solace for the partners.*

Recent theoretical studies by Whiting (1943), Sears (1948), Beller (1948) and Gewirtz (1948) have derived the conditions under which various types of dependent drives can be learned. In general, the derivations assume a certain consistency in the behavior of any given pair of parents toward their child. Measurements of both succorant and nurturant behavior in three- and four-year-old children by Gewirtz and of several kinds of succorance by Beller have shown that the kinds and amounts of these behaviors are reasonably consistent within any one child. This fact lends some support to the assumption that the parents provide consistent learning conditions.

Levy's careful analysis of maternal over-protection (1943) has indicated certain of the effects of very extensive reinforcement of some

* Succorant: seeking sympathy, help, protection, or indulgence. Nurturant: giving sympathy, help, protection, or indulgence.—*Eds.*

kinds of dependent behavior. He has shown, for example, that sub missive mothers have a tendency to create dominating children who nevertheless, are exceedingly dependent on having someone available for domination. The reverse likewise holds true; dominant mothers create submissive children. Symonds (1939), in another extensive study of parent-child relationships, has substantiated these findings and goes one step farther in the analysis of this latter principle. He was led to the conclusion that the apparent submissiveness of these children is in part a fearfulness of assuming the dominant role, and that as adults their pent-up aggression and compulsiveness create the same family pattern over again. They become dominating parents and create another generation of submissive children.

The data from Levy's and Symonds' studies are replete with instances of parental determination of childhood personality, and their merit stems in both instances from the care with which the relevant dimen sions of behavior have been isolated from the total matrix of child behavior. Levy's description of "over-protection" is a classic of careful psychological analysis.

The next steps in research appear to be in the direction of more extensive examination of parental attitudes and motives. The deriva tion of dominance and submission has been useful, but by no means exhausts the possibilities of inductive clustering of behaviors into defin able dimensions. In strict theory, every parent is unique in the particular repertory of motives that guide his behavior toward his child, but in practice, the task of the psychologist is to discover common patterns or clusters of motives that can be recognized and whose consequence in child personality can be predicted.

The importance of dependency in marriage and in other institutional settings, and the ease with which dependency can suffer frustration in American culture, gives these problems a high priority in research planning.

Sex and Affection

The development of sex behavior involves not only the learning of several complex forms of interpersonal activity, but also the establish ment of secondary drive systems for which particular kinds of persons must serve as the social agents in the process of securing gratification The newborn infant has the capacity to respond sexually to stimulation of his genital area, and from the beginning he is given various oppor tunities to make such responses, is rewarded for some and is punished or non-rewarded for others. Associated with the overt sex responsiveness is a process of discriminating among the persons in his social environment and developing an affectional reaction to them. Not only does he learn how to make various pleasurable responses, but he also learns to have affection for, to love, various people.

These two aspects of sex development are part of the same sequence of psychological events. In their study, most investigators have used Freud's theoretical formulation of sex development (1905) as the main starting point. A review of relevant research literature (Sears, 1943) reveals non-psychoanalytic investigative support for many of Freud's observations, and permits the following kind of summary of established facts to be made.

Sensitivity to genital sexual stimulation, with apparently pleasurable responsiveness, is present in the human organism from birth. In the first few months of life there is little evidence that sex behavior is socially oriented, but by the second year children show some signs of associating their pleasurable reactions to a social context. During the succeeding years, there is a constantly increasing interest in sexual play and the securing of sexual stimulation. This behavioral evidence of the existence of a genital sex drive increases steadily to the onset of adolescence, when the physiological maturation of puberty produces a sharp increase in sex-determined behavior (Kinsey, 1948).

During the preschool years, the social orientation of sex behavior becomes more pronounced. Its extent and kind are apparently largely a function of the amount and kind of permissiveness or restriction imposed by the parents. In those cultures in which sex play is accepted as a normal childhood activity (cf. Malinowski, 1927), there are evidences of a normal development of heterosexual behavior throughout childhood. In American culture, in which severe restrictions are placed on social sex behavior in the prepubertal years, there is evidence of suppression of the overt social expression of the sex drive. Freud's theory of the latency period, approximately coinciding with the secondary school years, is a not inaccurate description so far as public sex behavior or interest is concerned. Kinsey has shown, however, that during these years there is a considerable amount of private and socially hidden play that involves various deviations from heterosexual behavior as well as a relatively small amount of exploration with the opposite sex.

In the American culture, a considerable amount of shame and inhibition early become attached to the sex drive in most children. Sex matters are poorly verbalized by the child, he is ordinarily ignorant of the facts of sex and reproduction until he nears adolescence, and he associates sex behavior and sex drive with the same anxiety evoking class of events as elimination. During the two or three years immediately preceding puberty, the boy is likely to have homosexual play and to begin masturbating. This is less true of the girl.

Although Freud believed that all affectional attachments were based on sex, *i.e.,* that affectional behavior was a response to the sex drive, there is no clear evidence that this is the case. Strong love responses occur to parents, the preferred parent commonly being the mother for both boys and girls. Adult reports of childhood love affairs contain more reports of specifically sexual feelings related to cross-sexed siblings than to parents, however, and many childhood homosexual and heterosexual love affairs are apparently unaccompanied by any awareness of the sex drive or of other behavior that could reasonably be interpreted as deriving from that drive.

The complexity and variety of sex behavior in American society is so much greater than these meager facts indicate that it is surprising no more extensive investigation has occurred than these facts would indicate. This meagerness is no accurate reflection of the great amount of clinical observation that has been reported, but suggests that many such reports are repetitious.

What is most seriously needed at present is a detailed theory of the development of the social aspects of the sex drive. The very complexity of such behavior requires that research in this field be organized about a carefully constructed theory. While Freud's formulations have served as highly useful guides for clinical work, the total context of psychoanalytic theory has a logical character that is difficult to integrate with other systematic social science theories and methods of investigation. Much of Freudian theory can be translated into a more behavioral type of theory, however, and the next major theoretical step in the field of sex research will be the detailed elaboration of the conditions under which children learn the affectional and social behaviors that characterize growing children in American families. The general theoretical position that has been presented here in connection with the development of other secondary drives would serve as one useful framework within which such a task might be accomplished.

Although it is difficult to specify in advance of theory construction just what research will prove to be most crucial for the testing of the theory, the following general problems appear to have potential significance.

1. The effect of varying amounts of sexual stimulation in early childhood on the strength of the sex drive in later childhood, adolescence and adulthood. There is suggestive evidence that a high degree of stimulation, with consequent high frequency of gratification, increases the drive strength (*cf.* Sears, 1943, pp. 62-67), but information is lacking as to the relative effects of different kinds of stimulation. Further, there are no adequately controlled investigations in which drive strength has been measured independently of social controls.

2. The effects of differential strengths of attachment to parents and siblings on the kinds of sexual object-choices made in adolescence and adulthood. Although it is known in general that children of each sex may have strong preference for either parent, there has not been adequate analysis of matched groups of children with different patterns of childhood preference.

3. The effects of various kinds of restrictive and punishing parental behavior, directed at the child's sex instigated behavior, on the effective strength of the sex drive and the kinds of object-choices made in adolescence. There is a suggestion in clinical observations, as well as in the objective study of Hamilton (1929), that a history of punitive treatment of sex behavior is associated not only with sex anxiety but also with deviant sex behavior of various kinds. The factors responsible for such a development probably are related to the inhibitory effects of punishment and the consequent seeking for substitute and non-punishable forms of behavior.

4. The origins and effects of the process of identification. Little is known of the conditions under which children learn to identify themselves with other family members. The clinical literature is replete with instances, however, of strong childhood identifications which have served effectively to interfere with adult sexual adjustment of the kind demanded by American culture. The cross-sex identification of a girl with her older brother, for example, is not infrequently associated with ambivalent attitudes toward men to a degree sufficient to prevent a normal love relationship in adulthood.

These are but samples of the kinds of problems which will be posed by any systematic theory of social sex development. The details will have to wait upon the theory. The methods of research that will be required will undoubtedly run the gamut from careful individual analysis of developing children to statistical analysis of data from clusters of cultures whose values and behavior patterns permit cross-cultural comparisons. The interview method developed by Kinsey (1948) will, with some additions, be an unusually fertile technique for securing life history data that are sufficiently objective to be used in a quantitative manner. Clearly, the kinds of problems here envisaged will have to be dealt with in terms of far more complex indices of behavior and attitude than the simple orgasm, but there is nothing inherent in Kinsey's method which will prevent the use of as subtle and sensitive indices as an investigator may desire.

With respect to sexual development, the research problem of highest priority is one of theory construction rather than the development of methods of measurement, as was the case with the other secondary drive systems.

Conclusions

Research planning on the relation of personality development to family life must start with a careful consideration of the ways in which a child's behavior is influenced by his social environment. The specific nature of his acquired traits and motives is a function not only of the process of learning but of the social and emotional conditions under which this learning occurs. Many of the qualities of his personality, his wants and needs, his reactivity to others, and the kinds of social relationships in which he can find satisfaction, are determined by the rewards and frustrations of the family life in which he is reared.

Two main areas of research are important. One is the discovery of the influence of different methods of parental handling of the primary drives—hunger, sex, elimination, fatigue. The infant possesses ready-made action systems for satisfying his needs in these respects, but his methods are not always appropriate to social living. One of the major functions of the family is to teach him new methods, socially approved ones, for the satisfaction of these primary drives. This is the process of socialization. Research must be directed toward the discovery of what influences different methods of socialization have on the child's later personality.

A second area of research that is urgently needed is the analysis of the methods by which family living creates those important secondary drives that are based on the biologically inherent characteristics of parent-child relationships. These include the physical dependency between mother and child, the susceptibility to pain of the mother, and the unshareability of many of the goals that a child early learns to seek. The pervasive and socially important acquired drives of dependency, aggression, and competition appear to depend on these factors. These drives, likewise, are significant determinants of the kind of marital and family adjustment the child will make in his later life. It is therefore to be expected that considerable progress in understanding family life will ensue when there is available a more comprehensive theory and more complete body of knowledge concerning the family conditions under which such drives develop.

BIBLIOGRAPHY

Baldwin, A. L., Kalhorn, J., and Breese, F. H. 1945. Patterns of parent behavior. *Psychol. Monogr.,* 58; No. 268.

Beller, E. 1948. Dependence and independence in young children. Ph.D. Dissertation, State Univ. of Iowa Library.

Davis, H. V., Sears, R. R., Miller, H. C., and Brodbeck, A. J. 1948. Effects of cup, bottle and breast feeding on oral activities of newborn infants. *Pediatrics.,* 3, 549-58.

Davis, W. A., and Havighurst, R. J. 1947. *Father of the Man.* Boston: Houghton, Mifflin.

Dollard, J., *et al.* 1939. *Frustration and Aggression.* New Haven: Yale Univ. Press.

Fite, M. D. 1940. Aggressive behavior in young children and children's attitudes toward aggression. *Genet. Psychol. Monogr.,* 22, No. 2, 1-151.

Freud, S. 1905. Three contributions to the theory of sex. (Fourth edition.) Nervous and Mental Disease, Monograph Series, 1930, No. 7.

Gewirtz, J. L. 1948. Succorance in young children. Ph.D. Dissertation, State Univ. of Iowa Library.

Goodenough, F. L. 1931. *Anger in Young Children.* Minneapolis: Univ. of Minnesota Press.

Halverson, H. M. 1938. Infant sucking and tensional behavior. *J. Genet. Psychol.,* 53, 365-430.

Hamilton, G. V. 1929. *A Research in Marriage.* New York: A. and C. Boni.

Hull, C. L. 1943. *Principles of Behavior.* New York: Appleton-Century.

Huschka, M. 1942. The child's response to coercive bowel training. *Psychosom. Med.,* IV, No. 3.

Jones, H. E. 1943. *Development in Adolescence.* New York: Appleton-Century.

Kinsey, A. C., Pomeroy, W. B., and Martin, C. E. 1948. *Sexual Behavior in the Human Male.* Philadelphia: W. B. Saunders.

Levy, D. M. 1928. Fingersucking and accessory movements in early infancy. *Amer. J. Psychiat.,* 7, 881-918.

Levy, D. M. 1934. Experiments on the sucking reflex and social behavior of dogs. *Amer. J. Orthopsychiat.,* 4, 203-224.

Levy, D. M. 1937. Studies in sibling rivalry. *Amer. Orthopsychiat. Assn. Monogr.,* No. 2.

Levy, D M. 1943. *Maternal Over-Protection.* New York: Columbia Univ. Press.

Malinowski, B. 1927. Prenuptial intercourse between the sexes in the Trobriand Islands, N. W. Melanesia. *Psychoanal. Rev.,* 14, 20-36.

Merrill, B. 1946. Relation of mother-child interaction to children's social behavior. Ph.D. Dissertation, State Univ. of Iowa Library.

Miller, N. E., and Dollard, J. 1941. *Social Learning and Imitation.* New Haven: Yale Univ. Press.

Moloney, J. C. 1947. The Cornelian Corner and its rationale. In, M. J. E. Senn (ed.), *Problems of Early Infancy.* New York: Josiah Macy, Jr. Foundation.

Mowrer, O. H., and Kluckhohn, C. 1944. Dynamic theory of personality. In, J. McV. Hunt (ed.), *Personality and the Behavior Disorders.* New York: Ronald, Vol. I, pp. 69-135.

Pinneau, S. R. 1950. A critique on the articles by Margaret Ribble, *Child Development,* 21, 203-28.

Ribble, M. A. 1944. Infantile experience in relation to personality development. In, J. McV. Hunt (ed.), *Personality and the Behavior Disorders.* New York: Ronald.

Sears, R. R. 1943. *Survey of Objective Studies of Psychoanalytic Theory.* New York: Soc. Sci. Res. Council. Bull. 51.

Sears, R. R. 1948. Personality development in contemporary culture. *Proc. Amer. Philosoph. Soc.,* 92, No. 5.

Sears, R. R. 1951. A theoretical framework for personality and social behavior. *Amer. Psychologist.,* 6, 476-83.

Symonds, P. M. 1939. *The Psychology of Parent-Child Relationships.* New York: Appleton-Century.

Terman, L. M. 1938. *Psychological Factors in Marital Happiness.* New York: McGraw-Hill.

Whiting, J. W. M. 1944. The frustration complex in Kwoma society. *Man,* 115, 1-4.

Whiting, J. W. M., and Child, I. L. (In press.) *Child Training and Personality: A Cross-Cultural Study.* New Haven: Yale Univ. Press.

CHAPTER 9

The Adolescent: Familial and Non-Familial Relationships

HOLDING that adolescence is not necessarily filled with "storm and stress," Hollingshead presents a sociological interpretation of the age-category which the term denotes. Jones views adolescence as psychologically somewhat analogous to infancy and describes the emotional significance of the timing of the physical changes of puberty. While holding that the conflict between adolescents and parents may be overemphasized, Kingsley Davis analyzes the grounds for whatever antagonisms may exist. Noting the psychological significance of membership in social classes, Allison Davis describes important differences between the middle and lower classes in the expression of aggressive and sexual impulses among adolescents.

ADOLESCENCE: A SOCIOLOGICAL DEFINITION*

AUGUST B. HOLLINGSHEAD

In the past half-century physiologists, psychologists, educators, clergymen, social workers, and moralists have turned their attention to the physical and psychological phenomena connected with adolescence,

* Adapted and reprinted by permission of the author and publisher from *Elmtown's Youth*, New York, John Wiley & Sons, Inc., 1949, pp. 5-7.

and . . . of the millions of words written on the subject most have had a worried tone. This interest in the adolescent, with its emphasis on the "problems" of adolescence, can be traced to the monumental work of G. Stanley Hall.[1] Hall blended evolutionary theory, the facts of physical growth (as they were then known), instinct psychology, and a liberal sprinkling of ethnographic facts taken out of their cultural context with a set of strong moral judgments. He assumed that the individual in the course of his life recapitulates the evolutionary development of the human species.[2]

Hall conceived of adolescence as the period in the life cycle of the individual from age 14 to 24, when the inexorably unfolding nature of the organism produces a "rebirth of the soul" which brings the child inevitably into a conflict with society. This was believed to be a period of "storm and stress," of "revolution," in the individual. In the "new birth" the "social instincts undergo sudden unfoldment."[3] Hall also asserted that "the adolescent stage of life" is marked by a struggle between the needs of the organism and the desires of society, which is "biologically antagonistic to genesis."[4] "All this is hard on youth . . ."[5] This psychology of adolescence included in its scope physiology, anthropology, sociology, sex, crime, religion, and education. Needless to say, this is a broad area which only a system maker who ignored facts as they exist in society could cover in a single sweep.

Hall's prestige as a psychologist, educator, and university president was so great and his influence over students so dominant that his theories were accepted widely by psychologists and educators. Gradually, however, the weight of empirical information indicated that these views were largely doctrinal. But, even now, the idea that adolescence is a period of "storm and stress," of conflict between individual and society, is held by many people, in spite of the fact that this has never been demonstrated to be true. On the contrary, common-sense observation will cast grave doubts upon its validity. Nevertheless, a recent summary of the field of adolescent psychology insisted upon the "causal"

---

[1] G. Stanley Hall, *Adolescence, Its Psychology and Its Relations to Physiology, Anthropology, Sociology, Sex, Crime, Religion, and Education*, New York, D. Appleton and Company, 1904, two volumes.

[2] *Ibid.*, vol. I, p. viii.

[3] *Ibid.*, p. xv.

[4] *Ibid.*, p. xvi.

[5] *Ibid.*, p. xviii.

connection between the physical manifestations of adolescence and social behavior.[6]

Eventually, the conclusion was reached that, from the viewpoint of the sociologist, adolescence is distinctly different from psychologists', physiologists', and educators' concepts of it. *Sociologically, adolescence is the period in the life of a person when the society in which he functions ceases to regard him* (male or female) *as a child and does not accord to him full adult status, roles, and functions.* In terms of behavior, it is defined by the roles the person is expected to play, is allowed to play, is forced to play, or prohibited from playing by virtue of his status in society. It is not marked by a specific point in time such as puberty, since its form, content, duration, and period in the life cycle are differently determined by various cultures and societies. Sociologically, the important thing about the adolescent years is the way people regard the maturing individual. The menarche, development of the breasts, and other secondary manifestations of physical adolescence in the female, and the less obvious physical changes in the male connected with sex maturation, such as rapid growth, voice changes, the appearance of labial, axial, and pubic hair, derive their significance for the sociologist from the way they are regarded by the society in which the adolescent lives.

ADOLESCENCE IN OUR SOCIETY*

Harold E. Jones

The period of adolescence is sometimes referred to as a flowering and fulfillment, sometimes as a calamity. Taken literally, adolescence is the process of becoming adult, growing into maturity. But the term has gained other, less favorable meanings. These are implied when

[6] Wayne Dennis, "The Adolescent," in *Manual of Child Psychology,* edited by Leonard Carmichael, John Wiley and Sons, Inc., New York, 1946, pp. 633-666. We would agree with Dennis if he or any other psychologist demonstrated any "causal" connection between the physical phenomenon of puberty and the social behavior of young people during the adolescent period, irrespective of cultural milieu.

* Adapted and reprinted by permission of the author and publisher from *The Family in a Democratic Society: Anniversary Papers of the Community Service Society of New York,* New York, Columbia University Press, 1949, pp. 70-84.

we speak of adolescent "stress and strain," "growing pains," "teen-age troubles," "the silly phase," and other phenomena to which we attach the adjective "adolescent," sometimes in a resigned mood and sometimes in exasperation.

Many persons have raised the question of whether this process of growing up is naturally and inevitably a difficult one, or whether its painfulness is in some sense a disease of society, and therefore remediable through appropriate social changes. The answer to this question has varied widely according to the preoccupations of the person answering it. The biological answer stresses changes in hormone secretions, changes in the rate of skeletal growth, and temporary imbalances in body structure and function. It is these imbalances, we are told, which are the immediate source of adolescent maladjustment. The sociological and anthropological answer, on the other hand, stresses the conditions and demands of the culture in which the child is growing up. It is pointed out that the same processes of biological maturing that place a child in jeopardy in one culture may offer no special problems in another culture. Each of these answers is a partial one. Adolescence is not necessarily a period of acute disturbance. When disturbance occurs, the determining agencies lie in multiple form both in the organism and in society; we cannot hope to achieve understanding or control if we look at merely one of these two groups of factors.

It may be appropriate to begin this discussion with some account of the physical aspects of adolescence and of the developmental processes which set off this period so clearly from earlier childhood.

First, we know that at about eight or nine years of age on an average, in girls, and some two years later in boys, a change occurs in the rate of physical growth.[1] In the preceding years, ever since early childhood, growth has occurred at a fairly even and steady pace; growth in height, for example, involves gains of about 4 percent per year during these childhood years. But now, near the end of childhood, growth becomes slower; there is often a pause which marks the transition point between the slow, gradual development of childhood and the accelerated, more irregular growth changes of adolescence. It is as though the organism needed a little time in which to consolidate childhood gains, to mus-

[1] Frank K. Shuttleworth, *The Physical and Mental Growth of Girls and Boys, Age Six to Nineteen, in Relation to Age at Maximal Growth,* Washington, D. C., Society for Research in Child Development, 1939.

ter resources, and to get ready for the abrupt transformations that are now to take place. This is a figurative way of putting it, but it does appear that we have during this period an interval in which the growth controls of childhood are fading and the adolescent growth factors are not yet fully ready to function.

In some respects, the problems of adolescence bear a resemblance to the problems of infancy, so that adolescence is sometimes called a second infancy. Physiologically, this may in a way be justified, in view of the fact that infants show an instability in many physiological processes, and gradually win a greater degree of equilibrium. With the beginning of the puberal cycle we have a renewal of unstable conditions. Basal metabolism, for example, may show marked fluctuations at this time.[2]

In an adult such metabolic changes could readily be a matter of some concern; in an adolescent they are physiological in the sense that they are very commonly and perhaps normally shown in the process of adjusting to the new phase of more rapid growth and to new conditions in the internal environment. At the same time, changes are also occurring in other basal functions. Among girls, for example, in the three years just preceding the menarche the average pulse rate increases and then decreases; the systolic blood pressure increases and then levels off.[3]

It is not surprising that the adjustments in bodily processes should not always be smooth and orderly. The adolescent awkwardness, which we sometimes observe at the level of motor skills, may have its parallel in a kind of physiological awkwardness. The transition to a changed body economy may be difficult, and there may be further difficulties because of an interacting relationship with social and psychological transitions.

In a standard work on pediatrics the author observes that "the age of puberty is attended with many dangers to health. The changes in the organs are sudden. The heart grows larger, the blood vessels narrower. . . . At this time particularly mental disorders may develop and hereditary defects appear. Anemic conditions arise and may be followed

[2] Nathan W. Shock, "The Effect of Menarche on Basal Physiological Functions in Girls," *American Journal of Physiology,* CXXXIX, No. 2 (June, 1943), 288-92.

[3] Nathan W. Shock, "Basal Blood Pressure and Pulse Rate in Adolescents," *American Journal of Diseases of Children,* LXVIII, No. 1 (July, 1944), 16-22.

by constitutional diseases. . . ."[4] Such statements may cause unnecessary alarm and overemphasize the health hazards of adolescence, and yet it is true that the morbidity rate increases during the 'teens, and you have only to enter any classroom of adolescent youngsters to observe in posture, skin color, and, particularly, in skin conditions such as acne, abundant evidence of defects in the smooth course of adolescent maturing. Growth discrepancies also occur in the proportionate development of legs, arms, and trunk and in the deposition of fat. The timing of growth for different parts of the body may vary in different individuals, resulting in cases of poorly synchronized and markedly disproportionate development.[5]

Psychoanalysts have emphasized another way in which adolescence is like a second infancy, in that it involves a recurrence, in their terms, of infantile sexual impulses. The increased sexual drives of adolescence are countered by inhibitions; the adolescent may be afraid of these drives in the genital form in which they now appear, and may regress to more familiar infantile forms of sexuality. Fenichel points out that adolescence is often marked by contradictory psychological expressions: "Egoism and altruism, pettiness and generosity, sociability and loneliness, cheerfulness and sadness, silly jocularity and overseriousness, intense loves and sudden abandonment of these loves, submission and rebellion, materialism and idealism, rudeness and tender consideration—all are typical."[6] These contradictions as cited by Fenichel are related to the fact that in adolescence there appear side by side or following one another "genital heterosexual impulses, all kinds of infantile sexual behavior, and attitudes of extreme asceticism, which not only try to repress all sexuality but everything pleasant as well."[7] The intensification of the sexual impulses at puberty, and the resulting conflicts, mark the end of the relatively peaceful latency period. Fenichel expresses the view that all the mental phenomena characteristic of puberty may be regarded as reactions to these disturbances, and as attempts to re-establish the equilibrium of the latency period, and he

---

[4] John Diven, "Peculiarities of Disease in Childhood," in *Pediatrics,* ed. Abt, Philadelphia, Saunders, 1923, II, 192.

[5] Herbert R. and Lois M. Stolz, "Adolescent Problems Related to Somatic Variations," in *Forty-third Yearbook of the National Society for the Study of Education,* Chicago, University of Chicago, Department of Education, 1944, Part I, "Adolescence," pp. 80-89.

[6] Otto Fenichel, *The Psychoanalytic Theory of Neurosis,* New York, Norton, 1945, p. 111.

[7] *Ibid.,* pp. 110-11.

adds that "in a society that treated infantile sexuality differently puberty, too, would assume a different course."[8]*

In commenting upon this interpretation we may return again to our earlier statement that the difficulties of adolescence have a multiple origin and cannot be interpreted solely in terms of psychological, or cultural, or biological agencies. The student of child development is aware of many factors, by no means evidently related to sexual dilemmas or the Oedipus complex, which emerge at puberty to bedevil and perplex the child, his parents, and his teachers. Some of these factors have already been mentioned in connection with disturbances in physiological functions and in physical growth. Since adolescence is a period of increased susceptibility to psychosomatic disorders, no doubt a certain proportion of these cases of physiological disturbance trace more or less directly to the child's psychosexual development. A psychosomatic origin may also be found for some instances of disturbed physical growth. But we should not be too confident that all or even a majority of the physiological and physical anomalies which occur in adolescence have a primarily psychological source. The child's reaction to these apparent anomalies, the extent to which he tolerates them or is deeply worried by them, is a psychological matter, but their source and incidence seem quite as likely to depend upon intrinsic factors in the biological growth pattern as upon factors in the family situation or in the child's personality structure.

It is difficult to discuss the physical aspects of adolescence without reference to the factor of timing, and to differences in the age at which the puberal growth cycle begins. Let us consider first the facts as to the timing of puberty, and then the bearing of these facts upon adolescent problems. We shall see that it is of the first importance to know not merely what bodily changes are brought about by puberal growth, but also when these changes are induced.

In the case of girls, the most commonly used landmark for recording individual differences in puberal maturing is the menarche or the time of first menstruation. This occurs, of course, relatively late in the puberal growth cycle: a little more than a year after the adolescent

---

[8] *Ibid.,* p. 111.

* In psychoanalytic theory the *latency period* is a period of sexual quiescence between the repression of the Oedipus complex at about the age of six years to the onset of puberty at about thirteen. Studies by B. Malinowski, Margaret Mead, and A. C. Kinsey have thrown into question the universality of the latency period. *Cf.* R. R. Sears, "Personality Development in the Family," pp. 215-40 above.—*Eds.*

growth spurt has reached its peak, and a little more than three years after the beginning of the growth spurt.[9]

In our California sample the menarche coincides, on the average, with the beginning of the teen age, falling at thirteen years and one month. In some Eastern studies a somewhat later age has been indicated, nearer thirteen and a half or even fourteen. The question has been asked whether this difference is due to the stimulation of being near Hollywood, or whether it is an example of earlier maturing in a milder climate. The latter may be a factor, but we should point out the error in the popular idea that adolescence comes earliest in the Tropics. Adolescence is probably earliest in the Temperate Zone, and arrives somewhat later as we go north into the colder regions or south into tropical countries. For example, in a recent study in South America,[10] the average age of menarche directly under the equator, both in the mountains and in coastal areas, and for different ethnic groups, was found to be retarded almost a full year as compared with our California records.

We cannot be sure, however, that this is related to climate in any direct way rather than to general socio-economic conditions and conditions of health. Unfavorable living standards apparently tend to retard the beginning of adolescence; recent observers of child development in war-stricken areas of Europe have been impressed by this fact. A related finding may be the tendency for American children in the same social groups to mature earlier in this generation than was true fifty or a hundred years ago.[11] This is probably an illustration of the complex, biosocial nature of adolescence; for while earlier maturing may be attributable to gains in health and nutrition, these, in turn, rest upon social trends.

There is an implication here which may be worth noting. One effect of civilized living has been to extend the term of social adolescence, by delaying the time at which young people can begin to earn their own living. As society becomes more complex, educational demands increase, and more years must be devoted to preparation for adult life. One effect of this has been, of course, to delay the age of marriage and to lengthen the period of sexual postponements or com-

[9] Frank K. Shuttleworth, *Sexual Maturation and the Physical Growth of Girls, Age Six to Nineteen,* Washington, D.C., Society for Research in Child Development, 1937.

[10] Ulises D. Arrieta, "Menstrual Biology of the Peruvian Woman," *La Cronica Medica,* XLIX, No. 332 (October, 1932), 277-87.

[11] Clarence A. Mills, *Medical Climatology,* Baltimore, Thomas, 1939.

promises. But social adolescence is also being lengthened at the other end, by pushing the time of maturing down to an earlier age. It is probably safe to say that the period of social adolescence is now from two to three times as long as was the case in America several generations ago. Thus the improved conditions for healthy physical growth, which our society has gradually achieved, tend to make more difficult some of the adolescent problems of mental hygiene, because of the much greater length of time during which these problems must be faced.

Our chief purpose, however, is not to discuss the average age of maturing of various groups, but the great diversity within any group. In any normal sampling of schoolgirls we may expect to find some who reach the menarche at eleven years of age or even a little earlier; and some who are delayed until sixteen or even a little later. In terms of physical growth changes, some girls in a normal sample show the beginning of rapid puberal growth as early as nine years of age and others not until after twelve or thirteen. These extreme differences are not without important aftereffects. The early-maturing girl who reaches her peak of growth at eleven or even earlier also reaches an early limit of growth. By thirteen she has attained nearly her adult stature, and this adult stature is short.[12] The adolescent growth period is more or less abruptly brought to an end, epiphyses at the growing ends of the bones are closed, and no further increase in height is possible. If you plot the growth curves of early- and of late-maturing girls, you will find that the former are taller in childhood, even at six or seven years of age; they gain in relative height until the age of twelve, when they may be as much as four inches taller than the late-maturing, but by fifteen they are definitely in a shorter-than-average classification.

At the University of California we conducted a series of studies to determine the relationship of these early changes to problems of adjustment. In general, it appears that the very early-maturing girl, at least in an urban culture, is in many respects in a disadvantageous position. In one of our studies, not yet published, we selected two groups of early- and late-maturing girls, on the basis of skeletal maturity as read from X-rays. These were not clinical deviates nor cases of endocrine pathology, but merely the physically most precocious 20 per-

---

[12] Nancy Bayley, "Size and Body Build of Adolescents in Relation to Rate of Skeletal Maturing," *Child Development*, XIV, No. 2 (June, 1943), 47-90; Shuttleworth, *The Physical and Mental Growth of Girls and Boys Age Six to Nineteen in Relation to Age at Maximal Growth.*

cent and the physically most retarded 20 percent in a normal sample of girls from a public school. The two groups were similar in intelligence, in socio-economic status, in racial background, and in their childhood health records. When we compared them, however, with regard to various social traits, as noted by careful observers in a long series of records, we found that the early-maturing were below the average in prestige, sociability, and leadership; below the average in popularity; below the average in cheerfulness, poise, and expressiveness. In the opinion of their classmates, as judged from a reputation test, they were considered to be rather submissive, withdrawn, and lacking in assurance.

These deficiencies in social attitudes and behavior may indeed be interpretable in terms of deeper layers of personality, but before seeking a more recondite explanation we may point out certain obvious and external ways in which the early-maturing girl is handicapped. The first thing to note is that she finds that she has become physically very conspicuous, at a time when conspicuousness is not valued. She finds herself embarrassingly tall and heavy; she is embarrassed by a greater breast development than seems to her to be normal; she is handicapped when she attempts to participate in the active playground games which are still within the interests of her classmates—for in the case of girls, sexual maturing, although it brings greater strength, often leads to a decreased skill in physical activities involving running and jumping.

The early-maturing girl quite naturally has interests in boys and in social usages and activities more mature than those of her chronological age group. But the males of her own age are unreceptive, for while she is physiologically a year or two out of step with the girls in her class, she is three or four years out of step with the boys—a vast and terrifying degree of developmental distance.

Sometimes the early-maturing girl manages to escape into an older age group, and to associate with other adolescents in her neighborhood who are nearer her own physiological level. In doing this, however, she may encounter other problems that are even more serious. Some of these may be involved in the attitudes of her parents, who are scarcely prepared for this sudden jump into young womanhood. . . .

In the case of girls, however, the late-maturing appear to need no special aids or compensations, unless their growth lag is so great as to imply a pathological condition. In the study mentioned above, the girls who were late-maturing were not only superior to the early-maturing but also superior to the average in a great number of the characteristics included in our social observation schedules. They were significantly higher than the early-maturing in traits related to personal appearance and attractiveness, in expressiveness and activity, in buoyance, poise, and cheerfulness, and also in sociability, leadership, and prestige. We are here, of course, speaking of each group taken as a whole; individual cases can be found which do not by any means conform to these generalizations.

Several points may be noted in explaining the apparently better status of so many of the late-maturing girls. The first is a physical advantage. Because of lateness in sexual maturing and in the closing of the epiphyses at the growing points of the bones, she has a long time in which to grow. Her growth is less sudden, less abrupt, than in the early-maturing, seldom reaches as great a velocity at the peak of growth, and involves fewer hazards of physiological imbalance and physical dis-proportion. The longer period of growth affects particularly the legs, and the late-maturing girl is therefore long-legged, and tends to con-form closely to our American standards of beauty of figure, which in the present code of commercial advertising must always be long-legged and usually a bit hypofeminine.

Moreover, in this slower process of adolescence, the parents and the girl herself have a longer time in which to get used to the new interests, new impulses, and new requirements as to behavior. One further point is probably rather important. The late-maturing girl is more nearly in step with the boys in her age group than is the case with the early- or average-maturing girl. The two-year lag in the average maturity pat-terns of boys as compared with girls is reduced or eliminated among those girls who mature late, and their interests in mixed social activities, when they emerge, are more immediately satisfied.

If now we consider what adolescence may mean to the early- or the late-maturing boy, we find results quite the reverse of those reported for girls. The early-maturing boy enters adolescence at a time when girls in his age group are appreciative of male acquaintances who no longer insist upon being children. He also acquires traits of strength and athletic ability which give him prestige with his own sex. He is likely to be nearer the Apollonian build than the boys who mature later.

He wins friends and influences people through the mere fact of physiological precocity, and through the physical dominance which follows.[13]

This is, of course, not without its hazards. The hazard lies partly in discrepancies in different aspects of growth, and discrepancies between what a boy is prepared to do and what his parents and other adults expect and demand of him. The boy who at thirteen is as tall as an adult may be assigned tasks beyond his years. His teacher chooses him for positions of responsibility. The athletic coach grooms him for the first team. His parents expect him to carry a larger share of the family burdens. A thirteen-year-old may not be ready for all this. Muscular development tends to lag somewhat behind skeletal development, and although he is strong, the early-maturing boy is not so strong as he looks. These new demands fall upon him at a time when he is already carrying a heavy load of adjustment to a changed physical structure, a new body image, and new interests and impulses. Nevertheless, in spite of these handicaps, and his very rapid rate of physical change, the early-maturing boy may readily find more advantages than disadvantages in his position. Moreover, unlike the physically precocious girl, his growth is not arrested at an early age; he reaches an average height as an adult, and somewhat better than average strength and general physical ability.

On the other hand, the boy who matures late, like the girl who matures early, is out of step with all the others in his age group. At fifteen or even sixteen he may still be a little boy, ignored by other boys and girls alike, and unable to compete effectively in playground games. . . . Many of our late-maturing boys adjust by withdrawing from competition, becoming submissive and self-effacing. Others may take a more positive line of action; these are the active small boys, noisy, aggressive, and attention-getting. When at long last the late-maturing boy attains his growth spurt he is likely to reach normal height, but he may be slow to recover from the psychological scars of the period when he was a deviate. . . .

We have mentioned the sex difference in puberal maturing, which inducts girls into adolescence a year or two earlier, on the average, than boys. Another sex difference has been pointed out from one of our other studies by Dr. Caroline Tryon. Achieving manhood or womanhood in our society,

[13] Harold E. Jones, *Motor Performance and Growth*, Berkeley, University of California Press, 1949.

is a long, complex, and often confusing learning task. . . . For the most part boys and girls work at these tasks in a stumbling, groping fashion, blindly reaching for the next step without much or any adult assistance. Many lose their way. It seems probable that our adult failure to give assistance derives as much from ignorance about this developmental process as it does from the extensive taboos on sex which characterize our culture.[14]

One of the aspects of this developmental process is that, at least in an urban American culture, girls appear to have a greater problem than boys in adjusting to changing social requirements. In the adolescent culture itself girls encounter many changes in the conception as to what constitutes desirable behavior, changes and even reversals in the value system and in the relative ranking of traits which are important for popularity and prestige. Perhaps the principal single change which we have found in our California group is that at the beginning of adolescence the group standards for conduct among girls emphasize a quiet, demure, rather lady-like demeanor. By the age of fifteen this has altered, and we find that the girls who are now most popular in their set are active, talkative, and marked by a kind of "aggressive good fellowship." These traits, which may in part be adaptations to the hesitant and immature social approaches of boys, must again undergo considerable change in the later years of adolescence, if a girl is to maintain her status in the group. Dr. Tryon points out that boys, by comparison, seem to have a somewhat more consistent set of criteria to meet in developing their sex roles during this growth period. . . .

We have touched on only a few aspects of adolescence in our society. The motive in this selection has not been to cover the whole range of topics or, necessarily, the most important ones, but to discuss a few of the problem areas with which we must deal. Some of these are primarily social, others primarily biological in origin, but they all become expressed in the adjustment of the adolescent as a biosocial organism. There was a time when we referred quite frequently to the Four Freedoms. For the adolescent there must be another freedom, the freedom to become adult. Modern society imposes many restrictions on this freedom, and throws many hazards and delays in the path of growing up. Our own task as adults is to lend the adolescent a helping

[14] Caroline M. Tryon, "The Adolescent Peer Culture," in *Forty-third Yearbook of the National Society for the Study of Education,* Chicago, University of Chicago, Department of Education, 1944, Part I, "Adolescence," p. 234.

hand as he struggles toward maturity, always remembering, however, that it is he who must do the growing, and in his own way.

THE SOCIOLOGY OF PARENT-YOUTH CONFLICT*

Kingsley Davis

It is in sociological terms that this paper attempts to frame and solve the sole question with which it deals, namely: Why does contemporary western civilization manifest an extraordinary amount of parent-adolescent conflict?[1] In other cultures, the outstanding fact is generally not the rebelliousness of youth, but its docility. There is practically no custom, no matter how tedious or painful, to which youth in primitive tribes or archaic civilizations will not willingly submit.[2] What, then, are the peculiar features of our society which give us one of the extremest examples of endemic filial friction in human history?

Our answer to this question makes use of constants and variables, the constants being the universal factors in the parent-youth relation, the variables being the factors which differ from one society to another. Though one's attention, in explaining the parent-youth relations of a given milieu, is focused on the variables, one cannot comprehend the action of the variables without also understanding the constants, for the latter constitute the structural and functional basis of the family as a part of society.

* Adapted and reprinted by permission of the author and publisher from the *American Sociological Review*, 4 (1940), 523-35.

[1] In the absence of statistical evidence, exaggeration of the conflict is easily possible, and two able students have warned against it. E. B. Reuter, "The Sociology of Adolescence," and Jessie R. Runner, "Social Distance in Adolescent Relationships," both in *Amer. J. Sociol.*, November 1937, 43: 415-16, 437. Yet sufficient nonquantitative evidence lies at hand in the form of personal experience, the outpour of literature on adolescent problems, and the historical and anthropological accounts of contrasting societies to justify the conclusion that in comparison with other cultures ours exhibits an exceptional amount of such conflict. If this paper seems to stress conflict, it is simply because we are concerned with this problem rather than with parent-youth harmony.

[2] *Cf.* Nathan Miller, *The Child in Primitive Society*, New York, 1928; Miriam Van Waters, "The Adolescent Girl Among Primitive Peoples," *J. Relig. Psychol.*, 1913, 6: 375-421 (1913) and 7: 75-120 (1914); Margaret Mead, *Coming of Age in Samoa*, New York, 1928, and "Adolescence in Primitive and Modern Society," 169-88, in *The New Generation* (ed. by V. F. Calverton and S. Schmalhausen, New York, 1930; A. M. Bacon, *Japanese Girls and Women*, New York and Boston, 1891 and 1902.

The Rate of Social Change

The first important variable is the rate of social change. Extremely rapid change in modern civilization, in contrast to most societies, tends to increase parent-youth conflict, for within a fast-changing social order the time-interval between generations, ordinarily but a mere moment in the life of a social system, becomes historically significant, thereby creating a hiatus between one generation and the next. Inevitably, under such a condition, youth is reared in a milieu different from that of the parents; hence the parents become old-fashioned, youth rebellious, and clashes occur which, in the closely confined circle of the immediate family, generate sharp emotion. . . .

The Birth-Cycle, Decelerating Socialization, and Parent-Child Differences

Note, however, that rapid social change would have no power to produce conflict were it not for two universal factors: first, the family's duration; and second, the decelerating rate of socialization in the development of personality. "A family" is not a static entity but a process in time, a process ordinarily so brief compared with historical time that it is unimportant, but which, when history is "full" (*i.e.,* marked by rapid social change), strongly influences the mutual adjustment of the generations. This "span" is basically the birth-cycle—the length of time between the birth of one person and his procreation of another. It is biological and inescapable. It would, however, have no effect in producing parent-youth conflict, even with social change, if it were not for the additional fact, intimately related and equally universal, that the sequential development of personality involves a constantly decelerating rate of socialization. This deceleration is due both to organic factors (age—which ties it to the birth-cycle) and to social factors (the cumulative character of social experience). Its effect is to make the birth-cycle interval, which is the period of youth, the time of major socialization, subsequent periods of socialization being subsidiary. . . .

Physiological Differences

Though the disparity in chronological age remains constant through life, the precise physiological differences between parent and offspring vary radically from one period to another. The organic contrasts between parent and *infant,* for example, are far different from those between parent and adolescent. Yet whatever the period, the organic differences produce contrasts (as between young and old) in those desires which, at least in part, are organically determined. Thus, at the time of adolescence the contrast is between an organism which is just reaching its full powers and one which is just losing them. The physiological need of the latter is for security and conservation, because as the superabundance of energy diminishes, the organism seems to hoard what remains.

Such differences, often alleged (under the heading of "disturbing physiological changes accompanying adolescence") as the primary cause of parent-adolescent strife, are undoubtedly a factor in such conflict, but, like other universal differences to be discussed, they form a constant factor present in every community, and therefore cannot in themselves explain the peculiar heightening of parent-youth conflict in our culture....

Psychosocial Differences: Adult Realism versus Youthful Idealism

Though both youth and age claim to see the truth, the old are more conservatively realistic than the young, because on the one hand they take Utopian ideals less seriously and on the other hand take what may be called operating ideals, if not more seriously, at least more for granted. Thus, middle-aged people notoriously forget the poetic ideals of a new social order which they cherished when young. In their place, they put simply the working ideals current in the society. There is, in short, a persistent tendency for the ideology of a person as he grows older to gravitate more and more toward the status quo ideology, unless other facts (such as a social crisis or hypnotic suggestion) intervene. With advancing age, he becomes less and less bothered by inconsistencies in ideals. He tends to judge ideals according to whether they are widespread and hence effective in thinking about practical life, not according to whether they are logically consistent. Furthermore, he gradually ceases to bother about the *untruth* of his ideals, in the sense of their failure to correspond to reality. He assumes through long habit that, though they do not correspond perfectly, the discrepancy is not significant. The reality of an ideal is defined for him in terms of how many people accept it rather than how completely it is mirrored in actual behavior.[3] Thus, we call him, as he approaches middle age, a realist.

---

[3] When discussing a youthful ideal, however, the older person is quick to take a dialectical advantage by pointing out not only that this ideal affronts the aspirations of

The young, however, are idealists, partly because they take working ideals literally and partly because they acquire ideals not fully operative in the social organization. Those in authority over children are obligated as a requirement of their status to inculcate ideals as a part of the official culture given the new generation. The children are receptive because they have little social experience—experience being systematically kept from them (by such means as censorship, for example, a large part of which is to "protect" children). Consequently, young people possess little ballast for their acquired ideals, which therefore soar to the sky, whereas the middle-aged, by contrast, have plenty of ballast. . . .

Sociological Differences: Parental Authority

Because of his strategic position with reference to the new-born child (at least in the familial type of reproductive institution), the parent is given considerable authority. Charged by his social group with the responsibility of controlling and training the child in conformity with the mores and thereby insuring the maintenance of the cultural structure, the parent, to fulfill his duties, must have the privileges as well as the obligations of authority, and the surrounding community ordinarily guarantees both.

The first thing to note about parental authority, in addition to its function in socialization, is that it is a case of authority within a primary group. Simmel has pointed out that authority is bearable for the subordinate because it touches only one aspect of life. Impersonal and objective, it permits all other aspects to be free from its particularistic dominance. This escape, however, is lacking in parental authority, for since the family includes most aspects of life, its authority is not limited, specific, or impersonal. What, then, can make this authority bearable? Three factors associated with the familial primary group help to give the answer: (1) the child is socialized within the family, and therefore knowing nothing else and being utterly dependent, the authority of the parent is internalized, accepted; (2) the family, like other primary groups, implies identification, in such sense that one person understands and responds emphatically to the sentiments of the other, so that the harshness of authority is ameliorated;[4] (3) in the intimate

---

the multitude, but that it also fails to correspond to human behavior either now or (by the lessons of history) probably in the future.

[4] House slaves, for example, are generally treated much better than field slaves.

interaction of the primary group control can never be purely one-sided; there are too many ways in which the subordinated can exert the pressure of his will. When, therefore, the family system is a going concern, parental authority, however inclusive, is not felt as despotic.

A second thing to note about parental authority is that while its duration is variable (lasting in some societies a few years and in others a lifetime), it inevitably involves a change, a progressive readjustment, in the respective positions of parent and child—in some cases an almost complete reversal of roles, in others at least a cumulative allowance for the fact of maturity in the subordinated offspring. Age is a unique basis for social stratification. Unlike birth, sex, wealth, or occupation, it implies that the stratification is temporary, that the person, if he lives a full life, will eventually traverse all of the strata having it as a basis. Therefore, there is a peculiar ambivalence attached to this kind of differentiation, as well as a constant directional movement. On the one hand, the young person, in the stage of maximum socialization, is, so to speak, *moving into* the social organization. His social personality is expanding, *i.e.*, acquiring an increased amount of the cultural heritage, filling more powerful and numerous positions. His future is before him, in what the older person is leaving behind. The latter, on the other hand, has a future before him only in the sense that the offspring represents it. Therefore, there is a disparity of interest, the young person placing his thoughts upon a future which, once the first stages of dependence are passed, does not include the parent, the old person placing his hopes vicariously upon the young. This situation, representing a *tendency* in every society, is avoided in many places by a system of respect for the aged and an imaginary projection of life beyond the grave. In the absence of such a religio-ancestral system, the role of the aged is a tragic one.[5]

Let us now take up, point by point, the manner in which western civilization has affected this *gemeinschaftliche* and processual form of authority.

1. Conflicting Norms. To begin with, rapid change has, as we saw, given old and young a different social content, so that they possess

---

Authority over the former is of a personal type, while that over the latter (often in the form of a foreman-gang organization) is of a more impersonal or economic type.

[5] Sometimes compensated for by an interest in the grandchildren, which permits them partially to recover the role of the vigorous parent.

conflicting norms. There is a loss of mutual identification, and the parent will not "catch up" with the child's point of view, because he is supposed to dominate rather than follow. More than this, social complexity has confused the standards *within* the generations. Faced with conflicting goals, parents become inconsistent and confused in their own minds in rearing their children. The children, for example, acquire an argument against discipline by being able to point to some family wherein discipline is less severe, while the parent can retaliate by pointing to still other families wherein it is firmer. The acceptance of parental attitudes is less complete than formerly.

2. **Competing Authorities.** We took it for granted, when discussing rapid social change, that youth acquires new ideas, but we did not ask how. The truth is that, in a specialized and complex culture, they learn from competing authorities. Today, for example, education is largely in the hands of professional specialists, some of whom, as college professors, resemble the sophists of ancient Athens by virtue of their work of accumulating and purveying knowledge, and who consequently have ideas in advance of the populace at large (*i.e.,* the parents). By giving the younger generation these advanced ideas, they (and many other extrafamilial agencies, including youth's contemporaries) widen the intellectual gap between parent and child.[6]

3. **Little Explicit Institutionalization of Steps in Parental Authority.** Our society provides little explicit institutionalization of the progressive readjustments of authority as between parent and child. We are intermediate between the extreme of virtually permanent parental authority and the extreme of very early emancipation, because we encourage release in late adolescence. Unfortunately, this is a time of enhanced sexual desire, so that the problem of sex and the problem of emancipation occur simultaneously and complicate each other. Yet even this would doubtless be satisfactory if it were not for the fact that among us the exact time when authority is relinquished, the exact amount, and the proper ceremonial behavior are not clearly defined. Not only do different groups and families have conflicting patterns, and new situations arise to which old definitions will not apply, but the different spheres of life (legal, economic, religious, intellectual)

---

[6] The essential point is not that there are other authorities—in every society there are extrafamilial influences in socialization—but that, because of specialization and individualistic enterprise, they are *competing* authorities. Because they make a living by their work and are specialists in socialization, some authorities have a competitive advantage over parents who are amateurs or at best merely general practitioners.

do not synchronize, maturity in one sphere and immaturity in another often coexisting. The readjustment of authority between individuals is always a ticklish process, and when it is a matter of such close authority as that between parent and child it is apt to be still more ticklish. The failure of our culture to institutionalize this readjustment by a series of well-defined, well-publicized steps is undoubtedly a cause of much parent-youth dissension. The adolescent's sociological exit from his family, via education, work, marriage, and change of residence, is fraught with potential conflicts of interest which only a definite system of institutional controls can neutralize. The parents have a vital stake in what the offspring will do. Because his acquisition of independence will free the parents of many obligations, they are willing to relinquish their authority; yet, precisely because their own status is socially identified with that of their offspring, they wish to insure satisfactory conduct on the latter's part and are tempted to prolong their authority by making the decisions themselves. In the absence of institutional prescriptions, the conflict of interest may lead to a struggle for power, the parents fighting to keep control in matters of importance to themselves, the son or daughter clinging to personally indispensable family services while seeking to evade the concomitant control.

4. Concentration within the Small Family. Our family system is peculiar in that it manifests a paradoxical combination of concentration and dispersion. On the one hand, the unusual smallness of the family unit makes for a strange intensity of family feeling, while on the other, the fact that most pursuits take place outside the home makes for a dispersion of activities. Though apparently contradictory, the two phenomena are really interrelated and traceable ultimately to the same factors in our social structure. Since the first refers to that type of affection and antagonism found between relatives, and the second to activities, it can be seen that the second (dispersion) isolates and increases the intensity of the affectional element by shearing away common activities and the extended kin. Whereas ordinarily the sentiments of kinship are organically related to a number of common activities and spread over a wide circle of relatives, in our mobile society they are associated with only a few common activities and concentrated within only the immediate family. This makes them at once more instable (because ungrounded) and more intense. With the diminishing birth rate, our family is the world's smallest kinship unit, a tiny closed circle. Consequently, a great deal of family sentiment is directed toward a few individuals, who are so important to the emotional life that complexes easily develop. This emotional intensity and situational instability increase both the probability and severity of conflict.

In a familistic society, where there are several adult male and female relatives within the effective kinship group to whom the child turns for affection and aid, and many members of the younger generation in whom the parents have a paternal interest, there appears to be less intensity of emotion for any particular kinsman and consequently less chance for severe conflict.[7] Also, if conflict between any two relatives does arise, it may be handled by shifting mutual rights and obligations to another relative.[8]

5. Open Competition for Socioeconomic Position. Our emphasis upon individual initiative and vertical mobility, in contrast to rural-stable regimes, means that one's future occupation and destiny are determined more at adolescence than at birth, the adolescent himself (as well as the parents) having some part in the decision. Before him spread a panorama of possible occupations and avenues of advancement, all of them fraught with the uncertainties of competitive vicissitude. The youth is ignorant of most of the facts. So is the parent, but less so. Both attempt to collaborate on the future, but because of previously mentioned sources of friction, the collaboration is frequently stormy. They evaluate future possibilities differently, and since the decision is uncertain, yet important, a clash of wills results. The necessity of choice at adolescence extends beyond the occupational field to practically every phase of life, the parents having an interest in each decision. A culture in which more of the choices of life were settled beforehand by ascription, where the possibilities were fewer and the responsibilities of choice less urgent, would have much less parent-youth conflict.[9]

6. Sex Tension. If until now we have ignored sex taboos, the omission has represented a deliberate attempt to place them in their proper context with other factors, rather than in the unduly prominent place

[7] Margaret Mead, *Social Organization of Manua,* 84, Honolulu, Bernice P. Bishop Museum Bulletin 76, 1930. Large heterogeneous households early accustom the child to expect emotional rewards from many different persons. D. M. Spencer, "The Composition of the Family as a Factor in the Behavior of Children in Fijian Society," *Sociometry* (1939), 2: 47-55.

[8] The principle of substitution is widespread in familism, as shown by the wide distribution of adoption, levirate, sororate, and classificatory kinship nomenclature.

[9] M. Mead, *Coming of Age in Samoa,* 200 ff.

usually given them.[10] Undoubtedly, because of a constellation of cultural conditions, sex looms as an important bone of parent-youth contention. Our morality, for instance, demands both premarital chastity and postponement of marriage, thus creating a long period of desperate eagerness when young persons practically at the peak of their sexual capacity are forbidden to enjoy it. Naturally, tensions arise —tensions which adolescents try to relieve, and adults hope they will relieve, in some socially acceptable form. Such tensions not only make the adolescent intractable and capricious, but create a genuine conflict of interest between the two generations. The parent, with respect to the child's behavior, represents morality, while the offspring reflects morality *plus* his organic cravings. The stage is thereby set for conflict, evasion, and deceit. For the mass of parents, toleration is never possible. For the mass of adolescents, sublimation is never sufficient. Given our system of morality, conflict seems well-nigh inevitable.

Yet it is not sex itself but the way it is handled that causes conflict. If sex patterns were carefully, definitely, and uniformly geared with nonsexual patterns in the social structure, there would be no parent-youth conflict over sex. As it is, rapid change has opposed the sex standards of different groups and generations, leaving impulse only chaotically controlled.

The extraordinary preoccupation of modern parents with the sex life of their adolescent offspring is easily understandable. First, our morality is sex-centered. The strength of the impulse which it seeks to control, the consequent stringency of its rules, and the importance of reproductive institutions for society, make sex so morally important that being moral and being sexually discreet are synonymous. Small wonder, then, that parents, charged with responsibility for their children and fearful of their own status in the eyes of the moral community, are preoccupied with what their offspring will do in this matter. Moreover, sex is intrinsically involved in the family structure and is therefore of unusual significance to family members *qua* family members. Offspring and parent are not simply two persons who happen to live together; they are two persons who happen to live together because of past sex relations between the parents. Also, between parent and child there stand strong incest taboos, and doubtless the unvoiced possibility of violating these unconsciously intensifies the interest of each in the

10 *Cf., e.g.,* L. K. Frank, "The Management of Tensions," *Amer. J. Sociol.,* March 1928, 33: 706-22; M. Mead, *op. cit.,* 216-217, 222-23.

other's sexual conduct. In addition, since sexual behavior is connected with the offspring's formation of a new family of his own, it is naturally of concern to the parent. Finally, these factors taken in combination with the delicacy of the authoritarian relation, the emotional intensity within the small family, and the confusion of sex standards, make it easy to explain the parental interest in adolescent sexuality. Yet because sex is a tabooed topic between parent and child,[11] parental control must be indirect and devious, which creates additional possibilities of conflict.

Summary and Conclusion

Our parent-youth conflict thus results from the interaction of certain universals of the parent-child relation and certain variables the values of which are peculiar to modern culture. The universals are (1) the basic age or birth-cycle differential between parent and child, (2) the decelerating rate of socialization with advancing age, and (3) the resulting intrinsic differences between old and young on the physiological, psychosocial, and sociological planes.

Though these universal factors *tend* to produce conflict between parent and child, whether or not they do so depends upon the variables. We have seen that the distinctive general features of our society are responsible for our excessive parent-adolescent friction. Indeed, they are the same features which are affecting *all* family relations. The delineation of these variables has not been systematic, because the scientific classification of whole societies has not yet been accomplished; and it has been difficult, in view of the interrelated character of societal traits, to seize upon certain features and ignore others. Yet certainly the following four complex variables are important: (1) the rate of social change; (2) the extent of complexity in the social structure; (3) the degree of integration in the culture; and (4) the velocity of movement (*e.g.,* vertical mobility) within the structure and its relation to the cultural values.

Our rapid social change, for example, has crowded historical meaning into the family time-span, has thereby given the offspring a different social content from that which the parent acquired, and consequently

---

11 "Even among the essentially 'unrepressed' Trobrianders the parent is never the confidant in matters of sex." Bronislaw Malinowski, *Sex and Reproduction in Savage Society,* London, 1927, p. 36n. *Cf.* the interesting article, "Intrusive Parents," *The Commentator,* September 1938, which opposes frank sex discussion between parents and children.

has added to the already existent intrinsic differences between parent and youth, a set of extrinsic ones which double the chance of alienation. Moreover, our great societal complexity, our evident cultural conflict, and our emphasis upon open competition for socioeconomic status have all added to this initial effect. We have seen, for instance, that they have disorganized the important relation of parental authority by confusing the goals of child control, setting up competing authorities, creating a small family system, making necessary certain significant choices at the time of adolescence, and leading to an absence of definite institutional mechanisms to symbolize and enforce the progressively changing stages of parental power.

If ours were a simple rural-stable society, mainly familistic, the emancipation from parental authority being gradual and marked by definite institutionalized steps, with no great postponement of marriage, sex taboo, or open competition for status, parents and youth would not be in conflict. Hence, the presence of parent-youth conflict in our civilization is one more specific manifestation of the incompatibility between an urban-industrial-mobile social system and the familial type of reproductive institutions.[12]

CLASS DIFFERENCES IN SEXUAL AND AGGRESSIVE BEHAVIOR AMONG ADOLESCENTS*

ALLISON DAVIS

Before comparing middle-class and lower-class adolescents, a warning must be interjected. We recall that the long, indulgent nursing period of lower-class infants does not prevent their developing marked fear of starvation in later childhood and adulthood. This fact means that new situations, if strongly organized physically or socially, make new be-

[12] For further evidence of this incompatibility, see the writer's "Reproductive Institutions and the Pressure for Population," *(Brit.) Sociol. Rev.;* July 1937, 29: 289-306.

* Adapted and reprinted by permission of the author and publisher from "Child Rearing in the Class Structure of American Society," *The Family in a Democratic Society: Anniversary Papers of the Community Service Society of New York,* New York, Columbia University Press, 1949, pp. 56-59. Originally appeared in *Social-Class Influences upon Learning,* Inglis Lecture, Cambridge, Harvard University Press, 1948, pp. 32-37. Permission has also been granted by Harvard University Press.

havior. This is a cardinal principle of the new integrated science of social psychology. Basic learning can and does appear at any age level, provided that society or the physical environment changes the organization of its basic rewards and punishments for the individual.

Secondly, we should not be so naïve as to think that lower-class life is a happy hunting ground, given over to complete impulse expression. Slum people must accept all the basic sexual controls on incest, on homosexuality, on having more than one mate at a time, and on marital irresponsibility. In fact, there is evidence to indicate that slum people are more observant of the taboos upon incest and homosexuality than are those in the upper class. Furthermore, the same pattern which holds in their food intake—deprivation, relieved by peaks of great indulgence—is typical of lower-class sexual life. Lack of housing, lack of a bed for oneself, frequent separations of mates or lovers, the hard daily work of mothers with six to fourteen children, the itinerant life of the men, all make sexual life less regular, secure, and routine than in the middle class. In the slum, one certainly does not have a sexual partner for as many days each month as do middle-class married people, but one gets and gives more satisfaction, over longer periods, when one does have a sexual partner. With this reservation in mind, we may proceed to examine adolescent behavior in the two classes.

The aggressive behavior of adolescents is a crucial case in point. In the middle class, aggression is clothed in the conventional forms of "initiative," or "ambition," or even of "progressiveness," but in the lower class it more often appears unabashed as physical attack, or as threats of, and encouragement for, physical attack. In general, middle-class aggression is taught to adolescents in the form of social and economic skills which will enable them to compete effectively at that level. The lower classes not uncommonly teach their children and adolescents to strike out with fist or knife and to be certain to hit first. Both girls and boys at adolescence may curse their father to his face or even attack him with fists, sticks, or axes in free-for-all family encounters. Husbands and wives sometimes stage pitched battles in the home; wives have their husbands arrested; and husbands, when locked out, try to break in or burn down their own homes. Such fights with fists or weapons, and the whipping of wives, occur sooner or later in most lower-class families. They may not appear today, nor tomorrow, but they will appear if the observer remains long enough.

The important consideration with regard to physical aggression in lower-class adolescents is, therefore, that it is learned as an approved and socially rewarded form of behavior in their culture. An interviewer recently observed two nursery school boys from lower-class families; they were boasting about the length of their fathers' clasp knives! The parents themselves have taught their children to fight, not only children of either sex, but also adults who "make trouble" for them. If the child or adolescent cannot whip a grown opponent, his father or mother will join the fight. In such lower-class groups, an adolescent boy who does not try to be a good fighter will not receive the approval of his father, nor will he be acceptable to any play group or gang. The result of these cultural sanctions is that he learns to fight and to admire fighters. The conception that aggression and hostility are neurotic or maladaptive symptoms of a chronically frustrated adolescent is an ethnocentric view of middle-class individuals. In lower-class families, physical aggression is as much a normal, socially approved, and socially inculcated type of behavior as it is in frontier communities.

There are many forms of aggression, of course, which are disapproved by lower-class as well as by middle-class adolescents. These include, among others, attack by magic or poison, rape, and cutting a woman in the face. Yet all these forms of aggression are fairly common in some lower-class areas. Stealing is another form of aggression which lower-class parents verbally forbid, but which some of them in fact allow—so long as their child does not steal from his family or its close friends. The model of the adolescent's play group and of his own kin, however, is the crucial determinant of his behavior. Even where the efforts of the parent to instill middle-class mores in the child are more than half-hearted, the power of the street culture in which the child and adolescent are trained overwhelms the parental verbal instruction. The rewards of gang prestige, freedom of movement, and property gain all seem to be on the side of the street culture.

Like physical aggression, sexual relationships and motivation are more direct and uninhibited in lower-class adolescents. The most striking departure from the usual middle-class motivation is that, in much lower-class life, sexual drives and behavior in children are not regarded as inherently taboo and dangerous.

There are many parents in low-status culture, of course, who taboo these behaviors for their girls. Mothers try to prevent daughters from having children before they are married, but the example of the girl's own family is often to the contrary. At an early age the child learns of common-law marriages and extra-marital relationships of men and women in his own family. He sees his father disappear to live with other women, or he sees other men visit his mother or married sisters. Although none of his siblings may be illegitimate, the chances are very high that sooner or later his father and mother will accuse each other of having illegitimate children; or that at least one of his brothers or sisters will have a child outside marriage. His play group, girls and boys, discuss sexual relations frankly at the age of eleven or twelve, and he gains status with them by beginning intercourse early.

With sex, as with aggression, therefore, the social instigations and reinforcements of adolescents who live in these different cultures are opposites. The middle-class adolescent is punished for physical aggression and for physical sexual relations; the lower-class adolescent is frequently rewarded, both socially and organically, for these same behaviors. The degree of anxiety, guilt, or frustration attached to these behaviors, therefore, is entirely different in the two cases. One might go so far as to say that in the case of middle-class adolescents such anxiety and guilt, with regard to physical aggression and sexual intercourse, are proof of their normal socialization in their culture. In lower-class adolescents in certain environments, they are evidence of revolt against their own class culture, and possibly of incipient personality difficulties.

The point which these considerations seems to make clear, and which seems to be borne out by many detailed life histories of adolescents of each class, is as follows: The social reality of individuals differs in the most fundamental respects according to their status and culture. The individuals of different class cultures are reacting to different situations. If they are realistic in their responses to these situations, their drives and goals will be different. This basic principle of comparative psychology implies that in order to decide whether an individual in American society is normal or neurotic, one must know his social class and likewise his ethnic culture. He may be quite poorly oriented with regard to middle-class culture, simply because he has not been trained in it and, therefore, does not respond to its situations. If his behavior is normal for lower-class culture—which clinicians, teachers, and guidance workers do not usually know—he may appear to them to be maladjusted, unmotivated, unsocialized, or even neurotic. In dealing with such cases, the reference points of social reality of the teacher or psychologist must be set up with regard to the basic demands of lower-class culture upon its members.

CHAPTER 10

The Adult: Familial and Non-Familial Relationships

WE HAVE NOW CONSIDERED the child in the familial setting from the stage of fetus through the period of adolescence. As the offspring enters adulthood, he is expected to marry and to have children. For both sexes this involves finding a suitable and willing marriage partner (see chapters 12-15).

For the middle-class male there is the additional expectation that he will show promise of occupational success. After examining a number of business executives, Henry concludes that being emotionally "weaned" from parents is a necessary condition of success.

The article by Whyte, which appeared in *Life,* is an abridged form of two articles which were originally published in *Fortune.* Having conducted a number of interviews with executives, Whyte finds that for the upwardly mobile man in a large corporation the acceptability of his wife to his superiors (and their wives) is a consideration of some importance. Disadvantage, according to Whyte, falls to the man whose wife's social behavior is not appropriate to the social class which he is seeking to enter. The approval of the higher echelons is bestowed upon the wife who is not troublesome, who stays out of the way, and who is a good hostess. Whyte suggests that the ambitious junior executive would be well advised to marry a girl of social standing above his own. A later article, however, will report that marital adjustment is not particularly good when the man "marries upward."[1]

[1] J. Roth and R. F. Peck, "Social Class and Social Mobility Factors Related to Marital Adjustment," pp. 471-85 below.

An overdrawn, if telling, analogy may be made between the obligations of the traditional Japanese husband and those of the corporation husband. In neither case is the prime obligation of the man to his wife. It will be recalled that in traditional Japan a man's parents came first and that the point was dramatized by the fact that if his parents demanded it, he would be expected to divorce his wife.[2] Similarly, Whyte points out that the demands of the corporation are great, as are its powers to dispense rewards.

The article by Henry notes certain characteristics of personality which are rewarded in business: acquisitiveness and achievement, self-directedness and independence of thought. These are not characteristics which, according to Whyte, are approved in the "company wife," nor do they seem to constitute a good description of the maternal role. Thus, since marriage and career seem to require and to reward different patterns of response in women, it would be helpful if our girls were able to choose—or at least to know in advance—which it would be. As it is, many girls of the American middle class train for a career while looking for a husband. The confusion which this situation creates with respect to the feminine sex-role is described explicitly by Komarovsky and is implicit in the report of dissatisfaction over the masculine sex-role among college girls at Syracuse University.

THE BUSINESS EXECUTIVE:
A STUDY IN THE PSYCHODYNAMICS OF A SOCIAL ROLE*

William E. Henry

The business executive is a central figure in the economic and social life of the United States. His direction of business enterprise and his participation in informal social groupings give him a place of significance in community life. In both its economic and social aspects, the

[2] R. F. Winch, "Some Observations on Personality Structure in Japan," pp. 60-61 above.

* Adapted and reprinted by permission of the author and publisher from *The American Journal of Sociology* 54 (1949), 286-91.

role of the business executive is a highly visible one sociologically. It has clearly definable limits and characteristics known to the general public. These characteristics indicate the function of the business executive in the social structure, define the behavior expected of the individual executive, and serve as a guide to the selection of the novice.

Social pressure, plus the constant demands of the business organization of which he is a part, direct the behavior of the executive into the mold appropriate to the defined role. "Success" is the name applied to the whole-hearted adoption of this role. It assumes that the individual behaves in the manner dictated by the society and society rewards the individual with "success" if his behavior conforms to the role. It punishes him with "failure" should he deviate from it.

The participation in this role, however, is not a thing apart from the personality of the individual participant. It is not a game that the person is playing, it is the way of behaving and thinking that he knows best, that he finds rewarding, and in which he believes.

Thus, the role as socially defined has its counterpart in the personality structure of the individuals who participate in it. To some extent the personality structure is reshaped to be in harmony with the social role. The extent to which such reshaping of the adult personality is possible, however, seems limited. An initial selection process occurs in order to reduce the amount of time involved in teaching the appropriate behavior. Those persons whose personality structure is most readily adaptable to this particular role tend to be selected to take this role, whereas those whose personality is not already partially akin to this role are rejected.

This paper describes the personality communalities of a group of successful business executives. The research upon which it is based was undertaken to explore the general importance of personality structure in the selection of executive personnel. Many aptitude tests have been employed in the industry to decrease the risk involved in the hiring of untried personnel and to assist in their placement. These tests have been far less effective in the selection of high level executive personnel than in the selection of clerical and other non-administrating persons. Many business executives have found persons of unquestioned high intelligence often turn out to be ineffective when placed in positions of increased responsibility. The reasons for their failure lie in their social relationships. No really effective means has yet been found to clarify and predict this area of executive functioning. It is to this problem that our research[1] was directed.

From the research it became clear that the "successful" business executives studied had many personality characteristics in common. It was equally clear that an absence of these characteristics was coincident with "failure"[2] within the organization. This personality constellation might be thought of as the minimal requirement for "success" within our present business system and as the psychodynamic motivation of persons in this occupation. Individual uniqueness in personality was clearly present but despite these unique aspects, each executive had in common this personality pattern.

Achievement Desires

All show high drive and achievement desire. They conceive of themselves as hard working and achieving people who must accomplish in order to be happy. The areas in which they do their work are clearly different, but each feels this drive for accomplishment. This should be distinguished from a type of pseudo-achievement drive in which the glory of the end product alone is stressed. The person with this latter type of drive, seldom found in the successful executives, looks to the future in terms of glory it provides him and the projects that he will

[1] The research undertaken will be described in its entirety in a subsequent report. In summary it involved the study of over 100 business executives in various types of business houses. The techniques employed were the Thematic Apperception test, a short undirected interview and a projective analysis of a number of traditional personality tests. The validity of our analyses, which was done "blind," rested upon the coincidence of identical conclusions from separately analyzed instruments, upon surveys of past job performance, and the anecdotal summary of present job behavior by the executive's superiors and associates. . . .

[2] Success and failure as here used refer to the combined societal and business definition. All of our "successful" executives have a history of continuous promotion, are thought to be still "promotable" within the organization, are now in positions of major administrative responsibility, and are earning salaries within the upper ranges of current business salaries. Men in lower level supervisory positions, men who are considered "failures" in executive positions, and men in clerical and laboring jobs show clear deviations from this pattern. This suggests, of course, that this pattern is specific for the successful business executive and that it serves to differentiate him from other groupings in industry. The majority of these executives come from distributive (rather than manufacturing) businesses of moderately loose organizational structure where cooperation and teamwork are valued and where relative independence of action is stressed within the framework of a clearly defined overall company policy. In organizations in which far greater rigidity of structure is present or where outstanding independence of action is required, it is possible that there will be significant variations from the personality pattern presented here. We are currently extending our data in these directions.

have completed—as opposed to the achievement drive of the successful executive, which looks more to the sheer accomplishment of the work itself. The successful business leader gets much satisfaction from doing rather than merely from contemplating the completed product. To some extent this is the difference between the dreamer and the doer. It is not that the successful executives do not have an over-all goal in mind, nor that they do not derive satisfaction from the contemplation of future ease, nor that they do not gain pleasure from prestige. For more real to them, however, is the continual stimulation that derives from the pleasure of immediate accomplishment.

Mobility Drive

All the successful executives have strong mobility drives. They feel the necessity to move continually upward and to accumulate the rewards of increased accomplishment. For some the sense of successful mobility comes through the achievement of competence on the job. These men struggle for increased responsibility and derive a strong feeling of satisfaction from the completion of a task. Finished work and newly gained competence provide them with their sense of continued mobility.

A second group rely more upon the social prestige of increased status in their home communities or within the organizational hierarchy. To them the real objective is increased status. Competence in work is of value and at times crucial. But the satisfactions of the second group come from the social reputation, not from the personal feeling that necessary work has been well done. Both types of mobility drive are highly motivating. The zeal and energy put into the job is equal in both instances. The distinction appears in the kinds of work which the men find interesting. For the first group the primary factor is the nature of the work itself—is it challenging, is it necessary, is it interesting? For the second group, the crucial factor is its relation to their goals of status mobility—is it a step in the direction of increased prestige, is it appropriate to my present problem, what would other people think of me if I did it?

The Idea of Authority

The successful executive posits authority as a controlling but helpful relationship to superiors. He looks to his superiors as persons of more advanced training and experience whom he can consult on special problems and who issue to him certain guiding directives. He does not see the authority figures in his environment as destructive or prohibiting forces.

Those executives who view authority as a prohibiting and destructive force have difficulty relating themselves to superiors and resent their authority over them. They are either unable to work smoothly with their superiors, or indirectly and unconsciously do things to obstruct the work of their bosses or to assert their independence unnecessarily.

It is of interest that the dominant crystallization of attitudes about authority of these men is toward superior and toward subordinates, rather than toward Self. This implies that most crucial in their concept of authority is the view of being a part of a wider and more final authority-system. In contrast, a few executives of the "Self-made," driving type characteristic of the past of business enterprise maintain a specific concept of authority with regard to Self. They are the men who almost always forge their own frontiers, who are unable to operate within anyone else's framework, to whom cooperation and teamwork are foreign concepts. To these men, the ultimate authority is in themselves and their image does not include the surrounding area of shared or delegated power.

Organization and Its Implications

While executives who are successful vary considerably in their intelligence test ratings, all of them have a high degree of ability to organize unstructured situations and to see the implications of their organization. This implies that they have the ability to take several seemingly isolated events or facts and to see relationships that exist between them. Further, they are interested in looking into the future and are concerned with predicting the outcome of their decisions and actions.

This ability to organize often results in a forced organization, however. Even though some situations arise with which they feel unfamiliar and are unable to cope, they still force an organization upon it. Thus, they bring it into the sphere of familiarity. This tendency operates partially as a mold, as a pattern into which new or unfamiliar experiences are fit. This means, of course, that there is a strong tendency to rely upon techniques that they know will work and to resist situations which do not readily fit this mold.

Decisiveness

Decisiveness is a further trait of this group. This does not imply the popular idea of the executive making quick and final decisions in rapid fire succession, although this seems to be true of some of the executives. More crucial, however, is an ability to come to a decision among several alternative courses of action—whether it be done on the spot or whether after detailed consideration. Very seldom does this ability break down. While less competent and well organized individuals may become flustered and operate inefficiently in certain spots, most of these men force their way to a conclusion. Nothing is too difficult for them to tackle at least and try to solve. When poorly directed and not modified by proper judgment, this attitude may be more of a handicap than a help. That is to say, this trait remains in operation and results in decision-making action regardless of the reasonableness of the decision or its reality in terms of related facts. The breakdown of this trait (usually found only in cases where some more profound personality change has also occurred) is one of the most disastrous for the executive. As soon as this trait shows disturbance, the executive's superiors become apprehensive about him. This suggests an interesting relationship to the total executive constellation. Whenever a junior executive loses this quality of decisiveness, he seems to pass out of the socially defined role. It is almost as though the role demanded conviction and certainty as an integral aspect of it. The weakening of other aspects of the ideal executive constellation can be readily reintegrated into the total constellation. The questioning of the individual's certainty and decisiveness, however, results in a weakening of the entire constellation and tends to be punished by superiors.

Strong Self-Structure

One way of differentiating between people is in the relative strength or weakness of their notions of self-identity, their self-structure. Some persons lack definiteness and are easily influenced by outside pressures. Some, such as these executives, are firm and well-defined in their sense of self-identity. They know what they are and what they want and have well developed techniques for getting what they want. The things they want and the techniques for getting them are of course quite different for each individual, but this strength and firmness is a common and necessary characteristic. It is, of course, true that too great firmness of sense of self-identity leads to rigidity and to inflexibility. And while some of these executives could genuinely be accused of this, in general they maintain considerable flexibility and adaptability *within the framework of their desires and within the often rather narrow possibilities of their own business organization.*

Activity and Aggression

The executive is essentially an active, striving, aggressive person. His underlying personality motivations are active and aggressive— although he is not necessarily aggressive and hostile overtly in his dealings with other people. This activity and aggressiveness are always well channelized into work or struggles for status and prestige. This implies a constant need to keep moving, to do something, to be active. This does not mean that they are always in bodily movement and moving physically from place to place (though this is often true), but rather that they are mentally and emotionally alert and active.

This constant motivator unfortunately cannot be shut off. It may be part of the reason why so many executives find themselves unable to take vacations leisurely or to stop worrying about already solved problems.

Apprehension and the Fear of Failure

If one is continually active and always trying to solve problems and arrive at decisions, any inability to do so successfully may well result in feelings of frustration. This seems to be true of the executives. In spite of their firmness of character and their drive to activity, they also harbor a rather pervasive feeling that they may not really succeed and be able to do the things they want. It is not implied that this sense of frustration comes only from their immediate business experience. It seems far more likely to be a feeling of long standing within the executives and to be only accentuated and reinforced by their present business experience.

This sense of the perpetually unattained is an integral part of this constellation and is part of its dilemma. It means that there is always some place to go, but no defined point at which to stop. It emphasizes the "self-propelled" nature of the dynamics of this role and highlights the inherent need to always keep moving and to see another goal always ahead. This also suggests that cessation of mobility and of struggling for new achievements will be accompanied by an inversion of this constant energy. The person whose mobility is blocked, either by his own limitations or by those of the social system, finds this energy diverted into other channels. Psychosomatic symptoms, the enlargement of interpersonal dissatisfactions, and the development of rationalized compulsive and/or paranoid-like defenses may reflect the re-direction of this potent energy demand.

Strong Reality Orientation

The successful executives are strongly oriented to immediate realities and their implications. They are directly interested in the practical and the immediate and the direct. This is of course generally good for the immediate business situation, though an overdeveloped sense of reality may have secondary complications. If a man's sense of reality is too highly developed, he ceases to be a man of vision. For a man of vision must get above reality to plan and even dream about future possibilities. In addition, a too strong reality sense that does not find the realities in tune with individual's ambitions may well leave a further sense of frustration and unpleasantness of reality. This happens to many executives who find progress and promotion too slow for their drives. The result is often a restlessness rather than activity, a fidgetiness rather than a well channelized aggression, and a lack of ease that may well disrupt many of their usual interpersonal relations.

The Nature of Their Interpersonal Relations

In general, the mobile and successful executive looks to his superiors with a feeling of personal attachment and tends to identify with them. His superior represents for him a symbol of his own achievement and activity desires and he tends to identify himself with these traits in those who have achieved more. He is very responsive to his superiors— the nature of this responsiveness of course depending on his other feelings, his idea of authority, and the extent to which his sense of frustration is present.

On the other hand, he looks to his subordinates in a detached and impersonal way seeing them as "doers of work" rather than as people. He treats them impersonally, with no real feeling of being akin to them or having deep interest in them as persons. It is almost as though he viewed his subordinates as representatives of things he has left behind, both factually and emotionally. Still uncertain of his next forward step, he cannot afford to become personally identified or emotionally involved with the past he has left behind. The only direction of his emotional energy that is real to him is upward and toward the symbols of that upward interest, his superiors.

This does not mean that he is cold and treats all subordinates casually. In fact he tends to be generally sympathetic with many of them. This element of sympathy with subordinates is most apparent when the subordinate shows personality traits that are most like those of the superior. Thus, the superior is able to take pride in certain successful young persons without at the same time feeling an equal interest in all subordinates.

The Attitude Toward His Own Parents

In a sense the successful executive is a "man who has left home." He feels and acts as though he were on his own, as though his emotional ties and obligations to his parents were severed. It seems to be most crucial that he has not retained resentment of his parents, but has rather simply broken their emotional hold on him and been left psychologically free to make his own decisions. We have found those who have not broken this tie to be either too dependent upon their superiors in the work situation, or to be resentful of their supervision (depending of course upon whether they have retained their dependent parental ties or rather they are still actively fighting against them).

In general, we find the relationship to the mother to have been the most clearly broken tie. The tie to the father remains positive in the sense that he views the father as a helpful but not restraining figure. Those men who still feel a strong emotional tie to the mother have systematically had difficulty in the business situation. The residual emotional tie seems contradictory to the necessary attitude of activity, progress, and channelized aggression. The tie to the father, however, must remain positive—as the emotional counterpart of the admired and more successful male figure. Without this image, struggle for success seems difficult.

The Nature of Dependency-Feelings and Concentration Upon Self

A special problem in differentiating the type of generally successful executive is the nature of his dependency-feelings. It was pointed out above that the dependency upon the mother-image must be eliminated. For those executives who work within the framework of a large organization where cooperation and group-and-company loyalty are necessities, there must remain feelings of dependency upon the father-image and a need to operate within an established framework. This does not mean that the activity-aggression need cannot operate or that the individual is not decisive and self-directional. It means only that he is so within the framework of an already established set of over-all goals. For most executives this over-all framework provides a needed guidance and allows them to concentrate upon their achievement and work demands with only minimal concern for policy making of the entire organization. For those executives who prefer complete independence and who are unable to work within a framework established by somebody else, the element of narcissism is much higher and their feelings of loyalty are only to themselves rather than to a father-image or its impersonal counterpart in company policy. These feelings differentiate the executives who can cooperate with others and who can promote the over-all policy of a company from those who must be the whole show themselves. Clearly there are situations in which the person of high concentration upon self and low dependency-loyalty feelings is of great value. But he should be distinguished in advance and placed only in such situations where these traits are of value.

The successful executive represents a crystallization of many of the attitudes and values generally accepted by middle-class American society. The value of accumulation and achievement, of self-directedness and independent thought and their rewards in prestige and status and property are found in this group. But they also pay the price of holding these values and by profiting from them. Uncertainty, constant activity, the continual fear of losing ground, the inability to be introspectively leisurely, the ever-present fear of failure, and the artificial limitations put upon their emotionalized interpersonal relations—these are some of the costs of this role.

THE WIFE PROBLEM*

William H. Whyte, Jr.

Over the last few decades American corporations have been evolving a pattern of social community able to provide their members with more and more of their basic social wants. Yet, the corporation now

* Adapted and reprinted by permission of the author and publisher from *Life,* January 7, 1952, 32-48.

concedes, one of the principal members of its community remains officially almost unnoticed—to wit, the Wife. For the good of the corporation, many executives believe, it is time the matter was remedied. "We control a man's environment in business and we lose it entirely when he crosses the threshold of his home," one executive says mournfully. "Management, therefore, has a challenge and an obligation to deliberately plan and create a favorable, constructive attitude on the part of the wife that will liberate her husband's total energies for the job." Others, though they might not put it quite so baldly, agree that the step is logical.

Just how to do this is a problem that has many a management understandably baffled. On one very basic matter, however, management is not in the slightest baffled. It knows exactly what kind of wife it wants. With a remarkable uniformity of phrasing, corporation officials all over the country sketch the ideal. In her simplest terms she is a wife who (1) is highly adaptable, (2) is highly gregarious, (3) realizes her husband belongs to the corporation.

Are the corporation specifications presumptuous? It would appear not. The fact is that this kind of wife is precisely what our schools and colleges—and U.S. society in general—seem to be giving the corporation.

Let us define terms: we are discussing the wives of the coming generation of management, whose husbands are between 25 and 40, and in junior or middle echelons of management or with logical aspirations of getting there. There is, of course, no sharp dividing line between age groups, but among older executives there is a strong feeling that this younger generation of wives is the most cooperative the corporation has ever enlisted. "Somehow," says one executive, "they seem to give us so much less trouble than the older ones." "Either the girls are better or the men are marrying better," says another. "But whatever it is with these people, *they get along.*"

The Negative Role

Perhaps it is merely that this generation of wives has not yet grown older and more cantankerous. Perhaps. But there is evidence that this group-mindedness is the result of a shift in values more profound than one might suppose. The change is by no means peculiar to the corporation wife but by the nature of her job she may be the outstanding manifestation of it. And a preview, perhaps, of what is to come.

First, how do the wives conceive their own role? Critical literature has been answering the question rather forcefully, with the result that many Americans (and practically all Europeans) assume that the wife of the American businessman not only is the power behind the scenes but wants to become more so. The picture needs considerable revision. For the striking thing that emerges from wives' comments is the negativeness of the role they sketch. As they explain it, the good wife is good by *not* doing things—by *not* complaining when her husband works late; by *not* fussing when a transfer is coming up; by *not* engaging in any controversial activity. Moreover, they agree heartily that a good wife can't help a husband as much as a bad wife can hurt one. And the bad wife, clearly, is one who obtrudes too much, whether as a "meddler," a "climber," a "fixer" or, simply, someone who "pushes" her man around.

Resolutely antifeminist, the executive wife conceives her role to be that of a "stabilizer"—the keeper of the retreat, the one who rests and rejuvenates the man for the next day's battle.

This stabilizing calls for more than good homemaking and training the kids not to bother daddy before dinner. Above all, wives emphasize, they have to be good listeners. They describe the job somewhat wryly. They must be "sounding boards," "refueling stations," "wailing walls." But they speak without resentment. Nurturing the male ego, they seem to feel, is not only a pretty good fulfillment of their own ego but a form of therapy made increasingly necessary by the corporation way of life. Management psychologists couldn't agree more. "Most top executives are very lonely people," as one puts it. "The greatest thing a man's wife can do is to let him unburden the worries he can't confess to in the office."

A Social Operator

In addition to listening she can do some judicious talking. If she is careful about it she can be a valuable publicity agent for the husband. "In a subtle way," says one executive, "they put in a plug for the husband. They tell things he wouldn't dare tell for fear of seeming immodest." In similar fashion they can humanize him if he's a boss. "About the time I get fed up with the bastard," says a junior executive, "here I am, going over to dinner at his house. And she's so nice. She jokes about him, kids him to his face. I figure he can't be so bad after all."

Low-key "stabilizing," then, the wife sees as her main task. There is another aspect to her role, however, and it is considerably less passive. For the good corporation wife must also be a social operator, and when husbands and wives sketch out the personal characteristics of the ideal wife it is the equipment for this role that comes first to their minds. What they ask for, more than any other quality, is gregariousness, or a reasonable facsimile. Here are some of the ways in which they spell it out.

EXECUTIVE: "She should do enough reading to be a good conversationalist. . . . Even if she doesn't like opera she should know something about it so if the conversation goes that way she can hold her own. She has to be able to go with you if you're going to make a speech or get an award, and not be ill at ease."

EXECUTIVE: "The hallmark of the good wife is the ability to put people at their ease."

WIFE: "The most important thing for an executive's wife is to know everybody's name and something about their family so you can talk to them—also, you've got to be able to put people at their ease."

EXECUTIVE: "Keeping herself so she is comfortable with people on the boss's level is important. I don't think reading and music and that kind of stuff are vital."

EXECUTIVE: "The kind you want is the kind that can have people drop in any time and make a good show of it even if the baby's diapers are lying around."

WIFE: "It's a very worthwhile bunch we have here. Edith Sampson down on Follansbee Road is sort of the intellectual type, but most of the gang are real people."

For the corporation wife, in short, being "sociable" is as important as stabilizing. Like the army wife, an analogy she detests, she must be a highly adaptable "mixer." In fact, she needs to be even more adaptable than the army wife, for the social conditions she meets are more varied. One year she may be a member of a company community, another year a branch manager's wife, expected to integrate with the local community—or, in some cases, to become a civic leader, and frequently, as the wife of the company representative, to provide a way station on the route of touring company brass.

"It Makes Me Laugh"

As a rule, she is inextricably bound up in the corporation "family," often so much so that her entire behavior—including what and where she drinks—is subtly conditioned by the corporation. "It makes me laugh," says one wife in an eastern city dominated by one corporation. "If we were the kind to follow the Pattern, I'll tell you just what we would do. First, in a couple of years, we'd move out of Ferncrest Village (it's really pretty tacky there, you know). We wouldn't go straight to Eastmere Hills—that would look pushy at this stage of the game; we'd go to the hilly section off Scrubbs Mill Pike. About that time, we'd change from Christ Church to St. Edwards, and we'd start going to the Fortnightlys—it would be a different group entirely. Then, about 10 years later, we'd finally build in Eastmere Hills." It makes her laugh, she says, because that would be the signal to everybody that she had become a wife of the top-brass bracket. Which she probably will.

Few wives are as articulate as that on the social role, but intuitively they are generally superb at it; their antennae are sensitive, and they know the rules of the game by heart. Second nature to the seasoned wife, for example, are the following:

Don't talk shop gossip with the Girls, particularly those who have husbands in the same department.

Don't invite superiors in rank; let them make the first bid.

Don't turn up at the office unless you absolutely have to.

Don't get too chummy with the wives of associates your husband might soon pass on the way up.

Don't be disagreeable to any company people you meet. You never know. . .

Be attractive. There is a strong correlation between executive success and the wife's appearance. Particularly so in the case of the sales wife.

Be a phone pal of your husband's secretary.

Never—repeat, never—get tight at a company party (it may go down in a dossier).

One rule transcends all others: *Don't be too good*. Keeping up with the Joneses is still important. But where in pushier and more primitive times it implied going substantially ahead of the Joneses, today keeping up means just that: keeping up. One can move ahead, yes—but slightly, and the timing must be exquisite. Whatever the move, it must never be openly invidious.

Perhaps it is for this reason that, when it comes to buying an auto, the Buick is so much preferred: it envelops the whole executive spectrum and the jump from a Special to a Super, and from a Super to a Roadmaster, can be handled with tact. Not always, though. In one eastern steel town, where cars have always been the accepted symbol of rank, the chairman of the board has a Cadillac—certainly a high enough ceiling. The president, however, has taken to buying Buick Supers, with the result that people in the upper brackets are chafing because it would be unseemly to go higher. Except for the chairman, accordingly, only the local tradespeople drive Cadillacs and Roadmasters.

The good corporation wife, the rules continue, does not make friends uncomfortable by clothes too blatantly chic, by references to illustrious forebears or by excessive good breeding. And she avoids intellectual pretensions like the plague.

Are these rules of the game merely the old fact of conformity? In part, yes. But something new has been added. What was once a fact has now become a philosophy. Today's young couples not only concede their group-mindedness; they are outspokenly in favor of it. They blend with the group not because they fear to do otherwise but because they approve of it.

While few young wives are aware of the sacrifice involved, the role of the boss's wife is one that they very much covet. In talking about the qualities of the ideal wife—a subject they evidently had thought over long and often—they were at no loss. In one third of the cases the American woman's favorite cliché "gracious" came instantly to them, and in nearly all the others the descriptions spelled out the same thing. Theirs is a sort of First Lady ideal, a woman who takes things as they come with grace and poise, and a measure of *noblesse oblige;* in short, the perfect boss's wife. But how near do they come to the ideal?

What a Wife Faces

What, for example, of the listening job that wives take such pride in? How well can they listen? Consensus of a cross section of U.S. executives: not very well. ("And for God's sake, don't quote me.") There are excuses aplenty. "If he has had a rough day," says one wife, "I don't want to hear about it. He'd only get mad and say things the children shouldn't hear." The husband, however, may be the one chiefly to blame. He asks for active, intelligent listening, yet seldom wants advice ("Women just don't understand").

And how well does she handle the special social problem? In advancing the husband in the office, the corporation is quite likely to advance him socially as well. There is no easy out for the couple in such cases, and for the wife the inward tug of war between the social *status quo* and the prospect of advancement can be extremely poignant. "I must have made some terrible mistakes," laments one wife now in mid-passage. "I love people and I've made many intimate friends in the company, but since Charlie got his new job it's just been hell on us. He has so much control over their lives, and it's all gotten so complicated."

The fact that the office can spell sanctuary for the husband does not go unresented. Perhaps this is why the Christmas office party provokes such surprisingly bitter, if concealed, feeling from many wives. It dramatizes the wife's exclusion. Here, on this appointed day, is the world she can never share, and for all her brave little chuckles at the standing jokes of the office gang, she comes face to face with the fact. That is, if she's allowed to attend.

Burning though this exclusion may be to the wives, it is a topic they dislike intensely to talk about or to think about. And for them, indeed, the waters may well be better left muddy: to peer too deeply is to uncover an underlying point even more provoking. Where, the awful question comes up, does the man find his major satisfactions?

A common feminine observation is that a man's major satisfactions come from the home. If he's happy there, he can be happy in his work, and vice versa. The belief is probably necessary. Is it correct as well?

Item: As management psychologists note, the average executive shows a remarkable ability to repress his home worries while on the job; rarely, however, can he shut out office worries at home.

Item: The reaction to this Hobson's-choice question: "If you had to make the choice, which would you take: an increasingly satisfying work life and a proportionately souring home life—or the opposite?" The answers would surprise wives. "This business of doing it all for the family," as one husband confesses, "it's just a rationalization. If I got a windfall today I'd still knock myself out."

"Man's love is of man's life a thing apart," Byron once observed.

" 'Tis woman's whole existence." So, for all the group integration and communication skills she can muster, it will probably remain.

The schism between Home and Office has been even more accentuated recently. Thanks, in part, to the way the tax structure has accumulated, the corporation now provides the man with a higher standard of living in his work than in his home—and, it might be added, a higher one than his wife enjoys. From 9 to 5 he may be a minor satrap, guiding the destiny of thousands, waited on by secretaries and subordinates; back in his servantless home he washes the dishes. Nor is it merely the fact of his satrapy; the corporation virtually rigs it so that he can have more fun away from home.

The expense account has become a way of life. There is not only travel. There are also luncheon clubs, company retreats, special conventions, parties and perquisites, and, though the wife may be thrown an occasional convention as a crumb, the expense-account world rarely encompasses her. It is primarily a man's world—and if the man is at a low salary, he is likely to find the pattern of life at 7118 Crestmere Road dull in comparison.

"The company has spoiled Jim terribly," says one wife. "Even when he was only earning $7,500 a year he used to be sent to Washington all the time. He'd go down in a Pullman drawing room and as J. R. Robinson of the General Company, take a two-room suite. Then he used to be asked by some of the company officers to a hunting and fishing lodge that the company kept in the north woods. When he went to New York, he'd entertain at 21, the Barberry Room and the Chambord. Me, meanwhile, I'd be eating a 30¢ hamburger and, when we went away together on vacation, we would have to go in our beat-up old car or borrow my sister's husband's. This taste of high life gives some of these characters delusions of grandeur. Small wonder that they get to fidgeting after they have been home a couple of weeks."

"What the hell can you say?" says one executive. "Here I am eating high off the hog, meeting interesting people, while Jo is slaving back home. I get a big bang out of all this, but I also have a sort of guilty feeling, so I say to her, 'Gee, honey, I hate all this traveling, but I just have to do it.'" Of the wives FORTUNE interviewed, many mentioned, commiseratingly, how their husbands looked forward to coming home, how awful it was sleeping in hotel beds, rattling around on trains and eating bum food.

There are some things, however, that cannot be explained away. For more than sirloins and drawing rooms are at issue; over the long pull this disparity aggravates perhaps the most subtle problem of marriage: equality of growth. If marriage, as Sociologist Everett Hughes puts it, is a "mutual mobility bet," for whom are the cards stacked?

Growth can mean many things. To the younger generation of executives it seems to mean an increasing ability to handle and mix with people. And the terms are the same for the wife. "The wife who is not very sociable," goes a highly typical male observation, "might not affect the husband directly, but she can hurt him just the same. A lot of business is done weekends. If she doesn't go for this, her lack of growth can hold the man back." "I have seen it happen so many times," says another executive sadly. "He marries the kid sweetheart, the girl next door or a girl from the jerkwater college he went to. They start off with a lot in common. Then he starts going up. Fifteen years later he is a different guy entirely. But she's stayed home, literally and figuratively." Even the old idea of a wife as a sort of culture carrier is virtually dead; she is still expected to read and things like that, but for functional reasons. "Sure I want her to read good books and magazines," as one executive puts it. "I don't want her to make a fool of herself in conversation."

Fundamentally, of course, the problem goes back to whom the executive chooses in the first place. Is the moral that he should marry a girl "superior" to him? Thanks to the commonly accepted saw that a woman can pull a man up, but not vice versa, there are many who think he should. ("My best executives," remarks one boss, "are the ones who 'outmarried' themselves.") But the pitfalls are many. Her qualities may drive the man to preoccupation with office prestige in order to prove himself to her; furthermore, unless she is excellent at hiding her superiority—or lets it rest fallow—she can hurt his chances in a close "family" community. The Bryn Mawr accent can be absolute death for a career in some Midwestern corporations.

What kind of background for the woman, then, is the optimum? A serious career can be dismissed easily; there is almost universal agreement among wives, husbands and corporations on this score. Work before marriage, however, is generally approved. "I feel the fact that I worked before marriage," says one wife, "is a help. I know what goes on in an office and can understand what Charles is up against."

College? Here is the *summum bonum*. There are some obvious reasons; because virtually all executives now go to college, the couple in such cases starts off with shared values. But corporation people mention a reverse factor almost as much. It is not so important for the wife, they say, to have gone to college, but it is very important not to have *not* gone to college. If she hasn't, corporation people warn, she is prey to an inferiority complex that makes it difficult for her to achieve real poise. Some corporations, accordingly, make it their business to find out whether or not the wife has a degree.

More and more corporations these days are interviewing the wife before hiring an executive, and some are not uninterested in fiancées. There are many holdouts ("This railroad picks its executives and lets its executives pick their wives and so far it's been okay"), but roughly half of the companies on which FORTUNE has data have made wife-screening a regular practice and many of the others seem about ready to do so. And the look-see is not academic. About 20 per cent of its otherwise acceptable trainee applicants, one large company estimates, are turned down because of their wives.

Ordinarily, the screening is accomplished via "informal" social visits. Many executives, for example, make it a point to call on the wife in her own home. Louis Ruthenburg, board chairman of Servel (which never hires an executive without a look at the wife), likes to recall how one college president used to insist on eating breakfast with a candidate's family; the wife who didn't fix her husband a good breakfast, he used to say, wasn't a good risk. To help them spot such key indicators many executives rely heavily on their own wives. "My wife is very, very keen on this," says one president. "She can spot things I might miss. And if the gal isn't up to par with her, it's no go."

How to Screen a Wife

But the initial screening is only the beginning of the corporation's interest. In one way or another the corporation manages to keep an eye on the wife, and more and more the surveillance is deliberately planned. At the Container Corp. of America, for example, it is the duty of all vice presidents to get acquainted with their subordinates' wives, and on their travels they are expected to meet the wives of executives in the field. Thus, when a man's name comes up for promotion the company has the answers to these questions: What is the health of the family? What is their attitude toward parenthood? How does the wife run her home? Does she dress with taste?

The effect of all this surveillance on the husband's career is substantial. In the home office of an insurance company, to cite one not untypical example, the president is now sidetracking one of his top men in favor of a less able one; the former's wife "has absolutely no sense of public relations." In another company a very promising executive's career is being similarly checked; his wife, the boss explains, is "negative in her attitude toward the company. She feels that business is her husband's life and no part of hers." Wives who have donated income of their own to raise the family living standard may also call down sanctions on the husband. Says one president, "When a man buys a home he can't afford on his salary alone, we either question his judgment or feel that the wife wears the pants." In either case his career is not likely to profit.

So with alcohol. The little woman who gets tipsy in front of the boss is not quite the joke her celebration in cartoon and anecdote would indicate; indeed, it is almost frightening to find out to what degree executive futures have been irretrievably influenced by that fourth Martini. And it need happen only once. Recently, the president of a large utility felt it necessary to revise his former estimate of two executives. At the last company dinner their wives drank too many glasses of champagne. "They disported themselves," he says regretfully, "with utter lack of propriety."

Interestingly, divorce rarely disqualifies a man. Because of the phenomenon of the outgrown wife, the regret of most companies is tempered by the thought that the executive's next and, presumably more mobile, wife will be better for all concerned; one company, as a matter of fact, has a policy of sending executives away on extended trips if they need separating from nagging or retrograde wives.

One company has arranged for the team of consulting psychologists it retains to help out in delicate situations (currently they are making progress with an alcoholic wife). In most cases, however, the salvage task is up to the top man himself. "A lot of the 'company business' that presidents do," says one of them, "covers this sort of work. Take a situation I've got to wrestle with now. In one of our branch plants the wives of two vice presidents have started a feud. The men get along fine, but one of the wives is a real troublemaker. So I guess it's up to me to take a trip halfway across the continent—for other reasons, of course—and try and see what I can do about it."

Important as the wife-screening process may be, most executives realize that it is, at best, only a negative measure. For even with the most cooperative wives there can be much misunderstanding over such topics as travel and long hours. Therefore it is the company's duty, they argue, to *sell* the wife on the corporation's point of view. The result is an increasing use of such media as films, brochures and special mailings to drive home, in effect, the idea that the corporation isn't stealing her husband from her.

But something far more important is being brewed for the wife. It is not enough, in the view of many companies, that she merely be "sold" on the company; she should, they believe, now be integrated *into* it. "When a man comes to work for us," says William Given, chairman, American Brake Shoe Co., "we think of the company as employing the family, for it will be supporting the entire family, not merely the breadwinner." "The days of the strictly home wife," says a bank president, "are gone. She has become indispensable to our entire scheme of business." Among U.S. corporations, easily the most conspicuous and successful example of this kind of integration has been Thomas J. Watson's International Business Machines Corp. "Our wives," Watson explains, "are all part of the business. We started with just a few hundred people in 1914 and decided that no matter how large we grew we would carry it on in the family spirit. We always refer to our people as the 'I.B.M. Family' and we mean the wives and children as well as the men."

As a result the company can correctly claim that it makes available "complete social satisfactions." For $1 a year I.B.M. people enjoy a country club with swimming pool, bowling, 18-hole golf course, softball, tennis, picnics, and parties of all kinds. Even the children are integrated. At the age of 3 they may be enrolled in a special children's club, and at 8 go on to become junior members of the big club.

In keeping with the family spirit Mrs. Watson, a very gracious, modest woman, sets an example for other wives. "She's made my work play," her husband explains. "She has a great gift for human relations. I confer with her about personnel because she knows all the people. She has met them at luncheons where we hold a regular receiving line, and every year she goes to the 100-Percenter Club meetings." In addition to this, Mrs. Watson travels with her husband all over the world and keeps in touch with I.B.M. people; last year she traveled 38,046 miles and met 11,845 I.B.M. men and their wives.

Social integration, however, does not mean that the corporation necessarily *likes* the wife. A great many, as we have seen, do. But in some cases the corporation welcomes her largely as a means of defending itself against her. Amiable as it may be about it, the corporation is aware that the relationship is still triangular—or, to put it another way, if you can't beat 'em, join 'em. "Successes here," says one official, "are guys who eat and sleep the company. If a man's first interest is his wife and family, more power to him—but we don't want him." "We've got quite an equity in the man," another explains, "and it's only prudence to protect it by bringing the wife into the picture."

In fairness to the corporation wife, she must be recompensed somehow for the amount of time the company demands from her husband. Companies recognize the fact and are consequently more and more providing social facilities—from ladies' nights to special clubs—to hypo the sense of identification.

One corporation has gone considerably further. Via the wife of the heir apparent to the presidency, there has been set up, in effect, a finishing school so that the wives can be brought up to the same high standards. As soon as the husband reaches the $8,000-to-$10,000 bracket the wife becomes eligible for the grooming. It is all done very subtly: the group leader drops helpful advice on which are the preferred shops, where to dine, what to wear when doing it and, somewhat like a good cruise director, has a way of introducing newcomers to congenial people. "Her supervision is so clever and indirect," says one wife, "that the other wives appreciate it probably."

When the corporation turns to the Sales Wife, its attention becomes even more intense. As an economic lever on the salesman, companies have learned, there is no stimulus quite so effective as the wife, if properly handled. Some sales executives make a habit of writing provocative letters to the wife, reminding her of the sales-contest prizes her husband could win for her and how he is doing at the moment (not so well as he should be).

As an extra employee, the wife's potential is so great that with some concerns the "husband and wife team" is not only desirable but mandatory. And the wife is not always merely the junior member. "Wives can do a lot on their own," explains the president of a large paper-box company. "A lot of important business connections have grown from friendships between our wives and wives of executives of other companies. One of our executives' wives recently was down at Miami for two weeks, and a friendship she struck up with a woman there resulted in a big order from an account we hadn't been able to crack in 15 years."

Insurance companies, among the first to exploit this "team" potential, bear down heavily on the theme through a constant stream of literature addressed to wives. Through magazine articles penned by veteran wives they are told of the psychological requirements ("Earl Made a Believer of Me," Mrs. Earl Benton explains to wives in a typical article).

The question of integration is by no means simple. What we have been talking about so far is the kind of integration deliberately planned by companies. But there is another kind. Quite beyond the immediate control of the corporation there are forces at work to draw the bonds between wife and corporation even tighter.

Paradoxically, perhaps the greatest of these is the very decentralization of industry. Thanks to this growing trend, it is now a commonplace that the road to advancement is through transfer to the different seats of the corporation empire.

With their talent for adaptability, the younger generation of wives is in most respects well prepared for this new way of life. Most accept it philosophically, and a good many actually prefer it to staying put in one place. "Any time the curtains get dirty," says one wife, "I'm ready to move. I enjoy meeting new people and seeing new places. And it's kind of a vacation sometimes."

There are, nevertheless, some very real tensions produced. And for no one more than the wife. It is she, who has only one life in contrast to her husband's two, who is called upon to do most of the adjusting. The move at once breaks up most of her community friendships, severs her local business relationships with the bank and the stores, takes her from the house and the garden on which she worked so long, and if the move takes her to a large city it probably drops her living standards also.

But it is the effect on the children that concerns wives most. While the children are very young, most wives agree, the effect is not harmful; they make and forget friends easily. As they reach junior-high age, however, a transfer can become a crisis. Recalls one wife: "Every time my daughter made a place for herself at school with the other kids, we'd move, and she'd spend the next year trying to break in at another school. Last year, when she was a senior in high school, she had a nervous breakdown. She was sure she was an outsider." The effect is not often this drastic but, while most children sweat out their adjustment without overt pain, the process is one parents find vicariously wrenching. One executive who recently changed to a nontransferring company has no trouble recalling the exact moment of his decision. One night at dinner his little boy turned to him. "Daddy," he said, "where do you really live?"

While constant transfer exposes the couple to many environments, it is, nevertheless, one of the most powerful of all the forces for integration. Because moving makes their other roots so shallow and transitory, the couple instinctively clings all the harder to the corporation.

What are the wife's basic unadjusted feelings about all this? The answer is clear: she likes the way of life. To picture her as a helpless sort of being pushed around by the corporation would be to attribute to her a sense of plight she does not feel; she must be considered not only an object of the integration but a force for it in her own right. She has become such an ally of the corporation, in fact, that on several matters it would almost appear that she and the corporation are ganging up on the husband.

Whatever else she may think of the corporation, on three main points she and her sisters agree:

The corporation means opportunity. The big company, wives explain, plays fair. "We went over all the pros and cons of bigness before Jim joined Du Pont," says one wife, "and we've never regretted joining. The bigness holds out a challenge for you."

The corporation means benefits. "Eastman Kodak has wonderful goodwill policies," a wife explains. "I used to have to attend to all the home details like insurance and bills. Now the company has someone who does those things for you—they even plan vacations for you."

The corporation means security. "Some companies may pay more at the start, but employment is not so secure. Here they never fire anybody, they just transfer you to another department."

Few wives go on to articulate their image of "the Company." But there is an image, nonetheless, that of a beneficent "system," at once impersonal and warm—in a nice kind of way, Big Brother.

There is, of course, another side to the picture. Many companies that have extensive wife programs do not attempt social integration, and some not only look on the wife—to borrow one executive's explanation—as none of their damn business, but take active steps to see that she *doesn't* get close to them. A sampling of executive views—oil company: "We are just as happpy if we never see her at all." Tool company: "If wives get too close to management they always get too status-minded. That means trouble." Motor company: "Wives' activities are their own business. What do some of these companies want for their $10,000? Slavery too?"

In Praise of the Ornery Wife*

Having concluded the report, we find that some second thoughts are in order—one being a fleeting wish that we had never brought the subject up; too many wives read it.

But the news is out, and if it is even a half-way accurate representation of what is in store for the coming generation of management, it gives us the heebie jeebies. The picture that emerges, in brief, is that of a society in which the individualist, rugged or otherwise, seems to be out, definitely. What the modern corporation wants is "group integration"; to them, the "good" wife is the wife who subordinates her own character and her aspirations to the smooth functioning of the system; the wife, in short, who "adapts." And a small, but growing number of companies are taking active measures to bring the personal lives of their members within the corporation's domain.

This kind of thing is disturbing enough. But what is much more disturbing is the wife's reaction to it. For the fact is that the group-life is precisely what she seems to *like*. Getting along with people, she indicates—in a hundred different ways—has become more than mere expediency; it has become a dedicated purpose.

This devotion to group values is by no means peculiar to the corporation way of life; it shows there more, perhaps, but it does not stem from it. Some corporations, to be sure, have been giving it a powerful assist, but the basic forces behind "social integration" are far more universal. The wives who join the corporation come already equipped with an amenable philosophy. And in this, they are not only the reflector of the values of a whole generation, but the tutors of another, a preview perhaps, of what is to come.

By all indications, the philosophy they embrace is growing steadily in appeal. And if one word could define a philosophy, "adapt" would be it. Already, thanks in part to the growing impact of "social engineering" (a phenomenon FORTUNE will examine more closely in a future issue), "adapt" has been so well articulated and so intricately rationalized that its value as a guide to conduct is no longer questioned.

Which is just the trouble.

* Adapted and reprinted by permission of the author and publisher from *Fortune,* November, 1951.

The many virtues of adaptability, certainly, need no defense. But how much more are we to adapt? There is no ceiling in sight for the word. Indeed, it is becoming, in itself and without any qualification, an almost obsessive watchword. Whatever the circumstances, the good scout *adapts*. As The First Rule of "The Mental Hygiene Creed" (from the pamphlet, "The Doctor's Wife") typically enjoins: "I shall adapt to life, immediately, completely, and gracefully."

This is fatuous advice. "Adapt" is a meaningless word unless it is considered in relation to what one is supposed to be adapting to—and that tacit "life" needs lots of defining. To illustrate: there are a good many case histories at hand in which the husband has given up a job at a new post because his wife did not take to the community. Was she wrong? In the new lexicon of values, yes; as the obeisance paid "adapt" indicates, it is the environment that should be the constant; the individual, the variable. But might not she have been right after all? Some towns *are* stifling and backward, and one can adapt to them only by demeaning oneself. Should she, then, adapt? And if so, why?

Not only is the individual demeaned, but society as well. The status quo is institutionalized; the person who adapts can adapt only to something already existent. By extension, therefore, the advice implies that our creative capital is complete, and that we may live happily on the interest by merely refining and perfecting what we already have.

True, the very process of adapting may itself be dynamic. Many of our old notions of individual creativity are more sentimental than accurate; in "the well-adjusted group," as the social scientists have demonstrated, there is a total far above the sum of the individuals, and we have yet to exploit its full potential. With considerable persuasiveness, some go on to argue that the sheer working together by an increasingly group-minded people will furnish all the creative power society needs.

Just possibly, however, they may be wrong. We will go part way with their thesis; it is undeniably true that you don't have to be an s.o.b. to be creative. It is equally true, however, that a real advance in any field inevitably involves a conflict with the environment. And unless people temper their worship of environment, they may well evolve a society so well adjusted that no one would be able—or willing—to give it the sort of hotfoot it regularly needs. We would all be too busy participating and lubricating and integrating and communicating.

Several months ago a top official of one of the most group-integrating of corporations fell to musing over the death of a fellow official and his wife. It made him think a bit, he told one of his associates, of the drift of the company's personnel policy. "You know, they were terrifically stimulating people," he said. "They were the last *characters* I ever knew."

"I wonder," he added, thoughtfully, "whether we'll ever get any more."

It's not a trivial question.

CULTURAL CONTRADICTIONS AND SEX ROLES*

Mirra Komarovsky

Profound changes in the roles of women during the past century have been accompanied by innumerable contradictions and inconsistencies. With our rapidly changing and highly differentiated culture, with migrations and multiplied social contacts, the stage is set for myriads of combinations of incongruous elements. Cultural norms are often functionally unsuited to the social situations to which they apply. Thus, they may deter an individual from a course of action which would serve his own, and society's, interests best. Or, if behavior contrary to the norm is engaged in, the individual may suffer from guilt over violating mores which no longer serve any socially useful end. Sometimes culturally defined roles are adhered to in the face of new conditions without a conscious realization of the discrepancies involved. The reciprocal actions dictated by the roles may be at variance with those demanded by the actual situation. This may result in an imbalance of privileges and obligations[1] or in some frustration of basic interests.

Again, problems arise because changes in the mode of life have created new situations which have not as yet been defined by culture. Individuals left thus without social guidance tend to act in terms of

* Adapted and reprinted by permission of the author and editor from *The American Journal of Sociology*, 52 (1946), 184-89. This is one of the few sociological studies which has been repeated. See Paul Wallin, "Cultural Contradictions and Sex Roles: A Repeat Study," *American Sociological Review*, 15 (1950), 283-93.—*Eds.*

[1] Clifford Kirkpatrick, "The Measurement of Ethical Inconsistency in Marriage," *International Journal of Ethics*, XLVI (1936), 444-60.

egotistic or "short-run hedonistic" motives which at times defeat their own long-term interests or create conflict with others. The precise obligation of a gainfully employed wife toward the support of the family is one such undefined situation.

Finally, a third mode of discrepancy arises in the existence of incompatible cultural definitions of the same social situation, such as the clash of "old-fashioned" and "radical" mores, of religion and law, of norms of economic and familial institutions.

The problems raised by these discrepancies are social problems in the sense that they engender mental conflict or social conflict or otherwise frustrate some basic interest of large segments of the population.

This article sets forth in detail the nature of certain incompatible sex roles imposed by our society upon the college woman. It is based on data collected in 1942 and 1943. Members of an undergraduate course on the family were asked for two successive years to submit autobiographical documents focused on the topic; 73 were collected. In addition, 80 interviews, lasting about an hour each, were conducted with every member of a course in social psychology of the same institution— making a total of 154 documents ranging from a minimum of five to a maximum of thirty typewritten pages.

The generalization emerging from these documents is the existence of serious contradictions between two roles present in the social environment of the college woman. The goals set by each role are mutually exclusive, and the fundamental personality traits each evokes are at points diametrically opposed, so that what are assets for one become liabilities for the other, and the full realization of one role threatens defeat in the other.

One of these roles may be termed the "feminine" role. While there are a number of permissive variants of the feminine role for women of college age (the "good sport," the "glamour girl," the "young lady," the domestic "home girl," etc.), they have a common core of attributes defining the proper attitudes to men, family, work, love, etc., and a set of personality traits often described with reference to the male sex role as "not as dominant, or aggressive as men" or "more emotional, sympathetic."

The other and more recent role is, in a sense, no *sex* role at all, because it partly obliterates the differentiation in sex. It demands of the woman much the same virtues, patterns of behavior, and attitude that it does of the men of a corresponding age. We shall refer to this as the "modern" role.

Both roles are present in the social environment of these women throughout their lives, though, as the precise content of each sex role varies with age, so does the nature of their clashes change from one stage to another. In the period under discussion the conflict between the two roles apparently centers about academic work, social life, vocational plans, excellence in specific fields of endeavor, and a number of personality traits.

One manifestation of the problem is in the inconsistency of the goals set for the girl by her family.

Forty, or 26 per cent, of the respondents expressed some grievance against their families for failure to confront them with clear-cut and consistent goals. The majority, 74 per cent, denied having had such experiences. One student writes:

How am I to pursue any course single-mindedly when some way along the line a person I respect is sure to say, "You are on the wrong track and are wasting your time." Uncle John telephones every Sunday morning. His first question is: "Did you go out last night?" He would think me a 'grind' if I were to stay home Saturday night to finish a term paper. My father expects me to get an "A" in every subject and is disappointed by a 'B." He says I have plenty of time for social life. Mother says, "That 'A' in Philosophy is very nice dear. But please don't become so deep that no man will be good enough for you." And, finally, Aunt Mary's line is careers for women. "Prepare yourself for some profession. This is the only way to insure yourself independence and an interesting life. You have plenty of time to marry." . . .

A student reminisces:

All through high school my family urged me to work hard because they wished me to enter a first-rate college. At the same time they were always raving about a girl schoolmate who lived next door to us. How pretty and sweet she was, how popular, and what taste in clothes! Couldn't I also pay more attention to my appearance and to social life? They were overlooking the fact that this carefree friend of mine had little time left for school work and had failed several subjects. It seemed that my family had expected me to become Eve Curie and Hedy Lamar wrapped up in one.

Another comments:

My mother thinks that it is very nice to be smart in college but only if it doesn't take too much effort. She always tell me not to be too intellectual on dates, to be clever in a light sort of way. My father, on the other hand, wants me to study law. He thinks that if I applied myself I could make an excellent lawyer and keeps telling me that I am better fitted for this profession than my brother.

Another writes:

One of my two brothers writes: "Cover up that high forehead and act a little dumb once in a while"; while the other always urges upon me the importance of rigorous scholarship.

The students testified to a certain bewilderment and confusion caused by the failure on the part of the family to smooth the passage from one role to another, especially when the roles involved were contradictory. It seemed to some of them that they had awakened one morning to find their world upside down: what had hitherto evoked praise and rewards from relatives, now suddenly aroused censure. A student recollects:

I could match my older brother in skating, sledding, riflery, ball, and many of the other games we played. He enjoyed teaching me and took great pride in my accomplishments. Then one day it all changed. He must have suddenly become conscious of the fact that girls ought to be feminine. I was walking with him, proud to be able to make long strides and keep up with his long-legged steps when he turned to me in annoyance, "Can't you walk like a lady?" I still remember feeling hurt and bewildered by his scorn, when I had been led to expect approval. . . .

The final excerpt illustrates both the sudden transition of roles and the ambiguity of standards:

I major in English composition. This is not a completely "approved" field for girls so I usually just say "English." An English Literature major is quite liked and approved by boys. Somehow it is lumped with all the other arts and even has a little glamour. But a composition major is a girl to beware of because she supposedly will notice all your grammar mistakes, look at your letters too critically, and consider your ordinary speech and conversation as too crude.

I also work for a big metropolitan daily as a correspondent in the city room. I am well liked there and may possibly stay as a reporter after graduation in February. I have had several spreads [stories running to more than eight or ten inches of space], and this is considered pretty good for a college correspondent. Naturally, I was elated and pleased at such breaks, and as far as the city room is concerned I'm off to a very good start on a career that is hard for a man to achieve and even harder for a woman. General reporting is still a man's work in the opinion of most people. I have a lot of acclaim but also criticism, and I find it confusing and difficult to be praised for being clever and working hard and then, when my efforts promise to be successful, to be condemned and criticized for being unfeminine and ambitious.

Here are a few of these reactions:

My father: "I don't like this newspaper setup at all. The people you meet are making you less interested in marriage than ever. You're getting too educated and intellectual to be attractive to men."

My mother: "I don't like your attitude toward people. The paper is making you too analytical and calculating. Above all, you shouldn't sacrifice your education and career for marriage."

A lieutenant with two years of college: "It pleased me greatly to hear about your news assignment—good girl."

A Navy pilot with one year of college: "Undoubtedly, I'm old-fashioned, but I could never expect or feel right about a girl giving up a very promising or interesting future to hang around waiting for me to finish college. Nevertheless, congratulations on your job on the paper. Where in the world do you get that wonderful energy? Anyway I know you were thrilled at getting it and feel very glad for you. I've an idea that it means the same to you as that letter saying 'report for active duty' meant to me."

A graduate metallurgist now a private in the Army: "It was good to hear that you got that break with the paper. I am sure that talent will prove itself and that you will go far. But not too far, as I don't think you should become a career woman. You'll get repressed and not be interested enough in having fun if you keep after that career."

A lieutenant with a year and a half of college: "All this career business is nonsense. A woman belongs in the home and absolutely no place else. My wife will have to stay home. That should keep her happy. Men are just superior in everything, and women have no right to expect to compete with them. They should do just what will keep their husbands happy."

A graduate engineer—my fiancé: "Go right ahead and get as far as you can in your field. I am glad you are ambitious and clever, and I'm as anxious to see you happily successful as I am myself. It is a shame to let all those brains go to waste over just dusting and washing dishes. I think the usual home life and children are small sacrifices to make if a career will keep you happy. But I'd rather see you in radio because I am a bit wary of the effect upon our marriage of the way of life you will have around the newspaper."

Sixty-one, or 40 per cent, of the students indicated that they have occasionally "played dumb" on dates, that is, concealed some academic honor, pretended ignorance of some subject, or allowed the man the last word in an intellectual discussion. Among these were women who "threw games" and in general played down certain skills in obedience to the unwritten law that men must possess these skills to a superior degree. At the same time, in other areas of life, social pressures were being exerted upon these women to "play to win," to compete to the utmost of their abilities for intellectual distinction and academic honors. One student writes:

I was glad to transfer to a women's college. The two years at the co-ed university produced a constant strain. I am a good student; my family expects me to get good marks. At the same time I am normal enough to want to be invited to the Saturday night dance. Well, everyone knew that on that campus a reputation of a "brain" killed a girl socially. I was always fearful lest I say too much in class or answer a question which the boys I dated couldn't answer.

Here are some significant remarks made from the interviews:

When a girl asks me what marks I got last semester I answer, "Not so good—only one 'A'." When a boy asks the same question, I say very brightly with a note of surprise, "Imagine, I got an 'A'!"

I am engaged to a southern boy who doesn't think too much of the woman's intellect. In spite of myself, I play up to his theories because the less one knows and does, the more he does for you and thinks you "cute" into the bargain. . . . I allow him to explain things to me in great detail and to treat me as a child in financial matters.

One of the nicest techniques is to spell long words incorrectly once in a while. My boyfriend seems to get a great kick out of it and writes back, "Honey, you certainly don't know how to spell."

When my date said that he considers Ravel's *Bolero* the greatest piece of music ever written, I changed the subject because I knew I would talk down to him.

A boy advised me not to tell of my proficiency in math and not to talk of my plans to study medicine unless I knew my date well.

My fiancé didn't go to college. I intend to finish college and work hard at it, but in talking to him I make college appear a kind of a game. . . .

It embarrassed me that my "steady" in high school got worse marks than I. A boy should naturally do better in school. I would never tell him my marks and would often ask him to help me with my homework.

Mother used to tell me to lay off the brains on dates because glasses make me look too intellectual anyhow. . . .

How to do the job and remain popular was a tough task. If you worked your best, the boys resented the competition; if you acted feminine, they complained that you were clumsy. . . .

On dates I always go through the "I-don't-care-anything-you-want-to-do" routine. It gets monotonous but boys fear girls who make decisions. They think such girls would make nagging wives.

I am a natural leader and, when in the company of girls, usually take the lead. That is why I am so active in college activities. But I know that men fear bossy women, and I always have to watch myself on dates not to assume the "executive" role. Once a boy walking to the theater with me took the wrong street. I knew a short cut but kept quiet.

I let my fiancé make most of the decisions when we are out. It annoys me, but he prefers it.

I sometimes "play dumb" on dates, but it leaves a bad taste. The emotions are complicated. Part of me enjoys "putting something over" on the unsuspecting male. But this sense of superiority over him is mixed with feeling of guilt for my hypocrisy. Toward the "date" I feel some contempt because he is "taken in" by my technique, or if I like the boy, a kind of a maternal condescension. At times I resent him! Why isn't he my superior in all ways in which a man should excel so that I could be my natural self? What am I doing here with him, anyhow? Slumming?

And the funny part of it is that the man, I think, is not always so unsuspecting. He may sense the truth and become uneasy in the relation. 'Where do I stand? Is she laughing up her sleeve or did she mean this praise? Was she really impressed with that little speech of mine or did she only pretend to know nothing about politics?" And once or twice I felt that the joke was on me: the boy saw through my wiles and felt contempt for me for stooping to such tricks.

Another aspect of the problem is the conflict between the psycho-genetic personality of the girl and the cultural role foisted upon her by the milieu.[2] At times it is the girl with "masculine" interests and personality traits who chafes under the pressure to conform to the "feminine" pattern. At other times it is the family and the college who thrusts upon the reluctant girl the "modern" role.

While, historically, the "modern" role is the most recent one, onto-genetically it is the one emphasized earlier in the education of the college girl, if these 153 documents are representative. Society confronts the girl with powerful challenges and strong pressure to excel in certain

[2] Margaret Mead, *Sex and Temperament in Three Primitive Societies,* New York, Morrow & Co., 1935.

competitive lines of endeavor and to develop certain techniques of adaptations very similar to those expected of her brothers. But, then, quite suddenly as it appears to these girls, the very success in meeting these challenges begins to cause anxiety. It is precisely those most successful in the earlier role who are now penalized.

It is not only the passage from age to age but the moving to another region or type of campus which may create for the girl similar problems. The precise content of sex roles, or, to put it in another way, the degree of their differentiation, varies with regional class, nativity, and other subcultures.

Whenever individuals show differences in response to some social situation, as have our 153 respondents, the question naturally arises as to the causes. It will be remembered that 40 per cent admitted some difficulties in personal relations with men due to conflicting sex roles but that 60 per cent said that they had no such problems. Inconsistency of parental expectations troubled 26 per cent of the students.

To account for individual differences would require another study, involving a classification of personalities in relation to the peculiar social environments of each. Generally speaking, it would seem that it is the girl with a "middle-of-the-road personality" who is most happily adjusted to the present historical moment. She is not a perfect incarnation of either role but is flexible enough to play both. She is a girl who is intelligent enough to do well in school but not so brilliant as to "get all 'A's'"; informed and alert but not consumed by an intellectual passion; capable but not talented in areas relatively new to women; able to stand on her own feet and to earn a living but not so good a living as to compete with men; capable of doing some job well (in case she does not marry or, otherwise, has to work) but not so identified with a profession as to need it for her happiness.

A search for less immediate causes of individual reactions would lead us further back to the study of genesis of the personality differences found relevant to the problem. One of the clues will certainly be provided by the relation of the child to the parent of the same and of the opposite sex. This relation affects the conception of self and the inclination for a particular sex role.

The problems set forth in this article will persist, in the opinion of the writer, until the adult sex roles of women are redefined in greater harmony with the socioeconomic and ideological character of mode n society.[3] Until then neither the formal education nor the unverbalized sex roles of the adolescent woman can be cleared of intrinsic contradictions.

THE PROBLEM OF PANTS*

A challenging letter answered an editorial attack on coeds for wearing slacks. The female of the species had this to say:

"Before entering college we had great expectations concerning the college man. Needless to say we were gravely disappointed.

"What has happened to the rugged, outdoor man? He is no longer rugged. He eats soft food, sleeps too much, and considers the slightest physical exertion too much for him. He is never outdoors, his social life being centered around the parlor.

"An energetic game of chess or a snappy bull session is all the exercise he gets. . . . One glance at his apparel would make you doubt whether he is even a man.

"Masculine individuality has become a mirage. It seems that everything he does is inspired by the group to which he belongs. His aim in life is determined by what others have decided to be worthwhile goals. He no longer has the power to think and decide for himself.

"As an example, when he is on a date, the girl must be prepared to decide what movie they will see, what they will do afterwards, and she must even plan to spend the evening entertaining the man who has lost the power to take an active part in conversation.

". . . You denounced us girls for wearing slacks and jeans, etc. We would be only too glad to give them back to you, if you'd begin to earn your pants."

[3] See excellent discussions in Talcott Parsons, "Age and Sex in the Social Structure of the United States," *American Sociological Review*, VII (1942), 604-16, and in the same issue, Ralph Linton, "Age and Sex Categories," pp. 589-603, and Leonard S. Cottrell, Jr., "The Adjustment of the Individual to His Age and Sex Roles," pp. 617-20.

* Adapted and reprinted by permission of the editors from *The Daily Northwestern*, Exchange Section, May 9, 1952. Taken from the *Syracuse Daily Orange*.

CHAPTER 11

The Aged: Social Characteristics and the Problem of Support

ONE OF THE COROLLARIES of old age is dependence—financial, emotional, and physical. The core of the material in this chapter concerns financial dependence. The Federal Security Agency informs us that the aged are with us in ever-increasing numbers, that in 1950 70 percent of all women 65 years of age and older did not live with a spouse and that 59 percent of the aged male population is not employed. These data suggest that a considerable proportion of the aged population is financially dependent.

Dinkel implies that as the population becomes more urban and secular, adult sons and daughters become more reluctant to support their parents. It appears, therefore, that as the aged become a larger part of the population, their children are becoming increasingly reluctant to support them. Figure 7 of the F.S.A. article indicates one solution to this apparent dilemma. In 1951 almost seven out of every eight persons in the labor force were covered by some program of old-age benefits. These data indicate another case where a function previously fulfilled by the family is being taken over by another agency.

SOME STATISTICS CONCERNING OUR AGING POPULATION*

Number of Older Persons

Since 1900, the population of the United States has doubled, but the number of persons 45 to 64 years has tripled, while the number 65 years and older has quadrupled. There are now (early 1952) 13 million men and women 65 years of age and over. This number is increasing currently at the rate of about 400,000 a year.

Between 1940 and 1950 the country's population 65 years and over went up 36 percent. In California and Nevada the increase was 60 percent or more, in Arizona and Florida 80 per cent or more.

One in every 12 persons in the country is 65 years and over. This ratio varies in the States from about 1 in 19 in South Carolina to 1 in 9 in New Hampshire.

Women outnumber men 10 to 9 in the 65 and over age group. More than half of the women in this age class are widows. The majority of the men 65 years and over are still married, on the other hand.

Living Arrangements

Of the 13 million persons 65 years and over in the United States at the end of 1951:

Nine million, or 7 in 10, lived in their own households, of whom all but nearly 2 million had a wife, husband or some other relative living with them.

About 2¾ million others, or about 2 in 10, were living in the homes of relatives; 3 out of 4 in this group were women.

A little over half a million were roomers or boarders in families not related to them.

A little over 700,000 were living in institutions, hotels or large rooming houses.

* Adapted and reprinted from Federal Security Agency, Committee on Aging and Geriatrics, *Fact Book on Aging*, Washington, D.C., United States Government Printing Office, 1952.

Financial Status

Government estimates of what it cost an elderly couple to maintain a "modest but adequate" level of living in an urban area in October 1950 ranged from $1,602 a year in New Orleans to $1,908 in Milwaukee.

In 1950, 43 percent of the families headed by a person 65 years of age or over had a cash income of less than $1,500. Thirty percent had under $1,000. Fifteen percent had less than $500.

In the same year, more than three-fourths of all persons 65 years and over living alone or with nonrelatives had a cash income of less than $1,000. Nearly 40 percent had less than $500.

At the end of 1951, less than 1 in every 3 persons 65 years and over was receiving income from employment either as an earner or the wife of an earner. About 1 in 4 was in receipt of old-age and survivors insurance benefits; another 8 percent were getting benefits from the special retirement systems for railroad and government workers or from the veterans' program. One person in every 5 was on old-age assistance. Between 2 and 3 in every 10 aged persons were living solely on other types of income (investments, commercial annuities, industrial pensions, etc.) or were being supported completely by relatives.

Nearly 2 out of 3 families with a head 65 years and over own their own homes as against a little over half in the general population. Total indebtedness, including mortgage, tends to be smaller in families with an aged head, while total assets and net worth tend to be larger.

Employment

The proportion of men 65 years and over in the labor force declined from 68 percent in 1890 to 41 percent in 1952. Few changes have taken place, on the other hand, in the relative number of men 45-64 years in the labor force, while the labor force participation rates of older women have gone up.

Coupled with a parallel increase in longevity, the drop in work opportunities for older workers has made for a larger span of years in retirement. Between 1900 and 1940 the expected years in retirement for a man of 40 increased from 3 to 6 years.

In March 1952, nearly 3 million men and women 65 years and over were working. Forty percent were self-employed, of whom one-half were farm owners.

Health

Life expectancy at birth increased from 49 to 68 years between 1901 and 1949. The biggest improvement has occurred in the early years of life and becomes progressively smaller in the later years.

On a given day, 14 in every 100 persons 65 years and over are unable to perform their regular duties because of disability, as compared with 5 per 100 in the general population.

The leading causes of death in the later years are heart disease, cancer, cerebral hemorrhages and arteriosclerosis.

Most elderly persons cannot finance adequate medical care without outside help. In 1950 only 1 out of 4 had hospitalization insurance.

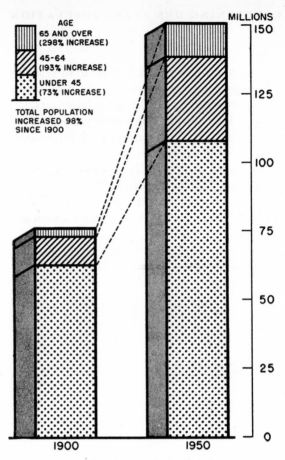

Figure 1. Our population is aging.

Source: Bureau of the Census, 16th Census of the United States, *Population,* Vol. II, Part 1, Table 8; *1950 Census of Population, Advance Reports,* Series PC-9, No. 1; un-published data. Figures on the number of persons 45 to 64 years and 65 years of age and over for 1950 are preliminary and subject to correction.

In 1900 the proportion of men and women 65 years of age and over in our total population was 1 in 25. Today it is around 1 in 12, and steadily increasing.

Equally significant is the increasing proportion of persons in middle age. In 1900, 1 person in 7 was 45 to 64 years of age. Today the ratio is 1 in 5.

The big increase in the relative number of older persons is the result largely of gains in the control of infectious diseases, other advances in the fields of prevention and medical care and of the general rise in the standard of living. Fewer people die in childhood or their early adult years; more live to reach their 60's and 70's.

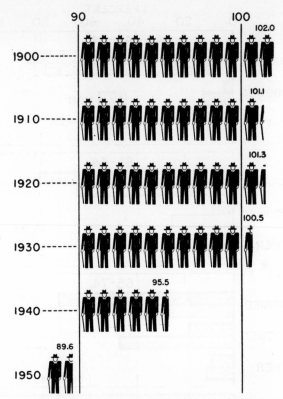

Figure 2. Aged women outnumber aged men.

Men per 100 Women (65 and over)

Source: Bureau of the Census, 16th Census of the United States, *Population*, Vol. II, Part 1, Table 8; *1950 Census of Population, Advance Reports*, Series PC-9, No. 1; unpublished data. Figures on the number of persons 45 to 64 years and 65 years of age and over for 1950 are preliminary and subject to correction.

The observation that women are tougher than men seems to be borne out by the facts. In 1950 there were 90 men 65 years of age and over in the country for every 100 women in those ages. Fifty years earlier the advantage in numbers among older persons ran the other way—102 men for every 100 women. The trend toward more older women than men is the result primarily of a more rapid decline in female than in male mortality. More boy babies are born than girl babies, but since in every age class the male death rate is higher than the female death rate, the male superiority in numbers, in a given generation, doesn't last very long.

The fact that until 1930 there were more aged men than women is attributable in part to the relatively large number of men among the immigrants who came to this country in the heavy immigration of the decades prior to World War I.

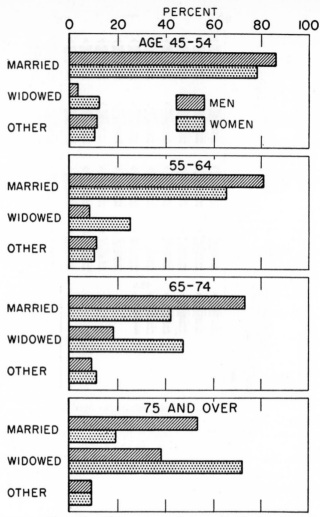

Figure 3. Changes in marital status with age.
Percent of Men and Women 45 and over, 1947.

Source: Bureau of the Census, *Current Population Reports, Population Characteristics* Series P-20, No. 10, Table 1.

The typical older man is married, the typical older woman is a widow. Because women have a lower mortality rate than men, age for age, and tend to marry men older than themselves, relatively more women than men lose a spouse through death. Remarriage following death of spouse is more frequent among men than among women. By the time they reach 70, more than half of all women are widows. At 70 almost 3 in 4 men are still married. It is not until they are 85 years or so that a majority of men are widowers.

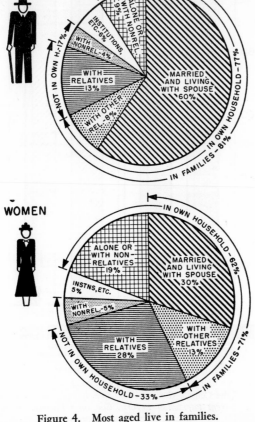

MEN

INSTITUTIONS, ETC.-6%
ALONE OR WITH NONREL.-9%
WITH NONREL.-4%
NOT IN OWN H.-17%
WITH RELATIVES 13%
WITH OTHER REL.-8%
MARRIED AND LIVING WITH SPOUSE 60%
IN OWN HOUSEHOLD-77%
IN FAMILIES-81%

WOMEN

IN OWN HOUSEHOLD-62%
ALONE OR WITH NON-RELATIVES 19%
MARRIED AND LIVING WITH SPOUSE 30%
INSTNS, ETC. 5%
WITH NONREL.-5%
WITH OTHER RELATIVES 13%
WITH RELATIVES 28%
NOT IN OWN HOUSEHOLD-33%
IN FAMILIES-71%

Figure 4. Most aged live in families.

Household Relationships of Men and Women 65 and over, 1950.

Source: Estimated by Social Security Administration from unpublished data of the Bureau of the Census.

Most older persons live in families; relatively few live alone; very few live in institutions.

In 1950 almost 7 in 10 persons 65 years of age and over maintained households of their own. Such persons typically had a spouse or other relative living with them. Most of those who didn't have a household of their own were living in the homes of relatives.

Altogether a little less than one-fourth of the persons past 65 years were not living in a family setting. This group included about 14 percent with households of their own but no relative present, 4 percent living as roomers or boarders with nonrelatives, and 6 percent in hotels, large rooming houses, and institutions.

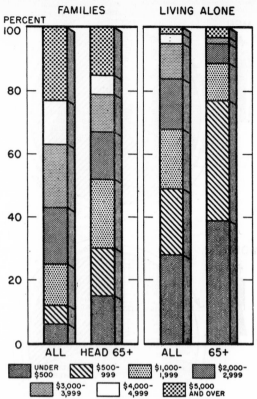

Figure 5. Aged have low incomes.
Income of Families and of Persons Living Alone, 1950.
Source: Bureau of the Census, *Current Population Reports, Consumer Income,* Series P-60, No. 9, and *Current Population Reports, Consumer Income,* Series P-60, No. 9.

Families with an aged head are by and large low-income families. If he is still working, the family head is past his peak earning period. If he is retired, his retirement income tends to be low. A relatively large number of families with an aged head are dependent on old-age assistance.

In 1950 half the families with a head 65 years or over had a cash income below $2,000. Three in every 10 families with an aged head had less than $1,000 in income. In that year the Bureau of Labor Statistics estimated that an aged retired couple living in a city would need from $1,600 to $1,900, depending upon the city of residence, to maintain an adequate level of living.

Older persons living alone tend to have smaller incomes than families with an older head. In 1950 half the persons aged 65 and over living alone or with nonrelatives had cash incomes below $650.

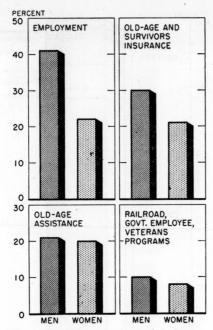

Figure 6. Where aged get their income.
Percent of Persons 65 and over, December 1951.
Source: Estimated by Social Security Administration from Bureau of the Census data and reports of agencies administering social insurance and related programs and old-age assistance. Estimates are preliminary.

In December 1951 three in every 10 persons 65 years and over were in receipt of earnings either as earners or the wives of earners. Old-age and survivors insurance benefits were going to 25 percent, while 21 percent, including some insurance beneficiaries, were on old-age assistance. About 8 percent were benefiting from the special programs for retired railroad and government workers and for veterans. Perhaps 5 or 6 percent were receiving payments under private insurance and annuity contracts, and 3 percent under private retirement plans. Income from investments, and contributions from children and other relatives constituted sources of income for an unknown number of aged. A large group, primarily widowed women, had no cash income at all, and were living with and being supported by children and other relatives.

The importance of these sources of income varied with age and size of income. By and large, persons past 75 years were more dependent upon social insurance benefits, annuities, public assistance and contributions from relatives, than persons in their late 60's or early 70's, more of whom depended on earnings. Earners tended to have higher incomes than retired persons with benefit or assistance income.

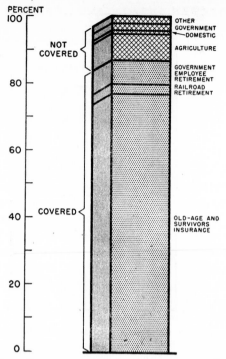

Figure 7. Most workers have old-age protection.
Coverage Status of Civilian Workers Under Public Programs, December 1951.
Source: Estimated by Social Security Administration from Census Bureau's *Monthly Report on the Labor Force.*

About 7 out of 8 of the 60 million persons in paid civilian employment in the United States in December 1951 had coverage under a public program providing old-age benefits.

A little over 3 out of 4 were under old-age and survivors insurance. About 10 percent were under the special programs for railroad and government workers.

Eight million paid workers, or 1 in every 8, had no coverage under these programs. Nearly 5 million were farmers or irregularly employed farm wage workers not covered by OASI; another million worked for State and local governments with no retirement system, and still another million were irregularly employed domestic workers.

Around 10 million workers had jobs in concerns with private pension plans. Almost all were also covered by OASI or railroad retirement. Since nearly all private pension plans require from 10 to 25 years' service for benefits, it is difficult to say how many of these workers, in a mobile labor market, will draw benefits at the time of their retirement.

ATTITUDES OF CHILDREN TOWARD SUPPORTING AGED PARENTS*

Robert M. Dinkel

Introduction

How satisfactory it may be for aged parents to live with their children[1] depends in part upon the attitude of the younger generation toward their responsibility for the care of their elders.[2] Children who did not want to accept the obligation, but who did so anyway, because of family tradition, community opinion, or legal requirement might carry out the role with such little grace or with such manifest ill will as to make the parents aware of not being wanted or as to lead to friction and major conflicts.[3]

The attitude of children toward taking care of aged parents also has implications for the law of support, for its administration, for public housing for old people, and for the medical care of mentally deficient or bedridden cases. These implications are particularly noteworthy if the assumption is made that there should be or eventually will be a definite relation between what the children want and what the law or its administration requires. If children do not believe they should extend home support to their aged parents, then, the question of what substitutes the State should provide becomes pertinent.

Two general hypotheses have been advanced: (1) Catholics and Protestants, urban and rural residents, males and females, college and high-school students, and persons of various ages differ significantly

* Adapted and reprinted by permission of the author and publisher from the *American Sociological Review*, 9 (1944), 370-79.

[1] Children of aged parents include persons of adult status.

[2] For the purpose of this study, persons 65 years of age and over are considered aged. References in this study to parents usually are intended to be limited to aged parents who are in need of assistance. It is estimated that about 30 to 40 percent of aged parents are supported wholly or in part by their children. Usually, support is in the form of the parent or parents living in the home of a child.

[3] This statement is one of the important assumptions of this study. It provides a justification of a study of verbal responses apart from whether or not children are consistent in what they say should be done and what they actually do when faced with the problem.

in their attitude with regard to the responsibility of children, and (2) the attitude of children toward giving an aged parent a home varies with the degree of physical or psychological hardship that they would experience in the situation.

The Opinionaire

Construction. A hybrid instrument was devised by combining several features of the Likert and Thurstone methods. One hundred and sixty items were rated on a five-point scale from "very favorable" to "very unfavorable" by 14 social workers. Only those statements were retained that 10 or more of the judges had put in the same scale position. Sixty-six propositions passed this test. They were given weights from plus two to minus two according to the category in which they had been classified by the judges.

Two preliminary forms with 20 items each were chosen from the 66 propositions. These two forms were so constructed that for every statement of a certain weight and subject matter in one there was a statement of the same weight and subject matter in the other.

They were given to 440 college students, using the Likert method of response. The first of the two forms was also given a second time with the instruction to answer by merely checking those statements with which there was agreement. The score for this type of response was the sum of the algebraic weights of the items that were checked.

Thirty of the 40 statements were found to have satisfactory discriminative value when tested by the Likert criterion. The two different methods of response correlated plus .86. This Pearsonian coefficient, based as it is on a small number of items, was considered sufficiently high to validate the simple-agreement type of response.

From the 30 statements of desired discriminative value, 20 were selected for the final form of the instrument. They were picked to give as well balanced an opinionaire as possible. Although the procedures used resulted in some tautology, there might be an appearance of greater duplication than is actually the case since the same subject matter may be found in positive and negative form and in both single and double weight.

Reliability. The instrument was given twice to a group of 90 students in sociology at the University of Minnesota. The second administration came three weeks after the first. Anonymity was assured by having the students use numbers known only to themselves instead of names on their opinionaires. The Pearsonian coefficient on test and retest was plus .874.

Validity. Validity has been largely assumed instead of proved. There are three main questions for which some answer would be desirable: (1) Do students have sufficient direct or indirect experience with the problem to have well-developed attitudes? (2) Does the opinionaire evoke the true opinions of the students? and (3) Do test scores assist one in predicting the degree of adjustment between the two generations when aged parents are taken into the home of one of the children?

Some fragmentary data were obtained on these questions. A group of 86 students in a beginning sociology class at the University of Minnesota were asked to write an essay on the subject of children supporting aged parents, citing whatever examples they could of their point-of-view. In 72 of the cases, the material was judged by the writer to be substantial and concrete, indicating sufficient background for the students to have a meaningful opinion on the problem. The essays were classified in five groups, depending on the degree of belief in the responsibility of children. An analysis of the variance of test scores was then made. A probability of less than .001 was obtained that the distribution was due to chance factors. Finally, in a case-history study of 50 families, the writer observed some relation between test scores on the opinionaire and conflicts between parents and children.[4]

It should be noted that the scope of validity has not been extended to include a relation between test scores and support behavior; that is, between opinon and practice. The case histories of the 50 families indicated that there is not a high correlation between the two.

Description of the Sample

The sample was composed of 1,006 college and 318 high-school students. The college students were in attendance during the academic year 1939-1940 at the colleges of St. Thomas and St. Catherine and at the Universities of Wisconsin, Minnesota, and Notre Dame. The high-school group consisted of rural boys from many sections of the state of Minnesota who happened to be members in the summer of 1939 of the annual Farm Camp of the Y.M.C.A. and of seniors of the 1939-

[4] For an analysis of these conflicts, see Robert M. Dinkel, "Parent-Child Conflict in Minnesota Families," *American Sociological Review*, August, 1943, pp. 412-19.

1940 class of University High School of Minneapolis and of Jackson High School, Jackson, Minnesota.

About 200 of the college sample were students who attended summer classes in 1939 at the Universities of Wisconsin and Minnesota. These persons were considerably older than the others, ranging in age from 22 to 45 years. The other college students were from 16 to 22 years, with an average age of a little more than 19 years. The high-school students were between 16 and 19 years, with an average of 17 years.

In the college group there was an approximately equal number of Catholics and Protestants: also included were 24 persons of the Jewish faith and 50 persons who stated that they had no religion. The high-school students were predominantly Protestant; there being five of such affiliation to every Catholic.

The sex distribution was well balanced for the sample as a whole. Among the rural residents, however, there were two females to every male in the college group and just the reverse ratio in the high-school group.

Group Differences

One of the hypotheses is that Catholics and Protestants, urban and rural residents, males and females, college and high-school students, and persons of various ages differ significantly in their attitude toward the responsibility of children for the support of aged parents. The influence of these factors upon the opinion of students was determined by comparing average scores. Four factors were held constant while ascertaining the influence of the fifth by the method of sub-grouping. For example, the score of 17-year-old Protestant males in their senior year of high school who had lived all of their life in rural territory was compared with that of 17-year-old Protestant females in their senior year of high school who had also lived all of their life in rural territory in order to determine in part the influence of sex upon student opinion.[5]

Religious Affiliation. Jewish, Catholic, and Protestant families are commonly supposed to differ in their degree of solidarity, traditionalism, authoritarianism, and related characteristics. These traits are probably correlated with opinion regarding family responsibility. Support of aged parents is, in fact, a form of family solidarity. That parents should be respected and assisted when in need is a provision of the

[5] Only some of the comparisons made have been selected for presentation in table form in the following pages.

traditional code of Christianity and Judaism. Finally, the more authoritarian the family system, the more the elders or patriarchs would be respected and provided for in case of need. Therefore, some association between religious affiliation and opinion regarding the obligation of children to give support is a reasonable hypothesis.

The order according to test score of the religious groups of the sample was Catholics, Jews, Protestants, and persons who professed having no religion. Catholics adhered most strongly and the persons of no religion the least to the belief that children should give support. The expected order was broken by the fact that the Jews instead of having the most favorable opinion toward the obligation of children had an average score between that of the Catholics and Protestants.

Table 1. Opinionaire Scores and Critical Ratios for Catholic and Protestant College Students According to Sex and Residence[6]

Sub-Group	NUMBER		AVERAGE SCORE*		Difference between averages	Critical ratio†
	Cath.	Prot.	Cath.	Prot.		
Male—urban	214	77	5.06	1.01	4.05	4.8
Female—urban	114	137	6.38	− .93	7.31	9.3
Male—rural	32	26	7.09	3.69	3.40	2.1
Female—rural	40	78	7.33	1.44	5.89	4.2

* The opinionaire has a theoretical range of 31 points, from minus 15 to plus 16.
† For a discussion and interpretation of the critical ratio, see Editors' Introduction, pp. 11-12 above.—*Eds.*

Differences between Catholic and Protestant college students in the extent of their acceptance of the individual statements of the opinionaire were large, averaging 17 percent and having a standard deviation of less than 3 percent. Differences between these two groups in average score (the algebraic sum of the weights of the statements agreed with) were tested by the standard error of the mean to determine their significance. Critical ratios for the four sex-residence sub-groups shown in Table 1 range between 2.1 and 9.3 with only one being less than 4.0. Clearly, these ratios indicate differences that are not due to chance.

An analysis of the Catholic sample showed gradations of opinion among the students of different institutions that attest further to the

6 Results for the high-school students have not been presented, because the number of Catholics in this part of the sample is very small. It should be noted, nevertheless, that the Catholic and Protestant high-school students differ in average score by only two and a half points.

existence of a definite association between religion and opinion. Women students at St. Catherine had a higher average score than the men at Notre Dame and St. Thomas. The Catholics in attendance at Minnesota and Wisconsin universities had an average score that was intermediate between that of the other Catholics and that of the Protestants at these two schools. That the students of St. Catherine should believe most strongly in the responsibility of children is believed to result from its imposing strict discipline and having the most rigid indoctrination of Catholic principles. That the Catholics at the state universities should have the lowest average score for persons of this faith follows from the secular character of these schools. In their cases, there is probably operating both a selective process that tends to attract Catholic students of weak religious belief in greater proportion than those of strong belief and a training process that modifies their original attitudes.

Residence. One of the widely used source books in the field of rural sociology states that the rural family is more integrated and has greater solidarity than the urban family. According to the authors, the bonds which hold the rural family together are quantitatively more numerous and qualitatively more intense than those holding the urban family together. From these and other distinctions that are drawn, the reader would infer that rural persons believe to a much greater degree than urban people that children should support aged and needy parents.[7]

In testing this hypothesis, residence was classified as rural or urban according to place of birth. This classification was found to be equivalent to predominant or continuous residence in rural or urban territory. About 70 percent of the college and nearly 100 percent of the high-school students had from birth continuous residence in one or the other type of place. Of the remaining 30 percent of the college students, 22 percent had lived from 75 to 95 percent of their years in the same type of place as that in which they had been born.

As shown in Table 2, rural residents uniformly had higher average scores than urban residents. Critical ratios for three sub-groups of high-school students were over 3.0 in every case, but for the college students, the ratios were only between 0.8 and 2.7. A single critcal ratio of less than three ordinarily is not considered as indicative of a significant difference. When there are several random samples from the same universe, each might have a critical ratio of less than three, but the ratios when com-

---

[7] Sorokin, Zimmerman, and Galpin—*Systematic Sourcebook in Rural Sociology,* Volume 2, Chapter X, "The Family as the Basic Institution," pp. 3-41.

bined would be significant. Although the conditions of sampling used in this study do not permit a mathematical determination of the collective influence of these critical ratios, the consistency in the results points to a rural-urban difference in student opinion that is not due to chance factors. . . .

Age and Education. Social, as distinct from biological aging, was thought to be associated with test score. This type of aging does not

Table 2.   Opinionaire Scores and Critical Ratios for Rural and Urban Residents According to Sex, Religion, and Educational Status

Sub-Group	NUMBER		AVERAGE SCORE		Difference between averages	Critical ratio
	Urban	Rural	Urban	Rural		
College Students						
Male—Catholic	214	32	5.06	7.09	2.03	1.9
Female—Catholic ...	114	40	6.38	7.33	.95	0.8
Male—Protestant	77	26	1.01	3.69	2.68	1.8
Female—Protestant ..	137	78	− .93	1.44	2.37	2.7
High-School Students						
Male—Catholic*	18	22	1.14	8.18	7.04	3.5
Male—Protestant	28	107	− .86	5.62	6.48	4.8
Female—Protestant ..	33	59	−3.21	3.14	6.35	4.2

* Third-year students added to urban group to obtain a larger number of cases.

take place year by year, but is more a matter of advancing from one social role or group to another. The age at which this is done is not fixed and uniform, but is only approximate. In age, therefore, the members of each group are not mutually exclusive.

Three age groups were recognized in the sample: (1) the high-school group, ranging between 16 and 19 years, but concentrated largely in the 17-year-old category; (2) the regular college group, ranging between 16 and 22, but with the great majority being either 18 or 19 years old; and (3) the summer-session adults, who were between 23 and 45 years of age.

An analysis of the test scores within each of the groups confirmed the validity of the classification. The variation according to year of age was slight within the first two and irregular within the third. The small number of cases in the third plus the high degree of heterogeneity in their social and economic characteristics made it impracticable to attempt to account for their fluctuations in score. These cases, therefore, have not been used in the major comparisons of this study. . . .

The expected difference in opinion between the two groups, however, was not found in the sample. Differences in test score were small and irregular.[8] While rural college students had lower average scores than rural high-school pupils, the relation was just the reverse for the urban groups. This negative finding may have been obtained for one or more of the following reasons: (1) no significant relationship exists; (2) additional factors would have to be controlled to demonstrate the correctness of the hypothesis; (3) the sample is not representative of the student groups tested; and (4) the true relationship is that indicated by the results and requires a different and more complex interpretation than the one that has been suggested.

Sex. Assuming that students either have insight into their future roles or are early conditioned according to them, more women than men students were expected to believe that children should support aged parents. This hypothesis followed from the fact that women usually are more dependent than men upon the family for economic security. One of the reasons for this greater vulnerability of women is that the care of children often makes it impossible for them to accept employment. When not tied down with this burden, women tend to experience greater difficulty than the other sex in obtaining a suitable position, because they have had less occupational training, because ordinarily they are discriminated against by employers in the recruiting of new workers, and because from early years they normally accumulate fewer years of job experience and job rights. In realization of these disabilities, a woman should be inclined to look to the family for the protection she often cannot earn for herself. A woman, furthermore, should find easier the acceptance of the status of dependency, since there is likely to be less reproach cast upon her than would be cast upon a man for failure to be self-supporting.

But the data do not bear out the hypothesis. Sometimes the males had a higher and sometimes a lower average score.[9] Critical ratios were all between one-half and two-and-a-half. This lack of association may, of course, be due to an error in assuming that student opinion has been molded in accordance with future economic role as has been

[8] The reader who is interested in the details may get them by re-arranging the data of Table 2.

[9] Again, a re-ordering of the facts of Table 2 will yield the details.

suggested above. Another explanation of the absence of a significant difference in opinion may be that some of the social factors in the situation balance the economic considerations. . . .

Summary. Religious affiliation and place of residence determine in part the extent to which students believe that children should support aged parents. Catholics more often than Protestants and rural more than urban residents believe in this obligation. In their acceptance of favorable or rejection of unfavorable statements, Catholics and Protestants differed on the average about 17 percent while rural and urban residents differed only about five percent. The factors of age, educational level, and sex, however, were not found to be related significantly to test score.

Replies of College Students to Individual Statements

The second general hypothesis of the study is that the attitude of children toward supporting an aged parent in their home depends upon the degree of physical and psychological hardship that would be experienced in the situation. This hypothesis has been tested by using the responses of the sample of college students to selected items of the opinionaire.

Several factors were controlled through verbal instructions in the administration of this instrument to the students. They were told to assume: (1) the children while able to give support would suffer a moderate degree of financial sacrifice by so doing; (2) if the children did not extend help, the parents would probably be able to get old-age assistance, which would meet their subsistence needs although it would not provide them with the comforts to which they had been accustomed; and (3) the parents were in reasonably good mental and physical health, being neither senile nor bedridden.

The opinionaire statements described various degrees of difficulty that would be present in taking an aged parent into one's home. Although the items are not finely graded, they are able to indicate the range in the percentage of students accepting or rejecting the obligation of children to give support as the circumstances vary from what might be considered normal to extreme hardship. The data are broken down by religious affiliation and residence since these two factors have been found to be significantly related to opinion.

Six of the 20 statements of the instrument are general in the sense that they do not specify either home care or financial aid as the method of giving support and make no mention of any difficulties that might be present in the situation. Two of these six statements, one positive and one negative, have been chosen as representative of this type of situation. The percentage of the college students agreeing with each of these two statements is shown in Table 3.

The statement that we should look to children to support aged parents puts the responsibility of the younger generation in the simplest of terms. No complications of unusual personality characteristics of the parents or unpleasant consequences to the home life of the children are introduced into the situation. About half of the Protestants and about three-fourths of the Catholics agreed with this statement.

Table 3. Percentage of Students by Religion and Residence Agreeing with Several General Statements of Obligation of Children to Support Parents

| | PROTESTANT | | CATHOLIC | |
Statement	Urban	Rural	Urban	Rural
We should look to children to support aged parents	49	53	74	71
Aged parents should understand they have to stand on their own feet without help from children	20	13	9	4

An unequivocal rejection of the responsibility of children is made in the statement that aged parents should understand that they have to stand on their own feet without help from children. This idiomatic language puts the denial of an obligation in blunt terms that are almost harsh in their flat finality. There is scarcely any room for misunderstanding the attitude of a person who would so express himself. From 4 to 20 percent of the college students agreed with this proposition.

Now see how these percentages change as different degrees of hardship are mentioned as part of the situation. From the remaining 14 statements, 11 were chosen for this analysis. They all refer to the specific method of helping parents by taking them into one's home. The first five presented below in Table 4 are positive in the sense that agreement with them indicates a favorable attitude toward assisting parents. . . .

. . . the belief of the college students in the responsibility of children dropped 30 to 40 percent as the circumstances varied from those that might be considered approximately normal to those of extreme hardship. The high point was reached when 49 to 74 percent agreed that children should give support. The low point showed only from 16 to 33 percent continuing in this opinion.

The extent to which students reject the obligation of children also varies considerably with the particular circumstances of extending help. The negative statement which was the least agreed with was that aged parents should understand they have to stand on their own feet without help from children. As shown in Table 3, only 4 to 20 percent of

Table 4. Percentage of Students Checking Each of Five Positive-Specific Statements According to Religion and Residence

| | PROTESTANT | | CATHOLIC | |
Statement	Urban	Rural	Urban	Rural
Children should overlook the trouble that aged parents might cause in the home ..	43	50	69	68
Children should put up with any inconvenience in their family life in order to help aged parents	23	31	44	48
Children should give a home even to aged parents who interfere a lot in family affairs	20	24	44	46
No matter how crabby, critical, and interfering aged parents are, children should give them a home	17	22	42	40
Children should be willing to give a home to an aged parent who is an extremely jealous busybody	16	19	33	33

the students checked their agreement with this item. That these percentages can be materially increased by reference to specific difficulties is demonstrated by the responses to the six statements described in Table 5.

The four conditions of the parents getting in the way, being unpleasant, being a nuisance, and being quarrelsome did not change substantially the percentage of students in agreement with the general negative statement that has been said to have been the least agreed with of this type. It would appear, therefore, that when students are of the general opinion that parents should not be supported it is because they believe that their elders would be unpleasant, quarrelsome, etc. How extreme, then, do the difficulties have to be before a significantly greater percentage agrees that children should not have this responsibility?

There is a moderate increase in the extent of agreement with the negative side of the case when the condition is that of the parents interfering in family affairs. Then from 21 to 45 percent of the students believed that the parents should not be given a home. There was a very marked increase in the percentages when taking care of the parents was said to make for squabbling and turmoil all the time. From one-

Table 5. Percentage of Students Checking Each of Six Negative-Specific Statements According to Religion and Residence

	PROTESTANT		CATHOLIC	
Statement	Urban	Rural	Urban	Rural
Aged parents who keep getting in the way should not be given a home by their children	21	15	7	3
If aged parents are unpleasant, children should not give them a home	25	16	12	7
If aged parents are a nuisance in the home, children should refuse to take them in	24	23	15	4
Children should not give a home to aged parents who are quarrelsome	34	18	15	10
Aged parents who interfere with family affairs should be put out of your home	45	30	26	21
Children should not take care of aged parents if it makes for squabbling and turmoil all the time	67	64	40	32

to two-thirds of the students were then of the opinion that assistance should not be required of children. This appears to be the upper limit of student rejection of this obligation of the offspring when the circumstances are within reason.

Summary. The hypothesis of this section has been that student opinion on the subject of children supporting parents varies according to the degree of hardship present in the situation. This hypothesis has been confirmed for the sample group. The sensitivity of opinion to this factor has been demonstrated for each of the several sub-groups of college students. The number of students accepting the responsibility of offspring decreased about 36 percent and the number rejecting such obligation increased about 39 percent as the circumstances changed from those that might be considered normal to those of extreme hardship. Many more students accepted than rejected the obligation of children when the situation did not present unusual difficulties. The division of opinion was about even when the hardship was a severe one. Under extreme circumstances, the balance swung sharply to the side opposed to the support of parents.

Implications

The obligation of children to support aged and needy parents is apparently no longer well established in the mores. This fact has an important bearing upon the psychological security that parents obtain from the family which they rear. In the past, elders were fairly certain that come what might in the history of their personal relations with their offspring the latter would be willing to give assistance if it were necessary. Now, the children often take into consideration the nature of their personal relations with parents in order to come to a decision as to whether or not to help them. Parents, therefore, cannot be sure of obtaining support no matter how smooth their interaction with children happens to be at a particular time.

This change in family organization would be less significant if the States had universal pension laws as is the case in England. But the means test is still applied in this country, so old-age assistance is supposed to be given only to those persons whose children cannot afford to take care of them. Furthermore, the application of this test tends to stigmatize the recipient of the assistance to the extent that old people often feel that it is not respectable to take the money. The result is that parents who are in doubt about being helped by their children sometimes are equally uncertain about being able to qualify for assistance from the State or look upon it as an unacceptable alternative.*

That the parents have less psychological security than they would have under a system of universal pensions is, of course, not a conclusive argument for changing the support laws of the States. Since the responsibility of children is upheld by more than a majority of the students, it might well be maintained that these laws still have sufficient strength of opinion behind them to justify their retention. However, the data suggest the desirability of liberalizing their administration. Not only should the financial ability of the children to give support be taken into consideration in deciding whether an individual qualifies for aid, but weight should also be given to the nature of the personal relations between the two generations. Some administrators, more or less on

* As a progressively greater proportion of the aged becomes eligible for Old-Age and Survivor's Insurance, however, the author's point will lose its force.—*Eds.*

their own responsibility, are already allowing old age assistance instead of pressing the legal obligation of children when to do so would lead to a bad family situation. This approach should be recognized as a valid one and should be adopted more generally.

But more assurance of financial assistance from the State is not enough to replace the loss the old person has probably suffered as a result of the change in family organization. One of his chief fears is often that of becoming physically or mentally infirm and either being an unwanted burden on his children or cast out without being able to get elsewhere the type of care he needs. In the past, families more often accepted the nursing problems that this kind of case involved. Now, they are much less willing to do so. Parents are then left to shift for themselves or are put in institutions that have inadequate facilities. What is necessary to provide for these cases and to eliminate the worry of old people is a State system of properly financed and properly supervised hospitals. One approach to building up adequate care for the bedridden and psychologically deficient cases is the conversion of the county poorhouses into rest homes, clinics, sanatoria, and similar institutions.

CHAPTER 12

Familial Roles: Summary

IN CHAPTERS 7, 8 AND 9 we have considered the manner in which the family functions in socializing the individual at different stages of development. In chapter 10 we have considered certain consequences of socialization in terms of the adjustment of the individual to adult social roles. Chapter 11 concerned the aged and certain aspects of their rejection as a dependent group by young adults. The article which makes up the present chapter summarizes the emphases of these previous chapters and elaborates the point that the dynamics of role development at each level are dependent on previous levels and are anticipatory of some, but not all, later levels.

In his article Parsons asserts that the two social categories which are primary determinants of social roles are age and sex but that they do not operate with equal importance at each level. Adolescence he characterizes as a period of the "glamour girl" and the "swell guy," a period typified by a youth culture which is different from the patterns characteristic of both childhood and adulthood. It is a period dedicated to irresponsibility and to glamour. Transition to adult roles requires the sloughing off of many of the elements of glamour which typify the youth culture and the acceptance of status based on occupational specialization for males and the reflected status of the mate for females.

The article asserts that there is a particular period of development toward which earlier roles are geared. Parsons believes that in the Western world it is the period of youth which is idealized. Parsons suggests that as social roles become more anticipatory of a particular age period, preparation for later periods becomes more inadequate. From this we may infer that in American society there is a decided lack of preparation for age categories which succeed youth. In making this point, Parsons emphasizes the extreme isolation of the aged, a condition studied by Dinkel in the last chapter.

AGE AND SEX IN THE SOCIAL STRUCTURE OF THE UNITED STATES*

TALCOTT PARSONS

In our society age grading does not to any great extent, except for the educational system, involve formal age categorization, but is interwoven with other structural elements. In relation to these, however, it constitutes an important connecting link and an organizing point of reference in many respects. The most important of these for present purposes are kinship structure, formal education, occupation, and community participation. In most cases the age lines are not rigidly specific, but approximate; this does not, however, necessarily lessen their structural significance.[1]

In all societies the initial status of every normal individual is that of child in a given kinship unit. In our society, however, this universal starting point is used in distinctive ways. Although in early childhood

* Adapted and reprinted by permission of the author and publisher from the *American Sociological Review*, 7 (1942), 604-16. . . . The present paper will not embody the results of systematic research but constitutes rather a tentative statement of certain major aspects of the role of age and sex in our society and of their bearing on a variety of problems. It will not attempt to treat adequately the important variations according to social class, rural-urban differences, and so on, but will concentrate particularly on the urban middle and upper-middle classes.

[1] The problem of organization of this material for systematic presentation is, in view of this fact, particularly difficult. It would be possible to discuss the subject in terms of the above four principal structures with which age and sex are most closely interwoven, but there are serious disadvantages involved in this procedure. Age and sex categories constitute one of the main links of structural continuity in terms of which structures which are differentiated in other respects are articulated with each other; and in isolating the treatment of these categories there is danger that this extremely important aspect of the problem will be lost sight of. The least objectionable method, at least within the limits of space of such a paper, seems to be to follow the sequence of the life cycle.

the sexes are not usually sharply differentiated, in many kinship systems a relatively sharp segregation of children begins very early. Our own society is conspicuous for the extent to which children of both sexes are in many fundamental respects treated alike. This is particularly true of both privileges and responsibilities. The primary distinctions within the group of dependent siblings are those of age. Birth order as such is notably neglected as a basis of discrimination; a child of eight and a child of five have essentially the privileges and responsibilities appropriate to their respective age levels without regard to what older, intermediate, or younger siblings there may be. The preferential treatment of an older child is not to any significant extent differentiated if and because he happens to be the first born.

There are, of course, important sex differences in dress and in approved play interest and the like, but if anything, it may be surmised that in the urban upper-middle classes these are tending to diminish. Thus, for instance, play overalls are essentially similar for both sexes. What is perhaps the most important sex discrimination is more than anything else a reflection of the differentiation of adult sex roles. It seems to be a definite fact that girls are more apt to be relatively docile, to conform in general according to adult expectations, to be "good," whereas boys are more apt to be recalcitrant to discipline and defiant of adult authority and expectations. There is really no feminine equivalent of the expression "bad boy." It may be suggested that this is at least partially explained by the fact that it is possible from an early age to initiate girls directly into many important aspects of the adult feminine role. Their mothers are continually about the house and the meaning of many of the things they are doing is relatively tangible and easily understandable to a child. It is also possible for the daughter to participate actively and usefully in many of these activities. Especially in the urban middle classes, however, the father does not work in the home and his son is not able to observe his work or to participate in it from an early age. Furthermore, many of the masculine functions are of a relatively abstract and intangible character, such that their meaning must remain almost wholly inaccessible to a child. This leaves the boy without a tangible meaningful model to emulate and without the possibility of a gradual initiation into the activities of the adult male role. An important verification of this analysis could be provided through the study in our own society of the rural situation. It is my impression that farm boys tend to be "good" in a sense which is not typical of their urban brothers.

The equality of privileges and responsibilities, graded only by age but not by birth order, is extended to a certain degree throughout the whole range of the life cycle. In full adult status, however, it is seriously modified by the asymmetrical relation of the sexes to the occupational structure. One of the most conspicuous expressions and symbols of the underlying equality, however, is the lack of sex differentiation in the process of formal education, so far, at least, as it is not explicitly vocational. Up through college, differentiation seems to be primarily a matter on the one hand of individual ability, on the other hand of class status, and only to a secondary degree of sex differentiation. One can certainly speak of a strongly established pattern that all children of the family have a "right" to a good education, rights which are graduated according to the class status of the family but also to individual ability. It is only in post-graduate professional education, with its direct connection with future occupational careers, that sex discrimination becomes conspicuous. It is particularly important that this equality of treatment exists in the sphere of liberal education since throughout the social structure of our society there is a strong tendency to segregate the occupational sphere from one in which certain more generally human patterns and values are dominant, particularly in informal social life and the realm of what will here be called community participation.

Although this pattern of equality of treatment is present in certain fundamental respects at all age levels, at the transition from childhood to adolescence new features appear which disturb the symmetry of sex roles while still a second set of factors appears with marriage and the acquisition of full adult status and responsibilities.

An indication of the change is the practice of chaperonage, through which girls are given a kind of protection and supervision by adults to which boys of the same age group are not subjected. Boys, that is, are chaperoned only in their relations with girls of their own class. This modification of equality of treatment has been extended to the control of the private lives of women students in boarding schools and colleges. Of undoubted significance is the fact that it has been rapidly declining not only in actual effectiveness but as an ideal pattern. Its prominence in our recent past, however, is an important manifestation of the importance of sex role differentiation. Important light might be thrown upon its functions by systematic comparison with the related phenomena in Latin countries where this type of asymmetry has been far more sharply accentuated than in this country in the more modern period.

It is at the point of emergence into adolescence that a set of patterns and behavior phenomena which involve a highly complex combination of age grading and sex role elements begins to develop. These may be referred to together as the phenomena of the "youth culture." Certain of its elements are present in pre-adolescence and others in the adult culture. But the peculiar combination in connection with this particular age level is unique and highly distinctive of American society.

Perhaps the best single point of reference for characterizing the youth culture lies in its contrast with the dominant pattern of the adult male role. By contrast with the emphasis on responsibility in this role, the orientation of the youth culture is more or less specifically irresponsible. One of its dominant notes is "having a good time" in relation to which there is a particularly strong emphasis on social activities in company with the opposite sex. A second predominant characteristic on the male side lies in the prominence of athletics, which is an avenue of achievement and competition which stands in sharp contrast to the primary standards of adult achievement in professional and executive capacities. Negatively, there is a strong tendency to repudiate interest in adult things and to feel at least a certain recalcitrance to the pressure of adult expectations and discipline. In addition to, but including, athletic prowess, the typical pattern of the male youth culture seems to emphasize the value of certain qualities of attractiveness, especially in relation to the opposite sex. It is very definitely a rounded humanistic pattern rather than one of competence in the performance of specified functions. Such stereotypes as the "swell guy" are significant of this. On the feminine side there is correspondingly a strong tendency to accentuate sexual attractiveness in terms of various versions of what may be called the "glamour girl" pattern.[2] Although these patterns

[2] Perhaps the most dramatic manifestation of this tendency lies in the prominence of the patterns of "dating," for instance among college women. As shown by an unpublished participant-observer study made at one of the eastern women's colleges, perhaps the most important single basis of informal prestige rating among the residents of a dormitory lies in their relative dating success—though this is by no means the only basis. One of the most striking features of the pattern is the high publicity given to the "achievements" of the individual in a sphere where traditionally in the culture a rather high level of privacy is sanctioned—it is interesting that once an engagement has

defining roles tend to polarize sexually—for instance, as between star athlete and socially popular girl—yet on a certain level they are complementary, both emphasizing certain features of a total personality in terms of the direct expression of certain values rather than of instrumental significance.

One further feature of this situation is the extent to which it is crystallized about the system of formal education.[3] One might say that the principal centers of prestige dissemination are the colleges, but that many of the most distinctive phenomena are to be found in high schools throughout the country. It is of course of great importance that liberal education is not primarily a matter of vocational training in the United States. The individual status on the curricular side of formal education is, however, in fundamental ways linked up with adult expectations, and doing "good work" is one of the most important sources of parental approval. Because of secondary institutionalization this approval is extended into various spheres distinctive of the youth culture. But it is notable that the youth culture has a strong tendency to develop in directions which are either on the borderline of parental approval or beyond the pale, in such matters as sex behavior, drinking, and various forms of frivolous and irresponsible behavior. The fact that adults have attitudes to these things which are often deeply ambivalent and that on such occasions as college reunions they may outdo the younger generation, as, for instance, in drinking, is of great significance, but probably structurally secondary to the youth-versus-adult differential aspect. Thus, the youth culture is not only, as is true of

occurred a far greater amount of privacy is granted. The standards of rating cannot be said to be well integrated, though there is an underlying consistency in that being in demand by what the group regards as desirable men is perhaps the main standard.

It is true that the "dating" complex need not be exclusively bound up with the "glamour girl" stereotype of ideal feminine personality—the "good companion" type may also have a place. Precisely, however, where the competitive aspect of dating is most prominent the glamour pattern seems heavily to predominate, as does, on the masculine side, a somewhat comparable glamorous type. On each side at the same time there is room for considerable difference as to just where the emphasis is placed—for example as between "voluptuous" sexuality and more decorous "charm."

(For an extended discussion of this point see Willard Waller, "The Rating and Dating Complex," see pp. 371-80 below.—*Eds.*)

[3] A central aspect of this focus of crystallization lies in the element of tension, sometimes of direct conflict, between the youth culture patterns of college and school life, and the "serious" interests in and obligations toward curricular work. It is of course the latter which defines some at least of the most important foci of adult expectations of doing "good" work and justifying the privileges granted. It is not possible here to attempt to analyze the interesting, ambivalent attitudes of youth toward curricular work and achievement.

the curricular aspect of formal education, a matter of age status as such but also shows strong signs of being a product of tensions in the relationship of younger people and adults.

From the point of view of age grading, perhaps the most notable fact about this situation is the existence of definite pattern distinctions from the periods coming both before and after. At the line between childhood and adolescence "growing up" consists precisely in ability to participate in youth culture patterns, which are not for either sex the same as the adult patterns practiced by the parental generation. In both sexes the transition to full adulthood means loss of a certain "glamorous" element. From being the athletic hero or the lion of college dances, the young man becomes a prosaic business executive or lawyer. The more successful adults participate in an important order of prestige symbols but these are of a very different order from those of the youth culture. The contrast in the case of the feminine role is perhaps equally sharp, with at least a strong tendency to take on a "domestic" pattern with marriage and the arrival of young children.

The symmetry in this respect must, however, not be exaggerated. It is of fundamental significance to the sex role structure of the adult age levels that the normal man has a "job" which is fundamental to his social status in general. It is perhaps not too much to say that only in very exceptional cases can an adult man be genuinely self-respecting and enjoy a respected status in the eyes of others if he does not "earn a living" in an approved occupational role. Not only is this a matter of his own economic support but, generally speaking, his occupational status is the primary source of the income and class status of his wife and children.

In the case of the feminine role the situation is radically different. The majority of married women, of course, are not employed, but even of those that are a very large proportion do not have jobs which are in basic competition for status with those of their husbands.[4] The majority of "career" women whose occupational status is comparable

[4] The above statement, even more than most in the present paper, needs to be qualified in relation to the problem of class. It is above all to the upper-middle class that it applies. Here probably the great majority of "working wives" are engaged in some form of secretarial work which would, on an independent basis, generally be classed as a lower-middle-class occupation. The situation at lower levels of the class structure is quite different since the prestige of the jobs of husband and wife is then much more likely to be nearly equivalent. It is quite possible that this fact is closely related to the relative instability of marriage which Davis and Gardner (*Deep South*) find, at least for the community they studied, to be typical of lower-class groups. The relation is one which deserves careful study.

with that of men in their own class, at least in the upper-middle and upper classes, are unmarried, and in the small proportion of cases where they are married the result is a profound alteration in family structure.

This pattern, which is central to the urban middle classes, should not be misunderstood. In rural society, for instance, the operation of the farm and the attendant status in the community may be said to be a matter of the joint status of both parties to a marriage. Whereas a farm is operated by a family, an urban job is held by an individual and does not involve other members of the family in a comparable sense. One convenient expression of the difference lies in the question of what would happen in case of death. In the case of a farm it would at least be not at all unusual for the widow to continue operating the farm with the help of a son or even of hired men. In the urban situation the widow would cease to have any connection with the organization which had employed her husband and he would be replaced by another man without reference to family affiliations.

In this urban situation the primary status-carrying role is in a sense that of housewife. The woman's fundamental status is that of her husband's wife, the mother of his children, and traditionally the person responsible for a complex of activities in connection with the management of the household, care of children, etc.

For the structuring of sex roles in the adult phase the most fundamental considerations seem to be those involved in the interrelations of the occupational system and the conjugal family. In a certain sense the most fundamental basis of the family's status is the occupational status of the husband and father. As has been pointed out, this is a status occupied by an individual by virtue of his individual qualities and achievements. But both directly and indirectly, more than any other single factor, it determines the status of the family in the social structure, directly because of the symbolic significance of the office or occupation as a symbol of prestige, indirectly because as the principal source of family income it determines the standard of living of the family. From one point of view the emergence of occupational status into this primary position can be regarded as the principal source of strain in the sex role structure of our society since it deprives the wife of her role as a partner in a common enterprise. The common enterprise is reduced to the life of the family itself and to the informal social activities in which husband and wife participate together. This leaves the wife a set of utilitarian functions in the management of the household which may be considered a kind of "pseudo-" occupation. Since the present interest is primarily in the middle classes, the relatively unstable character of the role of housewife as the principal content of the feminine role is strongly illustrated by the tendency to employ domestic servants wherever financially possible. It is true that there is an American tendency to accept tasks of drudgery with relative willingness, but it is notable that in middle-class families there tends to be a dissociation of the essential personality from the performance of these tasks. Thus, advertising continually appeals to such desires as to have hands which one could never tell had washed dishes or scrubbed floors.[5] Organization about the function of housewife, however, with the addition of strong affectional devotion to husband and children, is the primary focus of one of the principal patterns governing the adult feminine role—what may be called the "domestic" pattern. It is, however, a conspicuous fact that strict adherence to this pattern has become progressively less common and has a strong tendency to a residual status—that is, to be followed most closely by those who are unsuccessful in competition for prestige in other directions.

It is, of course, possible for the adult woman to follow the masculine pattern and seek a career in fields of occupational achievement in direct competition with men of her own class. It is, however, notable that in spite of the very great progress of the emancipation of women from the traditional domestic pattern only a very small fraction have gone very far in this direction. It is also clear that its generalization would only be possible with profound alterations in the structure of the family.

Hence, it seems that concomitant with the alteration in the basic masculine role in the direction of occupation there have appeared two important tendencies in the feminine role which are alternative to that of simple domesticity on the one hand, and to a full-fledged career on the other. In the older situation there tended to be a very rigid distinction between respectable married women and those who were

---

[5] This type of advertising appeal undoubtedly contains an element of "snob appeal" in the sense of an invitation to the individual by her appearance and ways to identify herself with a higher social class than that of her actual status. But it is almost certainly not wholly explained by this element. A glamorously feminine appearance which is specifically dissociated from physical work is undoubtedly a genuine part of an authentic personality ideal of the middle class, and not only evidence of a desire to belong to the upper class.

"no better than they should be." The rigidity of this line has progressively broken down through the infiltration into the respectable sphere of elements of what may be called again the glamour pattern, with the emphasis on a specifically feminine form of attractiveness which on occasion involves directly sexual patterns of appeal. One important expression of this trend lies in the fact that many of the symbols of feminine attractiveness have been taken over directly from the practices of social types previously beyond the pale of respectable society. This would seem to be substantially true of the practice of women smoking and of at least the modern version of the use of cosmetics. The same would seem to be true of many of the modern versions of women's dress. "Emancipation" in this connection means primarily emancipation from traditional and conventional restrictions on the free expression of sexual attraction and impulses, but in a direction which tends to segregate the element of sexual interest and attraction from the total personality and in so doing tends to emphasize the segregation of sex roles. It is particularly notable that there has been no corresponding tendency to emphasize masculine attraction in terms of dress and other such aids. One might perhaps say that in a situation which strongly inhibits competition between the sexes on the same plane the feminine glamour pattern has appeared as an offset to masculine occupational status and to its attendant symbols of prestige. It is perhaps significant that there is a common stereotype of the association of physically beautiful, expensively and elaborately dressed women with physically unattractive but rich and powerful men.

The other principal direction of emancipation from domesticity seems to lie in emphasis on what has been called the common humanistic element. This takes a wide variety of forms. One of them lies in a relatively mature appreciation and systematic cultivation of cultural interests and educated tastes, extending all the way from the intellectual sphere to matters of art, music, and house furnishings. A second consists in cultivation of serious interests and humanitarian obligations in community welfare situations and the like. It is understandable that many of these orientations are most conspicuous in fields where through some kind of tradition there is an element of particular suitability for feminine participation. Thus, a woman who takes obligations to social welfare particularly seriously will find opportunities in various forms of activity which traditionally tie up with women's relation to children, to sickness and so on. But this may be regarded as secondary to the underlying orientation which would seek an outlet in work useful to the community following the most favorable opportunities which happen to be available.

This pattern, which with reference to the character of relationship to men may be called that of the "good companion," is distinguished from the others in that it lays far less stress on the exploitation of sex role as such and more on that which is essentially common to both sexes. There are reasons, however, why cultural interests and interest in social welfare and community activities are particularly prominent in the activities of women in our urban communities. On the one side, the masculine occupational role tends to absorb a very large proportion of the man's time and energy and to leave him relatively little for other interests. Furthermore, unless his position is such as to make him particularly prominent his primary orientation is to those elements of the social structure which divide the community into occupational groups rather than those which unite it in common interests and activities. The utilitarian aspect of the role of housewife, on the other hand, has declined in importance to the point where it scarcely approaches a fulltime occupation for a vigorous person. Hence the resort to other interests to fill up the gap. In addition, women being more closely tied to the local residential community are more apt to be involved in matters of common concern to the members of that community. This peculiar role of women becomes particularly conspicuous in middle age. The younger married woman is apt to be relatively highly absorbed in the care of young children. With their growing up, however, her absorption in the household is greatly lessened, often just at the time when the husband is approaching the apex of his career and is most heavily involved in its obligations. Since to a high degree this humanistic aspect of the feminine role is only partially institutionalized it is not surprising that its patterns often bear the marks of strain and insecurity, as perhaps has been classically depicted by Helen Hokinson's cartoons of women's clubs.

The adult roles of both sexes involve important elements of strain which are involved in certain dynamic relationships, especially to the youth culture. In the case of the feminine role marriage is the single event toward which a selective process, in which personal qualities and effort can play a decisive role, has pointed up. This determines a woman's fundamental status, and after that her role patterning is not so much status-determining as a matter of living up to expectations and finding satisfying interests and activities. In a society where such strong emphasis is placed upon individual achievement it is not surprising that there should be a certain romantic nostalgia for the time when the fundamental choices were still open. This element of strain is added to by the lack of clear-cut definition of the adult feminine role. Once the possibility of a career has been eliminated there still tends to be a rather unstable oscillation between emphasis in the direction of domesticity or glamour or good companionship. According to situational pressures and individual character the tendency will be to emphasize one or another of these more strongly. But it is a situation likely to produce a rather high level of insecurity. In this state the pattern of domesticity must be ranked lowest in terms of prestige but also, because of the strong emphasis in community sentiment on the virtues of fidelity and devotion to husband and children, it offers perhaps the highest level of a certain kind of security. It is no wonder that such an important symbol as Whistler's mother concentrates primarily on this pattern.

The glamour pattern has certain obvious attractions since to the woman who is excluded from the struggle for power and prestige in the occupational sphere it is the most direct path to a sense of superiority and importance. It has, however, two obvious limitations. In the first place, many of its manifestations encounter the resistance of patterns of moral conduct and engender conflicts not only with community opinion but also with the individual's own moral standards. In the second place, the highest manifestations of its pattern are inevitably associated with a rather early age level—in fact, overwhelmingly with the courtship period. Hence, if strongly entered upon, serious strains result from the problem of adaptation to increasing age.

The one pattern which would seem to offer the greatest possibilities for able, intelligent, and emotionally mature women is the third—the good companion pattern. This, however, suffers from a lack of fully institutionalized status and from the multiplicity of choices of channels of expression. It is only those with the strongest initiative and intelligence who achieve fully satisfactory adaptations in this direction. It is quite clear that in the adult feminine role there is quite sufficient strain and insecurity so that wide-spread manifestations are to be expected in the form of neurotic behavior.

The masculine role at the same time is itself by no means devoid of corresponding elements of strain. It carries with it to be sure the primary prestige of achievement, responsibility, and authority. By comparison with the role of the youth culture, however, there are at least two important types of limitations. In the first place, the modern occupational system has led to increasing specialization of role. The job absorbs an extraordinarily large proportion of the individual's energy and emotional interests in a role which often has relatively narrow content. This in particular restricts the area within which he can share common interests and experiences with others not in the same occupational specialty. It is perhaps of considerable significance that so many of the highest prestige statuses of our society are of this specialized character. There is in the definition of roles little to bind the individual to others in his community on a comparable status level. By contrast with this situation, it is notable that in the youth culture common human elements are far more strongly emphasized. Leadership and eminence are more in the role of total individuals and less of competent specialists. This perhaps has something to do with the significant tendency in our society for all age levels to idealize youth and for the older age groups to attempt to imitate the patterns of youth behavior.

It is perhaps as one phase of this situation that the relation of the adult man to persons of the opposite sex should be treated. The effect of the specialization of occupational role is to narrow the range in which the sharing of common human interests can play a large part. In relation to his wife the tendency of this narrowness would seem to be to encourage on her part either the domestic or the glamorous role, or community participation somewhat unrelated to the marriage relationship. This relationship between sex roles presumably introduces a certain amount of strain into the marriage relationship itself since this is of such overwhelming importance to the family and hence to a woman's status and yet so relatively difficult to maintain on a level of human companionship. Outside the marriage relationship, however, there seems to be a notable inhibition against easy social intercourse, particularly in mixed company.[6] The man's close personal intimacy with other women is checked by the danger of the situation being

[6] In the informal social life of academic circles with which the writer is familiar there seems to be a strong tendency in mixed gatherings—as after dinner, for the sexes to segregate. In such groups the men are apt to talk either shop subjects or politics whereas the women are apt to talk about domestic affairs, schools, their children, etc., or personalities. It is perhaps on personalities that mixed conversation is apt to flow most freely.

defined as one of rivalry with the wife, and easy friendship without sexual-emotional involvement seems to be inhibited by the specialization of interests in the occupational sphere. It is notable that brilliance of conversation of the "salon" type seems to be associated with aristocratic society and is not prominent in ours.

Along with all this goes a certain tendency for middle-aged men, as symbolized by the "bald-headed row," to be interested in the physical aspect of sex—that is, in women precisely as dissociated from those personal considerations which are important to relationships of companionship or friendship, to say nothing of marriage. In so far as it does not take this physical form, however, there seems to be a strong tendency for middle-aged men to idealize youth patterns—that is, to think of the ideal inter-sex friendship as that of their pre-marital period.[7]

In so far as the idealization of the youth culture by adults is an expression of elements of strain and insecurity in the adult roles it would be expected that the patterns thus idealized would contain an element of romantic unrealism. The patterns of youthful behavior thus idealized are not those of actual youth so much as those which older people wish their own youth might have been. This romantic element seems to coalesce with a similar element derived from certain strains in the situation of young people themselves.

The period of youth in our society is one of considerable strain and insecurity. Above all, it means turning one's back on the security both of status and of emotional attachment which is engaged in the family of orientation. It is structurally essential to transfer one's primary emotional attachment to a marriage partner who is entirely unrelated to the previous family situation. In a system of free marriage choice this applies to women as well as men. For the man there is in addition the necessity to face the hazards of occupational competition in the determination of a career. There is reason to believe that the youth culture has important positive functions in easing the transition from the security of childhood in the family of orientation to that of full adult in marriage and occupational status. But precisely because the transition is a period of strain it is to be expected that it involves elements of unrealistic romanticism. Thus, significant features in the status of youth patterns in our society would seem to derive from

[7] This, to be sure, often contains an element of romantization. It is more nearly what he wishes these relations had been than what they actually were.

the coincidence of the emotional needs of adolescents with those derived from the strains of the situation of adults.

A tendency to the romantic idealization of youth patterns seems in different ways to be characteristic of modern western society as a whole.[8] It is not possible in the present context to enter into any extended comparative analysis, but it may be illuminating to call attention to a striking difference between the patterns associated with this phenomenon in Germany and in the United States. The German "youth movement," starting before World War I, has occasioned a great deal of comment and has in various respects been treated as the most notable instance of the revolt of youth. It is generally believed that the youth movement has an important relation to the background of National Socialism, and this fact as much as any suggests the important difference. While in Germany as everywhere there has been a generalized revolt against convention and restrictions on individual freedom as embodied in the traditional adult culture, in Germany particular emphasis has appeared on the community of male youth. "Comradeship," in a sense which strongly suggests that of soldiers in the field, has from the beginning been strongly emphasized as the ideal social relationship. By contrast with this, in the American youth culture and its adult romantization a much stronger emphasis has been placed on the cross-sex relationship. It would seem that this fact, with the structural factors which underlie it, has much to do with the failure of the youth culture to develop any considerable political significance in this country. Its predominant pattern has been that of the idealization of the isolated couple in romantic love. There have, to be sure, been certain tendencies among radical youth to a political orientation but in this case there has been a notable absence of emphasis on the solidarity of the members of one sex. The tendency has been rather to ignore the relevance of sex difference in the interest of common ideals.

The importance of youth patterns in contemporary American culture throws into particularly strong relief the status in our social structure of the most advanced age groups. By comparison with other societies the United States assumes an extreme position in the isolation of old age from participation in the most important social structures and interests. Structurally speaking, there seem to be two primary bases

[8] Cf. E. Y. Hartshorne, "German Youth and the Nazi Dream of Victory," *America in a World at War,* Pamphlet, No. 12, New York, 1941.

of this situation. In the first place, the most important single distinctive feature of our family structure is the isolation of the individual conjugal family. It is impossible to say that with us it is "natural" for any other group than husband and wife and their dependent children to maintain a common household. Hence, when the children of a couple have become independent through marriage and occupational status the parental couple is left without attachment to any continuous kinship group. It is, of course, common for other relatives to share a household with the conjugal family but this scarcely ever occurs without some important elements of strain. For independence is certainly the preferred pattern for an elderly couple, particularly from the point of view of the children.

The second basis of the situation lies in the occupational structure. In such fields as farming and the maintenance of small independent enterprises there is frequently no such thing as abrupt "retirement," rather a gradual relinquishment of the main responsibilities and functions with advancing age. So far, however, as an individual's occupational status centers in a specific "job," he either holds the job or does not, and the tendency is to maintain the full level of functions up to a given point and then abruptly to retire. In view of the very great significance of occupational status and its psychological correlates, retirement leaves the older man in a peculiarly functionless situation, cut off from participation in the most important interests and activities of the society. There is a further important aspect of this situation. Not only status in the community but actual place of residence is to a very high degree a function of the specific job held. Retirement not only cuts the ties to the job itself but also greatly loosens those to the community of residence. Perhaps in no other society is there observable a phenomenon corresponding to the accumulation of retired elderly people in such areas as Florida and Southern California in the winter. It may be surmised that this structural isolation from kinship, occupational, and community ties is the fundamental basis of the recent political agitation for help to the old. It is suggested that it is far less the financial hardship[9] of the position of elderly people than their social

[9] That the financial difficulties of older people are in a very large proportion of cases real is not to be doubted. This, however, is at least to a very large extent a consequence rather than a determinant of the structural situation. Except where it is fully taken care of by pension schemes, the income of older people is apt to be seriously reduced, but, even more important, the younger conjugal family usually does not feel an obligation

isolation which makes old age a "problem." As in other connections we are here very prone to rationalize generalized insecurity in financial and economic terms. The problem is obviously of particularly great significance in view of the changing age distribution of the population with the prospect of a far greater proportion in the older age groups than in previous generations. It may also be suggested, that through well-known psychosomatic mechanisms, the increased incidence of the disabilities of older people, such as heart disease, cancer, etc., may be at least in part attributed to this structural situation.

---

to contribute to the support of aged parents. Where as a matter of course both genera-tions shared a common household, this problem did not exist.

CHAPTER 13

Romantic Love in the United States

IN CONTRAST to certain other cultures (*e.g.,* traditional Japanese), that of the United States seems to hold that a prerequisite for marriage is something which we speak of sometimes as love and sometimes as romantic love. Romantic love is variously viewed as balm for the heartaches of man and as the foe of marital happiness. In part such a disagreement reflects a real difference in viewpoint, but at times at least it reflects merely a difference in definition of the term.

Some would hold that any attachment between persons of opposite sex is a "romance." In this usage, however, romance becomes the equivalent of co-sexual love, and hence the term has little power of denotation. Elsewhere Winch has traced romantic love back to historical forms in western Europe and has described both the historical and the modern versions in terms of the lover's moonstruck suffering as he idealizes his inaccessible love-object.[1] Using the term in this latter sense, we find that romantic longing is resonant with feelings of insecurity and that the romantic lover demands great—indeed, almost total—gratification from the love-object. We may use the term "companionship love" to denote a relationship between lovers who are more secure and hence disposed to make fewer emotional demands on the love-object.

In the present chapter Beigel summarizes the historical roots and examines the present status of romantic love. Somewhat sardonically Folsom discourses on some psychosomatic correlates of romantic love.

---

[1] R. F. Winch, *The Modern Family,* New York, Holt, 1952, ch. 14.

In chapter 15 we shall summarize several studies of marital adjustment which seem to imply that a marriage based on companionship love stands a better chance of resulting in good adjustment than one based on romantic love.

LOVE: COURTLY, ROMANTIC, AND MODERN*

Hugo G. Beigel

Three phases of formalized love are discernible in Western culture. The first encompasses the origin of courtly love in the twelfth century, the second its revival at the turn of the nineteenth century, and the third its present state and significance for marital selection. . . .

Courtly love was the conventionalization of a new ideal that arose in the feudal class and institutionalized certain aspects of the male-female relationship *outside marriage.* In conformity with the Christian concept of and contempt for sex, the presupposition for courtly love was chastity. Being the spiritualization and the sublimation of carnal desire, such love was deemed to be impossible between husband and wife. By application of the religious concept of abstract love to the "mistress," the married woman of the ruling class, who had lost her economic function, was endowed with higher and more general values: gentleness and refinement. Unselfish service to the noble lady became a duty of the knight, explicitly sworn to in the oath the young noble-man had to take at the dubbing ceremony.[1] Part of this service was ritualized; by means of such formalization the aggressiveness of unfulfilled cravings was channeled into codes and causes. In this manner sexual covetousness was deflected and the marital rights of husbands were—theoretically at least—safeguarded. This was obviously an important provision in an age in which social rules prevented free choice of a mate for marriage with the result that basic human needs were left unsatisfied.

Courtly love—in retrospect called romantic love—consequently was

* Adapted and reprinted by permission of the author and publisher from "Romantic Love," the *American Sociological Review,* 16 (1951), 326-34.

[1] "Monumenta Germaniae" (leges II, 363) in E. Sturtevant, *Vom guten Ton im Wandel der Jahrhunderte,* Berlin, Bong, 1917.

not a whimsical play. In spite of the surface appearance of its aesthetic formulation, it sprang from vital needs, from a deeply felt desire for the ennoblement of human relations, and from culture-bred frustrations. It made *māze* (moderation) a masculine virtue.

The fact that it is in the first place the sexual drive that was frustrated in this love relationship suggests an analogy with adolescent love. We can assume that certain features in the development of an adolescent brought up in an earlier phase of our culture coincide with tendencies observable nowadays. Those produced by the physiological maturation of the organism, for instance, are universal, and medieval literature gives some evidence of the emotions involved in self-discovery and the experience of change at this age.[2]

While the sexual drive rises to its greatest intensity during adolescence, it is denied satisfaction. Abstinence and celibacy being among the highest religious ideals and sexual immorality being threatened with hellfire, conflicts are created that lead to feelings of guilt, depreciation of the ego, and a heightening of the ego ideal. The phantasy is quickened and the suppression of the intensified desires results in a high emotionality which seeks for vicarious outlets.[3] While sexual relations cannot be established before marriage, there is sufficient erotic stimulation from talk, from visual stimuli, and an occasional trespassing with females outside one's class to feed the hope for more. Unless hope is realized or relinquished, the adolescent strains his resources to impress any members of the opposite sex and one female in particular whose behavior allows anticipation of possible acceptance. The means are display of masculine skill and prowess which, under the influence of religious teachings, the group code, and the masculine ideal, are subordinated to socially acknowledged causes or such feats as can be interpreted as good causes. The striving to prove one's independence and manliness finds expression in the search for adventures. The female, being at the same time the weaker competitor, the object to be obtained, and the substitute for the mother, grows to be the ideal audience and the representative for the super-ego; this has the effect that softer virtues often take precedence over coarser forms of behavior. While, in general, the adolescent does not aim at permanent possession of the

---

[2] Chretiens de Troyes, *Percival* (Conte del graal); Wolfram von Eschenbach, *Parzival;* Hartmann von Aue, *Der arme Heinrich;* Wirnt von Gravenberg, *Vigalois.*

[3] K. C. Garrison, *The Psychology of Adolescence,* New York, Prentice-Hall, 1950; A. H. Arlitt, *Adolescent Psychology,* New York, American Book Co., 1933.

female, any sign of approval by her is interpreted as accepted and props up the wavering self-esteem. For this service she is idealized; even the refusal of sexual gratification is taken as an indication of greater self-control and moral strength. Such greatness, on the other hand, reflects favorably on the quality of the one accepted, who tries to live up to moral perfection and thus to the beloved's assumed higher standard. Vows of self-improvement alternate with feelings of unworthiness and moments of expansive self-feeling.

The adolescent's showing-off attitude has its counterpart in the medieval knight's search for adventures and in the tournaments he fought for his mistress. Love tests are frequent. Certain feats like those of Ulrich von Lichtenstein, who sent his little finger to his mistress and drank the water in which she had washed, or of Peire Vidal, who had himself sewn into a bear's hide and hunted,[4] have their parallels in the adolescent's obsessional yearning to impress the chosen female by valiance, self-sacrifice, and self-punishment. As do adolescent relations, courtly love provided partial satisfactions of the sexual desire. The lover having become a *drutz*[5] had the right to accompany his lady to her bedchamber, to undress her to the skin, and to put her to bed. Sometimes he was even allowed to sleep with her if he promised to content himself with a kiss. The love symbols are similar; the adolescent feels the one-ness with the beloved by wearing a lock of her hair or a ribbon near his heart as the knight felt it when he tied her veil around his armor; and as the mistress wore her gallant's blood-stained shirt so may a girl today wear her boy's pin, blazer, or baseball hat.

Such and many more similarities provoke the conclusion that courtly love represents the aesthetization of adolescent feelings which, though recognized as precious, are rarely experienced in adulthood with the same ardor. Under the influence of the cherished tales of oriental love refinement, the pyre of adolescent emotions was artificially kept burning, producing that subtler form of male-female relations that exploited the elations and depressions of enforced chastity for the ennoblement of the mind and gave the newly consolidated ruling class moral distinction over the crude indulgence of the masses.

The cultural significance of this concept lies in the fact that the

---

[4] H. Jantzen (*ed.*), *Dichtungen aus mittelhochdeutscher Fruehzeit; Goeschen,* 137, Leipzig, 1910.

[5] A. von Gleichen-Russwurm, *Kultur und Sittengeschichte aller Zeiten und Voelker,* Zurich, Gutenberg Verlag, 1920. The lover who has reached the fourth and highest state in the ritual of courtly love and is accepted.

idealization of the female initiated her social elevation and that it introduced voluntary fidelity, restraint, and the magnanimous gentleness of the male consciously into the relation between the sexes, qualities that were not considered essential or even possible in a marriage based on the semi-patriarchal concept of the Middle Ages. As the idea spread, it influenced greatly the emotional development of the group as a whole. This penetration became evident when romantic love, the bourgeois adaptation of courtly love, was propagated by the Romanticists.

Presupposing the knowledge of the historic and socio-economic roots of the Romantic movement,[6, 7] we limit ourselves again to an outline of those trends that have direct bearing on our subject.

In formulating the idea of romantic love, the Romanticists merely propounded a concept that had become a socio-psychological necessity. Starting in the fourteenth century, the dissolution of the broader family had progressed to the point where its economic, religious, and political functions were gone. With increasing urbanization the impact of social isolation made itself felt upon the individual. As a result of industrialization and mercantilization the father's authority had decreased and the children remained longer under the more emotionally-oriented care of the mother, a fact that, together with the child's loss of economic function, effected a gradual change in personality, especially in the male personality. Reformation, revolutions, and wars had shaken the foundations of beliefs and traditions. Being the first to feel the pinch of the technological development on the treasured ideology of individualism, the Romanticists rebelled against the progressing de-humanization, the all-devouring materialism and rationalism, and sought escape from these dangers in the wonders of the emotions. In the basic feelings of humanity they hoped to find security and a substitute for the eliminated cultural values.

Under the increasing discomfort in a changing civilization, the aristocratic class had found a way to alleviate the defects of a family-prescribed monogamous marriage by dividing duty and satisfaction; the woman reserved her loyalty for her husband and her love for her gallant. Continuing on the tracks laid by the concept of courtly love, the nobles of the seventeenth and eighteenth centuries in Austria, Spain, France, the Netherlands, etc. still adhered to the tenet that love and marriage were irreconcilable. Yet, love had dropped its cloak of sub-

[6] R. M. Meyer, *Die Literatur des 19. und 20. Jahrhunderts,* Berlin, Bondi, 1921.
[7] L. Walzel, *Romantik; Natur und Geisteswelt,* Leipzig, 1915, vols. 232, 233.

limation. The medieval concept had drawn a line between the spiritual and the animalic-sexual, between love and marriage. The court society of the Baroque[8] and the Rococo periods, by rewarding the gallant's deeds and duels with carnal favors, actually integrated sex and love—though only outside marriage. The adaptation noticeable in the ascending bourgeois class followed the same line—integration of sex and love—with the important difference that their economic struggle, their tradition of thrift, their religious ideas (which, reformed to further their purposes, gave them moral support in their ultimate contest with the group in power),[9] did not permit them to accept illicit relationships as a solution of the problem. Yet, they had not remained unaffected by the ideology of earthly love. The refined concept had filtered down from the castles to the cities. Marriage, to be sure, was still arranged on a family basis with an eye on business, and the status of the wife was by no means enviable. But the verbiage of courtly love had entered the relation of the sexes. However, it was addressed not to the married woman, but, for the first time, to the marriageable maiden. Of course, this was hardly possible before the betrothal since, as an anonymous writer, Ursula Margareta, wrote in her diary published posthumously in 1805,[10] "the association with the opposite sex was not yet invented then (about 1760) . . . and we were shielded from them as from chicken pox." But during the months between engagement and marriage the betrothed was expected to "court" the girl and to display his emotional fervor in conversation, gifts, and poetry.

Preceded by the English novelist Samuel Richardson (1689-1761), who is credited with having said first that love is needed for marriage, the men of letters of those days pointed out both the immorality of the aristocratic solution and the sterility of the bourgeois pattern. Visualizing love as an antidote to the insecurity produced by social and technological changes, they propagated its legitimization and thus its perpetuation in marriage. The model for the bond between the sexes was the complex of feelings so graciously depicted in medieval romances, and its realization was henceforth called romance or romantic love.

We thus encounter a third stage in the development of love relations. The first admitted certain formalized features of adolescent feelings

[8] M. Carrière, "Barocque," in Gleichen-Russwurm, *op. cit.,* vol. 11.

[9] R. H. Tawney, *Religion and the Rise of Capitalism,* Penguin Books, Harmondsworth, England, 1938.

[10] "Alte und neue Zeit; Taschenbuch zum geselligen Vergnuegen, 1805," reprinted in Sturtevant, *op. cit.*

into the adult relationship to bridge the dichotomy between sublimated sex desires and the prevailing sex-hostile ideology; the second justified with love adulterous sex relations to ease the burden of an unreformed monogamy; the third aimed at the integration of love and marriage. It was promulgated by the first spokesmen of the bourgois culture, who pleaded for the right of the young people to make their own choice for marriage on the basis of their feelings. No longer was there to be a cleavage between the spirituality of love and the marital sex relation, but the latter was to be sanctified by the former. This combination raised—though only ideologically at first—the woman of the middle class to the status which heretofore only the aristocratic lady had achieved in relation to the man.

Like courtly love, the concept of the Romanticists leaned noticeably on adolescent experiences. Though less ritualized than courtly love, romantic love acknowledged the value of certain pre-adult emotions. It established a hierarchy of characteristics that marked predestined affection. Foremost among them was emotional instead of rational evaluation, an attitude that contrasts clearly with the adult behavior normally aspired to, but is typical of adolescence, in which the rational powers do not operate at their optimum. Economic and status considerations were belittled. The female was idealized because of her ("natural" kindness, her intuition, and her nearness to nature. The male conceived of himself as a restless, striving, and erring deviate, spoiled by civilization, who, inspired by the female's love, might find the way back to his better self. This tendency corresponds to the adolescent's moments of magnified feelings of inferiority in the face of the female's greater poise and virtue and the elation when he is accepted nevertheless. While in the romantic concept the adventures of the mind were valued over fighting and fencing, conflict, self-recognition, sensitivity and the preservation of one's "true" and original self were elevated to moral qualities. The analogy to the adolescent's defensive attitude toward practical adult goals is evident.

The romantic love relationship itself was pervaded by melancholy and *Weltschmerz* (world-woe), another trend that is generally encountered in adolescence when the young person, having severed his emotional ties with his protective elders and craving new attachments, finds himself abandoned and, in comparison with the still child-like ego ideal, inadequate. From the same experience, on the other hand, results the claim to uniqueness and originality. Owing to his maturing mental powers, his broadening experience and knowledge, the adolescent frequently senses suddenly some of the discrepancies between reality and the moral teachings of his group, especially those which are antagonistic to the fulfillment of his desires. In this whirl of contradictions, wishes, rebellious emotions, and thoughts he feels like a castaway or like a revolutionary, chosen for the fight against either the traditions or the temptations, like a hero or like a sinner, full of defiance or full of resolutions to prove himself better than anyone else. Simultaneously proud and afraid of his discoveries, he seeks reassurance, someone to confide to, a companion who confirms the value of his ideas and thus of his personality.

Unable to turn to his parents, who in a quickly changing world are no longer considered revered guides but old-fashioned antagonists, he can find assurance only with a friend who seems to be shaken by similar convulsions and consequently "understands." After a period of homosexual friendships, the social conventions, the ideal of masculinity, and the sex drive usually direct the choice toward heterosexual relations, the same relations whose secrecy, mood of conspiracy, exuberations and depressions were the raw material for romantic love which, minimizing the sexual aspect, introduced friendship between the sexes.

By the end of the nineteenth century love had won its battle along the whole line in the upper sections of the middle class. It has since been regarded as the most important prerequisite to marriage. The American concept that considers individual happiness the chief purpose of marriage is based entirely on this ideology. . . . Is this love identical with the formalized concept of romantic love?

Certainly, the all-pervading melancholy is relatively rare among young adults; the mood of lovers, though still vacillating between joy and depression, is, on the whole, less sentimentally sad and, owing to their greater independence and the diminishing outside interference, is based more often on anticipation of marital joys, cooperation, "having fun together," and pursuit of common interests. As contact between the sexes is freer, partial sexual outlets are frequently provided. And while such activities may still be followed by feelings of guilt, these seem to be greatly attenuated by a presumed necessity caused by a socially cultivated sexual competition. Sex competition, on the other hand, particularly potent among girls, tends to blur the line between the excitations of love and those of an aggressive ambition. As a result of the prevailing dating convention and its concomitant early initiation of the sexes on a social basis, the over-idealization of the female (the keynote in both courtly and romantic love) is curbed. The love conventions of the twelfth and the nineteenth centuries were grants made by the man to the female; love in our day and in this country, conversely, has become a demand of the female, who is in the privileged position to extend or withhold sexual favors. Her own desire probably being lessened by culturally necessitated repressions, she frequently uses such favors to reward or stimulate emotional expressions without regard to her own sex drive. Thus, it appears that the modern love concept is not identical with romantic love, but is a derivative, modified in concord with the conditions of our age and based more on ego demands than on ideal demands.

But whatever form it takes, love is rarely the only consideration upon which marriage is contracted. Rather, it is one selective factor operating within the controls imposed upon the mates by our culture. These controls involve age, race, religion, ethnic origin, and class,[11] and the thus defined field is furthermore narrowed by regional proximity. . . .

THE ROMANTIC COMPLEX AND CARDIAC-RESPIRATORY LOVE*

JOSEPH KIRK FOLSOM

Cardiac-Respiratory or Excited Love

What does it feel like to be "in love"? If one has the sexual, the oral, and the dermal feelings all together toward another person, is he in love with that person? If you are a thoroughgoing introspector, you will find that something else is necessary. To be physiological . . . an element of *breathlessness* is necessary. "In-loveness" implies catching of the breath, a deep sigh, a feeling about the heart, as if it had stopped, followed by palpitation or rapid beating, a feeling akin to fear. Shivering and trembling sometimes accompany these reactions. Then there is the *thrill* reaction, which may be a kind of muscular trembling, or a

[11] A. B. Hollingshead, "Cultural Factors in the Selection of Marriage Mates," pp. 399-412 below.

* Adapted and reprinted by permission of the author and publisher from *The Family,* New York, John Wiley & Sons, Inc., 1934, pp. 68-76.

circulatory disturbance. Introspection localizes it in the chest, abdomen, and arms; it seems to involve a sudden increase of energy due possibly to liberation of endocrine hormones into the blood. Some persons, perhaps, have never experienced it, and have been good lovers in the other three ways.* But those who have experienced it know what it is. The writers of popular fiction have a deeper insight into some things than is usually credited to them. Again, why does ancient tradition locate love in the heart; not in the lips, skin, or genitals?

Let us call this cardiac-respiratory, or excited, love. In this state, we are excited, alert. Of course, the condition is not a continuous one. It flares up now and then, whenever some stimulus occurs reminding us of the loved one. It may last, however, in mild form, for considerable periods of time. Under these circumstances the feeling is likely to take on more the character of a dull ache, a feeling of pressure in the chest. This, again, is a cardiac-respiratory disturbance. The more acute symptoms are akin to fear, the more chronic symptoms to anguish. Careful examination of a person in the active state of excited love would probably reveal the sympathetic nervous system functioning more than the cranio-sacral. The behavior in general is allied to the defensive, unpleasant system. But, obviously, keen pleasure is derived from certain nuances, interludes, or results of the behavior and renders it quite worth while. The situation resembles somewhat that of bob-sled running and other physical "thrills." Fear is stimulated, yet keen pleasure is gained by the sudden or periodic relief of the fear. It is the pleasure of excitement.

In the moments and hours dominated by excited love there may be little of the other kinds of love feeling. The desire for sexual contacts seems remote. Extensive kissing and touching seem out of place: one does not want oral or genital pleasure particularly, one uses the occasional kiss merely to revive and intensify the cardiac-respiratory thrills. One thrills at the mere presence of the beloved person and at receiving her (or his) undivided attention. There is sometimes a feeling of elevation or "lift" like that experienced after climbing a mountain, when the forced breathing of the ascent gives way to the slower, deep breathing of comparative relaxation. There is a great deal akin to feelings of reverence, there is an attitude of submission, of "looking up to" the beloved. Sometimes the feeling is the same as that in religious ecstasy.

* Sexual, oral, and dermal. *Cf. ibid.*, pp. 64-68.—*Eds.*

The Temporary Nature of Cardiac-Respiratory Love: Infatuation

This cardiac-respiratory pattern is especially characteristic of the early stages of a love relationship, especially among young or unsophisticated persons. They may thank their lack of sophistication for this opportunity to experience one of life's keenest pleasures. It is often called "infatuation," "falling in love," "love at first sight," and so on. Popular parlance tries to make a distinction between "mere" infatuation and love. By "mere" infatuation is evidently meant an excited love attitude which fails to lead to the other kinds of love.* *Excited love cannot endure.* It is a transitory phenomenon. This is because it is essentially dependent upon the *novelty* of the stimulus. We have seen that it is a pattern belonging in part, at least, to the defensive system and innervated through the sympathetic. It is never entirely pleasant; the slightest hitch in the drama of events, the failure of something to happen when the emotions call for it, brings fear, anguish, and even anger. It is well known to interfere with the appetite, a fact which attests its defensive, sympathetico-neural character.

By the principle of psychic economy any such behavior tends to eliminate itself. Like fear, it diminishes in intensity as the stimulus becomes more familiar. Love grows less exciting with time, for the same biological reasons that the second run on a fast toboggan slide is less exciting than the first. The diminished excitement, however, may increase the real pleasure. Extreme excitement is practically the same as fear, and is unpleasant. After the excitement has diminished below a certain point, however, pleasure will again diminish, unless new kinds of pleasure have meanwhile arisen.

In the normal course of falling in love, these other kinds of pleasure increase as the excitement diminishes. For example, the brief occasional kiss for thrill only gives way to the more frequent and voluptuous kissing which yields oral, dermal, and genital pleasure. In the early stages the pleasure lies chiefly in the *thought* that "he (or she) actually did kiss me." In the later stages the pleasure lies more in the kissing itself. Scarcity values diminish while quantity values increase. Finally the lover finds himself bound to his partner by oral, dermal

---

* Noting the negative and positive connotations respectively of the terms *infatuation* and *true love*, Winch holds that *infatuation* merely denotes "a love relationship of which someone disapproves," while *true love* "designates the opposite, or approving, kind of value-judgment." R. F. Winch, *The Modern Family*, New York, Holt, 1952, p. 336.—*Eds.*

and genital love, but with the excited love vanished. The love reactions he now enjoys are not transitory and self-eliminating like excited love. They belong entirely to the appetitive system. They do not diminish through constant use any more than do the pleasures of eating decrease through years of familiarity.

Sometimes the decrease of excited love is not accompanied by the forging of these other love bonds. It may be because one partner refuses to permit sufficient oral, dermal, and genital stimulation (not necessarily through genital *contacts,* however). Or it may be that there is no lack of these pleasures, but that some feature of the behavior of one partner angers or disgusts the other, and these emotions of course tend to inhibit all pleasure reactions. It may be that the partners are not "suited," which means, essentially, that some aversion (previously conditioned reaction or attitude) of the one personality meets with just that characteristic in the other person which arouses it. Now their friends say that they were "just infatuated." But that "infatuation" was no different from the excited love which initiates many a successful courtship. The difference lay in the interaction process which followed the infatuation. To predict these would require a very wise person.

The Sequence of Love Reactions: Courtship and Marriage

In normal, conventional courtship, the oral pleasures are the first to develop as excited love cools. At first there will be pure oral pleasure. Then the oral stimulus will arouse more and more genital reaction. Under recent cultural attitudes this has been more true of the man than of the woman. The woman was inhibited against all genital excitement by early training; the man was trained to expect genital reaction but to conceal it from the woman, to keep it within certain bounds, and to seek no direct stimulus to it. If it came about through kissing and petting within certain conventional limits, it was all right, but one must not seek to intensify it by further bodily contacts. Today, we are aware, there is some change in cultural attitude in this sphere, so that the woman may conscientiously allow herself to *feel* passion to the same extent as the man, if she controls its expression.

In late courtship more extensive body caressing was tolerated, in which the whole pleasure was genital rather than oral, although any such pleasure was not supposed to be carried to the point of orgasm. In late years, there has been a growing attitude among some young people which tolerates this carrying out of passion to the climax, but through methods short of actual coitus, leaving the girl still a "technical virgin." This changed attitude is a matter of serious concern among sexologists. Some hold that it is harmful in that it trains people to bad habits of sexual satisfaction, that after marriage it will be more difficult to enjoy normal coitus. The change has one very beneficial corollary: namely, the attitude that whatever pleasures are obtained should be the same on both sides, and not mainly a masculine monopoly. But its total effect cannot be judged without much more serious investigation than has heretofore been given it.

After marriage, of course, the predominating source of pleasure becomes passion, stimulated by its more direct and normal methods. Oral pleasure becomes a preliminary and an adjunct. It is possible also that the tender attitude becomes stronger and more important after marriage than before, and that it intensifies with age, the partners coming to feel more and more toward each other as a mother feels toward her baby. This, however, is a matter of great individual differences.

One of the most interesting facts about married love is that the cardiac-respiratory love of the early days may be revived through novelties of circumstance, including reunions after temporary absences. It probably can never be as prolonged an experience as in the beginning, but its occasional revival may add much zest to life. In rare cases, marriage may not result and the partners may be separated for a long period; yet the love between them may be renewed at a later date under changed circumstances, with all the excitement that went with the first falling in love.

The Meaning of Constancy in Love

Thus, on the reaction side love is an ever-changing attitude. If "constancy" in love means faithfulness to the same person, then we must be prepared to accept a great inconstancy of physiological reaction. Those lovers who are most tolerant of such changes of feeling toward each other are the ones most likely to achieve permanency of love relationship. We must be prepared to accept the fading out of excitement, to accept the growing importance of passion even if at the expense of the "purer" and "more elevated" feelings and at the expense of the "innocent" kiss whose pleasure is entirely oral. We must be prepared for cyclical diminutions of passion itself, and for increases in "motherly" feelings. The beauty of all this is that, if we do not develop irritations about these changes, we often come back again and again, in cyclical fashion, to previous combinations of feeling. It is one of the supreme experiences of life to be told by one's partner on some occasion years after marriage, "I feel toward you now just as I did that day we had lunch in ——."

On the other hand are those persons, like the Don Juans, who are constant in the sense of being faithful to a particular feeling of love, while the identity of the beloved must continually change in order to maintain this same feeling. We may have our choice.

Tragedies Due to an Unscientific Ideology of Love

Our cultural attitudes are imperfectly adjusted to these facts of the love process. Two common kinds of tragedies result. One is that of the young people who marry because of excited love before they give the other kinds of love sufficient test. In this class also are those who, although they do not marry, yet grieve over the loss of something which in its very nature was transitory.

The other tragedy is jealousy because one's married or unmarried partner develops a new "infatuation." This new excitement does not necessarily mean the weakening of the permanent love. It is a reaction which in its very nature can occur only to a novel stimulus. It is conventional for the jealous partner to think that his (or her) failure of some sort is the cause of this new excitement. This is apt to be false; the more serious failure usually comes after jealousy has set in. The change of attitude, the withdrawing, the bitterness, on the part of the jealous one, cause the new excitement to develop into something more important than it would otherwise become. The triangle requires adjustments by all parties concerned. Culture has placed most of the burden of this adjustment upon the infatuated persons, whereas such a person is no more able to behave rationally than is a jealous one.

The Romantic Complex

With modern civilization we have the romantic complex, which is held by many to be an innovation in culture. It is generally assumed that there is some peculiar kind of love which gave rise to this romantic complex. Lester Ward and other sociologists have held that the chivalry complex of the Middle Ages was the source. Before that, mankind knew sexual love and the conjugal love of duty combined with sex, but did not know the modern romantic love of free choice. Later writers assign the specific origin to the French troubadour complex of the twelfth and thirteenth centuries, rather than to chivalry *per se*. Today we feel much less safe than did the early sociologists in identifying particular culture complexes with particular feelings. We are not at all sure that there is any new emotion in romantic love. There is no doubt, however, that a certain patterned combination of emotional attitudes, social relationships, and literary expressions originated in the late Middle Ages, and has in part formed the basis for modern romanticism. These sub-patterns seem to be especially characteristic:

1. The elevation of mate love to a plane of idealization higher than that of parental love, filial love, or other family love. The relationship between lovers takes precedence over obligations to the larger family group or the community. It, and not duty, is institutionalized in marriage.

2. Great stress on the excitement or cardiac-respiratory love, which is stimulated by novel, esthetic, and adventurous situations of first acquaintance, and which is supposed to be the beginning of all true love. The wish for adventure is closely tied to the wish for response.

3. Sexual love supposedly absent until excited, dermal, and oral reactions are well established. When it develops it is not given direct artistic expression as are the other three reactions, and is clothed with a symbolic rather than a sensory value. The sexual relationship is never recognized or alluded to except in idealized terms. Oral and tender love must be throughout marriage above the sexual. Theoretically there is perpetual courtship.

4. Free choice of mate, even in defiance of parental will. Difficulties overcome in achieving the union add to its emotional value. Each person is supposed to have an "affinity" who will be immediately recognized when met (love at first sight).

The Romantic Sequence of Love Feelings

There are certain practical consequences of this pattern. One is that romantic love is intensely monogamous at *any one time*. Yet, essentially, its loyalty is to *love* rather than to a person; so that, when two persons cease to maintain the romantic love relation, divorce is thought to be not only permissible, but a duty to the highest morality. Marriage without romantic love is anathema to the romanticist. Another consequence, and one responsible for much needless unhappiness, is the failure to recognize the many varied sequences of interaction which do lead to happy unions. Romantic love calls for this sequence: excited love, free choice, oral and dermal love, sexual love, marriage, then sexual intercourse but without abatement of excited, oral, and dermal love.

Any deviation from this sequence supposedly spoils the magic of romance. If choice is made coolly and intellectually without the preliminary "love at first sight," that is not romance. The newer romanticism cares less about the time of marriage in the process, but, still, it is intensely solicitous that intercourse should follow the other love reactions. It is only the attitude toward the importance of the marriage ceremony which has been changed in the last few years; the attitude toward the love process remains much the same.

Human experience reveals that "unromantic" love sequences can and do occur without preventing the growth of a thoroughgoing love. Successful love affairs occur in which the first emotion may be purely oral pleasure from a friendly experimental kiss, or a wave of tender feeling aroused by the other person's being in need of some help, or even pure passion. Tenderness may be a result as well as a cause of passion. Competent sexual intercourse tends to lead to tender feeling in both partners even if such feeling was absent at the outset, provided both are completely free from the guilt attitude in regard to their intercourse. Marriage does not always overcome this sense of guilt, when persons have been badly conditioned or educated in regard to sex. A mere intellectual acceptance of the rightness of sex will not necessarily do away with this guilt attitude. It goes deeper than that.

Romanticism Emphasizes Cardiac-Respiratory Love

If there is any type of love feeling that is especially characteristic of the romantic complex, it is excited love. Perhaps the significant feature is the presence of this kind of reaction in the male partner. Rarely before chivalry, or in non-European cultures, do we find such artistic and literary expression of an attitude of reverence and excited humility on the part of a man in response to a woman. In the popular literature today it is the thrill, the palpitation, the excitement of first acquaintance, the birth of love in a fear situation or a curiosity situation, which characterize our romanticism. D. H. Lawrence, who idealizes sexual behavior, definitely does not express this complex. But, also, a thoroughgoing description of tender feelings or of the emotions connected with caressing would be out of place in the popular romantic literature. It would seem that the only emotions whose literary description is really tolerated are the defensive emotions. Thrills, tremblings, palpitations, misgivings, fears, jealous "passions" (not passion at all, but anger), anguish, coldness, and bitterness may be dwelt upon at great length.

But these are merely emotions surrounding love; they are mostly sympathetic-neural patterns. The pleasant reactions stimulated through the cranio-sacral are not orthodox themes for literature; they are too "sensual." Yet it is only they which make love worth while except as an ephemeral thrill.

Puritanism and Romanticism Separated Sexual from Other Love

The typical male of our recent culture was trained to make a discrimination between sexual and tender feeling. Indeed, he learned, through masturbation, that the purely sensual gratification was possible without recourse to any person. If he tried to satisfy his sex desire through a personal object before marriage, he usually did so through the person of a prostitute. Culture did not let him develop tender feelings toward prostitutes. He learned, instead, to despise the very person who was the source of his gratification. Culture trained him to anticipate a higher, purer relationship with a wife. After attaining this nobler love, he might, on occasion, again revert to prostitutes. But this, the physical unfaithfulness, from the standpoint of the male sex, was not a real unfaithfulness, because the illicit action which he secretly indulged would be for the sake of a gratification of an entirely different kind. It would be better after marriage to do without the "lower" love but if one could not, one could keep it utterly separate from the "higher." The common result was that the man expected his wife to show sexual behavior of a much more restrained type than the prostitute, while he himself failed to awaken her full sex passion because of his perverted sense of delicacy. Married sex relations, in certain social classes, at least, became a tender but lukewarm ritual, in which the passion of the male only was regularly satisfied, and even his satisfaction obtained without resort to the more voluptuous and thoroughgoing stimulations.

One may assume, with Freud, that tenderness and sex are innately bound together, and have been forced apart by culture. Or one may assume that sex and tenderness, though innately separate, tend to become conditioned together on a subcultural level, and that culture here prevents this normal fusion. The practical result is the same. Our recent culture prevented the thoroughgoing union of these two reactions. But experience shows that they do tend to unite when the individual is left free to develop his wish goals without cultural restraint. Such a natural union would seem to offer a better chance of a harmonious, integrated love life.

CHAPTER 14

Dating and Courtship

WHERE marriages are agreed upon by the persons directly involved rather than by their families (*e.g.*, in traditional Japan), the culture must make some provision for pre-marital association and for mate-selection. In its context the American practice of dating (eventually leading to marriage for most persons) makes good cultural sense, a point developed in the piece by Winch. The diffidence of Elmtown adolescents on their first dates and the age-pattern in dating are described by Hollingshead. In an article which has become a sociological classic in vituperation Waller presents dating not only as a precursor to marriage but also as a means by which college students achieve status and exploit members of the opposite sex. Kirkpatrick and Caplow examine a number of dating relationships to determine their duration, how they came out, and how the persons involved felt about them.

FUNCTIONS OF DATING IN MIDDLE-CLASS SOCIETY*

ROBERT F. WINCH

Dating is a form of social interaction between a male and a female. The persons involved are usually unmarried, but actually or potentially

* Adapted and reprinted from *The Modern Family,* New York, Henry Holt & Co., 1952, pp. 435-41.

marriageable to each other. It is therefore an activity characteristic of adolescents and young adults.

The age at which dating begins is related to the subculture. Although we have little but impressionistic evidence on this point, it appears to begin earlier in urban than in rural areas. There is a general belief that the age has been lowered in many areas to coincide with the onset of puberty, and that in some cases it begins even earlier. The form of the social interaction is usually joint participation in some form of entertainment—movies, dances, parties, etc. For the duration of the date, which is usually no more than a few hours, the male and female are identified as constituting a pair.[1]

Insofar as it is related to marriage, dating is the "window-shopping" period—it carries no commitment to buy the merchandise on display. Dating in American culture has a number of functions, some of which are only indirectly or not at all related to marriage. In the first place, dating is a popular form of recreation, and thereby an end in itself. In the current setting, at least where the urban ethos prevails, a date carries no future obligation on the part of either party except, perhaps, for some reciprocation in entertainment.

A second function of the phenomenon of dating is that of socialization. It provides males and females with an opportunity to associate with each other, and thus to learn proper deportment and the social graces. It serves to eliminate some of the mystery which grows up about the opposite sex—a mystery which is fostered by the small-family system in which many children have no siblings of the opposite sex near their own age.

There is a third function, which is a corollary of the second. The opportunity to associate with persons of the opposite sex gives a person the chance to try out his own personality and to discover things about the personalities of others. The social situation of the adolescent causes persons of both sexes to be somewhat uncertain as to how successfully they will work through their various tasks of self-validation, especially that of achieving the appropriate sex-type. The dating process is a testing ground—both in the sense of providing repeated opportunities for the adolescent to ascertain his stimulus value to persons of the opposite sex, and of providing learning situations so that he can improve his

[1] This is different from the practice of "group dating" sometimes evidenced among younger adolescents. In the latter case boys go to some social function in a group, and the girls do likewise. In this situation there is no explicit pairing of boys and girls.

techniques of interaction. Dating allows him an opportunity to discover that potential love-objects are also insecure; thus the adolescent can universalize his insecurity and thereby reduce his own feelings of inadequacy. In the process of learning about the personalities of persons of the opposite sex, the male, for example, ceases to react to all females as "woman" and discovers that there are "women," *i.e.*, that females too are individuals and have idiosyncrasies.

This step is, of course, vital for the fourth function of dating, that of mate selection. Dating enables young men and women to test out a succession of relationships with persons of the opposite sex. One finds that he "gets along nicely" with some, not so well with others, that some relationships are thrilling—at least for a time—that others are satisfying, and still others are painful and laden with conflict. Through dating he can learn to interpret the behavior and thereby to diagnose the personalities of persons of the opposite sex. By noting with what kind of person his interaction is most gratifying he can learn the personality characteristics which he would find desirable in a spouse. Armed with this ability he is in a vastly improved position to set about the task of selecting a mate.

With the urban emphasis upon the need-meeting aspect of the marital relationship (in terms of affection, security, etc.), two or three dates barely allow the testing function to get under way. It is consistent with the urban setting, moreover, that the dating process should begin at increasingly early ages in order to extend the range of experience of each individual before he makes the ultimate choice.[2]

Although the meaning of dating is little understood and remains to be studied, it appears to vary with the situation. On some college campuses, for example, it is thought desirable to "fall in love" soon after arrival, and there is some tendency to idealize a couple who go together through their college years and marry on graduating. In other settings the practice of "going steady" is approved, but is not conceived as entailing any intent to marry. Here the relationship is regarded as a mutual convenience, since neither party needs to worry about getting a date for any social affair. There is still another variation, in which even "going steady" is regarded with disapproval, where there is more or less open hostility between the sexes, where one's

2 According to one reference it is necessary for a man to know twenty-five women in order to find one who would meet his needs. (*Cf.* C. R. Adams and V. O. Packard, *How to Pick a Mate*, New York, Dutton, 1946, p. 62.)

involvement in "love" seems tacitly to be regarded as betrayal of the sex-group, and where the "victim of love" receives punishment by the same-sex peer group in the form of hazing. An example of such hazing (which looks like retaliatory aggression) is the practice in one midwestern chapter of a fraternity of taking any member who has "put out" his pin to the campus pond, throwing him in, and making him run back to the chapter house clad only in shorts.

In some settings, especially in the school situation, dating serves the additional function of status-grading and status-achieving. In his famous article on "The Rating and Dating Complex"[3] Waller made the point that in campus dating there was exploitation in two senses: (a) each party tried to make the other fall in love "harder" and earlier, and (b) each was interested in the other for status considerations. So far as fraternity men and women are concerned, the latter point has been corroborated on the campus of one midwestern university by Ray, who asserts that dating is "one of the ways of gaining, maintaining or losing prestige for the house."[4] He found this to be considerably more true, however, of women's than of men's organizations, and pointed out that, while dating was one of the principal ways in which a sorority accumulated and maintained prestige, a fraternity had other avenues to prestige, such as athletics. Both in sororities and fraternities dating was found to be quite homogamous with respect to social status, but the men's dates tended to diverge more from their own statuses than did those of the women. In this kind of setting, moreover, considerable pressure to date is exerted upon those who would prefer not to. It is consistent with the directness and cruelty of adolescence that such pressure is often expressed in the form of group ridicule. The social conditions of college life, then, stimulate one (a) to date, and (b) to date the type of person approved by his social group. . . .

From the discussion of the pressures exerted by fraternities it follows that a date does not always signify a man's spontaneous and voluntary affectional interest in a girl. We have seen that young persons of both sexes in certain college situations are subjected to considerable pressure to show an interest in the opposite sex and to manifest that interest in an approved way. It should not be thought, however, that fraternities represent the only source of such pressure. Families are frequently

---

[3] See pp. 371-80 below.

[4] J. D. Ray, *Dating Behavior as Related to Organizational Prestige,* Department of Sociology, Indiana University, 1942, p. 42 (unpublished master's thesis).

interested in the courtship progress of their young people, and are traditionally disposed to encourage the mating interest of their spinster daughters, irrespective of whether the age of spinsterhood be defined as beginning at eighteen or twenty, as in Colonial times, or, a decade or so later, as in the college-trained groups of today.

Since courtship in American culture has the functions of personality-testing and mate selection, many (and at the college level the majority) of the relationships break up rather than continue into marriage. Burgess and Wallin report that 70 per cent of the men and women in their study of engaged couples had "gone steady" with at least one other person than the one to whom they were engaged.[5] A study by Kirkpatrick and Caplow may be interpreted as providing evidence that the breaking up of college love affairs is not generally traumatic to the persons involved. They obtained responses from 141 college men concerning 314 affairs, and from 258 women regarding 582 affairs. To the question, "How did you feel about the way it ended?" 50.5 per cent of the men's and 45.0 per cent of the women's responses fell into the categories: "indifferent," "relieved," "satisfied," and "happy." If the category "mixed regret and relief" is added, the proportions become 72.4 per cent for men and 66.1 per cent for women.[6]

DATING IN ELMTOWN*

August B. Hollingshead

Local folksways define picnics, dances, parties, and hayrides as date affairs at which a boy is expected to pair with a girl. The testimony of many students demonstrates that the vast majority have their first formal date on these occasions. Individuals recalled vividly whom the first date was with, where they went, who was there, and other details which marked this important step in the transition from childhood to adolescent life. The first date is often a cooperative enterprise which involves the members of two cliques of the opposite sex. Two illustra-

[5] From the forthcoming book on marriage by E. W. Burgess and Paul Wallin.

[6] Clifford Kirkpatrick and Theodore Caplow, "Courtship in a Group of Minnesota Students," pp. 381-97 below; cf. esp. p. 395.

* Adapted and reprinted by permission of the author and publisher from *Elmtown's Youth*, New York, John Wiley & Sons, Inc., 1949, pp. 223-27.

tions will be given to illuminate the process; both were taken from autobiographies of seniors. The first was written by a class III girl.*

I began to date in the eighth grade with boys I had played with all my life. I ran with a group of girls, and there was also a group of fellows we liked. At all social functions where boys and girls mixed, these two groups came together. We started running around in the fifth grade at Central School, but we did not date yet. We were always together at all school parties, and by the eighth grade we were having our own private parties to which these two groups and no one else was invited. We held these parties at the homes of the girls fairly frequently, usually on a Friday or Saturday night, sometimes on Sunday, but not often. We still did not have any regular dates until the end of the eighth grade.

[Then] Marion Stowe's mother had a party for us. She invited all the kids in both our groups. The fellows got together and decided they would have dates. Tom Biggers asked me to go to the party with him. I was so thrilled and scared I told him to wait until I talked it over with Mother. Mother thought I was too young to start having dates. I argued with her for two days. Dad couldn't see anything wrong with me going to the party with Tom; so Mother let me say "Yes." Tom's dad came by for us in their car and took us to the party, but we walked home. My next date was with Joe Peters during the summer before I started to high school.

Eddie Parker, a class IV junior, believed that his interest in dating went back to the seventh grade, when he and his friends began "to feel shy in the presence of girls," whereas they had been indifferent, aloof, or hostile to them before. His clique talked "a lot" about dates, girls they would like to date, and "women" in general, but no one was bold enough to make a date. This went on until the spring "we were in the eighth grade when all of us [his clique] decided one Saturday we would make dates with the girls in our class who lived in the neighborhood. We went around to their houses and asked them if they would go to the show with us. We made dates with five of them, and that night we all went to the show together." In this case, it would appear that the boys, and probably the girls as well, derived support from one another. If we accept student reports, common characteristics of these first dates

---

* Hollingshead divides Elmtown families into five social classes. Class I carries the most prestige, and class V, the least. Class III families, then, tend to cluster around the midpoint of Elmtown's prestige spectrum, while the generally "poor but honest" families of class IV are presented as distinctly lower in prestige than those of class III. For a description of the sub-cultural characteristics of Elmtown's five classes, see A. B. Hollingshead, *op. cit.*, chap. 5.—*Eds.*

are shyness, fear of doing the wrong thing, of making statements the other person will resent, and overcautiousness in the physical approaches of one partner to another. Both persons have been filled with so much advice by parents, usually the mothers, about how to act and what to expect from the date that both play their roles clumsily. They are told precisely what to say and do, when to come home, what they should not do, and what the consequences will be if they violate their instructions. As one class III girl said:

I was so scared by what Mother told me Jim might do I did not like the experience at all. He did not even try to hold my arm. I knew I was supposed to "freeze up" if he did and I was so ready to "freeze up" we walked all the way home without saying much. I knew he was afraid of me so we just walked along. I was so disappointed in that first date I did not have another for a year. I had several crushes on boys, but I couldn't bring myself to say "Yes" when they asked me for a date. In the latter part of my sophomore year, I had a crush on Larry Jacobs, and when he asked me for a date I said "Yes." We went together a few times when Frank Stone asked me for a date. I went to the Junior Play with him. After the play we went to Burke's [a popular restaurant] with the rest of the kids and then home. Oh, we had fun! Since then, I have had a lot of dates, and now I really enjoy them.

The more adventurous youngsters begin to date when they are 12 years of age—at picnics and family group get-togethers—and the parents are usually present. A definite dating pattern becomes clear during the fourteenth year; 20 per cent of the girls and 15 per cent of the boys report that they had their first dates when they were 13. A much larger number begins to date in the fifteenth year, and by the end of it approximately 93 per cent of both sexes are dating with some regularity. Among the sixteen-year-olds, dating is the accepted procedure, and the boy or girl who does not date is left out of mixed social affairs. Our data make it clear that between the beginning of the fourteenth and the end of the sixteenth years the associational pattern of these adolescents changes from almost exclusive interaction with members of their own sex to a mixed associational pattern similar to that found in adult life. In this period, certain activities, such as girls' "hag parties" and hunting and baseball among the boys, are organized on a single sex basis; and others, such as dances and parties, are almost exclusively mixed.

Forty-three per cent of the boys and 58 per cent of the girls report that they experienced the thrill of their "first date" before they entered high school. Dating before entry into high school is not related signifi- cantly to age, town or country residence, or class. On the contrary, it is associated with clique membership. Some cliques have a much higher ratio of dates than others, but we did not search for an explanation of this fact either within the cliques which dated or those which did not. The discrepancy between boys and girls with dating experience prior to entry into high school continues throughout the freshman year. This differential disappears in the sophomore year, and by the time the junior year is reached more boys than girls report dates. At this level only 1 out of 13 and 1 girl out of 10 claim they have never had a date. All senior boys report they have had dates, but 3 girls are still looking forward to this event.

About 51 per cent of 553 dates the students reported during April, 1942, were with other students who belonged to the same school class, that is, freshman with freshman, and so on.[1] When the dating partner belong to different school classes, the pattern is significantly different between the boys and the girls. One-third of the boys' dates are with girls who belong to a class *below* them in school, wheras 31 per cent of the girls' dates are with boys *above* them in school. This gives the freshman girl a wider opportunity for dates than the freshman boy, for she can be dated by a freshman or a boy from the sophomore, junior, or senior classes. Freshmen and sophomore boys are reluctant to ask a girl who belongs to a class above them in school for a date. Many girls do not like to date younger boys unless they possess specific prestige factors, such as athletic prowess, "family background," or "good looks." Only 15 per cent of the boys' dates are with girls from a higher school class than theirs. Almost two-thirds of these mixed dates (62 per cent) are between senior girls and junior boys; the remainder are between sophomore boys and junior and senior girls.

These figures bring out the effects of two customs on the dating relations of these young people. In the first place, the folkways of court-

[1] All statistical data on the dating pattern unless otherwise indicated, such as the figures on dates and no dates before high school, are derived from the analysis of the dates the students reported they had during April, 1942. April was selected as our sample month because by that time we knew the students personally and had asked them so many questions that we assumed, and correctly, that they would give us information about their dating behavior. A second reason for choosing April was the belief that by this late in the year the dating pattern of the student group would be well estab- lished. We also believed that it was better to attempt a complete study of dating behavior for a single month than to trust student memories over a longer period.

ship encourage a boy to date a girl younger than himself. The complement of this is that the girl expects to date a boy older than herself. The operation of this rule results in boys dating girls either the same age as themselves or younger. With the school classes graded principally along age lines, this means that the boys date girls from their own class or a lower class in school. Thus, the freshman, sophomore, and junior girls have more opportunities for dates than the senior girls. In the second place, the senior girls' dating chances are limited still further by an administrative rule which restricts to high school students any high school party at which there is dancing. This rule severely restricts the senior girls' dating field, and to a less extent the juniors', particularly in class IV, because boys at this level drop out of school sooner than girls. Thus, a shortage of senior boys, combined with the school rule that only students may attend high school dances, forces the senior girls to ask junior boys for dates or let it be known that they would like to go with a junior boy or not date at school affairs. Another effect of this aspect of the dating system is the limited opportunity open to the freshman boy to date girls. Within the high school, the only girls he can date readily are freshmen, and here he competes with sophomore and junior boys who have more prestige in the eyes of the girls than he does. Then, too, the older boys are more sophisticated, more experienced in the arts of love, usually have more money, and give the girls more status in their own eyes than a "green kid" whom they have known through years of close contact in elementary school. The net effect of these factors on dating is a significantly lower ratio of dates among freshman boys in comparison with freshman girls, and of more junior and senior girls dating younger boys or boys outside the student group.

THE RATING AND DATING COMPLEX*

Willard Waller

Courtship may be defined as the set of processes of association among the unmarried from which, in time, permanent matings usually emerge.

* Adapted and reprinted by permission of the author and publisher from the *American Sociological Review*, 2 (1937), 727-34.

This definition excludes those associations which cannot normally eventuate in marriage—as between Negro and white—but allows for a period of dalliance and experimentation. In the present paper we propose to discuss the customs of courtship which prevail among college students.

Courtship practices vary from one culture group to another. In many cultures marriage eventuates from a period of sexual experimentation and trial unions; in others the innocence of the unmarried is carefully guarded until their wedding day. In some cultures the bride must be virginal at marriage; in others this is just what she must not be. Sometimes the young are allowed no liberty of choice, and everything is determined for them by their elders. Sometimes persons marry in their own age group, but in other societies older men pre-empt the young women for themselves. Although there are endless variations in courtship customs, they are always functionally related to the total configuration of the culture and the biological needs of the human animal. It is helpful to remember that in a simple, undifferentiated, and stable society a long and complex process of choosing a mate is apparently not so necessary or desirable as in our own complex, differentiated, and rapidly changing society.[1]

The mores of courtship in our society are a strange composite of social heritages from diverse groups and of new usages called into existence by the needs of the time. There is a formal code of courtship which is still nominally in force, although departures from it are very numerous; the younger generation seems to find the superficial usages connected with the code highly amusing, but it is likely that it takes the central ideas quite seriously. The formal code appears to be derived chiefly from the usages of the English middle classes of a generation or so ago, although there are, of course, many other elements in it.

The usual or intended mode of operation of the formal mores of courtship—in a sense their "function"—is to induct young persons into marriage by a series of progressive commitments. In the solidary peasant community, in the frontier community, among the English middle classes of a few decades back, and in many isolated small communities

---

[1] James G. Leyburn quotes an old-fashioned Boer mother who said, "I am sick of all this talk of choosing and choosing . . . If a man is healthy and does not drink, and has a good little handful of stock, and a good temper, and is a good Christian, what great difference can it make to a woman which man she takes? There is not so much difference between one man and another." (*Frontier Folkways*, p. 129.) Such an attitude was possible in Boer society as it is not in ours.

in present-day America, every step in the courtship process has a customary meaning and constitutes a powerful pressure toward taking the next step—is in fact a sort of implied commitment to take the next step. The mores formerly operated to produce a high rate of marriage at the proper age and at the same time protected most individuals from many of the possible traumatic experiences of the courtship period.

The decay of this moral structure has made possible the emergence of thrill-seeking and exploitative relationships. A thrill is merely a physiological stimulation and release of tension, and it seems curious that most of us are inclined to regard thrill-seeking with disapproval. The disapproving attitude toward thrill-seeking becomes intelligible when we recall the purpose of such emotional stirrings in the conventional mores of courtship. Whether we approve or not, courtship practices today allow for a great deal of pure thrill-seeking. Dancing, petting, necking, the automobile, the amusement park, and a whole range of institutions and practices permit or facilitate thrill-seeking behavior. These practices, which are connected with a great range of the institutions of commercialized recreation, make of courtship an amusement and a release of organic tensions. The value judgment which many lay persons and even some trained sociologists pass upon thrill-seeking arises from the organizational mores of the family—from the fact that energy is dissipated in thrills which is supposed to do the work of the world, *i.e.,* to get people safely married.

The emergence of thrill-seeking furthers the development of exploitative relationships. As long as an association is founded on a frank and admitted barter in thrills, nothing that can be called exploitative arises. But the old mores of progressive commitment exist, along with the new customs, and peculiar relationships arise from this confusion of moralities. According to the old morality a kiss means something, a declaration of love means something, a number of Sunday evening dates in succession means something, and these meanings are enforced by the customary law, while under the new morality such things may mean nothing at all—that is, they may imply no commitment of the total personality whatsoever. So it comes about that one of the persons may exploit the other for thrills on the pretense of emotional involvement and its implied commitment. When a woman exploits, it is usually for the sake of presents and expensive amusements—the common pattern of "gold-digging." The male exploiter usually seeks thrills from the body of the woman. The fact that thrills cost money, usually the man's money, often operates to introduce strong elements of suspicion and antagonism into the relationship.

With this general background in mind, let us turn to the courtship practices of college students. A very important characteristic of the college student is his bourgeois pattern of life. For most persons, the dominant motive of college attendance is the desire to rise to a higher social class; behind this we should see the ideology of American life and the projection of parents' ambitions upon children. The attainment of this life goal necessitates the postponement of marriage, since it is understood that a new household must be economically independent; additional complications sometimes arise from the practice of borrowing money for college expenses. And yet persons in this group feel very strongly the cultural imperative to fall in love and marry and live happily in marriage.

For the average college student, and especially for the man, a love affair which led to immediate marriage would be tragic because of the havoc it would create in his scheme of life. Nevertheless, college students feel strongly the attractions of sex and the thrills of sex, and the sexes associate with one another in a peculiar relationship known as "dating." Dating is not true courtship, since it is supposed not to eventuate in marriage; it is a sort of dalliance relationship. In spite of the strength of the old morality among college students, dating is largely dominated by the quest of the thrill and is regarded as an amusement. The fact that college attendance usually removes the individual from normal courtship association in his home community should be mentioned as a further determinant of the psychological character of dating.

In many colleges, dating takes place under conditions determined by a culture complex which we may call the "rating and dating complex." The following description of this complex on one campus is probably typical of schools of the sort:

X College, a large state-supported school, is located in a small city at a considerable distance from larger urban areas. The school is the only industry of the community. There are few students who live at home, and therefore the interaction of the young is but little influenced by the presence of parents. The students of this college are predominantly taken from the lower half of the middle classes, and constitute a remarkably homogeneous group; numerous censuses of the occupations of fathers and of living expenses seem to establish this fact definitely. Nevertheless, about half of the male students

live in fraternities, where the . . . bill is usually forty-five or fifty dollars
a month, rarely as high as fifty-five. There is intense competition among the
fraternities. The desire for mobility of class, as shown by dozens of inquiries,
is almost universal in the group and is the principal verbalized motive for
college attendance.

Dating at X College consists of going to college or fraternity dances, the
movies, college entertainments, and to fraternity houses for victrola dances
and "necking"; coeds are permitted in the fraternity parlors, if more than
one is present. The high points of the social season are two house parties
and certain formal dances. An atypical feature of this campus is the unbalanced sex ratio, for there are about six boys to every girl; this makes necessary the large use of so-called "imports" for the more important occasions,
and brings it about that many boys do not date at all or confine their activities to prowling about in small industrial communities nearby; it also gives
every coed a relatively high position in the scale of desirability; it would
be difficult to say whether it discourages or encourages the formation of
permanent attachments. Dating is almost exclusively the privilege of
fraternity men, the use of the fraternity parlor and the prestige of fraternity
membership being very important. Freshman men are forbidden by student
tradition to have dates with coeds.

Within the universe which we have described, competition for dates
among both men and women is extremely keen. Like every other process of
competition, this one determines a distributive order. There are certain men
who are at the top of the social scramble; they may be placed in a hypothetical Class A. There are also certain coeds who are near the top of the scale
of dating desirability, and they also are in Class A. The tendency is for
Class A men to date principally Class A women. Beneath this class of men
and women are as many other classes as one wishes to create for the purposes of analysis. It should be remembered that students on this campus
are extremely conscious of these social distinctions and of their own position
in the social hierarchy. In speaking of another student, they say, "He rates,"
or "He does not rate," and they extend themselves enormously in order that
they may rate or seem to rate.

Young men are desirable dates according to their rating on the scale of
campus values. In order to have Class A rating they must belong to one
of the better fraternities, be prominent in activities, have a copious supply
of spending money, be well-dressed, "smooth" in manners and appearance,
have a "good line," dance well, and have access to an automobile. Members
of leading fraternities are especially desirable dates; those who belong to
fraternities with less prestige are correspondingly less desirable. I have been
able to validate the qualities mentioned as determinants of campus prestige
by reference to large numbers of student judges.

The factors which appear to be important for girls are good clothes, a smooth line, ability to dance well, and popularity as a date. The most important of these factors is the last, for the girl's prestige depends upon dating more than anything else; here as nowhere else nothing succeeds like success. Therefore the clever coed contrives to give the impression of being much sought after even if she is not. It has been reported by many observers that a girl who is called to the telephone in the dormitories will often allow herself to be called several times, in order to give all the other girls ample opportunity to hear her paged. Coeds who wish campus prestige must never be available for last minute dates; they must avoid being seen too often with the same boy, in order that others may not be frightened away or discouraged; they must be seen when they go out, and therefore must go to the popular (and expensive) meeting places; they must have many partners at the dances. If they violate the conventions at all, they must do so with great secrecy and discretion; they do not drink in groups or frequent the beer-parlors. Above all, the coed who wishes to retain Class A standing must consistently date Class A men.

Cressey has pointed out that the taxi-dancer has a descending cycle of desirability. As a new girl in the dance hall, she is at first much sought after by the most eligible young men. Soon they tire of her and desert her for some newer recruit. Similarly the coed has a descending cycle of popularity on the campus which we are describing, although her struggle is not invariably a losing one. The new girl, the freshman coed, starts out with a great wave of popularity; during her freshman year she has many dates. Slowly her prestige declines, but in this case only to the point at which she reaches the level which her qualities permanently assure her. Her descent is expedited by such "mistakes," from the viewpoint of campus prestige, as "going steady" with one boy (especially if he is a senior who will not return the following year), by indiscretions, and by too ready availability for dates. Many of the girls insist that after two years of competitive dating they have tired of it and are interested in more permanent associations.

This thrill-dominated, competitive process involves a number of fundamental antagonisms between the men and the women, and the influence of the one sex group accentuates these. Writes one student informant, a girl, "Wary is the only word that I can apply to the attitude of men and women students toward each other. The men, who have been warned so repeatedly against coeds, are always afraid the girls are going to 'gold-dig' them. The coeds wonder to what degree they are discussed and are constantly afraid of being placed on the black list of the fraternities. Then too they wonder to what extent they can take any man seriously without being taken for a 'ride'." Status in the one-sex group depends upon avoiding exploitation by the opposite sex. Verbatim records of a number of fraternity "bull sessions" were obtained a few years ago. In these sessions members are repeatedly warned that they are slipping, those who have fallen are teased without mercy, and others are warned not to be soft. And almost all of the participants pretend a ruthlessness toward the opposite sex which they do not feel.

This competitive dating process often inflicts traumas upon individuals who stand low in the scale of courtship desirability. "While I was at X College," said a thirty year old aluminus, "I had just one date. That was a blind date, arranged for me by a friend. We went to the dorm, and after a while my girl came down and we were introduced. She said, 'Oh, I'm so sorry. I forgot my coat. I'll have to go get it.' She never came down again. Naturally I thought, 'Well what a hit I made!'" We have already seen that nonfraternity men are practically excluded from dating; it remains to note that many girls elect not to date rather than take the dates available to them. One girl writes as follows: "A girl's choice of whom to fall in love with is limited by the censorship of the one-sex group. Every boy that she dates is discussed and criticized by the other members of the group. This rigid control often keeps a girl from dating at all. If a girl is a member of a group in which the other girls are rated higher on the dating scale than she, she is often unable to get dates with boys who are considered desirable by her friends. In that event she has to decide whether to date the boys that she can and choose girl friends who would approve, or she must resign herself to not dating."

Since the class system, or gradient of dating desirability on the campus, is clearly recognized and adjusted to by the students themselves, there are interesting accommodations and rationalizations which appear as a result of inferior status. Although members of Class A may be clearly in the ascendant as regards prestige, certain groups of Class B may contest the position with them and may insist upon a measuring stick which will give them a favorable position. Rationalizations which enable Class D men and women to accept one another are probably never completely effective.

The accommodations and rationalizations worked out by one group of girls who were toward the bottom of the scale of campus desirability are typical. Four of these girls were organized in one tightly compact "bunch." All four lived off campus, and worked for their room and board. They had little money to spend for clothes, so there was extensive borrowing of dresses. Members of the group co-operated in getting dates for one another. All of them accepted eleventh hour invitations, and probably realized that some stigma of inferiority was attached to such ready availability, but they managed to save their faces by seeming very reluctant to accept such engagements, and at length doing so as a result of the persuasion of another member of the bunch. The men apparently saw through these devices, and put these girls down as last minute dates, so that they rarely received any other invitations. The bunch went through "dating cycles" with several fraternities in the course of a year, starting when one of the girls got a date with one member of the fraternity, and ending, apparently, when all the girls had lost their desirability in that fraternity.

Partly as result of the unbalanced sex ratio, the boys of the group which we are discussing have a widespread feeling of antagonism toward the coeds. This antagonism is apparently based upon the fact that most of the male students are unable to date with coeds, at least not on terms acceptable to themselves. As a result of this, boys take great pride in the "imports" whom they bring in for house parties, and it is regarded as slightly disgraceful in some groups to date a coed for one of the major parties. Other men in the dateless group take on the role of misogynists—and read Schopenhauer.

During the winter term the preponderance of men assures to every coed a relatively high bargaining power. Every summer witnesses a surprising reversal of this situation. Hundreds of women school teachers flock to this school for the summer term, and men are very scarce; smooth, unmarried boys of college age are particularly scarce. The school-teachers are older than the boys; they have usually lost some of their earlier attractiveness; they have been living for some months or years within the school-teacher role. They are man-hungry, and they have a little money. As a result, there is a great proliferation of highly commercialized relations. The women lend their cars to their men friends, but continue to pay for repairs and gasoline; they take the boys out to dinner, treat them to drinks, and buy expensive presents for them. And many who do not go so far are available for sex relations on terms which demand no more than a transitory sort of commitment from the man.

The rating and dating complex varies enormously from one school to another. In one small, coeducational school, the older coeds instruct the younger that it is all right for them to shop around early in the year, but by November they should settle down and date someone steadily. As a result, a boy who dates a girl once is said to "have a fence around her," and the competition which we have described is considerably hampered in its operation. In other schools, where the sex ratio is about equal, and particularly in the smaller institutions, "going steady" is probably a great deal more common than on the campus described. It should be pointed out that the frustrations and traumas imposed upon unsuccessful candidates by the practice of "going steady" (monopolistic competition) are a great deal easier to bear than those which arise from pure competition. In one school the girls are uniformly of a higher class origin than the boys, so that there is relatively little association between them; the girls go with older men not in college, the boys with high school girls and other "townies." In the school which is not coeducational, the dating customs are vastly different, although, for the women at least, dating is still probably a determinant of prestige.

True courtship sometimes emerges from the dating process, in spite of all the forces which are opposed to it. The analysis of the interaction process involved seems to be quite revealing. We may suppose that in our collegiate culture one begins to fall in love with a certain unwillingness, at least with an ambivalent sort of willingness. Both persons become emotionally involved as a result of a summatory process in which each step powerfully influences the next step and the whole process displays a directional trend toward the culmination of marriage; the mores of dating break down and the behavior of the individuals is governed by the older mores of progressive commitment. In the fairly typical case, we may suppose the interaction to be about as follows: The affair begins with the lightest sort of involvement, each individual being interested in the other but assuming no obligations as to the continuation of the affair. There are some tentatives of exploitation at the beginning; "the line" is a conventionalized attempt on the part of the young man to convince the young woman that he has already at this early stage fallen seriously in love with her—a sort of exaggeration, sometimes a burlesque, of coquetry—it may be that each person, by a pretense of great involvement, invites the other to rapid sentiment-formation—each encourages the other to fall in love by pretending that he has already done so. If either rises to the bait, a special type of interaction ensues; it may be that the relation becomes exploitative in some degree and it is likely that the relationship becomes one in which control follows the principle of least interest, *i.e.*, that person controls who is less interested in the continuation of the affair. Or it may be that the complete involvement of the one person constellates the other in the same pattern, but this is less likely to happen in college than in the normal community processes of courtship.

If both persons stand firm at this early juncture, there may ensue a series of periodic crises which successively redefine the relationship on deeper levels of involvement. One form which the interaction process may assume is that of "lovers' quarrels," with which the novelists have familiarized us. A and B begin an affair on the level of light involvement. A becomes somewhat involved, but believes that B has not experienced a corresponding growth of feeling, and hides his involvement from B, who is, however, in exactly the same situation. The conventionalized "line" facilitates this sort of "pluralistic ignorance," because it renders meaningless the very words by means of which this state of mind could be disclosed. Tension grows between A and B, and is resolved by a crisis, such as a quarrel, in which the true feelings of the two are revealed. The affair, perhaps, proceeds through a number of such crises until it reaches the culmination of marriage. Naturally, there are other kinds of crises which usher in the new definition of the situation.

Such affairs, in contrast to "dating," have a marked directional trend; they may be arrested on any level, or they may be broken off at any point, but they may not ordinarily be turned back to a lesser degree of involvement; in this sense they are irreversible. As this interaction process goes on, the process of idealization is re-enforced by the interaction of personalities. A idealizes B, and presents to her that side of his personality which is consistent with his idealized conception of her; B idealizes A, and governs her behavior toward him in accordance with her false notions of his nature; the process of idealization is mutually re-enforced in such a way that it must necessarily lead to an increasing divorce from reality. A serious sentimental involvement develops, the individual comes to be increasingly occupied, on the conscious level at least, with the positive aspects of the relationship; increasingly he loses his ability to think objectively about the other person, to safeguard himself or to deal with the relationship in a rational way; we may say, indeed, that one falls in love when he reaches the point where sentiment-formation overcomes objectivity.

The love relationship in its crescendo phase attracts an ever larger proportion of the conative trends of the personality; for a time it may seem to absorb all of the will of the individual and to dominate his imagination completely; the individual seems to become a machine specially designed for just one purpose; in consequence, the persons are almost wholly absorbed in themselves and their affair; they have an *egoisme à deux* which verges upon *folie à deux*. All of these processes within the pair-relationship are accentuated by the changes in the attitude of others, who tend to treat the pair as a social unity, so far as their association is recognized and approved.

COURTSHIP IN A GROUP OF MINNESOTA STUDENTS*

CLIFFORD KIRKPATRICK AND THEODORE CAPLOW

This article reports an investigation made among students at the University of Minnesota inquiring into (1) courtship difficulties, (2) growth patterns in courtship experience, (3) conflict and confusion in student love affairs, and (4) the breaking of love affairs as a bereavement experience.

Our sample, like those utilized by most investigators in the study of the family, is by no means representative. The individuals, investigated in 1940, were not necessarily typical students, being drawn exclusively from sociology courses on the elementary or intermediate level. Cooperation on the part of the subjects was excellent; only three students

Table 1. The Distribution of Schedules by Sex

Affair	Male	Female	Total
First	135	251	386
Second	105	195	300
Third	56	106	162
Fourth	18	30	48
Total	314	582	896

refused to fill out a questionnaire in whole or in part. The study is based upon 399 questionnaires, reporting 896 serious love affairs. There were 141 questionnaires filled out by men reporting 314 affairs. There were 258 questionnaires filled out by women reporting 582 affairs. Of the serious affairs reported by men, 73.0 per cent had been broken up; and, of those reported by women, 71.0 per cent.

The mean age of the men was 22.0 years and that of the women 21.9 years. Both men and women had completed an average of 2.8 years of college work. Distribution by affairs is indicated in Table 1.

The rather elaborate and lengthy questionnaire was so prepared that responses could be indicated by writing simple numbers or by check-

* Adapted and reprinted by permission of the authors and publisher from *The American Journal of Sociology*, 51 (1945), 114-25.

ing appropriate items. The following presentation is a condensed statement of the findings.

Courtship Difficulties

Sociologists are increasingly interested in the conception of family life as a continuous ongoing pattern of social interaction, with causative factors operating from generation to generation. The family group provides both incentives and obstacles to its own self-perpetuation through courtship, marriage, and reproduction. More specifically, two hypotheses may be presented to which our data are relevant: (1) There is reason to think that complex and ambivalent emotional patterns within the family both facilitate and hamper the difficult transition from intrafamily interaction to the more mature interaction involved in courtship. (2) Many adolescents feel inadequate and isolated in

Table 2.   Attitudes of Father toward First Dating

ATTITUDE OF FATHER AS REPORTED BY STUDENTS	MALE		FEMALE	
	No.	Per cent	No.	Per cent
Prohibited or disapproved	...	8.5	...	18.0
Indifferent	...	70.7	...	62.3
Encouraged	...	20.8	...	19.7
Replying	130	...	239	...
Blank	11	...	19	...
Total	141	100.0	258	100.0

venturing into the courtship market. The difficulties may be due to the mere fact of adolescence, to ties and complexes acquired in the family group, to personal defects, or to external difficulties in the larger impersonal environment.

Certain of the findings bear upon the first hypothesis. The response of students to a question concerning their father's attitude toward first dating is indicated in Table 2. There is a bare suggestion in these figures that fathers, as the Freudian theory maintains, are more inclined to resist the threatened emotional loss of their daughters than of their sons. The difference of resistant fathers of daughters as compared with resistant fathers of sons is 9.5 per cent (18.0 − 8.5), and the corresponding critical ratio is 2.72. The corresponding responses in regard to mothers' attitudes are indicated in Table 3.

The most significant finding is a difference of 15.8 per cent (50.9 −

35.1) between the proportions of girls and boys who were encouraged by their mothers in initial courtship experience. The critical ratio is 3.0. There is a suggestion here—in accordance with Freudian theory—of a willingness on the part of mothers to eliminate potential rivals from the family group. But since mothers were more inclined than fathers to encourage the dating of sons as well, a Freudian hypothesis must be qualified by the recognition that mothers may simply be more interested than fathers in the mating process; they perhaps acquire vicarious experience through identification. The percentage difference between mothers and fathers in the encouragement of sons—14.3 (35.1 — 20.8)— has a critical ratio of 3.0.

Table 3. Attitudes of Mother toward First Dating

ATTITUDE OF MOTHER AS REPORTED BY STUDENTS	MALE		FEMALE	
	No.	Per cent	No.	Per cent
Prohibited or disapproved	...	7.3	...	9.5
Indifferent	...	57.6	...	39.6
Encouraged	...	35.1	...	50.9
Replying	137	...	240	...
Blank	4	...	18	...
Total	141	100.0	258	100.0

As to the second hypothesis—that of inadequacy and isolation in early courtship experience—two types of evidence might be cited, the first having to do with reported overt behavior, the second with evaluations. Only 5.7 per cent of the 141 men replying reported no dating. The corresponding percentage for 251 girls ($N = 258$) is 2.7. The mean number of individuals dated more than once by men was 10.3. In the case of girls, only 3 reported no repeated dating, but a rather suspicious number—56—left the question unanswered. For the 202 girls replying, the mean of individuals dated more than once was reported as 11.7.

Obviously, dating relationships vary tremendously in intimacy and significance. Out of the male sample ($N = 141$), 135 reported at least one important love affair, as defined in terms of "going steady, long duration, closeness to marriage, and emotional attachment." Of the female sample ($N = 258$), 251 reported at least one important love affair. The average number of important affairs reported for men is 2.23. The average number of important affairs reported for women is 2.26. It can only be speculated as to whether a given affair is really important or merely seems important to the student against a background of limited experience.

Indirect objective evidence concerning the adequacy of courtship opportunity may be obtained from "endogamous" courtship behavior of members of various religious groups. It might be expected that members of minority religious groups would have to accept "exogamous" affairs, that is to say, affairs with members of different religious groups.

A comparison of the religious groups in the first three affairs combined are found in Table 4. The critical ratio of the difference in endogamy between male Catholics and male Protestants (79.5 — 58.5) is 2.8. The most striking difference, however, is that between female Catholics and female Protestants (80.8 — 38.0), which has a critical ratio of 7.0.

Table 4.   Affairs "Endogamous" by Religious Affiliation (First Three Affairs)

RELIGIOUS AFFILIATION	MALES		FEMALES	
	No.	Per cent "Endogamous"	No.	Per cent "Endogamous"
Protestant	176	79.5	391	80.8
Catholic	53	58.5	71	38.0
Jewish	29	72.4	52	84.9
No preference or incomplete ..	38	. . .	38	. . .
Total	296	. . .	552	. . .

These rather surprising findings might conceivably be due to a greater tolerance by Catholics of premarital courtship relationships. More probably Catholics, particularly Catholic girls, are handicapped as a minority group in the courtship market and, rather than be left out, seek or accept relationships with persons of another religion. It might be argued that this latter hypothesis is refuted by the endogamy of the Jewish group. In this case, however, a stronger endogamous tradition with reference to Jew and Gentile may prevail over the willingness of a numerically smaller religious group to seek courtship partners outside their own religious circle.

Taking up the student's evaluation of the adequacy of his courtship experience, certain findings are presented in Table 5. It would seem that over a third of the college students in the sample did feel that they had difficulty in initial participation in the courtship market.

Table 5. Difficulty in Making the Acquaintance of Members of the Opposite Sex in Early Adolescence

RESPONSE	MALE		FEMALE	
	No.	Per cent	No.	Per cent
Yes	...	10.7	...	13.7
No	...	53.6	...	48.0
To some extent	...	35.7	...	38.3
Replying	140	...	256	...
Blank	1	...	2	...
Total	141	100.0	258	...

That the students are not merely indulging in gloomy recollections concerning past difficulties is suggested by evidence in Table 6. This evidence that a surprising proportion of students in even a coeducational college lack opportunity to meet persons of the opposite sex is borne out by an extensive survey made at the University of Minnesota in 1934.[1]

Table 6. Participation in Present Formal Social Activities

RESPONSE	MALE		FEMALE	
	No.	Per cent	No.	Per cent
Extensive	...	4.2	...	3.1
Considerable	...	14.2	...	21.5
Average	...	36.9	...	41.4
Little	...	36.9	...	30.5
None	...	7.8	...	3.5
Replying	141	...	256	...
Blank	0	...	2	...
Total	141	100.0	258	100.0

Student reactions to their present opportunities to meet members of the opposite sex are fairly well indicated in Table 7. The reasons alleged for such inadequacy as given by the 35.1 per cent of the men and the 40.6 per cent of the women who checked "inadequate" are presented in Table 8. It would seem fair to conclude that, from one cause or another, at least a third of the sample of Minnesota students find their opportunities to meet members of the opposite sex inadequate.

Does such a situation described above imply frustrated romantic

[1] Clara Brown, Anne Fenlason, *et al.*, "Student Social Life at the University of Minnesota," I (February 2, 1935), 38, 45, and 57. (Mimeographed.)

Table 7.   Present Opportunities to Meet Members of the Opposite Sex

RESPONSE	MALE		FEMALE	
	No.	*Per cent*	*No.*	*Per cent*
Adequate	...	64.9	...	59.4
Inadequate	...	35.1	...	40.6
Replying	139	...	255	...
Blank	2	...	3	...
Total	141	100.0	258	100.0

longing or is there a practical eagerness to find realistic adjustments? Subjects were asked whether they would patronize a dating bureau established by a respectable agency. To this "yes-or-no" question, of the 136 men replying ($N = 141$), 79.4 per cent said "No"; of the 250 girls answering ($N = 258$), 84.4 per cent replied in the negative. The coefficient of mean-square contingency between willingness to patronize

Table 8.   Reasons for Inadequacy of Present Opportunities to Meet
Members of the Opposite Sex*

RESPONSE	MALE ($N = 141$)	FEMALE ($N = 258$)
No time	42.9	36.9
No money	61.2	11.7
Meet wrong kind	72.2	13.6
Personality limitations	10.2	11.7
Lack social contacts	21.1	48.5
No fraternity (or sorority)	18.4	19.4
Other reasons	12.2	14.6

* These percentages are based on a check list, hence responses may be incomplete or overlapping due to the wording of the question. The sum of percentages should not be expected to total 100.

a dating bureau and the adequacy of present social opportunities was found to be .00. Perhaps it is not just dates that students want but also success in competition for dates.

For the 139 men ($N = 141$) who replied concerning both adequacy of courtship opportunity and degrees of personal happiness, the coefficient of mean-square contingency is .37. The corresponding measure for 254 girls ($N = 258$) is .38. If happiness is good, then the courtship situation is bad for some Minnesota students.

Growth Patterns in Courtship

Quite aside from a possible trend toward increasing likeness in status, there is the possibility of growth trends, that is, that some developments are due to either biological or social maturation. They may imply progressively *either* greater or lesser similarity between the sexes. A number of hypotheses present themselves, none of which, to our knowledge, has ever been adequately tested.

1. It would be plausible to set forth the hypothesis that exclusiveness as an index of affair significance would increase with later affairs. The schedule called for an estimate as to what proportion of the relationship involved "going steady" (exclusively) with the affair partner. The exclusiveness continuum involved the following categories: "All the time; Three-fourths of the time; One-half of the time; One-fourth of the time; Less than one-fourth of the time; Not at all." Considering only the first three affairs—those involving an adequate number of cases—a trend toward exclusiveness would be indicated by a coefficient of mean-square contingency exceeding 0. This assumes that the flow of the scatter diagram is in the direction both of later affairs and of categories implying greater exclusiveness. There were altogether 296 first, second, and third affairs reported by men. For 295 of these, information was given concerning exclusiveness. The coefficient of mean-square contingency based on this sample of 295 cases was .35. There is evidence, therefore, of only a slight trend toward exclusiveness in later affairs reported by males. In the case of 541 of the 552 first three female affairs reported, information was given concerning exclusiveness. The corresponding coefficient was .16. In the case of female students, therefore, there is only an insignificant trend toward greater exclusiveness in later love affairs.

A rough index of exclusiveness would be a ratio of the proportion of students going more than half of the time exclusively with their partners, to the proportion of students going exclusively less than half of the time. The mean exclusiveness ratios are shown in Table 9. The evidence is in line with the coefficients of contingency and suggests a sex difference.

2. A closely related hypothesis is that later relationships would be regarded as relatively more important. Response categories to the question, "Did you feel that the relationship was the most important thing in your life?" were "Often," "Occasionally," and "Never." There

were 294 schedules ($N = 296$) reporting first, second, and third affairs of men which also gave information upon importance. The relationship between categories of importance and order of affair may be expressed concisely by a coefficient of mean-square contingency. The coefficient in this case is .45. There were 549 schedules ($N = 552$) concerning first, second, and third love affairs of female students which also gave information on importance. The contingency coefficient relating categories of importance to order of affair proved to be .12. By this criterion, there is some slight evidence of increasing significance of later affairs for males.

Table 9.   Mean Exclusiveness Ratios by Sex and Affair

Affair	Male	Female
First	.876	.638
Second	1.080	.807
Third	1.870	1.021

Another question in the schedule consisted of a check list of twenty-five emotional states. The proportion of men checking the item "Love" was: first affair, 56.3; second affair, 69.5; and third affair, 78.6. The difference between the first-affair percentage and the third-affair percentage (78.6 — 56.3) has a critical ratio of 3.0. In the case of girls there is likewise a tendency toward increasing expression of "love" from affair to affair. The percentages are: first affair, 46.6; second affair, 63.1; and third affair, 70.8. The critical ratio of the difference between the first and the third affairs on this item (70.8 — 46.6) is 4.3.

3. A final hypothesis concerning possible growth patterns in courtship might posit a progressive sex differentiation. In other words, beyond a certain point, unfolding courtship experience might follow one path in the case of men and another with women. Thus, Professor Waller assumes that a basic factor in biosocial sex differentiation in courtship would be differential maturity with reference to matrimony. Waller implies that men go through a period of dalliance in which there is an exploiting attitude toward women and an avoidance of entanglements which might lead to premature marriage.[2] In our culture, women tend to marry at a somewhat earlier age than men and are as yet less burdened with the problem of financial adequacy for marriage. The outstanding problem for girls is to find a mate. Men have to find both the mate and the means.

---

[2] Willard Waller, *The Family*, New York, Dryden Press, 1938, esp. pp. 223-25.

A more specific version of the hypothesis would then be that there is increasing conflict, sex frustration, and unhappiness for males as economic forces separate young men from girls in their own age group. Obviously, this aspect of the courtship drama will depend upon sex ratios, relative economic status, and range of social participation.

That the alleged "period of dalliance" is not altogether associated with superficial emotion on the part of men is suggested by our data concerning love. It will be recalled that the proportion of men reporting love increased with later affairs. The percentages tend to be higher

Table 10.   Causes of Conflict

Affair	Male $(N = 296)$	Female $(N = 552)$
First	1.8	2.0
Second	2.5	2.5
Third	2.7	2.0

than the corresponding percentages for girls, combining all schedules. The proportion of the 314 male schedules reporting love was 65.3; the corresponding proportion of the 582 female schedules was 57.9. This difference has a critical ratio of 2.2.

Again, we find by combining affairs that the proportion of men's schedules reporting melancholy is 19.4; the corresponding proportion of women's schedules is 8.9. The difference has a critical ratio of 4.2.

Another question on the schedule was: "Which, if any, of the following were causes of conflict between you?" The average number of sources of conflict reported by males and females is indicated in Table 10. The differences here are not significant, but they suggest that life does not become simpler for men with later affairs.

More conclusive evidence of increasing difficulty of adjustment for men struggling with a double problem of mate-finding and mate-supporting is found in the reports concerning emotions experienced in the affairs. For purposes of condensation, the twenty-five emotional states in the check list were arbitrarily classified as "Pleasant," "Unpleasant," and "Ambiguous." Three observers agreed independently upon the classification of all items, with the exception of one minor item ("Apathy"), listed as unpleasant rather than ambiguous by a two-thirds vote. The ratio of the number of pleasant emotions to the number of unpleasant emotions checked was calculated for each sex and affair group. The results are presented in Table 11.

Table 11. Ratios of Pleasant to Unpleasant Emotions

Affair	Male (N = 296)	Female (N = 552)
First	1.83	1.29
Second	1.57	1.56
Third	1.40	1.78

There is some evidence that men undergo increasing relative maladjustment because of their double burden of mate-finding and mate-supporting. On the other hand, there is little evidence in these data that young men protect themselves during social and economic immaturity by a casual attitude toward love relationships.

Conflict and Confusion

The so-called "older generation" has only a very hazy idea about the amount of conflict and confusion involved in the courtship of college students. All students of the family must seriously consider the brilliant analysis of ego-rivalries in courtship as made by Waller. His principle of least interest,[3] somewhat anticipated by E. A. Ross,[4] is a challenging one. Unfortunately, our own data do not bear too directly upon this principle. The students were asked, "Did you worry about being more deeply involved than he or she?" Since there was no pronounced trend, the four affair categories have been combined. The results are given in Table 12.

Table 12. Worry about Involvement

RESPONSE	MALE		FEMALE	
	No.	Per cent	No.	Per cent
Often	...	10.5	...	10.0
Occasionally	...	35.5	...	26.7
Never	...	54.0	...	63.3
Replying	313	...	577	...
Blank	1	...	5	...
Total	314	100.0	582	100.0

[3] *Ibid.*, chaps. x and xi.

[4] *Principles of Sociology*, New York, Century Co., 1921, p. 136; *cf.* Waller, *op. cit.*, p. 275.

There is a slight tendency, perhaps overcompensatory, on the part of the girls to insist that they did not worry about depth of involvement. The critical ratio of the difference in percentages $(63.3 - 54.0)$ is 2.7. Whether in these percentages evidence is found of a clash between love and pride depends merely upon the amount of conflict of this kind which is expected. The figures tell nothing, of course, about the actual dominance and subordination in the relationships.

Table 13. Percentages of Various Items Checked on Combined Schedules

Conflict item	Males ($N = 314$)	Females ($N = 582$)
Jealousy	28.0	23.2
Possessiveness	22.0	23.7
Criticism	21.0	17.9
Irritability arising from emotional tension	19.4	15.3
Dislike of friends	19.1	13.4
Accusations of loss of interest	15.3	14.1
Disagreement about the future	13.1	17.3
Dominance	9.6	8.9
Dependence	3.2	4.3
Exploitation	1.4	3.5

The schedule used in this study included a check list of possible causes of conflict in the relationship. The percentages of the combined schedules on which various items were checked are indicated in Table 13.

Aside from causes of conflict, a specific question was asked concerning the incidence of jealousy. The evidence is presented in Table 14. The difference between the proportion of males and females replying "Often" $(16.4 - 10.5)$ has a critical ratio of 2.4. The difference between

Table 14. Jealousy

RESPONSE	MALE		FEMALE	
	No.	Per cent	No.	Per cent
Often	...	16.4	...	10.5
Occasionally	...	55.1	...	49.5
Never	...	28.5	...	40.0
Replying	312	...	580	...
Blank	2	...	2	...
Total	314	100.0	582	100.0

the proportions of males and females replying "Never" (40.0 — 28.5) has a critical ratio of 3.5. The evidence of ego clash is not striking; but, considering the data on accusations of loss of interest, possessiveness, and jealousy, there is an implication that ego manifestations play a part in the courtship of college students.

There is the implication in Waller's discussion of "Rating and Dating" that under certain conditions, particularly when males are scarce, girls are forced to compromise in matters of sex morality in order to avoid the breaking of relationships by dominant males who are making the most of their period of dalliance. In view of our policy of avoiding questions concerned with sex, which might reduce student co-operation, we do not have data which bear specifically upon this hypothesis. The

Table 15. "Giving In"

RESPONSE	MALE		FEMALE	
	No.	Per cent	No.	Per cent
Often	...	4.5	...	3.0
Occasionally	...	28.7	...	16.3
Never	...	66.8	...	80.7
Replying	310	...	569	...
Blank	4	...	13	...
Total	314	100.0	582	100.0

students were asked concerning their affairs, "Did you give in on important theoretical or moral issues for fear of losing him or her?" The replies are indicated in Table 15, which shows that there is a striking tendency for women to deny giving in. The critical ratio of the difference between percentages responding "Never" (80.7 — 66.8) is 4.3.

It is unfortunate that definite general conclusions cannot be drawn. There is evidence of ego clash, which may or may not exceed expectations. The Ross-Waller principle of least interest is not verified by the present data—but neither is it refuted.

Pending the advent of a social engineer who can guide young people directly to their ideal mates, a more or less painful process of selection and rejection—of making and breaking courtships—must take place. Within certain limits, a willingness to look further implies the finding of straighter sticks. There is some danger that an individual may lag in his search through inertia, lack of confidence, guilt feelings, or excessive sympathy. Sometimes there is the feeling that too much has been invested in even an unsatisfactory relationship to justify its rupture. One gambles, as it were, on the possibility of success in the old relationship because of one's share in the "jackpot." To test the general hypothesis of inertia, subjects were asked, "Did you have a feeling of being trapped in the relationship?" All affair schedules are combined in Table 16.

The difference between the percentages of men and women replying "Often" (7.1 — 5.4) has a critical ratio of only 1.0. On the other hand, the difference between the percentage of men replying "Never" and the percentage of women so replying (79.4 — 69.8) has a critical ratio

Table 16. "Feeling Trapped"

RESPONSE	MALE		FEMALE	
	No.	Per cent	No.	Per cent
Often	...	7.1	...	5.4
Occasionally	...	23.1	...	15.2
Never	...	69.8	...	79.4
Replying	312	...	574	...
Blank	2	...	8	...
Total	314	...	582	...

of 3.1. Stating the matter in positive terms, the difference between the percentages of males and females replying "Often" or "Occasionally" (30.2 — 20.6) has a critical ratio of 3.1. This evidence corroborates the prior statement of sex differentiation in courtship patterns and may reflect the vague perception by the men of the double burden of finding and supporting a mate. . . .

Another item diagnostic of confusion in roles was the question, "Did the girl take the initiative in telephoning, visiting, and so forth?" The findings are given in Table 17.

All the sex differences appear to be statistically significant. The critical ratios of the differences in percentage responses are: "Never," 8.1; "Occasionally," 4.3; "Often," 3.9; and "Very often," 3.4. There is, again, no absolute proof of confusion of roles in view of the fact that the girls in the sample were not necessarily courtship partners of the boys questioned. One does, however, conclude that there is no longer close conformity to standardized courtship roles and that there is probably a sex difference in the interpretation of whatever actually does take

Table 17. Initiative-in-Dating

RESPONSE	MALE		FEMALE	
	No.	*Per cent*	*No.*	*Per cent*
Never	...	29.4	...	56.5
Occasionally	...	54.8	...	39.5
Often	...	11.3	...	3.6
Very often	...	4.5	...	0.4
Always	...	0.0	...	0.0
Replying	313	...	564	...
Blank	1	...	18	...
Total	314	100.0	582	100.0

place in the initiating and financing of courtship activities. This second conclusion is, of course, less well founded than the first. In view of prior evidence concerning worry about involvement, initiative in courtship, and moral issues, one feels that the women in the sample like to present themselves in a conventional, respectable, and sought-after role.

The Breaking of Love Affairs

Courtship selection as it now operates involves the making and breaking of love affairs. Much trouble might be spared the human race if first love were the right love, but such is not yet the case. . . .

We gain more insight into the actual or pretended roles played by women as compared with men when causes responsible for the breakup are considered. The students were asked, "Who or what was responsible for the breakup?" . . .

Table 18. Cause of Breakup Checked by Males

Cause of breakup	*Male* (N = 230)	*Female* (N = 414)
Parents	5.2	8.6
Friends	3.1	5.8
Subject's interest in another person	15.1	32.2
Partner's interest in another person	29.7	15.3
Mutual loss of interest	46.9	38.1
Total	100.0	100.0

It is clear from the figures that the happy circumstance of mutual loss of interest is the one most commonly mentioned, yet differential loss of interest—the chief source of heartache—is implied in nearly half of the responses. It is interesting to note the frequency with which men as subjects admit loss of interest, as compared with women. The difference between the percentages (32.2 — 15.1) has a critical ratio of 4.7. The same implication is found in the critical ratio of 3.7 between the percentages of male and female responses (29.7 — 15.3) accusing their partners of loss of interest. Again we find evidence that the girl student in our sample either enjoys the role of being sought after or wishfully identifies herself with this role.

Shock and Readjustment

The preceding discussion makes pertinent a more specific inquiry into the emotional consequences and adjustive mechanisms associated

Table 19. Emotional State

Reaction	Male (N = 230)	Female (N = 414)
Bitter	5.9	4.4
Hurt	10.0	14.3
Angry	3.3	3.5
Remorseful	6.6	6.7
Crushed	1.8	5.0
Indifferent	19.4	16.2
Relieved	15.2	16.8
Satisfied	11.5	8.5
Happy	4.4	3.5
Mixed regret and relief	21.9	21.1
Total	100.0	100.0

with the breakup of love affairs. The students were asked concerning their affairs, "How did you feel about the way it ended?" Their responses by category are again expressed in Table 19 as percentages of the *total number of responses,* since an individual might indicate more than one emotional state.

By way of check upon bitterness, rationalization, and overcompensation, the subjects were asked the question, "Do you feel that you were more honest and straightforward than he or she?" The results are presented in Table 20. The more striking implication of the evidence is a general tendency to moral self-justification regardless of sex or affair. The only way to avoid this interpretation is to assume that both the men and the women have courtship partners morally inferior to those included in the sample, although not inferior in social status, intelligence, income, or education.[5] College students, like other mortals, perhaps need ability to see themselves as others see them.

While relatively few of our sample verbally admit serious emotional complications in the breakup, one should remember the evidence of overcompensation found by Waller in his study of divorced persons.[6] We have just noted evidence of moral self-justification; another question brings evidence suggestive of repression and frustration. There were 488 responses made by men to a check list of adjustive reactions,

Table 20. Judgments of Relative Honesty*

JUDGMENT	PER CENT REPLYING		
	First affair	*Second affair*	*Third affair*
	Males ($N = 230$)		
More	25.5	29.3	37.2
Equally	62.0	58.5	43.1
Less	12.5	12.2	19.7
Total	100.0	100.0	100.0
	Females ($N = 414$)		
More	26.9	33.3	36.7
Equally	59.6	59.5	46.6
Less	13.5	7.2	16.7
Total	100.0	100.0	100.0

* Only completed schedules for first three affairs included. Very few broken affairs were fourth affairs.

and 977 responses made by women. The percentages *of responses* falling in various categories are indicated in Table 21.

It is interesting to note that between a fifth and a third of the responses indicate either nocturnal dreaming or daydreaming about the former courtship partner. It is also interesting to note the incidence of the wishful illusion of recognizing the former partner. This phenomenon has been noted in the case of divorced persons by Waller. Waller likewise has noted, in his analysis of the alienation process, that a definite break tends to set up a certain glorification of a severed relationship. Our data show a greater tendency to remember pleasant than unpleasant things. In the case of men, the difference between

[5] Supporting data not here included.
[6] *The Old Love and the New*, New York, Liveright, 1930.

Table 21. Adjustive Reactions

Behavior	Male (N = 230)	Female (N = 414)
Frequenting places with common associations	11.3	10.0
Avoiding places with common associations	2.9	3.4
Avoiding meetings	4.7	5.1
Attempting meetings	5.9	4.3
Remembering only unpleasant things	2.3	3.9
Remembering only pleasant things	15.6	15.8
Dreaming about partner	15.5	11.2
Daydreaming	14.3	11.4
Imagining recognition	6.4	7.9
Liking or disliking people because of resemblance	5.5	5.4
Imitating mannerisms	1.8	2.1
Preserving keepsakes	7.0	10.8
Reading over old letters	6.8	8.7
Total	100.0	100.0

percentages (15.6 — 2.3) has a critical ratio of 7.8. In the case of women, the corresponding difference (15.8 — 3.9) has a critical ratio of 6.7.

Perhaps the most direct evidence concerning actual severity of a possible trauma following breakup is found in the length of time required for readjustment. The subjects were asked, "How long was the period of readjustment after the breakup?" The results are reported in Table 22.

Table 22. Adjustment Duration

ESTIMATE	PER CENT REPLYING	
	Males (N = 230)	Females (N = 414)
None	51.4	49.4
Several weeks	33.6	19.5
Several months	7.7	19.5
A year	5.0	6.3
Several years	2.3	5.3
Total	100.0	100.0

The data based upon combined affairs leave unaltered the implication that about one-half the students have no readjustment problem. Again, it may be noted that any evaluation of the findings depends in part upon preconceptions about heartbreak.

CHAPTER 15

Cultural and Psychic Determinants
in Mate-Selection

FROM LOVE and courtship we turn to a consideration of mate-selection and address the question: who marries whom? Students of marriage have formulated two responses to the question: (1) like seeks like, and/or (2) opposites attract. The two formulations have been labelled homogamy and heterogamy respectively.

The articles by Hollingshead, Glick and Landau, and Koller support the hypothesis that mate-selection is homogamous with respect to such social characteristics as race, religion, ethnicity, social class, age, and residence. Ktsanes and Ktsanes view homogamy in social characteristics as creating a field of eligible mates for each person, but they further hypothesize that within the field of eligibles mate-selection operates on the theory of complementary needs. This means that rather than select a mate psychically similar to oneself, a person tends to select a mate whose pattern of needs is complementary to his own.

CULTURAL FACTORS IN THE SELECTION
OF MARRIAGE MATES*

August B. Hollingshead

The question of who marries whom is of perennial interest, but only during the last half-century has it become the subject of scientific research. Throughout American history there has always been a romantic theory of mate selection, supported by poets, dramatists, and the public at large. Social scientists, however—a group of jaundiced realists, by and large—have little faith in this pleasant myth as an explanation for the selection of marriage mates.[1] Their theories can be divided between (1) the homogamous and (2) the heterogamous.[2] The theory of homogamy postulates that "like attracts like"; the theory of heterogamy holds that "opposites attract each other."

Certain aspects of each theory have been investigated by psychologists and sociologists. The psychologists have confined their attention almost exclusively to individual physical[3] and psychological[4] characteristics. Sociologists have focused, in the main, upon factors external to the individual. As a consequence, sociological research has stressed such things as ethnic origin,[5] residential propinquity,[6] race,[7] religion,[8] socio-

---

* Adapted and reprinted by permission of the author and publisher from the *American Sociological Review*, 15 (1950), 619-27.

[1] For a discussion of this theory and some facts to refute it see A. B. Hollingshead, "Class and Kinship in a Middle Western Community," *American Sociological Review*, 14 (August, 1949), 469-475.

[2] E. W. Burgess and Paul Wallin, "Homogamy in Social Characteristics," *American Journal of Sociology*, 49 (September, 1943), 109-124.

[3] J. A. Harris, "Assortive Mating in Man," *Popular Science Monthly*, 80 (1912), 476-492. This is the earliest review in the literature that tries to give a scientific explanation of the question of who marries whom. The studies reviewed primarily dealt with physical characteristics: deafness, health, longevity, age, stature, cephalic index, hair and eye color.

[4] Harold E. Jones, "Homogamy in Intellectual Abilities," *American Journal of Sociology*, 35 (1929), 369-382; E. L. Kelly, "Psychological Factors in Assortive Mating," *Psychological Bulletin*, 37 (1940), 493 and 576; Helen M. Richardson, "Studies of Mental Resemblance Between Husbands and Wives and Between Friends," *Psychological Bulletin*, 36 (1939), 104-120.

[5] Bessie B. Wessel, "Comparative Rates of Intermarriage Among Different Nationalities in the United States," *Eugenical News*, 15 (1930), 105-107; Bessie B. Wessel, *An Ethnic*

economic status,[9] and social characteristics in general.[10] While all of these researches have used empirical data, only a few of them have attempted to measure the significant cutural factors that impinge upon mate selection against the background of the theories of homogamy and heterogamy. We shall attempt to do this in this paper.

My attack upon this problem will be to state the theoretical limits within which mate selection may take place, then turn to a body of data to determine how, and to what extent, specific factors influence the selection of marital partners.[11]

Survey of Woonsocket, R.I., Chicago, University of Chicago Press, 1931; James H. S. Bossard, "Nationality and Nativity as Factors in Marriage," *American Sociological Review,* 4 (December, 1939), 792-798; Ruby Jo Reeves, *Marriages in New Haven since 1870 Statistically Analyzed and Culturally Interpreted,* doctoral dissertation Yale University (unpublished), 1938; Ruby Jo Reeves Kennedy, "Single or Triple Melting-Pot? Intermarriage Trends in New Haven, 1870-1940," *American Journal of Sociology,* 39 (January, 1944), 331-339; Milton L. Barron, *Intermarriage in a New England Industrial Community,* Syracuse, Syracuse University Press, 1946. Barron has a good bibliography of studies in this area, pp. 355-366.

[6] James H. S. Bossard, "Residential Propinquity as a Factor in Marriage Selection," *American Journal of Sociology,* 38 (1932), 219-224; Maurice R. Davie and Ruby Jo Reeves, "Propinquity in Residence Before Marriage," *American Journal of Sociology,* 44 (1939), 510-517; Ruby Jo Reeves Kennedy, "Pre-Marital Residential Propinquity and Ethnic Endogamy," *American Journal of Sociology,* 48 (March, 1943), 580-584; John S. Ellsworth, Jr., "The Relationship of Population Density to Residential Propinquity as a Factor in Marriage Selection," *American Sociological Review,* 13 (August, 1948), 444-448.

[7] Romanzo Adams, *Interracial Marriage in Hawaii,* New York, The Macmillan Co., 1937; Otto Klineberg, *Characteristics of the American Negro,* New York, Harper, 1944, especially Part V where Negro-white intermarriage and the restrictions on it imposed by law are discussed; U. G. Weatherly, "Race and Marriage," *American Journal of Sociology,* 15 (1910), 433-453; Robert K. Merton, "Intermarriage and the Social Structure," *Psychiatry,* 4 (August, 1941), 371-374; Constantine Panunzio, "Intermarriage in Los Angeles, 1924-1933," *American Journal of Sociology,* 47 (March, 1942), 399-401.

[8] Reuben R. Resnick, "Some Sociological Aspects of Intermarriage of Jew and Non-Jew," *Social Forces,* 12 (October, 1933), 94-102; J. S. Slotkin, "Jewish-Gentile Intermarriage in Chicago," *American Sociological Review,* 7 (February, 1942), 34-39; Ruby Jo Reeves Kennedy, "Single or Triple Melting-Pot?" *op. cit.*

[9] Richard Centers, "Marital Selection and Occupational Strata," *American Journal of Sociology,* 54 (May 1949), 530-535; Donald M. Marvin, "Occupational Propinquity as a Factor in Marriage Selection," *Publications of the American Statistical Association,* 16 (September, 1918), 131-156; Meyer F. Nimkoff, "Occupational Factors and Marriage," *American Journal of Sociology,* 49 (November 1943), 248-254.

[10] Walter C. McKain, Jr., and C. Arnold Anderson, "Assortive Mating in Prosperity and Depression," *Sociology and Social Research,* 21 (May-June, 1937), 411-418; E. W. Burgess and Paul Wallin, "Homogamy in Social Characteristics," *American Journal of Sociology,* 49 (September, 1943), 109-124.

[11] For purposes of this paper we shall rely upon tests of significance and measures of association to tell us what cultural factors are of greater or lesser importance in the determination of who marries whom.

Viewed in the broadest theoretical perspective of democratic theory, the choice of marriage mates in our society might be conceived of as a process in which each unattached biologically mature adult has an equal opportunity to marry every other unattached biologically mature adult of the opposite sex. Viewed from the narrowest perspective of cultural determinism, biologically mature, single males or females have only limited opportunity to select a marital partner. The first proposition assumes complete freedom of individual choice to select a mate; the second assumes that mates are selected for individuals by controls imposed on them by their culture. If the first assumption is valid we should find no association between cultural factors and who marries whom; if the second is descriptive of the mate selection process we should expect to find a strong association between one or several cultural factors and who marries whom. The second proposition, however, allows for individual choice within limits of cultural determinism; for example a Jew is expected to marry a Jew by the rules of his religion; moreover, he is more or less coerced by his culture to marry a Jewess of the same or a similar social status, but he has a choice as to the exact individual.

In the remainder of this paper I shall test five factors—race, age, religion, ethnic origin, and class—within the limits of the theories of homogamy and heterogamy and the abstract model I have outlined. The data utilized to measure the influence of these factors on the selection of marriage mates were assembled in New Haven, Connecticut, by a research team during the last year through the cooperation of the Departments of Vital Statistics of the State of Connecticut and the City of New Haven. All marriage license data on marriages in New Haven during 1948 were copied. Then parents, relatives, in some cases neighbors, were asked in February, 1949, to supply the addresses of each newly married couple. Addresses were obtained for 1,980 couples out of a total of 2,063 couples married in the city in 1948. Nine hundred and three couples, 45.8 per cent, had moved from the city, and 1,077, 54.4 per cent, were living in it in February, 1949. A 50 per cent random sample, drawn by Census Tracts from the 1,077 couples resident in New Haven, was interviewed with a schedule. The interview, which lasted from about an hour and a quarter to three hours, took place in the home of the couple, usually with both the husband and wife present, and occurred most generally in the evening or late afternoon.[12] In addition, twenty-eight census-like items such as age, occupation, birthplace, residence, and marital status, were available on all of the 1,980 couples.

The 523 interviewed couples were compared with the 1,457 non-interviewed couples, census item by census item, to determine if the interviewed group differed significantly from the non-interviewed group. No significance of difference was found at the 5 per cent level for any item, except where the husband and wife were both over 50 years of age.[13] Having satisfied ourselves that the interviewed group was representative of the total group, we proceeded with a measure of confidence to the analysis of our data.

Race

Our data show that the racial mores place the strongest, most explicit, and most precise limits on an individual as to whom he may or may not marry. Although interracial marriages are legal in Connecticut, they are extremely rare; none occurred in New Haven in 1948. Kennedy's analysis of New Haven marriages from 1870 through 1940 substantiates the rule that Negroes and whites marry very infrequently. Thus, we may conclude that a man's or woman's marital choice is effectively limited to his or her own race by the moral values ascribed to race in this culture. Race, thus, divides the community into two parts so far as marriage is concerned. Because there were no interracial marriages in 1948, and because of the small percentage of Negroes in New Haven, we will confine the rest of our discussion to whites.

Age

Age, like race, is a socio-biological factor that has a definite influence on marital choice. The effects of cultural usages and values on the selection of a marriage partner may be seen by a study of Table 1. While there is a very strong association between the age of the husband and the age of the wife at all age levels, it is strongest when both partners are under 20 years of age. Men above 20 years of age tend to

[12] Eighty-seven per cent of the interviewing was done by senior undergraduates and graduate students, 5 per cent by an assistant, and 8 per cent by the writer. Six per cent of the interviews were checked for reliability from one month to four months after the original interview.

[13] The principal reasons for this deviation were (1) twice as many older couples refused to be interviewed as those below fifty years of age, and (2) the age gap between interviewers and potential interviewees influenced the situation.

select wives who are in the same 5 year age group as they are, or a younger one. After age 20 the percentage of men who marry women younger than themselves increases until age 50. After 50 the marital partners tend to be nearer one another in age. Table 1 indicates further that controls relative to age rather effectively limit a man's choice to women of his age or younger, but that the woman cannot be too much younger or counter controls begin to operate. Evidence accumulated in the interviews shows it is widely believed that a young woman should not marry "an old man." The effects of this belief and practice are reflected in the lower left hand section of Table 1. There we see

Table 1. Age of Husband and Wife by Five-Year Intervals for New Haven Marriages, 1948

Age of husband	Age of wife								
	15–19	20–24	25–29	30–34	35–39	40–44	45–49	50 & up	Total
15–19	42	10	3						55
20–24	153	504	51	10	1				719
25–29	52	271	184	22	7	2			538
30–34	5	52	87	69	13	5			231
35–39	1	12	27	29	21	2	3		105
40–44		1	9	18	17	8	2	1	56
45–49	1		3	6	16	16	7	1	49
50 & up			1	4	11	15	21	43	95
Total	254	850	365	168	86	47	33	45	1848

$x^2 = 2574.8905$ $P < .01$ $C = .76$ $\bar{C} = .80$.

$C =$ The coefficient of contingency.

$\bar{C} =$ The corrected coefficient of contingency corrected for broad grouping by the formula given in Thomas C. McCormick, *Elementary Social Statistics*, McGraw-Hill, 1941, p. 207.

that only 4 men above 45 years of age, out of a total of 144, married women under 30 years of age. The age-sanctions that impinge on a woman with reference to the age of a potential husband narrow her marital opportunities to men her age, or to slightly older men. This usage is reflected in the upper right corner of Table 1, where marriages between older women and younger men are conspicuous by their absence. In short, differences in the customs relative to age and marital partners place greater restrictions on a woman's marital opportunities than a man's. Nevertheless, it is clear that the values ascribed to age restrict an individual's marital opportunities within narrow limits; and a woman's more than a man's.

Religion

The effects of religious rules on an individual's marital choices were very clear.[14] Next to race, religion is the most decisive factor in the segregation of males and females into categories that are approved or disapproved with respect to nuptiality. Ninety-one per cent of the marriages in this study involved partners from the same religious group. In the case of Jews, this percentage was 97.1, among Catholics is was 93.8 per cent; it fell to 74.4 per cent for Protestants. The differences in percentage, we believe, are a reflection of the relative intensity of in-group sanctions on the individual in the three religious groups. A striking point that emerged from our data is that the effects of religion on marital choice has not changed between the parental and present generation.[15] Table 2 shows that the number of Catholics who married Catholics, and Jews who married Jews, was almost the same in both generations. The number of Protestants who married Protestants dropped in the present generation, but not significantly in terms of the numbers involved.[16] The influence of religious affiliation on the selection of a marriage mate is obviously strongest in the Jewish group and weakest in the Protestant. This is reflected in the number of mixed marriages. On this point, we would remark that there is no consistent bias between sex and mixed Catholic-Protestant marriages; either partner is likely to be a Catholic or a Protestant. On the other hand, in Jewish-Gentile marriages it has been a Jewish male who has married a Gentile female.

I shall point out, in passing, that the very high association we found between religion and marriage is not unique. Burgess and Wallin reported a coefficient of contingency of .75 for the 1,000 engaged couples they studied in Chicago;[17] our data revealed a coefficient of contingency of .77 in the present generation. This is not essentially different from theirs. Because religion is so effective a control in the selection of

[14] R. J. R. Kennedy, "Single or Triple Melting-Pot? Intermarriage Trends in New Haven, 1870-1940," *op. cit.*

[15] Our discussion on this and subsequent points includes only white marriages where the religion of the couple and of their four parents was known. Moreover, the tabular materials include only white cases where the specific data called for by the table were complete. "Unknown" cases were eliminated in particular instances.

[16] The religious affiliation of marital partners in the present and parental generations was tested for significance; none was found; $\chi^2 = 6.7015$ with 8 degrees of freedom.

[17] E. W. Burgess and Paul Wallin, *op. cit.*, p. 115.

Table 2. Religious Affiliation in the Parental and Present Generations

A. *Wife's Father and Mother**

WIFE'S FATHER	WIFE'S MOTHER		
	Catholic	Protestant	Jewish
Catholic	274	11	0
Protestant	9	75	0
Jewish	2	1	65
Total	285	87	65

$$x^2 = 522.4592 \quad P < .01 \quad C = .74$$

B. *Husband's Father and Mother*

HUSBAND'S FATHER	HUSBAND'S MOTHER		
	Catholic	Protestant	Jewish
Catholic	273	12	0
Protestant	14	70	0
Jewish	0	0	68
Total	287	82	68

$$x^2 = 494.4359 \quad P < .01 \quad C = .73$$

C. *Husband and Wife*

HUSBAND	WIFE		
	Catholic	Protestant	Jewish
Catholic	271	20	0
Protestant	17	61	0
Jewish	1	1	66
Total	289	82	66

$$x^2 = 636.0297 \quad P < .01 \quad C = .77$$

* The religious affiliation claimed by the interviewees is used here.

marriage mates I shall hold it constant and analyze other factors in
terms of it.

Ethnic Origin

New Haven remained almost wholly Protestant religiously, and
British ethnically, from its settlement in 1638 until the late 1830's. Be-
ween 1830 and 1880 Irish arrived by the hundred; Germans and
Scandinavians by the score. The Irish and a minority of the Germans
vere Catholic and they soon established themselves in this burgeoning
railroad and manufacturing center. An expanding economy, coupled

with political and economic unrest in Southern and Eastern Europe, resulted in the influx of thousands of Polish and Russian Jews, and tens of thousands of Italians between 1890 and 1914. After 1914, the stream of immigration became a trickle that has never again been allowed to run freely. Thus, today, New Haven is composed mainly of three large religious groups and seven European-derived ethnic stocks: British, Irish, German, Scandinavian, Italian, Polish, and Polish Jewish.[18]

We cannot discuss how ethnicity is related to the selection of a marriage mate apart from religion, because religion and ethnic origin are so closely related. Observation of . . . Tables 3 through 6 . . . will show that ethnicity within a religious group has been a very potent factor in influencing the mate selection process in both the parental and the present generations, but it was stronger a generation ago than it is now. Although ethnic lines are crossed within the Catholic and the Protestant faith more frequently in the present than in the parental generation, this is not true for the Jews. Furthermore, ethnic lines in both generations were crossed, for the most part, within religious groups. This means that the Catholics are becoming a mixture of Irish, Polish, and Italian as a result of intermarriage between these groups, but there is still a large block of unmixed Italian stock in New Haven and smaller blocks of Irish and Polish. The Protestants, on the other hand, select marriage partners mainly from the British segment of the city's population; a minority choose a partner from a Northwestern European group, and in some cases both partners will be of German or Scandinavian descent. Kennedy discovered this process in her study of New Haven marriage records from 1870 to 1940, and developed her theory of the triple melting-pot in terms of it.[19]

. . . Table 6 . . . indicates that, in most cases, marriages across religious lines involve the mixing of ethnic stocks. This is true whether Catholics and Protestants marry, or Jews and Gentiles, because the members of each religious group came from such different parts of Europe. From the viewpoint of assimilation, marriages across religious lines are crucial if the triple melting-pot is to become a single melting-pot. But as Kennedy's and our data show, we are going to have three pots boiling merrily side by side with little fusion between them for

[18] We are excluding Negroes from our discussion.

[19] For a discussion of this theory see Ruby Jo Reeves Kennedy, "Single or Triple Melting-Pot? Intermarriage Trends in New Haven, 1870-1940," *op. cit.*

Table 3.† Per cent of Interethnic and Intra-ethnic Marriages in the Present and Parental Generations among Catholics*

	Couples	Parents
Intra-ethnic	56	84
Interethnic	44	16
	100 (N = 271)	100 (N = 542)

Table 4.† Per cent of Interethnic and Intra-ethnic Marriages in the Present and Parental Generations among Protestants*

	Couples	Parents
Intra-ethnic	34	68
Interethnic	66	32
	100 (N = 61)	100 (N = 122)

Table 5.† Per cent of Interethnic and Intra-ethnic Marriages in the Present and Parental Generations among Jewish*

	Couples	Parents
Intra-ethnic	100	100
Interethnic	0	0
	100 (N = 66)	100 (N = 132)

Table 6.† Per cent of Interethnic and Intra-ethnic Marriages in the Present and Parental Generations among Mixed Religions*

	Couples	Parents
Intra-ethnic	18	86
Interethnic	82	14
	100 (N = 39)	100 (N = 78)

* The religious affiliation claimed by the interviewees is used here.
† Adapted from texts.—Eds.

an indefinite period. Furthermore, if the rules relative to mixed marriages in the Roman Catholic and Jewish churches were followed strictly there would be no mixing of the contents of one pot with those of another. To be sure, ethnic intermixture would occur, but within each respective religious group.

Class

Our discussion of the relationship between social class and marriage will be based on cases where the husband, the wife, and both parental families were *de facto* residents of New Haven.[20] The analysis of 1,008 marriages where the husband, the wife, and their families were residents of New Haven revealed that the class of residential area in which a man's or a woman's family home is located has a very marked influence on his or her marital opportunities. In 587 of these 1,008 marriages, or 58.2 per cent (see Table 7), both partners came from

Table 7.   Residential Class of Husband and Wife for Residents of New Haven

Class of husband	Class of wife						Total
	I	II	III	IV	V	VI	
I	13	7	1	0	3	1	25
II	8	56	8	12	13	8	105
III	1	4	15	5	7	7	39
IV	0	8	4	55	35	38	140
V	0	12	8	30	252	87	389
VI	0	5	9	40	60	196	310
Total	22	92	45	142	370	337	1008

$$x^2 = 1045.0605 \quad P < .01 \quad C = .71 \quad \overline{C} = .77$$

the same class of residential area. When those that involved a partner from an adjacent class area were added to the first group the figure was raised to 82.8 per cent of all marriages.

Careful study of the data presented in Table 7 will reveal that the residential class in which a family has its home has a different effect on a woman's marital opportunities in comparison with a man's. While the modal, as well as the majority, of marriages at all levels united class equals, when class lines were crossed the man selected a woman from a lower class far more frequently than was true for women. For instance, if you look at Table 7 you will see that 12 men from class I married women from lower ranking areas, and four of the twelve

[20] The index of class position used here was developed by Maurice R. Davie on the basis of the ecological analysis he had made of the city of New Haven. Davie has ranked the 22 natural ecological areas that are primarily residential into six classes. Class I is the best and class VI the worst type of residential area. For a discussion of the project on which these ratings are made, see Maurice R. Davie, "The Patterns of Urban Growth," *Studies in the Science of Society*, G. P. Murdock, *ed.*, New Haven, 1937, pp. 133-161.

married girls from class V and class VI areas. On the other hand, 9 women from class I areas married men from lower ranking areas, but 8 of the 9 came from a class II area and 1 from a class III area. No man from class IV, V, or VI areas married a woman from a class I

Table 8. Residential Class of Husband and Wife by Religious Groups

A. *Catholic*

RESIDENTIAL CLASS OF HUSBAND	RESIDENTIAL CLASS OF WIFE	
	I-III	IV-VI
I-III	16	7
IV-VI	12	161
Total	28	168

$$x^2 = 74.8413 \quad P < .01$$

B. *Protestant*

RESIDENTIAL CLASS OF HUSBAND	RESIDENTIAL CLASS OF WIFE	
	I-III	IV-VI
I-III	12	4
IV-VI	1	18
Total	13	22

$$x^2 = 18.0923 \quad P < .01$$

C. *Jewish*

RESIDENTIAL CLASS OF HUSBAND	RESIDENTIAL CLASS OF WIFE	
	I-III	IV-VI
I-III	24	2
IV-VI	3	15
Total	27	17

$$x^2 = 26.6687 \quad P < .01$$

area. If you follow down the successive class levels on Table 7 you will see that this tendency is repeated all the way to class VI. It is clearest, however, in classes IV and V. In class IV, only 12 women from classes II and III combined married men from class IV. On the other hand, class IV men married 35 class V and 38 class VI women, for a total of 73. Fifty class V men married women from classes II, III, and IV, but 87 married class VI women. These figures reveal that the man has a wider range of choice than a woman, but he tends, when he goes outside of his own class, to marry a woman in a lower class. From whatever way we view Table 7, it is evident that the class posi-

Table 9. Years of School Completed by Husband and Wife by Religion

A. *Catholic*

YEARS OF SCHOOL HUSBAND	9 & less	YEARS OF SCHOOL WIFE	
		10–12	13 & more
9 & less	35	19	1
10–12	33	128	27
13 & more	5	15	19
Total	73	162	47

$$\chi^2 = 80.9784 \quad P < .01$$

B. *Protestant*

YEARS OF SCHOOL HUSBAND	9 & less	YEARS OF SCHOOL WIFE	
		10–12	13 & more
9 & less	11	3	0
10–12	10	26	7
13 & more	3	6	16
Total	24	35	23

$$\chi^2 = 38.9932 \quad P < .01$$

C. *Jewish*

YEARS OF SCHOOL HUSBAND	9 & less	YEARS OF SCHOOL WIFE	
		10–12	13 & more
9 & less	0	0	0*
10–12	0	22	11
13 & more	0	8	26
Total	0	30	37

$$\chi^2 = 12.6033 \quad P < .01$$

* The zero cells were not included in the χ^2.

tion of a family is a factor that exerts a very important influence on the marriage choice of its children.

Now that we have seen the larger picture, we will look at it from the special perspective of a combination of religion and residential class. Because the number of cases where we knew both religion and class level was small in some residential areas, we have combined classes I through III, and classes IV through VI in Table 8. Table 8 indicates very clearly that the class factor operates independently of religion, and with about equal force in each religious group. What is especially significant is that the effects of class position on who marries whom are so strong in each religious group.

Education operates in the same way as residence to sort potential marriage mates into horizontal status groups within the confines of religion. Within each religious group men with a particular amount of education married women with a comparable amount of education in very significant numbers. This tendency was strongest in the Jewish and weakest in the Catholic group. The strong association between the educational level of the husband and the wife, so evident in Table 9, is not a new development. We compared the education of husbands and wives in the parental generation by religious groups and found that for both the husband's parents and the wife's parents the association held. Moreover, the coefficients of contingency for each set of parents by religion were almost the same, as the following tabulation shows:

Religion	Husband's parents'	Wife's parents'
Catholic	.57	.58
Protestant	.58	.59
Jewish	.59	.59

These coefficients indicate that education, along with religion, has influenced the mate selection process for at least two generations.

In summary, this paper has attempted to throw light on three questions: *first,* does a biologically mature unattached adult have an equal opportunity to marry an unattached mature adult of the opposite sex? *Second,* what restrictions are placed on his choice by society, and *third,* how effective are certain selected restrictions in limiting his choice? These questions become meaningful only when we relate them to the two propositions outlined in the introduction. There I set up a model with theoretical limits of absolute freedom of individual choice in the selection of a marital partner at one pole, and no choice at the other.

The data presented demonstrate that American culture, as it is reflected in the behavior of newly married couples in New Haven, places very definite restrictions on whom an individual may or may not marry. The racial mores were found to be the most explicit on this point. They divided the community into two pools of marriage mates and an individual fished for a mate only in his own racial pool. Religion divided the white race into three smaller pools. Persons in the Jewish pool in 97.1 per cent of the cases married within their own group; the percentage was 93.8 for Catholics and 74.4 for Protestants. Age further subdivided the potential pool of marriage mates into rather definite age grades, but the limits here were not so precise in the case of a man as of a woman. The ethnic origin of a person's family placed further restrictions on his marital choice. In addition, class position and education stratified the three religious pools into areas where an individual was most likely to find a mate. When all of these factors are combined they place narrow limits on an individual's choice of a marital partner. At the moment we cannot go beyond this point and assign a proportionate probable weight to each one.

In conclusion, I think the data we have presented strongly support the proposition that one's subculture, and one's race, age, and class positions in the society effectively determine the kind of a person one will marry, but not the exact individual. In a highly significant number of cases the person one marries is very similar culturally to one's self. Our data clearly support the theory of homogamy, rather than that of heterogamy, *but* a generalized theory of the precise influence of cultural and individual factors on the selection of marriage mates remains to be formulated. This is an objective for sociologists to work toward.

AGE AS A FACTOR IN MARRIAGE*

Paul C. Glick and Emanuel Landau

Age is one of several important factors that tend to limit the choice of a marriage partner. There is a general tendency in American society for men to marry for the first time when they are in their twenties and for them to marry a wife a few years younger than they are. Age at first marriage varies over a relatively limited number of years for most men and women, and the difference between the ages of most spouses likewise is subject to a small range of variation. There is the

* Adapted and reprinted by permission of the authors and publisher from the *American Sociological Review*, 15 (1950), 517-29.

additional tendency for the difference between the ages of the spouses to be greater if either or both are marrying for the sceond or subsequent time.

However important age may be in marital selection, other factors, such as propinquity of residence, quite often outweigh it. Furthermore, age at marriage is associated with the age at which physical maturity is reached, the age at which marriageable persons of the two sexes are concentrated, the age at which education is completed, the age at which self-support begins, the age at which children can be borne, and the like. Some, if not all, of these items vary from one racial, religious, or economic group to another and among persons within any one group.

Nor is age at marriage a tendency that is independent of the times. There is evidence that the median age at marriage has declined since 1890. On the basis of census data on marital status and age, the estimated median age at first marriage for men who had ever been married at the time of the 1890 census was 26.1 years; it dropped to 24.3 years for 1940, and to 22.7 years for 1949. For women, the corresponding figures were 22.0 years for 1890, 21.6 years for 1940, and 20.3 years for 1949.[1] Furthermore, age at marriage differs from prosperity to depression[2] and from peacetime to wartime. Marriages may be postponed

[1] The 1940 figure for females is based on census returns on age at marriage. It is quoted here because it has been used in several other publications and because it differs so slightly from the 1940 figure (21.5 years) based on the same method used in calculating the other estimated medians cited here. Estimated median ages at first marriage for persons enumerated in each census from 1890 to 1940 and the methods by which the medians were obtained were published by the Bureau of the Census in *Population—Special Reports*, Series P-45, No. 27, "Age At First Marriage." The figures for 1949 are based on statistics published in the Census Bureau's *Current Population Reports*, Series P-20, No. 26, "Marital Status and Household Characteristics," and supplemental data for men in the armed forces. See also the article by Paul C. Glick, "The Family Cycle," pp. 81-92 above. Nation-wide data on age at marriage are not available from statistics based on marriage records. Statistics for 23 states on age at marriage were published in the Census Bureau's *Vital Statistics—Special Reports*, 17: 85-108, "Marriage Statistics—Resident Brides and Grooms by Age: Collection Area, United States, 1940," March 1943 (out of print). Marriage statistics are now collected by the National Office of Vital Statistics. Figures for selected states on age at marriages during recent years will soon be published by that agency. See Samuel C. Newman, "The Development and Status of Vital Statistics on Marriage and Divorce," *American Sociological Review*, 15 (June 1950), 426-429.

[2] Evidence of such variation in age at marriage and especially of a decline in the difference between the ages of spouses at marriage during the depression of the 1930's is presented by Walter C. McKain, Jr., in an unpublished thesis, "Assortative Mating in Prosperity and Depression, with Special Reference to Ages, Residences, and Occupations of the Contracting Parties." See also Walter C. McKain, Jr., and C. Arnold Anderson,

or set forward, depending on the level of economic activity and psychological factors that prevail. Furthermore, practices with regard to age at marriage are commonly known to differ widely from country to country. Child marriages in India and late marriages in Ireland are cases in point.

It is beyond the scope of this paper to treat all of the ramifications of the subject that have been introduced. The paper is essentially an analysis of national data collected at one point in time. The value of the results would have been improved if more of the factors mentioned above could have been taken into account.

In April 1948, the Bureau of the Census included several supplemental questions on the schedule used in its monthly sample survey of a cross-section of about 25,000 scientifically selected households in 68 counties or groups of counties throughout the nation. In addition to questions asked each month on age, sex, employment status, occupation, and industry, the schedule included questions, as in April 1947 and earlier surveys, on income and marital status; and, for the only time during the 1940's, the sample survey included questions on number of times married and duration of present marital status. From the last three items, age at present marriage, widowhood, or divorce was also derived. The present paper deals primarily with some of the results obtained from this survey. Since the figures are based on a sample, they are subject to sampling variability. Therefore, the smaller figures, as well as small differences between figures should be interpreted with particular care. Nevertheless, the relationships revealed by the data should be useful for analytical purposes.

The first topic discussed is age of men and of women at marriage and remarriage. This is followed by a consideration of the differences between the ages of husbands and their wives. Finally, each of these subjects is treated in relation to selected socio-economic characteristics.

Age at Marriage and Remarriage

The period when half of the men have entered their first marriage is between the ages of about 22 and 28 years, according to the results

"Assortative Mating in Prosperity and Depression," *Sociology and Social Research,* 21 (May 1937), 411 ff.; Otis D. Duncan, "The Factor of Age in Marriage," *The American Journal of Sociology,* XXXIX (January 1934), 469 ff.; and James H. S. Bossard, "Age Factor in Marriage: A Philadelphia Study, 1931," *The American Journal of Sociology,* XXXVIII (January 1933), 536 ff.

of the 1948 survey. One-half of the men who were still married to their first wife had married sometime during the six-year span. (This span is described statistically as the difference between the first and third quartiles of the distribution of ages at first marriage.) Furthermore, as many had married before they had reached their 22nd birthday as had married after they had passed their 28th birthday. (See Figure 1.)

The average (median) age at first marriage for the men who were still married to their first wife at the time of the 1948 survey was 24.2 years.[3] It does not follow, however, that 24 was the modal age at marriage, that is, that more of the men married when they were 24 years old than at any other age. As a matter of fact, only 9 per cent of the men married for the first time when they were 24. There were about as many men reported as having married at age 21, 22, or 23 as at age 24. Only 9 per cent were first married before they were 20 and 7 per cent after 35. At each year of age after 24, the number marrying for the first time tapered off, gradually at first and then relatively more sharply.

Age at first marriage for women is lower, of course, and even more narrowly restricted in range than that of men. One-half of the women surveyed in 1948 who were still in their first marriage had entered matrimony between the ages of about 19 and 24—a span of 5 years. The median age of women at first marriage was 20.9 years. The peak years at which women entered their first marriage were from 18 to 21, inclusive; about 10 or 11 per cent of the women were reported as having married at each of these four ages. At the extremes, only 15 per cent of the women were first married before they were 18 years old and 7 per cent after they were 30.

This background serves as a basis for certain observations and con-

---

[3] This figure constitutes a revision of the corresponding figure, 24.7 years, published in Table 11 of the Census Bureau's *Current Population Reports,* Series P-20, No. 23, "Marital Status, Number of Times Married, and Duration of Present Marital Status: April, 1948." All of the medians presented in that table should be reduced by one-half year, because the medians were derived as if age at entry into present marital status had been obtained by a direct question in the survey, instead of being obtained indirectly in response to a question on duration of present marital status. The uncorrected figures were cited on page 728 of the article by Paul C. Glick, "First Marriages and Remarriages," *American Sociological Review,* 14 (December, 1949), 726-734. Earlier in this paper figures on the estimated median age at first marriage for 1949 based on the marital status and age distribution of the population were cited. Since the methods used in obtaining the 1948 and 1949 figures are not the same, the reader should not interpret the apparently marked difference between the figures given for these two years as indicating the amount of change during the intervening period in age at first marriage.

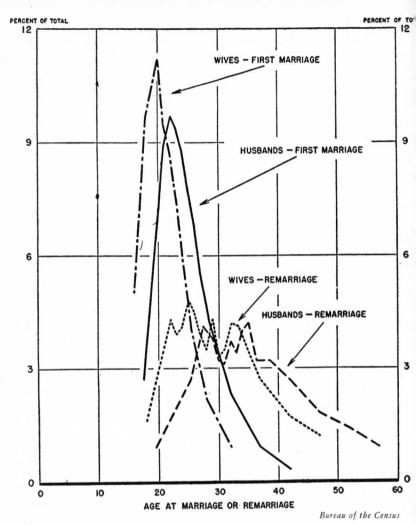

Figure 1.   Husbands and wives by age at first marriage and remarriage:
United States 1948.

clusions. First, there is a relatively narrow age period during which
the majority of men and women enter their initial marriage.

Second, although the range of age at first marriage is rather narrow,
there is enough variation to warrant giving more attention to the dispersion, and less to the central tendency, with regard to age at first

marriage, than has been given in some earlier treatments of the subject.

Third, changes in the average age at which education is completed have not affected the average age at marriage very seriously. In spite of the great increase in the proportion of persons who complete high school or who attend college, there has been no apparent repercussion on the average age at marriage. A counteracting factor that may have operated to encourage earlier marriage, on the other hand, is the wider dissemination of knowledge and practice with respect to family limitation.

Fourth, the period when men first marry may be compared with the corresponding period when men enter the labor force. A study made by the Bureau of Labor Statistics showed that half of the men enumerated in the 1940 census started their participation in the labor force between the ages of 15.3 and 18.1 years, with as many starting before age 15 as after age 18. Since so many reservations must be recognized because of differences in the base dates and other problems of comparabilty, however, further study is needed before a definitive statement can be made as to what proportion of the husbands precede their entrance into marriage with a given number of years of labor force participation.

Color differences and urban-rural differences in age at first marriage are not available from the 1948 sample survey, but they were obtained in the tabulations of the 1940 census data on the fertility of women. The 1940 tabulations on age at first marriage were based on a sample of about 3½ per cent of all women in the United States.[4]

Nonwhite women who had ever been married were about two years younger, on the average, than the corresponding group of white women at the time of first marriage. The median age at first marriage for nonwhite women was 19.3 years and that for white women, 21.1 years. These figures undoubtedly reflect well-known differences in the average income and occupational level of the two color groups. (See section below on classifications by socio-economic characteristics.)

Urban women were about 1 year older, on the average, than rural women at the time of first marriage, according to the 1940 figures.[5]

---

[4] The statistics on age at first marriage by color and residence presented here are from the Census Bureau's *Population—Special Reports*, Series P-45, No. 7, *op. cit.*

[5] Data for 1910 show a similar urban-rural differential in age at first marriage. See Frank W. Notestein, "Differential Age at Marriage According to Social Class," *The American Journal of Sociology*, XXXVII (July 1931), 22-48. In his study, the universe was limited to women who had been married five to nine years and who were under forty years of age at first marriage.

Age at entry into first marriage was about the same, on the average, for rural-nonfarm and rural-farm women. The somewhat older age of urban women at first marriage is very likely associated with the fact that women in cities are more likely to work for wages or salaries outside the home before marriage than women in rural areas.

Let us turn now to an analysis of age at remarriage. Of the 35 million married men in 1948, about 4½ million, or 13 per cent, had been married more than once. Their median age at remarriage was 36.5 years. A comparison of this figure with that for the median age at first marriage, 24.2 years, shows a substantial difference, namely 12 years. A comparison of the distribution of age at remarriage with that of age at first marriage is likewise very striking. The central one-half of the ages at remarriage for men cover the 17-year span from about 29 to 46 years of age. The corresponding span for age at first marriage was only 6 years.[6] (See Figure 1.)

About as many women as men in 1948 were remarried, but the women remarried at a considerably earlier age. The median age at remarriage for the 4½ million women who were still married at the survey date was 30.8 years. Once again the dispersion of ages at remarriage is very large. The central one-half of the ages at remarriage cover the 14-year span from about 25 to 39 years.

One of the gaps in our knowledge is the contribution of previously divorced persons, as compared with previously widowed persons, to the numbers of remarriages at different age levels. We have an indication, however, that about three-fifths of those who were remarried in 1940 had been previously divorced.[7] With the increase in the number of divorces between 1940 and 1948, it is likely that the ratio of previously divorced persons to previously widowed persons has risen at all ages of remarriage. Certainly most of those remarrying at the earlier ages are persons whose first marriage was broken by divorce and most of those remarrying at the later ages are persons whose previous marriage

[6] See Census Bureau's *Current Population Reports*, Series P-20, No. 23, *op. cit.* See comment on revised medians in footnote 4.

[7] See Census Bureau's *Vital Statistics—Special Reports*, 17: 128-129, "Marriage Statistics—Resident Brides and Grooms by Previous Marital Status: Collection Area, United States, 1940," March 1943; also see the discussion of available figures on previous marital status presented in *The American Family*, a report on the Inter-Agency Committee for the National Conference on Family Life, May 1948, U. S. Government Printing Office, 1949, p. 21.

was broken by death of the spouse. These facts would lead one to expect that the distribution of ages at remarriage was bimodal.

As pointed out above, women who remarry do so at a much younger age, on the average, than men do. This tendency suggests that the period between the dissolution of marriage and remarriage is briefer for women than it is for men. Statistics are not available on a national scale, however, to demonstrate this point. If it is true, a plausible explanation would probably include reference to the greater dependence of women on someone else for financial support.

Another hypothesis, on which there is some evidence from independent studies based on selected samples, is that women who marry at an extremely young age are more likely than those who marry at a more mature age to have their marriages dissolved by divorce;[8] such women would be expected to remarry subsequently at a relatively young age.

Again, women whose marriages are broken when they are past middle age, usually by widowhood, apparently have poorer remarriage prospects than men whose marriages are broken when they are past middle age. One reason for this is the fact that many widows would lose their pension rights or their inheritances if they remarried. This reason may be less important a factor, however, than other factors in accounting for the ratio of three widows for every widower in the United States. These other factors include the younger age of women at first marriage, with the consequence that women usually outlive their husbands; and also the more favorable survival rates of women at all ages. Because widows so greatly outnumber widowers and thus so often hold the life's earnings of the family, a large part of the wealth of the country is in the hands of widows. . . .

Differences Between Ages of Husbands and Wives

In our society there is a well-established pattern of differences between the ages of spouses, namely, the husband is generally a few years

---

[8] See Howard Becker and Reuben Hill (eds.), *Marriage and the Family*, Boston, D. C. Heath and Company, 1942, pp. 462-463; Meyer F. Nimkoff, *Marriage and the Family*, Boston, Houghton Mifflin Company, 1947, pp. 546-547; Andrew G. Truxal and Francis E. Merrill, *The Family in American Culture*, New York, Prentice-Hall, Inc., 1947, pp. 701-703; Metropolitan Life Insurance Company, "The Chances of Marriage and of Remarriage," *Statistical Bulletin*, January 1944. Statistics on divorce rates and marital death rates are presented in an article by Paul H. Jacobson, "Total Marital Dissolutions in the United States: Relative Importance of Mortality and Divorce," in *Studies in Population*, Princeton University Press, 1949, pp. 3-16.

older than his wife. This is not a rigid pattern, inasmuch as there is variation from couple to couple and also inasmuch as the pattern is not the same in remarriage as it is in first marriage. We shall return to

Table 1. **Number of Years Wife Was Younger or Older than Her Husband, for Married Couples, 18 to 74 Years Old, by Number of Times Married, for the United States: Civilian Population, April 1948**

(A minus sign for a quartile indicates that the quartile fell among wives who were younger than their husbands)

Years wife was younger or older than her husband	Husband and wife married once	Husband and/or wife married more than once
Number*	27,164,000	6,110,000
Per cent	100.0	100.0
Wife younger than husband	77.8	74.9
10 years or more younger	7.9	27.6
6 to 9 years younger	16.7	18.0
5 years younger	7.7	5.5
4 years younger	9.4	5.9
3 years younger	11.2	5.7
2 years younger	12.5	6.3
1 year younger	12.4	5.9
Wife same age as husband	10.2	6.5
Wife older than husband	12.0	18.6
1 year older	5.4	4.6
2 years older	2.7	3.0
3 or 4 years older	2.4	4.3
5 years or more older	1.5	6.7
Quartile		
First (years)	− 5.4	− 10.2
Second (median years)	− 2.8	− 4.7
Third (years)	− 0.7	− 0.5

*Married couples with both spouses living together. Excludes 1,015,000 married couples with one or both spouses under 18 years old; both 75 or over; or one between 18 and 74 and the other under 18 or over 74.

Source: Bureau of the Census.

some reflections on the possible reasons for the pattern, or patterns, after we have set forth some of the facts.

This part of the 1948 study is necessarily limited to married couples still living together at the survey date. Some of the findings are limited to persons 18 to 74 years of age (thereby omitting 3 per cent of the couples) and others are limited to couples with both spouses married only once (thereby omitting 19 per cent).[9]

The findings in Table 1 indicate that the average wife was 2.8 years younger than her husband,[10] where both the husband and his wife were married only once and where the median was used as the measure of the average.

However, the average wife, strictly speaking, was one of a small minority; only 11 per cent of all wives were just 3 years younger than their husbands. Half of the wives' ages fell below those of their husbands by about 1 to 5 years. In fact, 78 per cent of all wives were younger than their husbands and only 12 per cent were older; the remaining 10 per cent were the same age as their husbands. (See Figure 2.)

The figures just cited pertain to married couples living together in their first marriage. Quite a different picture is portrayed for couples with one or both spouses married more than once. Here the average wife was 4.7 years younger than her husband. In other words, marital unions involving at least one partner with a previously broken marriage tended to comprise husbands and wives whose ages were 2 years farther apart than those involving no partner with a previously broken marriage. Moreover, couples involving remarriages had a far wider scatter of the differences between the ages of the spouses, as indicated by the fact that the central one-half of the age differences included wives about 1 to 10 years younger than their husbands. The corresponding range for first marriages was 1 to 5 years younger.

Now let us consider some implications of the differences between the ages of spouses that we have set forth. Some of the factors in marital selection, such as propinquity and relative ages of men and women at physical maturation, were mentioned at the outset of the paper. In addition, the fact that three-fourths of the husbands are older than their wives seems to reflect the fundamental tendency for the hus-

[9] For 1948 statistics on age of husband by age of wife not shown in the present paper, see the Census Bureau's *Current Population Reports,* Series P-20, No. 26, *op. cit.*

[10] This figure is one-half year less than the difference between the median age of men at first marriage and the median age of women at first marriage for all married persons married only once (24.2 years minus 20.9 years). There is no mathematical requirement that the figures should be approximately equal, but familiarity with the subject matter would have led one to expect them to be nearly alike.

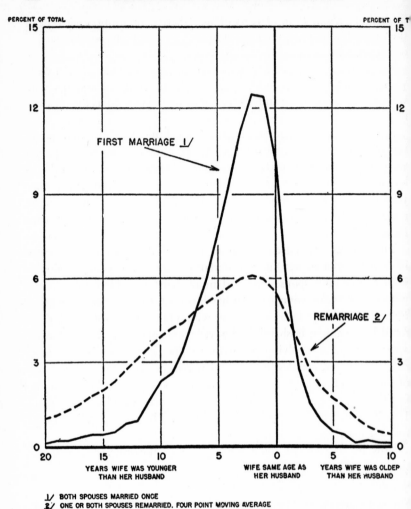

PERCENT OF TOTAL

PERCENT OF T

FIRST MARRIAGE 1/

REMARRIAGE 2/

| 20 | 15 | 10 | 5 | 0 | 5 | 10 |

YEARS WIFE WAS YOUNGER
THAN HER HUSBAND

WIFE SAME AGE AS
HER HUSBAND

YEARS WIFE WAS OLDER
THAN HER HUSBAND

1/ BOTH SPOUSES MARRIED ONCE
2/ ONE OR BOTH SPOUSES REMARRIED. FOUR POINT MOVING AVERAGE

Bureau of the Census

Figure 2.   Years wife was younger or older than her husband: United
States 1948.

band to be the sole, or at least primary, provider of economic support of
the family. In order for him to prepare for his role as provider, he
usually spends several years of apprenticeship at his job or profession.
Again, a young woman may be expected to prefer as a marital partner

a man who is somewhat older than she is and therefore likely to furnish a better livelihood than one who is her own age or younger.

The underlying factors, whatever they may be, that influence men to select wives a few years their juniors and that influence women to select husbands a few years their seniors may also operate in drawing together persons with extreme differences in age, as does happen in a minority of the cases. To illustrate, the young woman who places more than the usual amount of emphasis on material comforts or social status may be more readily attracted by the man who chooses to postpone marriage for a longer period of time than usual in order to be able to acquire more wealth, earning capacity, and social status before marriage than one who does not choose to do so.

Social pressures no doubt serve to restrain couples with large gaps in age from marrying.[11] In the case of first marriages, these pressures are augmented by the relative abundance of young adult single persons of nearly the same age. Moreover, persons marrying for the first time tend to select as a partner one who is also marrying for the first time; whereas those who remarry tend to select a partner who has been previously married.[12] In so doing, the person who is approaching first marriage tends to choose a mate more nearly his or her own age than the person does who is approaching remarriage. The difference between these two patterns seems to be the result of the interaction of the factors of selection and availability.

Another approach to the analysis of differences between the ages of spouses is found in the figures presented in Table 2. This table shows the median difference between the ages of husbands and their wives according to how old the husband (or wife) was at the survey date. The figures show that for successively older husbands, the median difference in age increased. The increase was much less pronounced for first marriages than for remarriages. Thus, among first marriages, the wife was only about 1 year younger, on the average, where the husband was between 18 and 24 years old, but the wife was 4 years younger, on the average, where the husband was 65 to 74 years of age. By contrast, among remarriages, the difference in age of the spouses was negligible where the husband was 18 to 24 years old but the wife

[11] For a study of the tendency for husbands and wives to have similar characteristics, see Ernest W. Burgess and Paul Wallin, "Homogamy in Social Characteristics," *The American Journal of Sociology*, XLIX (September 1943), 109-124.

[12] See Table 7 in the Census Bureau's *Current Population Reports*, Series P-20, No. 21, "Characteristics of Households, Families, and Individuals: April, 1948."

was about 10 years younger, on the average, where the husband was 65 to 74.

Before proceeding to comment on these figures let us note how unlike the figures just cited are the corresponding figures by age of

Table 2. Median Difference between Age of Husband and Age of Wife, by Age at Survey Date, for Married Couples, 18 to 74 Years Old, by Number of Times Married, for the United States: Civilian Population, April 1948

Subject	Husband and wife married once	Husband and/or wife married more than once
Median Years Wife Was Younger Than Her Husband		
Total*	2.8	4.7
Husband 18 to 24 years old	1.0	0.1
Husband 25 to 34 years old	2.3	2.1
Husband 35 to 44 years old	2.9	4.3
Husband 45 to 54 years old	3.4	6.1
Husband 55 to 64 years old	3.8	7.3
Husband 65 to 74 years old	4.3	9.7
Median Years Husband Was Older Than His Wife		
Total	2.8	4.7
Wife 18 to 24 years old	2.9	6.4
Wife 25 to 34 years old	2.7	5.4
Wife 35 to 44 years old	2.8	5.6
Wife 45 to 54 years old	3.1	4.4
Wife 55 to 64 years old	2.6	2.3
Wife 65 to 74 years old	1.3	0.3

* See footnote in Table 1.
Source: Bureau of the Census.

wife. Among first marriages, the median differences in age vary around 3 years for women in age groups up to 45 to 54 years, then they diminish. Among remarriages, the median differences diminish more or less steadily as the age of the wife increases.

The kind of figures shown in Table 2 illustrate a weakness of census-type data in the study of age at marriage. The data for the youngest age groups at the survey date reflect relatively current marriage experience but not lifetime experience. By comparison, those for the older groups, most of whose marriages took place several years ago, reflect almost the entire lifetime marriage experience but not very much current experience. The very oldest groups are also affected by selective factors in survival. Joint survival of both spouses is more likely if their ages are not far apart.

Classifications by Socio-Economic Characteristics

This brings us to the concluding section, in which we shall report briefly on some findings from the 1948 survey on age at marriage in relation to income and occupation of the husband and on differences between the ages of spouses in relation to occupation of the husband.[13] The universe covered was all married couples with the husbands married once. Occupation detail was obtained only for the couples with the husband employed.

The information on age at marriage was tabulated by broad groupings according to duration of marriage. The results for married couples that had been married fewer than 5 years are regarded as more appropriate for the present study than those for couples married for a longer time. Concentrating the attention on these men with fairly recent marriages as of the time of the survey reduces the effects on the results of improvement in earning capacity and of occupational mobility after marriage.

The median age of husbands at first marriage was, in general, progressively higher among husbands with progressively higher incomes; this generalization applies to husbands married less than 5 years. Those with less than $2,000 income were about 23 years old at first marriage, whereas those with $2,000 to $2,999 were about 24, those with $3,000 to $4,999 were about 26, and those with $5,000 or more were about 30 years old at first marriage. (See Table 3 and Figure 3).

These figures show clearly that the earning power of a man during the first few years of marriage is much greater for those who postpone their marriage longer than the average. The greater earning capacity may be explained in part as a result of a longer period of training or more experience in the labor force before marriage, or both. In addition,

[13] The findings from the 1948 census study generally confirm on a national scale the findings of other studies for smaller areas. See Frank W. Notestein, *op. cit.;* Walter C. McKain, Jr., *op. cit.;* Meyer F. Nimkoff, "Occupational Factors and Marriage," *The American Journal of Sociology,* XLIX (November 1943), 248-254; and Richard Centers, "Marital Selection and Occupational Strata," *The American Journal of Sociology,* LIV (May 1949), 530-535.

the same sociological factors that prompt some men to postpone marriage until they have exceeded the average earning capacity of men at marriage no doubt continue to operate after marriage to their financial advantage.

Table 3.   Median Age of Husbands at First Marriage, by Total Money Income of Husband in 1947, Major Occupation Group of Husband, and Duration of Marriage, for the United States: Civilian Population, April 1948

Major occupation group of husband and total money income in 1947	MEDIAN AGE AT FIRST MARRIAGE (YEARS)	
	Married less than 5 years	*Married 5 years or more*
Total Money Income in 1947		
All incomes	23.9	24.2
$6,000 and over	31.5	25.5
$5,000–$5,999	29.5	24.3
$4,000–$4,999	25.7	24.5
$3,000–$3,999	25.8	23.8
$2,000–$2,999	23.8	23.9
$1,000–$1,999	22.7	24.0
Under $1,000*	22.7	24.5
Employed Husbands		
Total employed husbands†	24.2	24.1
Farmers	25.6	23.8
Proprietors	25.4	24.4
Professional workers	25.2	25.5
Service workers	24.8	24.7
Clerical workers	24.6	24.7
Craftsmen	24.0	23.6
Operatives	23.4	23.3
Laborers, except farm	22.9	24.0
Farm laborers	22.8	23.0

* Including loss and no money income in 1947.
† Includes employed husbands married once and living with their wives.
Source: Bureau of the Census.

The figures on occupation of husband reveal tendencies that are consistent with those on income. The survey provided enough cases to establish two classes of occupation groups with relatively higher and lower median ages at marriage. Tests of statistical significance show,

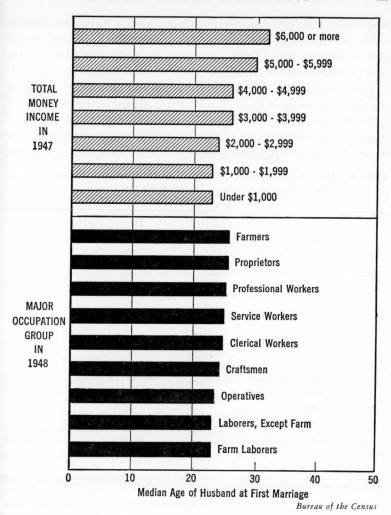

Median Age of Husband at First Marriage

Bureau of the Census

Figure 3. Median age at first marriage for husbands married less than 5 years, by income in 1947 and occupation in 1948: United States.

however, that some of the medians in one class were not clearly different from some in the other class.

In the former group (those with higher ages at marriage) were the white-collar workers—proprietors, professional workers, and clerical workers—and also farmers and service workers. The median age at first marriage for men in these occupation groups was about 25 to 26 years. The remaining occupation groups were manual workers—craftsmen, operatives, and laborers. The median age at first marriage for men in these groups was about 23 to 24 years.

These results show that in general the men in occupations requiring the acquisition of more financial resources or the pursuit of more specialized training tend to delay their first marriage for approximately 1 to 3 years past the age at which men in most of the other occupations first marry. In certain occupation groups, such as farmers, service workers,

Table 4. Median Difference between Age of Husband and Age of Wife, by Major Occupation Group of Husband, for the United States: Civilian Population, April 1948

Major occupation group of husband	Median years wife was younger than her husband
Total employed husbands* .	2.7
Clerical workers	2.4
Professional workers	2.5
Craftsmen	2.5
Operatives	2.7
Proprietors	2.7
Service workers	3.0
Laborers, except farm	3.1
Farmers	3.2
Farm laborers	3.4

* Includes employed husbands living with their wives, where both spouses were married once.
Source: Bureau of the Census.

and laborers, successive generations often follow the same type of work. It is possible that attitudes toward age at marriage may vary from one occupation group to another and may be passed on from one generation to another.

The analysis of differences between the ages of spouses by occupation of the husband was restricted to couples with both spouses married once. Unfortunately, in this part of the study, duration of marriage was not controlled. This fact may have obscured the relationships rather seriously. The figures in Table 4 show, however, that one of the occupation groups with relatively high ages at first marriage—professional workers—was among the groups with the smallest differences between the ages of husbands and their wives, about 2½ years. It appears, therefore, that professional men tended to marry relatively late and to marry wives comparatively near their own ages. At the other extreme, it was found that laborers were among the youngest at marriage and among those with the largest differences between the ages of the spouses. Standardizing the figures by age of the wife did not change the conclusions drawn from the unstandardized results presented in the table.

RESIDENTIAL AND OCCUPATIONAL PROPINQUITY*

Marvin R. Koller

Pioneer work by James Bossard in Philadelphia, 1931, suggested that residential propinquity of mates at the time of marriage is a factor in mate selection. Dr. Bossard examined five thousand consecutive marriage licenses in which one or both of the applicants were residents of Philadelphia. The study found that one out of four couples lived within two city blocks of each other; one-third of the couples lived within five blocks or less of each other. In an apt statement, Dr. Bossard concludes: "Cupid may have wings, but apparently they are not adapted for long flights."[1] Follow-up studies by Maurice R. Davie and Ruby Reeves in New Haven, Connecticut, 1931; Dr. W. A. Anderson in Genessee County, New York, 1934, and Carmella Frell in Warren, Ohio, 1947, confirmed Dr. Bossard's original hypothesis.

It was the purpose of the present study to apply more rigorous techniques to determine the validity of residential propinquity as a factor in mate selection in Columbus, Ohio.

The first refinement of Bossard's study was to shift the years of study away from the "Depression" of the early thirties. The possibility that the economic conditions of 1931 were responsible for Dr. Bossard's findings had to be eliminated. By selecting 1938 as a year well removed from the trough of the economic cycle and yet not a year closely con-

* Adapted and reprinted by permission of the author and publisher from the *American Sociological Review*, 13 (1948), 613-16.

[1] J. H. S. Bossard, *Marriage and Family*, Chapter Four. Philadelphia, University of Pennsylvania Press, 1940, "Residential Propinquity as a Factor in Marriage," pp. 79-92.

nected with World War II and 1946 as the post-war year, this possibility was eliminated. The war years themselves were not used, since residence was often waived as a licensing requirement. If a high degree of residential propinquity showed itself in these years, then its long run effect could be presumed.

The second change from Bossard's study was to discard information relating to Negroes as far as possible. Dr. Bossard had included them in his study, admitting that one-ninth of the city's population was Negro. The elimination of Negroes from our sample was done because Negroes do not have the freedom to move about a city compared to whites and hence are forced to live in segregated areas.

A third refinement was to employ the standard city block equal to one-eighth of a mile as the unit of measurement rather than to count individual city blocks "as if" they were equal. City blocks vary in length within cities and between cities. The use of the standard city block enables future studies to secure comparative data upon which we shall finally base our conclusions concerning the importance of residential propinquity as a factor in mate selection.

Dr. Bossard's study dealt with the first five months of the year and did not deal with those people who married during the last seven months of the year. To make sure that all couples in all twelve months would have a chance to be selected for study, a sampling technique of selecting the first fifty couples each month, starting with the first of the month and an additional fifty couples starting with the fifteenth of the month, or one hundred couples per month was employed.

A fifth refinement was to study solely the couples who were both residents of the city of Columbus, Ohio, and adjacent incorporated suburbs. A pilot study preliminary to defining the universe was run to determine how many of the couples marrying in Franklin County, the county in which Columbus is located, were both residents of the city. Over 70 per cent of those applying for a marriage license at the Franklin County Courthouse were both city residents. It was therefore decided to study only those couples who were both city residents rather than mix an urban and a rural study of distance between the homes of couples about to be married.

Lastly, Dr. Bossard's work was carried a bit further by investigating two factors which might possibly help explain whatever residential propinquity was found. These were the age and occupation of the male. The age of the man was used because there is the greater probability of accuracy with men due to the alleged tendency of women to under- or over-state their age. Occupation for men was regarded as more important since the occupation of the woman tends either to end with marriage or to be less permanent.

Summarizing the hypotheses implemented by the study.

1. Residential propinquity is a factor in mate selection for white mates who were both residents of the city of Columbus, Ohio, 1938 and 1946.

2. Residential propinquity is in part a function of (a) age and (b) occupation of males in Columbus, Ohio, 1938 and 1946.

It was possible to succeed in the original plan to take twelve hundred cases in 1946 as there were adequate numbers. In 1938, however, the numbers were considerably smaller and therefore the sampling in 1938 yielded only one thousand, one hundred and thirty-two cases. The total cases handled by the study amounted to two thousand, three hundred and thirty-two cases. . . .

The residences of both the male and female on each license were pinpointed on a large map of Columbus from the Office of the City Engineer. The closest possible distance in standard city blocks was desired. In the face of obstacles such as rivers, railroad tracks, golf courses, large estates, undeveloped areas, and large state institutions it was necessary to measure around them. For example, a couple whose residences faced each other across the river could not be measured in city blocks directly across the river but rather around the river to the nearest bridge and thence to the residence of the individual concerned.

The assembled data indicated very clearly that the refinements of Dr. Bossard's study when applied to Columbus, Ohio, for 1938 and 1946 sustained Dr. Bossard's original findings. The men tended to select women in the city who lived near the men's homes. Criticism that Bossard's study might have been influenced by the "Depression," by the inclusion of Negroes, by the treatment of all city blocks as equal, or by the sampling technique is not supported by this study in Columbus. In 51 per cent of the 1,132 cases studied in Columbus, Ohio, 1938, the men selected a girl living within 12 standard city blocks. In 1946, 50 per cent of 1,200 men selected a girl living within 15 standard city blocks. Combining the cases of 1938 and 1946, a total of 1,205 or 51 per cent of 2,332 cases chose a mate living within 14 standard city blocks.

Analysis of the frequency distributions found for both years into quartiles yields the following table.

Table 1.   Residential Propinquity of Mates in Standard City Blocks in Columbus, Ohio, 1938, 1946, and Total, by Quartiles

Quartiles	1938	1946	Total
Q_1	2.85	3.34	3.14
Q_2	11.75	14.69	13.33
Q_3	31.00	31.53	31.72
Q_D*	14.08	14.05	14.29

* Q_D (semi-interquartile range) $= \dfrac{Q_3 - Q_1}{2}$ —*Eds.*

There appears to be little difference in the degree of residential propinquity in the samples for 1938 and 1946. . . .

The potential criticism, that residential propinquity as found by this study might be nothing more than the operation of chance due to the selected nature of the sample universe, needs to be answered. Would any group of women and men with the common characteristics of being white, both city residents, and marriage license applicants in a given year on the basis of chance also select each other as future mates? If a close degree of residential propinquity was found for people who had these characteristics and yet had not selected each other as mates, the operation of the residential propinquity factor by sheer chance would be established.

The case records used in the study were thoroughly shuffled and two hundred cases were taken at random for each year. By plotting the residence of the male of the first card and the residence of the female on the second card, one hundred men and one hundred women who did not select each other as mates and yet who possessed the three common characteristics mentioned above were measured relative to their degree of residential propinquity. The degree of residential propinquity of these "chance couples" varied markedly from the degree of residential propinquity found for those couples who had actually selected each other as future mates. One-fourth of the "chance couples" lived within 17 standard city blocks whereas one-fourth of the actual couples lived within 3 standard city blocks of each other's homes. The median for the chance sample was about 29 blocks whereas for the couples who selected each other the median was about 13 blocks. The upper quartile for the chance sample was about 43 blocks whereas the couples about to be married had an upper quartile of 32 blocks. These findings indicate that something other than chance explains the close degree of residential propinquity found between the couples studied.

Analysis of the frequency distributions of the various age groups and occupations of the men studied in 1938 and 1946 indicates possible factors operative in the degree of residential propinquity.

Table 2.   Rank Order of Medians of Age Groups by Standard City Blocks, 1938 and 1946

1938		1946	
Age group	Median	Age group	Median
24–27	16.21	24–27	18.00
32–35	15.00	20–23	15.30
28–31	14.83	28–31	13.88
20–23	10.64	32–35	13.25
Over 35	6.66	Over 35	7.83

Dividing the frequency distributions for age groups in quartiles reveals again the close degree of residential propinquity for each age group for each year . . . the results varying with each age group. The age group 24-27 consistently demonstrated the greatest distance in standard city blocks. The age group Over 35 consistently demonstrated the closest degree of residential propinquity. The group 28-31 consistently remained in the middle between the age group 24-27 and the age group Over 35. Other age groups were erratic in their behavior. . . .

Table 3.   Rank Order of Medians of Occupational Groups by Standard City Blocks, 1938 and 1946

1938		1946	
Occupational group	Median	Occupational group	Median
Clerical and Sales	17.38	Professional and Managerial	18.50
Professional and Managerial	15.94	Clerical and Sales	15.25
Skilled	10.30	Skilled	13.90
Semi-skilled	9.33	Service	13.33
Service	8.63	Semi-skilled	11.17
Unskilled	2.83	Unskilled	4.79

A similar study of the occupations of the males yielded more significant data. In general, the higher a man ranged on the occupational scale the greater the distance in standard city blocks in which he selected his future mate. The lower the occupational position, the greater the degree of residential propinquity found. Professional and Managerial men had a median frequency of about 16 to 18 standard city blocks between themselves and their future wives, whereas the Unskilled men married girls living within three to five standard city blocks.

The findings of this study sustain the original hypothesis, namely, that residential propinquity is a factor in mate selection for white mates who were both city residents of Columbus, Ohio, 1938 and 1946 and that residential propinquity is explainable, in part, as a function of (a) age and (b) occupation of males in Columbus, Ohio, 1938 and 1946. Generalizations applied to age and occupational groups are not wholly correct unless one specifies which age group or which occupational group in a given year he means.

What interpretation should be given these findings? What social inference can we find here? If our findings are correct, then some of Bossard's original ideas that there are "social types in urban communities" who tend to marry may be correct. It is further suggested that because residential propinquity is operative in the city, the parents of boys and girls of marriageable age have unconsciously helped select their son's or daughter's mates by choosing to live in a given urban area. There appears to be a stronger than fifty-fifty chance that a young boy or girl in the city will marry someone living very close to his residence. Here, we might have a predictive device of great value.

We must be very cautious, however, before we generalize too freely about residential propinquity. Thus far the studies have dealt with marriage license applications. The findings must be supplemented by additional research, such as interviews, to determine if the residential propinquity reported in the documents is more apparent than real. More research using similar methods to this one should be undertaken to check these findings in Columbus. More researches using different methods are also welcomed as they might reveal discrepancies that cannot appear in a statistical study.

With Bossard then, we repeat, "Yes, Cupid has wings but he doesn't fly very far. . . ."

THE THEORY OF COMPLEMENTARY NEEDS
IN MATE-SELECTION*

Thomas and Virginia Ktsanes

Who Marries Whom?

The question of "who marries whom" is one which has aroused "common sense" as well as scientific interest. The common sense answer is paradoxical, for while everyone knows that "like marries like" and that "birds of a feather flock together," it is also equally clear that "opposites attract." As is frequently the case in folk wisdom, both assertions are probably true depending upon the characteristics considered. If by "like" one means similarity in regard to a variety of social characteristics such as ethnic origin, religion, occupation, residential location, and social status, then indeed the view that mates tend to be similar seems correct. If, on the other hand, "like" is used to denote similarity in a variety of psychological attitudes, traits, tendencies, or needs, then the situation is by no means clear. This being the case, it is in order to take a brief look at some studies which have attempted to answer the question of the degree to which homogamy or heterogamy prevails in marital choice. The tendency of persons to select mates who have certain characteristics similar to their own is called homogamy or assortative mating. Conversely, heterogamy refers to the selection of mates who are opposites or are merely different. We shall begin with a brief review of the research literature on homogamy. Later we shall present the theory of complementary needs as a special type of heterogamy.

Homogamy in Social Characteristics. Interest in the problem of assortative mating is probably an analogical extension out of the field of biology where for lower animals there seems to be a trend toward similarity in size and vitality. On the human level also there is some slight evidence for homogamy in physical characteristics.[1] With human

---

* Original Manuscript. The theory of complementary needs was first set forth by Robert F. Winch. For a more detailed exposition of the theory see his book *The Modern Family*, New York, Holt, 1952, pp. 209-13, chap. 12, and esp. chap. 15.

[1] In Mary Schooley, "Personality Resemblance Among Married Couples," *Journal of Abnormal and Social Psychology*, 31 (1936), 340-47, some low positive correlations were found to exist between mates on height, weight, visual acuity, and appearance.

beings, however, physical similarity has not been the principal concern. Most work on assortative mating has concerned a variety of social characteristics. We shall now briefly examine some of this evidence.

In an early study by Marvin[2] it was noted that there was a greater than chance tendency for marriages to occur between persons with similar occupations. More recently Centers[3] has pointed out that there tend to be no wide differences in the occupational statuses of spouses. Burgess and Wallin[4] have shown that there is homogamy in educational level. Further, basing their conclusions on the ratings by the couple of the social status of their parents and on their report of the present income of their fathers, Burgess and Wallin state ". . . it is clear that there is a considerable excess over chance for young people to fall in love and become engaged to those in the same social and economic class."[5] Kennedy[6] has indicated that there is a strong trend toward homogamy in regard to religious affiliation and a tendency, though less marked, toward homogamy in ethnic origin.

Bossard,[7] in a study repeated by subsequent researchers, showed that people usually select their mates from those who live nearby. In Bossard's classic study more than half of the marriages in his sample were between persons living within twenty blocks of each other. However, the effect of this factor of mere spatial propinquity must not be overemphasized for it overlaps with the factors discussed before. The various ecological areas of the city are characterized by heavy concentrations of certain socio-economic classes, ethnic and religious groups; and these groups as noted above tend to be endogamous.[8]

In summary, the studies reviewed indicate that persons who marry tend to be similar in regard to a variety of characteristics such as social class, ethnic background, educational level, religion, occupation, and area of residence. However, these findings actually bear little direct

[2] Donald Marvin, "Occupational Propinquity as a Factor in Marriage Selection," *Journal of the American Statistical Association,* 16 (1918-19), 131-50.

[3] Richard Centers, "Marital Selection and Occupational Strata," *American Journal of Sociology,* 54 (1949), 530-35.

[4] E. W. Burgess and Paul Wallin, "Homogamy in Social Characteristics," *American Journal of Sociology,* 49 (1943), 109-24.

[5] *Ibid.,* p. 114.

[6] R. J. R. Kennedy, "Single or Triple Melting-Pot? Intermarriage Trends in New Haven, 1870-1950," *American Journal of Sociology,* 63 (1952), 56-59.

[7] J. H. S. Bossard, "Residential Propinquity as a Factor in Marriage Selection," *American Journal of Sociology,* 38 (1932), 219-24.

[8] Endogamy refers to marriage within the group.

relationship to our problem. They are of some interest in that they give us a notion of the limits within which another principle of selection may operate. As we interpret them, these factors tend to define a field of eligibles from which a mate may be selected on psychological grounds.

Homogamy in Psychological Characteristics. Psychological characteristics which have been studied with respect to homogamy include a long and varied list. Characteristics investigated by means of "paper-and-pencil" personality inventories include neuroticism, dominance, self-sufficiency, etc. One early study[9] found moderately high correlations between mates on neurotic tendency and dominance. Burgess and Wallin[10] in their more recent study of 1000 engaged couples found homogamy in regard to a few traits. Their correlations, however, were of a rather low order and are therefore not too convincing. In regard to various "content" attitudes, e.g., religious and political attitudes, there is some evidence for similarity.[11] These similarities, however, may have developed after marriage. The results in this area are thus considerably short of being definitive. Stagner in reviewing the studies on homogamy in psychological characteristics has pointed out that correlations indicating similarity are higher with respect to intellectual, interest, and attitude scores, but that measures of temperament do not show this tendency as clearly.[12] The measures of temperament referred to by Stagner are those estimates of various traits such as dominance, self-sufficiency, etc., which are arrived at by means of paper-and-pencil tests. Confidence in paper-and-pencil tests is vitiated by the fact that subjects can "fake" their responses and thereby create what they regard as favorable impressions.[13] When we try to get behind the picture of personality which the subject wants us to accept, and more particularly, when we want to understand a subject's motivational patterns of which he may be only partially aware, we find no systematic research on the question of homogamous vs. heterogamous mate-selection.[14] In the

[9] E. L. Hoffeditz, "Personality Resemblances Among Married Couples," *Journal of Abnormal and Social Psychology,* 5 (1934), 214-27.

[10] E. W. Burgess and Paul Wallin, "Homogamy in Personality Characteristics," *Journal of Abnormal and Social Psychology,* 39 (1944), 475-81.

[11] T. M. Newcomb, and G. Svehla, "Intra-family Relationships in Attitude," *Sociometry,* 1 (1937), 180-205.

[12] Ross Stagner, *Psychology of Personality,* New York, McGraw-Hill, 1948, p. 387.

[13] *Cf.* Albert Ellis, "The Validity of Marriage Prediction Tests," pp. 494-95 below.

[14] A few individual cases have been reported at this "deep" level of analysis, but they have been neurotic patients and the authors' reports have lacked experimental control. *Cf., e.g.,* C. P. Oberndorf, "Psychoanalysis of Married Couples," *Psychoanalytic Review,* 25 (1938), 453-57.

absence of experimental evidence various writers have been theorizing on this problem.

Toward a More Adequate Theory

Ideas about types of harmonic intermeshing of needs have been suggested by various theorists and researchers. Many of these owe a debt to Freud, who made a distinction between "anaclitic" and "narcissistic" love.[15] By the anaclitic type Freud meant a love which was expressed in attitudes of self-derogation and reverential admiration toward the love-object. In this type of love one is dependent on the loved one toward whom he can express his need to revere and admire. Narcissistic love is essentially self-love but the narcissist has a great need to be admired by others as well as himself. Thus in his formulation of the narcissistic-anaclitic typology, Freud posited a type of complementary relationship, *i.e.*, the dependent person who has the need to revere and admire is attracted to the narcissistic person who has a great need to be admired and receive adulation.

Following the suggestion that persons with complementary psychic make-ups are attracted to each other, several psychoanalysts have proposed that matching occurs between those who are complementarily neurotic.[16] According to this hypothesis, for example, a dependent male with unresolved emotional ties to his mother would be attracted to an aggressive and dominant woman burdened with conflicts over her sex role. As a general theory of mate-selection, however, this literature is inadequate because the writers have explained attraction only in terms of the highly individualized neurotic patterns of their patients. What we are seeking is a theory which will be generally applicable, not merely to Freud's anaclitic and narcissistic types of persons, not merely to dependent people who marry nurturant people, not merely to neurotics, but to all kinds of personalities.

Gray[17] has used a broader approach to this problem. He hypothesized that mate-selection would be complementary with respect to the types

[15] Sigmund Freud, "On Narcissism: An Introduction," in *Collected Papers,* vol. 4, London, Hogarth, 1925, pp. 30-59.

[16] *Cf., e.g.,* C. P. Oberndorf, *op. cit.;* Edmund Bergler, *Unhappy Marriage and Divorce* New York, International Universities Press, 1946; and Bela Mittleman, "Complementary Neurotic Reactions in Intimate Relationships," *Psychoanalytic Quarterly,* 13 (1944) 479-91.

[17] *Cf., e.g.,* H. Gray, "Psychological Types in Married People," *Journal of Social Psychology,* 29 (1949), 189-200; and "Jung's Psychological Types in Men and Women," *Stanford Medical Bulletin,* 6 (1948), 29-36.

of personality formulated by Jung (extrovert-introvert, etc.). His empirical findings, however, were not convincing.[18]

Other theorists have tried to identify various motivation-linked aspects of interaction. Bernard, for example, suggests various dimensions of love.[19] She notes the usual dimension of dominance and also dwells upon the desire for response or acceptance and on the differential ability of persons to "give" as she calls it. As we shall see later, these are similar to some of the "needs" in our conceptual scheme. Bernard did not systematically state that attraction occurred between persons who were complementary in regard to these dimensions. Others, however, have come very close to this notion. Ohmann[20] stated this idea by saying that we are attracted to those who complete us psychologically. We seek in a mate those qualities which we do not possess.

Taking leads from all of the foregoing, Winch attempted to pull them together. He began by defining love in terms of needs:

Love is the positive emotion experienced by one person (the person loving, or the lover) in an interpersonal relationship in which the second person (the person loved, or love-object) either (a) meets certain important needs of the first, or (b) manifests or appears (to the first) to manifest personal attributes (*e.g.*, beauty, skills, or status) highly prized by the first, or both.[21]

Then he hypothesized that mate-selection would take place according to what he called the theory of complementary needs:

In mate-selection each individual seeks within his or her field of eligibles for that person who gives the greatest promise of providing him or her with maximum need gratification.[22]

Perhaps this can be phrased more simply by hypothesizing that the personality needs of marriage partners tend to be complementary rather than similar. Two points require further clarification: (a) What

[18] Winch applied tests of significance to some of Gray's data. These tests showed that the selection of mates in terms of Jung's types was not significantly greater than might have been expected by chance.

[19] Jessie Bernard, *American Family Behavior*, New York, Harper and Brothers, 1942, pp. 435-56.

[20] Oliver Ohmann, "The Psychology of Attraction," in Helen Jordan (*ed.*), *You and Marriage*, New York, Wiley, 1942, chap. 2.

[21] Robert F. Winch, *The Modern Family*, New York, Holt, 1951, p. 333.

[22] *Ibid.*, p. 406. In the phrase "field of eligibles" Winch takes account of the previously noted homogamy with respect to such social characteristics as race, religion, and social class.

are personality needs and which needs are germane to our problem? and (b) What exactly is meant by the term "complementary"?

Needs. One can think of the term "need" as meaning a goal-oriented drive. Goal in this sense refers not only to such things as material objects and status in the social structure but more particularly to such things as the quality and kind of response desired in interpersonal situations. Examples of the latter are the desire to give help or adulation to others, the desire to take care of others, the desire to control, etc. When these goals are attained, the need is gratified. However, gratification is a dynamic process, and a need once gratified does not cease to function. Patterns of behavior which are tension-reducing tend rather to be reinforced. In a marriage, for example, a woman who finds in her interaction with her spouse gratification for a need to control will continue to want to control him. One further characteristic of needs should be noted. Needs function at both the conscious and unconscious levels. A person may be conscious, partly conscious, or not at all conscious of the goals he desires.

Henry A. Murray has defined "need" in a more formal way:

A need is a construct . . . which stands for a force . . . which organizes perception, apperception, intellection, conation, and action in such a way as to transform in a certain direction an existing, unsatisfying situation.[23]

Further, he has elaborated an extensive list of emotional needs. However, because Murray's list is so detailed, we found it necessary to depart from it in a number of ways. The following list of needs[24] is nevertheless based upon Murray's scheme.

Needs

n Abasement[25]	To accept or invite blame, criticism or punishment. To blame or harm the self.
n Achievement	To work diligently to create something and/or to emulate others.
n Approach	To draw near and enjoy interaction with another person or persons.

[23] H. A. Murray, *et al., Explorations in Personality,* New York, Oxford University Press, pp. 123-24.

[24] R. F. Winch, *op. cit.,* pp. 408-409.

[25] The notation "n" before the name of a variable is used as a shorthand form for the term "need," and where it is found on following pages, that is what it represents.

n Autonomy	To get rid of the constraint of other persons. To avoid or escape from domination. To be unattached and independent.
n Deference	To admire and praise a person.
n Dominance	To influence and control the behavior of others.
n Hostility	To fight, injure, or kill others.
n Nurturance	To give sympathy and aid to a weak, helpless, ill, or dejected person or animal.
n Recognition	To excite the admiration and approval of others.
n Sex	To develop an erotic relationship and engage in sexual relations.
n Status Aspiration	To desire a socio-economic status considerably higher than one has. (A special case of achievement.)
n Status Striving	To work diligently to alter one's socio-economic status. (A special case of achievement.)
n Succorance	To be helped by a sympathetic person. To be nursed, loved, protected, indulged.

General Traits

Anxiety	Fear, conscious or unconscious, of harm or misfortune arising from the hostility of others and/or social reaction to one's own behavior.
Emotionality	The show of affect in behavior.
Vicariousness	The gratification of a need derived from the perception that another person is deriving gratification.

A study to test this theory has been undertaken with a group of middle-class subjects. Because striving for upward mobility (or higher socio-economic status) is so central to the middle-class value system, it was decided to include two variables pertaining to status.

Complementariness. To explain this theory let us imagine two person, A and B, interacting with each other. Let us assume that both are deriving gratification from this interaction. Then the interactional sequence will be in accordance with the theory of complementary needs if:

1. the need or needs in A which are being gratified are *different* from the *need* or needs being gratified in B; or

2. the need or needs in *A* which are being gratified are very *different* in *intensity* from the same needs in *B* which are also being gratified.

An example of (1) is found in the case of a person desirous of attention and recognition (n Recognition) who finds gratification in relationship with a person who tends to bestow admiration on the former (n Deference). Alternative (2) is illustrated in the interaction between a person who wants others to do his bidding (high n Dominance) and one lacking the ability to handle his environment who is looking for someone to tell him what to do (low n Dominance). It will be recognized that this definition of complementariness embraces two forms of heterogamy.

Points Requiring Further Elaboration. At present the theory of complementary needs is a hypothesis enunciating a general principle of mate selection when both spouses are given some freedom of choice. (It is clear that the theory would not be applicable under such a system of arranged marriages as has been traditional in Japan.[26]) This principle is now under empirical investigation, but the results of this study will not be available for some time.

There are a few points to be noted about the theory before the results of the research are known. First, although marriage is viewed as a major source of gratification, it is a matter of common observation that most married people derive gratification from social interaction with other persons as well as with their respective spouses. To the degree that this is true it is not necessary to hypothesize that marriage partners will be totally complementary in their need-patterns. The theory also hypothesizes, however, that if there is not a minimum degree of complementariness in the need patterns of the two persons, they will tend to regard the relationship as unsatisfactory. Their dissatisfaction would probably be registered as follows. Either the relationship would be broken during the dating or engagement periods, or if the couple should be married, their marriage would have more than the average probability of ending in divorce.

At this time the minimum degree of complementariness, referred to in the above paragraph, is unknown, and some criteria are required concerning the number of needs sufficient to hold a relationship to-

---

[26] See the discussion of the system of arranged marriages in the traditional Japanese family, chap. 2 above.

gether. Other questions which may be raised but which cannot yet be answered are as follows:

First, can matching which occurs only on one need in each spouse hold the marriage together? It seems logically possible that only one need of each member of the couple might be met in a relationship. This need, however, might be so important that it would set the tone of the whole relationship.

Second, when a person exhibits two needs which are in conflict, for which of these needs is gratification sought in marriage? For example, in the case of a woman who is upwardly mobile and is also very dominant, does she marry an aggressive type male who will get for her the status she desires but who will not submit to her domination, or does she marry a dependent male who will give in to her but who lacks the initiative to achieve status? It would be interesting to determine how frequently this type of problem is resolved by the individual's directing one need towards the marital partner and the other towards interaction with other persons. On the other hand, it may be that many persons with this type of conflict never achieve a satisfactory solution and that hence the intrapsychic conflict becomes a source of conflict in marital interaction.

Third, in persons who show a marked disparity between needs which are expressed overtly (or directly) and those which are expressed covertly (or indirectly), on which level does matching occur? Persons may behave overtly in a fashion quite different from, or even opposite to, their more basic wishes. We all have known insecure persons whose bold and aggressive exterior is an attempt to convince themselves and others that they are really unafraid. In this situation it may be that matching at the covert level would be more important than at the overt level, but this we do not know as yet.

Illustration of the Theory

To illustrate the theory of complementary needs we have chosen a case from a sample of middle-class married couples and have attempted to show how these two partners complement each other need-wise. It will be noted that in this case the male shows some dependent trends. We do not feel that this case is atypical of our middle-class sample. Dependent needs in the personality of the middle-class male are probably more frequent than is popularly supposed.[27] It is to be emphasized that the man and wife discussed here are a normally functioning couple.

The Case of Anne and Frank Hamilton.[28]   Before we can understand how individual needs function for mutual gratification in a marital relationship, it is first necessary to present the personalities involved. We shall consider first the wife and then the husband before we attempt to understand their relationship to each other.

Anne Hamilton is best described in build as "hefty." Her outstanding features facially are her large mouth and rather prominent teeth. That her mouth is so noticeable the interviewer attributes to the fact that "it never seems to be still." She talks loud and fast. She punctuates her words by dramatic use of her hands and facial expressions. Even when she is listening, her face does not relax. She smiles broadly or raises her eyebrows or in some other way responds aggressively to what is said.

Anne's energy is also evident in her capacity to work. To finish college in three years, she carried extra courses each term and still sailed through her undergraduate work. She earned most of the money to pay her college expenses even though her family was able and willing to pay them. But she just liked to keep busy, so not only did she work and keep up her grade average, but she also held responsible positions in numerous extra-curricular affairs. She was so efficient in getting ads for the school yearbook that for the first time that publication had a financial surplus.

Going along with this terrific need to achieve, there is a high need to

[27] For further elaboration on this point, *cf.,* for example, Arnold Green, "The Middle Class Male Child and Neurosis," *American Sociological Review,* 11 (1946), 31-41; and Talcott Parsons, *The Social System,* Glencoe, Ill., The Free Press, 1951, esp. pp. 262-69.

[28] This case represents one of those being studied in a project under the direction of Dr. Robert F. Winch at Northwestern University. This investigation is supported by a research grant, MH-439, from the National Institute of Mental Health, U. S. Public Health Service.

The material upon which the case analysis was done consists of a case-history type interview, Thematic Apperception Test protocols, and a second type of interview designed to get at the more behavioral aspects of personality. The full case analysis was made by the research staff of this project which consists of Dr. Winch, Mrs. Sandra K. Oreck, Dr. Oliver J. B. Kerner, and the authors of this article. The present report is a synopsis of their findings, which cannot be presented in their entirety because the analysis runs to about two hundred pages of manuscript. Much of the documentation for generalizations must be omitted. All names and identifying characteristics have been changed in order to preserve the anonymity of the couple without impairing the crucial facts of the case. It is our desire to present the case as simply as possible for the purpose of illustrating the theory.

dominate others, which Anne describes as "a certain element of bossiness in me." She feels that her way of doing things is best and she wants people to do things "in the manner I so designate."[29]

She does not like to be "stepped on" nor does she admire people who can be pushed around. Such people she cannot respect. "People that I cannot look up to, I have a tendency to shove out of my way or to trample on, just shove, push." Thus we see in Anne little need to feel sympathy for other persons (n Nurturance) but rather a hostile attitude towards them.

She tends to be critical of other people and apparently because of this she has encountered some difficulty in forming close friendships. She says that people usually like her if they can overcome their first impression which frequently is one of antagonism. She says on this point, "I'm very quick spoken and rarely stop to think that I may be hurting somebody's feelings or that they are not going to take it just the way I meant it." But she needs people and she wants them to like her.

The competitiveness and the need to manipulate people undoubtedly indicate compensatory behavior for feelings of insecurity at some level. There is some evidence to indicate that these feelings stem from her doubts about her being a feminine person. She tends to be jealous of pretty women. She is contemptuous towards them when their attractiveness and "poise" win them positions of prestige which they are not equipped to handle because of a lack of the "executive ability" that she possesses. All her life she states that she wanted to be like her mother who is pretty and sweet and "gives a lot, perhaps too much." She feels, however, that she has not succeeded in becoming this sort of woman. She regards herself as a person who is "quick, uneventempered and impatient, ambitious . . . ready to tell others how to do things." Evidence that she rejects this "masculine" component in her personality is her view that she would not want a daughter to be like herself, but "more like Mother."

The postulation of such a conflict helps to explain why Anne did not continue with her career plans. She took a master's degree in advertising the year following her undergraduate work. She then set out to make a career in this field, but there were no jobs immediately available. Employers did not want college graduates who had their own

---

[29] Shortly we shall note that this domination of others occurred very early in her life in her relationship to her parents and other members of the household.

bright ideas about the business, and, according to her account, they were unwilling to employ her for menial jobs which she was willing to take because they felt she was too intelligent and soon would become disinterested.

At this point Anne's career drive began to fluctuate. She took a job in an office. While there and while formally engaged to another man, she met Frank. She and Frank were married six months after their meeting, and they moved to a city where she had obtained a good job and where he enrolled in college. At the end of a year she became pregnant and stopped working for awhile. By the third month of her pregnancy, however, she became bored with "sitting around home" and took a job as a waitress, much against the doctor's orders. She lost the child three months later. She stated that she wanted the child very badly and that she was broken up over her loss. This wish would be consistent with the feminine desire to be a "mother." In addition to the conscious desire to be feminine, it seems probable that she had an unconscious wish to abort and to deny willingness to play a feminine (maternal) role.

Perhaps if we look into Anne's background for a moment we can see more clearly the circumstances which led to the development of her pattern of aggressive behavior and the confusion over appropriate sex-role behavior.

Anne was the only child in a family of four adults. Her father was a self-made man, one who built up a trucking business to the point where it netted him an income of around $700 monthly even during the depression years. She describes him as being a short man, one who was hot-tempered and stubborn. He was 30 when Anne was born and her mother was only 18. The mother is described as being even-tempered, calm and dependent. The third adult was Anne's maternal grandmother who came to live with the family shortly after Anne was born. She managed the house and Anne's mother and apparently Anne's father as well. Anne says her grandmother often warned the father against his outbreaks of wrath in front of the child. The grandmother brought with her one of her sons who was about the age of Anne's father and who was similar to Anne's mother in temperament. He was very good to Anne and gave her everything she wanted. He married for the first time and left the household when he was 50 years old.

Anne was the center of attention for these four persons. What she could not get from one, she could get from another. This pattern of relationships was conducive to her manipulation of persons and the need for recognition from them which we have noted earlier.

Grounds for the competitiveness may also be found in this network of relationships. Anne's mother was very young and still dependent upon her mother who looked upon Anne as "her youngest child." Thus the relationship between mother and daughter resembled sibling rivalry, not only for the "mutual mother's" love but for the husband-father's love as well. Here were two bases for Anne to dislike her mother, but her mother was such a sweet young thing that she never gave Anne any rationalization for hating her. This left Anne with an unexpressed hostility which apparently has been partially sublimated into an achievement drive and partially displaced onto "feminine" women like her mother. Her mother was better looking than she, so Anne could not compete with her on these grounds but had to seek other means of achieving superiority.

To strive in an aggressive manner was satisfactory in another way too because the father, who wanted a son, approved of such behavior in his little tomboy. Further, grandmother was a model of aggressive behavior. Anne's gratifying relationship with her fostered an identification. The aggressive pattern was fairly well set by the time Anne reached adolescence as is evident in her report that, in junior high school, teachers commented on it. One teacher advised her to change her ways or she would never get a husband. Father also changed his mind about what he wanted and began to look upon her as "feminine" and wanted her to become dependent on him while she was in college. These undoubtedly are the sources of some of the ambivalence we note in her picture, especially concerning career and motherhood.

Although she had doubts about her "feminine appeal," Anne apparently had little trouble in finding dating relationships. Though she confesses she was not the most popular girl on campus and that her weekend calendar was not always filled, she dated from the time she first entered high school. She had only one serious relationship before meeting Frank. This was an engagement to a man described as "suave and smooth . . . and with nice manners." It apparently was a stormy affair, off and on several times. The engagement was broken finally over the issue of whether or not there should be a formal wedding. Anne wanted one, but her fiancé's family did not.

Frank is unlike Anne in many ways. Whereas she gets much gratification from work and positions of responsibility, he much prefers just loafing and being with people. He is now in college, at Anne's request, and very much looks forward to the time when he will be through. College is just a means to an end for him; the less work he has to do to get through, the happier he will be. He wants the degree, however, because it will facilitate his getting a good job. He looks to the job to bring him status and prestige and to provide a large income so that he can buy sporty cars and a big house. Nevertheless, he does not like to work for such a position and is just as content if someone gets it for him.

Frank likes people and he gets along with them very well. It is important to him that they like him and give him attention. He loves to talk and to joke, and generally he is successful in winning friends. "I'm an easy person to get along with . . . I do a fair job of amusing people although I feel that people don't regard me as entirely full of nonsense." His physical appearance contributes to his acceptability for he is a good-looking man, tall and slightly heavy. His build is somewhat athletic but his muscles seem to lack the firmness and tonus of a well-developed athlete. He is light-hearted, pleasure-oriented, and loves to eat.[30]

To achieve acceptance Frank relates to people in a deferent manner. He consciously admires and accepts his allies almost uncritically. He shows no tendency to control them nor to compel them to do what he wants; in other words, he reveals no need to dominate. Though he likes very much to have the spotlight himself, he is willing to share it with others and even to concede it without resentment to people who are better attention-getters than he. He tends to establish friendships with such persons and to identify with them. Thus he receives vicarious gratification for his own need for recognition. This is illustrated in the fact that he joined the fraternity to which most of the "big wheels" on campus belonged though he himself was not a big wheel. Merely through association he felt he was able to share in their glory.

It is interesting to note that Frank does not limit his struggle for

---

[30] In terms of the Freudian stages of development, this aspect of his personality would place him at the "oral" stage, the stage at which the infant, for example, does little more than *receive* love, care, and attention from the mother. The passive-dependent trends which we note in Frank's personality are considered the psychological counterparts of this stage of development. We shall note, however, that this characteristic is by no means the whole picture and that he is considerably more active than is implied for this stage.

recognition to a few fields or a select group of persons as mature adults generally do. He is almost child-like in his willingness to perform. Once when drunk, he paid the singer in a night club twenty-five dollars to let him sing with her in front of the microphone. He still wears the badge that he received when he was deputized a sheriff for a week in his hometown. The importance of this incident was shown when Frank flipped his lapel so the interviewer could see the badge.

In addition to recognition, Frank seems to want love and affection. He tells that he was the "mascot" of a sorority at the first college he attended, and he was chosen "king of the prom" one season. If he feels blue, which he says is rare, he can be cheered by having women, peers or the mothers of peers, tell him how handsome he is.

Apparently since high school Frank always got along well with women because he always had a girl. He tended to date one girl at a time and to go with her pretty "seriously." He expected the same of her, and as a result most of these relationships broke up by his becoming jealous when the girl would date another fellow. He became jealous he says because he wanted "all her attention." The girls he dated were all short and very attractive. They conformed to his "ideal" of "one other fellows thought highly of, a popular girl in other words." Apparently a girl of this type brought vicarious recognition to Frank in the same manner as did the "big wheels" in the fraternity.

Now let us consider Frank's background. Frank was the third son in a family of four boys, all of whom were born during a period of eight years. His father, who was 57 when Frank was born, was a successful salesman until the depression. After losing everything in the depression, the father stopped working. The major burden of supporting the family then fell upon his mother who was about 28 years younger than the father. In time this responsibility was shared by the oldest son. The mother was a petite and good-looking woman.[31] She was a very hard-working, efficient sort of person who, besides working at a full-time job, kept her house, herself, and her sons immaculately neat and also found time to participate in a few club activities. She had considerably more education than her husband in that she had a B.A. degree whereas he completed only the eighth grade. Frank remembers her as being undemonstrative in her affections and as a reasonably impartial judge in the children's quarrels but with a tendency to side with the underdog. Frank had little to say about his

[31] It will be recalled that the girls he dated were of similar stature.

father's personality. Though the man had died only two years before the interview, Frank gave the impression that his father had participated little in family affairs. Frank's few descriptive comments portrayed an opinionated man, harsh in his judgments.

Among the seemingly more important aspects of this family is the absence of daughters. Having two sons already, both parents had desired that the next children be girls. Indeed Frank can remember the time when his mother gave him a girl's haircut. It would appear therefore that this attitude on the part of his parents, and especially his mother, laid the groundwork for the passive-dependent trends we have noted in his personality. It seems logical that Frank wanted the love and attention that is given to the baby. At the age of two years, however, he could no longer be gratified in these desires because of the arrival of the fourth and final brother. It appears that Frank resented this brother greatly. In one two-hour interview he mentioned both of the older brothers but not this one. Undoubtedly as a consequence of this situation Frank has developed a fear of rejection to which he has responded by always doing what is expected of him and by endeavoring to please people in order not to be rejected by them. Frank did not react to his feeling of rejection by rebellion. Perhaps this was because the mother never actually rejected him; she just did not give him all the affection he desired. To avoid losing what he did receive and to try to get more he reacted by being a "good boy."

But Frank was not a sissy in the common use of the term. He was interested in athletics and became captain of his high school football team. He liked mechanics and cars. Currently he is studying mechanical engineering and hopes someday to become a salesman for some large engineering firm.[32]

These masculine interests are very important for understanding Frank's personality. We have shown the tendency towards dependency in his personality which culturally is considered "feminine." Generally, males in our culture who tend to be passive experience some conflict if they are not able to live up to the cultural imperatives that they be assertive and "masculine." Frank shows little anxiety on this score, however, and appears to be very well adjusted. His not having developed a conflict on this score may be due to his having achieved such

[32] It is not surprising that Frank wants to become a salesman because he enjoys so much talking with people and feels certain that he is able to get along with them well.

successful identifications with male authority figures that he consciously never questions his "maleness."

Undoubtedly, the oldest brother is a significant figure in understanding these identifications with males. Very early this brother became a counsellor to the mother. Frank felt ambivalent towards him. He was jealous because this brother played such an important role with the mother. On the other hand, if he hated his brother, then the mother would reject him completely; but if he were like his brother, he would get his mother's attention and at the same time establish a good relationship with the brother, who was moderately successful in his own business and popular with people. Thus, the brother became an ego-model for him and at the same time was a person who could meet some of Frank's dependent needs.

Thus, we now see Frank as an amiable, non-anxious person who does not have a great deal of ambition but who has the knack of relating himself to people who can do things for him.

Up to this point we have attempted to describe both Anne and Frank with very little reference to each other. Now we shall discuss their case with relation to complementary need theory.

Frank says that he was attracted to Anne because "she's probably the smartest woman I've run into, and I admired her a great deal I think before I truly loved her." On the other hand, Anne admired his easy-going manner and his ability to get along with people. Knowing what we do about each of them individually, we can see in these two remarks alone some ground for their complementary matching. First of all, we have pointed out that Anne has had some difficulty in getting along with people and that she would like to be able to do so more easily. Frank's ability to attract friends and to keep them facilitates Anne's social relationships in that he attracts their mutual friends. For Frank, Anne's initiative and her ability to attain the financial and other goals she sets for herself complements his lack of drive. The question is open, however, whether or not this particular pattern of interaction which is now mutually gratifying will continue to be so if Frank becomes a successful salesman.

In their interaction with each other we note that Anne has the authority. She handles their finances, and she decided that he should go back to school. As we have seen, this is the way she likes to do things and we have also noted that Frank shows little need to dominate and he accedes quite willingly to her plans.

Anne tends to be a very emotional person who is easily aroused and upset. At such times Frank's calm and easy-going manner is consoling to her. He has a good shoulder to cry on and he is willing to listen to her problems. She feels that he is helping to calm her down.

About the only thing that disturbs Anne about Frank's personality is that he does not have as much ambition as she would like to see. Indeed she has been somewhat bothered by his rather lethargic attitude towards school work. She would prefer to see him as excited about it as she has always been, but she feels that she is learning to accept his attitude that graduation is the important thing and that the level of one's performance in school is soon forgotten.

Occasionally Frank is a little perturbed by Anne for sometimes he is embarrassed when she pushes ahead in a crowd and drags him along with her, but he goes along and says nothing about it. Undoubtedly he is ambivalent about her aggressiveness. On the one hand, her behavior and her drive facilitate the realization of such desires as the new car which they recently bought. On the other hand, Frank fears that the same aspects of Anne's personality may put him in a position of stepping on other people which might result in their rejecting him. However, this aggressiveness does not constitute one of the things he would change about her if he could push a button to change anything. He would want to modify only her quick temper and her heaviness.

Anne is very different from the girls that Frank dated. The other girls were like his mother in physical characteristics in that they were all short and attractive. Anne has none of these physical characteristics, but does resemble Frank's mother in her efficiency. Although very different from Anne's father, Frank tends to be more like Anne's uncle and Anne's mother who are calm, easy-going, and dependent.

Both Anne and Frank desire considerable recognition from other people. Frank is attentive to Anne and considerate of her. She undoubtedly regards his submissiveness to her as admiration. Anne does not pay as much attention to Frank as he would like. It would seem that although Frank would like more in the way of demonstrated "hero-worship," he does not feel too deprived because she facilitates his getting the symbols (*e.g.,* the new sports car) which enable him to attract attention from other persons.

There is one other thing about Frank which Anne finds gratifying and which is worthy of mention here. Frank's attractive appearance and engaging manner enable Anne to compete successfully on a feminine basis with other women. Although this appeal on his part is gratifying to her in one sense, in another sense it threatens her. She mentioned that she is jealous if he pays too much attention to other women at parties. He also becomes jealous when she has occasion to lunch with another man. This mutual jealousy is understandable in terms of the marked need for recognition which each of them exhibits. On Frank's part, it undoubtedly is a manifestation of his fear of rejection; and from Anne's point of view, the insecurity stems from doubts about her feminine ability "to hold a man."

The complementariness that is described in this couple can be summarized generally as a case of a passive-dependent male finding gratification in relationship with a striving aggressive woman (and vice versa). Indeed, they are not complementary on all counts, *e.g.,* neither is willing to surrender his own desire for recognition in favor of the other. However, it would seem that the mutual choice that has been made satisfies the major, predominating trends within the personalities of each.

CHAPTER 16

Results of Studies in Marital Adjustment

NOT ALL who marry live happily ever after. For some years students of marriage have been trying to find out why—or more precisely, they have been searching for the correlates of "marital happiness" and "marital adjustment." In the 1930's two major pioneering studies were published: one by Terman and his associates, and the other by Burgess and Cottrell. Summary extracts from both of these studies appear in the present chapter. From these two studies we learn that "happiness" or "adjustment" is positively correlated with (1) generally non-neurotic personalities of the spouses, (2) cultural homogeneity of the spouses, (3) their moral conservatism, (4) amicable relations between each spouse and his parents, and (5) the marital happiness of the spouses' parents. By implication these studies condemn romantic love as a basis for a happy marriage.

Roth and Peck have made a further analysis of some of the data of Burgess and Cottrell. This study reports that high marital adjustment is correlated with equality of social status in the two spouses. Conversely, low adjustment is correlated with differences in social status—especially with the situation wherein the wife's social status is higher than the husband's. The force of this finding is to offset the attraction of the "wife-higher" situation which Whyte implies facilitates the upward mobility of the junior executive in the large corporation.[1]

More recently two other studies of marital adjustment have appeared: one by Locke, which is summarized here, and the other by Georg

[1] "The Wife Problem," pp. 286-88 above.

Karlsson,[2] which was done in Sweden. In the next chapter we shall see that the two earlier studies have been subjected to serious methodological criticism. While the reader is encouraged to postpone his evaluation of the studies in the present chapter until he has read the next chapter, it may be noted that the more recent studies on quite different subjects support the general findings of the earlier studies. This is of particular interest in the case of Karlsson's study since it was based upon a more rigorously drawn sample of a European population.

PSYCHOLOGICAL FACTORS IN MARITAL HAPPINESS*

Lewis M. Terman *et al.*

An examination of recent contributions to the literature on marriage reveals a great diversity of opinion about the factors most responsible for marital success or failure. On practically every aspect of the problem the pronouncements by leading authors are highly contradictory. The explanation of this situation lies partly in the bias of authors, partly in their willingness to generalize from inadequate data, and partly in the use of faulty techniques in the collection of information.

The fact that most of the earlier and many of the later investigations were made by members of the medical profession has led to excessive emphasis upon the importance of the sexual factors and to a corresponding neglect of psychological factors. The studies of Bernard, the Mowrers, Cottrell and Burgess, and other sociological workers have accomplished something toward the correction of this misplacement of emphasis, but ours is the first publication to report a major investigation of marital happiness from the more strictly psychological approach.

In a preliminary study of 341 married couples and 109 divorced couples, evidence was sought regarding the relationship between marital happiness and scores on 12 personality traits, including dominance, self-sufficiency, neurotic tendency, masculinity-femininity, interest ma-

---

[2] *Adaptability and Communication in Marriage: A Swedish Predictive Study of Marital Satisfaction*, Uppsala, Almqvist & Wiksells Boktryckeri Aktiebolag, 1951.

* Adapted and reprinted by permission of the author and publisher from *Psychological Factors in Marital Happiness*, New York, McGraw-Hill Book Co., 1938.

turity, and 7 types of interest constellations. The most important conclusion from this preliminary study was that the "traits" in question, as measured by the tests used (the Bernreuter personality inventory and the Strong occupational interest test) are little correlated with marital happiness, but that the particularized attitudes expressed by subjects in response to many of the individual items in the two tests are significantly related to the happiness scores.

A second study was accordingly planned which would investigate for a larger number of subjects the relationship between happiness scores and a great variety of possible factors, including not only personality factors, but also background factors and factors having to do with sexual adjustments in the marriage. By the use of an improved technique for assuring anonymity of response, data were secured on these three sets of variables from 792 married couples who filled out the information schedules in the presence of a field assistant. The group studied represents a reasonably good sampling of the urban and semiurban married population of California at the middle and upper-middle cultural levels, though the sampling appears to be somewhat biased in the direction of superior marital happiness.

The Measure of Happiness Used

The marital happiness score which was computed for each subject was based upon information regarding communality of interests, average amount of agreement or disagreement between spouses in 10 different fields, customary methods of settling disagreements, regret of marriage, choice of spouse if life were to be lived over, contemplation of separation or divorce, subjective estimates of happiness, direct admission of unhappiness, and a complaint score based upon domestic grievances checked in a long list presented. Graded weights were assigned the various possible responses to these items on the basis of intercorrelations, and the total happiness score of a given subject was the sum of the weights corresponding to his individual responses. The resulting numeral score is a serviceable index of the degree of satisfaction that a subject has found in his marriage even though it cannot be regarded as a precise quantitative measure of such satisfaction.

The happiness scores ranged from practically zero to a maximum of 87 points, with a mean of 68.40 for husbands and 69.25 for wives. The respective σ's of the distributions were 17.35 and 18.75. The distributions for husbands and wives agreed closely throughout and were markedly skewed in the direction of high happiness. The scores of husbands and wives correlated to the extent of approximately .60, showing that the happiness of one spouse is to a surprising degree independent of the happiness of the other. This finding is new and perhaps rather significant. Its newness is probably explained by the fact that no previous investigation based upon a large group of subjects had secured its data by methods which prevented collaboration between husband and wife in filling out the information schedules. It is significant in the suggestion it carries that the degree of satisfaction which one finds in a marriage depends partly upon one's own characteristic attitudes and temperament and so need not closely parallel the happiness of one's marital partner.

Personality Correlates of Marital Happiness

The information schedule that was filled out by the subjects contained 233 personality test items dealing with interests, attitudes, likes and dislikes, habitual response patterns, and specific opinions as to what constitutes the ideal marriage. Of these, approximately 140 were found to show an appreciable degree of correlation with the happiness scores of either husbands or wives. The various possible responses to the valid items were then assigned score weights roughly in proportion to the extent to which they differentiated between subjects of high and low happiness scores. This made it possible to compute for each subject a "personality" score, which was merely the sum of the weights corresponding to the responses the subject had given. The personality score may be thought of as in some degree an index of the subject's temperamental predisposition to find happiness rather than unhappiness in the marital relationship. . . . This index correlates approximately .46 with the marital happiness scores of each spouse. Evidently the attitudes and emotional response patterns tapped by the personality items are by no means negligible as determiners of marital happiness.

By noting and classifying the individual items that differentiate between subjects of high and low happiness, it has been possible to piece together descriptive composite pictures of the happy and unhappy temperaments. For example, it is especially characteristic of unhappy subjects to be touchy and grouchy; to lose their tempers easily; to fight to get their own way; to be critical of others; to be careless of others' feelings; to chafe under discipline or to rebel against orders; to show any dislike that they may happen to feel; to be easily affected by praise or blame; to lack self-confidence; to be dominating in their relations with the opposite sex; to be little interested in old people, children, teaching, charity, or uplift activities; to be unconventional in their attitudes toward religion, drinking, and sexual ethics; to be bothered by useless thoughts; to be often in a state of excitement; and to alternate between happiness and sadness without apparent cause.

The above characterizations hold for the unhappy of both sexes. In many respects, however, the differences between the happy and unhappy follow a different pattern for husbands and wives. For this reason it has been necessary to present four composite pictures, rather than two, in order to make clear the contrasting happy and unhappy temperaments as we find them in both men and women . . .

The qualities of personality that predispose a person to happiness or unhappiness in his relations with others are of course far from being the sole cause of success or failure in marriage. Their importance, however, is so obvious from our data that the problem calls for further investigation, preferably by a combination of the statistical and clinical approaches.

Background Correlates of Happiness

Background factors which in these marriages were totally uncorrelated with happiness scores, or for which the correlation was so small as to have almost no practical significance, include family income, occupation, presence or absence of children, amount of religious training, birth order, number of opposite-sex siblings, adolescent popularity, and spouse differences in age and schooling. Nearly all of the factors in this list have been regarded by one writer or another as highly important, especially presence or absence of children in the home and differences between husband and wife in age and schooling.

It is doubtless true that the presence of children often prevents the breaking up of a marriage, but the evidence indicates that it has little effect on the general level of marital happiness. Childless women past middle age do show a slight tendency to be less happy than the average, but childless men of this age tend to have happiness scores above the average. If there are individual marriages that are made more happy by the presence of children, these appear to be offset by other marriages that are made less happy.

From the vantage point of our data it appears that much nonsense has been written about the risks entailed by marrying on inadequate income or by marrying out of one's age or educational class. The correlation of income with happiness scores is zero. The happiest wives in our group are those who are from 4 to 10 years older than their husbands; the happiest husbands are those who are 12 or more years older than their wives. Moreover, the spouses of these subjects rate as happy as the average for the entire population of subjects.

As for religious training, if this was ever a factor in marital happiness it appears no longer to exert such an influence.

It is encouraging to know that marital happiness as here measured shows little tendency to decrease with the passing of years. The scores are a trifle above average for the couples married less than 3 years, and there is a slight depression in the curves of mean happiness at 8 to 10 years after marriage and another at 15 to 17 years. It should be noted, however, that our study includes only marriages that had not been broken by separation or divorce.

We may designate as of slight importance the factors that show a barely significant relationship to the happiness of one or both of the spouses. This list includes age at marriage, absolute amount of schooling, rated adequacy of sex instruction, sources of sex information, age of learning the origin of babies, number of siblings, circumstances of first meeting between the spouses, length of premarital acquaintance, length of engagement, attractiveness of opposite-sex parent, resemblance of subject's spouse to subject's opposite-sex parent, amount of adolescent "petting," and wife's experience of sex shock or her age at first menstruation. No factor in this list is sufficiently related to marital happiness to warrant a prediction weight of more than one point for either husbands or wives. There has been a vast amount of exaggeration about the risks to marital happiness of early marriage, brief premarital acquaintance, inadequate sex instruction, adolescent "petting," and a history of sex shock on the part of the wife.

Expressed desire to be of the opposite sex tends to be associated with unhappiness in wives but not in husbands. A premarital attitude of disgust toward sex is unfavorable to happiness, and more so in men than in women. Frequent or severe punishment in childhood is reliably associated with unhappiness in both husbands and wives. The items mentioned in this paragraph carry a maximum prediction weight of two points for at least one of the spouses.

Next are five items carrying a maximum weight of three points for one spouse and two points for the other. They are: the relative mental ability of husband and wife, parental attitudes toward the subject's early sex curiosity, amount of conflict with father, and amount of attachment to both father and mother.

As to relative mental ability, the most favorable situation is equality or near equality. Marked mental superiority of husband makes for happiness in the wife but for unhappiness in the husband; marked inferiority of husband makes the wife unhappy but does not greatly affect the husband.

Subjects whose parents rebuffed or punished them because of their early sex curiosity are definitely less happy than the average, this effect being somewhat more marked in husbands than in wives.

Strong attachment to either parent is markedly favorable to happiness, especially in the case of husbands. Conflict with the father is unfavorable to happiness, especially in the case of wives.

We come now to the four most important of the background items: happiness of parents, childhood happiness, conflict with mother, and type of home discipline. All of these carry a maximum weight of four or five points.

Happiness of parents rates highest, with a maximum weight of five points for husbands and four for wives. This item is more predictive of success or failure in marriage than a composite of half a dozen items such as income, age at marriage, religious training, amount of adolescent "petting," or spouse difference in age or schooling.

Hardly less important is the rated happiness of respondent's childhood, with a maximum weight of four points for each spouse. Carrying the same weights is absence of conflict with mother. It appears that a record of conflict with mother constitutes a significantly greater threat to marital happiness than a record of conflict with father.

Childhood discipline that is firm, not harsh, is much more favorable to happiness than discipline that is lax, irregular, or excessively strict.

The 10 background circumstances most predictive of marital happiness are:

1. Superior happiness of parents.
2. Childhood happiness.
3. Lack of conflict with mother.
4. Home discipline that was firm, not harsh.
5. Strong attachment to mother.
6. Strong attachment to father.
7. Lack of conflict with father.

8. Parental frankness about matters of sex.

9. Infrequency and mildness of childhood punishment.

10. Premarital attitude toward sex that was free from disgust or aversion.

The subject who "passes" on all 10 of these items is a distinctly better-than-average marital risk. Any one of the 10 appears from the data of this study to be more important than virginity at marriage.

Sex Factors in Marital Happiness

Our study shows clearly that certain of the sex factors contribute materially to marital happiness or unhappiness. It shows no less clearly that others which have long been emphasized by sexologists as important are practically uncorrelated with happiness scores. The data in fact indicate that all of the sex factors combined are far from being the one major determinant of success in marriage.

Among the items yielding little or no correlation with happiness are both reported and preferred frequency of intercourse, estimated duration of intercourse, husband's ability to control ejaculation, methods of contraception used, distrust of contraceptives, fear of pregnancy, degree of pain experienced by wife at the first intercourse, wife's history of sex shock, rhythm in wife's sexual desire, ability of wife to experience multiple orgasms, and failure of the husband to be as dominant as the wife would like him to be in initiating or demanding intercourse.

The sex techniques that many writers regard as the primary key to happy marriage may be worth cultivating for their immediate sensual returns, but they exert no appreciable effect upon happiness scores. Their absence or imperfection is evidently not a major source of conflict or a major cause of separation, divorce, or regret of marriage. What is even more surprising, it appears that such techniques have no very marked effect on the wife's ability to experience the orgasm . . . On the other hand, the wife's happiness score (though not her husband's) is reliably correlated with the amount of pleasure that she experienced at her first intercourse, and the husband's happiness is reliably correlated (negatively) with the wife's tendency to prudishness or excessive modesty.

Five of the sex items that correlate quite markedly with the happiness scores are: number of sexual complaints checked, rated degree of satisfaction from intercourse with spouse, frequency with which intercourse is refused, reaction of the spouse who is refused, and frequency of desire for extramarital intercourse. The correlations, however, probably do not mean that the factors in question are to any great extent actual determiners of happiness or unhappiness. It is more likely that they are primarily symptoms. The discontented spouse rationalizes his (or her) unhappiness by finding fault with the sexual partner and at the same time develops longings for extramarital relationships.

Among the sex factors investigated are two that not only correlate markedly with happiness scores but are in all probability genuine determiners of them: *viz.,* the wife's orgasm adequacy and husband-wife difference in strength of sex drive.

Two measures were available on relative strength of sex drive. One of these was the ratio (computed for each subject) between actual and preferred number of copulations per month; the other was based on husband's and wife's ratings of their relative passionateness. The two measures agree in showing that equality or near equality in sex drive is an important factor in happiness. As the disparity in drive increases to the point where one spouse is in a more or less chronic state of sex hunger and the other in a state of satiety, the happiness scores of both drop off significantly. Even so, this factor is apparently less important than parental happiness, childhood happiness, or amount of conflict between child and mother.

First in importance among the sex factors is the wife's orgasm adequacy, which correlates about .30 both with her own and with her husband's happiness score. This is slightly higher than the correlation yielded by parental happiness. It is of special interest that orgasm inadequacy of the wife affects her husband's happiness almost as unfavorably as her own. Between wives of the "never" group and wives of the "always" group, there is a difference of 16.3 points in mean happiness, and a difference of 13.0 points in the mean happiness scores of their husbands. Nevertheless, one finds every grade of happiness both in the "never" group and the "always" group. Adequacy of the wife in this respect favors happiness but does not guarantee it, while on the other hand a considerable minority among the inadequates have happiness scores above the general average.

The Mystery of Orgasm Inadequacy

Almost exactly a third of the wives fall in the inadequate group, attaining orgasm either "never" (8.3 per cent) or only "sometimes" (25.1 per cent). Adequates include the "usually" group (44.5 per cent) and the "always" group (22.1 per cent). These figures are in fairly close agreement with those reported by other investigators in Europe and America. Why is it that one woman out of three rarely or never succeeds in reaching the normal climax of sexual intercourse?

. . . we have analyzed a large amount of data in the effort to throw some light on this mystery, but the resulting picture is far from clear. In this connection we investigated the relationship between wife's orgasm adequacy and both wife's and husband's responses to each of more than 300 items in the information schedule. Significant relationships were found for a large number of items. On the other hand, many factors that have been regarded as causative of orgasm inadequacy are uncorrelated with it in our data. These include attachment to father or to mother, conflict with father or with mother, amount of education, extent of religious training, sources of sex information, sex shock before the age of ten years, age at first menstruation, amount of childhood punishment, type of home discipline, happiness of childhood, premarital attitude of disgust toward matters of sex, admitted homosexual feelings, pain at first intercourse, methods of contraception used, fear of pregnancy, sleeping arrangements, date of birth, relative age of spouses, relative mental ability of spouses, length of marriage, and number of children.

Among the items most reliably associated with inadequacy are a goodly number of the Bernreuter and Strong type which appear to indicate neurasthenic tendencies, diminished responsiveness, and lack of zest, vigor, or colorfulness of personality. The picture is one that suggests the possible involvement of constitutional factors. In view of this picture and in view of our failure to find convincing evidence of the influence of emotional conditioning, we would raise the question whether the causes of orgasm inadequacy in women may not be biological rather than psychological, perhaps largely of genetic origin.

Whatever the causes may be, they are apparently deep seated, for our data show (1) that the tremendous cultural shift from the prudish sex attitudes of the 1890's to the liberal and frank attitudes of the 1930's has not appreciably reduced the proportion of inadequates among the younger wives of our group as compared with the proportion among the older; and (2) that if the orgasm is not established within the first year of marriage it is unlikely ever to be. In line with this is the opinion of Hamilton that the condition is rarely improved by a change of sexual partner.

The Relative Importance of Sexual and Psychological Compatibility

Our data do not confirm the view so often heard that the key to happiness in marriage is nearly always to be found in sexual compatibility. They indicate, instead, that the influence of the sexual factors is at most no greater than that of the combined personality and background factors, and that it is probably less. The problem is complicated by the fact that the testimony of husband and wife regarding their sexual compatibility is influenced by their psychological compatibility. Couples who are psychologically well mated are likely to show a surprising tolerance for the things that are not satisfactory in their sexual relationships. The psychologically ill-mated show no such tolerance but instead are prone to exaggeration in their reports on sexual maladjustments. The two sexual factors of genuine importance are wife's orgasm adequacy and relative strength of sex drive in the two spouses.

The Evidential Value of Marital Complaints

An important by-product of our investigation is the light thrown on marital complaints as evidence regarding the causes of domestic discord. The expression of numerous complaints is highly symptomatic of the presence of unhappiness, but the specific nature of the complaints made tells very little about the causes of unhappiness. It has been shown that some of the things most frequently complained of have little or no correlation with happiness scores. Inadequate income is the outstanding example. On the other hand, some of the things rarely complained of are usually quite serious when they are present. The clearest example of this is the wife's slovenliness in appearance.

The problem is important because of the use made of complaint data by domestic relations experts in the adjustment of marital difficulties. "Experts" is hardly the word, for usually such workers are able to claim success in only a small minority of cases treated. Our suspicion is that one cause of failure is the misleading information secured by the type of questioning so commonly used in clinical procedures. . . .

PREDICTING SUCCESS OR FAILURE IN MARRIAGE*

ERNEST W. BURGESS AND LEONARD S. COTTRELL, JR.

At the conclusion of a study the . . . following questions are almost always asked, and they are always well worth attention:

1. What, if any, contributions have been made to knowledge?
2. What is the significance of these contributions?

An attempt will be made . . . to answer the . . . questions by summarizing briefly the major findings of the study and by indicating their significance for an understanding of the way in which men and women adjust to each other in marriage.

Wives Make the Major Adjustment in Marriage. An outstanding, if not the most significant, finding of this study is that the background items of the husbands are much more important for adjustment in marriage than are the background items of the wives.

Why should the premarital characteristics of the husband be so much more closely correlated with marital adjustment than those of the wife? Perhaps in marriage the wife, on the average, makes much more of an adjustment to the husband than he makes to her.

On first thought the explanation that wives in the United States make the major adjustment in marriage is directly in contradiction to the American conception that marriage is a "fifty-fifty proposition" in which husband and wife make equal adaptations to one another. It might have been assumed that husbands in this country more than anywhere else in the world are disposed to cater to and comply with the wishes, attitudes, and even whims of their wives. European visitors to the United States are quick to point out the dominant position of the American wife in the home and the subservient or secondary role of her husband.

The findings of this study regarding the relatively greater weight of the characteristics of the husband in determining marital adjustment suggest that too much emphasis has been placed upon the superficial aspects of the American marital relationship. These aspects appear

* Adapted and reprinted by permission of the authors and the publisher from *Predicting Success or Failure in Marriage*, New York, Prentice-Hall, Inc., 1939.

greater by contrast with the obvious and definite subordination of woman to man in Old-World marriages. . . .

In the United States, where the mores sanction equality in the marriage relation, the superficial forms of the husband's behavior may hide the actual situation. Since the mores do not demand the obvious display of the husband's dominance, wide individual differences in the marital relation are apparent. In many unions the wife is in fact, and not merely seemingly, superordinate. The domineering wife and the "henpecked" husband, to mention an extreme illustration, are much more evident in the United States than in Europe. The dictatorship of wives, however, is undoubtedly limited to a relatively small proportion of marriages. The majority of wives must still achieve their aims in subtle and indirect ways which evidence the dominant position of their husbands.

The statistical findings of this study deal with averages and obscure individual differences. Our problem is, then, to explain why so great an average discrepancy exists between the greater inferred adaptability of the wife than of the husband.

Two explanations are at hand which may operate independently or in conjunction. First, it may be assumed that the new mores emphasizing equality of the sexes in marriage have not as yet entirely displaced the old attitude that the husband should be dominant. Second, it may be asserted that the trait of dominance is, on the average, more marked in the male, and that of submission in the female. To the extent that this is true, the wife would be disposed to be subordinate and the husband superordinate.

To state that at present in American society dominance is in general a male, and submission a female, trait is not to imply that this difference is necessarily biological. It may, in fact, be social, not in the sense that it is commanded by the mores, but in that it persists in the attitudes arising out of our self-consciousness of sex differences and our conception of what is expected in the behavior of boys and girls, men and women.

Further research will be necessary to clarify the points raised by the discussion of these findings. If they actually measure present differences in the amount of adjustment made by man and woman in marriage, then it should be possible to determine the varying differences in adjustment between the husbands and wives in different sections of the United States. Comparative studies might be made to verify assumed differences between the East and the West, the North and the South, or between different districts within the city, as between equalitarian-family areas, semipatriarchal immigrant districts, and the matricentric suburban neighborhoods. It would be assumed, for example, that the Southern wife makes a greater adjustment in marriage than the Western wife, and that the immigrant wife living in the semipatriarchal-family neighborhood is more submissive to her husband than is the wife who is herself gainfully employed and residing in the apartment-house area with its equalitarian standards of family life.

The Affectional Relationships of Childhood Condition the Love Life of the Adult. The response patterns of relationships established in childhood appear to be the dynamic factor determining the expression of affection in adult life. This finding is derived from the examination of 100 case studies in this investigation. It corresponds more or less closely to the conclusions reached by other workers in their clinical analysis of material obtained over a prolonged period by intensive psychiatric interviews. It is corroborated by the statistical evidence provided by this study.

Two general effects of the familial affectional environment upon the adjustment in marriage of young people have been independently established by Terman's study and by the present research:

1. Happy marriages of parents are correlated with happiness in the marriage of their children. This relationship is the outstanding association noticed in the study of the relation between background items of both husbands and wives and their adjustment in marriage.

2. Close attachment in childhood to father and mother and absence of conflict with them is positively correlated with the person's adjustment in marriage.

These two conclusions indicate the general correlation that obtains between a happy family relationship in childhood, with close attachment between parents and children, and a satisfactory adjustment as an adult in the marriage relationship itself.

Our case-study data enable us to proceed a step further and to make a specific formulation of a theory of childhood affectional attachment in relation to marital adjustment, as follows:

1. In childhood the person builds up a response relationship to the parent of the opposite sex which markedly influences his response to and selection of a love object in adult life.

2. If the childhood affectional relation to the parent of the opposite sex has been a satisfying one, the person will tend to fall in love with

someone possessing temperamental and personality characteristics similar to those of the loved parent.

3. If the childhood affectional relation has been unsatisfactory, he is more likely to fall in love with a person of opposite temperamental and personality characteristics. An exception occurs where the relation in childhood has been one of frustration rather than of conflict, so that as a consequence of idealization the person seeks all the more in a loved one the personality type of the parent of the opposite sex. Where the attitude is ambivalent, then there may develop alternating attitudes of love and hatred toward the affectional object.

4. The childhood response fixation is generally, but not always, upon the parent of the opposite sex. It may under certain conditions be centered upon the parent of the same sex or upon a brother or sister.

5. The actual complex of attitudes in affectional relationships in adult life tends to reproduce all the significant response patterns of childhood. Thus the adult unconsciously strives to act in his love life not only his childhood role with regard to his sex-opposite parent but also his childhood roles with regard to his parent of the same sex, to his older brother or sister, and to his younger brother or sister. Where the relation has been ambivalent, as in the case of submissive and rebellious behavior, this pattern also tends to be expressed in the marital relation.

This theory of the nature of early childhood affectional relationships as determining the dynamics of adjustment in marriage is of such great significance, if correct, that systematic effort should be made to verify or disprove it by objective methods. Its validation would greatly simplify the understanding of a great field of behavior that otherwise seems to be hopelessly complex, complicated, and often contradictory.

Socialization of the Person Is Significant for Adjustment in Marriage. A group of background items constituting what may be called the social factor in marital adjustment is found to be significantly related to success in marriage. Among these items are: higher level of education; objective evidence of religious activity, such as duration and frequency of attendance at Sunday school and church; the number and sex of friends; participation in social organizations; and residence in neighborhoods of single-family dwellings. These items taken together may be regarded as an index of sociability, or of socialization in respect to the degree of participation and achievement of the person in the activities of the community and its chief cultural institutions—the family, the school, and the church.

The impress of social institutions upon a person may be measured in terms of his conformity to social rules, his respect for conventions, and his stability of character. The socialization of the person which results prepares him for adjustment in marriage.

The Economic Factor, in Itself, Is Not Significant for Adjustment in Marriage. A finding quite unexpected by the writers, and almost certain to be surprising to the public, is the virtual disappearance of the premarital economic items from the group of items significant in marital adjustment. It is true that several economic items such as moderate income, savings, occupations characterized by stability and social control, and regularity and continuity of employment are positively correlated with adjustment in marriage. But all these combined add very little to the effectiveness of the prediction that can be made without them. In fact, by the method of partial correlation whereby other factors are held constant, the discovery is made that the correlation of the economic factor with the prediction score is only .04 in comparison with .20 for the psychogenetic factor and the response factor, respectively; .18 for the socialization factor; and .14 for the cultural-impress factor.[*]

The explanation for the very low weight to be assigned to the economic items in marital adjustment is that they add very little to the items included under psychogenetic, cultural-impress, social-type, and response factors. It may, indeed, be argued that the economic behavior of the person, at least so far as it affects adjustment in marriage, is an expression of these noneconomic factors. Economic items such as moderate income, savings, occupations characterized by stability and social control, regularity and continuity of employment, may all be taken as indicating a stabilized and socialized personality which readily adjusts to the marriage situation. But this is a type of personality which is also strongly indicated by psychogenetic, cultural-impress, social-type, and response factors. The economic behavior of the person may there-

---

[*] In zero-order correlation both variables are allowed to vary. In partial correlation, however, one or more additional variables are explicitly held constant. In this problem, when all of the other four factors were held constant, each resulting partial correlation was less than the corresponding zero-order correlation. Following is, first, the zero-order correlation, and, second, the partial correlation of each factor with marital adjustment score: psychogenetic, .39 and .20; cultural impress, .36 and .14; social type, .46 and .18; economic role, .32 and .04; and response patterns, .40 and .20.—*Eds.*

fore be thought of as the resultant of these noneconomic influences. In fact, the trait of personality which all our items are measuring may turn out to be *adjustability* or *socialization* that makes for adjustment in society, in industry, and in marriage. However, it must be remembered that the sample on which this study is based does not cover the entire range of economic groups in our culture.

With the Majority of Couples, Sexual Adjustment in Marriage Appears to Be a Resultant Not so Much of Biological Factors as of Psychogenetic Development and of Cultural Conditioning of Attitudes Toward Sex. This finding is derived from case studies and, while rather clearly indicated, should not be taken as conclusively established. It is in harmony with the obvious generalization that the biological growth and maturation of the individual takes place in association and interaction with his emotional, intellectual, and social development. The understanding of any one of these aspects of human growth is necessarily to be arrived at in the context of the others.

Prediction Before Marriage of Marital Adjustment Is Feasible and Should and Can Be Further Developed Through Statistical and Case-Study Techniques. This study has demonstrated the feasibility of predicting adjustment in marriage and has indicated the course of future research to improve the accuracy and significance of prediction.

With present methods it is entirely practicable to indicate the risk group into which any engaged person will fall, with a definite statement regarding the statistical probabilities of success or failure in marriage. This is, however, group prediction, as with life-expectancy tables which are used by life-insurance companies. But the prediction of marital adjustment has one advantage over that of a life-expectancy table: our study indicates that statistical prediction for all practical purposes can be applied to particular individuals at the two extremes where all, or at least 99 out of 100, persons assigned to the highest and to the lowest risk group will either succeed or fail in marriage, according to the predictions. . . .

In conclusion, a recapitulation of the findings of this study shows the following:

1. Contrary to prevailing opinion, American wives make the major adjustment in marriage.

2. Affectional relationships in childhood, typically of the son for the mother and the daughter for the father, condition the love-object choice of the adult.

3. The socialization of the person, as indicated by his participation in social life and social institutions, is significant for adjustment in marriage.

4. The economic factor in itself is not significant for adjustment in marriage, since it is apparently fully accounted for by the other factors (impress of cultural background, psychogenetic characteristics, social type, and response patterns).

5. With the majority of couples, problems of sexual adjustment in marriage appear to be a resultant not so much of biological factors as of psychological characteristics and of cultural conditioning of attitudes toward sex.

6. Prediction before marriage of marital adjustment is feasible, and should and can be further developed through statistical and case-study methods.

In short, the outstanding factors in marital adjustment seem to be those of affection, temperamental compatibility, and social adaptability. The biological and economic factors are of less importance and appear to be largely determined by these other factors.

SOCIAL CLASS AND SOCIAL MOBILITY FACTORS RELATED TO MARITAL ADJUSTMENT*

Julius Roth and Robert F. Peck

In any stratified social order, marriage usually implies equality of status. Although the American class structure considered in this paper is not so rigid as the caste system discussed by Kingsley Davis in "Intermarriage in Caste Societies,"[1] the fact remains that strata exist and the family is placed in the class structure as a unit. This means that if a man and woman of different social levels marry, there must generally be a shift of status for one or both of them.

The question arises: Does this necessary shift of status affect the subsequent adjustment of the spouses? Ruesch, Jacobson, and Loeb point out the feelings of stress, frustration, and confusion which often

* Adapted and reprinted by permission of the authors and publisher from the *American Sociological Review*, 16 (1951), 478-87.
[1] *American Anthropologist*, 43 (1941), 376-395.

accompany the acculturation of immigrants.[2] The greater the degree of culture difference, the greater the maladjustment of the individual is likely to be. The differences in the characteristics of the social classes in our society indicate that these classes are different cultural groups. A person moving from one class to another must go through a process of acculturation similar to, though perhaps not so extreme as, that of an immigrant.

In some cases a shift of status of one or both spouses has taken place before marriage. A certain amount of stress and insecurity in social situations may thus be brought into the marriage relationship by one or both partners. This possibility suggests a second major problem: Do the premarital mobility patterns of the spouses affect the subsequent marital adjustment?

A fairly large group of cases which had some rating of marital adjustment and some good indication of the subject's social class was needed in order to examine these problems. The schedules Burgess and Cottrell used in their study of marital prediction provided such a group of cases.[3] Each of their 526 cases had a marital adjustment score which they had worked out with the help of statistical techniques. Most of the cases had data which made possible an estimate of the social class level of the subjects.

No detailed account of the collection of the data and the characteristics of the group will be given here, since Burgess and Cottrell have already presented this information in Chapter II of their book.[4] It is important to note that the great majority of the subjects were in their twenties or early thirties and that the time since marriage was fairly short (less than seven years) in all cases.

Social Class Ratings and Adjustment Index

The McGuire-Loeb modification of W. L. Warner's Index of Status Characteristics (I. S. C.) was used to determine the class status of each subject.[5] The schedules of 523 couples were consulted. Only those

2 Jurgen Ruesch, Annemarie Jacobson, and Martin B. Loeb, *Acculturation and Illness,* Psychological Monographs, vol. LXII, No. 2, 1948.

3 Ernest W. Burgess and Leonard S. Cottrell, *Predicting Success or Failure in Marriage,* New York, Prentice-Hall, Inc., 1939.

[See also pp. 465-71 above.—*Eds.*]

4 *Ibid.*

5 The calculation of Warner's I. S. C. and the rationale on which it is based are presented in Part III of W. Lloyd Warner, Marchia Meeker, and Kenneth Eells, *Social Class in America,* Chicago, Science Research Associates, Inc., 1949. The McGuire-Loeb

cases were used where a single, definite class placement could be made with reasonable confidence.[6] This provided a maximum total of 428 husbands and 417 wives. Some of the tables included here have a smaller number of subjects, since they pertain to questions or classifications which did not apply to all the subjects.

Four social class levels—upper-middle (UM), lower-middle (LM), upper-lower (UL), and lower-lower (LL)—had a sufficient number of cases to be useful in most of the tabulations.

The concept and measurement of marital adjustment used by Burgess and Cottrell, as well as the adjustment scores which they derived for each of their cases, were assumed without modification. The scores were likewise classified into the same GOOD (160-199), FAIR (120-159), and POOR (20-119) adjustment categories which Burgess and Cottrell used in almost all of their tables in *Predicting Success or Failure in Marriage*.[7]

Social Class and Marital Adjustment

Table 1 shows an evident trend in the case of both the husbands and wives for the marital adjustment score to increase as we move up the social class scale. Testing this trend by the Chi-square method in comparison with a hypothesis of no relationship between social class and adjustment shows a significance at the 1 per cent level.

This finding is essentially in agreement with some of those of Burgess and Cottrell. Although they did not use any over-all measure of social class for comparison with adjustment, Burgess and Cottrell did examine many of the individual factors which are known to be related to class level. Education,[8] amount of organizational membership,[9] character of neighborhood,[10] and degree of economic security[11] are all positively correlated with class level. That is, in each case the part of the scale related to higher class status (e.g., more advanced education) included

---

version may be found in Carson McGuire, "Social Status, Peer Status, and Social Mobility," Memorandum for the Committee on Human Development and supplement to *Social Class in America*, 1949, pp. 7, 8.

[6] This rigorous approach reduced the size of the sample; however, it appeared that the results of the analysis could be stated with more confidence if the composition of the groups being compared was fairly uniform.

[7] Burgess and Cottrell, *op. cit.*

[8] *Ibid.*, pp. 121, 391.

[9] *Ibid.*, p. 126.

[10] *Ibid.*, p. 132.

[11] *Ibid.*, p. 261.

more couples who are well-adjusted than appear in the lower end of the scale (e.g., little education). The relationship of occupation to adjustment is less clear, because Burgess and Cottrell used an occupational classification which is only loosely related to the prestige value of the occupations. Executives and managers of large businesses and professional people, especially school teachers, show slightly better scores than clerical, sales, small business, and skilled trades people.[12] Terman also

Table 1. Distribution of the Husbands and Wives According to Social Class and Adjustment Index

Social class at marriage		ADJUSTMENT SCORES OF COUPLES							
		Number				Percentage			
		Good	Fair	Poor	Total	Good	Fair	Poor	Total
Husbands	UM	98	58	32	188	52.1	30.9	17.0	100.0
	LM	62	44	49	155	40.0	28.4	31.6	100.0
	UL*	27	17	28	72	37.5	23.6	38.9	100.0
	LL*	3	5	5	13	23.0	38.5	38.5	100.0
Total		190	124	114	428‡	...	...	...	....
Wives	UM	63	32	25	120	52.5	26.7	20.8	100.0
	LM	106	71	53	230	46.1	30.9	23.0	100.0
	UL†	16	15	28	59	27.1	25.4	47.5	100.0
	LL†	1	2	5	8	12.5	25.0	62.5	100.0
Total		186	120	111	417‡	...	...	...	....

* The cells in these two rows were combined in the Chi-square analysis.

† The cells in these two rows were combined in the Chi-square analysis.

‡ In this and in subsequent tables the total number of cases is less than 523 because the "unknown" and "indeterminate" cases are omitted.

found a slight positive relationship of marital happiness to education,[13] but no certain relationship to occupation[14] (again occupation was not classified according to prestige level).

When the social class background of each individual subject (that is, the social class of the spouse's parents) is tabulated, no class level trend in relation to adjustment is apparent (Table 2). The only fairly sharp difference lies between the lower-lower class and the remainder of the group. Lower-lower status has a slight negative relationship with

[12] *Ibid.*, p. 136.

[13] Lewis M. Terman, *Psychological Factors in Marital Happiness*, New York, McGraw-Hill Book Co., 1938.

[14] *Ibid.*, p. 169.

marital adjustment. It thus appears that the social class of the spouses' parents *per se* has little relationship to the adjustment of the spouses.

Social Class Difference and Marital Adjustment

In over half the cases in this study in which the difference or similarity of the social class of the spouses was established, the spouses were of the same social class at the time of marriage. (See Table 3.) Burgess and Cottrell state[15] that marriage tends to take place within a given

Table 2.   Relationship of the Social Class of the Parental Family to the Adjustment Index of Each Subject

Social class at marriage	ADJUSTMENT SCORE OF EACH SUBJECT							
	Number				Percentage			
	Good	Fair	Poor	Total	Good	Fair	Poor	Total
Subject's parents								
UM	67	43	40	150	44.7	28.6	26.7	100.0
LM	106	70	74	250	42.4	28.0	29.6	100.0
UL	87	54	45	186	46.8	29.0	24.2	100.0
LL	17	5	25	47	36.2	10.6	53.2	100.0
Total	277	172	184	633*	...	...	...	....

* Of the 1,046 subjects (523 husbands and 523 wives) only 633 gave sufficient information about their parents to permit class ratings to be made. Each parental family was status-identified by the man's occupation, source of income, and education.

cultural group and this has probably been the common finding in studies of marriage.[16]

Although most of the marriages take place within a given class, a substantial number of cross-class marriages are represented in Table 3. How do they compare in adjustment to same-class marriages? According to the hypothesis previously discussed, the cross-class marriages are likely to cause greater stress to the persons involved. How does this reflect on their relative adjustment? The percentage distribution in Table 3 shows that the adjustment scores tend to be higher in the case of same-class marriages. Testing this relationship by the Chi-square

15 Burgess and Cottrell, *op. cit.,* p. 77.

16 Robert T. McMillan, "Farm Ownership Status of Parents as a Determinant of Socio-economic Status of Farmers," *Rural Sociology,* 9 (June, 1944), 151-160. McMillan reports a strong tendency of farmers to marry within their own status group (defined by farm ownership) even where a marked disparity of the sex ratio made such pairing difficult.

Table 3. Distribution of Total Cases According to Adjustment Index and Similarity or Difference of the Social Class of the Spouses

| Social class at marriage | ADJUSTMENT SCORE OF EACH SUBJECT | | | | | | | |
| | Number | | | | Percentage | | | |
	Good	Fair	Poor	Total	Good	Fair	Poor	Total
Spouses of same class at time of marriage	115	56	44	215	53.5	26.0	20.5	100.0
Spouses 1 class apart at time of marriage	56	50	54	160	35.0	31.2	33.8	100.0
Spouses more than 1 class apart at time of marriage	3	8	10	21	14.3	38.1	47.6	100.0
Total	174	114	108	396	...	...	...	....

method[17] shows a significance at the 1 per cent level. This result suggests that the stress of a rapid shift in class values required by a cross-class marriage has a negative influence on the adjustment of that marriage.

In a cross-class marriage either the husband or the wife may be of the higher social class at the time of marriage. Does the effect on marital adjustment differ with the sex of the spouse of superior status? In Table

Table 4. Comparison of the Husband-High Cross-Class Marriages with Those in Which the Wife Is of the Higher Class

| Social class at marriage | ADJUSTMENT SCORE OF EACH SUBJECT | | | | | | | |
| | Number | | | | Percentage | | | |
	Good	Fair	Poor	Total	Good	Fair	Poor	Total
Husband 1 or more classes higher than the wife at marriage	41	38	37	116	35.3	32.8	31.9	100.0
Wife 1 or more classes higher than the husband at marriage	18	20	27	65	27.7	30.8	41.5	100.0
Total	59	58	64	181	...	...	...	....

[17] The corresponding cells for "1 class apart" and "more than 1 class apart" had to be combined because of the very small number of cases in the "more than 1 class apart" category.

4 the direct comparison is made of all the cases in which the husband was of the higher class at marriage, with all those in which the wife was of the higher class at marriage. The wife-high cases seem to be more unfavorable to marital adjustment than the husband-high cases, although both show a tendency to lower scores than same-class marriages. Using the Chi-square technique we may test the hypothesis: Cross-class marriages in which the husband is of the higher social class generally show better adjustment than those in which the wife is of the higher class. The level of significance proves to be very low $(0.30 < P < 0.50)$. The relationship is obscured by the fact that the class differences represented can have different origins. For example, a woman may have been mobile before marriage past the level of her future husband or she may have acquired her higher status from her parents. This problem will be further discussed in the section on mobility patterns.

Despite the low statistical significance of the relationship between wife-high and husband-high cross-class marriage, the relationship is in keeping with findings on this point in other studies. McMillan finds that in the case of marriages across class lines, it was most often the wife who "married up" the status ladder.[18] To put it another way, the men seemed to be more willing than the women to accept a lower status spouse. Terman found that in his subjects the wives who were markedly superior to their husbands in education[19] had low happiness scores, while the scores were much higher in cases where the husbands were markedly superior in education.[20] James West points out that in all of the cross-class dating in "Plainville" the boy is of the higher class A boy dating a girl of a lower class is frowned upon, but "for an upper-class girl to have a date with a lower-class boy would be inconceivable."[21]

Why is adjustment smoother when the man enters marriage at the higher status than when the woman does so? An important finding of Burgess and Cottrell gives a clue for further study on this point. The major adjustment, in fact almost the entire adjustment in mos marriages, is made by the wife.[22] Since an upward shift in class statu

18 McMillan, *op. cit.*

19 Education may serve as a crude index of class level.

20 Terman, *op. cit.*, p. 191.

21 James West, *Plainville, U. S. A.,* New York, Columbia University Press, 1945. In this rural village dating is generally looked upon as a forerunner to marriage.

22 Burgess and Cottrell, *op. cit.*, p. 341.

carries some rewards and also entails fewer punishments than a downward shift, we would expect less stress in those cases where the wife had to move upward (that is, the husband-high marriages) than in those where she was expected to shift her values downward (that is, the wife-high marriages).

In the case of differences in class background the results were unexpected. Table 5 shows no relationship of the adjustment scores of the

Table 5. Distribution of Adjustment Scores of Couples in Terms of the Social Class Difference of Their Parents

| Social class at marriage | ADJUSTMENT SCORE OF EACH SUBJECT | | | | | | | |
| | Number | | | | Percentage | | | |
	Good	Fair	Poor	Total	Good	Fair	Poor	Total
Couples' parents of same class	44	24	32	100	44.0	24.0	32.0	100.0
Couples' parents 1 class apart	48	30	30	108	44.4	27.8	27.8	100.0
Couples' parents more than 1 class apart	25	16	20	61	41.0	26.2	32.8	100.0
Total	117	70	82	269	...	...	...	....

spouses to the social distance of their respective parents. That is, the adjustment of the spouses does not seem to be affected by the fact that their parental background is of the same or different class level.

The results presented in Table 5 indicate that the difference in the parental social status *per se* does not affect the marital adjustment of the spouses. This is a direct contradiction of the finding of Burgess and Cottrell that the closer the similarity of the family background, the better the marital adjustment of the spouses.[23] Why the difference? It is important to note that Burgess and Cottrell used a method of estimating parental status level which is different from the one used in this study. The latter uses Warner's social class concept and relies largely on the Index of Status Characteristics with the items: occupation, source of income, and education. Burgess and Cottrell used a numerical index of similarity in family backgrounds based on the weighted items: parents' religious preference, their church participation, their education, the father's occupation, the respondent's rating of their economic status, and the respondent's rating of their social status. The

[23] Burgess and Cottrell, *op. cit.,* pp. 82-85.

last two items are subjective ratings which appeared rather unreliable when compared to the objective data provided by the schedules. Some attempt was made to examine the biases in the methods of determining status level to account for the apparently contradictory results. This examination was inconclusive. The difference in the results of the two studies probably lies in a difference of classification of occupation, education, and religion and a different weighting of these factors.

Social Mobility and Marital Adjustment

Social mobility is defined in this study as the distance which a subject moved from his parents in terms of social class level. Thus, if the subject were of the same social class as his parents at the time of his marriage, he is classed as "non-mobile," if he is of a higher social class he is "upward mobile," and if he is of a lower social class he is "downward mobile." In over half the cases in which the mobility pattern could be identified one or both of the spouses were upward mobile. This high proportion probably results from the fact that Burgess and Cottrell included in their study a large number of subjects with advanced education.

The high proportion of cases including downward mobile subjects is harder to explain. Although no accurate estimates of downward mobility have been made, the 20 per cent of cases involving downward mobility in this study seems exceptionally high. It is likely that some of these are cases of "age-graded" mobility.[24] An example of age-graded mobility is the situation in which a man has established himself in a high status level, but his son is forced to start his business or professional career at a lower occupational level. The schedule data were not adequate for distinguishing between age-graded and permanently downgraded persons, so they had to be lumped together in the "downward mobile" category. This fact should be kept in mind wherever the downward mobile group is used in later analysis.

Earlier in this paper the problem was posed: How does mobility prior to marriage affect later adjustment? Does the stress of this earlier culture shift make marital adjustment more difficult? In order to examine this problem the major mobility groups—non-mobile, upward mobile, and downward mobile—were compared to the total group.

The non-mobile group has almost the same proportional distribution as the total group. The upward mobile group actually shows better

[24] McGuire, *op. cit.,* pp. 3, 19.

adjustment than the total group, although this difference proves to be non-significant when the Chi-square test is applied. The stress of the earlier upward culture shift does not appear to affect marital adjustment adversely. It must be remembered that at the time of marriage an upward movement in status has already been achieved. The upward mobile person has largely or entirely assimilated the values of his new position. If he (or she) marries a person of this new social level, he is likely to make his relatively new position more secure and thus improve his general social adjustment. If he has moved up quickly through the educational and occupational ladder, but has not yet assimilated the values of his new position, his marriage to a person at this level may facilitate the learning of new behavior. In their discussion of the acculturation of immigrants, Ruesch, Jacobson, and Loeb point out that the migrant who marries a native partner acculturates much faster than his fellow migrants. "Constant exposure to a model, and reward in terms of affection, apparently accelerate the acculturation process."[25]

The downward mobile group, on the other hand, shows a distribution of significantly lower scores (P<0.02) than the total group, despite the probable dilution of "age-graded mobility" cases.[26]

The tables in the previous section indicated that spouses of the same social class level at the time of marriage scored higher in adjustment than those who were at different levels at marriage. Does this hold true regardless of the spouses' mobility patterns or do the mobility patterns contribute unequally to this relationship? To examine this question the cases within each of the major mobility groups were divided into those who were at the same level at marriage and those who were at different levels.

The "non-mobile" and "one spouse upward mobile" categories show a marked tendency for same-class marriages to have good adjustment compared with cross-class marriages. The Chi-square test shows that this relationship is significant at the 1 per cent level. The "both spouses upward mobile" group shows the same relationship, but the number

25 Ruesch, Jacobson, and Loeb, *op. cit.*, p. 23.

26 The strong social disapproval of downward mobility may make the intimate relationship of marriage less stable. More likely, perhaps, the downward mobile person is apt to be a rebel against convention, and to be a person who rejects responsibilities. His downward mobility would then be a symptom of difficulties in maintaining stable emotional relationships with others. In this case, the unsatisfactory marital relationship would be only one reflection of a general personality pattern.

of cases is too small for statistical analysis. The "downward mobile" group, on the other hand, shows no marked difference between the same-class and cross-class marriages. The slight trend toward better adjustment favoring the same-class marriages proves to be of low significance $(0.30 < P < 0.50)$. It appears that the unfavorable influence of downward mobility upon marital adjustment is so strong that the relationship of the class levels of the spouses is relatively unimportant.

Breaking the total group into a large number of mobility patterns left so few cases in each category that a further breakdown into "husband high" and "wife high" or "husband mobile" and "wife mobile" groups would make statistical analysis impossible. Nevertheless, some of the figures suggest explanations of relationships discussed earlier.

In the previous section it was noted that in cross-class marriages adjustment generally appeared poorer when the wife was of the higher class, than when the husband was of the higher class. The different mobility types are found to contribute very unequally to this relationship.

In the category "one spouse upward mobile, passing level of the other" the distribution is as follows:

	Good	Fair	Poor
Husband mobile	12	7	7
Wife mobile	2	2	8

Although the numbers are small the difference in distribution of "husband mobile" and "wife mobile" cases is extreme. When the wife is upward mobile and of higher class at marriage, the adjustment is markedly poor. That this poor adjustment is due primarily to the class difference rather than the mobility is shown by comparison with the tabulation of the category "one spouse upward mobile, reaching the level of the other":

	Good	Fair	Poor
Husband mobile	25	8	4
Wife mobile	15	5	0

In this tabulation the cases where the wife alone was upward mobile show no skewing toward poor adjustment; in fact, not a single one of the twenty cases falls in the "poor" classification. Also, in those cross-class marriages where there was no upward mobility on the part of either spouse before marriage, the distribution of adjustment scores is about the same for the husband-high and wife-high cases.[27]

Speculations and Suggestions for Future Research

In this paper marital adjustment has been examined in terms of certain relationships with the social class levels and mobility status of the spouses at marriage. Of these factors the one that appears to be of primary importance is the similarity or dissimilarity of the social class level of the spouses at marriage. In other words the chief question is: Are the spouses of the same social class or of different class levels at marriage? The former case is favorable to good adjustment, the latter unfavorable, in the population studied here. Whether the spouses are non-mobile or one or both are upward mobile, whether they are of the higher or lower classes, whether their parents are of the same or different social class levels, the most important factor is still the similarity of the class level of husband and wife at the time of marriage.

This does not mean that the other factors can be ignored. The social class level of the husband and wife in itself is related to adjustment. The subjects show progressively higher adjustment scores as we go up the social class scale. The values of the various social classes concerning marriage and family life may differ in such a way as to make for better adjustment between the spouses at the higher levels. Perhaps Burgess's concept of "companionship"[28] in marriage is found more often at the higher class levels. Downward mobility has a strong unfavorable influence on marital adjustment which tends to obscure other factors. Since in these cases the person was already downward mobile at the time of marriage, it is possible that the person is rebellious and rejects responsibility. His marriage relationships will therefore be unstable. Since the downward mobile group in this study is almost certainly diluted with cases of age-graded mobility, the unfavorable

[27] This might suggest that women who were upward mobile before marriage find the adjustment to a lower status husband more difficult than those who were not upward mobile. We may speculate that a young woman who moves upward in class status before marriage by means of the educational and occupational ladder is likely to desire a role other than (or in addition to) that of housewife and mother. If she marries a man of lower status, her position will appear to be one of superiority over her husband. Since most men in our culture find such a position ego-shattering and since a downward shift in status on the part of the originally upward-mobile wife is similarly difficult, such a marriage is likely to prove unsatisfactory.

[28] Ernest W. Burgess and Harvey J. Locke, *The Family,* New York, American Book Co., 1945.

effect of downward mobility is probably even greater than appears in the analysis presented in this paper.

Surprisingly, difference in the social class background of the spouses (that is, the social class of their respective parents), does not appear to affect their adjustment. Neither does the husband's or wife's social class background *per se*, except for a possible unfavorable effect in the case of lower-lower class parents. Of course, the class level of the parents has an indirect influence insofar as it affects the class levels of the spouses. But the actual levels of the spouses at marriage, whether they have been inherited directly from the parents or have been moved into through some mobility route, seem to determine the success of the marriage.

Our data show this pattern, but do not explain it. Why should it exist? In attempting to account for it, it seems reasonable to assume that it is the present, operating values of the husband and the wife which determine how they behave and how they evaluate each other's behavior. Thus, it would not be the sociological fact of their social status which makes them happy or unhappy. Rather, it would be the class-typical day-to-day behavior which would tend to harmonize in the case of same-class marriages, and conflict in cross-class marriages.

These data further suggest that there is no necessary, mechanical inheritance of values from the parental family. Instead, they suggest that it is possible to learn a whole way of life which is different from that of the family one is born into; and to do it successfully, by the standards of the new social group. Thus it is not some mysterious, automatic reproduction of asociological pattern; not some inexplicable, but inescapable, "background factor" which determines adult behavior and adjustment. Rather, the evidence indicates, as does so much other evidence, that the socially significant aspects of human behavior are largely learned. While the impress of childhood training is a powerful influence (and many of our mobile subjects may have been trained by a father or mother who envisioned and encouraged upward mobility), it remains that much of the acquisition of values and behaviors could and probably did occur outside the parental home. In the case of our well-adjusted subjects with disparate backgrounds but similar class-status at the time of marriage, some such process seems to be the most likely explanation.

Thus, a fatalistic prediction that the children of Park Avenue and Railroad Street could not marry happily appears untrue. Some of them can and do learn to be a different kind of person than their parents were, and live the new role successfully with a marriage partner of the new class.

On the other hand, it may be that the ability or willingness to learn a new pattern of life declines after marriage. Those subjects who had been mobile, but married a person of a different social class (as of the time of marriage), did not show the same success in adapting to their marriage that they displayed in adapting to their new social position.

It may be that one's pattern of behavior is largely set by the time one marries. *On the average* (for this is a statistical deduction that should not be applied uncritically to a specific case), it may be that it is not nearly so easy to learn new behavior patterns after marriage as it was in the earlier years. This might be a function of increasing psychological rigidity with age.

There is another explanation, however, which may fit the facts better. We know that there are cases in which husband and wife jointly move up the social ladder *after* they are married. The ability to achieve the complex learning this requires does not disappear at the point of the nuptial ceremony. Acculturation to a new group can still occur. In a sense, the adjustment to a marriage partner might also be considered an acculturation process, insofar as it involves the modification of behaviors and attitudes. Yet, our data point out that the same people who successfully acculturate to a new social class find it harder to adapt to a spouse of a different social status. Cross-class marriages, even among the mobile, are a poorer risk than same-class marriages. It may be that the motivation to adapt to a higher social class is actually stronger, and that the rewards appear more desirable to the individual, than is the case in adapting to the way of life of one's spouse.* This is an unromantic explanation, but it seems very possible. Put bluntly, people may be more willing to change themselves in order to be successfully mobile than to make the changes necessary for a satisfying, stable marriage.

If nothing more, these data suggest certain deep differences among the different social classes; deep enough to make it relatively hard for two people of different classes to live together happily as man and wife. To illustrate, a person who believes in accumulating property and providing economically for the future (middle class, especially upper-

---

* This point is considered in greater detail by Whyte in "The Wife Problem." See pp. 279-95 above.—*Eds.*

middle) would scarcely be able to agree in money matters with a person who prefers to spend all his money for immediate satisfactions (lower class, especially lower-lower). A person who seeks rather compulsively to impose "proper" behavior and attitudes on his children (middle class) would have difficulty in agreeing on child rearing problems with a person who had a more indulgent approach (lower class).[29]

As usual, a relatively small study such as this, using only statistical comparisons of groups, raises more questions than it answers. One hopes that they are different questions, based on a larger and clearer fund of knowledge than one had at the outset. The next step would preferably be an intensive study of married individuals, gathering the fullest possible information about childhood experiences and training, and the later influences and events that ultimately produce the adult behavior-value pattern present at the time of marriage. Further, we would need to know the crucial behaviors and attitudes that each partner shows within the successful and unsuccessful marriage. . . .

PREDICTING ADJUSTMENT IN MARRIAGE*

Harvey J. Locke

Science holds as one of its tenets the view that the conclusions of any study must be verified by repetitions of the experiment. This subjection of the conclusions of a study to continued investigation is particularly needed in the social sciences. The following conclusions from the present study, while presented in the form of rather dogmatic statements concerning the relationship between given behavior or situations and marital adjustment, are to be viewed as hypotheses for future research.

1. Marital adjustment ranges along a continuum from very great to very little adjustment. Happiness in marriage, as judged by an outsider, represents adjustment, and divorce represents maladjustment.

---

[29] Of course, middle-class parents often hold a conscious philosophy of permissiveness, but the weight they give to "proper training," in practice, still contrasts markedly with lower-class parents.

* Adapted and reprinted by permission of the author and publisher from *Predicting Adjustment in Marriage: A Comparison of a Divorced and a Happily Married Group,* New York, Henry Holt & Co., 1951, pp. 358-60.

2. The alienation process is generally a slow cumulation of conflicts and disagreements, accompanied by the psychological withdrawal of one or both spouses. If the course of the alienation process is far advanced, the spouses tend to express derogatory attitudes toward each other, tend to have many complaints about the mate and the marriage, and tend to exaggerate the deficiencies of the mate and the marriage.

3. The development of binding ties of affection, common interests and activities, similar attitudes and values, along with respect for the individuality of the partner, begins prior to the marriage ceremony and continues afterwards. Consequently, the experiences during the period of courtship and engagement are likely to be potent forces making for or against the success of a marriage. The longer the courtship the greater the probability that the uniting process will be well advanced prior to marriage and will continue after the ceremony.

4. Marital adjustment involves adaptation not only to the mate, but also to the mate's parents. The type of home atmsophere, revealed by such things as the degree of happiness in childhood and the happiness of the marriage of the parents, determines, in part, the *readiness* of a person to make the necessary adjustments to the behavior of others in the marriage situation. Some emancipation from the parental home prior to, as well as after, marriage increases the chances that one will be able to adjust to the behavior of the mate and of the in-laws.

5. Sexual relations in marriage are to be considered in terms of conflict, or lack of conflict, between the behavior of the individual and cultural values. They are also to be considered as an intimate form of communication. When there is a wide difference between the sexual behavior of a person and the cultural expectations relative to sex, such as the expectation that intercourse will be confined to the marriage relationship, the conflict will be reflected in the relationships between the spouses. Sexual intercourse, when coupled with affection, satisfaction, and enjoyment of the sex act, is one of the most subtle and potent forms of communication between the persons involved, and tends to weld them together.

6. There is no relationship between the presence or absence of children, or the size of the family, and marital adjustment. There is, however, an association between marital adjustment and those personality characteristics which are reflected in a desire for children.

7. Marital adjustment is associated with directorial ability, as measured by the ready acceptance of responsibility, strictness in dealing with

children, leadership, the ability to make decisions readily, determination, and not being too easily influenced by others.

8. Marital adjustment is associated with a general personality pattern of adaptability. It can be measured by such traits as yielding in arguments, not being dominating, slowness in getting angry, and quickness in getting over anger.

9. The capacity to give and receive affection, as measured by replies to questions on affectionateness and demonstration of affection, is associated with success in marriage.

10. Sociability, or the tendency to join with others for companionship, is highly associated with marital adjustment. It can be measured by such personality traits—as rated by oneself or by the mate—as sociability, enjoyment of belonging to organizations, some concern with what people say and think, and a sense of humor. It also can be measured by the number of friends of the husband or wife before marriage, after marriage, and in common during marriage. . . .

11. Conventionality is highly associated with marital adjustment. It can be measured by such things as having the marriage ceremony performed by a minister or priest, attendance at Sunday school up to a certain age, and affiliation with, and attendance at, church.

12. The companionship family, defined as having intimate communication, sympathetic understanding, common interests, mutual respect on the basis of equality, democratic behavior, and shared rather than individualistic behavior, is highly associated with marital adjustment.

13. Certain economic factors, such as economic security and stability, certain values associated with homemaking, appreciation of the efforts of the husband to provide for the needs of the family, appreciation of the work of the wife in homemaking, and other variables related to economic factors, are associated with marital adjustment.

14. The gainful employment of the wife outside the home is not associated with marital adjustment or maladjustment. On the other hand, the approval by the husband of the wife's working is associated with marital adjustment.

15. Bereaved persons and divorced women make as satisfactory an adjustment in subsequent marriages as the adjustment of persons who have been married only once.

CHAPTER 17

Discussions of Studies in Marital Adjustment

IN CHAPTER 1 we presented a set of criteria which we encouraged the reader to apply to the articles in this book. It is unfortunate that scientific literature generally, and especially that of the social sciences, contains so little systematic criticism of published studies.[1] If there were more criticisms in the literature, students would have an opportunity to see how experienced scholars utilize criteria such as those set forth in chapter 1, and, incidentally, the authors of the original studies would stand to benefit. We are glad to be able to publish a criticism by Ellis of the two major pioneering studies in marital adjustment. It should be noted that the more recent studies noted in the introduction to chapter 16 (those of Locke and of Karlsson) had not been published at the time Ellis wrote his critique, and hence his omission of any reference to them does not imply his judgment that they are invulnerable to criticism.[2]

We begin this chapter with a statement by Burgess on methods of measuring and predicting marital adjustment. Next is Ellis' critique

[1] Some years ago the Social Science Research Council took note of this lack and inaugurated a set of critiques. See, *e.g.,* Herbert Blumer, *Critiques of Research in the Social Sciences: I. An Appraisal of Thomas and Znaniecki's* The Polish Peasant in Europe and America, New York, Social Science Research Council, 1939.

[2] Since the data in the Roth-Peck article in chapter 16 are from the Burgess-Cottrell study, the critique and the defense in this chapter are generally applicable to that paper as well.

)f the Terman and Burgess-Cottrell studies, followed by a defense by Terman and Wallin, the latter of whom is collaborating with Burgess in a further study of marital adjustment.

METHODS OF PREDICTING MARITAL ADJUSTMENT*

Ernest W. Burgess

History and Nature of Predictive Methods

The first attempt to discover factors predictive of success or failure in marriage was made by Katharine B. Davis in 1926. In the intervening two decades a large number of studies have been made correlating factors assumed to be predictive of success in marriage with some criterion of success such as "happiness," "permanence of the union," "satisfaction," and "adjustment." The findings of many of these studies and a detailed analysis of them have been prepared by Clifford Kirkpatrick and published under the title *What Science Says About Happiness in Marriage*.

While in a sense all these studies could be termed predictive, they fall into two broad groups. The first are those which consider only single items and indicate their individual relation to the selective criterion of success in marriage. The second group are those which deal with several items combined into an expectancy table of the probabilities of marital success. The principal studies of the latter type have been those made by Terman[1] and his associates, by Burgess and Cottrell,[2] and by Burgess and Wallin.[3]

Our main emphasis in this paper will be upon studies dealing with a combination of factors as related to an index of success and failure in marriage. The studies of factors considered singly are not unimportant, particularly, as we shall see later, because they corroborate the findings of studies dealing with a combination of factors.

* Adapted and reprinted by permission of the author and publisher from "Predictive Methods and Family Stability," *Annals of the American Academy of Political and Social Science*, 272 (1950), 47-52.

[1] Lewis M. Terman, *Psychological Factors in Marital Happiness,* New York, McGraw-Hill Book Co., 1938.

[2] Ernest W. Burgess and Leonard S. Cottrell, *Predicting Success or Failure in Marriage,* New York, Prentice-Hall, 1939.

[3] Unpublished study of 1,000 engaged and 700 married couples.

Steps in Prediction

What are the steps in prediction? They involve the following:

1. The Selection of a Criterion of Success in Marriage. In the studies by Terman, by Burgess and Cottrell, and by Burgess and Wallin, the criterion is an index of success composed of answers of husband and wife to a large number of questions dealing with self-reports on happiness, satisfaction, agreements and disagreements, and common interests. By giving a numerical value to answers to these questions, a total score representing the degree of success of the union is obtained.

2. The Choice of Items Assumed to Be Predictive. These may be taken from the literature on human behavior, from previous research in the field of marital relations, and from the theories and hunches of the investigator. Appropriate questions are devised to be answered by the members of the engaged or married couples.

3. The Correlation of These Items Assumed to Be Predictive with the success score. Certain items are found not to be correlated, and only those which show correlations are retained.

4. The Construction of an Expectancy or Experience Table of the Probabilities of Marital Success. This is accomplished by getting a total prediction score for each couple on a basis of the answers which they give to the items that are found to be associated with success in marriage. This total prediction score for each person is then correlated with his corresponding success score. It is then possible to relate groups of prediction scores to the percentage of those who will succeed or fail in marriage. Such an expectancy table was prepared by Burgess and Cottrell[4] for a group of 519 couples, and is reproduced here in adapted form.

It will be noted in the study that husbands and wives with the highest premarital prediction score (700 to 779) have no cases with a very low marriage-success score, while those with a very low prediction score (220 to 229) have no cases with high or very high marriage-success scores.

5. Application of the Expectancy Table to a New Group of Cases. This was done by Burgess and Cottrell for a new sample of 155 couples with the same general socioeconomic level of the first group. The test of its validity was a correlation of .48 between the correlations of pre

[4] *Op. cit.,* p. 284.

narital prediction scores and success scores as compared with a correlation of .51 in the original sample . . .*

Questions of Application

Certain questions have been raised about the practical application of prediction tests. These may be taken up in the following order:

1. Are the Findings of These Predictive Studies Representative of the General Public? It is true that the studies by Terman and Burgess and Cottrell had a higher proportion of couples at the college and

Table 1. Relation Between Prediction Scores and Marriage-Success Scores (Percentage Distribution)

Premarital prediction score	MARRIAGE-SUCCESS SCORE			
	Very low	Low	High and very high	No. of cases
700 to 779	0.0	10.0	90.0	10
620 to 699	1.5	12.1	86.4	66
540 to 619	5.8	21.9	72.3	137
460 to 539	27.6	29.4	43.0	170
380 to 459	39.8	31.1	29.1	93
300 to 379	57.2	25.7	17.1	35
220 to 299	75.0	25.0	0.0	8
Total				519

high school level than that in the general population. On the other hand, they did include persons of only grade school training, and a larger number who had not completed high school. Other studies have been made where the sample included predominantly those who had not completed the grades or had not completed high school. Clarence Schroeder made a study of divorced and nondivorced couples, in a midwest city of 100,000, who were predominantly of low economic, low educational, and low social status. Locke compared background factors of divorced and nondivorced couples in the county in which was located a city of 400,000. They were also predominantly of low economic, low educational, and low social status. Both Schroeder and Locke found, however, that the same chief background factors were correlated with divorce and nondivorce as Terman and Burgess and Cottrell found associated with success or failure in marriage.

* A test, based upon the z transformation, of the significance of the difference between these two correlations yields a t of 0.325. This implies that the two correlations do not differ significantly from each other.—*Eds.*

An unpublished study in a small city indicates that the majority of background factors operate in the same way with southern Negroes as with white couples previously studied. Differences in predictive factors are perhaps not so great by social class and by region of the country as had been expected. This preliminary finding needs, however, to be checked by further research.*

2. Are Background and Personality Information Secured After Marriage Truly Predictive? The answer to this question is flatly, No. They can only be tentatively held as predictive until they are corroborated by studies of these items in the engagement period. Even then, they should be tested on a new sample to determine whether they are efficient predictors.

This point applies particularly to personality traits. Burgess and Wallin find that personality characteristics as measured by self-reports are subject to some change after marriage. For example, a person with a relatively high neurotic score in the engagement period may have a low score three years after marriage. The reverse is also the case. Research in the future should be directed to securing, if possible, personality characteristics that are not subject to change and are also predictive of marital success.

3. Are Not Statistical Methods of Prediction in Terms of Probabilities of Success for a Group of Cases Rather Than for the Individual? It is evident from Table 1 that the prediction is by risk groups. For example, a premarital prediction score of 700 to 779 may be interpreted to mean that 90 per cent of engaged persons will have a high or very high marriage-success score. But it is not possible to state from the premarital prediction score above whether a given person will fall in the 10 per cent with a low marriage-success score or in the 90 per cent with a high marriage-success score. The prediction is in terms of probabilities and not of certainties.

4. Can a Statistical Prediction Score Take Account of the Particular Configuration of Factors Operating in Every Engagement Relation? It cannot at the present stage of development of statistical prediction. It should be possible over a long period of research to convert more and more case-study findings into quantitative expression. For the time

* Burgess's argument that other studies based upon other kinds of subjects yield essentially comparable findings is further supported by a more recent study done in Sweden. *Cf.* Georg Karlsson, *Adaptability and Communication in Marriage: A Swedish Predictive Study of Marital Satisfaction,* Uppsala, Almqvist & Wiksells Boktryckeri Aktiebolag, 1951.—*Eds.*

being, however, a predictive factor indicates the way it operates in the majority of cases. In particular cases, under certain conditions, a factor may have the reverse influence.

These different objections need to be kept in mind in any attempts at the practical application to the solution of family problems of predictive factors or expectancy tables. . . .

THE VALUE OF MARRIAGE PREDICTION TESTS*

ALBERT ELLIS

Although marriage prediction tests are hardly new to sociological thinking or practice, they seem recently to have been applied on a much larger scale than ever before. Their increased use may be attributed to several different factors: increased interest and enrollment in college courses dealing with engagement and marital problems; widespread publicity in popular magazine articles and in books like Clifford Adams' *How to Pick a Mate;*[1] and the mushrooming of marital counseling facilities, with a concomitant search for short-cut methods of premarital guidance.

That effective marriage prediction tests would have an enormous practical value is indubitable. Our current divorce rates are generally considered to be alarmingly high; and any technique which might help to weed out doomed marriages before they were actually consummated would be enthusiastically welcomed by most front-line participants in these marriages, as well as by innumerable members of our society who are less directly concerned with the longevity of specific marriages. This very wish for some trustworthy prognosticator of connubial felicity is, no doubt, father to much of the hopeful application of existing marriage prediction scales.

Since, however, untrustworthy or false marriage prediction may well be more harmful than no prediction at all; and since many—if indeed not most—of those who are now applying marriage prediction tests and enthusiastically espousing them in the popular literature have but

* Adapted and reprinted by permission of the author and publisher from the *American Sociological Review*, 13 (1948), 710-18.

[1] Clifford Adams and Vance O. Packard, *How to Pick a Mate,* New York, Dutton, 1946.

meager training in test construction and administration; it seems well to inquire just how valid, from a theoretical and a practical standpoint this type of testing instrument is likely to be. It is to this inquiry that the present article is directed.

The Content of Existing Marriage Prediction Scales

One of the first steps in the appraisal of any sociological or psychological testing instrument is an examination of the content of the questions or techniques employed in the instrument. How, for example, were its questions originally chosen? What kind of item validations went into their selection? What was the theory behind choosing one type of question rather than an entirely different kind? When queries of this nature are raised in connection with existing marriage prediction tests, the following points are revealed.

1. Many of the prediction scales include conventional personality inventory items as an integral part of the test. Thus, Terman's[2] scale includes items taken from the Bernreuter Personality Inventory; the Burgess and Cottrell[3] prediction study used items from the Thurstone personality Inventory; and Adams[4] employed items from the Adams Lepley Personal Audit. Unfortunately, however, it is precisely this type of personality inventory which has proved to be of dubious value on several different counts: (a) Validation studies have shown that this type of inventory has given a satisfactory clinical diagnosis in only about one out of every two times it has been experimentally used to differentiate between clinical *groups*. This means that in the prediction of *individual* clinical diagnoses its validity is indeed questionable, and that its prognostic value is limited to special purposes, samples, and interpretive skills.[5] (b) This type of personality inventory, as has been known for years, is notorious for its inability to prevent sophisticated respondents from giving dishonest responses if for any reason they feel motivated to do so. Thus, in forty-two studies designed to show whether lying took place on this kind of inventory, thirty-six investi

[2] Lewis Terman and Others, *Psychological Factors in Marital Happiness*, New York McGraw-Hill, 1938.

[3] Ernest W. Burgess and Leonard S. Cottrell, Jr., *Predicting Success or Failure in Marriage*, New York, Prentice-Hall, 1939.

[4] Clifford Adams, "The Prediction of Adjustment in Marriage," *Educational and Psychological Measurement*, VI (Winter, 1946), 185-193.

[5] Albert Ellis, "The Validity of Personality Questionnaires," *Psychological Bulletin* XLIII (Sept., 1946), 385-440. Albert Ellis, "Personality Questionnaires," *Review of Educational Research*, XVII (Feb., 1947), 53-63.

gators found that respondents did tend to be dishonest in their inventory answers, while only six investigators failed to find such dishonesty.[6] (c) On none of the personality inventories used in the existing marriage prediction scales was an outside clinical criterion used in the original validation of the inventory. On the contrary, only internal consistency criteria were employed, and no attempt at clinical validation was made.

2. On several of the existing marriage prediction scales, some of the items included in the scales are *post*-marital rather than *pre*-marital ones. That is to say, the respondents in investigations (such as the Terman and Burgess and Cottrell studies) were asked, among other things, about their mutual interests after marriage, their handling of finances, their philosophy of life, their manner of dealing with in-law questions, and so on. While the correlation between the subjects' answers to such items as these and their avowed degree of marital happiness may be both interesting and important, it may have relatively little relation to the problem of predicting the success of a marriage *which has not yet taken place*.

Where the questions on a prediction scale are entirely of a pre-marital nature, they were given, in several of the reported studies, only to *post*-marital groups of respondents. That is, the respondents were asked about their family backgrounds, pre-marital relations with their spouse, number of friends they had at marriage, etc., only *after* they were already married; and it was assumed, as Burgess and Wallin point out, "that postmarital reports upon premarital variables would not be affected by postmarital experience."[7] This is an assumption for which adequate supporting evidence is hardly as yet available.

3. Many of the prediction scales were validated against a happiness adjustment score that was derived from rather naïve attitudinal questions. Thus, husbands and wives were asked how frequently they quarreled with each other, how often they kissed their spouse, how many times they regretted marrying, and similar questions. But such items suffer from doubt on at least two points: (a) At best, they tap only the most conscious and accepted attitudes of the respondents, while they fail to tap unconscious or unfaced feelings of hostility, affection, or ambivalence which may be more germane than the consciously

[6] *Ibid.*, 414-420.

[7] Ernest W. Burgess and Paul Wallin, "Predicting Adjustment in Marriage," *American Journal of Sociology*, XLIX (March, 1944), 324-330.

accepted feelings in determining a respondent's marriage adjustment score. (*b*) There is no safeguard, when items like these are asked of a respondent, that he will not quite consciously lie in his answers to them.

4. Some of the special questionnaires now being widely distributed and used as marriage prediction scales or adjuncts are composed of items which seem to have no statistical validation whatever. This is particularly true of several of the short questionnaires included in Adams' *How to Pick a Mate*. A search through this volume, as well as through all Adams' professional publications, failed to reveal any published validity (or even reliability) figures for several of these short questionnaires.

Thus, on page 46 of his book, Adams asks, "Are you grown up emotionally?" and gives eighteen questions, with the notation that "If you honestly answer YES to fourteen of these or more you are more mature emotionally than the average person. If you answered YES to sixteen or more you should have an exceptionally good chance for a happy marriage." There is no indication in the text that these eighteen questions were selected on other than an armchair basis, or that any statistical validation was done to show that people who have sixteen or more YES's definitely make happy marriages, while those who have less than sixteen YES's definitely do not.

Again, on page 54, Dr. Adams asks: "Are you really in love?" And he then gives twenty-four questions, with the claim that a "correct" answer to twenty or more means that "we would judge you to be solidly in love." Statistical validation is most conspicuously absent.

Still again, Dr. Adams, this time on the basis of ten or more "incorrect" answers, claims to be able to tell his readers whether their mate is a neurotic (page 164); and with fifteen out of eighteen "correct" answers he claims to be able to tell them that "you are a warm, ardent person and should be able to work out a satisfying sexual adjustment" (page 73). Statistical proof of these crucial cutting scores? None.

In sum: the content of the existing marriage prediction scales invites little trust in the prognostic value of these scales, since the questions contained in them sometimes include personality inventory items which are of questionable value for this purpose, post-marital items which have dubious relevance to pre-marital prediction tests, happiness adjustment items which probe only the most consciously accepted atti-des and feelings toward the respondent's spouse, and some special hort questionnaires which appear to be entirely unvalidated.

The Sampling Procedures Used in Marriage Prediction Studies

Marriage prediction scales, if they are to be generally applied, must f course work effectively when used with large segments of our opulation. Moreover, before the coefficients of correlation or critical atios on which their validations are based can be properly evaluated, ve must know something about the sampling procedures employed 1 their validity studies. These sampling procedures will therefore now e scrutinized.

An analysis of the sampling methods employed to date in marriage rediction studies reveals the following interesting facts:

1. All the validity studies appear to have used volunteer respondents; nd these volunteers seem to have been but a small proportion of the otal number of the potential respondents who were circularized. Thus, n the Burgess and Cottrell study, seven thousand questionnaires were listributed, and only 19 percent of the distributees actually returned heir filled-in questionnaires.

2. Virtually all the reported marriage prediction studies, as their uthors frankly point out, used samples which were heavily weighted vith college level respondents and with professional people. Thus, 8 percent of Terman's husbands and 38 percent of his wives were ollege graduates; 60.5 percent of Burgess and Cottrell's husbands and 5.7 percent of their wives were college graduates or had an under-graduate education; and three-fourths of Burgess and Wallin's hus-ands and about two-thirds of their wives were at the college level. While samples of this kind are serviceable for pioneering marital pre-liction studies, it is to be wondered whether prediction scales which re exclusively validated on them are clinically applicable to wider egments of our population.

3. The samples employed for validation purposes have consisted of ligh proportions of happily married couples. According to their own tatements, the samples used by Terman, Burgess and Cottrell, Burgess nd Wallin, and Adams all were heavily skewed in the direction of appy marriages. Moreover, some of the studies dealt with respondents vho were married only a short length of time, and never more than ix years. But, as one study after another has shown, happiness in narriage seems to vary inversely with the length of the marriage: so

that these studies could hardly help being weighted in favor of happil
married respondents. While this kind of sampling is perhaps acceptabl
in *initial* studies, it is to be wondered, again, whether prediction scale
based on such atypical samples can be safely applied to the very wid
varieties of individuals with whom such scales are apparently bein
clinically used today.

4. The samples used in the prediction studies were usually quit
small. Adams' study contained only a hundred married couples; an
the Terman and Burgess and Cottrell investigations, though containin
several hundred respondents each, broke these down into subsample
which soon became quite small. Since, as stated above, these sample
were far from random or unbiased ones in the first place, the fact o
their being so small can hardly enhance our faith in the reliability o
the validity coefficients obtained with their use.

In sum: the samples used in the existing marriage prediction studie
have been atypical, non-random, and small; and there is a possibilit
that some of the obtained results were in part a function of the sam
pling, and are consequently non-transferable to marital predictio
situations where the scales are used with many different kinds an
classes of counselees.

The Validation Procedures Used in Marriage Prediction Studies

The validity of marriage prediction scales may only be determine
by submitting them to proper validation procedures, and thereby de
riving an estimate of their practical value. Since validation procedure
differ widely, an inquiry into the nature and extent of those employe
in the most popular and publicized marriage prediction scales woul
seem to be in order.

Unfortunately, few of the published scales have used any objectiv
or outside performance criterion on the validation studies which hav
been done on them. Instead, they have employed methods which giv
results similar to those obtained by internal consistency validation
That is to say, the scale constructors have given a group of respondent
a set of questions to determine these respondents' marital adjustmen
scores: to determine, in other words, how happy or unhappy th
respondents have been in their *already existing* marriages. Then the
have given these very same respondents another set of questions cor
cerning the respondents' personality traits, attitudes, and pre-marita
backgrounds. On the basis of these two sets of questions, the scal

constructors have correlated the "marital adjustment scores" with the "predictor" questions, have eliminated those "predictor" questions which showed a low correlation with the "adjustment scores," and have called the remaining questions, which showed higher correlations with the "adjustment scores," their final "marital prediction scale." Thus, the Burgess and Cottrell and the Terman scales were mainly validated in this manner.

But this validation procedure proves, in effect, that the questions finally "validated" in the "prediction scale" are consistent with the scale-derived definition of "marital adjustment," which is also set up by the same "validation" procedure. Moreover, if—as has sometimes been the case—the criterion group which is given the "prediction" questions is the *same* group—rather than a fresh sample—on which the "adjustment" scale has been standardized, then (unless the number of cases employed is quite large) spuriously high coefficients of correlation between the "prediction" and the "adjustment" scales will tend to be found.

The proper method of validating a marriage prediction scale is (*a*) to devise a set of suitable prediction questions; (*b*) to test each one of these questions against a reliable outside performance criterion, such as several years of happily married life attested to by external observers as well as by the married participants; (*c*) to eliminate by item analyses all the non-discriminating questions; (*d*) to try the revised prediction scale on an entirely *new* group of subjects, again using a strict performance measure as a criterion of success; and (*e*) to repeat this procedure a sufficient number of times so that either high validity coefficients are obtained for the prediction scale, or it is deemed worthless for future experimentation.

Only a few of the published marriage prediction scales have used suitable independent performance criteria in their validation procedures; and then the strictness of these criteria has left much to be desired. Thus, Adams[8] gave his own Personal Audit, the Terman Prediction Scale, and the Guilford-Martin Personnel Inventory to 4,000 students; and later he found one hundred of the tested couples who had been married *six months or longer,* and determined their marital adjustment scores by questionnaire responses. Unfortunately, Adams does not report how many couples he had to query before he obtained his cooperative hundred; and he does report that his married couples

[8] Clifford Adams, *op. cit.*

were, at the time of their second questioning, married only for an *average of 2.36 years*. The criterion group here is hardly strictly selected or controlled.

Again, Burgess and Wallin[9] questioned 526 couples while they were engaged, and questioned the same group three years after their marriage, to determine the correlation between a marriage prediction scale and a post-marital adjustment scale. But they found that their respondents tended to be very happily married, in general—which is quite predictable from the fact of their (*a*) being voluntary respondents and (*b*) being married only for a relatively short length of time. Here again the performance measure used to check the validity of the marriage prediction scale is of dubious value.

In a somewhat different kind of study, Jessie Bernard[10] gave an instrument for the measurement of success in marriage to various respondents who had already been studied intensively by Paul Popenoe and she correlated their test scores with Popenoe's case study rating of the respondents. She found a rank correlation of .891; but had only thirteen cases in her sample. What is more important, her cases consisted of respondents who had voluntarily consulted Dr. Popenoe because of their marital difficulties, and who therefore would be expected to answer Mrs. Bernard's questionnaire in the same manner as they answered Dr. Popenoe's interview questions dealing with the same troubled areas of their lives. That is to say: the one neurotic in, let us say, a hundred who voluntarily goes for psychiatric or psychological counseling will quite expectedly give neurotic responses to a personality inventory; and the one troubled wife or husband in perhaps a thousand who voluntarily goes to Dr. Popenoe's clinic with his problems will be expected to admit the very same troubles on a marriage prediction scale like Mrs. Bernard's. Consequently, Mrs. Bernard's obtained validity coefficient, even though an outside performance measure was used in this instance, is tautological and meaningless.

In sum: virtually all the validation studies which have been made on marriage prediction scales have failed to use adequate outside performance measures in the evaluations of these scales. Either no attempt to provide such measures has been made; or those which have been

9 Burgess and Wallin, *op. cit.*

10 Jessie Bernard, "An Instrument for the Measurement of Success in Marriage," *Publications of the American Sociological Society*, XXVII (Dec. 28-31, 1932), 94-106.

provided have been inadequate for the purpose for which they were intended.

The Possibility of Differential Subgroup Bias

Underlying practically all the published studies on marital prediction scales has been the implication that the obtained correlations between marriage adjustments and premarital factors are substantial proof of causal connections. That is to say, it has been implied—though rarely baldly stated—that if a high correlation is found between, say, an individual's happiness after marriage and the happiness of his parents in *their* marriage, the latter variable is causally related to the former, and may therefore be used as a predictor of the former.

If this were not the implication behind marriage prediction scales, it is difficult to see what rationale could exist for them. Thus, if it is found that happily married men *do* tend to have parents who were also happily married, and it is *not* implied that the latter event tends to cause the former, this item will be perfectly useless in a marriage prediction scale. For it may be that happiness in marriage is associated with happiness in one's parents' marriage not because the two are causally related but because—let us say—people who claim (with perhaps no basis whatever in fact) that their own marriages are happy are the same kind of people who claim (with equally little basis in fact) that their parents' marriages were happy. If *this* were so, the obtained high correlation between self-happiness and parents' happiness in marriage would not only be meaningless as a marriage prediction item, but would in fact be entirely misleading.

Lest this assumption seem fantastic, the hypothesis will now be seriously raised that the obtained correlations between "marriage prediction scales" and "marriage adjustment scores" which have been frequently found by different researchers are better explicable in terms of what may be called *differential subgroup bias* than in terms (implied by nearly all the studies thus far referred to in this paper) of true causal relations. By *differential subgroup bias* is meant the tendency of one biased subgroup of a sample population to consistently answer questionnaire variables in the direction of their biases, and for another biased subgroup of the sample population to consistently answer the same questionnaire variables in the direction of *their* biases: thus leading to (partly or wholly) artificial correlations.

To illustrate this possibility, let us suppose that all respondents to a marriage prediction scale and a marriage adjustment scale may be divided into two subgroups: those who are ashamed to admit that there is anything seriously wrong with their marriages, and those who are not ashamed to do so. Under such circumstances, those individuals in subsample A—who are ashamed to admit that there is anything wrong with their marriages—will doubtlessly tend to (*a*) gloss over the defects of their marriages, and hence to obtain high marriage adjustment scores; and (*b*) to exaggerate the virtues of their parents marriages, and of other premarital background factors in their lives and thus to obtain high premarital adjustment scores. At the same time, those individuals who are in subsample B—who are not ashamed that there is something wrong with their marriages—will doubtlessly tend to (*a*) admit the defects of their marriages, and hence to obtain relatively low marriage adjustment scores; and (*b*) to admit the defects of their parents' marriages, and of other pre-marital background factors in their lives, and thus to obtain relatively low pre-marital adjustment scores. Under such circumstances, there would be a sort of double-barreled artificial correlation effect which would almost certainly lead to substantial "validity" coefficients between the entire sample's marriage adjustment and pre-marital adjustment scores; and a "marriage prediction scale" would probably result which proved only, in point of fact, that individuals who are ashamed to admit that there is anything wrong with their marriage receive consistently different questionnaire scores than individuals who are not ashamed to make such admissions.

To get down from the realm of sheer speculation to more specific hypothesis, it will now be hypothesized that the obtained "validity" coefficients for the existing marital prediction scales seem to mirror differential subgroup bias rather than causal connections between pre-marital background factors and post-marital adjustment; and, more specifically, that the factor common to the pre-marital and post-marital test items seems to be the *conservatism* of the individuals answering both sets of items.

The main evidence in favor of this hypothesis is the nature of the items on which substantial coefficients of correlation between pre-marital and post-marital questions have generally been found. Thus, it has been found that respondents who say that they are happily married—or who answer post-marital adjustment questionnaires so that they obtain relatively high scores on them—show greater attachments to their parents, come from homes in which the parents were happily married, come from generally good family backgrounds, have a history of childhood happiness, and claim to be virginal or almost virginal at marriage.[11] But these traits, obviously, are precisely those one would expect to find in, or expect to find claimed by, conservative and conventional respondents.

Again, it has been found that people who obtain the highest marriage adjustment scores, tend to attend Sunday school till relatively late in their lives, attend church regularly, be married in church, have long engagements and acquaintanceships before they marry, seldom change their residences, and go with few persons of the opposite sex before marriage.[12] But this is exactly, is it not, what one would expect to find conservative and conventional respondents doing or claiming to do?

Still again: it has been found that people who say that they are happily married tend to come from professional classes, frequently to be ministers or college professors, be rural dwellers, live in small communities, be home owners, and be relatively well-off financially.[13] Is not this, too, a fairly clear-cut picture of what the conservative and conventional individual in our society is?

Because of this close correspondence between conventionalism and conservatism on the one hand, and the traits that happily married couples have empirically been found to possess, or to say they possess, on the other hand, it seems clear that the obtained correlations between marriage adjustment and pre-marital traits and histories may *not* imply causal relationships at all, but may very well be the result of common factors like conservatism-radicalism or shame-about-marital-shortcomings and lack-of-shame-about-marital-shortcomings. Which means, of course, that the obtained "validity" coefficients which have been brought forth in support of existing marriage prediction scales may actually have little or nothing to do with predicting success in marriage.

11 Terman, *op. cit.;* Burgess and Cottrell, *op. cit.;* Paul Popenoe and D. Wicks, "Marital Happiness in Two Generations," *Mental Hygiene, XXI* (1937), 218-223; C. W. Schroeder, *Divorce in a City of One Hundred Thousand Population,* Peoria, Ill., Bradley Polytechnic Library, 1939; Katharine B. Davis, *Factors in the Sex Life of 2,200 Women,* New York, Harper, 1929; G. V. Hamilton, *A Research in Marriage,* New York, Boni, 1929.

12 Terman, *op. cit.;* Burgess and Cottrell, *op. cit.;* Schroeder, *op. cit.;* Howard E. Wilkening, *Attitudes toward Marriage and Divorce,* Ph.D. Thesis, New York University, 1941.

13 Terman, *op. cit.;* Burgess and Cottrell, *op. cit.;* Schroeder, *op. cit.*

The Predictive Power of the Obtained Validity Coefficients

While the obtained validity coefficients in marital prediction studie have been fairly promising as far as *group* differentiation has beer concerned, they have not been very high in terms of *individual* pre diction. Thus, in the Burgess-and-Cottrell and Terman studies, validity coefficients of .56 and .50 respectively were obtained between the tota prediction scale and marital happiness or adjustment scores. But wher translated into E, the coefficient of forecasting efficiency, correlation: of this magnitude mean that there is only about 15 percent better than chance odds of one's being able accurately to predict the good or bad marriage adjustment of a given individual who takes such a prediction test before he is married. Or, as Terman has noted, "in terms of the accuracy of prediction that one would like, the present scale would have to be considered very unsatisfactory indeed. A correlation of .50 between personality-background and happiness accounts for at most only a fourth of the happiness variance, leaving three-fourths entirely unaccounted for."[14]

In the Burgess and Wallin and the Adams studies, where outside performance measures of pre-marital attitudes and post-marital adjust ment were used, the obtained validity coefficients were somewhat lower than in the Terman and Burgess and Cottrell studies. Thus, Burgess and Wallin obtained correlations of .43 and .41 for husbands' and wives' engagement and marriage scores. And Adams obtained validity coeffi cients ranging from .25 to .38 when testing the Terman scale, the Hamilton scale, and the Burgess and Cottrell scale against marriage performance measures. Adams also obtained low correlations of from .33 to —.10 when using the Adams-Lepley Personal Audit, and of .21 to —.02 when using the Guilford-Martin Personnel Inventory in an attempt to predict actual marriage performance adjustment ratings.

It is clear, therefore, that in those studies where adequate perform ance measures of marital adjustment were not used, the obtained "validity" coefficients were encouragingly high for group, though not necessarily, individual prediction; while in those studies where more adequate performance measures of marital adjustment were employed, the obtained validity coefficients tended to be distinctly lower. It is true, as Terman points out, that "even the faintest light cast on a future darkened by the proverbial blindness of love may be of incalculable

[14] Terman, *op. cit.*, 362.

value to the persons concerned."[15] It is true, as well, that the existing scales, in the light of their obtained validity coefficients, show definite promise of *future* predictive accuracy, and that they certainly warrant continued experiment and research. Such continued research is, in fact, one of the outstanding needs in the area of courtship and marriage problems. At the same time, it must be realistically acknowledged that the manner in which existing marriage prediction scales have been standardized, and the validity coefficients which have thus far been obtained with their use, warrant little faith in the practical value of these scales, at present, as prognosticators of individual marital happiness. Only in the case of extreme high or low scorers on these scales can they be expected, today, to be of practical prediction value.

Summary and Implications

In examining the practical value of existing marriage prediction scales, their limitations are shown by several facts:

1. The scales often consist of items many of which have been selected on an armchair basis without benefit of item validations, and some of which are of questionable relevancy to the problem of marital prediction.

2. The validity studies made on the prediction scales have been almost invariably done with small, atypical, biased samples.

3. The validation procedures used with the scales have frequently been inadequate, and have especially failed to employ suitable outside performance measures of success or failure in marriage.

4. There is an important possibility that, because of the factor of differential subgroup bias, the obtained validity coefficients of the prediction scales give little factual and much artifactual evidence of causal connections between the pre-marital background factors and the post-marital adjustment factors that the scales purport to measure; and that consequently the obtained validity coefficients provide little or no evidence of success in marriage prediction.

5. The obtained validity coefficients of the marriage prediction scales, even assuming that they give genuine evidence of prediction possibilities, are certainly high enough to warrant continued experimentation with this kind of a testing instrument; but, as yet, they are far from being sufficiently high to have much practical value in predicting the marital adjustment of normal individuals.

[15] Terman, *op. cit.*, 364.

In view of these points, the present-day widespread use of marriage prediction scales for individual marriage counseling practice cannot be scientifically encouraged. It would appear that, at best, the existing scales are fit to be used as minor supplements to counseling interviews. It would also appear that they are definitely not valid enough to be published in books or magazines intended for lay audiences, or to be blithely given, in terms of a simple PASS-FAIL test score, to premarital counselees. If they are employed at all in a counseling process, they should be used only for the counselor's information; and his prognosis of a given individual's or couples' marriage, even when partly based on such prediction scale scores, should not be given to the client in terms of the score itself, but should only be given as an integral part of an extended discussion based on the gathering of considerable interview and/or test evidence over and above the giving of such a prediction scale.

As for future research and validation of marriage prediction scales, the following recommendations are in order:

1. In the construction and perfection of such scales, special care should be given to the selection of suitable *prediction* questions, rather than merely to questions which seem to be intimately related to marriage adjustment.

2. When suitable prediction questions are selected for a marriage prediction scale, every care should be taken for the proper validation of both the individual items and the entire scale. Adequate sampling, the pre-testing of items, repeated item validations, test validations with fresh samples, and adequate outside performance measures of validity should all be properly arranged for and effectively carried out.

3. When prediction scales are finally standardized, they should also be re-standardized on important subgroups of the population with which they are to be used. If necessary, separate standardizations should be made for college and non-college respondents, rural and city dwellers, religious and regional subgroupings, and so on.

4. Marriage prediction scales should be designed realistically for the practical purposes for which they seem to be most logically applicable, namely, for supplementing intensive and extensive marriage counseling interviews, rather than for attempting to act as a clinical substitute for them.

THE VALIDITY OF MARRIAGE PREDICTION AND MARITAL ADJUSTMENT TESTS*

LEWIS M. TERMAN AND PAUL WALLIN

This article concerns itself with some important methodological questions about marriage research recently raised by Ellis.[1] Ellis' criticisms of studies of the prediction of marital success were made largely to emphasize the limitations of their findings and the harm which might result from their misuse in counseling or in popular writing by inadequately trained persons. While fully in sympathy with Ellis' purpose we would like to call attention to some of his criticisms which are questionable or at best partially valid.

1. Ellis deals first with what he calls "the content of existing marriage prediction scales" and because of considerations relating to their content, he concludes that the prediction scales are of dubious prognostic value. The considerations cited, however, do not support the conclusion. Thus he holds that the inclusion in a marriage prediction of many items identical with, or similar to, items in the Bernreuter and Thurstone personality inventories is unwarranted in view of the fact that such tests are usually found to be wrong about half the time when they are ". . . used to differentiate between clinical *groups.*" It is true, as Terman and Buttenweiser reported in 1936,[2] that *trait scores* yielded by the Bernreuter test differentiate only slightly between happily married subjects and unhappily married or divorced subjects. It does not follow, however, that *individual items* in such a test may not be predictive of good or poor marital adjustment. As a matter of fact, Terman has found about 40 items of the Bernreuter type predictive of scores on a marital happiness test in two different populations numbering respectively, 792 and 567 couples. Similarly, in the Burgess-Wallin study the majority of the 42 items in the abbreviated Thurstone neurotic inventory (and the total score on the inventory) were found to be

* Adapted and reprinted by permission of the authors and publisher from the *American Sociological Review,* 14 (1949), 497-504.

[1] Albert Ellis, "The Value of Marriage Prediction Tests."

[2] L. M. Terman, and P. Buttenweiser, "Personality Factors in Marriage," *Journal of Social Psychology,* VI, 268 ff.

associated with adjustment in engagement (1000 couples)[3] and predictive of marital success (666 couples).[4]

Ellis errs factually in stating that the Burgess-Cottrell and Terman *prediction* scales are made up in part of post-marital items. The items he cites (handling of finances, manner of dealing with in-laws, etc.) are legitimately included in the scales measuring marriage *success or happiness.*

Ellis further questions the prediction scales as validated against marriage success scores derived from "rather naive attitudinal questions" such as how often husbands and wives quarreled, how many times they regretted their marriage and how often they kissed each other. Actually, these particular questions pertain to reported *behavior* of the spouses and, naive or not, they do discriminate different degrees of marital success. Admittedly, the marital happiness tests, in greater or lesser degree, "fail to tap unconscious or unfaced feelings of hostility, affection, or ambivalence which may be more germane than the consciously accepted feelings in determining a respondent's marriage adjustment score."[*] Unfortunately, however, it is not feasible for research or counseling purposes to put large numbers of persons through psychoanalysis or some other kind of prolonged clinical study that would bring to light the unconscious mechanisms affecting their marital adjustments. What we are up against is the necessity of devising an instrument that will give us more reliable and more valid evidence about a subject's marital adjustment than can be obtained in the same time by unsystematic and unstandardized methods of questioning. The adjustment tests now used by Terman and by Burgess and Wallin are, on the whole, reasonably satisfactory for this purpose, though doubtless they could be materially improved.

Ellis also objects to the validation of prediction tests against marital happiness scores on the ground that answers on which the latter are based can be faked by subjects who for any reason prefer to answer the questions untruthfully. This is undoubtedly true of both the marital happiness test and the marriage prediction test, just as it is true of a majority of personality tests. It would seem unlikely, however, that many subjects would deliberately respond falsely when they volunteer

[3] R. F. Winch, "Personality Characteristics of Engaged and Married Couples," *American Journal of Sociology,* 46 (1941), pp. 686-697.

[4] E. W. Burgess, and P. Wallin, *Engagement and Marriage,* to be published.

[*] See pp. 495-96 above.—*Eds.*

freely to participate in the research under conditions of strict anonymity as in the case of Terman's 1938 study or when they have the option of remaining entirely anonymous as in the Burgess-Cottrell and Burgess-Wallin investigations. Nonetheless, as a check on subjects who for any reason do not answer the test questions with complete frankness, it would be desirable to explore the possibility of devising a marital happiness test based on projective techniques.

Finally, Ellis notes that some of the special questionnaires now being widely used as marriage prediction scales seem to have no statistical validation whatever. We, too, deplore the use of such prediction tests, but it should be clear that their existence is completely irrelevant in judging scientific research in marriage prediction.

2. Ellis' second major basis of criticism of existing prediction scales is that they have been validated with small samples of volunteer subjects, who were predominantly of college level and happily married. It is argued that consequently the scales may not be applicable to the population at large. We are entirely in accord with this judgment. The fact of restriction of the findings of any scientific study to the universe from which its sample is drawn is, of course, taken for granted by the competent investigator. It was explicitly stated by Burgess and Cottrell[5] and heavily stressed by Terman.[6]

Notwithstanding the probable influence of cultural factors in determining what items will be predictive of marital success in markedly different social groups, it is interesting that the same items have been found to have predictive value in such dissimilar groups as the native Americans of the Burgess-Cottrell sample and young urban, middle class, Chinese couples living in southern China.[7] Some of the results obtained with college subjects were also secured for a sample composed of less urban persons, more nearly representative in education of the general population.[8] Moreover, Terman's prediction test and marital happiness test yielded almost the same results for gifted subjects having a mean intelligence score nearly a sigma above the average college

[5] E. W. Burgess, and L. S. Cottrell, *Predicting Success or Failure in Marriage,* New York, Prentice-Hall, 1939, p. 29.

[6] L. M. Terman, *et al., Psychological Factors in Marital Happiness,* New York, McGraw-Hill, 1938, pp. 13-14.

[7] L. S. C. Smythe, *Marriage Study,* a preliminary (mimeographed) report of a study by a seminar on the Chinese family at the University of Nanking, 1936.

[8] Harvey J. Locke, "Predicting Marital Adjustment by Comparing a Divorced and a Happily Married Group," *American Sociological Review,* 12 (April, 1947), pp. 187-191. [See also pp. 485-87 of this volume.—*Eds.*]

graduate as for their spouses whose schooling and intelligence averaged considerably less. In the marital happiness test used with some 600 gifted subjects and their spouses, there were 7 test items which had previously been used with a far less selected group of 792 couples. On every one of these seven items the distribution of responses was almost exactly the same for the less selected group as for the gifted group.

It is important that a determined effort be made to extend marriage research to the non-college segment of the population. One investigation has shown that dependence on volunteers does not necessarily bias findings,[9] but the question should be systematically explored with larger samples. Similarly the effect of weighting prediction studies with more happily married couples should be studied. It may well be that samples made up of subjects with a greater spread of marriage success scores will reveal higher correlations between the prediction and the marital success scores.

3. Ellis presents and discusses at some length the hypothesis that ". . . the obtained 'validity' coefficients for the existing marital prediction scales seem to mirror differential sub-group bias rather than causal connections between pre-marital background factors and post-marital adjustment; and more specifically that the factor common to the pre-marital and post-marital test items seems to be the *conservatism* of the individuals answering both sets of items."[*]

In developing this hypothesis Ellis states that "Underlying practically all the published studies on marital prediction scales has been the implication that the obtained correlations between marriage adjustments and pre-marital factors are substantial proof of causal connections." And he adds: "If this were not the implication behind marriage prediction scales, it is difficult to see what rationale could exist for them."[†] The first of these statements is largely untrue and the second rests on a logical fallacy.

The former statement hardly requires refutation for readers with even a modicum of statistical training. Correlations between predictive items and marital adjustment scores, like correlations in any area of human behavior, are not in themselves presented as, or implied to be, *proof* of a cause-and-effect relationship. Ellis illustrates the implication

[9] Paul Wallin, "Volunteer Subjects as a Source of Sampling Bias," *American Journal of Sociology*, LIV (May, 1949), pp. 539-544.

[*] See p. 502 above.—*Eds.*

[†] See p. 501 above.—*Eds.*

of causality he imputes to prediction studies by referring to the relation found between marital happiness of parents and that of their children. This in spite of the fact that the Burgess-Cottrell study which had this as one of its findings reported it as follows: "The conclusion reached, then, is that the domestic happiness of the parents does appear to be definitely correlated with the marital adjustment of the children. *The nature of the association* (italics ours) remains, however, undetermined. Three hypotheses may be offered which independently or in conjunction may explain this association."[10] Terman's volume explicitly warns against the causality interpretation in at least a dozen places. The chapter on domestic grievances and the discussion of sexual complaints—to cite two instances—both expose at length the absurdity of regarding the fault which a respondent attributes to his or her spouse as actual causes of the respondent's marital unhappiness, however high a correlation with unhappiness the item may have. It is especially easy to show that sexual complaints charged against the spouse by an unhappy respondent can never be safely interpreted as *causes* of the respondent's marital dissatisfaction. As often as not they are merely alibis for already existing dissatisfaction.

Causal relationships are notoriously difficult to establish in almost any field of the social sciences, and nowhere more so than in studies of marriage. Even relationships between personality characteristics and marital unhappiness, relationships which on the surface are suggestive of causality, cannot be thus construed. For example, the wife who admits that she usually tries to get her own way even if she has to fight for it is definitely more likely to be unhappy in her marriage than the wife who responds to this item in the negative. Does this mean that readiness to fight for her own way *causes* her unhappiness, or is this personality characteristic an index of an unhappy temperament which causes both her domestic unhappiness and her willingness to fight for what she wants? Obviously, the correlation here is no proof of causal connections.

The contention that marriage prediction tests have no rationale unless correlates are assumed to reflect cause-and-effect becomes patently absurd when we consider a relationship such as that between early marriage and the probability of divorce. Even an untutored layman would hesitate to impute the marital failure to the fact of early marriage itself. Early marriage is simply an index of one or more conditions

10 *Op. cit.,* p. 101.

of marital unhappiness. As such it is an indirect measure of some undetermined influences (such as recklessness or willingness to flout social pressures) which in part may account for variation in marital happiness. Prediction items can in this way be valid and useful even though not causally related to marital happiness. Nevertheless, it should be stressed that the nearer research comes to discovering predictive items which *are* causative of marital happiness (in the sense that they measure *directly* the factors which more immediately influence the marital relation) the better prediction tests will be.

Although Ellis is wrong in his assumption that the marriage studies imply predictive items are causally connected with marital success, this of itself does not invalidate his hypothesis of "differential sub-group bias." The hypothesis proposes two interpretations of how correlations found between pre-marital factors and marital success could be largely artifactual. The first is in terms of the possibility that certain individuals ". . . who are ashamed to admit that there is anything wrong with their marriages will doubtlessly tend to (a) gloss over the defects of their marriages and hence to obtain high marriage adjustment scores; and (b) to exaggerate the virtues of their parents' marriages, and of other pre-marital background factors in their lives, and thus to obtain high pre-marital adjustment scores."* On the other hand, persons not ashamed of their marital shortcomings ". . . will doubtlessly tend to (a) admit the defects of their marriage and hence to obtain relatively low marriage adjustment scores; and (b) to admit the defects of their parents' marriages, and of other pre-marital background factors in their lives, and thus to obtain relatively low pre-marital adjustment scores."†

Another example of a differential response-bias hypothesized by Ellis is that the correlations may represent a consistency of response on the part of conservative, conventional subjects to questions about their marriage and pre-marital history. The evidence cited in support of this interpretation is that items found to be predictive of marital success (parents happily married, greater attachment to parents, happiness in childhood, good family background, Sunday school attendance, marriage in church, et cetera) are ". . . precisely those one would expect to find in, or expect to be claimed by, conservative or conventional respondents."‡ These observations suggest that conventional, conserva-

* See p. 502 above.—*Eds.*
† See p. 502 above.—*Eds.*
‡ See p. 503 above.—*Eds.*

tive subjects are disposed to exaggerate both the success of their marriage and the virtues of their pre-marital history, thereby giving prediction scales a fictitious validity.

The possibility that differential response-biases, such as those cited, could, if present, affect the correlations is admitted, but their existence can neither be proved nor disproved by speculation. To the extent that they are real their effect would be to reduce the efficiency of marriage prediction scores and marital happiness scores in forecasting divorce or separation. The fact that such scores are, as will presently be shown, predictive of marital break-up to a considerable degree despite possible attenuation of the correlations by differential response-biases, suggests that this influence is probably not great. It is conceivable that a prolonged clinical study of a large married population would throw light on the reality of the hypothetical factor and on the extent to which it affects correlations. In the absence of data, however, further discussion of its role would be profitless.

4. Ellis' criticism of the procedure of validating prediction items with subjects already married is methodologically sound. As he says, items correlated with the marital adjustment scores of married groups might not be predictive if given prior to marriage. They *might* not, though it seems a reasonable hypothesis that many, if not most of them, probably would. In any case, the burden of proof is on the investigator. The prevailing practice has been dictated too often by considerations of convenience. It is difficult enough to get a large married population to take both the prediction test and the adjustment test, but it is far more so to give the prediction test to engaged couples and then follow them up to learn how successful their marriages have been. The latter procedure was attempted by Dr. Lowell Kelly more than a dozen years ago, when he administered the prediction items which Terman was then using, together with many others, to some 300 engaged couples with the idea of giving them a marital adjustment test from time to time after they were married. Unfortunately, the follow-up of Kelly's group was later interrupted and thus far has not been resumed. Some of his early follow-up results are summarized in the following quotation:[11]

"I have computed the total prediction score (personality plus background) for 82 of my couples who have been married 2 years, and I have computed

11 E. L. Kelly, "Concerning the Validity of Terman's Weights for Predicting Marital Happiness," *Psychological Bulletin,* vol. 36, no. 3, 1939, p. 202.

for these couples the correlation of the prediction score with marital happiness score at the end of 2 years. The resulting raw correlations are .26 for husbands and .30 for wives. When adjusted to allow for the extremely narrow happiness range[12] of my group, these became .50 for husbands and .56 for wives. The corresponding correlations reported by Terman for 200 couples were .54 for husbands and .47 for wives.

"In spite of the theoretical objections to assigning 'prediction' weights on the basis of mere 'correlation,' Terman's weights seem to be valid for an entirely different population, which responded to the items before marriage."

Burgess and Wallin have carried through a study similar to Kelly's in many respects and dealing with a larger sample of couples. They began with 1000 engaged couples and have restudied almost 700 of them after an average of three years of marriage. The follow-up study has shown that most of the items associated with the marital success scores are also associated with these scores when information on the items is secured before marriage. This is particularly striking for personality items which when answered by married persons might be expected to be influenced by their marital happiness or unhappiness.

Ellis' criticism of the Burgess-Wallin report of the correlation between adjustment in engagement and adjustment after three years of marriage on the ground that the subjects tended to be happily married is in the nature of a *non sequitur*. The finding of a correlation *despite* this weighting of the group with the more happily married and the consequent relatively narrow range of marital success scores argues all the more strongly for the validity of the obtained relationship.

Some 200 *unmarried* subjects in Terman's gifted group were given his marriage prediction test (camouflaged under the title "Personality and Temperament"). Most of these have since married and plans are under way to give the married ones a marital happiness test in the near future. Eleven of those who married after taking the prediction test in 1940 are known to have become divorced by the end of 1948. Of these 11 (7 men and 4 women), all but one had scored on the prediction test below the mean of all subjects who took the test. The men averaged .93 S.D. and the women 1.5 S.D. below the mean of the men and women subjects respectively. The number of cases here is very small and the results are only of suggestive value.

Ellis points out that prediction tests must be validated not only

[12] The narrow range of happiness scores in Kelly's group was presumably due to the fact that many of the marriages were still in the "honeymoon" period.

against marital adjustment scores, but also, and preferably, against an outside criterion of marital success. He suggests as a criterion ratings of the happiness of each marriage by friends or acquaintances. Although overlooked by Ellis this very criterion was in effect used in the Burgess-Cottrell study since their marital adjustment items were validated against subjects' ratings of their marital happiness which in turn were validated against independent ratings by friends of the happiness of the marriages.[13] Ratings by friends of the subjects are also being used in the Burgess-Wallin study.

It should be noted incidentally that, although marriage ratings by friends may be valid when the subjects are roughly homogeneous in social and economic status, they may be considerably less so for markedly heterogeneous subjects. In the latter case the rating might be distorted by the halo effects of occupational prestige.

A potentially valuable outside criterion is the kind of information that could be obtained by the clinical study of marriages. Unfortunately, such studies are so time-consuming that years would be required to obtain the number of cases needed for statistical evaluation of marriage prediction items. Unfortunately too, clinicians have their own biases which sometimes predispose them to find what they are looking for. One very able physician known to us told the students in a college class on marriage that from his clinical experience he estimates that 95 percent of divorces are caused by sexual incompatibility. This physician is a specialist in obstetrics! His figure is even higher than that of Kinsey who (according to a recent press report of one of his public addresses) is said to place his estimate at 75 percent. The psychiatrist in a Chicago Domestic Relations Court blamed divorces chiefly upon dementia praecox and feeble-mindedness.

The fact is that at present there is no completely satisfactory outside criterion for checking on the validity of either marriage prediction tests or marital happiness tests. Apart from ratings by friends, the only criterion available is the break-up of a marriage by separation or divorce, and the inadequacies of this criterion are obvious. The break-up of a marriage is an all-or-none score and cannot be known until long after the prediction test has been given. Still more serious is the limitation that it is at best a crude measure of marital dissatisfaction. Some persons resort to separation or divorce at the slightest provocation,

[13] Ratings of subjects and friends gave a tetrachoric coefficient of correlation of .91. The coefficient of contingency was .68. See Burgess and Cottrell, *op. cit.*, p. 41.

others for religious or ethical reasons will endure almost any amount of marital unhappiness rather than break up the home. Despite the inadequacies of separation or divorce as a criterion, the follow-up of subjects in the Burgess-Wallin[14] and Terman studies reveals that the prediction tests and marital happiness tests are predictive to a considerable degree of the break-up of marriages.

Terman's marital aptitude (prediction) test and his marital happiness

Table 1.   Marital Happiness Scores and Marital Aptitude Scores as Predictive of Divorce within Eight Years

| | MEANS* | | | |
Scores	Divorced	Non-divorced	C.R.†	r. bis.†
Happiness Scores				
Husbands	49.79	63.81	4.38	.349
Wives	48.73	66.68	5.78	.462
Composite	49.31	65.43	5.79	.468
Aptitude Scores				
Husbands	82.38	91.48	3.46	.253
Wives	69.16	80.00	5.32	.408
Composite	75.53	85.67	5.53	.455
Aptitude + Happiness Scores				
Husbands	132.19	155.33	5.09	.355
Wives	118.23	146.86	6.41	.517

* Happiness score means are for 52 divorced and 591 non-divorced husbands and wives. Means on marital aptitude (and on aptitude and happiness scores combined) are for 52 divorced and 580 non-divorced couples.

† C.R.'s are for the differences between means of divorced and non-divorced subjects. The biserial correlation is for test scores and marital failure measured by divorce.

test were administered in 1940 to more than 600 of his gifted subjects and their spouses. The median length of marriage when the tests were given was 4.1 years, and the median age at the time was approximately 26.2 years for husbands and 23.8 years for wives. Over a period of eight years after the tests were given, 52 couples were divorced and 591 were not. Table 1 compares, for husbands and wives separately, the scores of these two groups on marital happiness and marital aptitude.

The marital happiness test and the marriage prediction test used

[14] The Burgess-Wallin engagement adjustment scores were found to be predictive of broken engagements. (See E. W. Burgess, and P. Wallin, "Predicting Adjustment in Marriage from Adjustments in Engagement," *American Journal of Sociology,* 49 (1944) p. 329.) The findings of the follow-up study of couples who divorced and those who did not will be reported in the forthcoming volume *Engagement and Marriage.*

ith these subjects were revisions and extensions of those used by Terman with his less selected 1938 population. The reliability coefficient f the happiness test is .89 for each spouse; the reliability of the prediction test is .86 for husbands and .82 for wives. The content of both tests nd the method of deriving response weights have been described elsewhere by Terman and Oden.[15]

The data of Table 1 indicate clearly that the divorced and non-ivorced subjects differ significantly both on their aptitude and marital appiness scores.

These findings for divorced and non-divorced couples constitute lefinite proof that both the marital happiness test and the marital prediction test are predictive of relatively long-range marital success r failure. In evaluating the significance of these findings considerable llowance must be made for the fact that divorce (or separation) is, as tated earlier, a very rough criterion of the degree of marital dissatisaction, a circumstance which acts to attenuate the correlations. In other vords, the true predictive value (validity) of the prediction scales as neasured by a more refined external criterion of marital success would inquestionably be greater than is indicated by the correlations presented n the table.

We regard it as very promising for the future of marriage prediction ests that notwithstanding the severe limitations of the divorce criterion he biserial correlation between husband-wife composite marital aptiude score and this measure of marital failure is .455, which is only lightly lower than the (Pearsonian) correlation between the better cholastic aptitude tests and grade-point average in high school or college. Even so, we agree with Ellis that prediction tests, as yet, offer very uncertain guidance in the choice of a mate or in the determination of one's chances for marital happiness unless the score is either well above or well below the average. Moreover, the tests are actuarial n nature in that they merely indicate roughly the *chances* of marital success. This is where the competent counselor can be helpful since by taking into account both the clinical evidence and the test evidence he can better orient the subject toward his marital prospects than would be possible on the basis of the clinical data alone. The prediction test could also be used as a basis for pointing out to the individual what attitudes or behavior patterns unfavorable to marital success have been

---

[15] L. M. Terman, and M. H. Oden, *The Gifted Child Grows Up; Twenty-five Years Follow-up of a Superior Group,* Stanford: Stanford University Press, 1947, Chapter XIX.

revealed by the responses given to individual items in the test. A attempt can then be made to remedy them. We believe that despite th present somewhat limited validity of prediction tests they can serve the useful purposes. If they reduce by the slightest fraction the enormou gamble marriage is today their employment is justified.

CHAPTER 18

Dissolution of Marriage:
Death and Divorce

r is common knowledge that over the past half-century the divorce
ate in the United States has risen dramatically. Less widely known
s the fact that the rise in the divorce rate has been more than offset
y a decline in the death rate with the consequence that the rate of
marital dissolutions from both causes combined has been declining.[1]
acobson presents these and other facts about divorce, including the
bservation that divorces are not as heavily concentrated among child-
ess couples as has been the general impression.

Goode presents evidence to show that the incidence of divorce is
negatively correlated with social status as indicated by the occupation
of the husband. He also reports reactions of a sample of divorced
women concerning some economic consequences of divorce.

[1] Conclusions regarding marital dissolutions are necessarily qualified by the fact that
ata on desertions and other informal dissolutions are lacking.

DIFFERENTIALS IN DIVORCE BY DURATION OF MARRIAGE AND SIZE OF FAMILY*

PAUL H. JACOBSON

Trend of Marital Dissolutions

... As is well known, the divorce rate has risen with few interruption throughout our history. Shortly after the Civil War, the rate was le than 2 per 1,000 married couples; before the turn of the century, was 3; by the outbreak of World War I, it was up to 5; and in 194 it was close to 12.

Not as well known is the fact that, for the past 60 years at least, th upswing of the divorce rate has been more than offset by the steadi declining mortality rate. Thus, the annual frequency of marriage-di solutions by the death of one of the partners has decreased from 3 per 1,000 couples in 1890 to about 19 in 1948. In consequence, the aggre gate rate of marital dissolutions by death and divorce is somewhat lowe now than it was before the turn of the century.

The trend of marital dissolutions for the years 1890 to 1948 is show in Figure 1. From 1890 to 1915, the total rate of marital dissolution decreased from 33 per 1,000 couples to 29. It is evident that this declin reflected the improvement in mortality conditions. In sharp contrast wa the explosive rise in marriage-dissolutions in 1918, caused almost entirel by the influenza pandemic which struck in the autumn of that year The rate of dissolutions in 1918 jumped to 40 per 1,000 couples—the highest point in the past 60 years.

From the end of World War I to the beginning of World War II the rate of marital dissolutions fluctuated somewhat, but showed n definite upward or downward trend. It is noteworthy, however, tha during the depression years 1932-1933 the rate dropped to the lowes point of the entire series—very likely the lowest in our history. Through out World War II marital dissolutions rose rapidly as a result of the mounting divorce rate, and reached a high of 38 per 1,000 in 1946.

* Adapted and reprinted by permission of the author and publisher from the *American Sociological Review* 15 (1950), 235-44. The final report on this subject will appear in the author's forthcoming book on marriage and divorce, to be published by Rinehart & Co.

Vith the readjustment to peacetime life, however, the divorce rate eceded so sharply that in 1948 the total dissolution rate was almost ·ack to the prewar level.

It is evident from the foregoing that mortality has been decreasing in mportance in the disruption of conjugal ties, while divorce has been ›laying an increasingly important role. In 1890 divorce accounted for

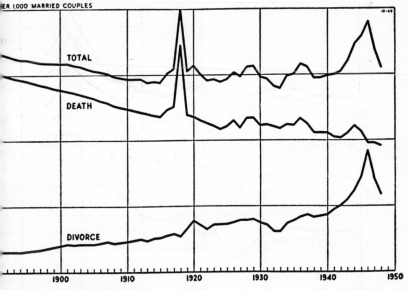

Figure 1. Marital dissolutions by death and divorce: United States, 1890 to 1948.

Note. The figures for divorce include annulments, and those for mortality include deaths overseas during World Wars I and II.

less than one-tenth of all marriage-dissolutions; in 1948, for almost four-tenths.

Trend of Divorce by Duration of Marriage

In view of the sharp rise of divorce in recent years, it is of interest to examine the trend of the divorce rate at various periods of married life. Figure 2 shows these rates by five-year marriage-duration groups for the period 1922 to 1948. It is evident that the recent upswing of the divorce rate was sharpest among those married less than five years—

essentially those married during the war. From 1941 to 1946, the divorce rate more than doubled for couples married up to five years. Increases also occurred among couples at the later durations, but the relative rise was smaller for each successive five years of marriage. However, even among those married 20 years or longer, the rate in 1946 was fully two-fifths higher than in 1941. Although divorce declined sharply after

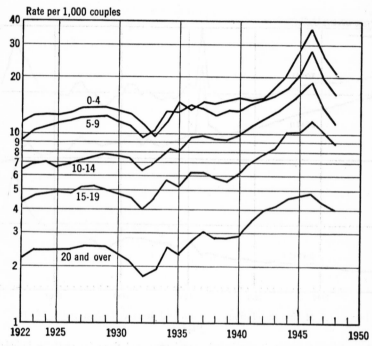

Figure 2. **Divorce rate by duration of marriage: United States, 1922 to 1948.**
Note. Includes annulments. Rates for 1948 are provisional.

1946, the duration-specific rates in 1948 were still above the prewar level. This was especially true for couples married less than five and from 15 to 19 years.

In general, the divorce-frequency is highest in the early period of married life. In 1948, the rate was at a maximum of 26 per 1,000 couples in the third year of marriage (duration 2-3 years), dropped sharply through the seventh year, and thereafter declined less rapidly but almost steadily with each advance of matrimonial duration. By the twentieth vedding anniversary, the rate was down to 8 per 1,000. Even after the golden wedding anniversary, some marital ties were dissolved by divorce.

Children in Divorce

About 313,000 children under the age of 21 were involved in the 421,000 divorces and annulments granted in 1948, or roughly three children for every four marriages dissolved. However, close to three-fifths of the divorced couples had no children. This means that more than two-fifths had children, and among them there was an average of 1.78 children per couple.

The proportion of divorces involving children varies considerably with the duration of marriage. According to the experience in 1948, the proportion rises from as little as 10 per cent among the marriages ended before the first year, to a maximum of 65 per cent in the eighteenth year of marriage (Figure 3). Beyond that duration, however, the proportion drops almost without interruption, reflecting the fact that the children of these marriages have matured.

It is noteworthy that in 1948, children were involved in more than one-half of all divorces granted to couples married 7 to 23 years. The fact that a large proportion of the total decrees do not involve children is explained primarily by the heavy concentration of divorces and annulments in the early years of marriage. In 1948, for example, about 55 per cent of the total decrees were granted to couples married less than 7 years.

It is also evident from Figure 3 that, among families with children, the average number of children increases with the duration of marriage prior to dissolution.[1] The average per parent-couple climbs from somewhat less than 1.2 children for marriages dissolved after the first year to a maximum of 2.5 for those broken in the nineteenth through the twenty-second year of marriage.

As a consequence of the above, the ratio of the number of children to the total number of divorces increases rapidly to a maximum of 1.6 in the nineteenth year of marriage, that is, at duration 18-19, and thereafter declines. The actual number of children involved, however, is at a

[1] The ratio of 1.3 children per family with children in the first year of marriage appears to indicate that the divorce rate was relatively high among the remarried with stepchildren. In this connection, see the lower curve in Chart 5.

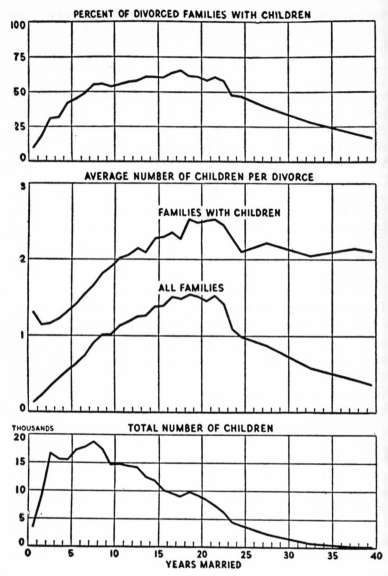

Figure 3.   Children under age 21 in families dissolved by divorce: United States, decrees granted in 1948.

Note. Includes annulments. Figures are provisional.

maximum in a much earlier period of married life (see the curve in the lowest tier of Chart 3). In fact, the divorces at durations 5-9 years in 1948 accounted for close to 28 per cent of the total children.

The concentration of divorce-children in the early years of marriage helps to explain the relatively young age reported for these children. Marshall and May,[2] for example, in their investigations in Maryland and Ohio for the period around 1930, found that 63 per cent of the children were under 10 years of age—a much higher proportion than prevailed among children in the families of the general population. More recent statistics for Multnomah County, Oregon[3] and Cook County, Illinois[4] indicate that the proportion at ages under 10 is currently somewhat larger—about 69 per cent. This increase in the proportion of younger children affected by divorce probably results from the relatively larger number of divorces now granted in the early years of marriage. In other words, it is likely that the age distribution of children involved in divorce at a specified duration of marriage has changed little if any in the past two decades. . . .

Trend of Children in Divorce

Apparently the average number of children per family reporting children has not changed. It was 1.8 in 1948 as well as during the period 1922 to 1932. However, the proportion with children rose from 38 per cent in the earlier years, to 42 per cent in 1948. As a result, the number of children per divorce increased from 0.68 to 0.74. Thus the total number of children affected has risen even more rapidly than the number of divorces. . . .

Divorce Rate by Size of Family

It is widely believed that the presence of children in a family acts as a powerful deterrent to divorce. This view probably had its origin in the high proportion of divorces to couples without children, but it has also received undocumented support from our technical literature. For exam-

[2] Leon C. Marshall and Geoffrey May, *The Divorce Court;* vol. 1, *Maryland,* 1932, p. 83, and vol. 2, *Ohio,* 1933, p. 115, Baltimore: The Johns Hopkins Press.

[3] Read Bain *et al.,* "Divorce and Children of Divorce," *Portland City Club Bulletin,* 30 (June 17, 1949), 350.

[4] Analysis by Judge Edwin A. Robson of 11,300 divorce cases heard by him in Superior Court from September 1945 to July 2, 1948; and cases filed in Superior and Circuit Courts from 1940 to 1946.

ple, consider this statement in one of the college textbooks on the family:

". . . where there are children the chances of divorce are much less than where there are no children; indeed, the chances in the first instance are only one nineteenth as great as in the second."[5]

For documentation, the reader is referred to a published dissertation from one of our leading universities. When we turn to that source, we read that

". . . 71 per cent of childless marriages in America end in divorce, while only 8 per cent of married couples with children eventually are divorced.'

Clearly, if this is the basis for the first statement, then the likelihood of divorce is only nine times greater in childless marriages than in those with children.

But even this ratio of nine is so much greater than that reported for other countries, namely, 2.0 for Amsterdam in 1929-1932[7] and 2.2 for Sweden in 1933,[8] that it is desirable to review the statistical basis for the last quotation. This statement is based on the erroneous assumption that if 17 per cent of American married women never bear children 17 per cent of the marriages existing in 1928 had no children. Obviously if 17 per cent of married women reach the end of their reproductive life span without ever having borne children, then the proportion in the early years of marriage who do not have children is much greater than 17 per cent. Moreover, not all children survive. Also, at the later years of marriage, an increasing proportion of the children reach adulthood, marry, or leave their families for other reasons. Therefore, the proportion of married couples without children was much greater than 17 per cent. Actually, the figure in 1928 was about twice as large, according to estimates made by the author from 1930 Census data. Using these population estimates, and including annulments with the divorces, we find that the divorce rate in 1928 was approximately 15.0 per 1,000 for couples without children and about 4.4 for the parent-couples. In other

[5] Meyer F. Nimkoff, *Marriage and The Family,* Boston: Houghton Mifflin Company 1947, p. 631.

[6] Alfred Cahen, *Statistical Analysis of American Divorce,* New York: Columbia University Press, 1932, p. 113.

[7] J. H. van Zanten and T. van den Brink, "Population Phenomena in Amsterdam," *Population, The Journal of the International Union for the Scientific Investigation of Population Problems,* August 1938, p. 30.

[8] Carl-Erik Quensel, "Frequency of Divorce with Special Regard to the Number of Children," *Annex No. 6,* Statistical Institute in Lund, 1938, p. 202 (in Swedish).

words, the divorce rate was only 3.4 times greater for the couples without children—not 19 times or even 9 times greater.

At this point, it is appropriate to ascertain whether the data for 1948 can throw any additional light on this question. Surveys by the Bureau of the Census in 1948 provide data from which it is possible to estimate the distribution of existing marriages according to number of children under 18 years of age.[9] The divorce data, however, are by number of children under 21 years of age. It is necessary, therefore, to translate the divorce data into their distribution by number of children under 18 years of age. This was accomplished by means of the statistics by Marshall and May on the age distribution of children in divorce according to marital duration.[10] In making this adjustment, it was assumed that the ratio of the children under 18 to those under 21 at any one specified duration of marriage was independent of the number of children in a family.[11]

The divorce rates per 1,000 married couples according to number of children under age 18 are shown in Figure 4. It is evident that the relative frequency of divorce varies inversely with the number of children in the family. For couples without children, the divorce rate in 1948 was 15.3 per 1,000. Where one child was present, the estimated rate was 11.6 per 1,000. The figure thus continues to decrease, and in families with four or more children, it was 4.6. Altogether, the rate for couples with children was 8.8 per 1,000. In other words, the rate for "childless" couples was almost double the rate for families with children, which is very much like the situation in the other countries previously noted.

Before drawing any conclusions from these rates, it is important to

[9] Bureau of the Census: *Current Population Reports,* Series P-20, Numbers 21 and 23, December 19, 1948 and March 4, 1949.

[10] Leon C. Marshall and Geoffrey May, *The Divorce Court,* vol. 1, p. 81 and vol. 2, p. 115.

[11] Actually, 12 per cent of the divorces and annulments were reported in this survey by number of children under 18 years of age, and 88 per cent by children under 21. In the preceding sections of this paper, the statistics on children under 21 included the data for those under 18 adjusted to ages under 21; in the sections which follow, the statistics on children under 18 include the data for those under 21 adjusted to ages under 18. Obviously, the statistics for children under 21 are less subject to error from this adjustment. However, it should be noted that the ratio of children under 18 to children under 21 does not deviate substantially from unity until about the twentieth year of marriage, when the frequency of divorce and the number of children fall off rapidly. It is unlikely, therefore, that the rates in Figure 4, or those in Figure 5, especially for the first 20 years of marriage, could be materially affected by the adjustment.

ascertain whether the differential results from the fact that "childless" marriages and those with children are of different composition with regard to duration. In other words, how does the divorce rate for the two groups compare at specified durations of marriage? These rates for the first 40 years of marriage are shown in Figure 5. It is readily apparent that the differential in the divorce rate between "childless" couples and

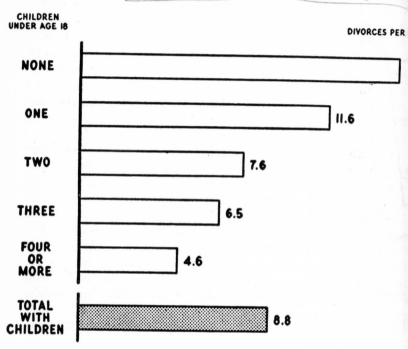

Figure 4. Divorces per 1,000 married couples according to size of family: United States, 1948.

Note. Includes annulments. Rates are provisional.

those with children is not uniform throughout married life. Rather, divorce is much more frequent among those without children in the early years of marriage, and the differential diminishes rapidly thereafter. The divorce rate for parent-couples climbs to a maximum of 15 per 1,000 at duration 3-4 years, whereas the rate for couples without children reaches a peak of 44 per 1,000 one year later. The chances for divorce among the "childless" fall off so much more rapidly after the peak that the ratio between the rates for the two groups drops from about 3½ after four years of marriage, to 3 by the tenth year, and to 2 by the twentieth year. Indeed, after the thirtieth wedding anniversary, the two rates are practically identical.

Thus, it is evident that refinement of the divorce rates according to duration of marriage does not eliminate the differential between

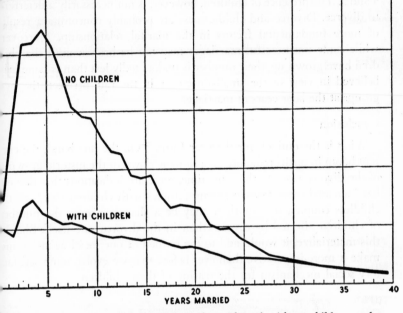

Figure 5. Divorce rate for married couples with and without children under 18, first 40 years of marriage: United States, 1948.

Note. Includes annulments. Rates are provisional.

"childless" and parent couples. Rather, the duration-specific rates indicate that the differential itself varies with the period of married life. What effect other uncontrolled variables have on the findings cannot be ascertained from the data now available. For example, the couples in the divorced group undoubtedly were separated for an average of about one year prior to divorce. Also, relatively fewer divorced couples are from rural areas where the fertility rate is comparatively high. Would divorce rates corrected for the actual period of marriage prior to separation and for urban-rural residence eliminate part or all of the differential?

For the present, one can only point to Quensel's estimates for Sweden,[12] namely, that the differential between the two groups was cut almost in half when he allowed for these variables. It is likely, therefore, that the chances for divorce in our country are also only somewhat greater for families without children than for those with children; perhaps the difference is only one-half that indicated by the data in Figure 4 and 5. The presence of children, however, is not necessarily a deterrent to divorce. Divorce and childlessness are probably concomitant results of more fundamental factors in the marital relationship. Moreover, while some unsuccessful marriages may not be broken until the children have grown up, their number is undoubtedly less than is popularly believed in view of the small difference in the rate between the two groups at the later years of marriage.

Conclusion

What is the outlook for the near future? On the one hand, the current boom in births may foretell a slowing down of the historic upswing of the divorce rate. At the same time, there are indications that divorce has increased more rapidly among families with children than among childless couples, so that there may be a sharper rise in the number of children affected by divorce than in the divorce rate itself. Should this materialize, it would add to the burden of our social agencies and make it more imperative than ever before that we evolve some satisfactory social mechanism for the rearing of these children.

ECONOMIC FACTORS AND MARITAL STABILITY*

William J. Goode

Economic Position and Divorce Rates

. . . The cumulative evidence seems overwhelming that there is a rough *inverse correlation between economic status and rate of divorce.* By absolute numbers and by rate, the lower economic strata experience

---

[12] Carl-Erik Quensel, "Frequency of Divorce with Special Regard to the Number of Children," *op. cit.*, p. 206.

* Adapted and reprinted by permission of the author and publisher from the *American Sociological Review* 16 (1951), 802-12.

more divorces than the upper. This fact has many implications for family theory, but only one need be given as an example: Many of the supposed characteristics of the divorced may not be entirely due to the divorce experience itself. Perhaps, instead, they may be seen at least in part as attributes of lower socio-economic strata, regardless of divorce. Among such characteristics are lower life expectancy, higher psychosis rate, higher rate of juvenile delinquency, etc.

Instead of exploring such implications, let us rather marshal the evidence for this apparent inverse correlation, and analyze some aspects of the social meaning of economic factors in the divorce process. The evidence for this correlation may be understood in these terms: (a) Economic factors do have an effect on divorce, and, possibly, marital conflict; (b) But their effect is interactional in character, not one of simple, direct causation; (c) Therefore, we do not expect to find high correlations but fairly low associations—yet they should appear in almost all studies of approximately random populations; (d) Because so many other variables are also in close relationship to the economic, and because our measures of all of them are crude, even partial correlational analysis may not consistently discriminate the *exact* effect of such economic factors. We can, however, specify the *direction* of their effect, and in the second section of this paper we shall attempt an exploration of the dimensions of the process. Thus, a firmer basis can be laid for later research.

Economic Distribution of Divorce

Bossard's Philadelphia study placed 5,644 divorced women in 404 census tracts for the year 1930. This was essentially an ecological study, using data from the 1930 Census, and it demonstrated clearly the relationship between low income and high divorce rate. High mobility, dense population, and anonymity characterize the tracts with high divorce rates, and it is almost unnecessary to point out that these are also areas of low income. Bossard and others have thought of this association as being due to "drifting," but such a hypothesis is unnecessary, even though it is true that *after* divorce some women do move into low income areas (the net direction of movement has not, to my knowledge, been calculated by anyone).[1]

[1] J. H. S. Bossard, "Spatial Distribution of Divorced Women," *American Journal of Sociology*, 40 (1935), 503-507. The Census data, of course, furnished no data on movement.

Schroeder's study shows similar results.[2] Burgess refers to Schroeder's sample as "predominantly of low economic, low educational, and low social status."[3] Since Schroeder does not present the data which would be necessary to check the sample, this conclusion need not be questioned for the field interview sample. However, an apparently satisfactory sample of 1,163, obtained from the complete divorce records for the period March, 1930 to March, 1934 was also used by Schroeder in an ecological approach which related divorce to various social variables, by enumeration districts. Because of the tracing technique used (City Directory), any bias would have overrepresented the upper-class groups, while correspondingly more losses would have occurred in the lower strata. Without attempting to present details, we may note that the following correlations were found:[4]

Factors correlated with divorce	r
Delinquency	.69
Relief cases	.61
Average rent	—.29
Average annual income	—.32
Percentage home ownership	—.53

Similarly he notes (p. 63) with reference to two districts with very low divorce rates, "In practically all the measurable factors they produce an opposite picture from those with the high rates."

Weeks' study used questionnaires from an almost complete sample of secondary school children in Spokane, Washington, relating divorce to occupation with this result:[5]

[2] Clarence W. Schroeder, *Divorce in a City of 100,000 Population*, Peoria: Bradley Polytechnic Institute Library, 1939.

[3] Ernest W. Burgess, "Methods of Predicting Marital Adjustment," p. 491 above.

[4] Schroeder, *op. cit.*, pp. 50-51. Against these it should be noted that (p. 56) he also calculated several partial correlations, and for one of them (delinquency held constant) the relationship between divorce and relief becomes very low. This is not surprising, however, since delinquency and divorce are also in close association, and one would not expect striking further gradations of association between divorce and relief. "Controlling" delinquency, then, "controls" divorce—within Schroeder's plan of organization—and thus the further variance is likely to be small. Moreover, most of the partial correlations do show the association between low income indices and high rates of divorce.

[5] H. Ashley Weeks, "Differential Divorce Rates by Occupations," *Social Forces*, 21 (1943), 334-337.

Number of divorces per 100 families, by occupation

Professional	6.8
Proprietary	8.4
Clerical	10.4
Skilled	11.6
Semi-skilled	13.4
Unskilled	7.3

Glick's study was taken from sample surveys done by the Census Bureau, and refers to the "remarried."[6] A somewhat similar pattern emerges, with the remarried falling into somewhat lower strata than the never remarried.

Sample Surveys of the Census Bureau utilize a random, national sample of about 25,000, and the "divorced" category (roughly 2 percent) will ordinarily be no more than 400, so that the sampling error is large. However, these studies have shown the same pattern as that described here. For April, 1949, to cite an example, the major urban occupational categories exhibited the following indices of "proneness to divorce":[7]

Professional, semi-professional	67.7
Proprietors, managers, officials	68.6
Clerical, sales	71.8
Craftsmen, foremen	86.6
Operatives (semi-skilled)	94.5
Service workers	254.7
Laborers (except farm and mine)	180.3

My own data resulted in the following indices of "proneness to divorce," ranked by occupational category:[8]

[6] Paul C. Glick, "First Marriages and Remarriages," *American Sociological Review*, 14 (1949), 726-734. Most of these remarried, but not all (the widowed) are also "ever divorced."

[7] The index expresses the relationship between the proportion of "Other Marital Status" (than single or married) in any given occupational category, to the proportion of "Married, Wife Present" in that category: %OMS/%MWP. See *Current Population Reports, Labor Force*, Series P-50, Nos. 11 and 22, December 23, 1948 and April 19, 1950, Tables 4 and 5 respectively. The above calculations were made from Table 5. *Current Population Reports, Population Characteristics*, Series P-20, No. 23 (March 4, 1949), p. 17, has similar figures. The rankings from the 1940 data differ from the above only in that "Professional" and "Proprietary" shift places (Table 5, Series P-50, No. 22).

[8] The procedure which was used above for the Sample Survey data was followed. The index was:

$$\frac{\% \text{ divorced husbands in any given occupational group}}{\% \text{ male in that category, Metropolitan Detroit}}$$

Professional and Proprietary	62.6
Clerical, Sales, Service	63.3
Skilled, foremen	89.9
Semi-skilled, operatives	142.4
Unskilled	166.7

This result is closer to the Sample Survey figures than Weeks', and both differ from Weeks' ranking only with respect to the unskilled which seems partially explicable in terms of (1) the absence of Negroes in Weeks' sample. Because the divorce rate is higher among Negroes than among Whites, a national random sample of urban populations will show a slightly higher representation of the unskilled among the divorced than for cities with low Negro populations.[9] Further, (2) since many of the lower-class children drop out in or during secondary school, there would be a slight bias toward the upper strata in his study.

Hollingshead, focusing on "marital instability" rather than divorce, suggests that the greater instability is found in the "working" and lower classes (presumably, upper-lower and lower-lower), with the lower-upper (the "fast set") coming next in order.[10]

William Kephart indicates an inverse correlation, too, in complete accord with the Survey data.[11] Kephart used occupational data from a 4 per cent random sample of Philadelphia divorces granted between

The data would be more satisfactory if the labor force data had been broken down by marital status. These data were obtained from *Current Population Reports, Labor Force* "Labor Force Characteristics of the Detroit, Michigan Metropolitan District, April, 1947," Series P-51, No. 19, July 28, 1947, Table 3. For an outline of the research plan of my own study, see William J. Goode, "Some Problems in Postdivorce Adjustment," *American Sociological Review*, 14 (1949), 394-401. A random sample design was followed, and randomness was approximated closely in field operations. A number of tests of these operations have been carried out, indicating a very slight but reliable lower-class bias for the 425 urban mothers, aged 20-38 at the time of the divorce.

[9] The data for the higher Negro divorce rate are conclusive, although there is considerable folk belief to the contrary. Cf. Ernest R. Groves and William F. Ogburn, *American Marriage and Family Relations* (New York: Holt, 1928), p. 372; T. Earl Sullenger, *A Study of Divorce and Its Causation in Douglas County, Nebraska*, University of Nebraska Bulletin, March, 1927, p. 9; Glick, *op. cit.*, p. 733. *Current Population Reports, Population Characteristics*, Series P-20, No. 10 (Feb. 6, 1948), pp. 14-15 as well as other tables, yield conclusive data. My own study gives a similar result.

[10] August B. Hollingshead, "Class Differences in Family Stability," pp. 105-15 above. There are no data given for the design of these aspects of his larger study.

[11] William M. Kephart, "Divorce—A Philadelphia Project," paper read at meeting of the Eastern Sociological Society, New Haven, March 31, 1951.

1937-1950, under these categories: professional-proprietary, clerical, skilled, semi-skilled, and labor service; and the "rates" of divorce rise in that order. Thus, Bossard's, Schroeder's, Weeks', my own, Kephart's, and the Sample Survey data agree on the generally *inverse* relationship between economic position and proneness to divorce.

A Contrary Study

One study has been cited innumerable times, usually with the interpretation that the differences between the divorce rates by occupation are only the result of differences in social and geographical mobility and in chaperonage.[12] Because no major Census study of this kind has been carried out since that time, it must be considered here.

Occupation was indeed recorded for 226,760 husbands, 24 per cent of the males divorced during the period 1887-1906. For three states, New Jersey, Pennsylvania, and South Dakota, this datum was recorded for over 50 per cent of the cases. Unfortunately, there is an unspecifiable bias toward occupations with higher incomes (p. 44), since occupation was more likely to be recorded when alimony was granted, and this is correlated with higher income.

The rankings of occupations by tendency to divorce vary from state to state, underlining the remark (p. 42) of the then Director of the Census, S.N.D. North: "Returns so incomplete can hardly be accepted as typical. . . ."

Although my own repeated attempts at recalculating these data have resulted in no discernible sociological order, the fact that there is some consistency between specific occupation-divorce rankings for the nine states suggests that the original sources might be more productive. Until the task is done, however, this study of fifty years ago remains a contrary case.

A Tentative Conclusion

Whatever the pattern of interaction, whether direct, indirect, or caused by still more fundamental factors, it is clear that when a study approximates a satisfactory sample, a rough *inverse* correlation between economic position and tendency to divorce is exhibited. The relationship is expected to be only rough, since this is a complex set of factors

12 *Marriage and Divorce 1867-1906*, 2 Vols., Washington: U. S. Bureau of the Census, 909.

in interaction, not clearly delineated, just as the population segments are not. It is likely, for example, that divorce rates for specific occupations are highly variant within any socio-economic level: psychiatrists as against patent lawyers, radio repairmen as against die sinkers. Nevertheless, we have to take the fact into account, and in sociological terms It is to this point that the following sections are devoted.

Social Meaning of Economic Factors

The statistical results at least suggest what common sense asserts that economic factors may be of importance in marital stability. We are not surprised, then, that economic matters occupy the top position in Terman's list of husband-wife complaints, or that Schroeder's list of "real causes" of divorce gives economic factors as No. 2 or No. 1 depending on how they are regrouped.[13] Burgess and Cottrell, with a predominantly middle-class, nonrandom sample, similar to that of Terman's, failed to find any such importance, but this was done by factoring out personality traits, cultural backgrounds, social participation, and response patterns. As noted before, however, it is possible that economic factors may have had some effect within any of these items, and the difficulties of discriminating between them, for purposes of partial correlational analysis, leaves the question of interaction basically unanswered.[14] Income stability is granted by Burgess and Cottrell to be important, but it should be remembered that (a) the stability of income is not unrelated to size of income, and (b) neither of these, stability and size, exhausts the dimensions of economic factors as they are experienced in marital relations.

[13] Lewis M. Terman, *Psychological Factors in Marital Happiness*, New York: McGraw-Hill, 1938, p. 105; Schroeder, *op. cit.*, p. 106. The studies of W. P. Meroney, Ernest R Mowrer, E. T. Krueger, etc., in spite of different emphases, also suggested at times the importance of such factors. Again, obviously, an "economic complaint," may hide something deeper. It is not good research practice to *assume* the deeper something. The orthodox Freudian dictum, "Things are never what they seem; indeed: the opposite seems almost a cynical response to observation."

[14] Ernest W. Burgess and Leonard S. Cottrell, *Predicting Success or Failure in Marriage* New York: Prentice-Hall, 1939, pp. 261 ff. An earlier study, by Richard O. Lang, *A Study of the Degrees of Happiness or Unhappiness in Marriage as Rated b Acquaintances of the Married Couples*, M.A. thesis, University of Chicago, 1932, with ove 22,000 couples rated, shows a striking association between occupation level and happine rankings. Harvey J. Locke's *Predicting Happiness or Divorce in Marriage*, New York Holt, 1951, finds economic factors of less significance, but with a nonrandom sampl For the design of sample, see pp. 13 ff.

Further dimensions are to be found in the *symbolic* character of income, *i.e.,* its social meaning.[15] That is, we must explore some of the sociological dynamics involved in the impact of economic factors on marital conflict and divorce, even though this must be considered a tentative beginning.

Perhaps the most fundamental symbolic relationship is that between economic support, the unity of the family, and the role of the husband as breadwinner. Even with the largest number of females in the labor force in our history, there seems little evidence that the female *as breadwinner* is beginning to emerge as a social role. It is true, of course, that families do survive even when the male head fails in this task, but it is indicative of our common sense observation and social definitions that we phrase the statement in this fashion.[16] When the female works, the work has a negative social value except under specified conditions of need or unless redefined in non-bread-winning terms. A crisis situation redeems such work, of course. For the upper strata, the work may be defined in terms of "expressing the wife's personality," or "giving us a wider area of experience," etc.[17] For the lower strata, the wife's work must be defined in terms of "saving a nest egg," or "to pay off the furniture," or even "we can't get along without it"—an auxiliary and

[15] This theme is also used in Komarovsky's study of depression families, indicating that loss of income had a weakening effect on the stability of certain types of families, while strengthening that of other types. *Cf.* Mirra Komarovsky, *The Unemployed Man and His Family,* New York: Dryden, 1940; and S. A. Stouffer and P. F. Lazarsfeld, *Research Memorandum on the Family in the Depression,* New York: Social Science Research Council, 1937. This relationship illustrates the frequent experience in research, that simple correlations are often low or nonexistent because our underlying categories have not been discriminated with sufficient clarity. In this case, it is the *meaning* of the income loss which discriminates. In other terms, the income factor *is* important, but interactionally, not as a simple, direct causal element.

It is worth emphasizing that (1) item analysis such as simple correlational or associational analysis gives a specious sense of security when one rejects a given factor as unimportant because it exhibits no high associational order. Moreover, (2) unless each item is clearly differentiated in the original schedule questions themselves, there is overlap in meaning and cause, and its individual importance remains somewhat ambiguous or approximate. Finally, (3) the differential contribution of most individual social factors may not be great, so that low correlations are to be expected until the sub-classes have been regrouped according to more crucial variables.

[16] Reminiscent of Benjamin Franklin's suspicion of the frequently formulated homily that people can be "just as happy" if they are poor.

[17] And, in such terms and for such groups, it is possible that marital adjustment is at least as good in families with an employed wife. *Cf.* Harvey J. Locke and Muriel Mackeprang, "Marital Adjustment and the Employed Wife," *American Journal of ociology,* 54 (1949), 536-538.

supposedly temporary activity, however long it may continue. It does call, however, for explanation or redefinition.

Similarly, the failure of the male head to play his role adequately calls for definition and explanation, if he and the family are not to undergo censure: "Joe has been sick for quite a while;" "He's studying for his journeyman's tests right now;" etc. On the other hand, no explanation at all is called for and no redefinition in terms of "higher" values is required if he is earning an adequate income, *i.e.,* is fulfilling his role, and his wife is not working. Even in those small groups in which it is felt that the wife *ought* to work, this ethic is distinguished from breadwinning.

Furthermore, the income is supposed to be earned for *all* the family. The male head of the family is responsible, in terms of our values, for the support of the entire group, and legal prescriptions underscore this in law. This legal responsibility carries correlative headship rights with it, and while the actuality is much more complex and often contradictory, open and public denials of this headship must be explained away or they will be censured. We have, indeed, a number of deprecatory terms in our slang to describe this situation (*e.g.,* "henpecked," "Milquetoast").

Now, it is obvious that personality problems can be projected onto economic problems. As the simplicist formulation of parlor psychoanalysts has it, the "stable personality" will not be affected by economic strain, while the immature will complain of economic factors in the marriage when the "real" trouble is emotional. However, in a society whose pervasive material values are less skewed within the economic strata than is income, it should be obvious that: (1) Economic strain may possibly be greater in the lower strata; and (2) Economic strain may in turn be expressed in ("projected on") non-economic situations such as sex and marital adjustment.[18] A general theory of psychodynamics must be able to utilize the Freudian patterns even when the source of strain is economic, or hunger, or glandular deficiency, not alone when it is sexual or "personality."

However, the complexities of such processes mean that interviewing on such subjects is peculiarly difficult. Although economic strain may

[18] Skewness of income is less important, of course, when different strata have material goals more in accord with their economic ability. The same interaction is to be seen in certain types of criminal activities and class opportunities: the juvenile delinquent who sees crime as the sole opportunity for obtaining the material goals desired throughout the society.

use considerable marital conflict, the statement of the respondent that effect is no guarantee of its accuracy, even when the respondent ishes to tell the truth. Consequently, pending deeper and more phisticated probings of marital discord than are now available, we ay have to work with some such crude category as "theme of complaint" made by the parties concerned.

Within such terms, the cumulative contribution of economic strain the marital discord which ends in divorce seems quite clear. The attern of this cumulative process, or developing spiral, of conflict was shrewdly analyzed by Waller, using thirty-three predominantly middle-class cases.[19] The same process is expressed in economic terms at least half of our Detroit cases, a more representative sample.[20] or, as discord from whatever source becomes systematic and chronic, withdrawal of economic support becomes a major expression of waning loyalty. The recurrence of this theme led us to develop the coding ategory, "The Complex," which may be defined as "drinking, staying ut, and helling around." The words varied, and sometimes one or nother of the components (gambling, adultery, etc.) might be missing, ut the complaint expressed a fairly constant charge: the husband was pending his time and money elsewhere. Withdrawal of economic upport was often answered by the wife's withdrawal of sexual favors. he comments ranged from frank remarks such as "What's the good f having a husband, if he won't support you?" to "When I saw that e wasn't interested in his home any more, I decided he was no good." Emphasis was not placed on the economic difficulties which resulted, uch as inability to pay bills, but on the strains in the marital relationhip which were induced by the unwillingness to support. Thus, failure o fulfill economic and affectional roles becomes cumulative, and approchement correspondingly difficult.

At lower-class levels this withdrawal of economic support is laden vith less guilt than might be supposed, because one of the components f the attitudinal complex of the lower-class divorced father toward is children is a tendency to think of them as belonging more to the nother than to himself. They are primarily her task and responsibility, nd her waning loyalty relieves him of at least some of his guilt con-

---

[19] Willard Waller, *The Old Love and the New*, New York: Liveright, 1930.

[20] A full analysis of these complaints and their class structure is not possible here. This proportion is to be found in our own study. For comparative results, see the studies previously cited.

cerning the children. If she no longer "deserves" his support, the neither do they.[21] The lower-class attitudinal structure concerning the points is very complex, however, and especially so in that the basic valu pattern regarding divorce itself is not decisive or clear.

Nonrandom interviews with middle-class divorced fathers sugge that this is also a component in their attitudes toward the childrer though possibly not so intense (and more strongly prevented by othe proscriptions from actional expression). It is especially evident when th middle-class divorcé is allowed little or no contact with his childrer

It is clear that this process, in the post-divorce phase, is equall cumulative. The divorced mother who fails to receive adequate suppor feels a decreasing attachment to the former spouse, while the ex-hus band feels a lesser need to help in economic crises that are increasingl defined as "hers."

The divorce decree formalizes this separation of the husband from th wife and children. The husband expects the children to remain witl the wife, and in 96 per cent of our cases this did happen. However, th separation, in accord with the above suggestion, does not increase th willingness of the husband to give his economic support to that unit The consequence is a measurable fact: even in Detroit, with consider able machinery to enforce support payments, only 34 per cent of thes husbands "always" made the payments ordered by the court, with a additional 14 per cent who "usually" did so. Thus over one-half of th husbands failed to keep up regular support payments for their children

The difficulty of the ensuing economic situation may be seen in th fact that for 43 per cent of these cases the total weekly payment per chilc (1946-1948) was supposed to be $7-$11, while the average number o children per divorce was 1.8.

Two further dimensions of the economic enter as sociological ele ments: *stability* of income, and *control* over income. Even with a lowe money income, in general these women had a more stable income and of course the spending of it was in their hands alone. Consequently even while voicing complaints about economic difficulties, the post

[21] Our liberal bias in favor of the "good" qualities of the lower class leads us to idealize its "warm, sympathetic" social life, as it leads us to a similar set of emotions regarding rural life. We are not referring here to love of children but to the definitions of sexual roles, and these are less equalitarian at the lower-class levels than in the middle-class groups. The general proposition could be tested easily enough by observing the circumstances under which the husbands of different strata are willing to "take over" wifely roles and duties.

ivorce period was not unanimously viewed as being one of financial deterioration. Indeed, from a comparison of *level* of income as against the *meaning* of that lowered income in adjustment terms, the following tabulation resulted:

	Per cent stating period of highest income to be:	Per cent judging "best" period financially to be:	% Difference
Group I (divorced 2 months)			
During marriage	50.9	37.7	−13.2
Final separation	8.8	7.9	− 0.9
Time of interview	30.7	42.1	+11.4
No difference	9.6	12.3	+ 2.7
	100.0	100.0	
Group II (divorced 8 months)			
During marriage	52.7	30.8	−21.9
Final separation	7.7	14.3	+ 6.6
Time of interview	34.1	46.1	+12.0
No difference	5.5	8.8	+ 3.3
	100.0	100.0	
Group III (divorced 14 months)			
During marriage	39.1	26.4	−12.7
Final separation	10.9	16.4	+ 5.5
Time of interview	44.5	50.0	+ 5.5
No difference	5.5	7.3	+ 1.8
	100.0	100.1	
Group IV (divorced 26 months)			
During marriage	30.9	22.7	− 8.2
Final separation	6.4	8.2	+ 1.8
Time of interview	53.6	59.1	+ 5.5
No difference	9.1	10.0	+ 0.9
	100.0	100.0	

Since each group numbers approximately one hundred, the sampling error is fairly large when comparing two percentages. Further, the judgments have complex socio-psychological components, so that those being singled out would not be expected to show sharp contrasts. Nevertheless, the consistency of the differences makes a number of conclusions tentatively acceptable:

1. The steadily increasing proportion who consider the time of interview to be better financially than during the marriage indicates the

degree of economic adjustment at various periods after divorce. Slightly more than half of Group IV has remarried, some receiving both child support from the ex-husband and income from the present husband. Thus approximately the same trend of steady increase is seen in the proportion stating the time of interview to be the period of highest income.

2. With a single exception, each of the comparisons between percentages consistently points to the same conclusion: From each time perspective after divorce, the marriage period is judged to have been worse, and the postdivorce period is judged to be better, than the income level alone would indicate.[22] From *no* time perspective is the marriage period judged by even half of the respondents to have been financially the best. Even the "no difference" group may be interpreted consistently: more are willing to admit differences in income than are willing to admit differences in economic well-being.

These data are corroborated and interpreted by the unstructured comments on income and economic adjustment: "I don't have much money to spend, but at least it's regular." "As long as I keep working, I know that I'll get along." "It's nice to know that the money is going to keep coming in now. Before, I never did know." Such comments emphasized the importance of *stability of income,* in the feeling of economic adjustment.[23]

Other comments on *control of income* came out in response to questions about present activities, goal achievement, and wishes for the future, indicating that the respondents were able to buy or obtain things which were not possible during the marriage. "At least now I know where the money's going." "Now I can buy things for the children. I couldn't afford them, before." "Since I'm the one who's doing the spending, I can plan for the future."[24]

---

[22] Of course, many families may earn a high income during a boom period without considering themselves to be better off financially. Such families would be distributed at random in this group, and the marriage-divorce comparisons would not exhibit such consistency as is shown here.

[23] The interviewing problem of retrospective falsification needs considerable analysis, since the restructuring of reality is certainly part of the adjustment process for almost every participant in an emotional crisis. Whether this type of falsification would account for the patterns exhibited seems doubtful.

[24] In addition to the possibly greater "objective" economic strain in the lower strata, differences in class patterns of sharing and control of familial matters generally may also intensify these economic factors. This point seems eminently researchable, as a step toward outlining the basic value structure of the classes.

Summary

Family stability in our society seems to be positively correlated with economic position. Acceptance of this fact suggests a reassessment of the characteristics which are supposed to result *from* divorce, since at least some of these differences (as contrasted with the married) may simply be characteristic of the lower strata in which the divorces occur. Since, in addition, the Negro divorce rate is higher than the White, the direction of reassessment would be similar to that for the lower-class strata.

However, the full acceptance of this inverse correlation suggests that we reintroduce so-called "economic" factors into our sociological analysis. This merely requires that any factor ordinarily studied at other abstract levels (economic, political, biological, psychodynamic, etc.) may be viewed sociologically as well, by observing its social meaning.

We need not thereby escape into the simplicist versions of "economic causation," any more than into those of "personality causation," and neither of these is, *per se,* "more sociological" than the other. Both are different abstract levels, and if we are to use either type of data, we must look for the processes by which they take on social meanings and thus become converted into variables with sociological significance.

We have therefore attempted, in the final section of this paper, to depict some of the *social meanings* of income roles, income size, income stability, and income control, utilizing data from a study now nearing completion. The formal tabulations confirm the meaning of economic factors as expressed by the female, divorced respondents. The meaning of these dimensions of the economic point to some of the reasons why the strata under great economic stress in our society exhibit a higher rate of divorce.

Additional clarification of these points can be achieved by research which is pointed toward these problems: (1) Specification of the further sociological dimensions of economic factors in familial relations; (2) Determination of the relative economic pressures on various strata in the population, as felt by those strata;[25] and (3) Separation of the socio-economic from the occupational factors in marital relationships. The present suggestions are presented, then, as tentative steps in these directions.

[25] An excellent beginning, showing the expected skew, may be found in Arthur Kornhauser, "Analysis of 'Class Structure' of Contemporary American Society—Psychological Bases of Class Divisions," *Industrial Conflict*, S.P.S.S.I., 1939, esp. pp. 242 ff.

CHAPTER 19

The Persistence of Attitudes and Behaviors Learned in the Family

THE FAMILY has been called a "primary group" in the sense that it provides contacts among its members which are intimate and face-to face. It is also primary in the sense that it is normally the first setting in which the child engages in social interaction.[1] In earlier sections we have considered patterns of interaction characteristic of the family husband-wife, parent-child, and sibling-sibling. The patterns of behavior which are learned in these relationships appear to persist and to be discernible in behavior which occurs outside the setting of the family. To a Freudian it is commonplace to observe that the affection and/or distrust a man has for his boss is frequently influenced by the attitudes he had in childhood toward his father and that the degree to which he competes with his peers is related to the rivalry he had with his siblings.

The persistence of parent-child relations in the child's later attitude might be illustrated from a variety of aspects of social life. Kardiner and Linton have traced the continuity of childhood disciplines into the religious attitudes of adults, and Lasswell and Erikson have interpreted political attitudes of adults in terms of the familial experiences of childhood.[2] Pointing out that industry is organized along authoritarian

[1] C. H. Cooley, *Social Organization*, Scribner's, New York, 1909, pp. 23-28.

[2] Abram Kardiner, Ralph Linton *et al.*, *The Psychological Frontiers of Society*, New York, Columbia University Press, 1945; H. D. Lasswell, *Psychopathology and Politics* Chicago, University of Chicago Press, 1930; E. H. Erikson, "Hitler's Imagery and German Youth," *Psychiatry*, 5 (1942), 475-93.

nes, McGregor observes that the subordinate is "dependent upon his superiors for his job, for the continuity of his employment, for promotion with its accompanying satisfactions in the form of increased pay, responsibility and prestige, and for a host of other personal and social satisfactions to be obtained in the work situation."[3] This dependence, he reasons, places the subordinate in the relation of child to the superior. To give the subordinate a sense of confidence and security on his job, McGregor holds that the superior should create an "atmosphere" of approval, should maintain a system of consistent discipline, and should create an opportunity for the subordinate to participate in the solution of problems. Such advice savors very strongly of the recommendations currently being given to parents concerning procedures for rearing their children.

To draw this book to a close we are presenting two selections to illustrate the persistence of attitudes and behaviors learned in the family: one on the "out-group" attitudes of adolescents and another on neuroses precipitated in combat. Frenkel-Brunswik reports that "prejudiced" adolescents (as contrasted with the relatively "unprejudiced") tend to have parents who are authoritarian, socially marginal, and greatly concerned over their own social status. Strictly speaking, the inference may not be drawn from the evidence here presented, but it appears highly plausible that the attitudes which these children exhibit toward members of "out-groups" are in large measure determined by the manner in which their parents have reared them.

Grinker and Spiegel saw military duty as psychiatrists with the United States Army Air Force in the Mediterranean and European theaters during World War II. They view the man-to-man relationship among airmen as similar to, and in many cases repetitions of, experiences these men had in their childhood with their own siblings. Their relations with superior officers seemed at times to show displacements of feelings which the men had had about their own fathers. The form and content of the emotional disturbances which these men suffered

[3] Douglas McGregor, "Conditions of Effective Leadership in the Industrial Organization," in T. M. Newcomb and E. L. Hartley (eds.), *Readings in Social Psychology,* New York, Holt, 1947, pp. 427-35. Quotation is from p. 428.

under the stress of combat are reported by the authors as being ge.
erally traceable to the experiences of childhood with members of the
families.

A STUDY OF PREJUDICE*

Else Frenkel-Brunswik

A Research Project on Ethnic Prejudice in Children and Adolescents

A research project designed to throw light on the determinants c
susceptibility to racial or ethnic prejudice and allied forms of undeme
cratic opinions and attitudes in children is being conducted at th
Institute of Child Welfare of the University of California in Berkeley

The age levels studied range from eleven to sixteen. The source c
our present report includes attitude and personality tests as well a
interviews with children and their parents. A total of about 1,500 boy
and girls of varied socio-economic background were studied and 12
of those found extremely prejudiced or unprejudiced were interviewe
according to a schedule prepared in advance. The parents of the chi
dren interviewed were visited and likewise interviewed.

In general, the results indicate that already at these age level
children's reactions to statements about men and society as well a
their spontaneous formulations about these topics form a more or les
consistent pattern. This pattern, in turn, seems to be related to certai
personality features of the child. Though there can be little doub
about the existence of these relationships, there is evidence that they ar
not as consistent and rigid as those found with adults in an earlie
similarly conceived Public Opinion Study, also conducted in Berkeley.

We shall point out the differences in the personalities of the ethnicall

---

* Adapted and reprinted by permission of the author and publisher from "A Study o
Prejudice in Children," *Human Relations*, 1 (1948), 295-306.

[1] The project on social discrimination in children was initiated by the present write
in collaboration with T. W. Adorno and Harold E. Jones under the sponsorship of the
Research Department of the American Jewish Committee. Donald Campbell, Murra
Jarvik, Joan Havel and Milton Rokeach have been likewise members of the staff an
contributed to the present paper.

[2] A detailed report of this project is given in T. W. Adorno, E. Frenkel-Brunswik
D. J. Levinson and R. N. Sanford: *The Authoritarian Personality*, New York, Harpe
& Brothers, 1950.

prejudiced and unprejudiced child. It will turn out that such prejudice is but one aspect of a broader pattern of attitudes. At the same time, we shall try to discover areas of possible modifiability in the personality structure of the prejudiced child. As a first step, a description will be given of the social and political beliefs of such children. Next, we shall present a composite picture of their personality structure. An attempt will be made to study their social opinions and attitudes in relation to their basic personality needs.

Establishment and Testing of Opposite Extremes

The initial classification of subjects was made on the basis of responses to a series of about fifty slogans of racial prejudice or tolerance as well as statements pertaining to more general social attitudes. A prejudice scale was thus constructed with items regarding the attitude of children toward five minority groups: Jews, Negroes, Japanese, Mexicans, and "outgroups" in general. It proceeds along established lines in that it covers such situations as eating in the same restaurant, living in the same neighborhood, participating at the same social affairs, letting in or keeping people out of the country, and stereotypical accusations of minority members such as cruelty of the Japanese, laziness of the Negroes, or radicalism and moneymindedness of the Jews.

It was found that some of the children tend to reveal a stereotyped and rigid glorification of their own group and an aggressive rejection of outgroups and foreign countries. The scale yielded split-half correlations of from .82 to .90 (uncorrected for length of test), indicating that ethnic prejudice is a consistent and firmly established pattern not later than at the earliest of the age levels studied. In the present paper, the term "unprejudiced" (or "liberal") refers to those 25 per cent of the children who were found to be in greatest agreement with tolerant statements, whereas those in the opposite extreme quartile will be called "prejudiced" or "ethnocentric." The last two terms especially are to be understood to refer not only to racial or ethnic prejudice in the narrower sense of the word, but to a certain extent also to include its usual accompaniments, such as clannishness or national chauvinism and even glorification of family and self, in correspondence with the varying scope of what is being experienced as "ingroup" in any given context.

The disjunctive statements made in this paper concerning other attitudes or personality traits found predominantly in one or other of the two extreme groups are all based on quantitative material gained from other tests or from the interviews. The tests involved were constructed on the basis of initial clinical data gathered from children with extreme standing on the prejudice scale. Aside from a separate scale for more general social attitudes, there was a personality test containing about 150 items. The interviews were evaluated in terms of a system of categories which had proved themselves to be especially relevant in this context.[3] Statistical significance (often at as high a level as 1 per cent or better) is established for all differences referred to in this paper between the two extreme groups, with respect to test items and in most cases also with respect to over-all interview ratings. Quotations of answers to interview questions are added informally by way of illustration. It must also be kept in mind that the results presented here are limited to extremes only. Furthermore, they may well be less pronounced in cultures or subcultures in which the choice between alternative ideologies of the type involved here is less clearcut.

In addition to revealing prejudice toward specific ethnic groups, the children classified as ethnocentric are in marked disagreement with such more general statements, also included in the defining scale, as the following:

> Different races and religions would get along better if they visited each other and shared things.
> America is a lot better off because of the foreign races that live here.

The liberal children endorse most of such statements with a considerable approximation to unanimity.

General Social Attitudes of Prejudiced and Unprejudiced Children

Along similar lines are the children's spontaneous reactions in the interviews to the question: "What is America's biggest problem today?" The liberal children can more readily remove themselves from their immediate needs and think in terms of a far-reaching social good. Examples of the problems they list are:

> ". . . the starving people in Europe, because the people in our country won't think of them and they should," or,

---

[3] For a discussion of the principles involved see E. Frenkel-Brunswik, Dynamic and cognitive categorization of qualitative material (two parts). *Journal of Psychology*, 25 (1948), 253-77.

"The atom bomb; how to do things about the atom bomb to keep peace in the world."

Ethnocentric children, on the other hand, are more concerned with things that affect their immediate welfare. They tend to give greatest prominence to such problems as:

"Taxes on everything, and the cost of living."

The question "How would you change America?" is answered similarly. Ethnocentric children tend to mention external things:

"Clean up the streets—all that garbage lying around! See that everything is in order."

Liberal children, on the other hand, tend to mention such things as:

"So the Negroes wouldn't be beaten up like they are down South," or "We should have a world police so that there would be no more wars."

We turn now to the test intended to ascertain even broader social attitudes. In this scale, as well as in the personality scales to be discussed next, differentiations are much more clearcut at the later age levels studied. Study of the interview suggests that this is in part due to a comprehension factor, but that there is also a genuine absence of the relationship in the younger children.

The following statements in this scale differentiate to a particularly significant degree between the prejudiced and unprejudiced children, with the prejudiced more often endorsing them:

If we keep on having labor troubles, we may have to turn the government over to a dictator who will prevent any more strikes.

It is better to have our government run by business men rather than by college professors.

The government is interfering too much with private business.

Paralleling the rejection of the outgroup is a naive and selfish acceptance of the ingroup. Thus above age 11 approximately two-fifths of the prejudiced extreme but only a scattered few of the opposite extreme group subscribe to the following two statements:

People who do not believe that we have the best kind of government in the world should be kicked out of the country.

Refugees should be thrown out of this country so that their jobs can be given to veterans.

A particularly narrow form of ethnocentrism is revealed in the tendency prominent in the prejudiced child, to agree with the following statement:

Only people who are like myself have a right to be happy.

The selfish orientation toward their own country and the indifference and hostility against other countries is furthermore expressed in the agreement of almost half of the ethnocentric children with the following statement:

We should not send any of our food to foreign countries, but should think of America first.

The rejection of foreign countries by the ethnocentric child, and the projection of his own hostility onto them, may be considered to contribute to his affinity toward war. Thus, our ethnocentric children subscribe almost twice as often as the liberal to the statement:

Most of the other countries of the world are really against us, but are afraid to show it.

There is, furthermore, the conviction—apparently deep-rooted in the personality structure of the prejudiced child—that wars are inevitable. Comparatively often he tends to endorse the following statement:

There will always be war, it is part of human nature.

In the interviews, where the children are able to express their opinions spontaneously, the ethnocentric children make remarks such as the following about war:

"One happens in every generation," or,
"The Bible says there will always be wars," or;
"Sure, we will have another war. Wars never end."

Anti-weakness Attitude of the Prejudiced Child

The aggression of the ethnocentric children is not limited to minority groups and other countries but is part of a much more generalized rejection of all that is weak or different. Statements from additional scales help to assess such more general personality traits. Thus the prejudiced child agrees more often than the unprejudiced with the statement:

The world would be perfect if we put on a desert island all of the weak, crooked and feeble-minded people.

It is especially the prejudiced girl who tends to disagree with the following statement:

It is interesting to be friends with someone who thinks or feels differently from the way you do.

The ingroup feeling is clearly expressed by her tendency to endorse the following statement:

Play fair with your own gang, and let the other kids look out for themselves.

Dichotomy of Sex Roles

Ethnocentric children tend to conceive of the other sex as outgroup, and tend toward segregation from, and resentment against, the other sex. Associations of masculinity vs. femininity with strength vs. weakness need no further elaboration.

Around adolescence, the prejudiced of both sexes tend to agree with the statement:

Girls should only learn things that are useful around the house.

On the whole, ethnocentric children tend toward a rigid, dichotomizing conception of sex roles, being intolerant of passive or feminine manifestations in boys and masculine or tomboyish manifestations in girls. Thus an ethnocentric girl, asked how girls should act around boys, answers:

"Act like a lady, not like a bunch of hoodlums. Girls should not ask boys to date. It's not lady-like."

Two of the liberal boys reply to the same question as follows:

"It depends on their age; the girls should not be so afraid of the boys and not be shy," and,
"Talk about the things you like to talk about, about the same as another boy would."

Asked what is the worst occupation for a woman, one of the ethnocentric boys answers:

"To earn her own living, usually the man does that.

On the other hand, a boy low on ethnocentrism answers to the same question

"What she doesn't like to do."

The intolerance the ethnocentric child tends to show toward manifestations of the opposite sex in himself or in others makes for bad heterosexual adjustment, as was also found in the study of adults. The rigid and exaggerated conception of masculinity and femininity further tends to lead to a strained relation to one's own sex role. Thus the few children who, in reaction to some indirect questions, show envy of the role of the other sex, are ethnocentric.

The liberal child, on the other hand, tends, as does the liberal adult, to have a more flexible conception of the sex roles as well as to face conflicts in this direction more openly. Boys in this group show less repression of feminine, girls less repression of masculine trends. At the same time there is on the whole a better heterosexual development and less rejection of the opposite sex. Tolerance toward the other sex and the equalitarian relationship between the two sexes seems to be an important basis for tolerance in general and thus should be fostered by coeducational measures. This is one of the places where thinking in dichotomies has to be broken down.

Power and Money

The contempt the ethnocentric child has for the weak is related to his admiration of the strong, tough, and powerful, *per se*. He tends to disagree with the statement:

Weak people deserve consideration; the world should not belong to the strong only.

And he relatively often agrees with the statements:

Might makes right; the strong win out in the end.
A person who wants to be a man should seek power.

The latter statement shows the ideal aspired to by the typical ethnocentric boy and demanded in men by the typical ethnocentric girl. This pseudo-masculine ideal often prevents a humanitarian outlook which is sometimes considered as soft and "sissified." The fear of weakness is expressed in the tendency of the ethnocentric boy to agree with a statement like:

If a person does not watch out somebody will make a sucker out of him.

In the same context belongs the orientation toward money as a means of obtaining power, material benefits, and sometimes even friends. In the interviews of prejudiced children appear such statements as the following:

"It means something if you want to buy a house or a car or a fur coat for your wife. No dollar, no friend; have a dollar, got a friend."

The over-libidinization of money leads not only to an exaggeration of its importance but also to an unrealistic fear of it as something evil. The following is typical of the statements made by some of the ethnocentric children:

"It helps make enemies. Money is the root of all evil, they say."

Ambivalent Submission to Parents and Teachers

The admiration the ethnocentric child tends to have for success, power, and prestige may be assumed to result from submission to authority based on his fear of punishment and retaliation. The originally forced submission to parental authority apparently leads to a continued demand for autocratic leadership, strict discipline and punishment, as exercised not only by parents but also by parent substitutes. Thus ethnocentric children, especially girls, tend to agree more often than liberal ones with the statements

Teachers should tell children what to do and not try to find out what the children want.
It would be better if teachers would be more strict.

This attitude is also mirrored in their spontaneous statements made in the interviews while talking about parents and teachers. They tend to refer to the authoritarian aspects of the parent-child relationship whereas liberal children tend to emphasize the cooperative aspects of this relationship.

Though there tends to be a surface submission to authority in the ethnocentric, there is often, at the same time, an underlying resentment against authority. Apparently, this resentment is repressed for two reasons: first, because of a fear of retaliation for any open expression of resentment; and second, because of a fear of being deprived of the material benefits which persons in authority can give, and upon which the typical prejudiced child seems especially dependent. For the ethno-centric more than for the liberal, parents and other adults are conceived of as the deliverers of goods.

The following quotations illustrate the attitude of the ethnocentric child toward the parents as well as toward teachers. Asked to describe the perfect father, one of the boys in this group says:

> "Does not give you everything you want, is very strict with you, doesn't let you do the outrageous things that you sometimes want to."

Typical of these children is the use of the negative in the characteriza-tion of the perfect parent and the references to the punitive and re-strictive aspects. Others of these boys say about the perfect father:

> "He spanks you when you are bad and doesn't give you too much money," or;
> "When you ask for something he ought not to give it to you right away. Not soft on you, strict."

Similar is the description of the perfect teacher by another ethno-centric boy:

> "She is strict, treats all children the same, won't take any nonsense of them, keeps them organized in the playground, in class, in lines."

About teachers who are not liked an ethnocentric boy says:

> "Those who tell you in a nice way instead of being strict and they don't make you mind."

The same group of children when asked how they would like to change their fathers sometimes reveal resentment and feelings of being deprived and victimized. One of the ethnocentric boys says:

> "He wouldn't smoke a pipe, would not eat too much, wouldn't take all the food away from his son."

Along the same lines is the answer of an ethnocentric boy to the ques-tion, "For what should the hardest punishment be administered?";

> "Should be for talking back to parents, it should be a whipping."

One of the girls in this group says:

> "Naturally for murder, the next is for not paying attention to her mother and father. She should be sent to a juvenile home for not paying attention to her parents."

Another ethnocentric boy asks for punishment too:

> "Talking back, not minding, for example, if you are supposed to saw a certain amount of wood in one hour and don't do it you should be punished for it."

Methodical clinical ratings of the interviews confirm the impressions gained from these quotations. The ethnocentric children tend to think in the category of strictness and harshness when telling about their fathers whereas the liberal children tend to think primarily in terms of companionship. The ratings also seem to indicate that ethnocentric children tend to complain more about neglect by their fathers. The interview ratings bear out the fearful submission to harsh punishment on the part of the typical ethnocentric child and the ability of the typical liberal child to assimilate punishment which is explained to them and for which their understanding is thus assured. Fear and dependency not only seem to prevent the ethnocentric child from any conscious criticism of the parents but even lead to an acceptance of punishment and to an "identification with the aggressor." The fact that the negative feelings against the parents have to be excluded from consciousness may be considered as contributing to the general lack of insight, rigidity of defense, and "narrowness of the ego." Since the unprejudiced child as a rule does not seem to have had to submit to stern authority in childhood (according to the interviews at least), he can afford in his later life not to long for strong authority, nor does he need to assert his strength against those who are weaker. The "anti-weakness" attitude referred to above seems thus to be directly related to the fearful submission to authority.

Parents' Concern with Social Status. Rigid Rules and Discipline

The hypothesis may be offered that it is this repressed resentment toward authority which is displaced upon socially inferior and foreign groups. As may be seen from the interviews with the parents, the liberal child, in contrast to the ethnocentric child, is more likely to be treated as an equal and to be given the opportunity to express feelings of rebellion or disagreement. He thus learns at home the equalitarian and individualized approach to people, as the ethnocentric child learns the authoritarian and hierarchical way of thinking. Interviews with parents of ethnocentric children show an exaggerated social status-concern. This may be assumed to be the basis of a rigid and externalized set of values. What is socially accepted and what is helpful in the climbing of the social ladder is considered good, and what deviates, what is different, and what is socially inferior is considered bad.

The parents of the ethnocentric children are often socially marginal. The less they can accept their marginality, the more urgent becomes the wish to belong to the privileged groups. This leads to the development of a kind of collective ego which is very different from genuine group identification and which must be assumed to contribute to ethnocentrism. With this narrow and steep path in mind such parents are likely to be intolerant of any manifestation on the part of the children which seems to deter from, or to oppose, the goal decided upon. The more urgent the social needs of the parents, the more they are apt to view the child's behavior in terms of their own instead of the child's needs. Since the values of the parents are outside the children's scope, yet are rigorously enforced, only a superficial identification with the parents and society can be achieved. The suppressed instinctive and hostile tendencies are apt to become diffuse and depersonalized and to lead an independent, autonomous life. In line with this the over-all clinical ratings seem to indicate the more diffuse and explosive nature of the aggression of ethnocentric children, as compared with milder and more ego-acceptable forms of aggression in the typical liberal child. Thus fascism and war must have a special appeal to ethnocentric children and adults, who expect liberation of their instincts in combination with approval by authorities.

Moralism and Conformity

The influence of the parents must be considered at least a contributing factor to the tendency, observed in the ethnocentric child, to be more concerned with status values than are liberal children. He expects —and gives—social approval on the basis of external moral values, including cleanliness, politeness, and the like. He condemns others for their non-conformity to such values, conformity being an all-or-none affair. The functioning of his superego is mainly directed toward punishment condemnation, and exclusion of others, mirroring thus the type of discipline to which he was exposed. Interview ratings show a tendency toward more moralistic condemnation on the part of the prejudiced child and greater permissiveness toward people in general on the part of the unprejudiced.

The trend to conformity of the ethnocentric child is expressed in his greater readiness to agree with the following statements:

There is only one right way to do anything.
Appearances are usually the best test.
One should avoid doing things in public which seem wrong to others even though one knows that these things are really all right.

Politeness, cleanliness, good manners appear again and again among the requirements of prejudiced children, especially the girls, for a perfect boy or perfect girl. Interview ratings indicate that ethnocentric children tend to mention in this connection purity, cleanliness and what corresponds to a conventional conception of good personality, whereas the liberal children tend to mention companionship and fun.

In the light of what has been said before about the attitude of the typical ethnocentric child toward parents, we may assume that the conformity to approved social values is based on fear of retaliation by society for disobedience rather than on a real incorporation of those values. In order to conform, he demands a set of inflexible rules which he can follow, and he is most at ease when he can categorize and make value judgments in terms of good or bad.

Intolerance of Ambiguities

Analysis of the interviews indicates that this inflexibility of the ethnocentric child is part of a broader texture of rigidity and incapacity to face ambiguous situations. Intolerance of ambiguity has been found above in his conception of the parent-child relationship and in his conception of the sex roles. It is also present in the organization of the perceptual and cognitive field.

That this rigidity represents a more generalized approach to the solving of problems even in fields where there is no social or emotional involvement has been experimentally demonstrated by Rokeach.[4] In solving arithmetic problems ethnocentric children show greater resistance to changing a given set which interferes with the direct and simple solution of a new task. Thus even in children rigidity tends to be a pervasive trait. It must be added that it is rigidity in thinking that is related to ethnocentrism, and not intelligence, *per se;* the IQ was

[4] M. Rokeach, "Ethnocentrism and a general mental rigidity factor" (Abstract). *Amer. cychologist,* 1946, 1, 451.

found to be only very slightly (negatively) correlated with ethno-centrism.

Our interpretation then could be that ideas and tendencies which are nonconforming and which do not agree with rigid, simple and pre-scribed solutions (such as submission to the strong) have to be repressed and displaced. When displaced into the social sphere, this is expressed in an overly moralizing, authoritarian or generally destructive manner, and it is here that the ethnocentric child becomes a potential fascist. The choice of simple solutions apparently helps to reduce some of the repressed anxieties. These anxieties are often more directly expressed in the liberal child, since he does not tend as much to deny possible weakness or shortcomings in himself and his group as does the ethno-centric child.

Catastrophic Conception of the World

The anxieties and insecurities of the ethnocentric child are expressed more indirectly, *e.g.*, in a greater readiness to conceive of dangers and catastrophes in the outside world, to feel helplessly exposed to external powers and to subscribe to bizarre and superstitious statements. Thus the ethnocentric child (as also in this instance the ethnocentric adult) relatively often tends to answer in the affirmative to the following three statements:

> Some day a flood or earthquake will destroy everybody in the whole world.
> There are more contagious diseases nowadays than ever before.
> If everything would change, this world would be much better.

The tendency to wish for a diffuse and all-out change rather than for definite progress indicates how relatively poorly rooted the typical ethnocentric child is in the daily task of living and in his object rela-tionships. Behind a rigid façade of conformity there seems to be an underlying fascination by the thought of chaos and destruction. A leader will thus be welcome who gives permission to this type of license. The ideal solution for this type of child and adult is to release what is dammed up, and thus remains unintegrated, under the protection of a leader representing the externalized superego.

We find dependency not only upon external authority but also upon inanimate external forces. Thus ethnocentric children subscribe signifi-cantly more often to such superstitious statements as:

The position of the stars at the time of your birth tells your character and personality.

It is really true that a black cat crossing your path will bring bad luck. You can protect yourself from bad luck by carrying a charm or good luck piece.

It seems to be important for the typical ethnocentric child to use devices by which he can get evil dangerous forces to join him on his side as a substitute for an undeveloped self-reliance. In general, his attitudes tend to be less scientifically oriented and rational than those of the liberal child, and he is likely to explain events for which he has no ready understanding in terms of chance factors.

Comparative Flexibility of Ethnocentrism in Children

As indicated above, the personality structure of the ethnocentric child is similar to that of the ethnocentric adult. But while this personality pattern seems quite firmly established in the adult, it appears in the child as incipient, or as a potential direction for development. This is indicated by correlations which are all-round lower than the analogous ones in adults. For instance, we often find in ethnocentric adults a highly opportunistic, exploitative and manipulative attitude toward other people. The ethnocentric child, however, in spite of showing tendencies in the same direction, still generally seeks more primary satisfaction of his psychological needs. Thus not only liberal minded children, but to a great extent children in general, tend to choose their friends from the standpoint of good companionship and "fun," whereas the ethnocentric adult tends to be more exclusively oriented toward status in his choice of friends. Furthermore, the ethnocentric child is more accessible to experience and reality than the ethnocentric adult who has rigidly structured his world according to his interests and desires. Finally, the child's position as a comparative underdog constitutes a possible resource for expanding the experimental basis for his sympathy for other underdogs.

In spite of all the differences between the ethnocentric and liberal child, it must be pointed out that with respect to many of the features mentioned above, such as superstition or conformity, children in general have more of a touch of the ethnocentric than of the liberal adult. In turn, the ethnocentric adult may be considered as more infantile than is the liberal adult with respect to these variables. The older the children become, the greater the differences between the ethnocentric and the liberal child. All this seems to indicate that some of the trends which are connected with ethnocentrism are natural stages of development which have to be overcome if maturity is to be reached.

Over-all Picture and Conclusions

Let us review once more the personality structure and the background of the ethnocentric child and compare this with that of the liberal child. As mentioned before, the parents of the ethnocentric child are highly concerned with status. They use more harsh and rigid forms of discipline which the child generally submits to rather than accepts or understands. Parents are seen simultaneously as the providers of one's physical needs and as capricious arbiters of punishment. On the surface the ethnocentric child tends, especially in his more general statements, to idealize his parents. There are, however, indications that the parent-child relationship is lacking in genuine affection. In many ethnocentric children underlying feelings of being victimized are revealed by specific episodes, told by the children, of neglect, rejection and unjust punishment. The pressure to conform to parental authority and its externalized social values makes it impossible for the child to integrate or to express his instinctual and hostile tendencies. This lack of integration makes for a narrow and rigid personality. Thus instinctual tendencies cannot be utilized for constructive purposes, such as genuine ability for love, or creative activities, for which both more permissiveness and more guidance on the part of the adult would be needed. Since the ethnocentric child often gets neither of these he presents the dual aspects of being too inhibited, on the one hand, and of having the tendency to join wild and rough games, on the other. The gang-oriented child may later conform to an "adult gang" without having acquired an internalized conscience which would control the direct and indirect expressions of aggression. When the inhibition is more pronounced we have to do with the conventional pattern of ethnocentrism. Whenever disinhibition dominates the picture, we have to do with the delinquent variety of the ethnocentric. Since, however, delinquency also often looms behind the surface of rigid conventionality the affinity of the two patterns should not be overlooked.

By contrast, the liberal child is more oriented toward love and less toward power than is the ethnocentric child. He is more capable of giving affection since he has received more real affection. He tends to judge people more on the basis of their intrinsic worth than does the ethnocentric child who places more emphasis on conformity to social mores. The liberal child, on the other hand, takes internal values and principles more seriously. Since he fears punishment and retaliation less than does the ethnocentric child, he is more able really to incorporate the values of society imposed upon him. The liberal child employs the help of adults in working out his problems of sex and aggression, and thus can more easily withstand hateful propaganda both in the forms of defamation of minorities and of glorification of war. By virtue of the greater integration of his instinctual life he becomes a more creative and sublimated individual. He is thus more flexible and less likely to form stereotyped opinions about others. The interview ratings point toward a better developed, more integrated and more internalized superego. The unprejudiced child seems to be able to express disagreement with, and resentment against, the parents more openly, resulting in a much greater degree of independence from the parents and from authorities in general. At the same time there is love-oriented dependence on parents and people in general which constitutes an important source of gratification.

This is not to say that the liberal child is necessarily always socially or personally better adjusted. He has more open anxieties, more directly faced insecurities, more conflicts. For the reduction of these conflicts he does not as a rule use the simple though, in the last analysis, inappropriate and destructive methods characteristic of the ethnocentric child. It may be precisely this lack of displacement and projectivity which enables the liberal child and adult to evaluate social and political events in a more realistic and adequate fashion. This makes it less likely that the paradoxical attitudes of depersonalizing human relationships and personally tinting political and social events will be developed. Glorification of the ingroup and vilification of the outgroup in the ethnocentric child recurs in the dimensions of power-weakness, cleanliness-dirtiness, morality-immorality, conformance-difference, fairness-unfairness, etc., thus mirroring some of the basic dimensions of their outlook and personality dynamics. Above and beyond this, stereotypes provide the individual enough latitude to project onto outgroups his specific problems, such as aggression, underlying weakness, or preoccupation with sex. Different minority groups thereby seem to lend themselves to different types of accusations.

From the point of view of society as a whole, the most important problem therefore seems to be the child's attitude toward authority.

Forced submission to authority produces only surface conformity coun-termanded by violent underlying destructiveness, dangerous to the very society to which there seems to be conformity. Only a frightened and frustrated child will tend to gain safety and security by oversimpli-fied black-white schematizations and categorizations on the basis of crude, external characteristics. Deliberately planned democratic par-ticipation in school and family, individualized approach to the child, and the right proportion of permissiveness and guidance may be in-strumental in bringing about the attitude necessary for a genuine identification with society and thus for international understanding.

MEN UNDER STRESS*

Roy R. Grinker and John P. Spiegel

. . . An examination of the work record and past history of a large number of fliers shows that, at the time they were accepted for training, they were still in the adolescent phase of testing themselves against the world and of developing confidence in themselves. From the stand-point of both practical achievement and psychological maturity they show a wide range of success. Many have retained considerable emo-tional and economic dependence on their families. Immediately prior to induction a great number were still living at home, where they were inclined to be spoiled by their mothers and dominated by their fathers. A large percentage of these youths have an emotional attachment to their mothers far more intense than their chronological ages should permit. In this regard they conform to the average contemporary product of our past decades, which is the result of an excessive grati-fication of children combined with an insincerity in instilling mature standards of conduct.

Among enlisted men and, to a smaller degree, among officers, a large number of broken homes have been responsible for a disturbed family life. Parents separated or divorced, stepfathers and stepmothers, familial discord, a drunken, sadistic father and other disturbing family settings give an unexpected view of a cross section of family life. The relation-

* Adapted and reprinted by permission of the authors and publisher from *Men Under Stress*, Philadelphia, The Blakiston Co., 1945, pp. 8-9, 21-25, 289-93.

hip of such specific factors to psychological disturbances arising out
of combat will be considered later. The general background considered
here can be delineated in this way: the men selected for flying training
are in the normal transition stage between the emotional and economic
dependence of their adolescent years and the self sufficiency of adult
life. In this process some of the men have had more than the usual
amount of economic difficulty because of either chronically poor family
circumstances or personal limitations, or both. Others have had more
than the usual amount of emotional dependence on their families. In
either case the circumstance is apt to lead to an interest in flying which
represents an overcompensation for and an escape from previous difficulties. This is entirely a quantitative matter, a question of how much
of an individual's motivation represents an overcompensation, how
much of his past history indicates excessive economic or emotional
dependence. The point he occupies on this spectrum, which shades
subtly from the normal to the seriously maladjusted, has a great significance for the future career of the would-be flier . . .

The impersonal threat of injury from the enemy, affecting all alike,
produces a high degree of cohesion so that personal attachments
throughout the unit become intensified. Friendships are easily made
by those who might never have been compatible at home, and are
cemented under fire. Out of the mutually shared hardships and dangers
are born an altruism and generosity that transcend ordinary individual
selfish interests. So sweeping is this trend that the usual prejudices
and divergences of background and outlook, which produce social
distinction and dissension in civil life, have little meaning to the group
in combat. Religious, racial, class, schooling or sectional differences
lose their power to divide the men. What effect they have is rather to
lend spice to a relationship which is now based principally on the
need for mutual aid in the presence of enemy action. Such powerful
forces as antisemitism, anticatholicism or differences between North-
erners and Southerners are not likely to disturb interpersonal relationships in a combat crew . . .

The most vital relationship is not the purely social. It is the feeling
that the men have for each other as members of combat teams and
toward the leaders of those teams, that constitutes the essence of their
relationship. It is an interesting fact that, although the members of
combat crews are thrown together only by chance, they rapidly become
united to each other by the strongest bonds while in combat. The char-

acter of these bonds is of the greatest significance in determining their ability to withstand the stresses of the combat situation.

In combat the center of activity shifts from one crewmate to another in accordance with the situation. . . . At one time it may be the waist gunner, at another, the tail gunner, upon whose skill and courage depend the lives of all the others. The combined efforts of all the crew may be wasted if the bombardier is incompetent or anxious and fails to line-up correctly on the target. All members of the crew are dependent upon each other to an unusual degree. Day after day, or mission after mission, this mutual dependence is made to pay dividends in safety and effectiveness of the combat crew. It is no wonder then that the emotional relationships between these fliers assume a special character. The men and their plane become identified with each other with an intensity that in civil life is found only within the family circle. Crew members habitually refer to each other as "my pilot," "my bombardier," "my gunner," and so on, and their feeling for their plane is equally strong, since its strength and reliability are as important as those of any human members of the crew. . . .

In this atmosphere of mutual dependence, the task of carrying out complex, highly coordinated maneuvers in the face of great danger imposes upon the men and their leaders a special relationship. The emotional attitudes the fliers take toward each other have less to do with the accident of their individual personalities than with the circumstances of their association. We have already described the intensity of their feeling for each other as resembling the closeness of relationship between members of the same family. In truth, they are brothers-in-arms in more than a figurative sense. They actually feel toward each other as if they were brothers. It is a very common thing to hear a flier say of his buddy, "He reminds me of my brother" or "I felt closer to him than to my own brother." The men in the combat teams are brothers by virtue of their constant enforced association, their dependence upon each other, their common ideals and goals, and their relation to their leaders. In the family circle of the combat group, the leader is in the position of the father. Again it is extremely common to hear a combat flier describe his commanding officer as reminding him of his father. As with the fraternal feelings of the men toward each other, this seems to have less to do with the physical appearance of the leader or his actual personality than with his relation toward the men in combat. From a psychological point of view, the combat leader is a father and the men are his children.

The men are in the position of children by virtue of the ordinary army administrative setup. As in the case of children, they must do what he says, whether they want to or not. He may give them what they want, or deny it, as he wills, rewarding them when they are good and punishing them if they are bad. But in combat the vital relationship derives less from the channels and routines of army administration than from the actual helplessness of the combat team without the aid and protection of the leader. He can lead them into certain death and destruction, or skillfully extricate them from a desperate situation. Their fate is in his hands; their future, their chance of survival, depend upon him. It is small wonder, then, that they feel, for better or for worse, that he is their father. Whether he is a good or bad father is reflected in the morale of the unit in a manner which will be described later. However, it is clear that in such a situation the type of combat personalities developed by the men greatly depends upon the character of the commanding officers and subordinate leaders. . . .

Case 41. Compulsive character precipitated into depression after injury and death of comrades; identified with brothers toward whom the patient had considerable repressed hostility.

This patient, a 24-year-old radio operator, entered the hospital with the complaints of nervousness, irritability, insomnia, battle dreams, and depression. He flew fifty combat missions in a B-25 in thirteeen months. He had trained as a radio operator and gunner, after he failed the physical examination for aviation cadet training because of an ocular defect. However, he made a good adjustment, liked to fly and took great pride in his ability as a radio operator. The patient had high patriotic ideals and felt that he really understood what he was fighting for. He felt that he was well adjusted during his combat tour until his twenty-fourth mission, which occurred in support of a landing. His formation approached from the sea through heavy flak. Stukas were diving through the patient's formation to bomb ships and troops below. A piece of flak penetrated the top turret and struck a gunner in the eye. This gunner was a very close friend and crew member of many months' standing. He descended from the turret and said to the patient, "No, no, this can't happen to me." The patient quickly applied a dressing and mounted into the top turret to cover his friend's position. He frantically called to the other crew members to come to assist the wounded gunner. He could look down and see the blood-smeared face of his buddy below him. He cursed the enemy planes and hoped for them to come in so he could shoot them. About this time there was engine trouble and his plane left its formation and soon landed on a nearby field. He carried his friend out of the plane and became blood-smeared himself in doing so. He then accompanied him in an ambulance to a hospital where his wounds were cared for. That night he couldn't sleep and was nervous and jittery, but became less tense and "settled down" in two or three days.

After completing his thirtieth mission, his organization was moved and there ensued an operational lull of about three months. During this time he noticed increased nervousness, apprehension, fear of flying, irritability, and insomnia. He developed recurrent battle dreams, particularly one in which he was covered with purple blotches, which he attempted to pick.

On resuming combat he "really began to sweat them out." He dreaded each mission. About the time of his forty-second mission a very good friend, not a member of his own crew, was flying with the patient's old copilot. Their plane was hit by flak and exploded. No parachutes were seen to leave the plane and the deaths of all the crew members were later confirmed. The loss of this friend caused the patient great concern and he became even more nervous and irritable.

He finished his fifty missions by forcing himself. He dreaded each of them, but, wanting to get through and get home, he continued to fly. When he received his orders, they read that he was to return for more combat after thirty days' leave. He felt that this was unfair, that he had done his tour and should go back for good. He complained bitterly to his superiors. He returned to the United States, went to his home for thirty days but was very depressed, anxious and upset because he knew he must go back to combat. He had planned to marry his girl but decided against it because of having to return.

The patient was the second child in a closely knit family of four children, with one older and two younger brothers. His father was in the construction business and of moderate means, a hard worker, who had encouraged his children to be morally straight and religious and to prepare themselves for later life by education.

In childhood the patient was a fat, healthy, "serious" youngster. He enjoyed his schooling. His father offered treats to the child who rought home the best report card and would take him to the rodeo, all game, etc. The patient became a consistent winner of these treats, until finally the father began taking the other boys anyway. His older brother was a source of some conflict. This brother would kid him bout being fat and would delight in provoking him and engaging him in arguments. He and this brother bought an automobile in partnership but the patient never drove it much, "to keep the peace." He always tried to run around with his brother's crowd but was unable o keep up with them.

After graduation from high school the patient decided to enter college and was proud of the fact that he could get a scholarship. He had always been ambitious to occupy an important place in society. He received little financial assistance, but got moral support from his parents. His older brother kidded him still and referred to him as "Joe College." During this time, the patient began to get the best of he arguments and thereafter his brother ceased chiding him. Because of the imminence of his induction, he did not teach after finishing college but worked in a factory until he entered the army nine months ater.

On the twelfth day of hospitalization, narcosis was induced with 0.4 Gm. of [sodium] pentothal, injected intravenously, and, after being stimulated by the question, "What about Sid?," he spoke with few interruptions always in the past tense.

He said, "No! No! Sid, it can't happen to me. He was hit in the eye." (Marked emotion with tears and squirming about on the couch.) "I prayed and prayed he would be all right and I cried. I asked the navigator to come back and look out for him. He was all blood—bleeding. He said, 'No! No!' I tried to help but I had to go up in the turret." He paused and then went on. "Flak! Flak! Sid was there. I couldn't see him. I called up Jack (navigator) and told him to get to Sid. I didn't know if he was alive or dead.

"I was crying up there. I was cursing those dirty bastards. I was hoping they would come near. He was all covered with blood. He was a good kid. I couldn't help him out. We left the formation. He looked rotten. I looked down from the turret and saw Sid's eye. His whole face was bleeding. I prayed. I carried him out of the plane. I was all covered with blood; he didn't say anything. At the hospital they were so damned slow. There was another fellow there, all full of holes. I told Jack to go tell them to hurry up. Then they finally came and X-rayed him and put him to bed. I told him I would see him again. I told him Mary (his girl) would love him anyway. He went to sleep then.

"At first, I didn't like him. He shot off his mouth too much. He did—he did shoot down a plane." (Pause) "All over my coveralls was his blood. All those stupid arguments we used to have. I always talked him down and put him in his place." He was then stimulated with "How about Al?" Whereupon he said "He was so crazy. He liked his women and his liquor and got both. He was grounded and didn' have to fly. He would trade cigarettes with the natives for eggs and had them for us when we were going on a long mission. He did so much for me; I did nothing for him. His plane exploded. I prayed that night. I was a heel. I would always tell him off. He didn't come back. I told Sid about it. He died for his country" (tears)—"he did so much for the crew; when he would get a package he'd head for me. I was such a dope. Told him he didn't have any sense. And now he is dead. Then Fred, he was put in another squadron. He was so good. He was married to a nice girl. We were on the mission he went down on There were fighters and flak up there. The plane started to go down and hit the damned mountain." (Pause) "I knew I couldn't get out.' (Pause) "The whole thing was crazy. My little brother is out there He is only a kid. He was only 18 when they took him out where those damned animals are. But what the hell does he say when he writes?—nothing. He's so young, so little. He hasn't lived. I used to always argue with him and tell him off. Once I had a fight with him. I was so smart. I was going to be a big shot. They upset my plans, those orders. I was afraid up there. They had no right" (speaking of ordering him on a second tour of combat). "I was going to show them how brave I was" (speaking of his family) "and make them proud of me. I'm not sure they are."

The following day, material concerning his friend Sid was reviewed. In simple terms his ambivalent feelings toward Sid were discussed. He accepted the explanation given him and seemed more cheerful at the close of the interview. Two days later the discussion was continued, this time about his friend Jack. Here again his ambivalent feelings were pointed out as a possible cause of his guilty feelings. He said he could understand but still felt badly about the way he had talked to his friend. He was asked if Jack reminded him of anyone in his family and he answered that he was something like his older brother. It was pointed out that the old rivalry among the children may have caused him to resent his brother in some way. He was quick to grasp insight into this interpretation, whereupon he was told that perhaps his behavior pattern of compulsive and aggressive rivalry with his brother was also to be found in his behavior with his combat crew "family."

He was next seen three days later and immediately began telling about his improvement. He had ceased to refer to himself as a social misfit. He continued to mix with other people of his own volition. His appetite was good. He was more cheerful. Occasionally he felt depressed for a short time but not so profoundly as at the time of admission. Later he was discharged to full duty.

. . . . .

Ambitious and conscientious, this patient had never been able to fuse his positive and negative feelings, toward brother figures, derived from his early sibling rivalry. His ego-ideal was very highly developed and rigid, as shown in social relations, his motivation for combat, and his conscientiousness toward his buddies who were injured. He had solved his negative feelings toward his rivals in the family by identifying with them as best he could, emulating his brother by going with his crowd. His identification with the injured friend was evidenced by his battle dreams in which *he* was covered with purple blotches like the gunner hit in the eye. Punishment for his negative feelings mobilized by the actual death of and injury to the brother figures was thus directed toward his own ego identified with these hostile rivals.

In spite of the powerful pull of the group toward cohesion of all its members, some fliers make a desperate attempt to avoid all close identifications and fight against the compulsion to recreate the family setting in combat. They frankly state they were afraid to make friends because of the terrific reaction if one of them were to be killed or hurt. . . .

Therapy consisted in a thorough abreaction of the guilty feelings, comparing them with reality, and forcing the patient to face his negative or hostile attitudes toward his friends. This was quickly followed by interpretation of similar feelings toward his real brothers. The result was a striking improvement.

In this case is shown the reaction of a man who under normal conditions has been able to handle his aggressive and hostile feelings but who, under the stress of the combat situation and the loss of his friends, has found his ego unable to cope with the quantity of these feelings, which resulted in anxiety and depression.

NAME INDEX

Italicized page references indicate selections contained in this volume.

SUBJECT INDEX

7